Maida Springer

Pan-Africanist and International Labor Leader

MAIDA SPRINGER

Pan-Africanist and International Labor Leader

Yevette Richards

UNIVERSITY OF PITTSBURGH PRESS

Copyright © 2000, University of Pittsburgh Press
All rights reserved
Manufactured in the United States of America
Printed on acid-free paper

10 9 8 7 6 5 4 3 2 1

Library of Congress Cataloging-in-Publication Data
Richards, Yevette.
Maida Springer : Pan-Africanist and international labor leader /
Yevette Richards.
p. cm.
Includes bibliographical references and index.
ISBN 0-8229-4139-2 (cloth : alk. paper)
1. Springer, Maida. 2. Women labor leaders—United States—Biography.
3. Women labor union members—United States—Biography.
4. Afro-American women—Biography. 5. International labor
activities—History. 6. Pan-Africanism—History. I. Title.
331.88'092—dc21   00-009652

Photographs of Maida Springer with Charles Zimmerman reproduced with the permission of
Photographs and Prints Division
Schomburg Center for Research in Black Culture
The New York Public Library
Astor, Lenox and Tilden Foundations

Photograph of Springer, James Kemp and A. Phillip Randolph reproduced with the permission of Ed Jackson.

To Paul and our daughter,
Amara Gabrielle Jordan

CONTENTS

Acknowledgments   ix
Abbreviations   xi
A Chronology of Maida Springer-Kemp's Life   xiii
Awards   xvi
Memberships   xvii
Introduction   1

1. "My Wonderful Young Mother": Springer's Formative Years   13
2. "My Union Was a Very Political Union": Springer Joins Local 22   36
3. The Dilemma of Race and Gender during World War II   57
4. The National and International Struggle against the Color Line   77
5. Dancing on the End of a Needle: African Connections   100
6. The Atlantic City Compromise   129
7. The Beginning of the Affiliation Struggle   176
8. Springer Joins the AFL-CIO Department of International Affairs   198
9. AFL-CIO Africa Programs   222
10. Crossroads   246
11. Continued Service   262

Notes   285
Bibliography   347
Index   357

ACKNOWLEDGMENTS

When I first began work on this project in 1989, I understood that I was privileged to research and write about many historically important events that had yet to be fully studied. Learning about this history has been an exciting adventure, and shaping it into a book has been a rewarding challenge. I could not have done it alone.

The many archivists who aided me in my research efforts include Lee Sayrs of the George Meany Memorial Archives, Brenda Square of the Amistad Research Center, Patrizia Sione of the Kheel Center for Labor-Management Documentation and Archives, Sylvia McDowell of the Schlesinger Library, and Carol Leadenham of the Hoover Institution. I was able to pursue this project thanks to a Ford Foundation postdoctoral fellowship, a grant from Carnegie Mellon University's Center for African American Urban Studies and the Urban Economy (CAUSE), a University of Pittsburgh postdoctoral fellowship, a Swarthmore College research grant, and a Yale University John F. Enders Special Research Assistance Grant.

I am deeply indebted to many friends, family members, colleagues, and mentors who helped sustain me through my research and writing. Above all others I thank Maida Springer-Kemp for the countless hours she spent with me discussing various aspects of her life and career. Through her, I was able to meet with a number of labor activists in the United States and Africa whose testimonies enrich this book. Her aid was also indispensable in adding context to many of the documents I came across.

David Montgomery gave me steadfast support and an incisive analysis of the dissertation from which this book emerged. Joe William Trotter, Jr., gave generously of his time and expertise in evaluating much of my manuscript. As a Ford fellow, I was associated with Carnegie Mellon University's CAUSE program. Part of the mission of CAUSE is to "consider the comparative experiences of blacks and other ethnic and racial groups, including relevant international comparisons" and to publish material that would be of interest to both academics and the general public. Others who analyzed sections of this manuscript and expressed a faith in me that was one of my many blessings include Joseph Adjaye, Hazel Carby, Barbara Lazarus, Vernell Lillie, Martin Morand, Brenda Gayle

Plummer, Marcus Rediker, and Diana Wylie. I also thank two anonymous readers of this book for their valuable criticisms, as well as the editors and anonymous readers of articles I published in the *Journal of Women's History* and the *International Journal of African Historical Studies*. "Race, Gender, and Anticommunism in the International Labor Movement" appeared in the *Journal of Women's History*, 11(2) and is adapted for this book with permission of Indiana University Press. "African-American Labor Leaders in the Struggle Over International Affiliation" appeared in revised form in the *International Journal of African Historical Studies*, 31(2). I am grateful to Sabiyha Prince for our many discussions about the challenges of writing. I thank my mother, Bobbie Richards, and my sister, Cynthia Richards, for being my loudest cheerleaders.

Most importantly, I thank my husband, Paul Jordan, who from the beginning of this project always put my needs first. He is a gem.

ABBREVIATIONS

AAFLI	Asian-American Free Labor Institute
AALC	African-American Labor Center, AFL-CIO
AAPC	All-African People's Conference
AATUF	All-African Trade Union Federation
ACOA	American Committee on Africa
ACWA	Amalgamated Clothing Workers of America
AFL	American Federation of Labor
AFRO	African Regional Organization
AFSCME	American Federation of State, County, and Municipal Employees
AID	Agency for International Development
ALP	American Labor Party
ANC	African National Congress
ANTUF	All-Nigeria Trade Union Federation
APRI	A. Philip Randolph Institute
ATUC	African Trade Union Confederation
BSCP	Brotherhood of Sleeping Car Porters
CELU	Confederation of Ethiopian Labor Unions
CIA	Central Intelligence Agency
CIO	Congress of Industrial Organizations
COSATU	Congress of South African Trade Unions
CP	Communist Party
CPP	Convention People's Party (Ghana)
DGB	Deutscher Gewerkschaftsbund (German Trade Union Federation)
FBSI	All-Indonesian Federation of Labor
FEPC	Fair Employment Practices Committee
GEB	General Executive Board
IAM	International Association of Machinists
ICC	Isthmian Canal Commission
ICFTU	International Confederation of Free Trade Unions
ILGWU	International Ladies' Garment Workers' Union

ILO	International Labor Organization
IPWF	International Plantation Workers' Federation
ITGLWF	International Textile, Garment and Leather Workers' Federation
ITS	International Trade Secretariat
KANU	Kenya African National Union
KFL	Kenya Federation of Labor
KTUC	Kenya Trade Union Congress
LEGCO	Legislative Council (Colonial Africa)
NAACP	National Association for the Advancement of Colored People
NALC	Negro American Labor Council
NCNW	National Council of Negro Women
NDP	National Democratic Party (Southern Rhodesia)
NED	National Endowment for Democracy
NLRB	National Labor Relations Board
NTUC	Nigerian Trade Union Congress
NUTA	National Union of Tanganyikan Workers
OATUU	Organization of African Trade Union Unity
OAU	Organization of African Unity
PAC	Pan-Africanist Congress
SCLC	Southern Christian Leadership Conference
SNCC	Student Nonviolent Coordinating Committee
SRATUC	Southern Rhodesia African Trade Union Congress
SRTGWU	Southern Rhodesian Textile and Garment Workers Union
SRTUC	Southern Rhodesia Trade Union Congress
TANU	Tanganyika African National Union
TEKSIF	Turkish Textile and Garment Workers Union
TFL	Tanganyika Federation of Labor
TUCN	Trade Union Congress of Nigeria
TUCSA	Trade Union Council of South Africa
Turk-Is	Confederation of Turkish Trade Unions
UAR	United Arab Republic
UAW	United Auto Workers
UN	United Nations
UNIA	Universal Negro Improvement Association
ULC	United Labor Congress (Nigeria)
USIA	United States Information Agency
WFTU	World Federation of Trade Unions
ZACU	Zimbabwe African Congress of Unions
ZANU	Zimbabwe African National Union
ZAPU	Zimbabwe African People's Union

A CHRONOLOGY

of Maida Springer-Kemp's Life

1910	(May 12) Birth in Panama
1917	(August 4) Immigration to New York City
1917	Attended St. Marks School
1918	Attended Public School 90
1923–1926	Attended Bordentown Manual Training and Industrial School for Colored Youth, Bordentown, N.J.
1926	Attended night school in New York
1927	Worked as receptionist at Poro School
1927	Married Owen Winston Springer
1929	Birth of Eric Springer
1929–1930	Lived in East Orange, New Jersey
1932	Began work in the garment industry
1933	(May) Joined the ILGWU Local 22
1935–1936	Participated in a variety of training classes
1937–1939	Represented union in union and community work
1936	Member of Committee on Prices, Local 22
1938–1942	Executive Board Member, Local 22
1940	Chair of Education Committee, Local 22
1942	Trained as first-aid teacher, ILGWU
1942	American Labor Party candidate for New York State's 21st Assembly District (Harlem)
1942–1944	Captain of Women's Health Brigade (ILGWU)
1943–1945	Educational Director, Local 132
1944	Member of the War Price and Rationing Board of the Office of Price Administration
1945	Labor exchange delegate to England
1945–1948	Staff member of the Joint Board of Dress and Waistmakers Union, ILGWU (in Complaint Department in 1945)
1946	(February 28) Executive director of Madison Square Garden Rally for a Permanent FEPC
1948–1959	Business Agent for Local 22

1950	(January 16) Local 22 representative in the NAACP delegation to the Washington, D.C., Civil Rights Conference
1951	(August–September) Studied workers' education in Sweden and Denmark
1951–1952	Urban League Fellow, Ruskin College, Cambridge University, England
1952	Observed labor conditions in France and Italy
1953	Local 22 delegate to the 49th annual convention of the NAACP
1954	Trade Union Committee member of the New York branch of the NAACP 1954 Fight for Freedom Campaign
1955	Divorced from Owen Springer
1955	(October–November) AFL observer to the ICFTU International Seminar, Accra, Ghana
1956	Among the prime coordinators of Madison Square Garden rally honoring heroes of civil rights
1957	(January 14–18) Observer at the first ICFTU African Regional Conference, Accra, Ghana
1957	(January–February) Visited East Africa at the invitation of the KFL and TFL, and visited the Belgian Congo
1957	(March 6) Attended independence celebration in Ghana
1957–1958	(October 18–January 29) Based in Tanganyika for the American Trade Union Scholarship Program for Africa
1958	(December 8–13) Attended All-African People's Conference, Accra
1958–1959	(December and January) Observed trade schools in Israel
1959	Ill for eight months and unable to work
1960–1966	(January 21) International representative for Africa, AFL-CIO International Affairs Department
1960	Attended independence celebration of Nigeria
1961	Attended independence celebration of Tanganyika
1963	Attended independence celebration of Kenya
1964	Advisor to the U.S. Worker Delegate at the 48th session of the ILO Special Commission of Women Workers in a Changing World
1965	(January 27–30) Advisor to the Liberian CIO at the First National Industrial Relations Conference
1965	Attended independence celebration of Gambia
1965	(April 29) Married James Horace Kemp
1965–1969	General organizer for the ILGWU, Southeast Region
1969–1973	Midwest director of the A. Philip Randolph Institute
1970–1974	Vice President of the NCNW

1973	Consultant to African American Labor History Center
1973–1976	Staff member of the AALC
1975	Attended world conference on the United Nations Decade for Women, Mexico City
1977–1981	Consultant for the AALC
1977–1981	Consultant for the AAFLI
1977	(November 18–21) Observer at National Women's Conference, "American Women on the Move," Houston, Texas
1977	Member of the South African Task Force of the NAACP Task Force in Africa
1977	(July 17–27) Co-coordinator of the Pan-African Conference on the Role of Trade Union Women: Problems, Prospects and Programs, Nairobi, Kenya
1980	AALC Trip to South Africa with Lester Trachtman
1985	(July 15–26) Attended World Conference on the United Nations Decade for Women, Nairobi, Kenya

AWARDS

Women of the Year Award, National Council of Negro Women

Trumpeter Award, National Consumer League, Washington, D.C.

Ad Hoc Labor Committee Award, National Council of Negro Women

Candace Award, National Coalition of 100 Black Women, New York

Bessie Abromowitz Hillman Award, Coalition of Labor Union Women, Metropolitan St. Louis Chapter

Afro-American Women Sojourner Truth Award, Coalition for Afro-American History Month, Salute, Pittsburgh

First Annual Rosina Tucker Award, A. Philip Randolph Institute, New Orleans

Featured in Women of Courage/East Photographic Exhibition, developed by the Schlesinger Library, Radcliffe College

Women's Rights Award of the American Federation of Teachers

Doctor of Humane Letters honorary degree, Brooklyn College of the City University of New York

Maida Springer-Kemp Collection on Women and Labor, Wright Library, La Roche College, Pittsburgh, Pa.

MEMBERSHIPS

(Past and Present)

Board member of the Neighborhood Day Nursery in New York
Trustee and member of the International Affairs Committee of the New York
    Urban League
Harlem Defense Recreational Center
A. Philip Randolph Institute
National Council of Negro Women
National Association for the Advancement of Colored People
YWCA
National Organization for Women
Coalition of Labor Union Women
Aurora Reading Club
Pittsburgh Urban League
Greater Pittsburgh Commission for Women

Introduction

I FIRST LEARNED OF MAIDA SPRINGER IN 1985, WHEN I saw a postcard showing a picture of her that had been taken in Timbuktu, Mali, in 1974.[1] Microphone in hand and wearing African garments, Springer was speaking about the massive drought in the Sahel. She was in Mali as a member of the African American Labor Center (AALC), one of the international auxiliaries of the American Federation of Labor–Congress of Industrial Organizations (AFL-CIO).[2] An avid student of African American history, I was astonished to discover this woman, a pioneer domestic and international labor activist, whom I had never heard of. Then, in 1987, I came across more information on Springer through Pauli Murray's posthumously published autobiography, *Song in a Weary Throat*, which she dedicated to Springer. I also discovered a collection of Springer's papers at the Schlesinger Library at Radcliffe College and the transcript of an interview of her conducted by the Black Women's Oral History Project.[3] Researching Springer's work with the International Ladies' Garment Workers' Union (ILGWU) and with the AFL-CIO in Africa suggested how many aspects of African American history have yet to be recorded.

I decided to contact Springer to learn more about her career in the international labor movement, and she graciously invited me to her Pittsburgh home for a weekend. After we spent a couple of hours reviewing the events in her life, she asked what I wanted of her. I explained my desire to write a dissertation on her career that would include oral-history segments. She replied that others had also asked for her help in writing her biography, but she was not interested. Accepting her explanation with some disappointment, I nevertheless insisted that she must at some point record the important history of her life's work. Later I learned that a number of labor and civil rights activists, including Pauli Murray, Caroline Ware, Julius Nyerere, and James Farmer, had similarly encouraged her to record her unique experiences. In 1973 Springer herself had launched an oral-history project to record the experiences of African labor leaders. Although the African American Labor History Center, formed to carry out this work, had the support of a wide range of renowned scholars and was under the aegis of the AALC, the project failed to obtain sufficient funding to carry out its work.

Springer responded that she was aware of the significance of her career to different histories. Then she looked at me and on the spot decided to collaborate with me on the dissertation. I had not expected her to change her mind, but I was pleased and honored that she had. Springer explained that others who had approached her had come with preconceived ideas about the roles she played, but she believed I would be fair.

At that time I knew little of the international Cold War struggle in the labor movement. Although I knew something about many of the people of African descent with whom Springer was connected, I knew nothing of the controversies surrounding white labor leaders like Charles Zimmerman, Jay Lovestone, and Irving Brown. I was also unfamiliar with the two rival world labor bodies, the non-Communist International Confederation of Free Trade Unions (ICFTU) and the Communist-run World Federation of Trade Unions (WFTU). During my preliminary research, I was surprised to discover that a fellow graduate student had heard of Springer's work. My reaction turned to shock when he asserted that she had been involved in international espionage activities designed to weaken and split African labor. This allegation was in complete contrast with what I knew about Springer from her collection of papers and other archival materials. I had read numerous letters from African labor and nationalist leaders expressing their complete trust and affection for her. Moreover, U.S. labor and government officials had made similar comments about Springer's influence. For example, Dan Lazorchick, who traveled to Africa in 1960 for the U.S. Department of Labor's Division of International Trade Union Organizations, remarked that his reception among Africans was greatly enhanced because of his connection to Springer.

I began to realize the extent to which the Cold War raged strong in scholarship about the AFL-CIO's role in Africa and elsewhere. By the time I had completed my research I knew how utterly inadequate much of this scholarship was in assessing international labor relations from the standpoint of African American labor leaders and the Africans with whom they worked. The African labor movements, particularly those in the British colonies, counted Springer, George McCray, and A. Philip Randolph as vital allies in the effort to advance their interests internationally. Randolph, who was Springer's lifelong mentor, encouraged her ascent in the ranks of labor's leadership, used her organizational and promotional skills in domestic civil rights activism, and, as a vice president of the AFL-CIO, supported her Africa programs.

My research and interactions with Springer have given me no reason to doubt that she has provided truthful portrayals of her experiences as she sees them. She does not claim to be objective, and I agree that complete objectivity is elusive. In this study, I have instead strived for balance by giving serious attention to all of the information I have gathered. In writing about the AFL-CIO's controversial foreign policy and Springer's role with respect to it, I have attempted to blend her assessment of events, historical documentation, and criticisms of the AFL-CIO's policies and practices into a cohesive yet multifaceted story.

At no time has Springer attempted to impose her views on me. For example, while she responded to criticisms of the AFL-CIO's role in Africa, she also suggested that I draw my own conclusions. She placed only two limitations on my writing. First, we agreed that this biography would focus on her public and not her private life. Springer is protective not so much of her own privacy as of that of her family. Still, she has provided evocative portraits of some family members. Second, after I had come across letters in her home revealing that a small number of African and U.S. labor leaders had acted in dishonest and self-serving ways at her expense, she requested that I not use this material. She did not want to appear vengeful or bitter; nor did she think her detractors deserved the attention. Moreover, she seemed not to want these negative incidents to overshadow some of the more positive aspects of her work with labor nor to serve the purposes of those whom she views as having a vendetta against labor without an attendant interest in building a more equitable labor movement. When controversial material of this kind was available in public archives, I have addressed these issues.

A unique feature of this biography is that it connects pan-Africanism, national and international labor relations, the Cold War, and African American, labor, women's, and civil rights history. In addition to documenting Springer's role in international labor relations, the biography examines a wide range of social movements and political leaders. Its principal goal is to understand Springer's role as a black woman working in the white male–dominated fields of the U.S. labor movement and international affairs and within the context of the Cold War. It addresses four major questions. First is what impact Springer's race, gender, nationality, and AFL affiliation had on her experiences within the American labor movement and how these factors influenced her relationships with African labor leaders, ICFTU leaders, and colonial government officials. Second is how her activism in Africa changes our understanding of the conflicts over international labor policy within the AFL-CIO and between the AFL-CIO and the British Trades Union Congress (TUC). The third question concerns Springer's role in the fiercely contested pan-African labor struggles over the nonalignment issue and the nation-building policies of independent African nations. Finally, the fourth question has to do with the way Springer negotiated her work within the ideological and structural parameters of the AFL-CIO's foreign policy.

Although Springer has begun to receive attention from scholars, no one has yet documented and analyzed the role of African American labor leaders in Africa during the Cold War and the various independence movements.[4] Pan-African scholarship and scholarship concerning the response of African Americans to U.S. foreign policy recognizes the vital role African labor played in anti-colonial struggles; less understood, however, are the ways in which the strong ties between African American labor leaders and African labor and independence leaders contributed to the independence struggles, the formation of AFL-CIO policy, and the development of stronger labor unions.[5] African labor scholarship also has largely ignored the tremendous influence African American labor leaders had in forging links between Africa and the West and the role that their strong professional and personal ties played in shaping the pan-African labor debate over the volatile issue of affiliation to non-African labor internationals.[6] Scholarship concerning AFL-CIO foreign policy has tended to concentrate on its role in Europe or the Americas.[7] Those scholars who have given some attention to Africa, including strong critics of AFL-CIO Cold War policies, have drawn little attention to the influence that blacks, both in the United States and in Africa, had on the direction, scope, and formation of AFL-CIO and ICFTU foreign policy.[8]

Springer's testimony and the wealth of papers concerning her career and the work of her colleagues open up a new arena of African American history and help to reshape the history of AFL-CIO activism in Africa. The paucity of information about Springer in labor, pan-African, and women's histories is largely due to the dearth of scholarship on the activities of the AFL-CIO in Africa; secondary factors are androcentrism in scholarship and Springer's own diffidence in promoting her achievements.[9] Her story demonstrates interconnections between the struggles for African liberation and the U.S. civil rights movement.

Scholars have noted that World War II, by opening up national boundaries, allowed for the domestic race question to be linked with international issues of colonialism. Brenda Gayle Plummer and Penny M. Von Eschen are among those who argue that the repression of the Cold War contributed to a general decline in anticolonial activism in the United States at the same time that opportunities for furthering the domestic civil rights agenda emerged.[10] Indeed the statements of Randolph and Springer during this period reflect the general optimism regarding progress in civil rights. Speaking before workers in Morogoro, Tanganyika, in 1958, Springer remarked, "Prejudice is a disease which my country has not been cured of entirely but Negroes and whites alike in my country are determined to rid ourselves of this cancer. It is easier said than done. But the progress we have made in the last 20 years while not compelling at least gives room for hope."[11]

Some American blacks were beginning to break through barriers to employment in the professions and other job categories. Legal supports for segregation in housing, transportation, eating establishments, hotels, and public education were gradually dropping. The negative effects of segregation on the world's perception of American democracy and the exploitation of the issue by the Soviets also served as a powerful stimulus for change.[12]

Penny Von Eschen's contention, however, that Randolph was among those African American leaders who began to emphasize their Americanness as a way of distancing themselves from Africa is inconsistent with his reputation as a staunch defender of African labor and nationalist movements. Both Springer and Randolph had a vital concern with Africa at a time when most African Americans were reluctant to identify with the continent because of the deprecation of all things African in U.S. culture. In 1952 Randolph called for the creation of a "world congress of Negro workers" that would fight both colonialism and communism. Scheduled to speak before workers in New Delhi and Burma in 1953, Randolph expressed a longing also to visit Africa, "where the workers are stirring in their struggle for status, freedom and dignity."[13] At the fifth ICFTU World Congress, held in Tunis in 1957, Randolph delivered a strongly worded anticolonial speech that validated the views of Africans present. In a letter written a few months later to the British TUC complaining about British labor representatives, the Ghana TUC quoted extensively from his speech.[14] As an AFL-CIO vice president, Randolph had the requisite stature to get the concerns of Africans a hearing before an international whose policies the AFL-CIO was attempting to align more with the concerns of African labor and anticolonial movements as well as with the concerns of U.S. labor in fighting communism.

Springer, Randolph, and McCray tried to manipulate the Cold War in service to African liberation. Yet the wholesale expulsion of Communists who played leading roles in organizing blacks into CIO unions and in fighting union discrimination contributed to an environment less receptive to black advances. Springer understood how the Communist Party (CP) could be a source of inspiration and comfort for African Americans such as Paul Robeson, W.E.B. Du

Bois, and CP leader Benjamin Davis. Her dilemma was to reconcile her disapproval of the curtailment of civil liberties and the persecution of black radicals with her distrust of the Communist Party.

In a 1953 discussion of Du Bois's book *The World and Africa*, Randolph voiced his concern about how the repressive climate of Cold War America wreaked havoc on struggles for equality and punished those who showed any pro-Communist views. He thought that Du Bois, whom he characterized as the "most competent person living to write an authentic book on Africa," might be "likely to slant this book in such a manner as to run into many difficulties from anti-Communist forces. I hope he doesn't. . . . In the present climate of the free world, even though a book might be well written and authentic in terms of facts, if it is weighted or oriented from the point of view of opinion in favor of the Communist world, it is doomed to a bad reception." Randolph's remark that Communists, if given the "slightest opportunity . . . would seek to capitalize on the great scholarship of Du Bois" demonstrated his own deep distrust of Communists. Yet he refrained from making statements about the political orientation of Du Bois, whose book he had not yet read, or of anyone else unless he knew them to be true. "Unfortunately, that is the trouble with many of the people who have become hysterical over Communists and Communism. They are ready to brand everybody as a Communist who is militant and stands up and fights for civil rights or any other kind of right."[15]

During Springer's own work in Africa, colonial sympathizers sometimes labeled her a Communist. Interestingly, the FBI kept a file on her from 1957 until 1970, when the New York office decided that a certain document indicated "in part" that she had an "anti-Communist philosophy" and her files revealed no "subversive activities."[16] Du Bois would eventually join the CP and move to Ghana in 1961. Springer and Randolph, however, were among those who viewed the system of Communist rule as oppressive and unlikely to foster a lasting liberation of black people. As bad as the case of human rights was in the "free world," Randolph held that they were completely dismissed in Communist countries.[17]

Former AALC deputy director David Brombart has stated that Springer and McCray were "too advanced in their thinking." They faced great difficulties in getting their programs and ideas a hearing in the labor movement because they were perceived as too radical. They wanted white labor leaders to denounce Western allies for colonialism as vociferously as they did the Soviet Union for communism. Ironically, they counted Jay Lovestone, a former Communist leader turned Cold Warrior, as their ally. McCray relied on Lovestone, who was a primary architect of the AFL-CIO's Cold War policy, to let him know how AFL-CIO leaders received his African reports. "One false move on my part," he averred, "and my stuff will end in the waste basket."[18]

Springer admired and respected Lovestone in part because she believed him to be honest in his dealings with her and not one who held a double standard regarding African and white Western labor movements. He was one of the few white labor figures who in the late 1940s took seriously her talk about the will of Africans to liberate themselves. She also appreciated small efforts he made on her behalf. For example, after she mentioned her desire to have Kenyan labor leader Tom Mboya meet with a group of ILGWU educational directors during his first U.S. visit in 1956, Lovestone made it possible for a luncheon to be held. In many other instances Springer entertained and hosted Africans at her own expense. In a rare interview given in 1978, Lovestone remarked that Springer had not "been given enough credit" for her work among African trade unionists. "She had a sound idea long before we had auxiliaries [the AFL-CIO international institutions]. . . . Her idea—I'll put it in my own language—it's one thing fellows hungry are given some fish and to eat and be satisfied. It's another thing to teach him how to be a fisherman. And she, without expressing it in that form, sensed that."[19]

Springer noted that Lovestone never tried to make her a Cold Warrior. In his disagreements with her and McCray over the AFL-CIO's concentration on communism in African policy, he was characteristically blunt but also respectful, a quality he did not show many who disagreed with him. Clearly, he otherwise valued their activism.

Randolph too considered Lovestone an ally in the cause of African liberation. He had first known Lovestone as a Communist leader. In early 1931 they were both scheduled as speakers in a roundtable discussion on unemployment at Abyssinian Baptist Church in Harlem.[20] In an interview with Springer, Randolph recalled Lovestone's street activism: "Street meetings represented one of our most effective educational agencies at that time, and I may say that our participants were not altogether black. We had some young white radicals who shared the soapbox with us in carrying the message and the fight against imperialism in Africa. . . . Jay Lovestone was a brilliant mind, and has a long record of struggle and propaganda for labor in general and world socialism in particular."[21]

In contrast, various labor leaders and historians have excoriated Lovestone along with Irving Brown and AFL-CIO president George Meany as virulent anti-Communist ideologues with connections to the Central Intelligence Agency (CIA). CIO leaders Walter and Victor Reuther helped to foster allegations of CIA involvement. There existed between them and Lovestone a mutual personal and professional hatred. When former CIA official Thomas Braden publicly upbraided the Reuthers for hypocrisy, Victor admitted with qualifications that he had received CIA money for the CIO's international activities in postwar Europe. Ironically, since CIO leaders were noted for their comparatively progressive stance in civil rights and foreign affairs, their opposition to Lovestone led them to support the policies of international labor leaders whom Africans viewed as having vested interests in maintaining colonialism.[22]

Although Meany and Lovestone always vociferously denied charges of CIA involvement, they did through the operations of the AFL's Free Trade Union Committee (FTUC) receive CIA funding.[23] In response to the FTUC's willingness to take money but not direction from the agency, the CIA reduced FTUC funding and diversified its labor contacts. Lovestone, however, maintained a long-standing personal and professional relationship with Jim Angleton, a CIA counterintelligence officer. Serving as field representative for the AFL and later the AFL-CIO from 1945 to 1962, Brown was instrumental in fighting Communist unions in Europe and helping to organize the anti-Communist Force Ouvrière (Worker's Force) in France. However, by the late 1950s he was spending increasing amounts of time in Africa.[24]

Unlike the case of postwar Europe, allegations of CIA involvement have not been as fully documented in the AFL-CIO's work in Africa. Such suspicions, in the context of Cold War antagonisms and power struggles, have nevertheless touched many labor leaders involved in international affairs. Based upon assertions made by the People's News Service in 1978, Barry Cohen alleged that Springer served as the CIA contact officer for Tom Mboya. Springer, who considered Mboya as her second son, retorted that the only truth to the charge was in the spelling of her and Mboya's names.[25] She also commented on the impossibility of disproving such allegations. However, the available documentation does not demonstrate that she had easy access to financial support for the programs and projects African labor leaders requested of her. She lobbied not only the AFL-CIO and its affiliates for financial and material support but nonlabor organizations as well.

Moreover, documentation shows that Brown and McCray were the principal figures lobbying the AFL-CIO for financial support of Mboya. In urging support Brown once stated, "Of course, this must be done very discreetly since he is subject to all sorts of attacks from both the colonial crowds and the Communists as being too friendly to the USA."[26] Brown distributed some of the funding Mboya eventually received for both union and political work.[27] The ultimate source and amount of some of these funds and the uses to which they were put are legitimate points of inquiry; however, the AFL-CIO at least by 1961 charged Brown with making funding decisions regarding African projects. He also recommended African projects for the ICFTU.

Allegations of CIA involvement could have far-reaching consequences. It cast other shadows over the work of Brown and Mboya. For example, two years after Mboya's assassination in 1969, his widow, Pamela Mboya, wrote Brown to

say their names had been implicated in a trial of twelve people accused of plot-
ting to overthrow the Kenyan government. Acknowledging that these allegations
would come as a "great shock and embarrassment" to him, she asked Brown for a
letter she had earlier written to him that would help "clear my name in this very
sorry affair."[28] The complete story of Mboya's assassination, including the possibility that Kenyan government officials plotted his death, has yet to be revealed.

Investigating the relationship between AFL-CIO leaders and the CIA is important in assessing their characters and the extent to which their actions undermined the U.S. and other labor movements in exchange for Cold War gains.
Current scholarship, however, which essentially dismisses AFL-CIO activism in
Africa as interventionist and in collusion with the CIA, fosters a narrow reading
of international labor relations during the Cold War. An examination of the relations between African and African American labor leaders and with white labor
leaders is essential for developing a more complex view of international labor relations.

Documents pertaining to the experiences of Springer, Randolph, and Mc-
Cray provide an alternative view of international labor relations and of the motives of Africans like Tom Mboya. Mboya remains a deeply controversial figure.
Colonialists considered him arrogant and resented his ability to focus the attention of the West on settler-held East Africa. He was respected by many Africans
but also despised because of his skill in outmaneuvering opponents and his tendency to act alone.[29]

Responding to Mboya's 1956 appeal, the AFL-CIO contributed a grant of
thirty-five thousand dollars toward the building of a headquarters for the Kenya
Federation of Labor (KFL), eventually called Solidarity House. Mboya biographer David Goldsworthy has suggested that the location of Solidarity House—on
the outskirts of town and in the African section, rather than in Nairobi's business
center—was self-serving for Mboya since Africans would be reminded in their
daily passings of what he had accomplished for African labor. Whether or not
this location served Mboya's political ambitions, documentary evidence shows
that the principal determinants of the building site were the colonial government's restrictions and the union's financial limitations. Even if the KFL could
have afforded and had desired a building in the center of Nairobi, it is doubtful
that the government would have allowed it there. A sign of white hostility to
Africans in the area at that time was the refusal of the Stanley Hotel to admit
Arthur Ochwada, KFL deputy general secretary, for an appointment with Randolph, who was staying there.[30]

Goldsworthy also suggests that, with respect to the financing of Solidarity
House and other matters, Mboya saw benefit in playing the Western labor organizations against each other. Motivated by Cold War concerns, he remarks, the

AFL-CIO leaders viewed their Solidarity House grant as a way to establish independent influence in Kenya. Springer's and Randolph's documents again provide an alternate view. Randolph's statements demonstrate that his assistance to the KFL was not part of the AFL-CIO's competition with the ICFTU to influence African labor. Indeed, he advised the KFL on how they might induce the ICFTU and its affiliates to give aid by offering to name rooms in Solidarity House in their honor. Springer also did not seek to compete with the ICFTU. She constantly hoped for more ICFTU participation in Africa, provided it came without paternalism and condescension.[31]

Disappointed in the ICFTU's continuing poor record in Africa and motivated by the appeals of numerous Africans, Springer and Randolph were largely responsible for the AFL-CIO's decision in 1957 to sponsor a scholarship program for Africans to study in the United States. Some accounts of the conflicts surrounding this program are narrow and misinformed. Incorrectly identifying the scholarship program as the Americans' "own independent Africa labour centre," Don Thomson and Rodney Larson hold that it competed with the ICFTU's plan to build an African labor school. However, as the documentation of Springer, Randolph, and McCray illustrates, the ICFTU's decision to build the labor school was based on persistent AFL-CIO pressure and came in exchange for the AFL-CIO's agreement to curtail its scholarship program and desist from bilateral projects with Africa. Neither Thomson and Larson nor Anthony Carew address the views of Africans who were desperate to preserve the scholarship program.[32]

Thomson and Larson also leave the impression that the British members of the ICFTU liked the idea of the AFL-CIO putting funds into the proposed school: "They accomplished more than even Geiger [the ICFTU's Swedish president] expected. The AFL-CIO plan to invest 50,000 dollars into the Africa labour centre was converted instead into a grant for the ICFTU scheme."[33] (Note that Thomson and Larson mistakenly identify the original beneficiary of the grant as the African labor center, when in actuality it was the scholarship program for Africa.) In a 1973 interview conducted by Springer, Randolph stated that the British opposed his lobbying the AFL-CIO for financial support of the proposed African labor school.[34]

Anthony Clayton and Donald C. Savage suggest that Tom Mboya supported Arthur Ochwada as a trainee in the scholarship program "to ensure that he would be out of the way." Ochwada was challenging Mboya for the leadership of the KFL, but whatever Mboya's motivation, Ochwada himself had lobbied Springer, Randolph, Lovestone, and Brown for a scholarship to the United States. Moreover, while on the scholarship program, he asked Mboya to see to it that his stay in the United States was extended. The labor centers had ultimate responsibility for choosing the candidate, and the KFL unanimously supported Ochwada.[35]

Barry Cohen's short account of AFL-CIO activities in Southern Rhodesia characterizes Springer and Brown's support of labor leader Reuben Jamela as underhanded and as serving to undermine the labor movement.[36] This portrait, however, is not consistent with much of the available evidence. Among those African leaders who eventually opposed Jamela and affiliation with the ICFTU were many who continued to seek AFL-CIO aid and had very friendly relations with both Springer and Brown.

Cohen remarked that Springer provided Jamela with the financial assistance to travel. Springer replied that she never gave Jamela as much as ten cents for his own use. What she had done, twice, was to send fifty dollars from the AFL-CIO for him to deliver to the detained labor leader Josiah Maluleke, who eventually opposed Jamela. Brown most likely was responsible for Jamela's travels. He wrote AFL-CIO international affairs director Michael Ross saying that he had "stuck his neck out" by inviting Jamela's trade union center to send a delegate to the third ICFTU African Regional Conference in Tunis that November 1960. The then-united leadership in the executive council chose Jamela. Brown would also advocate approaching foundations about providing aid to Southern Rhodesia and other English-speaking areas. He thought it a mistake for the United States to give the impression that Mboya was the only one who could win financial assistance.[37]

Springer years later commented on the conflicting assessments of AFL-CIO policy in Africa: "The ugly names I have been called, and harassment that I sometimes have been subjected to in pre-independence Africa, has been a small price to pay for the opportunity of having been an AFL-CIO Representative in Africa. Whatever the present policical intrepretations of the AFL-CIO in Africa may be, I can say without equivocation that I have never been asked to do anything by the AFL-CIO that was in conflict with the early stated aims of the African Trade Union Movement."[38]

The end of the Cold War affords scholars of pan-Africanism and labor the opportunity to move away from the simplistic polarities of communism and anticommunism in our understanding of the ILGWU and of the AFL-CIO's foreign policy in Africa. Springer's experiences provide one way to approach these histories from a fresh angle. By documenting the untold stories associated with her activism, this biography breaks new ground in the fields of pan-African studies and in African American and labor histories. It addresses the complex and controversial nature of Springer's activism by exploring the ways in which pan-Africanism, racism, and anticommunism affected her political development and her relationship with political and labor leaders in Africa, as well as with U.S. and European labor leaders. Although racism and sexism within organized labor created barriers to her obtaining institutional power, with the support of key leaders she pushed against those limitations and helped to garner support within the AFL-CIO for the agenda of African labor.

The U.S. labor movement's reputation in Africa was largely built on the work of Maida Springer, George McCray, and A. Philip Randolph. Although Springer's projects seldom won the immediate approval of European labor—indeed, often they were met with outright hostility—and although they also fell short of her own ambitions, as a pioneer she helped forge the early relationships between the AFL-CIO and African labor and also opened the door wider for those who followed her into international affairs.

1

"My Wonderful Young Mother"

Springer's Formative Years

B Y ALL ACCOUNTS ADINA STEWART'S SPARKLING personality was irresistible, and her culinary talents were legendary. Vivacious and engaging, she could hold the center of attention in any social setting. In contrast, young Maida was serious, sensitive, and shy. Noting her adult daughter's demure manner and penchant for subdued clothing, Stewart would say in jest that Maida did not have a "dash of paprika." However, Stewart did impart to her daughter important marks of her own personality and character. Both became renowned for their hospitality, generosity, commitment to struggle, and love for Africa.

The genesis of Stewart's strong feelings for Africa may have begun through her relationship with Nana Sterling, a midwife who functioned as a grandmother figure in her early life in Panama. According to the tales that were passed down to Springer, Nana Sterling had been captured into slavery as a young girl. Although Springer was too young to remember this woman, whom she considered her great-grandmother, Nana Sterling nevertheless made an imprint on her life. She delivered her into the world and was the source of the West African folktales that Stewart passed on to her.

Springer's formative years as an immigrant in Harlem helped hone her into a dedicated pan-Africanist and labor activist. Her childhood socialization included exposure to widespread racist discrimination and subjugation. Through her mother's influence she also entered the political world of New Negro radicals. A group of young activists, including Marcus Garvey, A. Philip Randolph, Chandler Owen, and Hubert Harrison, separated themselves from the black leaders whom they termed "Old Negroes." The New Negro demanded equal rights and social justice, while the Old Negro begged for consideration. The inspiring speeches of the New Negro radicals addressed the sufferings of blacks in the United States and globally.

Springer's youthful experiences were welded to a cultural and political life that affirmed black dignity and achievement and believed in the eventual triumph of the American ideal of equality. The existence of this oppositional culture in the midst of the dominant society's blatant racism points to some central dilemmas of black life. It also sheds light on Stewart's contradictory position as both a believer in the American ideal and an advocate of Garvey's Back to Africa movement. Pointing to the pride her mother had as a resident of the United States, Springer described her mother as a "real flag waver."[1] In her own later years, Springer confronted similar contradictions.

Early Family Life in Panama

Maida's life began on May 12, 1910, under inauspicious circumstances. She was born with her limbs folded tightly in upon her body, and her father reacted badly to the apparent deformities. After viewing the newborn, he threatened to harm his wife, whom he blamed for the condition. For a week Nana Sterling and Adina Stewart's mother, Eliza Anderson, continuously massaged the child's limbs until they unfolded properly.

Cultural differences between Harold and Adina Stewart were also a source of conflict between them. Harold, who had joined the largest Caribbean migration in history to work on the Panama Canal construction project, was from Barbados. Born and raised in Panama by parents who came there from the Caribbean, Adina identified as a Spanish-speaking Panamanian. As a Barbadian Harold believed in British cultural superiority, and he devalued the Panamanian culture of his wife, who was eleven years his junior. He even forbade her to speak Spanish in the house. His contempt for Latin culture might have received some support from British colonial teachings. British colonialists encouraged their subjects to view British culture as superior and promoted rivalry among the islands of the Caribbean. This strategy of divide and conquer was, as the historian Michael Conniff has observed, a preventative measure against the development of pan-Caribbean ties that might lead to anticolonial agitation.[2]

Eliza Anderson was born in Jamaica in 1870. Living in Panama since she was a child, she adopted Panamanian attitudes toward the Caribbean immigrant community that grew out of the canal construction project, first under the direction of France and later the United States. Describing her grandmother as a proud, aggressive, and fiercely independent woman, Springer recounted, "In the Spanish community, they called her Doña Luisa. In the West Indian community, Red Liza. To be derogatory, they called her Red Liza. She had big brown freckles and kind of copper-colored red skin from the sun."[3] According to the tales Springer's mother told, Doña Luisa was easily offended and was quick to seek recourse through the courts. Her aggressive and litigious nature made her a formidable opponent. Against her, a West Indian stood even less chance of receiving a fair hearing than a Panamanian. Doña Luisa's success in the courts was due to her peripheral relation to Panama's oligarchy. During her childhood she had been a servant companion to a child of one of the ruling families.[4]

The imperialist and racist rule of the U.S.-run Isthmian Canal Commission (ICC) helped to inform the intraracial hostility between black Panamanians and Caribbeans. Historian Walter LaFeber succinctly assessed the U.S. impact: "Panama's racial sensitivities needed no honing, but they were sharpened to a fine point by the Canal Zone's policies." Panamanian society recognized a variety of racial designations. Few Panamanians could legitimately claim sole Spanish descent, but those having a great degree of Spanish ancestry composed the small "white" oligarchy, whose families often intermarried. Blacks, on the bottom of the social hierarchy, were subdivided into the higher-status indigenous Spanish speakers and the lower-status Caribbean immigrants. The ICC upset this hierarchy by favoring Caribbean immigrants over black Panamanians for employment positions on the canal project.[5]

Regardless of nationality, however, virtually all blacks performed heavy, dirty, dangerous, unskilled labor and were paid according to the lower Panamanian silver standard. At the same time U.S. whites were favored for the highly skilled crafts and mechanical work and received wages based on the higher U.S. gold standard. Springer does not recall what her father did but remembers his wearing dress shirts and working at an office job. Although Stewart was among the 10 percent of the Caribbean labor force having white-collar positions, he like all blacks received less pay for the same work whites were doing.[6]

The wages, benefits, and privileges accorded to canal workers were overwhelmingly determined by race, although skill level and nationality also were factors. Deemed semiwhite, European workers from Spain, Italy, and Greece were put on the silver roll; but they were given higher wages than blacks for the same work and were allowed the "privilege" of racially separate mess halls and living quarters.[7]

The ICC's discriminatory practices, the extreme scarcity of food, and the exorbitant prices Panamanian grocers charged made food service for blacks precarious during both the French and American periods of canal construction. During Adina Stewart's childhood, Doña Luisa seized this opportunity to institute a profitable meal-service business. ICC actions between 1906 and 1912 to resolve the problem of access to food and also to monopolize meal service provisions could have ended Doña Luisa's business if it had been operating during this juncture. During these years the ICC opened a series of segregated mess halls and made mandatory deductions from paychecks for the cost of meals.[8]

Canal officials extended the Jim Crow system to cover all other aspects of life in the Canal Zone. In the separate school systems financed by the taxes of Caribbeans and Panamanians, white children were educated for college placement while black children received inferior educations intended to fit them for manual labor.[9] In the United States Maida would encounter directly the educational philosophies and structures that had been exported to Panama. In Panama her family had not resided in the Canal Zone.

A Caribbean friend of her father's prepared young Maida for the move to the United States by instructing her in basic math and by teaching her to read and write English.[10] Punishment was an integral part of the learning process. She recalled, "The training began with counting the braids on my head. If I missed one, I would get a crack on my knuckles with a ruler and my slow-wittedness would be reported to my father. I learned to read a little primer, and when I was slow in pronunciation or missed words, a dunce cap made of newspaper would be placed on my head and I would have to stand in a corner for a time. I think my mother was afraid of the West Indian teacher and would not intervene on my behalf."

Springer's sister Hélène, who was two and a half years younger, was a quick learner. Springer recalled Hélène as a precocious child who "walked early, talked early and intelligibly with a lisp which made her more adorable. She was very mischievous, and this only added to her charm. Hélène seldom played with children and only if she was the leader in whatever we were playing. Adults were her playmates and they loved to engage her fertile mind in conversation." In contrast to Hélène, Springer described herself as a "quiet, colorless, obedient child who would not fuss or fight unless provoked."

Springer noted that her grandmother, maternal Uncle Elisha, and godmother were the only ones who did not "succumb to [Hélène's] unusual personality"—that is, who did not let her have her way. Hélène's mischievousness, including soiling her fine clothes just before the family was to go out, only amused her father. Springer's grandmother and godmother, both accomplished seamstresses, made elegant clothes for her and her sister, which their father insisted they wear most of the time.

Tragically, Hélène's life was cut short by spinal meningitis a year and a half before the family immigrated to the United States. The words the three-year-old spoke the night of her death were the last sign of her adult ways: "Everybody got to die, somebody is going to die, and Hélène is going to die." Hélène's death was an irreparable loss to Harold Stewart, whose grief was the occasion for additional mistreatment of his family. Shortly after settling in Harlem, Adina and Harold ended their marriage. Although Adina faced a difficult time working and raising a child alone, the end of the marriage freed her and her daughter from a man who was often mean-spirited toward them. The pain her father caused influenced Springer to speak sparingly of him. In contrast Springer was very fond of Dalrymple Carrington, the stepfather she gained when her mother remarried in the early 1960s.

Springer recalled with awe and gratitude the struggle her mother waged as a single parent to raise her. They lived in Harlem during a turbulent period marked by post–World War I repression and Jim Crow segregationist practices. Despite Doña Luisa's concern for the hardships they might encounter in an unfamiliar land, Stewart had refused to leave her daughter with her in Panama until she could get settled.

First Impressions in a New Country: Harlem during World War I

Traveling to New York on the S.S. *Alianza*, the Stewart family joined an estimated 300,000 Caribbeans who immigrated to the United States between 1900 and 1930. The exodus from Panama was spurred by the declining job opportunities following the canal's completion, decreasing wages and rising costs, and Panamanian discrimination against Caribbeans.[11] Cultural considerations and perhaps prejudice against African ancestry played a role in the racial classification system employed on the ship's manifest. Under the category "Race or People" Maida was listed as "Spanish American," following the designation of her mother, while her father was designated as "African."[12]

Racial classifications, however, did not interfere with her family's relatively comfortable journey and the quick processing of their immigration papers when they reached Ellis Island on August 4, 1917. With pride Adina Stewart repeatedly told young Maida that they had been able to pay for their passage in full and consequently did not have to ride in steerage. In contrast, many of the Eastern Europeans who later became Springer's colleagues in the garment industry had horrific immigration experiences. Factors facilitating the Stewart family's entry into the United States included their facility with the English language as well as having proper documents and a sponsor. By using her skills of translation during their short stay at Ellis Island, Stewart helped less fortunate Spanish speakers, whose prospects for a quick resolution of their immigration problems were dim.[13]

Once they reached the mainland, however, the Stewarts' relative privilege was subsumed under a hierarchical racial classification system. Just as in the Canal Zone, foreign-born whites were not accorded equality with native-born whites, but they did have a higher status than all groups belonging to the African diaspora. Concerning the hostilities that developed out of the imposed hierarchy,

Springer commented, "We were all strangers. The black American, the black foreigner, and we did not like one another, and the white foreigner liked us less, and the white American hated all of us."[14]

In the 1920s one-fourth of the black population of Harlem was foreign born.[15] Hostility between African Americans and Caribbean blacks was at its worst during Springer's childhood years. Blacks divided along ethnic, color, and class lines as each group sought to distance itself from the pariah status to which American society consigned all blacks. Nevertheless, most had to struggle with high rents and food prices, poor education and health care, congested housing, and restriction to menial employment. As blacks from the American South, the Caribbean, and South and Central America continued to pour into Harlem after the war, Maida witnessed its change from a mixed-race community to a segregated, overcrowded, and neglected black community. Religious affiliation could serve as another means to separate the black community, both along class and ethnic lines. With humor Springer recalled that people made fun of the "high church" ways of many Caribbeans. The majority of Harlemites were Baptists and Methodists and regarded the services of the black immigrants, who were predominantly Episcopalian and Catholic, as staid, quiet, and reserved.[16]

Black church activities in general, however, could serve as a unifying force in the black communities by providing a forum for social and political commentary and artistic performance. In the Baptist church of her American friends Maida learned more about the rich heritage of African Americans. She was exposed to the accomplishments of George Washington Carver, the poetry of Countee Cullen, the voice of Marian Anderson, the voice and intellect of Paul Robeson, and the discourses of W.E.B. Du Bois.[17]

Maida's first connection with native-born blacks came through her friendship with next-door neighbor Dora Murray. The only blacks in their class at St. Marks Catholic School, the girls were placed together at a double desk and became best friends. Springer had fond memories of going to Dora's house on cold days and eating thick soup with chorice (spicy New Orleans beef or pork sausage) and crusty homemade bread. The Murrays, who were Louisiana Creoles, were responsible for socializing Maida into a pleasant side of American life. They introduced her to the circus, picnics, museums, and the library.[18]

One of Maida's experiences with the Murray family foreshadowed her later association with her mentor, A. Philip Randolph. Unaware of the import of their actions, Maida and Dora as ten-year-old children folded papers for Dora's father, who was a Pullman porter. Springer recalled that Murray would put the papers into one of his black work satchels. At the time they did not know that these papers had to do with the porters' early efforts at organizing. In order to avoid losing their jobs, the porters distributed these papers secretly as they traveled.

Joining forces with the Brotherhood of Sleeping Car Porters (BSCP) in 1925,

A. Philip Randolph headed the effort that eventually forced the Pullman Company to recognize the union. As a delegate from the dressmakers' Local 22 of the ILGWU, Springer marched with her young son, Eric, in the Brotherhood parade celebrating the 1937 contract victory. When as an adult activist she stopped by the Brotherhood offices, "Pops Murray," as she called him, took pride in her association with Randolph and repeated this story from her childhood. He would conclude, "Now this little ole Maida is a big union lady going to talk to the Chief" (Randolph).[19]

Stewart also had friends who introduced her to American culture, including the blues. Secretly listening to her mother's collection of records, Maida imagined herself becoming a blues singer while she sang along with great artists such as Bessie Smith. World War I, which the United States had entered four months before her family immigrated, was a subject of one of the songs she recalled entitled "Those Draftin' Blues." This song perhaps echoed a section of the black community's response to the war. For the women left behind, honor and patriotism hold sway, even though there is no enthusiasm for the war.

> When Uncle Sam calls out your man
> Don't cry, don't sigh, 'cause you know
> You're gonna lose,
> To hold him back, will make him slack
> Just say you've got
> Those draftin' blues.[20]

Maida witnessed the effects of the war on her Harlem community. In the years before strict segregation had congealed, her neighborhood was a diverse immigrant community in which the small store owners were predominantly European immigrants. Along with a live chicken market, a general grocery store, and a drugstore owned by Jews, and a bakery and florist shop owned by Italians was a pork store owned by a German, which was a favorite of Maida's. She fondly remembered the aroma of spices used to make pickles, sausages, head cheese, smoked meat, and sauerkraut. The owner would give the children of regular customers a sample of wurst and German potato salad. A rising anti-German prejudice, however, led many people to stop their patronage of German stores. Consequently a number of these businesses left the neighborhood. The "general consensus," Springer recalled, "was that Germans were very bad people."[21]

At St. Marks Maida and the other children supported the war effort by knitting woolen socks for "our brave soldiers over there." She was in school on November 11, 1918, when Sister Magellan announced to the class that the war had ended; in celebration school was dismissed. Maida then joined other children and adults who danced and marched in one of the impromptu parades that took place all over the city. She reported on the celebration and her mother's response to her participation:

> We were fed and loved as though we were one big happy family. I ended up far away from my familiar surroundings, but kindly adults directed me and other children back to our home areas. I arrived home dirty, bedraggled, and smelling like a chimney, the result of impromptu food vendors who set up shop along the line of march with kerosene stoves and coal posts. Adults bought delicious half cooked food for the children and we just kept eating. As I neared my house, I could see my mother weeping on the stoop of the building. She had just returned from the police station after reporting me missing. When she saw me, her anxiety and tears disappeared and she promised to give me the worst spanking I had ever had. A neighbor intervened and suggested that this was a time for forgiveness and prayers. My mother just hugged me as we walked up six floors to our apartment.[22]

As a politically active person, Stewart surely was aware of the debates in the black community concerning the war. With her daughter in hand, she proudly marched with the Black Cross Nurse contingent in the parades of Marcus Garvey's Universal Negro Improvement Association (UNIA). Attending Sunday meetings in the UNIA's Liberty Hall, she cheered the calls for African liberation made by UNIA speakers.

Just as their Panamanian home had been a gathering place for performing calypsos and playing instruments, their Harlem home was frequented by people who were active in the political life of the soapbox circuit and in the UNIA. As well as engaging in entertainment, they read to each other stories of black struggle and triumphs printed in black newspapers. African students, mostly Nigerians, spent summers as boarders with them. To young Maida's dismay, one named Said Ibrahim, who thought her youthful play was a frivolous waste of time, spoke to Stewart about her studying higher mathematics. Herbert Julian, a flamboyant aviator and an officer in the UNIA, also had plans for her. Jokingly, he suggested that Maida prepare herself to become the first black female aviator. As part of its program to build an independent African nation, the UNIA formed the Black Eagle Flying Corps.[23] Hearing visitors in her home and political figures in the UNIA and in the streets speak with bitterness about being treated as less than human left an indelible mark on young Maida.

Springer recalled that A. Philip Randolph and Frank Crosswaith were known as silver-tongued orators. Richard Parrish, a member of the American Federation of Teachers, reported that Crosswaith, known for wearing a fresh red rose in his lapel and carrying a box of raisins in his pocket, was called the "black Gene Debs," and that only Randolph and Garvey were in his league. Randolph also praised Crosswaith's speaking ability: "He had evident sincerity. When he spoke to an audience, he captured an audience—not only by his diction, his knowledge, and so forth, but by his dedication to the cause of Socialism and the struggle for Negro rights. I don't think there was anyone who [had] a higher record than he. . . . He was priceless, because he was one of the best speakers we had. The best orator, not only in the union, but one of the best orators in the country."[24] Randolph remarked that soapbox speakers covered a wide variety of subjects ranging from the "French Revolution, the history of slavery, to the rise of the working class." Orators also participated in organizing tenants' leagues, publishing Marxist and socialist journals, and speaking out against black participation in the war.[25]

Asserting that the German threat was a more formidable barrier than U.S. racism to the aspirations of blacks for freedom, equality, and democracy, Du Bois had urged blacks to join the war effort by "closing ranks" with whites and "forgetting their special grievances" for as long as the war lasted. In reaction, the New Negro accused Du Bois of being a sellout. As strident critics of lynchings, which were routine and frequent in this period, Randolph and Owen played upon the war slogan "make the world safe for democracy" to highlight the huge gap between American ideals and practice. Their opposition to the war and their assertions that they would prefer to "make Georgia safe for the Negro" and "make America unsafe for hypocrisy" caught the attention of public officials. The Lusk committee, appointed by the New York State legislature to investigate radicalism and sedition, branded Randolph "the most dangerous Negro in America."[26]

Black leaders' bitter denunciations of white America for its continued denial of equal opportunity and equal protection for people of African descent resulted in continued government surveillance following the war. Coinciding with increased repression of political dissent and labor demands in this period of the Red Scare and the Palmer Raids were a series of race riots in what was coined the Red Summer of 1919. Race riots and lynchings, even of black soldiers in uniform, served as a reminder that the American dream did not apply to blacks. Disillusioned by the postwar repression, Du Bois called for blacks to defend themselves.[27]

Strong ideological divisions among black leaders, however, prevented the emergence of a united front against segregation, discrimination, and lynching. The greatest division eventually developed between Garvey and his African American and Caribbean critics, including Randolph, Owen, Crosswaith, Du Bois, George Padmore, and Cyril Briggs. Supporting liberal, socialist, or communist interracial organizations, these critics disagreed with Garvey's increasing emphasis on racial separatism and racial purity, his advocacy of a limited capitalism, and his rhetoric of empire building in Africa. Yet his critics had to acknowledge Garvey's tremendous success. The growth of the UNIA, the largest mass black organization of its kind, reflected the extreme pessimism of its followers concerning conditions in the United States, their commitment to African liberation, and their attraction to the philosophy of racial pride and cooperation.[28]

The UNIA not only imparted racial pride to Maida but also provided her with models of female activism. Of all the UNIA speakers she heard, Henrietta Vinton Davis most captivated her. Davis, who could hold an audience as well as Garvey, was one of the UNIA's original thirteen founding members, and she held the positions of international organizer, fourth assistant president-general, and eventually secretary general. As historian William Seraile indicates, Davis's close relationship with Garvey is important in assessing Garvey's view of color. George Padmore and others believed that Garvey's experience in the extremely color-conscious Jamaican society made him "[hate] mulattos even worse than he hated white people," and oppose lighter-complexioned blacks in leadership positions in the UNIA. Perhaps sexism led them to overlook Davis, who was characterized as an octoroon.[29]

Garvey did not hold blacks responsible for the miscegenation that took place during slavery, but he spoke out sharply against voluntary interracial unions of his day. His stance reflected more than personal prejudice. He was reacting to sexist and racist ideology that espoused white male possession and protection of white women as a symbol of civilization and success. Many whites believed that blacks in interracial political movements were only interested in social equality, and specifically in black male access to white women. Interracial marriages were widely outlawed at the time. Bitterly feuding with his rivals, Garvey helped to perpetuate the belief that blacks in interracial organizations merely hankered after the company of whites.[30]

Garvey's bitter feuds with other black leaders eventually led him to associate with white supremacists, whom he regarded as true representatives of white America, including those whites who were involved in interracial organizations.[31] This association became a divisive issue both within and outside the UNIA. Adina Stewart stopped being active in the UNIA during these struggles.

Although black leaders often attacked one another's politics, Springer recalled that the adults who congregated in her home had great respect for all those who spoke out against black oppression. Springer, like many others, admired their courage and commitment to changing the degraded status of blacks in spite of the obstacles arrayed against them. In her childhood and adulthood many of them would influence her development. The Garvey movement reinforced her strong identification with Africa and pride in her heritage. Du Bois's life represented to her a supreme example of intellectual achievement and commitment to race advancement. Padmore would introduce her to the pan-African movement that would end African colonialism. Randolph would vigorously support her work on behalf of African labor development and independence.

Subjugation under the U.S. Educational System

At St. Marks and in public schools, Maida contended with a curriculum that denied black achievement and in general deprecated Africans and people of color. Educational institutions actively discouraged blacks from pursuing higher education, and standard textbooks perpetuated views of black inferiority. When Maida first enrolled at St. Marks, her advanced educational level was somewhat overshadowed by student and teacher prejudices against her race and foreign status. She recalled the racist interpretations of history and culture that were taught: "In teaching geography, Sister pointed to the map and talked about Central America, particularly Panama. She said among other things, that there were gold mines and cannibals in Panama. [The cannibals] had pierced ears in which gold rings were inserted, gold around their necks, bangles on their hands, and a gold ring in their nostrils. The only thing missing when the children looked at me was a ring in my nose. No doubt, the children thought I wore the nose rings at home."[32]

Ethnocentrism and the cruelties of children partly explain why Maida lost the use of Spanish, her first language. Her fellow classmates made fun of her pronunciation and English-language syntax. Referring to her transposition of words and phrases, children teased her for talking "upside down." In response Maida made a conscious decision to refrain from speaking Spanish: "I regret that when I was a child, I just wouldn't speak Spanish, because in a new country you wanted to be what you were here. And in the United States, people looked down their noses at foreigners, and my God, a black foreigner to boot."[33]

Springer recalled that she "learned not to cry out in class, or to expect the nuns to take my part" when the children mistreated her. One of their torments was to jerk her bushy hair into their ink wells. She decided to fight back when a boy placed ink on her collar and called her a name. Maida responded by butting him in the head and making his nose bleed.[34] The next day the boy's father demanded to know the identity of the brutish child who had attacked his son for no reason. Although Maida was short and her adversary was tall and bulky, school officials ignored the boy's provocative behavior and threatened to expel her. To prevent this Adina Stewart apologized to the boy's father. Realizing that her daughter's attire marked her as different, she also stopped dressing Maida in brass-toed shoes, starched drawers and petticoats, and the beautiful pongee dresses that her grandmother and godmother had painstakingly stitched and embroidered.

After the St. Marks incident, Stewart, following the advice of American friends, transferred her daughter to a public school. In order to fit in with the African American children at P.S. 90, Maida in private began imitating their speech patterns. She recalled one day when "I was in the bathroom practicing and my mother wanted to know why I was talking to myself and sounding as if my nose was clogged. I did not try to explain that this was how I perceived the Negro American speech pattern."

But racist treatment continued at the new school, where an all-white staff taught a predominantly black student body. When a teacher named McNulty, whom Springer described as a young, very pretty, red-headed woman, tried to curb the self-esteem and race pride Stewart had instilled in her, Maida defended herself. After dismissing the children at the end of the class, McNulty called Maida to her desk to ask why she did not say "yes ma'am" or "no ma'am," as the other children did. Instead Maida would say "yes, Miss McNulty" and "no, Miss McNulty." McNulty evidently believed that this response did not show the proper deference a child, and particularly a black child, should have for a white teacher. Springer explained: "I told her that I was taught that yes and no was English and adding her name was polite. She called me a smart little nigger and slapped my face. Just the two of us were in the room by this time. I did not say a word but kicked her leg. I was not wearing my fighting shoes with the thick soles and brass-plated front, and the kick was a glancing one which did not soil her dress or leave a mark. But her authority had been challenged."

Arrogant in her racism and believing that Adina Stewart would uphold her authority, McNulty accompanied Maida home. Maida walked the teacher around for an hour before arriving home, fearing the reaction of her mother. Upon finally meeting Stewart, McNulty implied that she was doing her a favor by coming to her first. Since Maida's grades were good and she was never late and did not play hooky, McNulty concluded that she must have good parents, and therefore she had decided not to report her to the principal. Stewart then asked for her daughter's explanation. After listening to Maida without giving a clue as to which side she favored, she turned to McNulty and proceeded to berate her with one of her familiar threats: "Miss Teacher, you curse my child and hit her! If you ever come here with a complaint, I will eat you whole and leave your head and hair hanging out." The teacher promptly left the house, and Maida continued not to say ma'am or sir.

When educational counseling began in the sixth grade, school officials encouraged Maida to lower her aspirations. Often counselors advised black parents that after the eighth grade their children should seek employment or transfer to a vocational school. This type of "counseling" was an integral part of the education system for generations of black students. However, Springer's mother was outraged at the advice: "[S]he resented the fact that a counselor or the teacher would tell me that there was no way I could do whatever it was I wanted to do at the time. . . . So my mother went to school and chewed that lady up and down, never using a vulgar word. No, not being abusive. No. That's what people very often do when they're angry, curse and be very vulgar. Not my mother. She said,

'Miss Teacher, how do you know? How do you know?' Because I had all good marks."[35]

Stewart again resolved to find a new school for her daughter, one that did not "low rate Negroes." Friends recommended the Manual Training and Industrial School for Colored Youth, a boarding school in Bordentown, New Jersey, that was staffed by black teachers and funded primarily by the state. In Maida's first four years in the United States, she had never had a black teacher. Popularly known as Bordentown, the school catered to single parents like Adina Stewart, struggling to raise a child alone while working. Looking like a teenager herself at age twenty-eight, Stewart hoped that her five-feet-four-inch, eleven-year-old daughter could pass for thirteen, the minimum age required for enrollment. Minnie E. Davis, the matron of girls, was not fooled. Recognizing that Maida was most likely underage since upon questioning she had no knowledge of menstruation, Davis rejected her application.[36]

Maida interpreted her mother's attempt to place her in a boarding school as evidence that she was a burden. Not fully understanding her mother's concerns, she became dejected and remained so for many weeks. Maida's spirits had begun to revive when suddenly it was her turn to worry. Stewart abruptly lost her sight two days after Christmas, the result of a neurological ailment. Maida withdrew from school for a term in order to look after her. To entertain her mother, whom Springer described as an absolute romantic, she read serialized pulp-fiction love stories to her. Under a doctor's care, Stewart recovered.

Maida's happiness when her mother's sight returned was short-lived because Stewart soon revived plans to enroll her in Bordentown when she turned thirteen. When Maida arrived on the campus, however, she was so taken by the grounds and the teachers that she stopped resisting her mother. Principal William R. Valentine once wrote about the positive affects that the scenic campus had on the students.

> Four hundred acres of campus, field and woodland, beautiful modern buildings situated on a bluff overlooking the Delaware River, carefully tended lawns, with trim hedges and walks, all combine in a scene of singular beauty that has made Bordentown a loved gathering place for thousands of visitors annually. In the midst of this dwell 400 boys and girls for ten months of the year; therein lies the secret of much of the success which the school has had. Their surroundings alone produce an inspiration and a supporting influence difficult to achieve through any other means. Mention "Bordentown" to any graduate, and watch his glow of pride.[37]

At Bordentown Maida was no longer subjected to a curriculum that denied black achievement. However, the school was limited by its adherence to the so-called Tuskegee model. In fact, Bordentown was labeled the "Tuskegee of the North," and Booker T. Washington had a direct influence on the curriculum after he visited the school in 1913. He advised the state to survey the types of occupations blacks held in New Jersey and then implement and emphasize the training of those skills and trades within the school. Aware that blacks resented the industrial-education model, Washington suggested that "one ought to be careful not to give the people the impression that the academic or mental training is going to be discarded or pushed aside." He advised school administrators to "dovetail" academic training to fit within the industrial-training structure.[38]

Although some of Bordentown's graduates pursued higher education, the school made no pretense of preparing students for that path. Year after year the school's bulletin emphasized that Bordentown's primary concern was teaching trades and not "blindly" following the curriculum of a conventional high school. Bordentown did not even offer a high school degree. Its curriculum only covered grades six through ten. Students who were not interested in the vocational aspects of the curriculum were discouraged from attending.[39]

Nevertheless, the faculty realized that the job prospects for their graduates were dismal. Industrial education could not keep up with the rapid pace of technological advance, and racial discrimination and trade-union exclusionism played a huge role in keeping Bordentown graduates in menial jobs. Facing these grim realities, the teachers sought to equip students with self-confidence, character, initiative, and ambition. They placed utmost importance on each student's "all-round training in thinking, adjusting, and attacking his [or her] personal problems." Students who could adapt readily to an unforeseen situation might have the edge in obtaining employment that, nevertheless, would most likely be of a menial character.[40] Valentine noted, "These teachers have had to work out a technique for training their youth in vocational methods, and at the same time equip them with a mental attitude that will keep up courage and self-confidence in the face of persistently unfair rebuffs when they seek jobs."[41]

Thus, the Bordentown administration placed heavy emphasis on students' attitudes, and strict discipline was an essential component of their educational philosophy. However, as an incident involving Maida demonstrates, disciplinary actions were sometimes misdirected. Within her first month she faced possible expulsion over an incident involving a male student whom she described as a popular football hero, a skillful basketball player, and a fine singer. When he put his hand on her backside as she was drinking at a water fountain, she reacted by spitting water into his face and on his clothes. He then had the audacity to report her behavior to the faculty. She noted that the "other girls thought she was 'loco in her coco'" because this was 'Mr. Wonderful.'"[42]

Faculty members were incensed at Maida's behavior and did not deem it necessary to seek out her explanation. Springer recalled that a prejudice against

New Yorkers existed at the school; students considered them smart alecks, and the adults perceived them as disrespectful. In later years, when Lester Granger was director of the National Urban League and collaborated with Springer in trade-union educational work, he said he had taken a dim view of her at Bordentown because of her "attitude" and the way she sharply answered yes and no. Apparently "sir" and "ma'am" were still not a part of her vocabulary. At Bordentown Granger served as extension agent, commandant over the boys, and a football coach.[43]

Minnie Davis, who had rejected Maida's initial admission request, saved her from expulsion because she knew how important it was to Stewart that her daughter remain. After listening to Maida's story of the incident, Davis told the Faculty Discipline Committee that she would take responsibility for disciplining her. Maida's punishment for defending herself against the improper advances of the popular student was to scrub the corridor and steps on her dormitory floor.[44]

If the faculty committee knew about the male student's behavior and believed Maida, according to their rules they should have suspended him. This was because the school kept strict rules concerning the separation of the sexes. Boys and girls sat apart in the classrooms and left the classroom buildings by separate doors. They could socialize together only during well-supervised special events. Alumni recall the secret name they gave Lester Granger was "Eagle Eye" because of his knack for observing students when they least expected it. If a male student put his foot on the curb bordering the stretch of lawn that separated the boys from the girls, Granger was sure to see this and have that student report to him. Granger once remarked that the school gave him good training for his later work with the Urban League, "from the standpoint of the old-fashioned neatness and politeness and regularity standards."[45]

Engaged in activities from breakfast, which was served at 6:30 A.M., to taps at 9:30 P.M., the students were so busy that they hardly had time for mischief. The school days were equally divided between learning a trade and academic work. Part of the students' training involved maintaining the school grounds and buildings, growing and cooking its food, operating the laundry, and maintaining faculty cars through the auto mechanics course. At 6:45 P.M. students and faculty gathered in the chapel for evening prayers and short inspirational talks. One of the popular sayings, reflecting the obstacles blacks faced, was "Not that you win, but how did you fight?" In the evenings before taps, students studied in their dormitories for two hours. On Saturday mornings they performed chores. Extracurricular activities such as participation in athletics, literary and social clubs, the YMCA and YWCA, bands and singing groups, were reserved for weekend evenings.[46]

Although segregated black schools, with their meager resources and downgraded curriculums, seriously limited their students' economic opportunities and career choices, paradoxically this discrimination helped to bring about at least some students' exposure to highly qualified black teachers and distinguished black visitors. The preference given to white teachers in the public schools and the lack of career options for educated blacks help to explain the high intellectual quality of some of the segregated black schools. Adept at teaching two or three different subjects, many of the Bordentown teachers were graduates of some of the country's best colleges, normal schools, and technical schools. Among the noted members of the Bordentown administration and faculty were William Hastie, Ben Johnson, and Charles Ray. Hastie, who would become governor of the Virgin Islands and the first black judge on the U.S. Court of Appeals, was Maida's science teacher. Both he and Granger were Bordentown alumni. Like Granger, Hastie became friends with Springer after she reached adulthood.[47]

Although Bordentown's alumni included a number of noted individuals, most students had poor educational foundations before coming to the school.[48] As a result of the Great Migration of the 1920s, a large influx of southern blacks enrolled in the school. Among this group was a large percentage of older students whose age prevented them from attending public schools. Granger reported that some of the faculty, frustrated with their limited employment options, believed they were wasting their talents.[49]

Two teachers, however, had a missionary zeal toward their students, and they greatly influenced Springer. She credits Frances Olivia Grant and Thomas Calvin Williams, both of whom began teaching at Bordentown in 1918, with expanding her worldview and imparting to their students confidence and pride in their African ancestry. Williams taught history and civics and served as the school's assistant principal. Alumni recalled their secret nickname for him was Blue Steel because of his dark color, commanding presence, and proud demeanor. Thomas Williams and William Valentine were in the same Harvard graduating class as Franklin Roosevelt.[50] Springer recalled of Williams:

> His talk fascinated me. I never learned anything in public school very much about ex post facto law and the slavery codes and what happened after the revolution. He made history, poetry. He was a giant of a man. He must have been six-three or four with great big lips and coal black and great big feet. When he walked across the room and talked about the history of the United States and the politics of black men and women like Sojourner Truth, I sat in awe with my mouth open. It was music. It was music.
>
> So at Bordentown the history of the American Negro became alive! The music of America which I had been introduced to in the Negro church was kept alive in this boarding school. And big names, people like Paul Robeson and Dr. Du Bois, walked across your stage, ate in the dining room. You

served them! If I was lucky and it was my week to work in the teachers' dining room, I saw all kinds of people. They made a circuit of the black schools. Although this was an industrial school, not for the supposed intellectual, the quality of the teachers as I continue to reflect on this was just amazing.[51]

Through the connections of Frances Grant, principal William Valentine, and his wife, Grace B. Valentine, and others the school frequently brought in renowned visitors. Grant recalled that the school's Sunday afternoon "monthly teas," attended by such notables as Robeson, Bud Fisher, E. Simms Campbell, Elmer Carter, Nella Larsen, and Richard B. Harrison, acted to "heighten student awareness of black achievement." Students were particularly enchanted with Robeson, who was personable with them.[52] Grant remarked on the necessity of instilling pride in the youth: "Belief in yourself—in this I go back to my early parents—and some pride in your own heritage, was so necessary in those days, when the students had been brought up to feel that Negroes didn't do anything, didn't have anything, couldn't go anywhere."[53]

A classics scholar and a magna cum laude graduate of Radcliffe College, Frances Grant devoted her teaching career to resisting the Tuskegee model, as she also resisted society's assignment of blacks to inferior positions. Lester Granger had a similar perspective. He was interested in preparing students for opportunities that might eventually open up to them. As the school's first extension agent, he spent two months during each summer screening applicants to Bordentown. He would visit their homes and study their communities, focusing on employment patterns and employment-referral systems. After students graduated, he performed follow-up studies. In 1934 Granger left Bordentown because of disagreements with William Valentine over his "social work" approach.[54]

Frances Grant also encountered resistance to change. She correctly viewed the school's curriculum as "impossible" since students could not earn a high school diploma. Grant was instrumental in devising a curriculum that required students to earn both a high school degree and a trade certificate. Included in this curriculum was a five-credit course in Negro history. Grant herself taught American history, Latin, and English. As a measure of the school's intransigence, ten years passed before Bordentown fully implemented the new curriculum. Maida, who attended Bordentown from 1923 to 1926, graduated a year before the curriculum was instituted. In 1928 the first students graduated with the four-year high school degree. Changes in the teaching staff and curriculum resulted in an increased number of successful graduates. By 1929 Bordentown was ranked as the leading vocational preparatory school in the country for "colored boys and girls."[55]

Still, Bordentown's vocational courses were quite limited, especially for girls, and racism drastically shrank employment options for its graduates. During

Maida's student years, girls could train in plain sewing, dressmaking, the essentials of housekeeping and cooking, and laundering. Boys could train in printing, steam-boiler operations, plumbing, electrical work, laundry operations, woodworking, agriculture, and auto mechanics.[56] Although Stewart was well aware of the extremely limited employment opportunities for black women, she hoped that Bordentown would help her daughter to go further than she had. Her ambitions conflicted with the proposal of the domestic science teacher, who recognized Maida's potential. Offering to pay Maida's tuition, the teacher wanted to train her as a cook. Stewart was horrified. Proudly referring to her adopted country as she always did, by its entire name, Stewart stated that she had not brought her daughter to the United States of America to become a cook.[57]

Yet Bordentown represented an important survival resource for Maida and other black youth. The school had reinforced the lessons she learned in the political world of Harlem concerning pride in race and culture. With this important foundation she and other students might maintain their ambitions, even while performing the menial work that white America considered their lot.

By 1948 Bordentown dropped the phrase "For Colored Youth" from its name, in compliance with a nondiscrimination clause in the new state constitution. New Jersey closed Bordentown in 1955 under the pretext that the school was not integrating fast enough. In the wake of the 1954 *Brown v. Board of Education* decision by the U.S. Supreme Court, some speculated that the closing had more to do with alleviating whites' fears that their children might be forced to attend a coeducational integrated boarding school. However, since many all-white schools delayed desegregation for years, taking advantage of the latitude of the Supreme Court's directive to desegregate with "all deliberate speed," others believed that the state's motive was to take away these choice facilities and land from blacks. Until 1992 the Bordentown site became the Johnstone Training and Research Center, an institution serving persons with mental retardation. The site is now part of the state juvenile corrections system.[58]

Employment Discrimination

Adina Stewart had immigrated to the United States expecting greater opportunities for her daughter in education and employment. However, she soon found that blacks faced a limited range of employment options. The concerted efforts of trade unions to exclude blacks from skilled positions and the racism of employers constricted the employment options of blacks. During the Jim Crow era the expanding opportunities in education and employment that became available to white women were largely closed to black women. By 1920, outside of agricultural work, 80 percent of black women workers held positions as maids, cooks, or washerwomen, work that received the least respect and remuneration.

The exploitation of black domestic workers, who constituted an increasing proportion of that employment field, was a national phenomenon. They worked long, backbreaking hours for low pay, and were at risk of sexual abuse by the white men of the household.[59]

Stewart's first job in the United States was as a day worker, domestic-service work that women preferred to being a live-in maid. She was so humiliated by the arduous work, the low pay of $2.10 per day, and the meager lunch she was provided that she soon quit. Springer explained:

> I think my mother worked as a day worker maybe for a month. Then she said, "Never! Never!" When she talked, she was very dramatic. She talked like that. I think what finally broke her back was this incident. After working for eight hours washing clothes—and I think this lady gave my mother a hard-boiled egg and a stale roll for lunch—my mother did not get paid at the end of the day. This lady told my mother that her husband had not come home and she could not pay her. My mother said, "No?" Then she went over to the lady's china closet and held it and began to shake it. The lady went into her bedroom and found $2.10 and got rid of my mother. That was her last day work.[60]

After that Stewart worked at a variety of jobs. Because she was quick and skillful, she made a good living at a Park Avenue laundry, where she ironed hand-pleated nightgowns and fine embroidered linens. After becoming a skilled cook, she prepared and served dinner parties two or three times a week for households that did not have full-time domestic staffs. During part of the time her daughter was in boarding school, Stewart worked as a chef in an exclusive club in Connecticut and stayed in a little house that was one of the perquisites of the job. During one of her summer vacations Maida acted as a helper in the club's kitchen.[61]

During other summer breaks, Maida tried to obtain work to help her unsuspecting mother. At the age of eleven she discovered that employers used employee or customer racism as an excuse for exclusion. Following the example of the working-class Irish youngsters she knew, she attempted to pass for a teenager and applied for employment with the New York Telephone Company. Although a female official told Maida that she had the best voice for the job, she pointed out that no white parent would want their child to sit next to her. Maida was devastated to learn that, despite her qualifications, race prejudice prevented her from obtaining the job. This was not an isolated incident. In 1920, a year before Maida's experience, the same company refused to hire any blacks for the thousand openings it had, because, as the assistant to the vice president stated, white women would object to working beside black women.[62]

Only after the 1935 Harlem riot did the New York City government begin to recognize the hardships experienced by Harlem residents stemming from inadequate housing, health care, education, relief aid, and employment opportunities. Yet public hearings held in 1937 by the state's Temporary Commission on the Conditions of the Urban Colored Population revealed that the New York Telephone Company and other businesses still argued that black employment in certain categories would disrupt a harmonious workplace and lead to customer dissatisfaction. During the early twentieth century, the Bell system was the largest employer of females in the country, and until the late 1930s it excluded blacks from any employment above the position of janitor.[63]

After her rejection by the New York Telephone Company, Maida held a few summer jobs in the garment industry, one of the few fields outside domestic work open to black females. In one factory she had worked for a week when her mother discovered what she was doing and learned that the employer had refused to pay her. Stewart stepped in to insure her daughter's rights. "My mother was small, but as she said, *pura Latina*, she was a pure Latin. . . . My mother did not use vulgarity, but she used her eyes and a way of stamping her feet. And when she would really take off, then she would tell him in Spanish what she wanted him to know. . . . He paid me. Never wanted to see me or my mother again."

White employer preferences exacerbated the issue of color consciousness among blacks and served to reinforce the class hierarchy associated with complexion. As a teenager Maida learned that she was too dark to work in a restaurant that was part of the Alice Foote MacDougall chain. The restaurants were set up on a plantation theme with light-complexioned waitresses playing the role of house servants. As Springer described the establishment, "All of the waitresses were dressed in Southern costumes with their heads tied in a bandanna. It was a plantation. And it never occurred to me that all of the girls were very light-brown skinned, very, very fair. . . . My neighbor, my mother's friend, her daughter was a waitress there. She went to college and made very good money, good tips, and so she asked me to come down and I went. . . . I was too dark to be a waitress in this place, and I was too dark to be the salad girl, and that was behind the counter helping to mix salads. . . . They were not secretive about it."[64]

Light-complexioned Pauli Murray, who would later become a close friend of Springer's, worked as a waitress for this same chain of restaurants in 1929. She did not observe that darker-complexioned blacks were excluded; she only saw the regular color line that was drawn between the higher-paying white and lower-paying black jobs. Only whites obtained positions as executives, hostesses, and cashiers, while blacks were relegated to waiting tables and kitchen work. The white staff chose meals from the menu and ate in the dining room, while blacks ate tasteless leftovers on bare tables in the basement. The chain refused service to black customers.[65] Any labor-market advantage that light-complexioned blacks had over dark-complexioned blacks, however, largely concerned access to menial and low-paying jobs. All blacks, regardless of physical features (except those who passed for white), were subject to pervasive and blatant employment discrimination and exclusion.

The hair-care business was another avenue of employment open to black women outside of domestic labor. Springer expressed great respect for her mother, who, despite her limited English education, took classes and passed the exam to gain state certification as a beautician. Stewart opened her own beauty parlor and never worked for anyone else. Envisioning a productive mother-daughter partnership in the beauty-culture industry, she was behind her daughter's gaining a beautician's license as well. However, while Adina Stewart had a great love for the profession, Maida hated it.

Maida earned her license during other summer breaks from Bordentown by attending Poro College on Seventh Avenue in Harlem, one of the schools of beauty culture run by the renowned black businesswomen Annie M. Turnbo Malone. Perhaps some of the training Maida received at Bordentown in poise and self-confidence helped to alert Malone to her potential. She gave Maida a job as a receptionist and offered her a job as a field representative for the school. However, Maida turned it down in part because she believed Malone might become disappointed that she did not share her deep religious beliefs and practices. Springer recalled:

> [E]veryday in the school, you stopped for midday prayer. . . . She was a soft-spoken woman, but very correct and very, very traditional. Just extremely correct. I thought too correct for my taste. But this is how she impressed me. When she spoke, you listened. She would dress as befitted a lady of her station, the head of an organization. She always had on hats and gloves and muted shades when she walked out. She wore no flamboyant colors and wore very nice things. You could look at her clothes and see that it was, as we say, "high class stuff." I remember her having a faint smell of lavender.[66]

Domestic Affairs

Maida's marriage to Owen Springer, who was from Barbados, temporarily ended her participation in the workforce. Among the Springers women did not work. Five years her senior, Owen first became enamored with Maida when she was a preteen. He then informed his mother that he would marry her when she grew up. As was the custom of the older neighborhood children, he looked after the younger ones; however, he gave special attention to Maida. At the time she was unaware of his intentions but took full advantage of his kindness. She recalled, "Owen worked in an ice cream parlor on the corner of our block. We went—Dora Murray and maybe another friend—down to the parlor, sat on the stool and had ice cream. I would eat pineapple temptations. Owen would buy ice cream for the three of us." Laughing, she added, "I'm sure he didn't go home with much money. If they paid him five dollars a week, I guess we ate two dollars a week."[67]

The two lost contact during Maida's years at Bordentown, but they renewed their friendship while she was working for Annie Malone. The relationship blossomed into romance, and the couple married in 1927. Maida opposed her mother's wish to have a large wedding because she did not want her to incur a debt that would take years to pay off. Instead they compromised with a small wedding and a large reception at a salon Madame C. J. Walker had established for blacks to use on such occasions. Madame Walker, who had died in 1919, had made her fortune in the hair-care business. She and Malone were America's first black female millionaires.[68] The young couple moved into the same building where Owen's mother and his sister's family lived.

Eager to be an adult in her own home, Maida was a proficient housekeeper; however, she was astounded to discover that her husband was extremely fastidious, even folding his dirty laundry before placing it in the hamper. Always gentle with her, he did not direct her to emulate his standards. When their son, Eric, was born two years later, Maida saw her husband blossom into a loving father. His family was the center of his world. For recreation he coached a basketball team called the Metro Diamonds that played warm-up games against a team whose style of play was similar to that of the later formed Harlem Globetrotters. On Sunday afternoons, he would take his young son in a stroller to the basketball practices.

Owen was able to support his young family comfortably on the salary he made repairing dental instruments for an English firm, Claudius Ash and Son. For a black man, he had a very good job. The firm recognized his great skill and intelligence and did not have to worry about customer prejudices because his primary contact with dentists was by telephone. They called from all over the country with questions concerning the intricacies of assembling, adjusting, and repairing the instruments. Only dentists who found the opportunity to visit the firm discovered he was black.

The Depression dramatically altered Maida and Owen's relationship.[69] Forced to accept a significant wage cut, Owen also had to accept the necessity of his wife's employment. Maida found work in the garment industry and soon became passionately involved in the labor movement. For a young man who desired their family to be the focus of Maida's energies, her active involvement with the labor movement was a blow. As the historian Alice Kessler-Harris has pointed out, the conjugal relations of many female activists in the garment trade either suffered or were nonexistent, and some formed unions with other women.[70]

Rigid gender roles supporting the activism of men in the public sphere more often absolved male leaders from having to pay such a heavy price.

The dressmaking skills Springer learned at Bordentown and narrow employment options led her to find work in dressmaking shops. By 1927 the garment trade was the leading industry in New York, employing a large percentage of New York City's working women. In turn women represented the majority of workers in the dress trade. The volatile garment industry, particularly in the lowest-paying sectors and categories, exploited all the workers regardless of race and ethnicity.[71] Conditions of employment and the garment workers' radical tradition kindled Springer's activist spirit. As she embraced a union career, the education she received from her mother and in the streets, church, and school had instilled in her a sense of hope and an appreciation for unified struggle.

2

"My Union Was a Very Political Union"

Springer Joins Local 22

NTIL SHE HEARD A SPEECH A. PHILIP RANDOLPH gave shortly before she entered the labor force in 1932, Springer had been unsympathetic toward organized labor. Randolph's analysis of the ways employers used racism as a means of dividing and exploiting all workers moved her to view the fight against union exclusion and discrimination as essential for black advancement. Springer's experiences in the garment industry soon reinforced her beliefs. For example, a contractor who had not paid her and the other workers for two weeks secretly moved the shop over a weekend. In May 1933, enraged over this kind of treatment, Springer joined Local 22 of the International Ladies' Garment Workers' Union. Because the ILGWU was, as she stated, "flat on its face" during these Depression years, she had to search for the union.

Springer's civil rights and labor activism became intertwined through her connections with Local 22 manager Charles "Sasha" Zimmerman, ILGWU president David Dubinsky, and black leaders A. Philip Randolph, Frank Crosswaith, and Lester Granger. The ILGWU was a strong financial backer of the Negro Labor Committee and a long-time supporter of the Brotherhood of Sleeping Car Porters. A conference composed of 110 black and white AFL delegates organized the Negro Labor Committee on July 20, 1935. Its headquarters was in the

Harlem Labor Center, which opened in November 1935 with the objective of organizing and educating black workers in "this sadly neglected working class section of New York City."[1] ILGWU organizer Crosswaith served as head of both the Negro Labor Committee and the Harlem Labor Center, and Randolph was a vice chairman of the Negro Labor Committee. Granger, who acted as chair of the Harlem Advisory Committee of the Workers Education and executive secretary of the National Urban League, was along with Springer a sponsor of the Negro Labor Committee.[2]

When Springer first joined the ILGWU, she was unaware that her activism would lead to an intimate association with black leaders whom she had admired since childhood. She explained, "I would have thought it inconceivable that I would become part of that inner circle of the Randolph family, that Randolph would be calling my union to say, 'Now, Sasha [Charles Zimmerman], now Dave [David Dubinsky], we would like to borrow Maydia' [Maida] to do whatever it was they were doing. I really began to know Randolph by 1936. And by the time the March on Washington was planned in 1941, I was on first-name basis; I could call him 'Chief.'"[3]

During Springer's early years of activism, competing radical groups vied for the allegiance of the union membership. Although she never joined any group, her friendship with Socialists like Randolph, Crosswaith, and Leon Stein, who was editor of the ILGWU organ, *Justice*, and his wife, Miriam, and Lovestoneites like Zimmerman, Jennie Silverman, Minnie Lurye, and Edward Welsh reinforced her distrust of the U.S. Communist movement. To place her ideological position in context, it is necessary to examine the ILGWU's radical tradition and particularly the activism of Charles Zimmerman. Expelled from the Communist Party (CP) in 1929 along with other allies of Jay Lovestone, the deposed head of the American CP, Zimmerman became one of Springer's early mentors and helped to sustain an anti-Communist alliance with black leaders in Harlem. Both he and Lovestone later were strong supporters of Springer's work in Africa.

Springer's experiences with Communists and former Communists in these early years provide a more complex picture of race relations and the nature of militancy within the ILGWU and particularly within Local 22. Some historians of the ILGWU hold that its Jewish male leadership tried to shape black and Puerto Rican members into a docile and nonmilitant body and begrudgingly yielded power to its membership only under pressure from a powerful Communist opposition. Without discounting the racism and sexism prevalent among the ILGWU leadership, Springer's experiences, and particularly her relationship with Zimmerman, do not fit these characterizations.[4] Nor should Springer's activism be viewed as merely an exception. A fuller story of the ILGWU has to explain the enthusiasm and loyalty of many of its members as well as the disaffection with the union that many of those same members exhibited.

The Lovestoneite Influence

Composed primarily of Jewish and Italian immigrants, many of whom had been radicalized by the revolutionary struggles of 1905–1920 in their countries of origin, the ILGWU had a large left-wing presence of Socialists, Communists, syndicalists, and anarchists. As refugees from political oppression and religious persecution, many were inspired by the success of the 1917 Bolshevik revolution in Russia.[5] Exploitative conditions within the U.S. garment industry also informed their radicalism.

Among these radicalized immigrants were Charles Zimmerman and Jennie Silverman. In 1913, at the age of sixteen, Zimmerman emigrated from Russia and began work in the New York garment industry. His commitment to social change led him to join the Amalgamated Clothing Workers as a charter member, the ILGWU in 1916, the Socialist Party in 1917, the Industrial Workers of the World in 1918, and the Communist Party in 1919.[6]

Jennie Silverman, who became a close friend of Springer's and a fellow Local 22 business agent, emigrated from the Ukraine in 1919 with eleven members of her family, following a pogrom that resulted in the deaths of all the males present in her village. Silverman's traumatic experiences led her to become a member of the Young Communist League. She reflected that in the party there was room for idealism and saving the world "because you came from a very bad world."[7]

Although women were subordinate in the leadership structure of the ILGWU, they largely set the pace for radicalism within the union. The female-dominated dress and waistmakers' Local 25, which Zimmerman called "*the* local in the International,"[8] led the 1909 strike that became known as the "Revolt of the Twenty Thousand." This strike firmly established a radical tradition within the ILGWU. The 1911 Triangle Shirtwaist Company fire, in which 146 young women died, provided a further stimulus for labor union agitation. Ironically, the Triangle Shirtwaist Company was the same garment factory where the Revolt of the Twenty Thousand had started.[9]

During the 1920s Local 22, created in part out of Local 25 in a move to dilute its radicalism, served as the center of ILGWU insurgency. The General Executive Board (GEB), the ruling body of the ILGWU that was composed of the president, secretary-treasurer, and vice presidents, changed the ILGWU constitution early in the decade in order to counter the insurgency of the left-wing locals. Divulging union proceedings to employers or nonmembers was made illegal, and membership in all leagues was deemed dual unionism and therefore illegal. These laws imperiled the position of left-wing union leaders who belonged to the garment section of the Communist-run Trade Union Education League (TUEL) and consulted with top CP officials about union strategy. The TUEL was the largest of the leagues, the strongest of which were formed to oppose the more conservative ILGWU leadership. The majority of the Local 22 Communist leaders who were expelled in 1923 on charges of dual unionism were women, as were the majority of Communist leaders expelled in 1925 from Locals 2, 9, and 22 on these same charges. The GEB replaced most of them with men.[10]

Zimmerman played a major role in the internecine union battles of the 1920s between a Communist-led left-wing movement and the largely Socialist ILGWU leadership. The most contentious struggle concerned the system of representation, which overwhelmingly favored the small and usually conservative locals. The ILGWU constitution allowed only a minuscule increase in representation for the large locals over the base number to which all locals were entitled. Since the selection of local delegates to the joint boards (governing bodies usually composed of a city or region-wide group of locals involved in the same industry) and to the biennial ILGWU conventions was based on this system, a minority was able to control the majority. Under a fairer form of proportional representation, the larger left-wing locals in New York City, where the bulk of the trade was centered, could have controlled the GEB by electing left-wing officers at the conventions.[11]

Even without a more equitable system of representation, a favorable outcome of the 1926 cloakmakers' strike could have resulted in Communist control of the ILGWU. The bitter factionalism raging inside the CP contributed to the decision of the Communist union leadership to reject a generally favorable agreement Zimmerman had worked out to end the strike early.[12] The defeat within the Soviet-led Communist International (Comintern) of those accused of right-wing deviation—that is, of supporting policies that were considered non-revolutionary or as collaborating with capitalists—informed the actions of American CP officials in this strike. In a meeting of dozens of Communist shop representatives, Joseph Boruchowitz made an off-hand remark that led all to believe that the agreement they had been about to approve was not good enough. The top rival officials of the American CP also were present at this meeting. Mindful of the Comintern's interest in the strike, each faction leader tried to present himself as being more revolutionary than the others, leading them all to reject the settlement. To Zimmerman's dismay, they then instructed him to negotiate a better deal. He could not. The resultant prolonged strike caused the ILGWU to accumulate a tremendous debt.[13]

With the membership demoralized by the strike, the factional fighting, and the economic downturn of the industry, the GEB took over the strike and expelled the left-wing leadership on charges of not following legal procedures for striking and, more dubiously, mismanagement of strike funds. The strike was concluded with an agreement significantly worse than the original one Zimmerman had negotiated.[14]

The factional fighting within the American CP continued after the strike and was directly related to the struggle within the Comintern between factions loyal to Russian leaders Joseph Stalin and Nikolai Bukharin. The policy differences between the two leaders stemmed from divergent analyses of the third period. In a report to the July 1928 Sixth World Congress, Bukharin divided the post–World War I capitalist order into three periods. He reported that the upcoming third period would represent a period of capitalist reconstruction. Based on this analysis he wanted to continue working with Socialists and within established unions.[15]

Stalin's faction correctly predicted that the third period would instead represent an era of global crisis in capitalism. Accordingly, they supported a policy of separation from established unions and the formation of a "united front from below" — that is, unity with the rank-and file union members coupled with an all-out attack on the leadership. This tactic, they held, would put Communists in positions of leadership during the expected revolutionary period.

Loosely aligned with Bukharin, Jay Lovestone, head of the American CP, and his supporters lost favor with Stalin. With Stalin's faction emerging as the more powerful force, the Lovestoneites also lost support among American Communists. The Executive Committee of the Comintern decided to reassign Lovestone to international work and place William Foster, the leader of the minority political faction, in control of the American CP. When Stalin's forces won final approval for their third-period policies in 1929, Lovestone, Zimmerman, and Edward Welsh were in Moscow appealing the decision of the Executive Committee. Welsh, who was black, gained some prominence for rejecting an overture by Stalin directly following the failure of the Lovestoneite appeal.[16]

Zimmerman remarked that his stand during this Moscow trip led American CP members to treat him "as a pariah." Nevertheless, he believed that Communists in the garment industry secretly agreed with him. Ben Gold of the International Furworkers Union told him that they must submit to the new policy because they could accomplish more from inside the party. Local 25 veteran Rose Wortis, whom Zimmerman later characterized as the ILGWU's *La Pasionaria* long before there was one in Loyalist Spain, declared her willingness to do anything the party told her no matter how repugnant. When Zimmerman continued to speak against separate unions, the people around him at a CP general membership meeting spat all over his coat.[17]

Despite what some Communists may have perceived as flaws in party policy, many were fiercely committed to the CP as the best means for creating a society free of capitalist oppression and catering to basic human needs. Communists in the garment industry formed the rival Needle Trades' Workers Industrial Union (NTWIU) in 1928. Zimmerman's continued disagreements with the Comintern policy landed him before the U.S. Communist Party Control Commission and led to his expulsion in October 1929. Lovestone had been expelled prior to him, first from the Comintern and then from the American CP. Still trying to change the Comintern policy, Zimmerman tried to work inside the NTWIU until 1930.[18]

When Zimmerman returned to Local 22 on May 15, 1931, and brought a few Lovestoneites with him, including Jennie Silverman and Minnie Lurye, CP members, who were operating in both unions, strongly ridiculed him for continuing to call himself a Communist. They also accused him of being in collusion with the bosses, introducing a "reign of terror" against those fighting to improve conditions, and participating in the expulsions of Communist executive board members, particularly from Local 9, "because they fought against piece work and the sweat shop."[19] Yet, Zimmerman later remarked that in 1931 he defended Barnet Cooper, the local's Communist manager, against expulsion. His defense of the right of at least this one Communist to hold office, however, in no way moderated his desire to "beat [Communists] ideologically." He stated that he fought against them "tooth and nail."[20]

Complying with the institution of the Comintern's United Front policies against fascism in 1934–1935, Communists officially quit the NTWIU and returned to the ILGWU. Although they held a strong base in the union, they failed to regain the widespread support they had commanded in the 1920s. Several factors contributed to their weakened position. Communists may have lost support as a result of their stance against the ILGWU before they officially returned to the union. When workers overwhelmingly supported the ILGWU during the August 1933 dressmakers' strike, Communists engaged in a futile effort to prevent workers from joining the ILGWU. The ILGWU leadership's move to ban permanent clubs to insure unification of a diverse ethnic membership as well as wipe out possible bases for Communist resurgence was a hindrance, as historian Nancy Green has demonstrated. The ILGWU was suspicious of subgroups that might become permanent centers of opposition, as the leagues of the 1920s were before they were outlawed. Union members could only form temporary clubs around an election. Lovestoneite power in Local 22, which for a period was renowned as the largest and most progressive ILGWU local, also stood in the way of the Communists. The influence of Lovestoneites, however, was greater than their numbers.[21]

Portraying themselves as "the best proletariats, comrades who founded and built the Party," Lovestoneites waged a twelve-year struggle to reform and reenter the CP. They even supported the increasingly despotic practices of the Stalin-led government. They sought to justify the first two Moscow show trials in which those deemed Stalin's enemies were forced to confess to crimes they did not commit and were subsequently executed. The third trial and execution of Bukharin and his associates in 1938, however, marked the beginning of the end of their pro-Soviet stance. The group irrevocably turned against Stalin following the 1939 Nazi-Soviet Non-Aggression Pact and disbanded at the end of 1940.[22] Zimmerman reflected:

> We began changing, questioning the idea of communism as interpreted by the Soviet Union. Not communism as an advanced stage of socialism. I did not question the basic theory of a socialist society. I changed the theory from dictatorship, dictatorship of the proletariat or dictatorship over the prole-tariat or this kind of dictatorship as portrayed by the Soviet Union, by the whole leadership of the Soviet Union. . . . It developed afterwards more on whether it is possible to have the kind of a dream that we have of a socialist society, whether it's possible to have it, under a collectivist system without guaranteeing rights.[23]

To the chagrin of some, Zimmerman refused to show contrition for his former Communist affiliation. Springer recalled that ILGWU president David Dubinsky would make a point of publicly chastising Zimmerman for his party membership. Dubinsky's dubbing him the "returned prodigal son" and assessment of his Communist past as "years of sin" clearly irritated Zimmerman. Recalling the struggles of the 1920s, Zimmerman remarked that he told the ILGWU leadership many times that the Communists' strong following was justified, given the ILGWU's intransigence, cynicism, and undemocratic hold on power. However, he believed that leftists lost the struggles of the 1920s because the "Communist Party forced extraneous matters that had nothing to do with conditions of unions."[24] Nevertheless, he did not regret having joined the party: "I could be more objective than others, because I am not one of those who bemoan my past. Just the opposite. I don't bemoan that. I think it was an important chapter in my life. And I learned quite a bit."[25]

Zimmerman's opposition to the CP did not mean that he turned into an un-bending Cold Warrior.[26] In contrast Lovestone became a virulent anti-Communist. The ILGWU eventually provided an opening for his reinvolvement in domestic and international labor affairs. During World War II he served as director of the union's International Relations Department before taking charge of the AFL-associated Free Trade Union Committee (FTUC) in 1944. Lovestone became a principal architect of AFL and later AFL-CIO foreign policy.[27]

Springer's relationship with Lovestone began in the late 1940s. At that time he was virtually the only prominent white leader who took her discussions of African aspirations seriously and who was in a position to advance her ideas to other officials. Lovestone was staunchly anticolonialist, both in principle and as a tactic for defeating what he considered the greater menace of Communist expansion. In consultation with Dubinsky and Randolph, he was responsible for bringing Springer into the International Affairs Department in 1960. Although Springer rarely displayed a concern for monitoring Communist influences in her international work, Lovestone's single-minded anti-Communism and his clandestine mode of operation had implications for how some domestic and international labor leaders viewed her activism.

The Union's Rebirth

The internecine struggles of the 1920s played a large role in the precipitous decline in the ILGWU membership. The onset of the Depression, the culmination of nearly a decade of slowing growth in the garment industry, however, was the most immediate reason for the ILGWU's weakness. Between 1920 and 1929 the ILGWU membership dropped by two-thirds, with half of the loss occurring after 1926.[28] After Charles Zimmerman returned to Local 22, Lovestoneites, Socialists, and anarchists formed the Committee of 25 to increase membership. By 1933 the ILGWU counted forty thousand members, up from the 1929 low of thirty-two thousand. Having joined Local 22 a month after Zimmerman became manager, Springer was among the new members of this still-weak union.[29]

Unions gained increased strength as a result of the passage of the 1933 National Industrial Recovery Act. Section 7a of the act acknowledged the right of workers to organize and bargain collectively. The celebrated strike of 60,000 dressmakers in August 1933, however, served as the catalyst for the union's rebirth. Bargaining from a position of strength, the dressmakers made better gains in hours and wages than the minimum codes the government recommended. Membership in the Dress Joint Board, composed of locals representing the cutters, pressers, dressmakers, and the separate Italian dressmakers, increased from 20,000 to 80,000, and the membership of Local 22 settled at around 30,000. Local 22's black membership increased from 600 to 4,000 members. By 1938 the ILGWU had a black membership of 12,000, and a total membership of 300,000, making it the third-largest union in the AFL.[30]

Springer was thrilled by the legitimacy and power that the 1933 strike conferred on the union. Having helped with the processing of new members following the strike, she recalled the celebration:

> It was an electrifying occasion. Thousands of new members, of which I was one, were attending their first trade union celebrations. I was awed by the participation of the celebrated artists of the Metropolitan Opera and the Jewish Theater. Union banners, American flags, flowers and huge plants decorated the hall. The huge orchestra was in place and union leaders were busy welcoming government officials. Luigi Antonini looked more like an impresario than a union leader, with his barrel chest, string tie and huge black fe-

dora. Small statured David Dubinsky, President of the International Ladies' Garment Workers' Union, was 10 feet tall. The Italian artists led us in the great Italian workers' song "Pan e Rose" [Bread and Roses]. I was intoxicated with the drama, beauty and importance of the occasion. As a result of this exhilarating experience, I proudly accepted more assignments and enrolled in more classes than was reasonable. My youth, enthusiasm, and the daily evidence of changes that the Union had wrought in our lives lessened the normal tedium of tasks.[31]

Owen Springer counseled his young wife against strong union involvement. Like many blacks who were suspicious of white overtures for union solidarity, he believed that the labor movement would only use and abuse her. Because he was five years her senior and she respected him, Springer listened to her husband. She recognized that a significant percentage of employers and ILGWU leaders perpetuated discrimination against black workers by confining them to the least skilled and lowest paying job categories. She asserted that up until the 1940s employers were particularly reluctant to hire black women as power-machine operators.[32] Most black women worked as pinkers, cleaners, examiners, and finishers, and were concentrated in shops making lower-priced dresses. Springer herself began working as a finisher, whose responsibilities included hand sewing of accessories such as buttons and trimming. Before becoming a union officer she worked for a time as a power-machine operator.

While conceding that her husband's opinion of union involvement for blacks might be correct, Springer was inspired by union triumphs and was swayed by Randolph's philosophy. Her union membership brought increased wages and access to health care, social activities, and labor education. In spite of her husband's disapproval of her union activities, Springer stated that she "was on fire with it." She attended classes or meetings three nights a week. Her mother, mother-in-law, and sister-in-law assisted her by caring for her young son.[33] Her volunteer assignments included serving on the education committee and the committee that settled piecework prices for shops doing contract work for the same manufacturer. By 1938 she served on the local's executive board and by 1940 was chair of its education committee.

At the Harlem Labor Center, Hudson Shore Labor School, Wellesley College Institute for Social Progress, and Rand School for Social Science (among other sites) she attended lectures dealing with the basics of parliamentary procedure, interpretation of contracts, the history of the AFL and the ILGWU, and current social history. She recalled, "They had some wonderful training classes about another world, another way, workers. Classes that kind of opened your eyes as you listened." Lovestoneite Edward Welsh, who had begun working as a labor organizer for Local 22 in 1930, particularly captivated Springer: "Here was this bronze god. He taught at the Harlem Labor Center, which offered history, philosophy and that wonderful word, dialectical materialism, an understanding about Communist theory. And Eddie Welsh taught some of those classes that provided an understanding of the worker's cause and the worker's right to be a part of the structure of society with dignity. Eddie Welsh was a Lovestoneite. I didn't know this when I was sitting there in awe as he was moving back and forth across the room with his six-foot-four self, this bronze Adonis."[34] Welsh, his wife, Miriam, and her sister Evelyn Scheyer later became friends with Springer. Welsh would work with labor unions in East Africa during Springer's period of activism on the continent.[35]

The ILGWU's radical political tradition, concern with international issues, and strong commitment to education and social welfare programs fueled the members' enthusiasm for the union. By the mid to late 1930s, when Springer was participating in classes, the ILGWU had developed a mass-education movement. In 1938 there were 620 educational groups attended by 22,050 students in fifty-eight cities. "Tool" courses included public speaking, parliamentary law, English, and trade-union techniques. "Background" courses included the economics of the garment industry, the history of the ILGWU and labor in general, and current events. In addition the ILGWU established lecture circuits and weekend and ten-day institutes and furnished films on the history and activities of the union, and songbooks and recordings of union songs. Within the union or at institutes workers formed athletic groups, participated in dances, parties, and hikes, attended concerts and plays, and visited museums.[36]

Local 25, out of which Local 22 was created, had pioneered in union education by instituting the first education department. A 1937 report claimed that Local 22 "was justly proud that no other union of the I.L.G.W.U. had drawn such a large proportion of its members into educational activities."[37] The education and social welfare programs helped to sustain union membership even as working conditions deteriorated. Reflecting on this period of activism, Zimmerman asserted, "We brought in that dynamism and that activity. [The local] was pulsating all the time, with all kinds of activities. We brought in many outside things, like civil rights, assisting refugees and other things in which members were interested. All kinds of things. The local was a beehive of all these activities and it involved a lot of members."[38]

Springer's later friend Minnie Lurye, whose involvement in the labor movement began in childhood, also attested to the spirit that engulfed Local 22 activists. To Zimmerman she once wrote, "It is no surprise to me that you get such fine response from our people in the ranks. The Progressive Group has given them an aim and purpose in life. It has taken an occupation of making dresses and transformed it into a purposeful life. It has given them an ideal to live by that transforms a drab and humdrum existence into actual *living*. They *are* a swell bunch!"[39]

By the mid 1940s the ILGWU educational department spent annually between $250,000 and $300,000. The department's director, Mark Starr, conducted various interracial classes, in which Negro history was one of the most important subjects. In the early 1960s Starr would spend some time in Tanganyika among Springer's friends in the nationalist and labor movements while he gave technical assistance to labor unions. Frank Crosswaith, who was connected with the ILGWU education department, attributed the solidarity among members to the union's educational work. Moreover, he gave inflated praise to the ILGWU, maintaining that it "has always stood 100 percent on the side of the Negro and has put forth every effort to advance his status in practically every phase of American life."[40]

Some in the ILGWU wanted to advance Springer into the entertainment arena by having her perform in a union play called *Pins and Needles*. With Local 22 members accounting for most of the cast, the play had a successful run from 1937 to 1941, which included a stint on Broadway and even a White House performance.[41] Springer believed that her race may have led some to presuppose that she had a natural talent for performing:

> Since I was one of the activists on this committee and that committee and every committee—a face that was familiar to them—they tried very hard to put me in the cast of *Pins and Needles*. My reaction to this was I could not dance, I could not sing and I wasn't pretty, and what did they want from me? . . . So eager was the union to involve what they thought was their potential and to have a very democratic show including Negroes and Hispanics. And I think in the back of their minds the assumption was that all Negroes dance and all Negroes sing, but I couldn't do either. My husband had told me early on that I had a good voice for cooling soup, because I would sing to this little boy [her son Eric] when he was a baby. So my opportunity to be in the theater was lost. That was one thing I was intelligent about.[42]

Communists recognized that the control of Socialists, Trotskyites, and Lovestoneites over the ILGWU educational apparatus, and particularly Lovestoneite influence in Local 22, was a great hindrance to their work. At the tenth New York State CP convention, held in 1938, one speaker named Josephine Martini commented that the strong active membership of the ILGWU was a result of its fine educational program, which included popular educational activities, sports, and forums. Other unions could learn a lesson from the ILGWU, she noted, but she bemoaned the fact that the educational department head was a Socialist (Mark Starr) and that the teachers included Trotskyites and Lovestoneites like Gus Tyler, Sam Friedman, and Minnie Lurye.[43] Max Steinberg, CP organization secretary for New York State, admonished Communists for not doing enough to counter the hegemony of Lovestoneites in the education field: "How are we Communists struggling against the Lovestoneites and Trotskyites? The results show that the struggle is by far insufficient. OUR COMRADES SEEM TO HAVE TOO LONG A PERSPECTIVE ON LOVESTONEITES, ESPECIALLY AMONG THE DRESSMAKERS, FIGURING THAT SOMETIME IN THE FUTURE THE UNION WILL BE RID OF THEM. Meanwhile the comrades go about their daily work in the union leaving the workers in the main to the education of the Lovestoneites in the union with their propaganda against the unity of the workers and the People's Front."[44]

ILGWU Alliance with Black Leadership

The ILGWU was one of a few AFL unions that took an early position against segregated locals and pay differentials based on race. With the growth of mass industry, the ILGWU in 1935 helped to form the AFL Committee for Industrial Organization, which was dedicated to both industrial and interracial organizing. Favoring the traditional and narrow organization of labor by crafts, the AFL old guard expelled the unions belonging to this committee in 1936, including the ILGWU. Two years later some of the rejected group formed the Congress of Industrial Organizations (CIO). Opposed to establishing a permanent rival federation, the ILGWU refused to join the CIO. For added measure ILGWU leaders disliked John Lewis, the CIO head, and opposed the CIO's tolerance of Communist participation. The union returned to the AFL in 1940 and helped to facilitate the merger of the two federations into the AFL-CIO in 1955.[45]

Within the ILGWU, Communists and anti-Communists vied for black support.[46] Since 1928 the Comintern recognized that in order to take full advantage of the third period it was essential to win the most subjugated group in the United States. This agenda entailed breaking with the old view of race as merely an extension of class and dealing seriously with racism within the American CP and the white working class.[47] Recruitment of Harlem's blacks became a major priority.

The success of the 1933 strike, which they had ardently opposed, forced party members into extraordinary efforts to woo black dressmakers. They railed against the Lovestoneites in general and Charles Zimmerman in particular, accusing him not just of failing to fight discrimination but of failing to recognize that it even existed. A CP-led group called the Negro Committee of the Left Wing launched similar attacks.[48] The strong connections Zimmerman developed with the black leaders and Local 22's progressive reputation helped him withstand the attempts of Communists to defeat his administration and to discredit his leadership among black dressmakers.

Zimmerman's interest in organizing black workers was in accordance with official ILGWU policy and may be seen as continuing the race work begun during his brief tenure with the Communist-run Needle Trades' Workers Industrial Union.[49] Throughout his career he engaged in numerous civil rights projects. The same month that Springer joined the ILGWU, he wrote a letter to the Urban League stating his two objectives. One was to get blacks, who were mainly employed in the lower-paid crafts, to join the union. The second was "to activize Negro workers in our Union. To draw them into the leadership of the union, so that they may have their say in the conduct of the organization, as well as in the solution of problems that we are faced with in the industry."[50] In pursuit of these objectives it was inevitable that he would come to recognize Springer as an exceptional candidate for union leadership. He promoted her as educational director of Local 132, the plastic, button, and novelty workers' union, in 1943; as an official in the complaint department of the Dress Joint Board in 1945; and as a Local 22 business agent in 1948.

During Springer's early years in the union, Communists repeatedly sought her support. Concerning the Communists' appeal, she remarked:

> "[T]hey were saying *all* of the right things. Very engaging. *All* of the right things. You cannot live in this society at that period and not at least listen. The structure of this society was *so* prejudiced. You couldn't have a job. You couldn't ride. You couldn't be employed as a bus driver. You could not be employed as a subway motorman. . . . You could not sit in the theater wherever you wanted. There were hotels and other places that you could not and didn't dare go. The Communist Party spoke of these things. . . . They had all of the angles for capturing the hearts of a disturbed and a downtrodden people."[51]

The post–World War II employment experience of Owen Springer exemplified the limited opportunities blacks still confronted. He worked in a subway token booth, a job that did not utilize his considerable talents but nevertheless represented one of the employment fields where blacks recently had waged a successful struggle against exclusion.

In the early 1930s the CP was probably the most vociferous of the nonblack organizations in condemning racism. Their tactics of mass action and confrontation in campaigns against discriminatory and inadequate relief payments, evictions, employment exclusion, police brutality, and lynchings, and the willingness of both black and white CP members to put their lives on the line in these campaigns, earned them the respect of many blacks. Their participation in the Scottsboro case, involving nine black youths falsely accused of raping two white females in Alabama, added to their prestige among a sizable number of blacks.[52]

Springer, however, resisted the Communist appeal. Among members of her Harlem social circle was a strong belief that the CP's concern for blacks was opportunistic. As an NAACP supporter, Owen Springer particularly had no sympathies for Communists and thought that the Scottsboro Boys' victimhood had been prolonged in order to advance party goals and achieve power. Maida Springer held a peculiar mix of distrust of Communist motives and enthusiasm for their exposure of racial injustice. When Communists came to her home unannounced on Sundays, her husband promptly and politely left the house. Unlike her husband, Springer would converse with them, but through these conversations she gained a negative opinion of Communists active in the ILGWU:

> I think the thing that offended me was that I always felt that I was being patronized. I think they loved me too much. And I'm always [suspicious]. I was here long enough to know that while this is the most wonderful place on earth, it leaves a great deal to be desired if you wear brown skin. But I didn't think that my Soviet colleagues would be any different. So I never bought that line.
>
> After we talked about fundamental things that I thought the union was doing and that I was a party to and that I was given an opportunity to serve, they would keep talking and then I would get nasty. I would ask them, "How many Colored people live in the building you live in?" Because it was time for me to do something with my child. It was time for me to cook my dinner. You know, it's Sunday! Maybe I've just washed the clothes. And then I would make it awkward sometimes by saying, "Don't you have anything to do in your house?" I'm looking at my watch, and I've got something to do. I have to clean my house. I've got to go to work tomorrow morning. I have this child's clothes to iron. Saturday, I went shopping or I worked half a day or I was at a union meeting. I washed Saturday night. So they were a nuisance.
>
> You could come to my house, you could come to my community to be with me. You would share things in *my* community. All right. I could not come into your community in the same way, because you may live in the house where the elevator man says, "You have to go to the back to the servants' entrance." There were some who shared your living and your problems with you, but that was a minority.[53]

Springer thought some of the representations of the Communists were unrealistic, such as their descriptions of the Soviet Union as a purely egalitarian society and a worker's paradise.[54] Moreover, she disagreed with their negative interpretation of the Dubinsky administration's every act. More receptive to the ideas of Socialists and former Communists, she commented, "Just as the Communists were busy proselytizing me, the group that I dealt with . . . had a very different concept of the world—certainly a social democracy which gave better opportunities to the working men and women, a more egalitarian society, one in which people voted for something, people had a voice in something, and which as much murder was not committed. You know, mine is the only right way [speaking of Communists]. You had, similarly, religious walls. Mine is the only right religion and everyone else is wrong."[55]

By the late 1930s Communists had given up trying to recruit Springer. During a Local 22 political campaign before Springer became a union officer, she was involved in a shoving match with a male Communist, which caused her to fall down a flight of stairs. More humorously, another Communist, his male pride apparently offended, once stalked out of a first-aid class she taught after she demonstrated the fireman's carry on him.

Later, as a business agent, Springer continued to have heated political discussions with some of her Communist shop chairs. Every day, she recalled, the Communists brought in articles from the *Daily Worker* attacking "everything that the union leadership said, from Dubinsky on down." She viewed their behavior as constantly seeking to create disorder. Although personally fond of some of these workers, she did not doubt that if there were any room for criticism of her work, they would try to undermine the confidence that workers had in her. For this reason she believed that she had to make an extra effort to attend to complaints in these shops.

Local 22 was involved with the Harlem community on issues concerning both labor and civil rights. An article in *Opportunity*, the organ of the Urban League, stated, "Local 22, under the guiding spirit of the militant Charles S. Zimmerman, has become the most progressive single local in the entire labor movement. With a membership of 30,000 including every racial group (with the exception of the Italians) in the New York City dress industry, it forms a model of unionism. The International Ladies' Garment Workers' Union has been in the forefront of American labor in working out the solution of the Negro-white labor problem. This is done through the leadership of Fannia M. Cohn and Mark Starr."[56]

Nevertheless, the cause of organized labor was not popular in Harlem because of the exclusion of blacks from many unions and jobs and the perpetuation of wage-scale differentials based on race. Granger, Randolph, Crosswaith, and Springer worked to change black perception of organized labor. With the Harlem Labor Center and the Brotherhood of Sleeping Car Porters located within a block of one another, Crosswaith and Randolph were particularly well situated to work closely together on the Negro Labor Committee.[57]

With their Bordentown ties as a foundation, Granger developed a friendship with Springer and relied on her for information and advice concerning the relationship between black workers and the ILGWU. He sometimes began letters to Dubinsky with the phrase "Talking with Maida the other day," and then proceeded to review a strategy that she had proposed for promoting unionism among black workers. In 1946, after Springer informed him of a shop composed mostly of blacks who were not interested in unionism, Granger suggested to Dubinsky that the Urban League's industrial relations department republish "The ABC's of Labor," a booklet explaining why Negro workers should join unions. Granger had prepared the booklet ten years earlier while serving as the Urban League's workers' education secretary. He held that the League's reputation of not being "'owned' by the labor movement" would give their arguments "extra authority" and would "represent the opinion of an outside agency interested primarily in the welfare of Negroes." This was not the first time he recommended that the Urban League act as a front for the labor movement. Recognizing the relative conservatism of a significant portion of the black community, he reasoned that the Urban League's reputation for supporting policy that was "far from 'radical'" would aid the organization's efforts to influence blacks on the labor question.[58]

Along with their support of organized labor, black leaders working with the ILGWU leadership were also committed to opposing Communist influence in Harlem. Although Springer had a negative view of Communist tactics and goals, the documentation does not show that she had a direct interest in challenging Communists. Instead, she seems to have served as a symbol of union progressivism while working to gain both middle- and working-class black support for organized labor.

After learning from Springer of Zimmerman's plans to prepare a leaflet of indoctrination for new and insufficiently active union members, Granger encouraged him in his efforts, citing Communist challenges and the danger that weak unionism posed for the struggle against racism. Claiming that Communists used catchwords to delude minorities, he asserted that union members needed to learn the difference between "progressive, constructive leadership, and the disruptive exploitative influences that masquerade under the title 'progressive.'" He also wanted the leaflets to identify "democratic heroes" whom Communists had subjected to "character assassination."[59]

Frank Crosswaith's view of communism barely wavered throughout his activist career. According to historian Mark Naison, he could work with Communists on an issue-by-issue basis but "regarded them as too politically and intellectually corrupt to entrust with leadership in black organizations." He believed that the CP was trying to make good on its pledge to "close up" the Harlem Labor Center by opening up organizations with similar names in the same vicinity. The Negro Labor Committee conducted a Negro Labor Assembly in the offices of the

Harlem Labor Center on 125th Street. Communists opened up an office on the same street from which they conducted a Negro Labor Victory Assembly. Perhaps this problem influenced Dubinsky's decision to tell the ILGWU Joint Boards to rely on Crosswaith's advice about whether organizations soliciting financial and moral support were Communist-supported ones claiming to work on behalf of black labor or "authentic" black ones.[60]

Until the 1939 Nazi-Soviet Non-Aggression Pact, A. Philip Randolph and the CP alternated between periods of hostility and cooperation. Supporting the Bolshevik Revolution until the 1921 split in the Socialist Party, he remained with the Socialists in opposition to the left-wing members, who then organized the American Communist Party. After U.S. Communists and their allies influenced the National Negro Congress to support the pact, Randolph resigned as the president of the congress and became unalterably opposed to Communists. He banned them from participating in the 1941 March on Washington Movement, which fought against segregation and discrimination.[61]

During World War II black protests combined with labor shortages opened up employment opportunities and unionism gained greater acceptance. Crosswaith gave some of the credit to the Negro Labor Committee, stating that nine and a half years of educational and organizational work had finally paid off. The Harlem Labor Center had helped to organize painters, butchers, building service employees, Pullman porters, cafeteria workers, and garment workers. In 1938 the Negro Labor Committee had 73 union affiliates and was responsible for twenty-five thousand blacks joining trade unions. By 1944 the number of affiliates increased to 110, representing both AFL and CIO unions.[62]

Crosswaith also proudly proclaimed that the ILGWU had placed blacks on most of its committees. As examples of ILGWU liberalism he specifically highlighted the recent appointments of Edith Ransome as business agent of Local 22 and Maida Springer as educational director of Local 132.[63] Granger also gave unabashed praise for the union's civil rights work: "There is no union in the country which has done more for a submerged group of workers, which has offered them a truer partnership in leadership activities, and which has more consistently fought reaction in the trade union fields and in politics than the International Ladies Garment Workers Union and many of its affiliated locals."[64]

Limitations of ILGWU Liberalism

ILGWU leaders often basked in what became a familiar litany of praise for their civil rights work and other progressive policies. Outside of public discourse, however, black allies occasionally criticized the ILGWU for not giving enough support to their leadership or the black working class. Twice Crosswaith wrote Zimmerman complaining of the absence of white ILGWU delegates at the monthly meetings of the Negro Labor Assembly.[65] Sustaining white participation in the interracial education classes offered at the Harlem Labor Center was also a problem. Springer assessed the situation partly in terms of convenience: "After the first excitement of winning the union contract, a lot of people fall off. You start with great excitement and then you stop going. The interest wanes. It's inconvenient to come to Harlem if you live downtown or in Queens or New Jersey. I'm sure people felt, I can do this downtown. Why should I go to Harlem?"[66]

Although his criticisms were not as sweeping as those of Communists, Granger suggested to Zimmerman that "Local 22 [could] well afford to improve its contact and influence among colored women in the dressmaking industry who live in Harlem."[67] He also faulted the ILGWU for not working aggressively enough to educate the Negro public about its deeds: "I say 'aggressive' because though the ILG has supported the Negro Labor Committee, has made intelligent use of some of its Negro officers, has generously backed not a few liberal activities in the Negro communities of New York, Chicago and elsewhere—though these things are true, such activities have been either of short duration or have been pushed forward only tentatively."[68]

In spite of the ILGWU's largely female membership, Jewish and Italian men predominated on the union's General Executive Board (GEB). People of color were unrepresented and women had only token representation. Dubinsky viewed this as a simple case of merit and not the perpetuation of white male privilege. ILGWU veteran Pauline Newman recalled Dubinsky's response to Crosswaith, when during the union's 1936 Chicago convention he ventured to criticize the lack of black representation. "Well, Dubinsky as usual got excited, and he said that the ILGWU never had any objection to having blacks on the executive board, but they've got to have ability to represent the ILGWU in every respect, and there are not many who can do that. If this was to happen today, I'm sure there are many members in the ILGWU who will say, 'But Mr. President, how can they get experience if they have no opportunities?' But in those days nobody said that."[69]

At the 1944 ILGWU convention in Boston, Rose Pesotta, at the end of her speech resigning her post as vice president, questioned why there was just one woman on the General Executive Board. Newman recalled that Pesotta's remarks made Dubinsky "mad as hell." He told Pesotta that women had to be capable in order to become a vice president. Springer too recalled hearing this argument from the male leadership, observing that many men who were not able nevertheless became members of the GEB. For many years thereafter the GEB still had only one female vice president.[70]

Jennie Silverman recalled that Maida Springer was loved and appreciated, "but that has never had anything to do with being treated equally." Silverman saw a terrible contradiction in the attitude of Communists, Socialists, and anarchists, who were proud of their stances against racism but only tolerated both black and white female leaders as long as their own positions were not threatened.[71] To illustrate the male leadership's entrenched sexist attitudes, Silverman told of an incident at a ceremony in which David Dubinsky was installing her, Springer, and others as newly elected officers. Springer's friend Pauli Murray was present as a guest. A man who was not a garment worker was also being installed as an officer, and Dubinsky did not understand he was insulting the women present when he commented on this fact. Silverman recalled, "He's talking to us! He says, 'You know, we're a union of women, and so sometimes we have to go for leadership outside the union.' And Pauli pinched me. We were ready to scream. But we shut up; he was our president installing us. . . . That's how deep-seated this attitude was. They weren't *aware* that they were discriminating against women."[72]

Silverman maintained that the ILGWU leadership's sexist practices included putting subtle pressure on female union officers to retire in order to get rid of them. She asserted that this happened to her when she was made to retire at age sixty-two and also to others.[73] Male leaders were not subtle in their attempt to force the retirement of Fannia Cohn, who in 1916 had the distinction of becoming the first female vice president of a major union. She also helped build and sustain the workers' education movement within the ILGWU and made a major contribution in support of other union and independent workers' schools.[74] Springer recalled the less than cordial relations between the ILGWU leadership and Cohn:

> Fannia . . . was critical of her male colleagues. I think she made life so uncomfortable for them that in due course she was not a vice president anymore. She irritated people because she was getting old, and I think many people thought she was out of step with the times. She was being isolated, and the young intellectuals were the movers and the shakers. She was an old intellectual who talked still with a heavy accent, and many people thought she was a nuisance. I guess this was in the forties.
>
> But Fannia was a woman who believed in books and believed in the power of thought. She was a force for many years in the whole educational structure of the ILG. Whenever you saw her, she'd hold your sleeve to talk with you about books. Many people looked at her as a bother sometimes, but she was a treasure for me. Fannia was a resource.[75]

Believing that Cohn's Old World ways and demeanor would not appeal to the changing ILGWU membership, Dubinsky hired Mark Starr in 1935 as educational director. Historian Annelise Orleck notes that Cohn continued to act as an ILGWU official and that she and Starr held a mutual dislike for one another. In August 1962 the union held a retirement party in order to force Cohn out of the union. Springer recalled that in response she thanked them very much and returned to work the next day. She died four months later. Although the ILGWU leadership failed to give Cohn proper recognition for her work, she gained respect and acclaim among ILGWU members and others involved in worker education nationally and internationally. Springer asserted that "Fannia Cohn, Pauline Newman, and a host of others were among the rambunctious, tenacious women who made themselves heard."[76]

Newman held that the ILGWU should have given women more opportunities to rise. She maintained that some had the chance "to rise somewhat," as organizers, business agents, and educational directors, but not as vice presidents. Some believed that the ILGWU leadership became more amenable to placing a black woman in the unofficial female spot on the GEB in order to make the minimal adjustment to demands for both black and female inclusion. Orlech commented that, in taking a position with the AFL-CIO International Affairs Department in 1960, Springer did not "wait around" to become a vice president. She also did not want the position.[77]

By 1963 Dubinsky offered Springer the opportunity to return to the ILGWU as a vice president at large. She declined this offer to become the union's first black vice president precisely because she was not a leader of a local. She understood that without a base of support her potential to make meaningful changes would be undermined. Her assessment of this position echoed Pesotta's three decades earlier. Bemoaning her decision under pressure to become the union's only female vice president, Pesotta remarked, "the voice of a solitary woman on the General Executive Board would be a voice lost in the wilderness."[78] As an ILGWU organizer in the mid 1960s, Springer argued for a broad inclusion of blacks in the entire union structure as opposed to symbolic representation. "Negro workers are aware of their need of a strong trade union movement but we need also to believe that the trade union movement has moved from the concept of a few chosen for their high visibility to an inclusiveness which makes unionism meaningful to all the workers in industry and at all levels."[79]

As Springer moved into leadership positions, *Justice* celebrated her success by featuring stories about her pioneering work. These stories never reported the racism she encountered from ILGWU members, their families, and from employers. Some of these incidents seemed to sustain Owen Springer's foreboding about union activism. Yet Springer remained committed to the ILGWU in large part because she credited the union with increasing the standard of living for all workers and because of the relationships she formed with leaders who were strong supporters of civil rights. Her relationship with these leaders also placed her on the side of anticommunism. Springer, however, did not become obsessed with anticommunism, as many union leaders did whose past was marked by bitter political battles. Her primary focus as a union officer was to fight discrimination, strengthen unionism through education, and develop female leadership.

In 1942 Springer visited Bordentown Manual and Industrial School for the first time since her graduation sixteen years earlier. Addressing the faculty and student body, she spoke of the organization of workers as the most important factor in the struggle against discrimination. A number of the faculty could not understand her enthusiastic support for unionism since graduates with good skills were not only denied jobs but also were met with contumely. While Springer recognized that a number of unions barred blacks, she still believed that unions on the whole were "liberalizing forces."[80] The ILGWU was among the better examples of unions that spoke out forcefully against discrimination.

3

The Dilemma of Race and Gender during World War II

ECAUSE OF THE PROMINENCE SPRINGER GAINED representing Local 22 in labor and community functions and through her volunteer position as chair of the local's education committee, the leaders of Local 132, the plastic, button, and novelty workers union, approached Local 22 manager Charles Zimmerman to inquire about her becoming the educational director. While remaining a Local 22 executive board member, Springer accepted this paid staff position with Local 132 in March 1943. The remarks of former Lovestoneite Minnie Lurye to Zimmerman following Springer's departure demonstrate that Springer stood out because her activism was stellar and because there were relatively few black activists. "I don't know the details, of course, but I've regretted the local's losing Maida. Couldn't you find some way of keeping her? She was by far the most intelligent and capable Negro woman we have yet drawn into union activities."[1]

Zimmerman had every intention of utilizing Springer's talents again. Planning to promote her to a paid staff position within Local 22, he believed her work in the smaller Local 132, which had only five paid staff workers, would be good preparation. Springer stated, "[Zimmerman] thought I had a special talent and wanted kind of a showcase to give me an opportunity and him an opportunity to see whether I had what they thought I had."[2]

Initially, however, Springer resisted the offer. A. Philip Randolph sought to allay her fears by encouraging her to view the position as an opportunity to be creative, including, if need be, in her dissent against racist practices.[3] The educational opportunities she provided workers included not only instruction in union procedures, labor contracts, and labor history but also promotion of racial tolerance and an appreciation for diversity. With mentors and role models such as Randolph, Charles Zimmerman, and a number of activist women in the garment unions and in the Women's Trade Union League (WTUL), she could count on a base of support.

For ILGWU women who represented the majority membership in a union whose leadership was dominated by men (Local 22's membership was 95 percent female), the WTUL was a valuable resource. Women from both AFL and CIO unions belonged to the WTUL. Springer was particularly close to women belonging to the CIO-affiliated Amalgamated Clothing Workers of America (ACWA). ILGWU president David Dubinsky and ACWA president Sidney Hillman, who was also a CIO vice president, battled each other for President Franklin Roosevelt's support and over issues of jurisdiction and Communist participation in the CIO and the American Labor Party (ALP).[4] Springer's relationships with women in the ACWA, however, centered around gender and race issues rather than the ideological debates around communism and other issues that preoccupied the male leadership.

Springer's activism during this period was also geared toward supporting the Allied cause in World War II. She recalled that some ILGWU members lost their lives working with underground forces to help people escape from Germany and Italy. She also saw new workers in Local 22 who had escaped from Nazi concentration camps. The ILGWU and other unions helped Norwegian underground forces, the French resistance movement, and European labor movements struggling against fascism. U.S. unions also supported the Committee to Defend America, which worked with the International Transport Workers Federation to fight fascism.[5] The ILGWU joined with the Organization for Rehabilitation and Training in helping to assist refugees.

Although Springer affirmed that "we [ILGWU members] were super patriots," racist practices did temper her activism in support of the war and pointed to serious shortcomings of Roosevelt's administration concerning racial justice.[6] While Springer's experience of racism may have tested her mettle, she did not change her belief in the role organized labor could play in fighting racial discrimination. She used her position to combat racism and stereotypes, create greater social awareness, and establish a basis for unity around the struggle for better working conditions, wages, and hours.

Racial, Ethnic, and Religious Conflict within Local 132

By 1943 when Springer became the Local 132 educational director, a diverse group of new workers had replaced the large numbers of white men who had gone to serve in the armed services. This new group included black and white Southerners and Jewish escapees from Hitler's death camps. Working alongside the newcomers were women and older men from European immigrant families. Springer recalled, "People worked together who were so strange to one another's cultures." Part of her strategy for building union strength was to help the workers understand the benefit of working together on issues that affected them all, a lesson she had originally learned from Randolph. A work environment that contained hazardous materials and machinery also required that workers develop a sense of responsibility for each other.[7]

In her work with Local 132, Springer instituted a library, arranged lectures, and began classes in public speaking, the union, its constitution, and the contract. At first many of the new union members attending these classes failed to realize that she was the educational director since she brought in white lecturers to help indoctrinate the new members. Workers often did not learn her identity until they had attended a class or two and were instructed to pick up their union book from the educational director. At that point their reactions varied from pleasure to shock. Springer recalled that an older white man who was a shop chair and a molder reacted with the most contempt: "[He] came into my office to pick up someone's union book. He said he wanted to see Springer. My name doesn't tell you anything nor does my voice. I was sitting at my desk in a big office all by myself, and I said, 'I'm Maida Springer.' He looked at me and said, 'You're Springer! Puh!' Spit on the floor and walked out."[8]

Considered the aristocrats in the local, the molders were of Polish, German, Swedish, and Italian background. Although members of these ethnic groups sometimes despised one another, they were united in their hatred of blacks.[9] Yet Springer had to work with this man who, as a shop chair, was part of the local's executive board. In efforts to organize new workers he worked with Springer and others issuing leaflets in early morning hours between shifts at an accessory plant. Six months after the incident in her office, he helped her in preparations for a Christmas party she planned by organizing a group of shop chairs to decorate the hall. Springer did not interpret his cooperation as a sign he was overcoming his racism: "People become accustomed to you. Work with you. And they may hate all other people of that nation, of that color, but you are different. Well, this is what happened to this chairman. He worked with me. I was therefore different. I wasn't like all those other people he hated whom he did not know. . . . I was one of those he worked with and served him well, served his shop well. And that was the priority. I never misunderstood."[10]

Springer would continue to meet with similar forms of racism in her work. Once a ILGWU staff member, whom Springer described as having dark coloring, thick lips, and an Eastern European accent, said in her presence, "We builded [sic] the union for the schwartzer?" (a Yiddish word meaning black that acquired a derogatory connotation in its use in the United States by English speakers). Springer remarked that incidents like these "burned her up inside," but instead of exploding in anger, she learned to respond in a way that emphasized the perpetrator's ignorance. In her work as educational director, Springer recognized that she might not change attitudes, but she could help influence workers to follow the enlightened self-interest that supported the union as a whole.

Among the challenges Springer confronted was a strike involving the followers of the powerful black cult leader and businessman Father Divine at a Local 132 waste-products plant in Manhattan. As a rebuke to the union's demands for a wage increase from thirty-five to fifty cents an hour, the employer hired strikebreakers, the majority of whom were Father Divine followers, at a wage of seventy-five cents an hour. Goons hired either by the Divine movement or by the employer drove the Divine followers to the plant in Cadillacs.

Although Divine sometimes directed his followers to cooperate with organized labor and other groups on issues he deemed important, he opposed their joining labor unions and engaging in strikes. He also counseled his followers not to accept what he regarded as charity or welfare, such as paid holidays and other benefits won in labor struggles.[11] Divine biographer Robert Weisbrot asserts that his position derived from his view of labor as violent and undemocratic. More importantly, he wished to preclude his followers from having outside commitments that could disrupt the cohesion of his movement. His followers viewed him as the embodiment of God.

Leader of the Negro Labor Committee Frank Crosswaith, who once called Divine "the religious clown of our time," opposed him for allowing his followers to work as strikebreakers and under sweatshop conditions.[12] His hostility toward Divine was so strong that he once refused to sit on the same platform with him at a rally against police brutality called by the United Front of Labor Unions.[13] Springer's approach was very different from Crosswaith's. In the Local 132 strike she became the main liaison between the union and the Divine movement. In dealing with the Divine followers, she applied the lessons she learned from her friend Layle Lane, an organizer and one of the first black vice presidents of the American Federation of Teachers. In the late 1930s, during pickets protesting the exclusionary policies of Harlem businesses, Springer observed Lane deal with difficult circumstances with patience, clarity, and a minimum of hostility.[14]

The employees of the embattled factory, which produced cleaning rags used to service large machinery in industrial plants, were Jewish refugees, Southern black migrants, and people recently released from prison. Their differences could have caused the failure of the strike if not handled sensitively. For example, Springer quickly learned that in providing food for the strikers during their lunch breaks from the picket line, the leadership had to insure that only workers who adhered to kosher standards bought and prepared the food, table, and utensils for the workers of that group. She remarked, "This is a part of the education that does not come in a book. You see what you are faced with and that you could lose the cohesiveness of a struggle you are in, if you do not understand the social implications. They picketed together. The common objective was better wages and recognition. There was no problem with this, but if we interfered with their social institutions, we could have destroyed that struggle."[15]

Another problem the union quickly resolved concerned the former prisoners, who numbered fewer than a dozen. If they participated in any visible way in the strike, they would violate the terms of their probation. Accordingly, Springer and business agent Samuel Eisenberg assigned them to work in the office "stuffing envelopes and mimeographing, preparing the leaflets."[16] Perhaps because the strikers were unusually diverse, ethnic and racial tensions did not inform the way they viewed the factory owner, who was Jewish, and the Divine strikebreakers and escorts, who were black.

Weisbrot maintained that Divine did not deliberately seek jobs for his followers in strike situations. His focus was on the availability of employment and not the conflicts between employers and unions.[17] Divine's willingness to ignore the full context in which followers sometimes worked explains the stance his representative took in a telephone conversation with Local 132 manager Martin Feldman. When Feldman broached the subject of strikebreaking, the representative responded in the unfamiliar language and concepts of the Divine movement. Feldman was dumbfounded. Springer's understanding of the Divine movement made her the best one to continue the negotiation process.

> I understood that you had to speak in terms of Father Divine. You dare not call them anything but angels, when you spoke to the Father's representatives, which I did three times a day. I gave Feldman a crash course in Father Divine language. That was difficult. When you call a representative or employer, you attempt to do a straightforward discussion. If you are angry, he's angry. But to be spoken to in nice soft tones about the children and heaven was bewildering. Feldman would hang up and say, "Springer, what is he talking about? These people are out there killing us." We laughed about this very often after that.[18]

The followers of Divine were called either angels or children. Angels gave all their property and donated their wages and labor to the movement in exchange for his ministry and food, shelter, and employment. As part of their total submission to Divine, followers renounced all familial relations and gave up sexual activity. Those classed as children were not willing to part with all their property, but they still followed his teachings and lived in the buildings and homes owned by the movement, called Peace Missions or heavens.[19]

Divine sent in his white followers to purchase choice properties in communities that adopted restrictive covenants, which were agreements not to sell property to blacks. The movement also owned successful rural farming cooperatives in New York's Ulster County and a number of businesses that provided inexpensive meals and services in Harlem and other areas. Springer knew a number of people in the Divine movement, both sincere believers and hustlers who sought personal advantage from the movement. About the latter she explained, "You ate a whole meal for five cents and you lived somewhere for very little and you did the minimum." [20]

In attempts to resolve the strike situation, Springer contacted a Divine follower, a lawyer who had been very successful in real estate.[21] Accompanied by someone in her community who was involved in the Divine movement, she also attended a number of Sunday meals presided over by Father Divine. Although Springer had been introduced to Divine and he knew the purpose of her visits, the two never conversed. The followers with whom she did speak lacked authority over decisions regarding the Divine workers at the waste-products plant.

The turning point in the strike happened as a result of the introduction of violence. One day Springer had positioned herself on a loading platform in order to address the men who were escorting the Divine strikebreakers. Her appeal concerned the disparity between the union's demands and what the employer was currently paying the strikebreakers. As she was speaking, someone hit Martin Feldman in the back of the head with a blackjack, leaving him lying in the street with traffic whirling by him. Just as she spotted Feldman, some of Divine's escorts restrained her while women kicked her. Both she and Feldman recovered, although Springer sustained permanent marks on her legs from the assault.

During another ILGWU strike involving Divine's followers, Crosswaith questioned the sincerity of the movement's commitment to nonviolence. He observed that Father Divine trucks, which brought in his followers as "scabs," were "guarded by dusky and husky male angels whose powerful arms and stout bodies testify as to their faith in the principle of Peace." Weisbrot maintained that the pacifist principles of Divine's followers were tested after they suffered assaults as scab labor.[22] Although Springer was unsure whether her attackers were Divine devotees, it is clear that the movement employed people who were not committed to nonviolence.

The introduction of violence quickly led the employer to call for negotiations. With the strike called off and negotiations in process, Local 132 leaders knew they still had to come to some accommodation with the Father Divine group. This was a difficult undertaking since Divine followers resisted both union membership and union gains, which they perceived as welfare. Negotiations were further hampered by the failure of Divine representatives to show up for scheduled meetings with Local 132 leaders. When the parties eventually met, the union had no choice but to allow some of the Divine followers to stay at the plant and accept that they would not adhere to union principles. All the followers, however, eventually left the plant.

An unexpected outcome of this strike was that Springer developed enough rapport with Divine representatives to allow her to bring workers from the Hudson Shore Labor School to a Divine mission located adjacent to the school. Spencer's Point, a five-hundred-acre estate across the Hudson River from the Hyde Park mansion of President Franklin Roosevelt, was the Divine movement's most celebrated acquisition. Landowners did not always realize that Father Divine was involved in the purchase of their property, but in this case the former owner, Howland Spencer, did know and apparently approached the deal with great relish, selling the property in 1938 for an incredibly low sum. As Weisbrot explained, Spencer, an eccentric millionaire, was a bitter enemy of Roosevelt and did not like his "socialistic" programs. By selling his estate to the interracial Divine movement, Spencer hoped to create a political problem for Roosevelt, particularly by offending Southern Congressmen, whom Roosevelt courted for passage of his New Deal policies. Roosevelt responded to the widespread publicity surrounding the Spencer's Point Peace Mission by making light of the situation.[23]

Springer viewed these visits as a way of providing workers with the opportunity to make a more informed assessment of a movement that also had an impact on organized labor: "You could not take pictures, but you could talk to people and you could walk around. Many people didn't believe, and particularly white workers, that the place could be orderly. I was able to take these workers and show them physically that people were being rehabilitated. And while this in my view was a cult, most of the people who went into Father Divine went there to change their lives into hope and they'd given their all to the work of Father Divine. It was another learning experience."[24]

Educating against Racism

Similar to the philosophy of the Bordentown industrial school Springer had attended, the ILGWU's education movement stressed the overall development of the individual and more importantly promoted group solidarity. As part of her work in building an appreciation for labor solidarity, Springer arranged weekend seminars for Local 132 workers at the Hudson Shore Labor School. In addition to recreational activities that included swimming, marshmallow roasts, cookouts, square dances, and singing, she also organized lectures. For example, Lester Granger spoke on prejudice and the problems of people who settled in an urban community.[25]

The ILGWU, Amalgamated Clothing Workers of America, and Women's Trade Union League were strong supporters of this residential school. It was founded by Hilda Worthington Smith in 1939 at her family's fifty-acre estate in West Park, in New York's Ulster County. Springer first became close to Smith through their activism in the WTUL. She credited WTUL organizer Rose Schneiderman with bringing "the women of wealth and prominence to understand the concerns and the problems of working women."[26] Springer was drawn further into the circle of upper-class women reformers after meeting Caroline Ware in 1945; Ware was also close to Smith. As a result of Smith's friendship with Eleanor Roosevelt, she was appointed to organize within the New Deal administration the Camps and Schools for Unemployed Women, the women's counterpart to the Civilian Conservation Corps for men, commonly called the CCC. The press then dubbed Smith's program the "She-She-She." With humor Springer recalled, "She-She-She camp was not its name, but the men mimicked it and called it that because women were not really accepted. They were not people."[27]

Located at the foot of the Catskill Mountains, Hudson Shore included three large houses that could accommodate sixty-five people in warm weather and forty-five in cool weather. Among those on the board of directors in the 1940s were Mark Starr, who would give technical assistance to unions in Africa in 1961, and Springer's good friends from the ACWA, Esther Peterson and Dollie Lowther Robinson. The Honorary Sponsoring Committee included Eleanor Roosevelt, Lester Granger, and CIO leaders James B. Carey and Walter Reuther. During Springer's period of activism in Africa, Carey and Reuther's opposition to Jay Lovestone had a negative impact on her work.[28]

The curriculum was a collaborative effort involving the WTUL, labor unions, and students. Some of the activities included putting on plays, hiking, going on picnics, swimming, dancing, singing, giving short speeches, making charts and graphs, and writing leaflets and articles. Robinson, who was among the many to receive WTUL scholarships for Hudson Shore, held that the teachers' use of the workers' experiences to teach subjects like economics and science was very effective.[29]

Lessons also were geared toward advancing racial equality. Smith's hope was that through work and play and a "skillful analysis of the problem [racism] in the objective atmosphere of the classroom," workers might devise techniques for achieving a harmonious community life. Interracial contact might open students to new understandings, which in turn could serve to illuminate "all personality and community relationships of the individual students, and of the groups to which they would return."[30]

Racial prejudices, however, nearly scuttled Springer's first attempts at full inclusion of union members. She recalled that distraught shop chairwomen, primarily from Greek, Polish, and German immigrant families, would tell her, "I want to go to Hudson Shore for the weekend, but my brother said or my father said or my mother said they'd kill me if I went anywhere with niggers." These families were shocked that their daughters might have a black female roommate and were horrified at the prospect of perhaps two black shop chairmen attending, whom they regarded as potential rapists. To her credit, Springer found ways to educate the women and their families without losing her self-respect or alienating them. On a number of occasions the daughters would invite her to dinner to allay the family's fears and correct their misconceptions. Springer described the interactions:

> [T]hey would be very honest and say . . . they heard that black men did this, that, and the other. I said most of the men who were in jail for rape and this, that, and the other are white. But you have to be able to say this without embarrassment and to have a few of your facts. In those days, I would always go with some facts. You had to stand your ground. . . . Among the things I learned was how important it was to be direct, to have respect for yourself, and not to let anyone disrespect you. Fortunately, I knew enough political history that I could cite simple examples of how prejudice played a part in their lives in the countries from which they came. And since I was also a foreigner, I think it was acceptable, grudgingly, because no matter what I did, no matter what I said, I still wore this brown skin.[31]

Springer recalled that perhaps only one family with whom she had dined remained adamant against their daughter's participation in the labor school. In response to the suggestion that her success may have been due to the families' perception of her as "a proper chaperone," Springer remarked, "I think it had to do more with a belief that I was one Negro that maybe, that they thought met their standards. Their standards were much lower than mine in most instances, but again, these are the prejudices you had to deal with."[32]

Some of the white women who attended the weekend institutes still worried about their families' response to their socializing with blacks. Springer recalled that they would say, "Please don't take pictures. I can't go home and let my mother and father see that I was sitting next to Negroes."[33]

Yet Hudson Shore's interracial setting provided the context for examining relations between diverse communities, especially between black and white work-ers. John Caswell Smith, Jr., executive secretary of the Urban League of Greater Boston, who led discussions on race relations at Hudson Shore in the early 1940s, concluded that the school up to that point had little success in changing atti-tudes. Smith, who was black, perceived that there was an "atmosphere of phony friendliness, the artificial part of which shines through occasionally whenever somebody's 'guard' slips for a moment." In his view, blacks did not feel relaxed around whites, feeling they always had to be on their best behavior. The white students, who were equally confused about living so close to blacks and also were condescending toward them, believed they were being the "good sports." One example of how traumatic this interracial experience was for some whites was re-vealed in Smith's story about a Southern woman named Mary. Mary explained, "When I first came to this school it was my first time in the North. . . . When I found out I had to sleep in the same room with some colored girls, my stomach turned over. I didn't want it to, but it did."[34]

The veteran white ILGWU leader Jennie Matyas recalled that the union began to have heightened racial problems when blacks migrated from the South in great numbers during World War II. Although the official position of the ILGWU was that all members were brothers and sisters, Matyas like Springer concluded that the rank and file was like any cross-section of society. As the num-ber of black workers increased in the industry, Matyas stated that whites devel-oped a fear that blacks would take over.[35]

In some respects Springer's experience in Local 132 diverged from the typi-cal black experience in industry during and after the war. Perhaps because the local's new Southern and European immigrant workers were largely inexperi-enced in factory production and were marginalized in the larger society, the be-lief that black workers were unsuited for factory work did not hold. And, unlike the experience elsewhere, the white men from Local 132 who had served in the war did not for the most part reclaim their old jobs, thereby replacing these new factory workers. Instead they took advantage of the GI educational bill and went to college, in the process tempering white fears of black advancement.

Women's Circles

Through union education programs and contact with the Women's Trade Union League and the Amalgamated Clothing Workers of America, Springer met and worked with women committed to the solidarity of labor, the develop-ment of female leadership, labor education, and civil rights. She has stated, "My own constant passion about the labor movement with all of its bumps and warts is because I came up at a time when there were so many role models." These role models included Charlotte Adelmond, an organizer and business agent for the Laundry Workers Joint Board; Dollie Lowther Robinson, educational director of the Laundry Workers Joint Board; Esther Peterson, ACWA educational director; Pauline Newman, educational director of the ILGWU Health Center and the union's first female organizer; Frances Perkins, Secretary of Labor under Roosevelt; Eleanor Roosevelt; Hilda Worthington Smith; Rose Schneiderman; and Fannia Cohn.[36]

Springer viewed the WTUL as a forum for women, an educational center, and a resource that promoted women's self-respect. The WTUL also taught her to lobby. In late 1945 the WTUL had her speak against the Equal Rights Amendment (ERA) before a judiciary subcommitee of the U.S. Senate. Elisabeth Christman, the secretary-treasurer of the National WTUL, congratulated Springer for making "a fine statement which expressed your conviction of the danger inherent in this vicious bill." The following year the Senate narrowly defeated the ERA. The WTUL opposed the ERA, which was first introduced in Congress in 1923, because it would overturn the protective laws for women governing hours and conditions of work. Labor opposition to the ERA slowly began to drop after the courts consistently ruled that Title VII of the 1964 Civil rights Act, barring sex and race discrimination, overturned state protective laws. Nevertheless, in 1982 the ERA died three states short of ratification.[37]

Springer's first introduction to Dollie Lowther Robinson and Charlotte Adelmond was through WTUL programs. By 1938 nine locals in the New York City area with a membership of nearly thirty thousand made up the Laundry Workers' Joint Board in which these women held office. Robinson and particularly Adelmond began the movement in New York City to organize laundry workers during a 1937 strike at the Colonial Laundry where they were both employed. The laundry workers were one of the lowest paid and most exploited labor groups. They were subjected to extreme heat, heavy lifting, and work that would make their hands crack and bleed. Some even had to work while standing in water.[38] At the Colonial Laundry, workers numbering three hundred labored seventy-two hours a week for six dollars. Robinson maintained that the supervisors, owing to their "nasty" attitudes, were the best organizers for the shop. Still, as Pauline Newman put it, the laundry workers needed somebody "to let employers know how little they paid for labor that was really unpleasant" and make them see the human side of their business. According to Robinson, New York mayor Fiorello La Guardia was willing to put pressure on the Colonial Laundry. He supported the striking workers by having the laundry's water turned off, which effectively shut down the business.[39]

Remembering Adelmond as an "unsung heroine, fiery, tenacious, and loyal," Springer remarked, "This proud West Indian black woman was uncompromising on any form of racial discrimination. I so admired her courage and I hope that a little of it rubbed off on me."[40] She viewed Adelmond, who was a Garveyite, and Robinson as a formidable team:

> Both of them were tall women and not thin women. Charlotte wore her hair in an Afro. She was a black nationalist. These kids today think they're nationalists? Shucks. They don't know. She was outspoken, outraged. . . . And Dollie Lowther came in as the highly educated, soft spoken, both physical and mental giant. They were giants in the labor movement. Giants. Fierce about workers' dignity. Fierce! These people who stand over big steam tubs and ironing tables and big machines with dirty clothes going around inside had a right to personal dignity and decent wages. When the shops were organized, Charlotte still would remind people that the flame was always burning, lest we forget, lest we relax our vigil, lest anybody get comfortable while someone does an under-the-table contract or somebody gets sloppy about their work. . . . One of the lost warriors. Talk about a pioneer. When she went back to Trinidad, I think she was a very sick woman, a very broken woman when she died. Oh God, strength, courage, she had it all. Nationalist to the core. Part of her undoing. This was so long ago and people couldn't accommodate that. And whether anyone said anything about it or not, this made angry people who couldn't accept her vigilance, her forthrightness. She was too much for them.[41]

Dollie Robinson, who praised Adelmond as one of her teachers, drew a similar portrait of her leadership. In the initial stages of organizing in 1936, Adelmond would use her own home as a meeting place, and she appealed to other unions for help.

> Charlotte was the one that was there early morning, late at night. Everything she did was for the workers. That was her life. She had no other life. None of us did. . . . [Among the leaders] Charlotte was the only woman and she was the strong one. And as I remember her, it was years ago, . . . to prove that she was strong, she wore a shirt and tie. And . . . before the Afro came in, she had her hair short, and she wore those felt hats. *Unbelievable* woman. The things she would have you do to organize a shop, I mean, were just sheer guts and grit. . . . I mean you just had to give every ounce of your time to it. . . . I guess she was the first person I ever saw that could knock a boss out physically and never raise her hand. And I never knew how she did it, and the workers would swear by her. The bosses were very abusive. They'd get very loud and raise their hands. And then you'd see he was really on the floor, and you never knew why and how. It was because Charlotte was from

the West Indies and knew how to butt. And they butt with the back of their head and they never raise their hands. And to the workers, at that point, that was strength, you see. They had been taking so much abuse, and even if a boss fought them they'd have to forego arresting him, because they wanted to work. And she was in a terrible area. Brownsville was where the little gangsters and the mobs were. But she was able to hold her own.[42]

Although Springer's relationship with Robinson and Adelmond was one of mutual respect and friendship, they had different assessments of some of the labor and political leaders based upon their individual experiences. Robinson was close to black political leader Adam Clayton Powell, Jr. As a U.S. congressman, Powell helped secure her appointment in the early 1960s as assistant to Esther Peterson in the Women's Bureau of the U.S. Department of Labor.[43] During that same period, when Springer was working for the AFL-CIO International Affairs Department, Powell investigated racial discrimination in the ILGWU as chair of the House Committee on Education and Labor. He showed up uninvited at a party AFL-CIO president George Meany was hosting in Geneva. Springer recalled, "Adam walked in wearing a short evening jacket—you know the way some wear them in the tropics—with a red cummerbund and black silk-striped pants. I was standing welcoming guests. Normally, he would have said hello and passed by me. But this evening he was effusive. And Mr. Meany was looking at me and looking at Adam. He had a *presence* that filled the room."[44] Powell exited only after he had succeeded in making all uncomfortably aware of his presence.

The hostile relationship between Powell and the ILGWU leadership began as early as 1944, when Powell's People's Committee, which had Communist support, campaigned for the defeat of the Zimmerman administration.[45] Springer both admired Powell and was ambivalent toward him because of the political differences between him and Zimmerman. She asserted, however, "beneath whatever the facade was, we were moving in the same direction and each of us in turn had our role to play."[46] Frank Crosswaith, on the other hand, considered Powell a demagogue.

Dollie Robinson criticized Powell's nemesis, Crosswaith, and Negro Labor Committee organizer Noah C. A. Walter. She remarked that they had been in the forefront of organizing for the laundry workers, until they "really went off key and didn't do and didn't fight." After the laundry workers gave up on them, she asserted that Socialist Party head Norman Thomas was the "one that kept the faith" with them. The ACWA made the laundry workers an affiliate after the ILGWU declined to take them in. The WTUL was concerned with organizing the laundry workers as well.[47]

Principally, these women loyally supported one another. Charlotte Adelmond's strength, pride, and leadership qualities clearly threatened the security of many of the white male leaders in the ACWA, who took for granted that it was their right and duty to lead. Unbeknownst to the ILGWU and ACWA leadership, in the early 1940s Adelmond used the mimeograph machine in Springer's office to print leaflets that were part of her challenge to the "seasoned leadership," as Robinson dubbed the ACWA administration.[48] Robinson recalled that although Adelmond's enemies were forced to respect her abilities, they still tried to undermine her: "She would win elections by an overpowering number of votes. I don't care who they put against her, or what methods they used, she would win those elections as the strong person. And, with proper guidance, probably never would have been out of the union. But, some people seeing strength, the weaklings hang on and tear down the strength."[49]

The circumstances that finally crushed Adelmond's spirit are unclear. However, she finally lost an election and left the labor movement. Unlike Adelmond, both Springer and Robinson had the support of higher officials. Robinson credited ACWA officer Bessie Hillman with helping her to survive and counted Bessie's husband, Sidney Hillman, as one of her supporters.[50]

The women in Springer's circle viewed with some amusement the rivalry between the leaders of the women's and men's garment unions. An occasional organizer for the ILGWU, Esther Peterson reported that when "things got tight" between the two unions, Hillman did not want her to help the ILGWU. Once he told her, "If you want to organize, you organize for the Amalgamated. And don't organize for our competitor." She responded, "Well, Sidney, you always told me that the thing to do was to organize the unorganized!"[51] Both Springer and Hillman were the godmothers of Robinson's daughter, Jan. Of her close relationship with Robinson and Adelmond Springer remarked, "We were supposed to be enemies, because . . . this was at a period when Sidney Hillman . . . and David Dubinsky . . . were vying for FDR's favor. Everybody who *worked* for them was either with them or 'agin 'em.' I was supposed to dislike everybody out of the Amalgamated. But this never happened to Dollie, it never happened to Charlotte and myself."[52]

Dubinsky and Hillman managed for periods of time to cooperate in support of Roosevelt. For his reelection campaigns, they worked through the American Labor Party to garner support from Socialists and other third-party members who refused to register as Democrats. The needle trade unions formed the American Labor Party in 1936 to compete with the Democratic candidates in New York State who were supported by the corrupt Tammany Hall machine.[53]

Stalin's execution in 1942 of the Polish labor leaders Henryk Ehrlich and Victor Alter exacerbated the differences between Hillman and Dubinsky over Communist participation in unions and the ALP. Ehrlich and Alter had been leaders of the Socialist Bund, from which Hillman, Dubinsky, and almost all Jewish Socialists in the United States traced their political roots. Many believed that the Soviet Union executed them on the trumped-up charges of being Hitler allies and Nazi supporters, because the Comintern was threatened by the prospect of their renewed activism in Poland after the war. After learning of the execution, a committee of 250 trade unionists headed by Dubinsky announced a mass meeting of protest. Dependent upon Communist support in the CIO and concerned for the sake of war unity, Hillman did not attend the memorial protest.[54]

The solidarity embraced by black trade union women, despite the rivalries of their leaders, is reflected in their actions in the 1942 election campaign. The Amalgamated Clothing Workers temporarily withdrew from the American Labor Party because Hillman supported a Tammany Hall nominee for governor over the ALP candidate, Dean Alfange. On the ALP ticket with Dean Alfange was Springer, the party's nominee for the state assembly from the Twenty-first District. The ACWA-affiliated Laundry Workers Union endorsed her candidacy and worked for her election.[55]

Springer's nomination gained her the distinction of becoming the first trade union member nominated from a Harlem district for an electoral office. She agreed to enter the race only because ALP supporters wanted a trade unionist on the ticket and they had assured her that she could not win the primary. Her platform included pledges to fight discrimination in industry, government, and the armed services, to crack down on labor unions that excluded blacks, to equalize rent levels in Harlem to those of other areas, to end the poll tax, Jim Crow and anti-Semitism, to equalize food prices with the rest of the city and control quality, to check juvenile delinquency, and to fight fascism and win the war. After winning the primary, Springer to her relief lost the election to the Democratic incumbent, William T. Andrews, whom she considered "a nice guy and a friend."[56]

The ALP right wing led by Dubinsky quit the party after Hillman's left wing, with the support of Communists, overwhelming defeated them in the 1944 spring primary. The former right wing group then formed the Liberal Party. Both the ALP and the Liberal Party supported Roosevelt's 1944 reelection.[57]

Dubinsky first took note of Springer's activism as a result of her participation in this campaign. Dubinsky had requested that union managers bring their educational staffs and active members to prepare mailings targeting ILGWU members living in New York, New Jersey, and Long Island. In response between fifteen and thirty-five workers came to ILGWU headquarters each night to help. When he sent out the call for all the locals to get as many volunteers as possible for the final mail drive before the election, only Springer showed up with twenty-five people from Local 132. Impressed by their activism, Dubinsky gave them the Council Room in which to work and told Springer to take herself and the workers to the finest restaurant for dinner. Seeking to shake up male egos, he then called various union managers and said, "I want you to see what a girl does." Dubinsky then began to pay attention to Springer's work and learned that other locals joined in the educational activities she planned.[58]

Race Relations and the War Effort

Springer's labor activism on behalf of the war involved educational, fund raising, and cooperative work. She served as a first aid instructor and a captain of the Women's Health Brigade, an ILGWU effort to support the war effort. As Local 132 educational director, she organized a club whose members wrote letters to Local 132 servicemen, edited a newsletter called "PX" for Local 132 servicemen, and in 1944 became a member of the New York City War Price and Rationing Board. Along with Robinson and Newman, she served on the New York State Minimum Wage Board, which monitored hours and general working conditions. They particularly were concerned with placing checks on the exploitation of women workers.[59]

The ILGWU war effort was coupled with an unabashed admiration for Franklin Roosevelt that dated to his tenure as governor of New York. Springer recalled becoming captivated with Roosevelt at the age of twenty-two: "I was standing in the living room of my small apartment running the carpet sweeper and listening to the President's inaugural address when I heard him say, 'You have nothing to fear but fear itself.' I just stopped my work and sat down to give full attention to the rest of that memorable speech."[60] Even Owen Springer worked for Roosevelt's election, believing that it represented the "crossing of the Rubicon for working people."[61] Otherwise, to his wife's consternation, he remained a staunch Republican. For him the Democratic Party was stigmatized as the party of the Confederacy and of the corrupt Tammany Hall.

During Roosevelt's presidency blacks en masse changed party affiliation from Republican to Democrat. His New Deal policies and particularly Eleanor Roosevelt's support of civil rights helped to spur the change. Although strong advocates of Negro rights worked within his administration, Roosevelt actually did little to alter the system of discrimination and segregation.[62]

During the war many blacks became increasingly vocal in their resentment of the discrimination that pervaded all sectors of American life, and they remained hostile to unionism. In a letter to Crosswaith's Negro Labor Committee, Charles Zimmerman acknowledged the role racist union practices played in the disaffection of black labor when he stated that the labor movement should take the leading role in promoting equality for blacks, as the ILGWU had done. Pointing to the hypocrisy of the U.S. disdain for Nazi doctrines of racial purity while it tolerated Jim Crow, he indicated that a critical national issue was economic, social, and political justice for "millions of Americans whose skin happens to be black." In 1942 the Negro Labor Committee was sufficiently alarmed about the threat that racism posed to a unified war effort to propose a conference to deal with the "high degree of racial tension." The committee acknowledged that anti-white and anti-Semitic feelings within the black community "may be understandable enough in view of the highly restricted employment opportunities." The following year a riot erupted in Harlem.[63]

To symbolize the need to fight both a domestic and foreign battle, African Americans transformed Winston Churchill's "V for Victory" sign into a double V, connoting victory over fascism abroad and victory over racism at home. They also supported A. Philip Randolph's March on Washington Movement. Its goals included abolishing the discrimination blacks faced in the war industries, the federal government, and the armed forces. Concerned over what a mass march of blacks would mean for the war effort, Roosevelt, six days before the scheduled event, signed Executive Order 8802 establishing the Fair Employment Practices Committee (FEPC) to abolish discrimination in the war industries and government for the duration of the war. The armed forces, however, remained untouched, and the FEPC's enforcement powers would prove to be weak.[64] Randolph had agreed to call off the march in exchange for the creation of the executive order. However, the movement continued. The aim of the now-expanded March on Washington Movement was to end discrimination and segregation in all phases of public life. Its motto was "Winning Democracy for the Negro is Winning the War for Democracy." Randolph and Norman Thomas noted, "The very thought of a jim-crow army fighting to break down Nazi race theories is an anachronism of policy and would be humorous were it not so tragically dangerous and destructive."[65]

Numerous articles and cartoons in *Justice*, the ILGWU organ, pointed out how race hatred at home was akin to Nazism abroad. A major story of the time concerned the case of Alton Levy, a white sergeant assigned to train black soldiers at an air base in Lincoln, Nebraska. An organizer for the ILGWU before his enlistment, Levy was court-martialed, demoted to a private, and sentenced to hard labor for protesting the treatment of black soldiers.[66] Yet *Justice* remained mute about one of the most egregious affronts to blacks during the war. By separating the blood donations of blacks and whites, the American Red Cross catered to white fears that blood carried racial traits. Without acknowledging this practice, *Justice* carried a plethora of stories praising ILGWU efforts to aid the Red Cross. Springer, however, refused to participate in Red Cross blood-donor drives. She was aware that the preeminent black surgeon Dr. Charles Drew, who had pioneered in the mass production and storage of blood plasma, resigned his position as the director of the Red Cross's blood bank in New York City because of these policies.[67]

When Dubinsky requested all ILGWU locals to organize blood drives, Martin Feldman concurred with Springer's decision not to participate; however, he suggested she find an alternative way of contributing. At her suggestion Local 132 members raised $1,100, which they used to buy a blood plasma machine for the Chinese blood bank located in New York. With the support of Shavy Lee, the mayor of Chinatown, Springer then arranged a drive for the Chinese blood bank. For these efforts the officers of Local 132 were celebrated in Chinatown. Ironically, however, given that the drive was organized to protest the racist practices of the Red Cross, the American Signal Corps saw in this event an opportunity to propagandize the ideals of democracy. They printed pictures of black and white blood donors with the caption "American democracy at work." *Justice* articles also commended Local 132 for being the first ILGWU local to donate to the Chinese Blood Bank. The *Justice* staff, however, either did not know or did not report Springer's role in these events, and did not mention her name. They did report, however, Zimmerman's praise for the efforts of this multiracial local and Feldman's praise for the heroism of the Chinese people.[68]

Dollie Robinson and Charlotte Adelmond also found the policies of the Red Cross disturbing. Along with Bessie Hillman and Esther Peterson, Robinson belonged to a national committee assigned to promote a blood drive for the Red Cross. Complaining that the blood segregation policy made it extremely difficult to convince blacks to donate, she convinced a reluctant Hillman to air these grievances at a meeting of the national Red Cross in Washington, D.C.[69] With her trademark forthrightness, Adelmond also refused to support the Red Cross at a meeting Civilian Defense leaders organized to request New York labor leaders to organize blood-donor drives. Civil rights activist Anna Arnold Hedgeman, who was working for the Civilian Defense at the time, reported:

> Adelmond, . . . a sturdy, thoughtful and dedicated unionist, rose and said: "I will give no blood to the war effort and will not appeal to my workers to give until the practice of the segregation of Negro blood is stopped." There was dead silence in the room for a moment and then a white union member said: "Charlotte, what if your brother in the Army in North Africa should need that blood you will not give, and die for lack of it?" Charlotte stood again and with head high said, "If that happens, at least I will know that he died for democracy." The meeting ended on that note. What could anyone say?[70]

Although the American Red Cross eventually began to hire black employees, the organization continued to segregate blood during the Korean War until United Nations employees protested.[71]

Another incident, involving the execution of the Virginia sharecropper Odell

Waller, pointed to the irony of blacks fighting a war to defend democratic ideals from which they were excluded. Springer was involved with the Waller case in only a tangential way; however, the case is important to her personal history in two respects. First, the activism surrounding the case provides a clear portrait of the solidarity of black female activists. Secondly, the case served as the context in which Springer first met Pauli Murray. On behalf of the Workers Defense League, Murray raised funds for Waller's appeal and increased the public's awareness of the case on a national scale.

In 1940 an all-white jury, ten of whom were farmers, convicted Waller of murdering his white landlord, Oscar Davis, in an altercation over their jointly owned wheat crop, which Davis had appropriated. Believing that Davis was about to shoot him, Waller had shot first. Waller's lawyers filed numerous appeals on the grounds that the jury, selected from poll-tax payers, violated his constitutional right to a jury of his peers. The poll tax was one means of disenfranchising practically all blacks and many poor whites in the South.[72]

Just prior to Waller's execution, Roosevelt declined to meet with a civil rights delegation that included Randolph, Crosswaith, Anna Arnold Hedgeman, Layle Lane, Mary McLeod Bethune, and others. A distraught Eleanor Roosevelt got no further with him. Although Roosevelt had in the past written to Virginia's governor requesting a commutation of Waller's sentence to life imprisonment, he refused to intervene further, claiming that the case was out of his jurisdiction.[73] Paradoxically, support for racial justice in the United States would harm the war effort against Nazism. Waller's life had to be sacrificed in order to promote cooperation between Southern congressmen and the president.

After Waller's execution on July 2, 1942, Randolph asked Murray to coordinate a silent parade to mourn his death and to protest the poll tax, two recent lynchings of blacks, and the brutal beating in Rome, Georgia, of the renowned black tenor Roland Hayes and his wife. Robinson, who knew Murray, was responsible for getting Springer and other trade unionists to participate in the march. Springer's introduction to Murray came at a preparatory meeting: "I walked into this meeting with Dollie and other trade union people, and we heard this little small person with cropped hair, wearing these white sailor pants and standing on the table. She was on *fire*, talking about social injustice and Jim Crow."[74] During the march Springer, Robinson, and Murray carried a huge banner reading "Jim Crow Has Got To Go." In her autobiography, Murray gave tribute to the black female activist community for their support: "Without money or organizational assistance, it was remarkable that we had any demonstration at all. With the help of two young women from labor's ranks—Maida Springer of the Dressmakers Union and Dollie Lowther from the Laundry Workers Union— from Bessie Bearden's Housewives League, and from Layle Lane, Anna Hedgeman, and a few recruits from youth groups in Harlem, we managed to mobilize the Waller Silent Parade, although it would go down in civil rights protest history as a 'very minor achievement.'"[75]

Murray believed that this march, which was sponsored by the New York office of the March on Washington Movement, was probably the only one that actually materialized out of the national movement. Five hundred protesters marched silently "with the faint throb of muffled drums" from 56th Street and 8th Avenue to Union Square at 14th Street. After a ceremony at Union Square, Springer and Murray joined other marchers in singing protest songs and chanting anti–Jim Crow slogans on a truck ride back to Harlem. Not until 1966, twenty-four years after Waller's execution, did the Supreme Court rule the poll tax unconstitutional.[76]

After the Waller march, Springer did not hear from Murray until four years later, when the National Council of Negro Women (NCNW) headed by Mary McLeod Bethune honored the two of them, and ten others, for their "devotion to the public good."[77] Sharing a commitment to civil rights, women's rights, and labor, Robinson, Springer, and Murray eventually enjoyed a three-way friendship. For a period in the 1940s and 1950s, Murray and Springer lived in the same Brooklyn neighborhood. Murray's work as a lawyer influenced Springer's son, Eric, to pursue legal studies.[78] Often contained in the correspondence of the African nationalists and labor leaders who visited Springer's home in the 1950s and 1960s were greetings not only for her mother and son but also for Dollie and Pauli. Ironically, Springer would not have become intimately involved in pan-African affairs in 1945 if not for a lesson Bethune taught her concerning how to deal with her anger and resentment over racist treatment. The circumstances surrounding Springer's fateful encounter with Bethune are the subject of the next chapter.

4

The National and International Struggle against the Color Line

S A PARTICIPANT IN A 1945 LABOR-EXCHANGE TRIP to England, Springer had the distinction of becoming the "first Negro woman to represent American labor abroad."[1] The governmental agencies promoting the exchange trip included the British Ministries of Information and Labor and, in the United States, the Office of Labor Production of the War Production Board and the Office of War Information (OWI). Springer was one of four delegates. Their responsibilities included meeting with British women working in the war industries, exchanging experiences concerning war work conditions, and discussing postwar plans. Newspaper coverage of the mission singled Springer out for special recognition, often including a picture of her beside the article.[2]

The implications of her appointment, however, went beyond her symbolic representation as a "Negro first." For many her appointment demonstrated that for African Americans the gap between democratic ideal and practice could be lessened. For anti-Communists, her appointment represented a partial antidote to Communist influence in the CIO and the international labor movement. For Springer personally, the appointment had far-reaching consequences in terms of her future activism on the African continent. The connections she made through her association with pan-African strategist George Padmore put her in a position to influence future AFL-CIO policy toward Africa.

For Springer the struggle against colonialism was connected to the struggle for civil rights at home. As a union officer she seized opportunities to promote blacks within the garment industry, work for civil rights, expand her international connections, and support political candidates sympathetic to labor and civil rights. Racism within the labor movement and the U.S. government's tolerance of segregation and discrimination sometimes provoked her to despair and rage. Nevertheless, the fight for civil rights was for Springer a necessary ingredient for the race's survival.

Labor Delegate to England

The ILGWU organ *Justice* provided extensive coverage of Springer's work on behalf of the union. Impressed by her activism in electoral politics, in trade union education, and on behalf of the war effort, David Dubinsky gave her name to AFL president William Green as a delegate for a 1945 good-will labor exchange trip with England. When Dubinsky's secretary, Hanna Haskel, tried to arrange a meeting so he could inform Springer of her selection, Springer ingenuously told Haskel that she was busy showing workers a film on venereal disease. Taken aback, Haskel asked when she would have time to see the president of the International. When Springer arrived late that afternoon, Dubinsky greeted her with humor: "Oh, you're sure you have time now?"[3]

In the context of the racist practices prevalent in the United States, African American leaders and interracial organizations appreciated the ILGWU's bold move in selecting Springer. The problems of race and gender inequality within the union were muted in the outpouring of praise for the union for taking such a monumental step. Springer herself, in applauding the union's fight against economic barriers based on color, stated: "Belonging to the union gave me the same kind of chance everybody else had. I don't think I could work hard enough or do enough to compensate for all this."[4]

Frank Crosswaith and A. Philip Randolph were effusive in their show of appreciation. In response to Crosswaith's letter stating that her selection was "quite in line with the steady integration of the Negro into the American labor movement," Charles Zimmerman declared, "In our local we practice what we preach. We are always anxious to bring to the forefront young rank and file workers, whether white or colored, Jew or Gentile." Moreover, he hoped that the successful completion of her mission would foster a better understanding between U.S. and English workers and "also help to eradicate completely whatever remnants of racial prejudice there may still exist in some unions of the AFL."[5] Mildred A. Keller of the Burlington, New Jersey, Inter-Racial Committee echoed this sentiment in a letter of commendation. "By choosing a qualified negro woman in this capacity, your union shows itself forward-looking and fair-minded. Your action should have a favorable effect on American workers, and we hope that it will help convey to the British the fact that racial discrimination, though widespread, is not universally practiced here."[6]

Springer's appointment made her a symbol of AFL and CIO rivalry over issues of communism and equality. She remarked that the two CIO delegates, Grace Woods Blackett from the United Auto, Aircraft and Agricultural Implement Workers of America (UAW) and Anne Murkovich from the American Federation of Hosiery Workers, were horrified because they viewed her selection as upstaging their federation. With great satisfaction, Randolph and Crosswaith conveyed to Dubinsky that Springer's appointment represented an embarrassment and a blow to Communists, whom they accused of working "overtime" in Harlem to misrepresent them and destroy sections of the labor movement they did not control.[7]

AFL leaders, however, questioned Dubinsky's wisdom in appointing a black delegate who was also relatively young and inexperienced in international affairs. They came from Washington to New York to confer with him. For union leaders, the central international conflict at that time concerned the AFL's opposition to the participation of the CIO—and, more importantly, the Soviet All Union Central Council of Trade Unions—in the London and Paris meetings of the World Trade Union Conference convened to establish the World Federation of Trade Unions (WFTU).[8] The AFL held that unions from Communist countries were government entities and did not truly represent workers. The leadership of the British Trades Union Congress (TUC) reluctantly acquiesced to the participation of these unions. Historian Peter Weiler contends that the sympathies of British workers for the Soviet Union, the willingness of the Soviets to make concessions to insure their participation, and the British government's priority of having a unified front against fascism forced the TUC leadership into compliance.[9] At the time of the trip some AFL leaders were skeptical of Springer's ability to meet any challenges to the unpopular AFL policy. Apparently, Dubinsky personally reassured them of her competence. She recalled, "I am told—I don't know this—that Dubinsky told them, 'Don't worry about Springer. She knows her way around the political world.' . . . They could not deny him the *right* to select me, nor did they try. . . . The AF of L and CIO were very hard-nosed people. They lived in a world of all men. They would understand a Julia O'Connor Parker. She was there with [Samuel] Gompers for the [founding of the] League of Nations, and she was a political war horse. I was not. And you throw in my color for good measure. Never leave that out."[10]

The AFL's other delegate, Julia O'Connor Parker, who was president of the Telephone Operator's Department of the International Brotherhood of Electrical Workers, was also concerned about Springer's lack of international experience. Moreover, Springer believed Parker "was extremely perturbed" to have a black woman as a colleague. Accordingly, a meeting between the two was arranged at a New York City hotel. Knowing that she was being tested, Springer was resentful: "[W]ho was she that she had to determine whether she would like to be my colleague or no?" Feeling hostile, Springer had expected that they would quarrel, but they did not. She recalled that Parker "was *formidable* to talk to, and she cut through niceties and went directly to what she wanted to talk about, trade unions. . . . She, of course, was very conversant with the politics of the labor movement, the broader context of problems and jealousies in regard to the CIO, which was considered the young avant-garde group. So in that context, she saw our duty was to hold our own and to work at being the most effective representatives that we could be. And so, we established an accommodation, not friendship."[11]

On the trip to England, aboard a ship on which she was the only black, Springer recalled that there was a "surface politeness" between her and the other three delegates. As union officials, she held, "We had a body of experience that we could speak about and have an interchange. So, on that level, we were fine." Personally, however, there was mutual dislike among the women. Given this inauspicious beginning, it is remarkable that by the conclusion of the trip, Springer and Parker had formed a "fast friendship." They would maintain contact with each other until Parker's death.[12]

U.S. Government Hypocrisy

On January 9, 1945, Dubinsky presided over a send-off luncheon in Springer's honor at the Park Central Hotel in New York City. Over one hundred labor and civil rights leaders attended. Among the speakers were AFL regional representative William Collins, NAACP secretary Roy Wilkins, and WTUL leader Rose Schneiderman. Afterwards Springer joined the other delegates in Washington, D.C. for three days of meetings with members of Congress, officials of various government agencies, and representatives of labor groups.[13]

However, the exclusion and discrimination she experienced in the nation's capital nearly caused her to withdraw from the labor delegation in anger. While the city had a long history of alignment with Southern racist customs and laws, it was still common for black visitors to Washington to be caught by surprise by the pervasive restrictions imposed upon blacks. With the advent of the Cold War in 1947, the Truman administration viewed segregation in the nation's capital as fodder for Soviet propaganda and as an acute embarrassment unexplainable to "friendly" governments. The Washington, D.C. office of the NAACP had even campaigned against placing UN headquarters in the nation's capital because of segregation.[14]

First was the matter of where Springer would stay. One of the nation's grandest hotels, the Statler, where Springer's colleagues had accommodations, drew the color bar, and Secretary of Labor Frances Perkins was unsuccessful in persuading any other hotel to admit her. Unlike the ILGWU, which refused to patronize hotels that discriminated against blacks, neither the government nor the labor federations had insisted on finding a hotel where all the delegates could stay. Instead, the government sought ways to accommodate Springer to the problem of exclusion by lodging her at Council House, Mary McLeod Bethune's home and the headquarters of the National Council of Negro Women. Unaware of the reason for this arrangement, Springer nevertheless suspected something was amiss.[15] "Under ordinary circumstances," she explained, "to have been invited to be the guest of Dr. Bethune was a great honor. [But if] I had known about the segregation I would face, I would never have gone to D.C. to be treated like that when I was going on an overseas trip for the Office of War Information! And I was selected [as] one of four people in the United States to go! Had I known that this might have been one of the conditions, no, I wouldn't have gone. I was too young and too warm-blooded to have accepted anything like this in advance."[16]

The Washington, D.C., trip was not the first time Springer experienced exclusionary practices. Some incidents in the "liberal" North involved New York restaurants. When the management refused to serve her and her white union colleagues because of her presence, her colleagues became indignant, left, and perhaps felt some gratification for their principled stand. Springer, however, remained humiliated and angry. Her personality was not like that of her contemporary and later associate, Edith Sampson, who in 1950 became the first black alternate delegate to the U.S. mission to the UN. When Sampson was refused meal service at one Washington, D.C., hotel following her return to the United States from a government-sponsored world tour, she ate a hearty meal at another hotel, where the other diners were less than pleased with her presence. She explained, "If I stopped eating every time something like this happened, I'd be thin as a rail."[17] Moreover, Springer was angered that behind the scenes the government was tolerating segregation and exclusion while publicly heralding her appointment and using her as a symbol of racial progress.

Government officials also were not sensitive enough to foresee that simple conveniences, such as taxis and meal service, would be unavailable to Springer. Her problems became apparent when she set out to attend the delegates' first briefing session at the Office of the United Nations Relief and Rehabilitation Administration (UNRRA).[18] She recalled:

> I walked out to take a taxi, and it was freezing, dreadfully cold, and *no* taxi. Nothing would pick me up. I was not aware of this. The Western Union man was delivering telegrams in their brown cars and kept driving around and around and around, and I'm still standing on the corner waiting. I don't know *anything* about transportation. I don't know where to go to take a bus or anything. Finally, the young white driver came over to where I was shiv-

ering. . . . He told me the white cabs would not pick me up, and there were very few black drivers and jitneys. So he drove me to the building where I was to go.[19]

Before entering the building for the meeting, Springer went into the coffee shop next door to warm up. There she encountered a black porter who identified with the proponents of segregationist policies.

> I went in and sat on the stool to get a cup of coffee. My teeth were chattering. I sat there and no one came to ask me for my order. Other people came, and they got their coffee and donuts. It was a greasy spoon. It was a very ordinary coffee shop. Finally, someone came over to me, a porter with his mop, and he said, "Us don't serve Colored in here." By that time I was nearly apoplectic.[20]

Late for the meeting, which included former New York governor Herbert Lehman, Springer explained what had happened and announced that she wanted to withdraw from the trip.[21] Lehman promptly apprised Bethune of the situation. In her work as head of the Negro Division of the National Youth Administration and in causes she championed, Bethune had a record of working for integrated opportunities when feasible and toward equal participation in separate programs when not. She took action on two fronts. First, she contacted Eleanor Roosevelt, who arranged for Springer to have a chauffeured limousine.[22] (Springer's colleagues benefited from this remedy; they joined her in using the limousine.) Second, after Springer had vented her pain, humiliation, and rage, Bethune undertook to suggest how Springer could channel her outrage in a more productive manner. Bethune gently lectured her, challenging her sense of responsibility for the "extraordinary opportunity" she had been given: "Daughter . . . you have a more important role to play than the concern for your good feelings. No matter how justified you are in your anguish, you have a responsibility, given the opportunity, to bring back and share with us what you have learned."[23]

Springer recalled, "Well, when that dear lady got through talking to me, I felt like a worm. . . . It was a very great lesson for me in terms of what you do to achieve things you want, or what you make of your resentment, your disagreement with how you're being treated. . . . I crawled back to my room. I had to have a deep conversation with myself."[24]

Springer's withdrawal from the delegation would have precluded her from developing the relationships with future leaders of Africa that helped make her a trusted and influential contact within the U.S. labor movement. Moreover, her role as a symbol and a pioneer carried a message of hope to many. During the trip *Justice* published numerous articles concerning her activities and afterwards featured a series of articles she wrote detailing her experiences. Following the trip, a wide variety of organizations held functions in which Springer, as the honored guest, related her experiences. Even her friend Dollie Robinson, on behalf of the Negro Women, Inc., organized a tea in her honor. Bethune, whose organization, the NCNW, encompassed women in various walks of life, would soon come to view Robinson and Springer as her labor women when she needed to consult someone on labor issues. In 1970 Springer became a NCNW vice president and also served as chair of its international division.[25]

Another person who helped Springer during the Washington visit was Caroline Ware, a social historian and Howard University professor. Esther Peterson was responsible for introducing Springer to Ware and her husband, Gardiner Means, both of whom were white. The Ware-Means home, a seventy-acre farm in Vienna, Virginia, was a refuge for students, writers, activists, and travelers. Springer asserted that if it were not for the time she spent there, she "would have snapped." She had braced herself for Ware to meet her with an air of condescension and the expectation that she should feel privileged to associate with whites. Instead, after hearing about Springer's humiliations, Ware actually helped her to be flexible and "not dwell on what was, but to deal positively with the issue at hand." Ware became a lifelong friend and a financial supporter of some of her labor projects. Pauli Murray also belonged to this circle of female activists, having met Ware in 1942 while attending Howard University Law School. Murray nicknamed her "Skipper" because she would often drive black guests between her farm and Washington so they could avoid the humiliation of segregated public transportation.[26]

Perhaps one gauge of the importance of framing Springer's selection as a symbol of racial progress is that no papers of that time chronicled her encounters with segregation. Understandably, the Office of War Information press release concerning the Washington meetings omitted such matters. Instead it reported her praise of the ILGWU and comments on the war effort.[27] Only later, after the trip had receded from public memory, did Springer document her experiences. She also noted the subtle ways that the British made accommodations for the prejudices of her colleagues. For example, in the hotels she might be assigned to a single room while her colleagues got a suite containing four beds.[28]

The War Effort in England

Only after their briefing in Washington was completed were the delegates given the details of their travel plans. They were admonished to keep the plans secret, even from family members, as a precaution against the information becoming known to wartime enemies. Springer's husband and their fifteen-year-old son, Eric, had said their good-byes when they put her on the train to Washington.

Owen Springer had misgivings about his wife serving as a delegate, knowing that the war put her life in danger. Still, he gave her encouraging words before she departed.

The trans-Atlantic voyage began with a train trip to Halifax, Nova Scotia. From there the group was to travel on an impounded Italian ship, but at the last minute their departure was delayed. The rumor circulated that their vessel, which had not been built for travel in cold waters, needed repairs. After they finally boarded, they spent seven harrowing days on the leaking ship, traveling as the lead vessel in a convoy with other ships. The omnipresent danger of German submarines made the war palpable. They learned in whispered conversations of other ships in their convoy being destroyed by submarine fire, and they witnessed planes taking off from and landing on aircraft carriers belonging to the convoy. After arriving in London, Springer wrote Dubinsky that their arrival was greatly delayed and that "the OWI had just about given us up, since no record of our travel was available until two days prior to landing." "Our voyage over," she concluded, "is one that I will never, never forget."[29]

The delegates also experienced firsthand the effects of the war in England. They saw and felt the German V-2 bombs as they exploded, shaking the earth and brightening the night sky. For Springer the saddest experience of the trip was witnessing the damaging effect of war on children at a nursery in Hampstead, named for and operated by Anna Freud, the daughter of Sigmund Freud. She was also moved by a garment worker who had an artificial arm because of war injuries. Standing on top of a table in a huge factory, she spied him in the midst of two thousand workers who were waving their arms while she led them in a union song.[30]

Springer declared that during the trip "*everything* was done to maintain the solidarity and the feeling of cooperation." The labor delegates and Springer in particular were heralded all over England. An OWI press release highlighted her discussion of rationing at a press conference with female newspaper writers, who, it was reported, showed great interest in American women's current clothing problems.[31] She had a brief discussion with Lady Astor, a U.S.-born member of Parliament, on the problems of blacks in the South, after which Springer believed that perhaps Lady Astor gained more insight.[32] On behalf of the ILGWU she gave a letter and money to a hostel to help support recreational facilities for women in the war. Springer also spent an evening at the Luton ILGWU Merchant Navy Club, where she was a big hit. The British War Relief Society informed her that "the boys . . . have never stopped talking of your visit to them, and wonder whether you will find the time to go there one entertainment evening." The ILGWU had founded the club in Luton with a gift of seventy-five thousand dollars before the United States entered the war.[33] Anne Loughlin, a general organizer of the National Union of Tailors and Garment Workers, was responsible for having branch representatives meet Springer during her tour of the country. And a week before her departure the executive board of the garment union gave a small luncheon in her honor. Loughlin informed Dubinsky, "Maida Springer charmed all the people she came into contact with; she was extremely interesting, and in addition well-informed. Naturally I was pleased as she represented a sister Union."[34]

In addition to learning about wartime conditions relating to security, rationing, diet, and housing, the delegates met with Clement Attlee, deputy prime minister under Winston Churchill; Ernest Bevin, the minister of labor; Jenny Lee, the youngest member of Parliament, representing the Independent Labor Party; the queen; and many women's and labor groups. They even met with the U.S. and Russian delegates to the London meeting of the World Trade Union Conference, which had convened at County Hall.[35]

AFL leaders' anxiety about Springer's ability to handle conflicts arising from their unpopular stance toward the WFTU turned out to be unnecessary. She wrote Dubinsky that there had not been "too much unpleasantness about our non-participation" in the labor conference.[36] It appears that people were more interested in her symbolic representation as a "Negro first" than as an exponent of AFL foreign policy.

The Pan-African Network

Soon after her arrival, Springer met the black staff members of the U.S. Embassy, the YWCA, and the Red Cross, and they made sure she met others with whom she had interests in common. She remarked that with them she never had to discuss racism because they understood it.[37]

Jamaican-born Una Marson, who was a pan-Africanist, playwright, journalist, and among the first Caribbean women to gain recognition as a poet, became an influential contact for Springer.[38] The two met after officials at the British Broadcasting Company (BBC), having read in Springer's dossier that she was born in Panama, asked her to participate in broadcasts to the Caribbean for the BBC World Service. Springer made her first international broadcast on Marson's program "Caribbean Voices," which helped to promote unity for the war effort. Marson and others, however, held that the price the allies should pay for this unity was black liberation.

In Marson's apartment located in a half-blown-out building, Springer met African and Caribbean soldiers who, like African Americans, were caught up in the dilemma of defending ideals that they were denied. Over Marson's Caribbean meals, she recalled, they would discuss the implications of the war. "They had no illusions about what they were doing and for the most part—because I think Una was very selective about the people she invited—these were men who had a vision of the future, and they were looking to the day when they were going to have a country, not a colonial dependency. So it was very good talk at night. Very explosive talk! Had they been heard, they would all have been court-martialed."[39]

Springer credits George Padmore for her "introduction to political Black England." Over the years he became her principal mentor on pan-African affairs. Like many of her mentors and associates, he was also a former Communist. Born in Trinidad, he attended Fisk and Howard Universities before joining the Communist Party, where he quickly rose to become head of the Negro Bureau of the Profintern (the Red International of Labor Unions). He used his position to build a global network of black labor and political activists. He broke with the Communist International following the rise of Hitler, accusing the leaders of downgrading anticolonial work in exchange for closer alliances with Western powers. Nevertheless, he continued to build this network, and his articles were widely published in the black press.

Padmore sought out Springer at a London press conference for the labor delegates. Springer recalled, "It was at a public meeting that I first met the acid-tongued writer and empire basher, George Padmore. I think we were in one of General Eisenhower's war rooms, where they were giving us a picture of the war effort, a very cursory thing in a big assembly room. And every newspaper reporter was there, asking us all of the foolish questions that they ask people who have no information. You know, you're there two days, and they ask, 'How do you assess the war effort?' and 'What do you think of the workers?'"[40]

To Springer's surprise, Padmore asked her a "very precise question about settlements of industrial disputes used only in ILG [the ILGWU]." She later learned that he and his colleague Ras Makonnen knew about the union through their contacts with Caribbean cutters, tailors, and sewing machine operators. They also knew ILGWU educational director Mark Starr, a Scotsman with "a fine reputation in workers' education in England." A year earlier Starr had participated in an OWI mission of educators to Britain.[41]

During the press conference, Padmore passed his card and a note to Springer, asking to meet with her. She quickly responded with a note of her own identifying her hotel. After a conversation with Padmore over tea, Springer returned to her hotel to discover that he had left her one of his books and a letter of introduction to meet Makonnen in Manchester. As soon as the delegation reached Manchester, she called Makonnen, who invited her to dine at one of his restaurants, which were money-making ventures for the pan-African cause. Later a small group of Africans, including Jomo Kenyatta of Kenya, joined them. Decades later Springer still recalled this first meeting with awe: "Jomo Kenyatta was the man with the most commanding presence—over six feet tall, a deep resonant voice—and eyes that seemed to set off sparks when he was animated."

When he asked her, "Young girl, what does the working class in America know of the struggle for liberation from colonialism?" she became embarrassed.[42] Her interest in Africa had been forged during her childhood years in the Garvey movement; however, the ILGWU—which prided itself on its radical tradition, diverse immigrant membership, and international activism—gave colonial oppression no official attention. Kenyatta's question altered her life profoundly; she began a new struggle to motivate U.S. labor leaders to support African demands for labor development and independence.

Kenyatta would attend the fifth Pan-African Congress scheduled to begin on October 15 in Manchester, directly following the Paris meeting of the World Trade Union Conference.[43] With the help of African and Caribbean delegates to the London labor conference, the founders of the Pan-African Federation, Padmore, Makonnen, and Peter McDonald Milliard, were laying plans for the pan-African meeting.[44] Although Springer would not attend, she later met many of the future African political leaders who did, including Kwame Nkrumah, Joseph Appiah, and Ako Adjei (from the Gold Coast, now Ghana), Wallace Johnson (from Sierra Leone), Peter Abrahams (from South Africa), and Hastings Banda (from Nyasaland, now Malawi). The only African Americans to attend were W.E.B. Du Bois, who had been a strong force at previous Pan-African Congress meetings, and Henry Lee Moon, a journalist, NAACP activist, and member of the CIO's political action committee.

Historian Brenda Gayle Plummer notes that the small role of the NAACP in planning the Pan-African Congress symbolized the end of African American stewardship of the movement for African liberation. African Americans thereafter were relegated to the roles of "onlookers or increasingly superfluous intermediaries for colonials who became daily more self-sufficient."[45] However, Springer, Randolph, and their fellow African American George McCray were very important intermediaries between African and Western labor during the 1950s. Within the U.S. labor movement, Springer made the earliest sustained connections with future leaders of independent Africa. Africans viewed her as a welcome alternative to trade unionists from colonial powers.

Springer's relationship to this pan-African network in 1945 was not entangled in the controversies surrounding the AFL's refusal to support the WFTU. African political and labor leaders were more concerned over their immediate oppression under colonialism and imperialism than in the dangers of communism or fascism. At the London labor conference, colonial delegates asserted that article 3 of the Atlantic Charter, declaring the right to self-determination for peoples under Nazi rule, should also cover people under colonial rule.[46] Moreover, the Charter of Labor for the Colonies that they adopted reflected the similarity of African and African American struggles. The charter called for the abolition of the color bar and all racial discrimination; establishment of equal pay for equal work regardless of race, color, creed, or sex; and abolition of laws excluding blacks from white labor unions.[47] With the suppression of labor rights connected to the political status of workers as colonial subjects, it stands to reason that the African labor movements would become one of the primary arms of the liberation struggles.

Having formed extensive pan-African connections in the seven weeks that she spent in England, Springer returned to Washington with her colleagues and the British exchange delegates. While on shipboard they learned of Roosevelt's death on April 12, which made them quite somber upon arrival. Labor secretary Frances Perkins hosted an international reception in their honor at the Statler Hotel while they marked the end of an era. Although Springer was one of the honored speakers, she still could not stay as a guest at the hotel.[48]

Political Involvement

The fight for equal opportunity in the United States, like the fight against colonialism, took off globally during World War II. Randolph's expanded March on Washington Movement sought "to popularize the slogan of a Free Africa and Free Caribbean." He was among the major figures who took up the argument Du Bois had made since the previous world war, that the status of U.S. blacks was inextricably tied to that of Africans and other people of color: "The problem of the Negro in the United States is no longer a purely domestic question but has world significance. It's integrated with the larger strategy of defeating the Axis. We have become the barometer of democracy to the colored peoples of the world, Africa, India, China, Latin America and the West Indies, all look to the United States."[49]

With the end of World War II, African Americans faced the demise of the movement's principal victory, the wartime Fair Employment Practices Committee (FEPC). In his efforts to build support for a bill sponsored by Representative Irving M. Ives and Senator Dennis Chavez to make the FEPC a permanently funded federal agency, Randolph proposed a mass rally at Madison Square Garden. He asked Dubinsky and Zimmerman to release Springer to work as the rally's executive secretary.[50] Once again she did not relish being put in a position of major responsibility. By nature modest to a fault, Springer was afraid that she lacked the necessary administrative and fund-raising skills required for this position. She recalled:

When my manager [Charles Zimmerman] approached me and said, "You know, Phil called today and he wants you to work with the committee, wants you to be the executive secretary," I said I'd die. I never raised money. I am not in public relations, or whatever we called it in those days. So he said,

"Randolph believes in you." Well, I was dead in the water then. "And we are going to release you. Your salary will be paid and you will go up and talk to Randolph." I said, "Sasha, I can't do it." He said, "You can't?" So I think it's finished, because I'm scared and I said I can't do it. I have said no from the president of the ILG[WU] on down.[51]

Springer, however, could not say no to Randolph. She recalls that he began his appeal to her by saying, "Now, Maida dear, the cause of social justice is at stake."[52] He sent her out of his office with promises of support from others and a check for six hundred dollars to begin the fund-raising drive to rent Madison Square Garden.

Among those working on the rally were Ben McLaurin and William Bowe of the Brotherhood of Sleeping Car Porters (BSCP), Socialist lawyer Max Delson, and Bill Sutherland, who later served as an organizer of the 1958 All African People's Conference, which Springer attended. Anna Arnold Hedgeman, who served as executive secretary of the National Council for a Permanent FEPC, worked from a base in Washington, D.C. Vivian Odems Lemon, secretary for Workers Defense League head Morris Milgram, worked closely with Springer. Freida Louise Andrews organized several hundred gospel singers, many of them domestic workers and post office employees, into a massive choir for the event and then had them sell tickets.[53] Springer recounted how she and Lemon would go to choir rehearsals to collect the ticket money: "I would go home on the subway with a thousand dollars in my pocket . . . and then to the office the next morning. And I wasn't afraid. Times have changed."[54]

The Madison Square Garden rally for a permanent FEPC was held on February 28, 1946, with 17,500 in attendance. The event was a tremendous success. About Springer's work, Pauli Murray noted, "Reverberations of the fine job she did reached me in California from sources not acquainted with her personally. . . . Often, like the story of the 'five loaves and two fishes,' she has wrought miracles in campaigns with nothing more at the start but her own determination and her 'begging hat.'"[55] Among those in attendance were Secretary of Labor Lewis B. Schwellenbach; Eleanor Roosevelt; Senators Denis Chavez of New Mexico and Wayne Morse of Oregon; former New York mayor Fiorello La Guardia; film and stage stars Orson Welles and Helen Hayes; renowned dancer and choreographer Katherine Dunham; Matthew Woll of the AFL; James B. Carey, secretary-treasurer of CIO; Milton Webster of the BSCP; and Roy Wilkins, secretary of the NAACP.[56]

Randolph averred that if Congress failed to pass the FEPC legislation, the fault would lie with the Truman administration and the unholy alliance of Republicans and Southern Democrats.[57] In fact, the rally did not generate enough pressure for Congress to pass the bill. The "unholy alliance" used a filibuster to forestall the vote, prompting a threat from Randolph to work for the defeat of senators who refused to vote for cloture. Another strategy to gain passage of the bill involved reviving the march idea. But Randolph's threat of a "silent, non-violent march on Washington of Negroes, Japanese-Americans, Mexicans, Protestants, Catholics and Jews, trade unionists, AF of L and CIO, men, women and children" did not prevent Congress from finally defeating the bill in 1950.[58] Although a number of states passed FEPC laws, national fair-employment legislation was not implemented until the passage of the 1964 Civil Rights Act. Randolph did achieve one federal concession out of the movement. In response to his call in 1948 for a civil disobedience campaign and nonviolent protest of the segregated armed services, President Truman issued an executive order calling for equal opportunity in the armed services. The armed forces gradually became integrated during the Korean War.

Springer's political activism during this period was also geared toward supporting candidates on the Liberal Party ticket. Her experience in organizing and her knowledge of Brooklyn politics became "decisive factors" in Pauli Murray's decision to run in 1949 on the Liberal Party ticket for a city council seat from Brooklyn's 10th Senatorial District. Caroline Ware also encouraged Murray to run as a step forward in women's rights. Springer, who served as Murray's campaign manager, recalled her experience as campaign manager for Ben McLaurin of the BSCP: "My candidate got beaten terribly. (laughter) I worked sixteen hours a day." Once again at Randolph's request, the ILGWU had released her from her duties to work on McLaurin's campaign.[59]

Unlike that campaign, Murray nearly won despite lack of money. She and Springer passed out copies of her platform at busy intersections and shouted themselves hoarse. Springer recalled that on one cold, windy, October night, Murray was on a street corner "waxing eloquent on the needs of the community" when a woman leaned out an apartment window, said something unintelligible, and then threw a pail of cold water on them. The two went home to "Mom's hearty food and sympathy." Despite such setbacks, Murray's campaign gathered sufficient momentum to worry the Democratic opponent, Sam Curtis, who began to engage in smear tactics. He charged that Murray, who at the time was a lawyer, was unqualified to hold office because of her occupational background as a waitress and a dishwasher. Surpassing many expectations, Murray in her defeat polled more than both the Republican and American Labor Party candidates. In a congratulatory note to Springer, the chair of the Liberal Party stated, "We feel that the large vote we obtained in your Assembly District is an indication that your organization did an excellent job in carrying our message to the people."[60]

Through their Liberal Party activism, Murray and Springer also campaigned for Franklin Roosevelt, Jr., and Jacob Javits in their successful congressional bids and for Harry Truman in his presidential campaign. The Liberal Party had endorsed these Democratic candidates. Murray claimed that she and Springer were among the few Truman supporters in their district to believe that he would defeat Thomas Dewey.[61] In the 1950s Springer worked with the Liberal Party in support of Democrat Adlai Stevenson's presidential campaigns.

Along with her campaign work, Springer continued to support a variety of civil rights projects associated with Randolph and the NAACP. Among these were the NAACP-sponsored 1954 Fight for Freedom Campaign under the directorship of Ella Baker; a 1956 Madison Square Garden rally honoring the heroes of civil rights, for which she served as co-coordinator; and a 1958 Youth March for School Integration. The goals of the 1956 rally included raising funds for the NAACP Legal and Educational Fund, the Montgomery Improvement Association, and for victims of economic boycotts in South Carolina and Mississippi.[62] Springer solicited the ILGWU's support for these projects by suggesting that NAACP leaders like Thurgood Marshall address the union's membership meetings and that efforts be made to get union members to become NAACP members as well. Her union and civil rights activism were intertwined.

Policing the Union Contract

In 1945, after Springer had served for two years as educational director of Local 132, Zimmerman told her, "Well now you've gotten your feet wet. You need to learn the internal mechanics." He then sent her to work in the Complaint Department of the Dress Joint Board, where her duties included handling workers' complaints concerning wages or treatment; enforcing contract provisions governing health services, vacations, retirement, and pensions; and maintaining a record of all shop meetings. This job was good preparation for her appointment in 1948 as business agent, to fill out the short term remaining in a vacated position.[63] Edith Ransome was Local 22's first black business agent; however, Springer became the local's first black business agent to control a district, an administrative unit containing a set number of garment shops. Ransome's position did not cover a whole district and did not cover all the workers in her shops. Springer's district consisted of two thousand workers employed in sixty shops, most of them small. In a section of the industry called the Better Makers, these shops made dresses of a quality considered middle range—that is, between low-priced and high-priced garments.

Springer's high regard for Zimmerman was partly because he refused to accommodate anyone who resisted working with her on account of race. Months after becoming business agent, she learned that her appointment had been opposed by representatives of the manufacturers' association whose job it was to work with the business agent in settling problems between the workers and management. When the association's officers declared they would not be seen with her, Zimmerman retorted, "You won't see *any of us*." Only one of the officers distanced himself from the protest, in a letter to Zimmerman stating that he would be pleased to work with Springer. Jennie Silverman, who recalled that all the people involved in the dispute were Jewish, indicated that Springer became good friends with this officer. After Springer finished the term of the vacated seat, Local 22 members elected her to the position. She continuously won reelection until she resigned her post in 1960 to work for the AFL-CIO International Affairs Department.[64]

Although 95 percent of the workers in her shops were white, Springer continued efforts she had begun while working in the Complaint Department to provide opportunities for blacks, who were concentrated in less-skilled positions, to move out of the dead-end, low-paying jobs. She was disheartened to discover in both her positions that she could not convince some black women to accept the training opportunities available to them as a union members. In cooperation with the Fashion Institute of Technology, for example, union officers supervised training programs that would allow members to improve their skills and move into better-paying jobs. Local 22 and the New York State Board of Education also sponsored classes at the Central High School of Needle Trades.[65] As an added inducement, Springer offered to place black workers who had completed training in shops where they could work at a slower pace and develop their skills without the threat of reprisals. "They would walk away from me and say to a friend who was with them, 'She's a *fool* if she thinks I'm going to take my time and go.' This used to make me very sad. . . . This has been my failure. I felt that I did not have the technique to reach them. . . . But I had a few successes."[66]

One of her success stories involved a Cuban friend of her mother named Melba Soloman, who eventually became a price adjuster for the union. Solomon's story also illustrates employer bias against black operators. Since the business agents knew the skills and capabilities of workers in the many shops they serviced, employers relied on them as referral agents to fill positions. Once when a contractor of a shop making high-priced dresses and gowns requested an operator, he had the audacity to say, "Springer, don't send me a *schwartzer*." She did indeed send him a black woman: Melba Solomon. Astounded by Soloman's skill, the contractor would say that she had golden fingers. Concerning this incident and others, Springer explained:

> You know, people become so accustomed to you, so that they forget for a minute that they are telling me something prejudiced. If you allow yourself to be seduced, to be told that you are different, you are psychologically in real trouble. Because there but for the grace of God go I, that person whom they are stereotyping and describing to me. When I was told that I was different, my blood pressure would rise, and I would become angry and illogical. And this same employer tomorrow I would have to work with, so I could

not walk out of the shop and give him some emotionally satisfying answer. So you learned the many ways of educating the people you dealt with.[67]

Silverman recounted cases in which employers would stipulate "don't send me a black" when asking a business agent for a chief examiner. Only with the approval of the chief examiner would contracting shops send their finished garments to the manufacturer who supplied the stores. Rather than head examiners, blacks tended to be lower-paid regular examiners, who looked at the garment for defects at the various stages of production. The head examiner only looked at the final garment. Silverman wrongly assumed that when Springer became a business agent, employers "couldn't very well tell her that."[68]

Because 90 percent of workers' wages were based on piecework, Springer was aware that shop chairpersons could discriminate against black workers by unfairly dividing the work.[69] Elected by their fellow employees, shop chairs also represented workers' interests to the contractor and on various union committees. Springer also recognized that, because of her race, sex, and position, she could not automatically assume the trust of shop chairpersons and other workers. She remarked that every shop represented a small government and that she "had to be cognizant of the [different] personalities." As a business agent she had to overcome the general suspicion that she would collude with employers. As both a black person and a woman, she had to overcome the suspicion that she was incompetent. According to Israel Breslow, later the manager of Local 22, Silverman was once rejected as a business agent by an all-female shop whose members perhaps believed that a male would have more power than she in representing their concerns. Part of Springer's strategy for building trust included observing basic courtesies such as greeting the shop chairperson on her arrival and including him or her in meetings with the employer. Despite the pressures of a heavy workload, she made a point of taking sufficient time to settle disputes.[70]

In a *Justice* article Springer detailed her typical workday as a business agent. After arriving at work at nine o'clock and checking messages and complaints, she would proceed to visit shops and handle complaints from ten o'clock to noon. At lunchtime she was inundated by various groups competing for her attention. Workers wanted to discuss their complaints. An employer might try to justify some action to her. A department manager might talk to her about a dispute in which the workers believed that they were not receiving fair treatment. Shop chairpersons and shop committees would seek her clarification on issues of authority. And urgently seeking permission for overtime, shop chairpersons and employers would call her. After lunch Springer would continue her rounds of visiting shops until she returned to her office at five o'clock, where at a more leisurely pace she met with workers who had special grievances or dealt with the endless paperwork.[71]

Springer also found it important for herself, and to help support Zimmerman, who contributed Local 22 funds to the NAACP, to educate her shop members about the plight of blacks in the South and the work of the NAACP. She held that many of them understood oppression in terms of pogroms and Hitler's Holocaust but not in terms of what American blacks experienced and the history of slavery. At her request, NAACP leader Walter White visited some of her shop meetings to address the workers about these issues.

It appears that from the beginning of her thirteen-year tenure as a business agent, Springer gained the trust and respect of most workers. A worker named Leo Heit, who was present at the first shop meeting she held, expressed to Zimmerman that it was a "pleasure and an honor to be a part of an organization with such a worthy person as Miss Springer."[72] Referring to the 1947 Taft-Hartley Act, which circumscribed the power of unions, Heit recalled: "It was with pride that I sat and listened to her lecture. . . . I do not believe a qualified labor attorney can define its laws [the provisions of the law] as she has done. She presided over the meeting with dignity, intelligence. It was an atmosphere of true unionism. . . . May our great union possess more 'Springers' as officers."[73]

Murray and Silverman witnessed the effect Springer had on the people with whom she worked. Murray offered this assessment: "Trying to settle petty disputes between workers and employers who screamed at one another Maida's gracious manner and sense of proportion made her a remarkably effective union representative."[74] Silverman remembered Springer showing her a gift she received from one of the pressers, a box of matchbooks with a different composer pictured on each. Silverman was impressed because the pressers had a reputation for being "tough guys" and less learned. The gift seemed to exemplify Springer's ability to draw out the kind of character that was normally hidden. Silverman added, "She was loved. For the simple reason, respect people and listen to them. . . . If I want to tell you what Maida's like, I'd tell you very easy in a sentence or two she's very bright. But more than that, she's understanding, she's considerate beyond anything. . . . I mean it's really rare. We had an immigrant membership. I said, 'Maida, you got to use shorter words; these are immigrants.' And that was O.K. There was no 'Why?'"[75]

Silverman recalled only one negative comment about Springer within the ILGWU. A white colleague tried to put her down by saying that she only had white friends. "So I said, how would you know? I said I've been to a dozen parties at her house, and I'm the only white person there. Sometimes there's another one. People always have to find something to pick on, and it was very hard to pick on Maida. Very hard."[76]

Long after Springer ceased to be active in the ILGWU, workers still remembered her. Having read an article about her in a 1986 issue of *Justice*, Francis Fimmano, a former shop chair, recalled Springer admiringly, even though he had lost contact with her in 1955.[77] Among African nationalists and trade union leaders Springer's work would engender similar admiration.

A Year Abroad

*"I had a hope that perhaps at some point I would be able to travel
more freely and go back to England when my son was out of school. But in
no way did I think I would be involved in international affairs in the way
that it developed in 1945. I surely didn't think that."*
Maida Springer, author interview, 1991

Although the coverage was not as extensive as for her 1945 trip, the announcement of Springer's 1951 foreign-study tour still met with fanfare. Under the auspices of the American-Scandinavian Foundation and the American Labor Education Service Office, she began the trip by studying workers' education in Denmark and Sweden. Afterwards she observed labor conditions in France and Italy, before settling down on an Urban League scholarship to study international labor relations at Oxford University's Ruskin Labor College.[78]

In accepting the opportunity to travel, Springer had assumed that she would have to forfeit her job. However, Zimmerman valued her service and safeguarded her post by temporarily dividing her district among three or four business agents. The manufacturers' association members, who initially had been so outraged at having to work with Springer, now bent every effort in praise of her services. In a celebration before her trip, they credited her with superior talents and held that no one could ever take her place.[79]

While in Scandinavia in August and September, Springer spent time in the home of her good friends Esther and Oliver Peterson, who had lived in Sweden since Oliver Peterson's appointment as labor attaché. Their presence became of particular value in helping her out of a predicament that immediately enveloped her. Attending a reception in her honor hosted by a group of professional women, Springer was unwittingly drawn into a national debate concerning differential pay based on sex. In addition to receiving less pay for the same work, Swedish women were in the unjust position of training males who were then promoted above them. Female journalists and teachers in particular, Springer recalled, "were inveighing against this differential." At the reception the journalists sought her opinion on the wage differential. Seeking to avoid implication in the national debate, she sidestepped the question by speaking instead about women's struggles in the United States and the ways in which work could be structured into sex-specific jobs with women receiving lower pay. The next day the newspapers printed that she had said she pitied the Swedish female workers because of the wage differential.[80]

Unaware of the content of the articles because of the language barrier, Springer knew something was amiss when she went to a large factory for her first appointment. She remarked that icicles were "hanging from everywhere" and that the workers bowed their heads and would not look at her. Both male and female workers felt that she had insulted them, the leader of the women's section of the labor movement refused to meet her, and the newspapers made carica- tures of her. The race and gender bias Springer confronted in the United States would have made her an unlikely candidate to pity Swedish workers, whose country was far advanced in areas such as care for children and the elderly. The reactions of Swedish workers, particularly women, to her alleged comments did not necessarily reflect support for the pay differential but resentment of an out- sider standing in superior judgment of another country.[81] If the statement that she pitied workers helped the movement for equal pay, it happened at the price of her reputation among workers.

The Petersons, who were well respected, came to Springer's rescue by invit- ing a hundred labor leaders to talk with her in their home. Esther Peterson, who had been with Springer at the reception, verified that she had not made any state- ment about pitying the Swedish workers. Moreover, the Petersons got the news- papers to make retractions.[82] To help counter any future incidents of this sort, Springer had two witnesses present at her public appearances who could verify her remarks. It appears that she was able to rehabilitate her image. Gunnar Hird- man, who acted as her interpreter, informed Eleanor Coit, the head of the Amer- ican-Scandinavian Foundation, that everyone had taken a "fancy" to her and that they all regretted that she could not stay longer. He particularly recalled with fondness singing labor songs with Springer and the Petersons.[83]

Although painful and embarrassing, the Swedish controversy provided Springer with a useful lesson for her career in international affairs. She became more aware of the way language could be manipulated to promote a cause or de- stroy the influence of an individual or a movement. Although she would not es- cape being misunderstood or misquoted, she learned to hone her diplomatic skills, choosing her words carefully and keeping alert to the overarching political context in which she worked.

In Africa, as in the United States, Springer was exercised about the pervasive disadvantages attached to being female. In countering sexism, however, she un- derstood that despite racial ties, her nationality made her an outsider. Starting at Ruskin Labor College, she privately spoke with African men about the necessity of improving the status of women in order for nation building to succeed. Lis- tening to her lectures and witnessing her work on behalf of women's causes caused some men to become more supportive of expanded opportunities for women. Others would intimate that she was making trouble.

As a black woman from the U.S. labor movement, Springer was viewed as a curiosity at Ruskin. However, she soon found a niche for herself among some of her classmates and met a number of future African and Caribbean leaders. Among them were Eric Williams of Trinidad and Ben Essumen, Richard Quarshie, and Alex Quaison-Sackey of Ghana.[84] She perceived that many of these men projected a facade of accepting the social order but were really revolutionaries, "busily working at changing the status quo."[85] Springer also renewed her relationship with George Padmore, with whom she had maintained an active correspondence since 1945. She remarked: "George Padmore, I considered, was my Ph.D. education without going to a university for it. In a half hour we would sit down and over a cup of tea and cognac he would—not discuss with me, because I wouldn't have known what I was discussing—but he would lay out to me part of the history of what he called Empire. So he was a great educator, and he didn't have a problem proselytizing me. I was a very willing subject."[86]

In his role as mentor Padmore also helped Springer with her lessons and encouraged her to challenge arguments concerning the "white man's burden." He would say, "Now let me mark this passage for you, and I want you to take a stand!"[87] Exposure to the political work of Africans and Caribbeans, however, led her to pay less attention to her classes on the international labor movement and European unions and focus more on colonial development. Listening to Padmore and other pan-Africanists discuss strategies to bring about independence for Africa and the Caribbean, attending the lectures on colonial history at Rhodes House and the debates of the Oxford debating society, and participating in "heated discussions at tea and sherry parties" became as much a part of her educational experience as her classes. Commenting on the Rhodes House lectures, she reflected, "It seemed altogether fitting, if a bit ironic, that these lectures should be given at Rhodes House; that the young Asians and Africans should be refining their skills to return home to serve their countrymen with ability, composure, dignity and insight, thus giving the lie to the Rhodes-Kipling concept of the 'White Man's Burden.'"[88]

Writer Benedict Anderson has addressed the importance of literacy and bilingualism to the development of nationalist sentiment among intellectuals. Paradoxically, the imposition of European languages and Western education on Africans served as unifying elements. They gave Africans access to the Western models of nationalism and democracy that were often used as weapons against colonialism. As Makonnen aptly observed, "[W]hen you look at the results of those Africans who had been to England, you wouldn't be far wrong in saying that England had been the executioner of its own colonial empire."[89] Tanganyikan leader Julius Nyerere, who pursued advanced education in Scotland, expressed the same sentiment to Springer in the late 1950s: "Our political philosophy is Western because Western Europe has been our teacher. We quote the Declaration of American Independence, we quote the lofty ideals of the French Revolution and the tradition of practice of British democracy. . . . Our complaint is the lack of them in our countries . . . those ideals are our greatest allies."[90]

The Africans and Europeans whom Springer encountered in England were well aware that these ideals did not match the black experience in the United

States. Makonnen indicated that "the prevailing mood in Britain, whether you were a cockney or a black seaman, was to look at the American scene as just a bunch of barbarians." Although compared to the United States there was a relative lack of racial violence in England, racial barriers and prejudices were still quite apparent. Both Makonnen and Springer commented on the problem blacks had in finding accommodations. Some newspaper ads for lodging, Springer noted, would bluntly stipulate, "No Africans."[91]

British society, like American society, rejected interracial relationships and children of mixed races. In partial response to the plight of hundreds of children who had been fathered by African American soldiers stationed in Britain and abandoned by their white mothers, Makonnen helped to found an orphanage and also to place some in homes in the United States. He remarked that, at that time, the Daughters of the American Revolution were lobbying for a bill prohibiting children fathered by African American men from entering the United States. Underlying their actions was a fear that black American men overseas might marry the English and Italian mothers of their children, bring their families home, and thus disrupt the racial order and damage white prestige. Historian Brenda Gayle Plummer states that publicity about the explosion of "brown baby" orphans was muted in the mainstream U.S. press. Military commanders recognized that publicity might lead to white demands for a reduction in the number of blacks deployed overseas, a position that would be roundly attacked by blacks, who demanded full inclusion in the national life. Racist military leaders also forbade black servicemen to marry European white women.[92]

Springer asserted that her discussions with Africans about U.S. racism were sharply different from those she had with some of her English associates. Africans were open to the information she provided them, including accounts of the civil rights activism of the NAACP and the National Council of Negro Women. But Springer was offended by the approach of a small British group. She felt that their criticisms of U.S. racism were based less on a real concern for blacks than on resentment of the postwar ascendancy of the United States as a world power and the corresponding decline in Britain's fortunes. Her perception that they pitied her was reminiscent of the reaction of Swedish workers toward her alleged remarks. She recalled:

> Sometimes I had issues with my young Socialist friends, not the ones who had some real understanding, but the ones who were snide, not decent. They were in the labor movement and were all on scholarship at Ruskin. I have had a young man say to me that wasn't I very glad I was here in England, so that I would not be faced as I was in the U.S. with lynchings. I then went on to give him some British history about where my father came from and that West Indian background. I wanted him to tell me the policies of the

British in the colonies. Then talk to me about the U.S. That usually made people quiet. And I would go further and say, "Tell me about Stepney and Shorditch." These were seaports where the relationships were very mean and bad and where there were a lot of blacks who were seamen. . . . Many of them had relationships with women, and they had children who were called "half caste."[93]

In a report to the Urban League on her stay in England Springer remarked that the emergence of an independent Africa and Asia will be, "the overwhelming problem" Europe and the United States will have to face in the near future. Therefore they needed to revise their conceptions of colonial people.[94] Most European and white American labor leaders with whom Springer had discussions, however, scoffed at the idea of African independence. They could understand Indians fighting for independence but not Africans, particularly those south of the Sahara. Their lack of respect for her view that Africa soon would be a center of anticolonial struggle is reflected in a statement she made in 1959: "Listening to men like Jomo Kenyatta as far back as 1945 in England, made it abundantly clear the West would be called upon to make some hard decisions on their territories. In those days I was a prophet without honor."[95]

Widespread cultural representations of Africans as primitive, inferior, and bereft of culture fed white ignorance of the extent of Africans' discontent with colonialism and even influenced the negative attitudes many African Americans had toward Africa. Plummer asserts that the paucity of general information about Africa, unbalanced reporting of African conflicts, and the filtering of African conflicts through the lens of Cold War security interests also had a negative impact on African American interest in the continent.[96]

Springer was among those who did not absorb the negative views of Africa prevalent in U.S. culture and who had access to people who were informed about the developing nationalist struggles. Optimistic that meaningful changes were on the horizon for people of African descent, Springer continued to expand her connections with African nationalist and labor leaders by hosting many who traveled to the United States. While Owen Springer supported African liberation, he saw this cause as one more obstacle to his desire for more of his wife's attention. His wife's 1951 trip abroad was a strong indication that they could not reconcile their differing expectations of family life. The couple divorced in 1955, the year that Springer began frequent travels to Africa.

5

Dancing on the End of a Needle: African Connections

AIDA SPRINGER FIRST SET FOOT IN AFRICA IN 1955, just before the merger of the two national federations into the AFL-CIO. She came to Accra as an observer for the AFL and the only woman attending a seminar held by the International Confederation of Free Trade Unions (ICFTU). The central conflict leading to the establishment of the ICFTU in 1949 was the opposition of Communist trade unions to the U.S.-sponsored Marshall Plan to rebuild Europe after World War II. Consequently, the CIO and noncommunist European unions withdrew from the World Federation of Trade Unions and joined with the AFL to form the ICFTU. As a direct result of colonialism, African labor centers, as well as other colonial labor bodies in Asia and the Americas, were brought into the ICFTU.

The political differences that plagued the international from its beginning had a detrimental effect on Springer's work in Africa. Internal fighting within the ICFTU contributed to the delay in setting up a regional organization for Africa. Regional organizations, which the ICFTU had already established in Asia and the Americas, were charged with promoting labor education and organizing. Nevertheless, colonial affiliates were not accorded full rights in the international and were dominated by the labor unions from the countries that ruled them. African labor centers looked to the staunchly anticolonialist U.S. labor movement for support. They perceived European ICFTU leaders as unwilling to address their needs fully, to treat them with respect, and to understand the importance of the nationalist struggle to the labor movements. Another point of division within the ICFTU affecting African policy was the AFL leadership's strident opposition to relations with Communist labor unions. Within European and CIO unions there remained a significant core of support for engagement with the labor movements from Communist countries. These divisions helped inform the constant friction among U.S. labor leaders after the merger, and contributed to disagreements over policy in Africa.

While carrying out her work in Africa Springer would feel that she was "dancing on the end of a needle" because of her desire to effect social change in face of European labor leaders' insistence that the African labor movements stay out of politics. Springer agreed with Africans that the problems many labor unions faced necessitated a political solution leading to the end of colonialism. After all, the colonial governments, which were also the largest employers in most African countries, passed labor legislation designed to shape, contain, and constrain the labor movements. Moreover, labor commissioners had a conflict of interest, acting both as colonial government representatives and advisors to the labor movement.

The insistence of European labor leaders on complete separation of political and labor issues was a constant source of tension in their relations with Africans. Many Africans held leadership positions in both labor and political organizations. Moreover, in places where political organizations were banned, people naturally looked to labor unions to help advance human rights and fight against colonialism. Consequently, many labor leaders became officials in the first independence governments.[1]

The House in Brooklyn

Springer's office and home were part of a circuit frequented by African and Caribbean visitors to the United States. They might come as guests of the government, labor movement, and other organizations; or they might visit in order to study or to petition the United Nations (UN). Springer particularly welcomed African labor leaders to drop in on Local 22 and observe the functions of the union. She herself had begun to spend a great deal of time at the UN attending meetings and developing relationships with others committed to African liberation. By 1959 Springer, along with Socialist leader Norman Thomas, served on the board of directors of the International League for the Rights of Man, a UN consultant agency whose responsibilities included pressuring governments to support human rights and aiding petitioners from trust territories.[2]

Springer's support for African independence was tied to her support of civil rights at home and her desire to bring Africans and African Americans into closer association. Ghana's independence, achieved on March 6, 1957, affected her more than that of any of the other countries that followed. Springer wept while she and Ras Makonnen stood on either side of A. Philip Randolph as the British flag was lowered and Ghana's flag was raised. In an article for the *Pittsburgh Courier*, she expressed envy for Africans, who she said always knew they had a country and always belonged. Colonialism had only temporarily controlled their lives. She hoped that "we American Negroes" were ready "to look outside ourselves and so learn something of the vast continent of Africa."[3]

Although many of Springer's African friends and colleagues who traveled to the United States had personal encounters with its pervasive system of discrimination and racism, they still looked favorably upon the country, particularly in contrast to the colonial powers. The reputation the United States enjoyed as a noncolonial power (in the traditional European sense), the AFL-CIO's strong anticolonial pronouncements, the cultural connection to Africa the United States had through its large black population, the perception that the status of African Americans was steadily improving, and the influence of African Americans within the AFL-CIO—all helped to account for the prestige of the U.S. labor movement in Africa.

One of the many Africans who stayed at Springer's home was Tanganyikan political leader Bibi (a title of respect) Titi Mohammed, when she arrived for a U.S. government–sponsored tour in June 1963. Having known Bibi Titi Mohammed since 1957, Springer went to her hotel and invited her to stay at her home. It was close by, she could have privacy during the day, and she could cook African meals. Bibi Titi Mohammed agreed to the switch and used Springer's home as a base while she traveled to other U.S. cities. She observed that people, particularly those of African descent, seemed to sense Springer's arrival home. They showed up at her house as soon as she returned from work.[4] Her home served as a refuge where they could congregate, relax, eat, and discuss plans for independence. Waiyaki Wambaa was one of the many students who frequented her home; he and his fellow students appreciated being able to use her house to hold meetings.[5]

Many of Springer's African friends, both inside and outside the labor movement, called her Mama or Mama Maida, reflecting both a familial sentiment and respect for her older age. They also referred to her mother as Mama. Through these visitors, Adina Stewart's engaging personality became well known in African labor and nationalist circles. Joseph Thuo, who worked for the U.S. Information Service in Kenya, once asked her how she managed so successfully to combine work and a sense of humor.[6] If Stewart could help their African guests with medical attention or any other form of aid, she made sure the services were provided free of charge in the name of "the cause." Reflecting on how her home became a pan-African center, Springer commented, "If you're involved in international trade union activities, there is a network. It is assumed that if you have something to give or contribute, you do it. All of us who worked in this area contributed what we could. I had a thirteen-and-a-half-room house, an old brownstone, nothing grand or special, but an old house with space and a back yard."[7]

Among Springer's earliest contacts were Maynard Mpangala, assistant general secretary of the Tanganyika Federation of Labor (TFL); Julius Nyerere, head of the Tanganyika African National Union (TANU); and Tom Mboya, the general secretary of the Kenya Federation of Labor (KFL). Through her friendships with these men and others, Springer developed a close affinity for the people of East Africa. While she was charmed by the people and pace of life there, she was exercised about the harsh conditions they lived under. In this region that attracted little publicity apart from British accounts of the horrors of Mau Mau, Springer became a witness to the deprivations under which Africans suffered as well as their struggles and triumphs. Until 1963 she considered moving permanently to Tanganyika (now Tanzania).

Mpangala was the first to inform Springer about the struggles of the TFL when they met in New York in 1956. The previous year, while engaged in efforts to form the TFL, he had attempted to break through the atmosphere of isolation in Tanganyika by writing to an ICFTU regional office, whose address he had discovered in some labor literature from Latin America. His letters were forwarded to ICFTU headquarters in Brussels, which dispatched Mboya to advise the Tanganyikan labor leaders.[8]

The ICFTU also sent Mpangala to an ICFTU seminar in Mexico. It was during a stopover in New York that he met Springer. After the ICFTU's New York office publicized his presence, she showed up at his hotel, introduced herself, and inquired about the conditions in his country. When he stopped in New York again on his way back from Mexico, Springer met him at the airport and took him home to meet her mother. In a 1991 retrospective on Springer's career, a Tanzanian labor paper stated of Mpangala's visit, "During their talks, Maida's mother was full of praise for her daughter, for her good heart, and the courage she had to fight for the weak, an act that was later to be recognized and appreciated."[9]

Although the Eisenhower/Stevenson presidential elections were commanding the attention of many in the United States, Springer managed to introduce Mpangala to a number of political and labor leaders, including Zimmerman and Randolph, so he could explain the work of TANU and the TFL. He also addressed the ILGWU council. During his stay, Mpangala asked Springer to help TANU leader and ex-schoolteacher Julius Nyerere in his quest for educational opportunities for Tanganyikans.[10]

In West Africa, where there was not a large settler class, it was to Britain's ad-

vantage to educate Africans to fill the subordinate positions in the colonial administrative apparatus. Tabora Government Secondary School was the only gov-
ernment-supported secondary school in Tanganyika. Makerere University College in Uganda was the only school of higher education in all of East Africa. The
large demand for educational opportunities made these schools highly competi-
tive and meant that few if any women could attend.[11]

Nyerere came to the United States in 1955 and June 1957 as a petitioner before the UN Trusteeship Council and in December 1956 as a speaker before the
UN Trusteeship Committee. His goals included setting a timetable for independence and winning support for universal suffrage. Nyerere would become
the first leader of independent Tanganyika and would hold power for twenty-five
years. He and Springer remained lifelong friends. She recalled that they first met
by chance at the UN in 1956: "I guess both of us had been described to one another [by Mpangala]. So as we walked toward one another . . . he said, 'You're
Maida Springer.' And I said, 'You're Julius Nyerere.' That's how we met. He was
going to an important meeting and I was going to some noise-making thing that I
was involved in, some protest involving Africa."[12]

Horace Mann Bond, the first African American president of Lincoln University, known as the "Black Princeton," happened to be attending a meeting at
the UN that day too. Springer, knowing of the thirst for education in Tanganyika
and Lincoln's long commitment to educating Africans, seized the opportunity to
introduce the two men. Kwame Nkrumah, Ako Adjei, and Nnamdi Azikiwe were
among the many Africans who had studied at Lincoln. Through the initial contact with Bond, Nyerere soon made many others.[13]

Donating her own money and other resources, Springer helped to educate
particularly young girls in Tanganyika but also Africans of all age levels studying
in Africa and the United States. Among the schools she helped was a Tanganyikan primary school started by Mary Theresa Ibrahim. In addition to personally giving the school two hundred dollars, which paid the fees of thirty-three
children, she put Ibrahim in touch with other groups that could aid her school.[14]

Sir Edward Twining, the governor of Tanganyika, reacted to Nyerere's attempts to obtain scholarships during the 1956 trip by attempting to stir up dissension among Africans. He suggested that students would get a substandard education in the United States that would not allow them to qualify for a government
job. Moreover, he stated that they would be taught nothing but evil and would
return defiant of tribal authority. Of course, his real concern was that they would
return defiant of colonial authority. Due to the nationalist fervor of Africans who
attended Lincoln University, British colonial officials held the school suspect.
According to Makonnen, colonial officials in neighboring Kenya were reluctant
to give passports to Africans who wanted to study abroad. They preferred them to
go to Lovedale in South Africa, where they would not be exposed to a different
sort of race relations.[15]

Nyerere complained to Springer that the British were proud to announce that after thirty-seven years in Tanganyika they had produced one African district officer. Because of the limited educational opportunities he did not find this situation surprising. He stated, "What would be surprising would be the acceptance by the African of this stupid propaganda that we should wait until the British educate us before we seek Self-Government." The colonial press condemned TANU's plan to build schools by claiming that a similar experiment in Kenya had served as a breeding ground for the Mau Mau rebellion, a predominantly Kikuyu anticolonial movement. The Kenyan government had banned the 127 Kikuyu schools. Nyerere rejoined that if the Tanganyikan government satisfied Africans' thirst for education, TANU would not build one school. Nyerere, who was called Mwalimu (Teacher), was the first Tanganyikan to receive a degree from a British University.[16]

Twining's warning about U.S. education most likely took place at a Conference of Chiefs at Mzumbe, near Morogoro. Nyerere informed Springer that at this conference the governor warned the chiefs "of the danger of 'a new political party composed largely of people whose tribal links have loosened, and who had not the proper respect for the Native Authority and Chiefs. Most of their ideas came from outside Tanganyika, put into their heads by people who did not have the true interest of the territory at heart and who wanted to apply methods which are not suitable to local conditions.'" Judging by her negative reception by the East African press and British TUC officials during her early 1957 tour of Africa, Springer was among those Twining would have classed as ignorant outsiders.[17]

The Tanganyikan government also sought to undermine Nyerere by publishing a pamphlet called "Some Comments on Mr. Nyerere's Speech to the Fourth Committee of the United Nations," with the aim of countering any sympathy his arguments for constitutional reform might have gained. The pamphlet attacked Nyerere and impugned his motives, asserting that he was primarily after self-glorification. In an attempt to gain sympathy from the West, the government conjured up a foreboding image of black domination as the end result of universal suffrage. Nyerere vowed to Springer that he was prepared to return to the United States and try to "minimise the harm that these people might do there."[18]

Mboya represented a second strong link Springer had with East Africa. In 1962 he became Kenya's minister of labor in the transitional government before independence was instituted in late 1963. Afterwards he served first as minister for justice and constitutional affairs and then as minister of economic planning and development. Mboya first came to the United States under the auspices of the American Committee on Africa (ACOA), arriving in New York on August 15, 1956, his twenty-sixth birthday. One of ACOA's objectives was to introduce him to American labor leaders. After having met Mboya in Brussels just before his U.S. trip, John Tettegah, general secretary of the Ghana labor movement, wrote Springer that he was "quite a nice Pan-African chap" and that she would find his personality interesting. The two men would later represent opposing forces in the struggle over international labor affiliation.[19]

Pauli Murray drove Springer to pick up Mboya. Springer recalled, "We took Tom to Brooklyn to my mother. And she fell in love with him immediately. Tom would sit in the back yard writing notes and doing other things, and she would take him a glass of cold milk and something to snack on. Oh, she loved Tom. Serious young man. He was this soft face, beautiful black young man, very black young man, whose mind was like a sword."[20] Springer, whose son, Eric, was Mboya's age, considered Mboya her second son. He in turn expressed a desire to keep in touch with Eric and attributed his successful trip to the United States in part to the hospitality of Murray, Springer, and her mother. "I enjoyed nothing more than the comfort of your home and reassuring company."[21]

During his 1956 tour of England and the United States, Mboya was the man of the hour. He countered colonialist scare stories about the Mau Mau rebellion led by the Kikuyu by exposing the oppression of Africans. He recounted how the colonial government had overseen the massive expropriation of African land without compensation. Europeans were given the most fertile land, which afterwards was called the "White Highlands," while Africans were crowded onto reserves occupying the worst land and were forced to work on European farms. The Kikuyu represented the greatest number among the landless.[22]

The Kikuyu, in particular, were subjected on a mass scale to suffering and torture. Under the state of emergency in effect since 1952 to suppress the Mau Mau rebellion, the government killed thousands, arrested well over a hundred thousand, and arbitrarily placed tens of thousands without trial in detention camps, where many died under atrocious conditions.[23] Several hundred thousand Kikuyus were forced into newly erected fortified villages, where they were subjected to curfew and forced labor. Under Operation Anvil the government in 1954 rounded up all the adult men in Nairobi. They permanently detained twenty-four thousand mainly Kikuyu in a restricted area surrounded by barbed-wire fences. Since the beginning of the emergency, the government had begun a pattern of residential ethnic separation in Nairobi. Although Tom Mboya was a Luo, they moved him to a house in the more restricted Kikuyu area in order to keep a better watch on him.[24]

The most famous detainee was Mzee (a title of respect meaning Old Man) Jomo Kenyatta. As head of the primarily Kikuyu political organization, the Kenya African Union (KAU), he was arrested in 1952 under the pretext of Mau Mau suppression. Unlike the armed struggle of the Land Freedom Army (dubbed the Mau Mau), the KAU advocated the nonviolent strategy for liberation popularized by the Indian national leader Mahatma Gandhi. KAU radicals, drawn mostly from a group of ex-soldiers, were unhappy with the KAU policy and helped to start the Mau Mau rebellion. The emergency would last until the end of 1959, but Kenyatta, who had not been part of the radical group within the KAU, would remain under detention until 1961.

Through Mboya, Springer later met Anselmi W. Karumba, a former detainee and a founder of Kenya's garment union. While in the United States on a 1961 study tour Springer had organized, he spoke to groups about his six-year experience in detention. He and others were confined naked in cells, without even blankets to sit or sleep on. One form of torture the colonialists used, which resulted in hundreds of deaths, was to deny detainees food and drink for four days and then supply them with more than they could consume. Karumba would counsel his fellow detainees to modulate their intake; however, some were so ravenous that they would not listen and consequently died. Karumba remarked that some in the United States were wary of him at first because they believed the British propaganda that represented the Mau Mau insurrection as irrational and composed of bloodthirsty savages.[25]

Possessing a sharp wit and quick intelligence, Mboya was adept at answering reporters' questions that revealed ignorance of the plight of Africans. Springer described him as a "very rare human being," a patient teacher who was tolerant of Americans who knew little about conditions in his country.[26] In her judgment, "Tom was his own best salesman." AFL-CIO executive council members invited him to Unity House, the ILGWU summer resort. At the meeting they promised financial assistance to help erect a trade union building for the use of the KFL and its affiliates. Shortly afterwards Randolph visited Kenya to ascertain the needs. During her early 1957 visit to the region, Springer helped Mboya to speak with governmental officials about possible locations for the center. That summer Randolph delivered to the KFL a thirty-five-thousand-dollar grant from the AFL, as a contribution toward building what would be called Solidarity House. Since Mboya had a close relationship with leaders of the United Auto Workers (UAW), he may have decided upon this name because the UAW's headquarters was also called Solidarity House.[27]

Like Nyerere, Mboya also sought educational opportunities during his 1956 visit. William X. Scheinman, head of Arnav Industries, a manufacturer of aircraft components, personally guaranteed the airfare for seventeen Kenyan students to come to the United States for an education. In order to present a different picture of the Kikuyus than that perpetuated by colonialists, Mboya designated Kamau Mwangi, a Kikuyu, as the first beneficiary of this education project. Before proceeding to Ohio Wesleyan University, Mwangi stayed at the Springer home and became another favorite of Adina Stewart's. She agreed to let Mwangi, whom Springer described as a fine artist, and his colleagues paint a map of Africa in the cemented center of their back yard. Afterwards this map provoked controversy among visitors from West and Central Africa, who argued that the representation of their countries was too small.[28]

Following his successful tour, Mboya soared in popularity among Africans and became the object of greater enmity from colonialists. A large African crowd converged on the airport to welcome him home with cheers and song, while a large number of police looked on. Mboya told Springer that Africans warned him to "look out for any suspicious European characters—some had decided I must be silenced permanently."[29]

In fact, however, Mboya's assassination thirteen years later came at the hands of a fellow Kenyan. The anxiety in political circles about the possibility of his succeeding Kenyatta as president of Kenya combined with rumors of his impending assassination have left the impression that the plot behind his murder has not been fully disclosed. Mboya's popularity in the United States, his occasional display of arrogance, his tendency at times to act on his own, and his success at political maneuvering became infused into the ideological conflicts, leadership rivalries, and jealousies among Africans. The Ghana TUC and the Convention People's Party attacked him as early as his first U.S. tour. They viewed his activities as a Kenyan as partly usurping Ghana's position of leadership in the continental struggle for liberation. Ghana TUC officer Joseph-Fio Meyers remarked, "Tom Mboya is a young boy whom Dr. Nkrumah wanted to train and put into the struggle for African liberation. Then the Americans offered him a scholarship to bring him into level with Dr. Nkrumah as a maneuver for causing dissension."[30] This view of Mboya as a youthful upstart would be persuasive in many African societies, where wisdom and leadership are equated with greater age.

Navigating through the Cold War

Opponents of the U.S. civil rights movement constantly tried to undermine it with accusations that it operated under the behest of, or in collusion with, international communism. Springer was among those who sought to put the Cold War in service of civil rights and anticolonialism, instead of allowing the prevailing political climate to undermine struggles for equality. The fact that anticommunist beliefs were shared by civil rights activists as well as staunch racists imparted contradictions and complexities to the struggle for civil rights. As despondent as she would become about U.S. race relations and the policies of the U.S. government, she never considered that an alliance with Communists to fight for civil rights was a better strategy.

The infrequency with which African communism is mentioned in the letters of African and African American labor leaders, however, demonstrates that their use of Cold War arguments was inspired not so much by real concern as by a strategy to manipulate the current political climate to their own ends. Springer expressed her ambivalence toward the Cold War in a letter to Nyerere in which she stated how much more desirable it would be if a fraction of the billions the U.S. invested in atomic weapons were spent on developing "the human potential of Africa."[31]

Before Western audiences Springer supported the leadership of Mboya and Nyerere and tried to place the debate over colonialism and communism in an African perspective. Instead of encouraging Africans' thirst for knowledge and demand for parliamentary democracy, she argued, the West mainly expressed "pious apprehensions that the African will fall victim to communism." Springer sought to allay Western fears by asserting that communism was at present not attractive to Africans.[32]

Springer reacted sharply to the procolonial sentiments expressed in the U.S. popular press. In unpublished letters to the New York Times, she urged the paper to "render a world service by presenting the case of the African by an African."[33] After she informed Nyerere about a procolonial article in the Times written by Elspeth Huxley, he responded, "She and her kind will learn rather late we cannot surrender fundamental freedoms to our immigrant neighbours for the sake of pleasing their supporters abroad. We are not asking for privilege, we are challenging their privilege and no body can stop us."[34]

After the Times printed a third article by Huxley in less than a year, the last one targeting Mboya, Springer wrote the Kenyan leader, "I have been forced to conclude that the Times has joined the Colonial Powers to create and maintain a certain kind of American public opinion about Africa and over African aspirations for the future." Mboya informed her that he had written a long response to the Times and also to Newsweek objecting to their printing inaccurate information.[35]

In Springer's letters to the Times, she tried to shift the terms of the colonial debate away from concerns about safeguards for white minority interests and the stabilization of foreign capital and toward what she considered the basic issues of minority domination, special privileges, and cheap labor.[36] She wrote, "Continued deprivation of rights—whether in Africa or the U.S.—is not the answer or solution to the demands for justice, freedom and equality. Nor will Apartheid serve to quell the nascent fires."[37] In response to Huxley's concern over the impact of Radio Cairo and Radio Moscow in East and Central Africa, Springer, having heard comments from the African communities, agreed on the effectiveness of the programs. However, she argued, the root problem was to be found in the attitudes of the colonial governments.[38] She added, "It seems self-defeating for the United States and Britain to skimp or deny support and aid to the Africans and then bemoan the threat of Red domination."[39]

When Life magazine published a series on African political movements in early 1959, Springer wrote Mboya that once again his actions had been portrayed in a "distorted fashion." Regarding the recent struggles in the Congo, she held that only the "blind and the smug" could fail to understand the African discontent.[40] Moreover, she was disturbed that Sir Roy Welensky, the premier of the Central African Federation, was popular among most Americans, who were charmed by his athletic prowess. Springer was dumbfounded that her fellow citizens did not understand that African social protest was a natural development against the oppressive Central African Federation.[41] Composed of Southern and Northern Rhodesia and Nyasaland (Malawi), and lasting from 1953 to 1963, the Federation strengthened white minority rule and the exploitation of African labor in the region's copper and agricultural sectors.

By late 1959 Springer reported to Mboya that at least some European political leaders now viewed Kenyan independence as "valid, foreseeable and, perhaps, not too unreasonable." After hearing that a white employer had been sentenced to death for the shooting death of an African who had thrown stones at his dog, she expressed hope that justice was moving toward some semblance of balance in Kenya.[42]

As for U.S. injustice against its black citizens, Communists used the more sensational cases of violence and the general resistance to civil rights as powerful evidence of U.S. hypocrisy.[43] After returning home from her stint at Ruskin College in England in the early 1950s, Springer reported that because the "dramatic instances of social injustice" in the United States were well known, many Africans had a misconception of the status of African Americans. They believed that lynchings, segregation, and unequal employment opportunities represented a uniform pattern throughout the country. She remarked that it was a "happy challenge" to inform them that the "Negro Problem," like the "Colonial Problem," was not static.[44]

By the end of the 1950s, Springer would become despondent over the plight of both Africans and African Americans. In 1960 she remarked to Mboya that although she was heartened by the student protests in the South, she was discouraged over civil rights bills that were so weak that they were hardly worth the hard work required to muster support for passage. Still, Springer was in favor of Africans having the opportunity to form their own opinions of the racial realities in the United States. When she was asked in a 1963 conversation with U.S. government and labor representatives what she would do if the Guinean delegation she was to host asked to see the South, she responded that she would rather have them go than develop highly distorted impressions.[45] The news stories of resistance to desegregation in the U.S. also were powerful propaganda tools for procolonial forces who wanted to put the U.S. labor movement in its place. Springer remarked that British colonialists got much satisfaction from viewing the great anticolonial power try to wiggle out of its racist contradictions. In a 1959 speech she once commented:

The fear of Communist expansion in Africa is not entirely unwarranted. Those of us who think we have some understanding of this evil doctrine can understand the concern of the West. However, the ever present examples of Western democracy as practiced in South, Central and East African make us apologists for the West, and [leave] us self-conscious about the Congo and Portuguese East Africa. This is not all. Our allies in democracy, to ease the burden of criticism of their colonial policies, never let us lose sight of our own color dilemma. Under such circumstances it comes with poor grace to tell Africans communism is worse.[46]

Regarding Mboya's 1959 visit to the United States, a writer for the *New Republic* suggested that the Kenyan settlers were "breathing fire at the American welcome to the 'arch extremist' Mboya, ascribing the whole expedition to guilt feelings by Americans who seek to justify to Africa that Little Rock ever happened." (In 1957, the United States sent 11,500 soldiers to the Arkansas capital to protect nine black students who were integrating Central High School.) As Mboya noted, "colonial powers are only too ready to use this sort of publicity to prove that where as they are wrong, they are not the only people who are always wrong."[47] Yet Mboya too used the segregation issue to point out Western hypocrisy and goad the West into practicing democracy.[48] Nonalignment, he explained, stemmed from the inconsistent standards of U.S. foreign policy:

The West condemns Soviet Russia for its interference in Hungary, but when France denies the Algerian people the same basic rights, the West remains silent. The West condemns Communist China for its actions in Tibet, but when the British shoot down 50 unarmed African demonstrators, it compromises. The West attacks Soviet Russia for her type of government, her regimentation, her slave labor camps, yet shares the same table with South Africa. The West condemns her for her slave labor camps in Siberia. Yet the West says nothing about the slave labor camps in the Portuguese territories in Africa.[49]

Nyerere counted on Springer to help interpret for the West the reasons Africans desired independence and to explain their positions and struggles in relation to the Cold War. In one letter he told her that he had wanted to express certain views in the United States but felt they would be misunderstood. Instead, he decided to tell her some of these, hoping that through her "a few of our friends may get some idea of what we are trying to do." Principally, he wanted the United States to take a more active interest in East Africa, and Tanganyika in particular, and to stand unequivocally on the "side of morality and democracy." He believed that the United States had "the means and the democratic tradition to enable" it to ally with Tanganyika against poverty and ignorance "without imperialist motive." But if help from the West were not forthcoming, Africa might turn to Communist countries "and rid herself of the immediate humiliation" of colonialism and later hope to deal with danger of communism. Anticipating the charge of blackmail, he answered, "Perhaps they should be reminded that Washington, London and Paris were allies of Moscow against Hitler. In desperation first things come first."[50]

In a 1960 AFL-CIO memorandum, Springer suggested that the United States could learn something from the Chinese. She may not have believed that the Chinese were free of racism; however, she used their treatment of African visitors as a standard to judge Western attitudes. The hundreds of Africans who visited Peking, she stated, felt welcomed, were not treated as curios, and were never humiliated in hotels and public accommodations, as they would be in the United States. Further, they were never asked such questions as when they had learned to speak English, whether they were comfortable in Western clothes, were they ready for self-government, and were they Mau Maus.[51]

The primary opposition Springer had to overcome in her work on behalf of African labor came not from Communists but from colonial governments and her Western colleagues. Whenever she arrived in Africa, they would ask her with evident pleasure about the serious problems in U.S. race relations. She particularly remembers the glee with which some approached her about the Emmet Till murder. She became physically ill afterwards in her hotel room. Although she refused to be an apologist for U.S. race relations and foreign policy, she quickly cited the sins of the colonial governments in order to counter what she called the double and triple standards they upheld. In order not to jeopardize any future opportunities for training and material aid African labor might receive, Springer often hid the bitterness she felt about the opposition of European labor leaders to her activism. The stress that resulted, coupled with the hectic work pace she kept, caused a flare-up of ulcers and bouts of depression.[52]

In dire need of basic office supplies, means of transportation, technical and educational support, and leadership development, the financially strapped African labor unions barely stayed afloat. Whereas the ICFTU was slow to act, U.S. labor, largely through the intercession of Springer and Randolph, gave financial support to strikers and labor and political activists facing trial or detention. In justification of their slow approach, ICFTU leaders pointed to the suspected or real misappropriation of funds by individual leaders and to poor accounting practices. They also argued that large amounts of external aid would blunt local initiatives to build support networks.[53]

While these arguments had some merit, ICFTU leaders failed to recognize fully the hardships experienced by African labor. Springer and others believed that fear of African nationalism played an even stronger role in the ICFTU's tendency to delay assistance, including the implementation of the international's own recommendations. ICFTU leaders, particularly those from the British TUC, resented Springer's relationships with Africans and sought to restrain the AFL-CIO from taking on a greater role in Africa.

First Conflict with the ICFTU

In 1955 Francis Edward Tachie-Menson, a government minister and president of the Gold Coast (later Ghana) Trades Union Congress, helped to arrange Springer's first visit to Africa. He first met Springer earlier that year, during his U.S. tour under the auspices of the State Department's International Education Exchange Program. Upon returning to Africa, Tachie-Menson wrote the ICFTU, an organization with which he was often at odds, that it was the "plea" of his colleagues that "this wonderful coloured American lady trade unionist of international fame" be invited to the ICFTU seminar. Remarking that she had the "magic color" (black), he hoped that she could help convince Gold Coast women to join the labor movement.[54] ICFTU officials attending the seminar would learn of Springer's extensive connections with African labor and political leaders.

While attending the seminar, Springer renewed friendships with Ghanaians whom she had met during her stay at Ruskin College, and she met other important leaders, including John Tettegah, the general secretary of the Ghana TUC. Joining Springer from the United States were two African Americans representing CIO unions, Hilton Hanna of the Butcher Workers and William Beckham of the UAW. Labor delegates and observers from seventeen countries in Africa and other parts of the world attended the three-week seminar.[55]

Springer was impressed by the commitment of the African delegates and the high level of discussions. Many delegates had struggled to gain an education through correspondence school, and some from Algeria had recently spent time in jail for their activism. Most of those in attendance were agricultural, mining, or government workers. The seminar addressed the abysmal working and living conditions of agricultural workers, problems of trade-union organization and administration, general labor conditions, workers' education, and the role of labor in Africa's future. Throughout Africa, there was a great disparity between wage rates and the cost of living, which in turn posed a problem for the financing of unions, including having resources to cover transportation, organization, education, and publicity.[56]

Springer's European colleagues were dumbfounded when Kojo Botsio, who at that time served as Ghana's minister of trade and labor, visited her at her hotel. Springer recalled that the sight of Botsio's official car, resplendent with waving flags, "had everybody's eyes popping and mine too." Having stopped in England on her way to Africa, she had a letter of introduction from George Padmore to meet Osagyefo (a title of respect meaning Redeemer) Kwame Nkrumah. As a preliminary check, Botsio invited her to dinner before introducing her to Nkrumah.[57]

At this seminar Springer played what would become a recurring role: she mediated between African labor and the ICFTU. She recalled that Tachie-Menson had some "very harsh things to say about [ICFTU] policy and its representative." Although he served as host of the seminar, he had been prepared to walk out and sever ties with the ICFTU. Springer wrote that she had "some small bit to do with their consideration not to withdraw."[58]

Springer's second trip to Africa began in January 1957. She came to attend the first ICFTU African Regional Conference, to meet with East Africans, particularly Kenyans regarding the plans for Solidarity House, and to attend Ghana's independence celebrations. The delegation to the conference, representing the now-merged AFL-CIO, included secretary-treasurer William Schnitzler, vice president Emil Rieve, European field representative Irving Brown, and Springer. Among the conference proposals were requests for the ICFTU to build a labor school in Africa and set up an African Regional Organization (AFRO) corresponding to those already in operation for Europe, Asia, and the Americas. Although the ICFTU executive board had approved the conference as a step to organizing a regional organization for the continent, they hesitated about following through on their own recommendations as well as about meeting other African requests.[59]

Springer formed strong relationships with many of the delegates, whom she described as earnest men, the majority of whom had suffered for their commitment to "independence, political and economic equality." Held at the newly built Ambassador Hotel, the conference served to showcase the Ghanaian government on the eve of independence. In the opening speech, Kwame Nkrumah recalled his membership in the Maritime Union while working in the United States as a steward on a passenger ship of the Clyde Mallory Line. Pledging his continuing commitment to independent and free trade unionism, he also averred that labor had a role to play in the larger development of Africa and in the anticolonial movements.[60]

Good rapport existed between African labor and government officials and the AFL-CIO delegation. During the conference they met with Nkrumah, who was interested in their ideas concerning outside capital investment in Ghana, which had been the primary subject of his opening-day speech. The delegation spoke of the experiences of Israel and Puerto Rico, and in particular Springer recalled that Brown, Rieve, and Schnitzler "kept ideas moving."[61]

Although the U.S. delegation was heartily welcomed by Africans, ICFTU representatives were angered by their presence. Based on conversations with the

American Jay Krane, who served as the ICFTU's assistant director of organization, Springer suggested that the European leaders were quietly seething over the AFL-CIO's decision to give the Kenya Federation of Labor a grant to help build Solidarity House. Krane offered the frequent charge of corruption as a reason for not giving aid. The AFL-CIO action, he proposed, would have a snowball effect by encouraging other African labor movements to make requests. Indeed, African labor leaders did make numerous appeals to the AFL-CIO. The AFL-CIO's later agreement to cease their independent work with African labor in favor of deferring to the ICFTU as the sole developer of African policy and programs would not stop the requests. Some leaders also appealed directly to Springer to tap into resources of AFL-CIO affiliates and find other sources of support.[62]

Krane informed Springer that the ICFTU, with its direct experiences with Africans, was in the best position to determine what projects were worthy of support and would not be swayed by the personality of the petitioner. This comment was an obvious swipe at the charismatic Mboya, who was absent from the conference because of his involvement in Kenyan elections. Mboya's decision to enter the political arena was a primary reason he decided to turn down an ICFTU position that would have afforded him further opportunities to travel and also would have provided, as he said, "personal security."[63] ICFTU officials were not happy with his political ambitions and resented the ties he had made within the U.S. labor movement.

The U.S. delegation arrived in Accra to discover that their status at the conference would be as guests and not observers. The ICFTU secretariat, and not the leaders of the African affiliates who were the conference delegates, had made this decision. Among the observers were one representative each from the ICFTU's Asian Regional Organization and Inter-American Regional Organization and four from its European Regional Organization. Moreover, at least three Europeans served as delegates representing African countries and others served on conference committees.[64]

ICFTU officials twice told Springer that her guest status meant that she had no right to participate formally in the conference proceedings.[65] Elaborating on the ICFTU position, Krane told Springer that although the ICFTU general secretary, Jacob Oldenbroek from Holland, had received a letter from AFL-CIO president George Meany stating that they were coming as observers, the ICFTU had decided against sending invitations to the U.S. delegation. Intimating that the ICFTU was being tolerant, he remarked that they did not object, however, when the U.S. delegation arrived.[66]

Nevertheless, the British, French, and Belgian observers openly disapproved of the U.S. presence and particularly of Springer's. She recalled that the head of the Belgian labor movement (FGTB), Louis Major, whom she described as "frigid, polite and venomous," was intent on humiliating her by making her lose her temper or break down and weep. During the conference, however, Major was the one who became outraged when the credentials committee discussed at some length whether he and fellow Belgian Raphael Bintou should represent Belgian Congo workers. Eventually, the committee approved them with a comment that in the future the Congo should be represented by an African, to which Springer noted that Major "made a vigorous protest." Springer concluded of Major, "His aggressiveness left some delegates with the feeling that his arrogance and superiority would hardly invite the confidence of many Africans."[67]

A heated exchange Major had with Tettegah and Mboya nearly two years later, at an ICFTU executive board meeting, substantiated Springer's assessment. Again the subject was the question of FGTB representation, this time in the proposed AFRO. In response to Mboya's insistence that African trade unions must be autonomous and independent, Major claimed that the FGTB had instituted autonomous unions with "absolute trade union rights," which was more than he could say of some "recently liberated countries." This was an obvious reference to the recent passage of Ghana's Industrial Relations Act, which limited labor independence and strike activity.[68] Mboya replied that while listening to Major speak, "he felt he was back in his country listening to the kind of talk received from colonial civil servants." Krane, however, backed up Major by stating that the FGTB had a right to be represented. According to Irving Brown, at a subsequent ICFTU meeting Major, while on a general tirade against nationalist struggles, "made the insulting remark that all that was needed for the Congo was to buy enough soap for the backward natives."[69] African American George Mc-Cray once reported that on a trip to the Congo, he talked with Africans who were preparing to withdraw from the FGTB because they asserted that the white members ran it for their "own special advantage." After reporting this information to the ICFTU, McCray did not receive an immediate reply.[70]

Marcel Babau from France, who served as both a delegate for French West Africa and an observer from the European Regional Organization, told delegates at the African regional conference "that they were 'wrong' to discuss 'general political problems'" at a labor conference. No one had dared openly criticize Nkrumah for his declaration of labor's political role. On the conference's last day, he accused the U.S. delegation of being interested in organizing political action. He also questioned their presence since the AFL-CIO did not contribute to the ICFTU regional fund that sponsored the conference.[71] Moreover, he reprimanded the ICFTU secretariat for not reviewing beforehand the speech Schnitzler made at the conference. It had included a tirade against Soviet aggression in Hungary, criticisms of U.S. foreign policy, and a ringing denunciation of colonialism.[72]

Schnitzler's speech caused panic among British authorities for some time.

Springer suggested that the speech contributed to European fear that the AFL-CIO was ready to take a "wider interest in the actual functions of these far-flung possessions, and that of course would be in extremely bad taste on our part and really unthinkable in their opinion."[73] No doubt the successful cocktail party that Springer had arranged for the U.S. delegation to give for conference participants and Ghanaian officials contributed to European fears. After all, they were learning just how close Springer already was to many Africans.[74]

Africans, on the other hand, were elated with Schnitzler's speech, which was reprinted in *The Ghana Worker* along with a photograph of Tettegah and Schnitzler shaking hands and surrounded by others, including Springer and Brown. Concerned that U.S. labor's position not be in any way offensive to Ghana on the eve of independence, Springer had shown a draft of the speech to Padmore in England on her way to the conference. Based on his assessment she then offered suggestions to Schnitzler regarding tone and nuance.[75]

Babau's remarks, which brought out into the open conflicts between the ICFTU and the AFL-CIO, provided an opening for Africans to voice their frustrations with the international. In response a Nigerian delegate strongly denounced the attack on the AFL-CIO, after which Springer requested permission to answer the charges. As a delegate, Babau could speak directly to the conference. Although observers could speak "during debates on certain conditions," both observers and guests like Springer had to make a written request to speak to the steering committee. Aware of the volatility of the situation, the committee, which included Krane and Tettegah, who served as chair, with some effort convinced her not to speak in exchange for registering her protests. Springer stipulated that if any further disparaging remarks were directed against the AFL-CIO, she would disrupt the meeting by speaking. In part she relented because she did not want her actions to lead ICFTU officials to retaliate against African labor by further restricting travel opportunities. Nor did she want the incident to become a precipitating factor in the possible development of a "minor race incident." "In the closing hour of the conference," she stated, "it would have been a pity to leave such a memory." Referring to the conference's conclusion as the end of the "deep freeze," Springer reflected, "We were most unwelcomed here and I confess that it was a good feeling to have the conference end."[76]

Greetings in East Africa

Following the ICFTU African Regional Conference Springer proceeded to East Africa, where she was heralded all over the region by Africans. Traveling hundreds of miles by train, truck, and car, and even a little on foot, she spoke before large crowds, attended feasts in her honor, was invited to sit in the councils of elders, and met with villagers, chiefs, and a wide variety of trade union leaders and members. Her schedule was hectic. "In one country in ten days," she wrote, "I attended 10 trade union and political meetings spoke at all of them visited four garment factories, saw several government officials and had time to attend three to four parties." Everywhere she went African labor wanted to know the experiences of U.S. unions with arbitration and negotiation and disputes over the firing of workers.[77]

Documents regarding Springer's activism in East Africa highlight the extreme suspicion and resentment British TUC and ICFTU officials exhibited toward her. She arrived in Dar es Salaam just ahead of others who had participated in the regional conference: Tanganyika Federation of Labor (TFL) general secretary Rashidi Kawawa; Walter Hood, head of the British TUC's Colonial Section for eight years; and Albert Hammerton, director for four years of the ICFTU's West African Trade Union Information Center, located in Accra. Hood and Hammerton came to Tanganyika in response to Kawawa's appeal while in Accra for help with a monumental labor crisis, which began with a strike by hostel workers. The colonial government and employers had combined forces in an attempt to destroy the young TFL. Kawawa also asked the U.S. delegation attending the ICFTU regional conference to allow Springer to be a part of this mission. Yet when she arrived in Tanganyika, she was not allowed to participate directly in negotiations with the colonial government, reportedly because she did not have official ICFTU sanction.[78]

When Hood voiced his annoyance at Springer's presence in Tanganyika, Kawawa made it clear that the TFL wanted her there, thus ending the discussion but not the resentment. Later, during a meeting at TFL headquarters, Springer noted that Hood and Hammerton referred to one another in their remarks and "pretended that I was not in the room with them." During her talk she made a point of saying that the AFL-CIO wanted to work with its Western colleagues in order to offer African labor "greater moral, spiritual and financial support." In the hotel where Hammerton and Hood had rooms next to Springer's, they continued to ignore her, exchanging only brief hellos in the hallway. After Springer left Tanganyika for Kenya, she remarked, "as far as my colleagues were concerned I still was not ever there." Africans who viewed her as a great resource and friend were incensed by the behavior of the British.[79]

In Kenya Springer witnessed the great deprivations Africans endured under the state of emergency. Bemoaning the increasing numbers of teenagers who were left on their own and poised to become a public menace, she noted that their parents were either in detention camps or dead. She also learned that on the reserves where Kikuyus were interned, they were required to perform ninety days a year of unpaid labor on the nearby farms of settlers. At a farewell dinner the KFL gave in her honor on February 20 at the Queen's Hotel in Nairobi, she witnessed the agitation of her hosts when they realized the time: They had just twenty minutes to meet their curfew and return to the segregated ethnic areas where they were assigned to live.[80] She later confessed that being in the country "was a shaking experience which I could not admit to my friends there. I had forgotten what it was like to be in an atmosphere of hate, to be so acutely aware of it that the small hair on the back of your neck begins to raise."[81]

Springer noted that her presence was the "subject of numerous broadcasts and news releases." Colonial supporters used the scandal of the Teamsters' union corruption and its alleged ties to organized crime to try to discredit the AFL-CIO and impugn her motives. One newspaper tried to impugn her connection to the AFL-CIO grant for Solidarity House, which Randolph would deliver to the KFL that summer, by stating that it represented blood money from the Teamsters. At the end of the year, the AFL-CIO would expel the Teamsters from the federation on charges of corruption. Teamsters' president Jimmy Hoffa would eventually be imprisoned and afterwards disappear mysteriously. Springer also reported that Kenyan newspapers had recently published a "Wicked Uncle" series, which portrayed the United States as using its economic strength to dominate others. Therefore the AFL-CIO grant was seen by many as "further proof of our Machiavellian motivations."[82]

A year later, a newspaper writer for the Kenyan Sunday Post accused the AFL-CIO of "representing all the filth and lack of civilization" that had been revealed by the McClellan Committee in Congress, which was in the process of investigating union corruption. Mboya took exception to the author's implication that the AFL-CIO as a whole represented a racket involved with "murder, graft, thuggery, extortion." He suggested that the author's attitude reflected that of many in Kenya, who became very disturbed when the United States showed any interest in the problems of Kenya.[83]

The article was written in response to the AFL-CIO's decision to give twenty-five hundred dollars for the defense of Mboya and six other African members of the colonial assembly, called the Legislative Council (Legco). Africans had recently won the right to elect a small number of representatives to the Legco. Those elected were brought up on charges of libel and conspiracy for calling another group of Africans "stooges, traitors and quislings" because of their willingness to run for Legco seats under a plan the colonial government supported which divided seats equally among Europeans, Arabs, and Africans. The defendants were found guilty on the charge of libel and fined a modest sum.[84]

Springer referred to the U.S. consulate in Kenya, where Africans were welcomed as an "oasis in this desert of hate." Although she averred that many in the consulate were good, she singled out vice consul Jack Mowrer and his wife, who gave a buffet party in her honor so that she could meet other consular heads and colonial officials.[85]

Upon Mowrer's advice, Springer made follow-up courtesy calls to the

Kenyan officials she had met. Posing as an ignorant American while Mboya sat silently next to her, she was able to get government cooperation on questions of concern to the KFL that Mboya had been hard-pressed to obtain. She remarked that the government made a complete about-face on some issues after having recently refused the simplest requests of the KFL. Springer recognized that government officials could very well be feigning politeness and cooperation, but she hoped that their posture "had more sincerity than diplomacy." Elsewhere she wrote, "I trust that their promises last for at least the next six weeks."[86]

The focus of the discussions Springer had with government officials were the plans for constructing Solidarity House. "[J]ust on the question of land" on which to build Solidarity House, Springer proclaimed, "the Federation could be tied up for the next year or two." She noted the heavy taxes on certain types of land and that land in the "African area" was limited. After delivering the AFL-CIO grant, Randolph stated that according to the KFL's assistant general secretary, Arthur Ochwada, the land they got was not the most desirable, "but, no doubt, it is the best they can get from the government."[87]

In contrast to the generally positive regard Springer had for U.S. consular officials in Kenya, in Tanganyika the U.S. consul, Robert L. Ware, gave her pause. The principal sources of information on which this relatively new appointee relied were government officials and the procolonial *Tanganyika Standard*, the only English language daily newspaper in the territory. She requested the TFL to send him some of their literature. Ware voiced a desire to meet with the African community, and Springer believed that if this did not occur he would succumb to settler attitudes and beliefs.[88] When she returned to Tanganyika eight months later, her fears were borne out.

In both Kenya and Tanganyika, Springer witnessed the African labor movements hamstrung by numerous restrictions on their activities, little recognition, and a membership impoverished by abysmally low wages. The few rooms that constituted TFL headquarters on 87 Livingston Street were shared with six TFL affiliates, which were supposed to contribute equally for the rent. The financial straits of these unions, however, made them unable to meet their obligations. The TFL itself could not count on obtaining the three cents in dues it charged its members each month. Sisal workers, who represented half of the African labor force and half the TFL membership, were the poorest paid, making only $3.80 a month, and their conditions had a depressing effect on all wages. Springer noted that neither casual and unskilled workers nor clerical and government workers, "who are presumably better paid," could not afford a midday meal.[89]

Repression by colonial authorities also included laws prohibiting strikes in the essential industries, which most of the industries were deemed to be. Public outdoor labor meetings were banned, and in Kenya microphones were not allowed in the indoor meetings. But these restrictions did not accomplish their aim. Springer noted that both political and union meetings always had "tremendous attendance," evidence of the determination of Africans to change the conditions under which they lived. At a meeting at which she addressed the dockworkers of Tanga, Tanganyika, she noted that of the eight hundred people in attendance, half waited outside the building because of lack of room.[90]

Regarding the Tanganyika labor movement, Springer averred, "There is a spirit of dedication in this country such as I have never seen in unions elsewhere."[91] For example, she witnessed the activism of the four young women who managed the office of the financially strapped Tanga dockworkers' union daily from eight to five without pay. Although the dockworkers, as the strongest and oldest union in the territory, were among the highest-paid Africans, Springer noted their wages were still woefully inadequate. Her concern that the office workers be shown at least a modicum of appreciation, however, led to the union decision to provide them with some pocket money every month.[92]

With her background of activism in the National Council of Negro Women, the Women's Trade Union League, and in the female-dominated ILGWU, Springer always included a concern for women's development in her relationship to Africa. Personal experiences served to remind Springer that she too faced restrictions due to her sex. The following month in Kano, Nigeria, for example, she learned that she could not enter a mosque: "it seemed that I was the wrong sex."[93] Wherever she traveled, she spoke to women about their needs and desires. Even if Western male labor leaders had an inclination to seek out the views of African women, cultural barriers militated against close association. African women felt comfortable in expressing their views to Springer and trusted her. In fact, Tachie-Menson had seen this potential in Springer back in 1955, when he requested her presence in Ghana.

Over the years Springer lobbied African labor, the International Labor Organization, the AFL-CIO, and the ICFTU to include women in trade union programs. Moreover, she promoted and organized numerous projects and programs aimed at opening up opportunities for African women, such as her support for Maendeleo ya Wanawake (Women's Progress), an East African cooperative committed to developing money-making ventures for women. Much of her work to benefit women, like her appeal on behalf of the young women in Tanga, was done quietly and on a small scale.[94]

African unions were not the only ones interested in Springer's advice and influence during her 1957 trip. While she was in Kenya, the Asian Railway Workers Union executive board sought her advice regarding their future prospects and how Africans viewed them. Indian immigrants performed skilled labor and belonged to separate unions that commanded higher pay for their members. Moreover, Indians owned many factories employing Africans and upheld an exploitative apprenticeship system. Under this system Africans were hindered from learning skills that could enable them to perform the complete operations of the trade. Yet Springer believed that Indians and Africans did not hate each other as Africans and settlers did.[95] In order to keep this buffer group aligned more with the interests of settlers than with Africans, however, Europeans fueled speculations about the horrible fate that would await them under an African government. The Indians' fears of impending disaster no doubt were fed by their knowledge that Indians in general had benefited from the exploitation of African labor.

The three-hour questioning Springer underwent with the executive board primarily centered on her opinions about the viability of Indians in Africa and the possibility of migrating in large numbers to the United States. They also asked about the relationship of black and white workers to union activity in the United States, including the question of equal wages. They were incredulous when she stated that blacks and whites went out on strike together. In response to their question about whether they should have discussions with Africans about the possibility of combining the racially based unions, she informed them she would approach the KFL about proposing a joint meeting.[96]

Observer of Political Movements

During both her 1955 and 1957 African tours, Springer observed the important but unsung roles of African women in the independence struggles, such as the West African market women and the Tanganyikan Muslim women. Springer commented on the irony of Muslims, who constituted a majority of the people in coastal areas like Dar es Salaam, having reputations as "obedient, docile and humble folk, especially the women who are hardly ever seen on the streets." Yet these women, who in 1957 formed about 30 percent of the membership of the Tanganyika African National Union, were a force to be reckoned with. Colonial oppression and hope for the opportunities that liberation could bring—particularly for their daughters, who might receive the education that had eluded them—spurred many Muslim women to become active in TANU. TANU women accepted primary responsibility for raising money for political work, including Nyerere's trips abroad. Once when Nyerere expressed concern to Springer about the cost of a prospective trip, he indirectly gave tribute to these women with the remark, "but my Members have a way of getting over these difficulties when the occasion warrants it."[97] During mass political meetings of thousands of people, Muslim women would form a large phalanx in front of the speaker's stand. They made an impressive sight. All were dressed in black-colored *bai bui*, a form of traditional Muslim dress (called *jilbaab* which is comprised of a headdress and robe) worn by Muslim women of East Africa when going out of the house.

During this trip, Springer made her first acquaintance with Bibi Titi Mo-hammed, the leader of the Muslim women in TANU and president of the United Women of Tanganyika (UMT). An early member of TANU, and the first woman to join, she played a major role in expanding the female membership and building the nationalist movement. With the female membership of TANU in 1955 greater than the male, women's activism became an impetus for men to join. One writer stated that "to many outsiders UMT deserved all the credit for bringing TANU to power." Bibi Titi became a Legco member in 1960.[98]

Two years after her 1967 resignation from the TANU executive committee due to health problems, she faced serious political problems. Charged along with six others with involvement in an alleged plot to overthrow the government, Bibi Titi was imprisoned until Nyerere pardoned her. Bibi Titi's activism cost her two marriages. Her first marriage ended before independence because her hus-band did not support her political work with TANU. Her second husband, Micky Ndoe, head of the Tanganyika Broadcasting Corporation, left her following her arrest. As historian Susan Geiger points out, a number of the Muslim women leaders faced divorce because their husbands were incensed about their commit-ment to the political struggle. The marriages of Springer and other labor women in the United States also were negatively affected by their strong commitment to activism.[99]

Among the non-African TANU supporters and sympathizers whom Springer encountered were an Indian couple, Zainy and Amir Habib Jamal, and Randal Sadleir, whom she identified as a rebellious Irish public relations officer. The colonial officials who had placed Sadleir in charge of all Swahili press and radio instructed him not to publish anything that the government would find embar-rassing or controversial. When he persisted in printing TANU news from the ma-jority African point of view in one Swahili newspaper, he was transferred to pro-motional work, and someone more amenable to the government's interests was named as publisher. With this change, Springer reported that the paper's circu-lation dropped from thirteen thousand to seven thousand.[100]

The Jamals, who introduced Springer to other Tanganyikan Indians, sup-ported TANU's protest against the parity system of compulsory tripartite voting. Under this system the country's three distinct racial groups—25,000 European settlers, 45,000 Asians, and 8 million Africans—would elect the same number of Legco representatives, who had to be of their own racial group. In 1958 Amir Jamal became a TANU-supported Legco member representing Asians and an ap-pointed unofficial minister for urban local government. After independence he held several ministerial portfolios and government positions.[101]

But the most damaging of Springer's social contacts, in the eyes of colonial authorities, was Springer's fraternization with Julius Nyerere, a man they labeled an "irresponsible agitator." Primarily for this reason she followed through on ad-vice she had gotten from the Gold Coast information office in London to have

Meany send to her while she was in Ghana letters addressed to Mboya and Mpangala stating her plans to visit their federations. She explained, "While the governments of these areas dislike visitors, they are reluctant to make an issue when it involves someone who has affiliation with an international body." Nevertheless, Springer's activities drew the continuous interest of the police. Although they did not directly question her, they questioned people in places where she traveled and was expected to travel.[102]

Springer's arrival in East Africa nearly coincided with Nyerere's return after five months in Britain and the United States, where he petitioned the UN Trusteeship Council. She was present at a mass meeting of fifty thousand Africans gathered at a park named Mwazi Moja (One Coconut) on January 27 to hear him speak of his UN mission and his search for scholarships, and answer the anti-TANU editorials in the *Tanganyika Standard*. Amazed at the discipline of the crowd, which Springer described as "[a]n absolute island" of men wearing red fezzes and women in black veils, she remarked, "They sat alternately through showers of rain and sun—these people sat, on the earth, lined the sidewalks, stood on balconies and roof tops."[103] The *Tanganyika Standard*, as expected, responded by ridiculing Nyerere's speech. It treated as extreme his estimate that independence would come in twelve years. Yet TANU would be successful in obtaining independence within four. In response to Nyerere's popularity and his success in gaining international attention, the government closed eleven TANU branches and banned Nyerere from speaking. Springer noted that these measures simply caused the TANU membership to swell.[104]

Interestingly, Springer was informed that Governor Twining, who had waged a long campaign to undermine Nyerere, secretly agreed with him about the need for independence but remained committed to the interests of the "diehard settler community." She hoped that the new governor slated to come in would act more autonomously. In July 1958, Sir Richard G. Turnbull, the former minister of internal security in Kenya during the emergency, became the new governor, and did indeed help smooth the transition to majority rule.[105]

The Princess Margaret Incident

Springer's lack of official ICFTU sanction to participate in Hood and Hammerton's mission did not prevent her from advising the TFL during its labor crisis. A Tanzanian labor paper reported in a 1991 retrospective on her work, "Despite that discrimination that she had suffered, Maida did not give up being a part of the people's struggle and kept working with the leaders of the TFL. She contributed her ideas and participated fully in the struggle to find solutions to the problems faced by the workers that had been raised during the strike."[106]

The labor crisis developed out of what became known as the Princess Margaret incident. In early December 1956, the manager of the Kinondoni Hostel fired four workers, alleging that they had been inebriated while working at a party held in connection with the visit of Queen Elizabeth's sister. When their shop steward interceded on their behalf he too was fired, along with forty hostel workers who had struck on his behalf. Next the Domestic and Hotel Workers struck, demanding reinstatement of all the dismissed workers as well as a wage increase. Two other unions called a two-day sympathy strike. In response employers followed the government's advice and fired all five thousand striking workers. The Tanganyika Federation of Labor and its affiliates quickly exhausted their funds through payments to the striking workers for food and rent.[107]

Describing the conditions of these workers, TFL assistant general secretary Maynard Mpangala noted that they worked from ten to sixteen hour days for less than subsistence wages. Their workdays tended to be longest under Asian employers. Some domestic workers were required to pay for food they consumed that was left over from the family dinner. They might sleep in the passways of the home or in outdoor sheds, where they had scant protection from the weather. Hotel employees might sleep in the foodstore, or three or more workers might share a room in the slum areas. Europeans deducted accommodation fees from wages, which then bound the worker to a form of indentured servitude. Workers and their families were often hungry, and their children, dressed in threadbare clothes, roamed the streets and beaches.[108]

In support of the workers, the industrial unions called for a general strike, and TFL general secretary Rashidi Kawawa went to London and Brussels to consult with British TUC and ICFTU leaders. The British TUC advised the TFL and the Colonial Office of the British government to approach the colonial government and employers with a proposal to return all fired workers and discuss putting in place arbitration and negotiation machinery in return for a cancellation of the threatened general strike. Seeking to break the two-year-old TFL, the government and employers remained unmoved.[109] As required by law, the TFL gave the Labour Commissioner a twenty-one-day notice of a general strike planned for February 11. The government reacted to the strike notice by threatening to institute a state of emergency.[110]

The *Tanganyika Standard* noted Hood and Hammerton's arrival with optimism and expressed satisfaction with their statement that they would approach the problem with an "an open mind." To cultivate that open mind, the paper suggested that they read through its recent issues in order to understand the positions of the TFL, Labor Commissioner, Chamber of Commerce, and the employers in the dispute. With this information the paper was sure that the two would learn "that there is ample good will on the part of the employers and Government" and that the demands of the TFL are "outrageous."[111]

A writer for the *Sunday News* also ridiculed the TFL's wage demands as extravagant. "The trade union leaders who drew up these figures," he remarked, "should be sent packing—not by expensive legislation but by a good swift kick in the pants." Moreover, he averred that African workers were being duped "by a handful of citizens" (that is, TFL leaders) who, if they were in England, "would be laughed out of existence at Hyde Park Corner."[112]

This view of the TFL demands contradicts those of Springer and Omer Bécu, general secretary of the International Transportworkers Federation (ITF) and the future successor to Jacob Oldenbroek as ICFTU general secretary. While in Kenya Springer had discussed the situation with Bécu, who was traveling through Africa as a representative of the ITF. Bécu indicated that he had no faith in the goodwill of the government or the employers. Although he was very supportive of the TFL leaders, he thought they were too polite, self-effacing, and perhaps too modest in their demands.[113]

The British TUC leaders generally were not trusted by Africans, in part because they advised the Colonial Office. Yet Springer and Mpangala commended Hood and Hammerton on the work they had done with the TFL's Emergency Committee to get the government and employers to be more open to TFL demands. An "uneasy truce" was established, and Springer believed the general strike could now be avoided. The TFL indeed called off the projected strike. However, the Tanganyika government and employers had only feigned a willingness to cooperate.[114]

After Springer's return to the United States, Mpangala wrote her that the labor movement was still in crisis. "Although those guys [Hood and Hammerton] came here to help us," he declared, nothing had changed. He reported that the TFL affiliates were bankrupt, people were still out of work, and many faced eviction and hunger. When Hammerton had returned to the territory to conduct a ten-day labor seminar, he had promised to ask the ICFTU for financial help. Since then they had heard nothing from him or the ICFTU, even after sending a reminder cable.[115]

Before receiving this letter, Springer had gotten Zimmerman to agree to create a small fund to help the TFL.[116] After hearing from Mpangala, she approached him in a panic. Zimmerman told her to write a memorandum about the crisis, which he would give to Randolph to present before the upcoming AFL-CIO executive council meeting. Springer followed Zimmerman's advice but also appealed to him to provide an immediate grant of five hundred dollars to the TFL while other options were being pursued. That money, she stated, would pay for about a week's ration for 175 families and help stave off evictions. Moreover, the grant would be a demonstration of world labor solidarity and give hope to the TFL to continue the struggle for recognition. By enlisting the aid of Randolph and Zimmerman, Springer was able to inform the TFL of an AFL-CIO grant for twenty-five hundred dollars.[117]

A Promise to Return

As grateful as the Tanganyika Federation of Labor was for the ILGWU's financial assistance, as well as for the educational material, plays, and songs she got the union to send, Africans expressed equal gratitude for Springer's visit. Kawawa wrote Meany that her presence symbolized the sympathy of U.S. workers with their plight and that they all wished she could have stayed longer. Both Kawawa and Mpangala wrote Springer that the impression she made was so great that she would never be forgotten. Kawawa assured her, "your name is always mentioned everywhere."[118]

During Springer's stay in East Africa, Africans had pleaded with her to convince AFL-CIO leaders to resist any pressure from the British TUC to withdraw their attention, and had her promise that she would return to East Africa. Kenyan labor pioneer Aggrey Minya, who wrote Springer a confidential letter while she was on tour in Kenya, told her, "if your organization wants to help us let it not be afraid of British Trade Union or anybody."[119] He warned her to show the letter only to Americans because of the repercussions Africans could face as "British subjects." Springer informed AFL-CIO leaders, "I have been asked over and over again by people who feel that the hope of the African in these territories and colonies is America—whether we are serious and will continue to have an interest in these vital areas or are we just putting on a show? Africans do not ask this—they just beg that we do not leave them to the mercy of the [British] TUC."[120]

The services of Hood and Hammerton were overshadowed by their contempt for Africans and their sympathies for colonial governments. The Ghana TUC complained to the ICFTU about comments demeaning to Africans that Walter Hood allegedly made in an unpublished interview dated November 29, 1956. The head of the British TUC's Colonial Section had allegedly portrayed African trade unionists as inferior to the British, criticized nationalist struggles, and referred to Africans as "pics" (short for pickaninnies). Hood also reportedly complained about Africans' hygienic inadequacies. Concerning the alleged remarks, Springer commented that while she could not "vouch for its authenticity," she had listened to Hood "enough to feel that most of it is factual."[121]

There were also complaints against Albert Hammerton, the ICFTU's representative in West Africa. At the fifth ICFTU congress held that summer, Africans asked that he be withdrawn from the continent. Ghanaian labor leader John Tettegah informed Springer than he told the European leaders that Africans would prefer her as a representative rather than those they suspected of "vested interest in the Colonial policy of their own movement." Kenyan leader Arthur Ochwada also mentioned that they had tried to have her appointed as a representative for Africa. Despite the protests of all the African delegates, according to Tettegah, the ICFTU reassigned Hammerton to Africa.[122] Concerning the suggestion that she might become an ICFTU representative, Springer responded, "If I told you that this idea is looked on with disfavor, you may consider that this is the understatement of the month. I could serve no useful purpose in an organization in which there are so many personality problems. Fortunately for me I have the confidence of many African leaders and my organization does not question my integrity." Although Springer recognized that relations with the ICFTU were at a low point, she still hoped that Africans would take their rightful place within the organization. She vowed to continue working constructively even if the ICFTU misunderstood her motives and those of others.[123]

Springer gained quite a reputation for her relentless efforts on behalf of African labor. Within labor circles, some would ask incredulously, "Did you get the latest Springer memo?" Although a few tried to temper her zeal, she would not heed their warnings. Instead Springer wrote a number of reports and spoke to anyone willing to listen about the urgent requests Africans had made for direct relationships with the AFL-CIO, financial and technical assistance, and above all educational opportunities. Her efforts would pay off temporarily.[124]

6

The Atlantic City Compromise

*We irritated and annoyed some of our more liberal trade union colleagues
around the world and some, the supposedly Socialist and socially-oriented trade
union leaders around the world whose governments had colonies, were
uncomfortable with some of the positions taken by the AF of L-CIO.*[1]

WITH TONGUE IN CHEEK SPRINGER MADE THIS comment. Although the AFL-CIO was considered conservative and even reactionary compared to European labor leaders on matters of economic philosophy and communism, on the issue of anticolonialism Africans viewed U.S. labor as their ally. Lack of opportunities for education and training were high on their list of grievances against the International Confederation of Free Trade Unions (ICFTU). For example, Kenyan labor leader Tom Mboya criticized ICFTU general secretary Jacob Oldenbroek for opposing his plan to send Africans to study at the ICFTU's Calcutta College with grant money Mboya had raised in Britain. Instead Oldenbroek requested that Mboya give the money to the ICFTU, which would decide how best to spend it. This kind of behavior on the part of ICFTU officials contributed to the African view of them as condescending and paternalistic.[2]

The AFL-CIO's 1957 Trade Union Scholarship Program for Africans brought to the fore British fears that racial bonds between African and African American labor were a threat to their colonial proprietorship, and that U.S. influence would supplant the British as the empire disintegrated. Under pressure from ICFTU and CIO leaders, including Walter and Victor Reuther and James B. Carey, the AFL-CIO at its convention in Atlantic City agreed to stop working independently of ICFTU channels in Africa.

On first sight it seems incongruous that CIO leaders, noted for a more progressive stance on foreign policy and civil rights issues, would oppose a program Africans were desperate to keep. Their opposition was a reflection of the power struggles that developed as the AFL and CIO merged into one federation. CIO leaders opposed the AFL's international anticommunism as too rigid. Jay Lovestone, head of the AFL-associated Free Trade Union Committee (FTUC), and George Meany held that any relations with Communist powers provided a cloak for Communists to advance their drive for world domination. The FTUC's opposition to India's embrace of Cold War neutrality and to labor exchanges with Communist countries pointed out fundamental difference between the FTUC supporters and a number of ICFTU and CIO leaders.[3]

CIO and ICFTU critics accused Lovestone and AFL-CIO European representative Irving Brown of either needlessly duplicating ICFTU work or pursuing policies contrary to those of the ICFTU. Lovestone insisted that "so-called independent work," did not conflict with ICFTU operations but served to supplement it. Moreover, he asserted, that if it were not for their operations, the ICFTU's prestige and influence would suffer. This certainly was the case in Africa in the 1950s.[4]

The Case for the AFL-CIO Trade Union Scholarship Program

After Springer's 1957 trip to Africa, Rashidi Kawawa, general secretary of the Tanganyika Federation of Labor (TFL), implored her to find a way for African labor leaders to come to the United States to study. He also suggested that someone like herself come to Tanganyika for a year to help the labor movement. The ICFTU did provide occasional short-term seminars that Africans, who had few opportunities to receive training, found useful. However, Springer agreed with Africans that these seminars were not sufficient to enable the labor movements to operate with competence and confidence.[5]

Springer also contended that for some European representatives, giving short seminars in Africa seemed to be a means of enjoying a vacation in the colonial possessions. Although she supported instituting programs through the ICFTU, she believed that British TUC leaders, in spite of their "professed convictions," would stand in the way. To reduce the friction between the AFL and the British TUC, the ICFTU earlier had agreed that only affiliates from small countries would head the organization. AFL leaders, however, believed ICFTU policy was still dominated by the British TUC with its large colonial representation. Having heard British labor leaders speak in discriminatory ways about Hungarians and Italians, Springer could well imagine what they thought of people of African descent.[6]

During the 1957 ICFTU African Regional Conference, Ghana TUC presi-

dent Joe-Fio N. Meyer stressed the need for immediate implementation of programs to train leaders. The conference proposal for an African labor school was
not a new idea. In 1951 African trade unionists, who had come together in
Douala, Cameroon, for a conference under the auspices of the ICFTU, had requested a labor school. For a number of years Mboya also had pressed for an educational facility. Cognizant of the ICFTU's predilection to respond slowly and
inadequately, if at all, to the urgent requests of Africans for educational development, Springer wrote A. Philip Randolph in April 1957 about possible roles U.S.
labor could perform.[7] About the possibility of a scholarship program she argued,
"The American labor movement could do a very challenging and rewarding
work in Africa. We could hasten the democratic process as urgently needed in
these countries. We could help raise the standards of human dignity. These
needs in Africa are as important as the full dinner pail from which the African is
still a long way."[8]

Springer suggested two purposes for the program. First, Africans could gain
valuable knowledge about bargaining and international agreements, giving them
the confidence to be better negotiators. Second, she believed that the young
leaders of these weak trade-union movements would benefit from an exposure to
labor relations outside the colonial context. Having witnessed the humiliations
and deprivations East African workers endured under a multiracial labor system,
and in a society in which they were the vast majority, Springer deemed it important for Africans to view another society where blacks worked in a multiracial
workforce.

As a long-time supporter of Randolph's campaigns against racist practices,
she was well aware that the AFL-CIO was not a model of racial harmony.
Springer also understood that no African American working in Africa could ignore the central dilemma of advocating Western democratic ideals for Africans
that in practice U.S. blacks did not fully enjoy. Unlike the labor situation in
Africa, however, there were examples in the United States of races working side
by side and of blacks in positions of authority. Both she and Randolph held that
it was the AFL-CIO's responsibility to foster antiracist democratic trade unionism, both within its own ranks and internationally. Springer once stated her belief that the British understood that the "struggle for equality" within the American labor movement gave U.S. labor the edge over European labor in Africa.
According to George McCray, later to become her associate, Nkrumah also saw
value in observing U.S. labor for comparative purposes. To demonstrate his belief in the possibility of increasing African labor productivity to a level of high
competitiveness, Nkrumah noted that African Americans worked just as effi-
ciently as their white co-workers.[9]

During Randolph's 1957 tour of the continent, Africans also stressed to him
the need for training programs.[10] In lobbying the AFL-CIO, he described the

driving spirit of East African workers to build labor movements despite an appalling lack of resources and trained leaders: "I observed the veritable thirst for knowledge among these workers who are pitifully poor. It is no exaggeration to say that they are in rags and live in squalor or privation and social misery. Yet, they possess the spirit of trade union workers and fighters for better standards of living and social conditions for their brothers."[11]

Due to Randolph and Springer's exertions, the AFL-CIO executive council at a Chicago meeting on August 12, 1957, approved a project to provide scholarships for ten to twelve Africans to attend the Harvard Labor-Management Industrial Relations Center. After they completed the program, the AFL-CIO would pay them a stipend for a year to organize workers in their countries. Randolph boasted that the Harvard Center was the best established labor-management school and had a worldwide reputation for its liberal philosophy on race. The scholarship program would enable Africans to attend the school for the first time. They were to spend thirteen weeks studying and twenty-six weeks visiting unions and government officials around the country. The AFL-CIO appropriated fifty thousand dollars for the program and requested that the ICFTU immediately lend its support.[12] The three members on the policy-making committee overseeing the program's implementation were Meany, Randolph, and Walter Reuther. The program was also to have a scholarship coordinator. The description of the coordinator's responsibilities contained no gender designations, suggesting that from the beginning Randolph had Springer in mind for the position. He calculated that the coordinator—who would in fact be Springer—should arrive in Africa by the middle of October in order to have trainees attending classes in the United States by January 1958.[13]

When by late August the AFL-CIO had not received a response from the ICFTU, they decided to have vice presidents Walter Reuther and Joseph Keenan, who would attend the British TUC convention in September, confer with the ICFTU officers who would be present about making the program a joint venture. After the convention Reuther was stricken for nearly a month with the flu, and Meany indicated that he was unaware of Reuther's discussions with the ICFTU. Although no agreement was reached, the ICFTU officers reportedly expressed a definite desire to participate.[14] The nature of that participation is unclear; however, based on subsequent actions of the ICFTU and British TUC, they evidently did not support an education program that entailed Africans coming to the United States. The lack of communication between Meany and Reuther concerning the logistics of this program points to their rivalry as leaders and possible attempts to undermine each other.

By the time Meany learned of the discussions, Springer was preparing to leave the United States in two days. She would first stop in London to consult with British TUC and government leaders regarding the program before going on to Tanganyika, where she would set up her headquarters. As coordinator of the program, Springer was to help facilitate the process by which African labor centers would make their selections. The labor centers slated for participation were in Tanganyika, Kenya, Uganda, Sudan, Liberia, Ghana, Nigeria, and the countries of the Central African Federation, Northern and Southern Rhodesia and Nyasaland. Afterwards, she planned to stay in Africa for a year, particularly to advise the Tanganyikan Federation of Labor (TFL).

Although some AFL-CIO leaders suggested delaying the trip, Meany decided to allow Springer to proceed since plans were already made for her to meet people in London and in Africa. Eleven days after she arrived in Africa, Meany wrote Oldenbroek to inform him of her appointment. The first trainees, he hoped, would arrive by December to attend the AFL-CIO convention. He calculated that any remaining differences among the Western labor leaders could be worked out during the AFL-CIO convention.[15]

During the three weeks of preparation before Springer flew to London on October 12, she met with various AFL-CIO officials, attended a State Department briefing, and met with the British labor attaché. She also attended functions for Ako Adjei, the visiting Ghanaian Minister of Justice. Unofficially she met with J. A. Rogers, a black historian and bibliophile, and Michael Scott, an Anglican minister and activist for Africa.[16]

Through Springer's influence, the AFL-CIO agreed that East Africa would be her base of operations. She preferred giving attention to this region because of its paucity of educational opportunities and its relative obscurity compared to West Africa. During her meetings in London, however, Springer got an inkling of just how worried the British were about having attention focused on this settler-held territory. They wanted to know "Why East Africa?" and "Why so much time in Tanganyika?"[17]

More civil than he had ever been to her, Walter Hood, head of the British TUC's Colonial Section, invited Springer to meet with him and other staff members. She recalled a man named Burke remarking "that being starry eyed about such a program would hardly bring the desired results." Springer answered him sharply, "so it was a little strained for a bit." She also learned in Hood's office that it was rumored that she planned to move to Tanganyika with her son, who would set up a law practice. She later remarked that this was "not a bad idea," but Eric might have other plans.[18]

She also met with the British TUC general secretary, Sir Vincent Tewson.[19] He reminded her of the importance of not duplicating ICFTU work and suggested that she should visit ICFTU headquarters. He finally agreed with her, however, that since she did not hold a policy-making position, consultation with Brussels was not her responsibility.[20] But even if this had been her assignment, she could not have changed the ICFTU's opposition to any project that entailed

Africans studying in the United States. Certainly, Springer would have gotten no further than Reuther had in August. While in London, she also met Sir Guild-hamm Myrdinn-Evans, the chief advisor on international affairs in the Ministry of Labor. She came to believe that he played a role in devising ways to remove her from Africa.[21]

Although Springer was aware that the British TUC and ICFTU leadership generally resented the U.S. presence in Africa, she looked forward to a year of success and concentrated on the beneficial impact the scholarship program could have on African development and U.S. domestic race relations. Julius Nyerere would share the hopes she voiced in a letter to him: "I can think of no sounder way to hasten the responsible growth of union leadership in Africa with a wider implication of easing racial tension at home and creating a greater awareness abroad. The fact that many criticisms are being put forward from the usual sources is not too troublesome to our union leadership. In time they will welcome the initiative we took and perhaps broaden the scope of the program."[22]

The Reaction of Colonial Governments

Upon her arrival in Dar es Salaam on October 18, 1957, Springer was subjected to a rigorous search in customs for subversive literature, a greeting that portended the treatment that would continue throughout her stay in East Africa. Ostensibly as a precaution against the riot her presence might provoke, the colonial government had also surrounded the airport with sand bags, "heavy duty emergency wagons and [a] full complement of African police and European officers." This show of force, presumably meant to intimidate, demonstrated their presumption that she was a destabilizing force in the area as well as their anxiety over the developing anticolonial movements. In contrast Nyerere, TFL general secretary Rashidi Kawawa, and about two hundred trade unionists greeted her at the airport with enthusiastic cheers. They came in spite of government warnings and threats of prosecution and job loss if any demonstrations were held. Their purpose was not only to celebrate her arrival but also to provide a show of support that might help her deal with the extremely hostile government. Their enthusiasm for the program convinced Springer that the effort was worth "double the trouble."[23]

With suspicion about her work looming large, Springer sent copies of the AFL-CIO scholarship proposal to the *Tanganyikan Standard*, the police department, and a number of government agencies.[24] Nevertheless, the East African governments, with a helping hand from the British TUC, carried out an extensive campaign of harassment against her. Tanganyikan officials pointedly wanted to know if she planned to discuss the program with Albert Hammerton, director of the ICFTU's West African Trade Union Information Center in Accra. She recounted her answer in a letter home: "In the area where he is stationed I would naturally talk with him, just as I have come directly to them."[25]

From the beginning of Springer's stay, the British and colonial governments were devising plans to revoke her visa, and the ICFTU began preparing to fight for the termination of the program at the upcoming AFL-CIO convention. Feeling under siege, Springer often wrote friends, family, and labor colleagues about the harassment and the mounting pressure to declare her a prohibited immigrant. Recognizing that the government probably read her mail and tapped her telephone, she conveyed her experiences with humor and light-heartedness that belied her real mood. In letters to her family she particularly was concerned about allaying her mother's fears.[26] Springer recalled:

> They did everything to make you uncomfortable while at the same time being very charming on the surface. For about a month many mornings I had to report to the principal immigration officer and he would say, "Mrs. Springer, it is not clear what you mean by" whatever it was I had written on my itinerary. If I had not been old and had a fairly steady head on me and conscious of what the Colonial Office would do to me in terms of sabotage, I would have been giddy out of my mind beyond belief, because there was constant harassment. You're resented *doubly* if you wear my paint job, because they make an assumption that the Africans are going to empathize with me and I with them.[27]

The harassment also included searches of hotel rooms where she stayed, police surveillance, the use of African informants, derogatory newspaper stories, and interventions with prospective landlords that made it difficult for her to find a place to live. A white government employee whose identity Springer never discovered assisted in getting her a temporary place to stay. He later sent word that she should continue being calm because the government was working to upset her. The colonial authorities finally agreed that S. J. Nasero Kiruka, a prominent African leader, could rent Springer his building on Wanyamwezi Street—provided he would spy on her. But the African community welcomed her presence and offered their support in myriad ways. One day, for example, a man approached her under the pretext of asking for money; he let her know that she was being spied on in the restaurant where she was eating. He had overheard the men talking about her, while they, seeing him only as a beggar, had paid no attention to him.[28]

The TFL moved from their cramped offices into her building, and members of the woodworkers' and carpenters' union volunteered their time to make nearly all her furniture, using her back yard as their workshop. Springer wrote her mother that the TFL leaders were like a large protective family and that they wanted to come to the United States to be pampered by her and eat her food as well as to receive training.[29] Admitting a bias, Springer described them as the "most tireless workers, self-sacrificing and humble men [she] had ever met."[30] Following a welcoming party the TFL gave in her honor, she reflected wistfully, "Most of these boys are deadly serious about fitting themselves for future leadership. They are not content to say we have been wronged and should be given our due. They are willing to compete for it with constitutional weapons. The language of logic and law. They cannot lose this struggle. It is a beautiful thing to watch these who are now in the front line. They are intelligent and have a sense of humor. A combination you just can not beat. And what is more they are young—so young."[31]

Observing their conduct at the third TFL Annual Conference, held November 25–28, 1957, Springer admired the leaders for their tolerance of dissenting views, their "ability to lose completely without rancor," and the relative absence of pomp and vanity among them. She feared that with their own increased age and greater financial stability within the union, the leaders might lose these "precious" qualities. To Ghanaian leader John Tettegah she intimated that the Tanganyikans could serve as role models for her "older and more sophisticated" Western colleagues. She also believed that the TFL could serve as a model for other young African labor federations.[32]

In contrast to the TFL, the Nigerian labor movement was badly fractured. The splits troubled Springer as she groped for a way to include this important territory in the scholarship program. Recognizing that favoring any single faction would exacerbate the situation, she enlisted Tettegah's help. With the scholarship program's future in jeopardy, she asserted, "History will prove the soundness of our judgment and I would like Nigeria to be included in that history." In spite of the difficulty the Nigerian situation posed, Springer thought that coordinating the program in West Africa would be a "relief" compared to her East African experiences.[33]

As a result of negative press coverage, Springer's face and name became recognizable among the settler population. Many of the articles criticized her, the AFL-CIO, and the African labor and nationalist movements. An excerpt from one article read: "That busy little American Negress who has done so much both in cash and in kind for Kenya's Federation of Labor, Mrs. Maida Springer, is active now in Tanganyika on a new 'goodwill mission.'" Springer reported that the government accused her of promising money or delivering threats in certain secret conversations. Through intermediaries her anonymous government supporter let her know that if she had brought money for the TFL, the government would have revoked her visa. She remarked, "Funny thing, I have never been given funds for any trade union organization or given the authority to pledge such funds." The government also was suspicious that the AFL-CIO might provide funds for a TFL building project.[34]

Government authorities and some ICFTU representatives believed the rampant rumors that Springer was distributing money. Probably referring to TFL president Michael Kamaliza and to the ICFTU assistant director of organization, Jay Krane, she once wrote, "Michael is one of the TFL men our American friend in Brussels would ask—'tell me honestly what did she promise you.'" These rumors found believers primarily because earlier in the year, and due to her efforts, the AFL-CIO had sent financial support to Tanganyikan strikers, and she had participated in discussions with the Kenyan government regarding Solidarity House. Springer was sure some of the British TUC representatives helped to spread these rumors.[35]

Hammerton was in the region during this time and was present at one of her meetings with Kenyan government officials. During this meeting the Minister of Lands and Labor suggested that the scholarship recipients spend a month in Britain. The next day, at another meeting in which Mboya was also present, labor commissioner Walter Coutts and the industrial relations officer reduced the proposed stay to one week. They wanted the trainees to observe British TUC operations as a point of comparison. While Springer responded that she would pass the information on to the AFL-CIO scholarship committee, she privately speculated that the proposal did not originate in the minister's office.[36]

Government officials invited Springer to "sundowners" or cocktail parties in order to place her in another forum where she could be tested. However, she never allowed them to provoke her into saying anything that could justify their revoking her visa or, more importantly, that would give them a pretext for jailing any of her associates from the TFL or TANU.[37]

Springer's association with Julius Nyerere was open. Bibi Titi Mohammed recalled that Springer traveled with Nyerere through all parts of Tanganyika because he wanted her to observe the conditions of the country and its people. She also observed his deft performance in the Legislative Council (Legco).[38] After Springer became aware that the government's negative assessment of Nyerere was shared by U.S. consul Robert L. Ware, she advised Ware in private:

"What you need to think about is those young Africans who are clerks in these offices, who watch you all go home to eat your lunch with all of these African people serving you. At lunch time these young Africans, wearing a clean shirt and khaki pants, go and sit on the beach with nothing to eat, because the salary is so poor they can't afford lunch." And while I never raised my voice, I was very serious about what I was saying. I was furious.[39]

As could be expected, the attitudes of government officials toward Springer were shared by their wives. After Zainy Jamal suggested inviting Springer to speak before the local branch of the International Council of Women, an organization in which Springer held membership, the wife of Governor Twining refused to sanction the event. Jamal was not allowed to use the branch's headquarters or the property of the British Red Cross Society for such a purpose. Instead, she used the occasion of a visit from an Indian musician to invite Springer to her home.

Courage or curiosity drew seventeen Asian and nine European women to attend this event. Some risked reprisals from the governor's wife, who could block their access to government social events and to positions within the women's organization. Wanting to avoid trouble for the women and concerned not to provide an excuse for the authorities to revoke her visa, Springer chose an innocuous subject; she spoke about American women in politics and briefly touched on the struggles of women pioneers during the Conestoga wagon days. She had considered talking about American women in labor unions but deemed that too radical. Nevertheless, the wife of the chief of police, whom Springer suspected of being a spy, took notes during Springer's talk. Springer believed that in this situation what made her so objectionable was not so much her color but the British association of her with U.S. foreign policy, African nationalism, and trade unionism. The next day, one newspaper reported that Springer wore silk gloves with a mailed fist, meaning that her talk was on the surface harmless, but underneath full of implications of danger.[40]

Meanwhile Joseph Thuo, a journalist with the U.S. Information Service in Kenya, wrote Springer's worried mother about her condition. He reported that while Springer worked under "clouds of suspicion," she remained cheerful. "I admire her stout heart, her desire for adventure, her love for African people, and, of course, I am not the only person who looks at her more than once. I am proud to be her brother."[41]

Government officials, however, attempted to use Springer's nationality to force a wedge between her and Africans. They suggested that, as an American, she "had a higher mental capacity than Africans." She explained, "Had I fallen for such an offensive flattery, life would have been much easier for me." Her "passport of a dark skin," she averred, allowed her to learn and share with the African community in a way that they "still can not do." She noted the similarity of U.S. and British colonial racial attitudes: "In relation to the more personal British resentment against me, I encountered an attitude reminiscent of many Americans, and more particularly Southerners, who, by virtue of close contact with Negroes feel sure that they alone know what Negroes want and what is best for them."[42]

The British did insist that they knew what was best for Africans, and they portrayed the American presence as counterproductive and interfering with their own efforts to develop trade unionism in East Africa. James Johnson, a British member of Parliament representing the Labor Party and a specialist in East African colonial affairs, reflected this opinion in a thinly veiled criticism of the scholarship program: "There has been some friction in East Africa, where the AFL-CIO decided to select ten African trade union leaders to go to courses in the U.S.A. There is need here for close cooperation with the British TUC in any such schemes for the Colonial Office has its own Labour Commissioners on the spot in close contact with Africans, and the British TUC leaders visit the territories to advise these young African unions."[43] Springer later learned in confidence that the Kenya Minister of Labor wrote the British TUC complaining that the AFL-CIO's influence was spreading too rapidly in Africa. As a remedy, he suggested that the TUC give more scholarships for Africans to come to England, a program the British government might well support financially.[44] The scholarships were forthcoming.

Resolving Conflicts

While in East Africa Springer became a valued advisor to the labor movements in their organization efforts and in resolving conflicts among themselves and with employers and the ICFTU. Employers in the important sisal industry, where the TFL was focusing great unionizing efforts, were particularly concerned with her presence. That year East Africa would report a record-producing sisal crop.[45]

Since the TFL's inception a main priority of its leaders was to organize agricultural workers, who represented the bulk of laborers, 300,000 out of a working population of 450,000. The sisal industry alone employed 200,000.[46] But conditions were not conducive to organizing. During his visit in the summer of 1957, Randolph noted that although the TFL received some financial assistance from the ICFTU plantation fund, the leaders still faced travel and communication problems. During her work on the scholarship program, Springer noted that one young organizer with a blanket and pillow traveled seventy miles by bicycle to hold meetings for farm workers. The workers lived in labor camps situated in the center of estates that might be as large as ten miles long by eight miles wide. Since employers forbade trade-union activity on the estates, the workers were forced to hold secret night meetings. By September 1957 only two agricultural unions were registered.[47]

Springer and Randolph's sympathies for the hardships of African labor contrasted to the more suspicious attitudes of ICFTU officials. The ICFTU's stance in relation to a strike on the Pongwe sisal estate serves as one example. In September 1957 Rashidi Kawawa, the TFL general secretary, requested ICFTU assistance to retain a lawyer from outside Tanganyika to defend arrested workers. The TFL had collected 150 pounds but needed to raise an additional 1,000 pounds.[48] ICFTU general secretary Oldenbroek asked if they had approached anyone else for assistance (possibly a reference to U.S. labor unions) and requested confirmation of the incident and additional details. Pondering the reason they needed so much money for a lawyer, he asked, "Are there no African lawyers willing to take on a service of this kind as something for their own people?"[49] Perhaps Olden-broek did not appreciate the severe limitations on educational opportunities for Africans. There were no African lawyers from Tanganyika. TFL assistant general secretary Maynard Mpangala complained that the unions, confronted with con-stant arrests and fines, found their own funds exhausted through the payment of excessive legal fees.[50]

In response to another of Kawawa's requests that summer, for financial assis-tance for a six-month effort to organize plantation workers, ICFTU director of organization Charles Millard questioned the necessity of the organizer's having a telephone and an office assistant. Such conveniences might induce the organ-izer to spend more time in the office than out in the field. Suggesting the organ-izer could use TFL offices, he praised Malayan plantation workers who had con-structed a building entirely financed by themselves. Moreover, Millard objected to the TFL's choice for the organizer and preferred Kawawa to take the position. He argued that it "should be clear" that the newly established International Plan-tation Workers' Federation (IPWF) should pick the organizer since the TFL was not paying the salary. The IPWF was an International Trade Secretariat (ITS) associated with the ICFTU. ITSs are international organizations that represent workers in the same industry.[51]

Kawawa replied to Millard that the TFL had followed the instructions of Hammerton by appointing an organizer immediately, and that he had already begun work. Moreover, he stated that the TFL did not have office space to ac-commodate the organizer, who absolutely needed an office in the center of op-erations. Kawawa concluded by welcoming the ICFTU to play an advisory role to the TFL Plantation Committee. At a meeting in July 1957, the TFL general council passed a resolution of no confidence in the ICFTU representative. They held that if the ICFTU sent a representative to be in charge of organizing, the TFL would not receive him.[52] East African labor centers insisted on autonomy in their organizational efforts.

Soon after Springer's arrival in Tanganyika that fall, the head of the sisal growers' organization made a speech stating that he supported union develop-ment but would not tolerate outside interference. Pro-colonialists in general, Springer remarked, used "the handy device of name-calling in an attempt to dis-credit the American Labor Movement in the eyes of Africans." The name-calling included labeling her a dictator, a Communist, and a demagogue. In an effort to dispel the distortions of her role, Meany eventually sent a telegram confirming that she represented the AFL-CIO.[53]

Some who were sympathetic to settler interests also accused Springer of being a reactionary anticommunist. An article in a 1958 issue of the London

Economist made an apparent reference to Springer and Randolph in charging that AFL-CIO representatives who came to Africa combined "fierce anti-communist fervour with no less fervent anti-colonial messianism." Moreover, the article stated that these representatives were even less knowledgeable than ICFTU officials about what sort of labor organizations were best suited for African workers.[54] Springer's letters, however, did not reflect a concern about communism. Rather, she was totally preoccupied with the treatment she and her African colleagues experienced under colonialism.

The *Economist's* reference to suitable forms of labor organization may have been an oblique comment on the way plantation workers were being organized. The TFL resisted the demand of the Tanganyika Sisal Growers Association that the sisal workers form a union separate from other agricultural workers. Among the reasons the TFL wanted a union to cover all plantation workers was the difficulty of differentiating types of agricultural workers since they did not limit their work to only one crop.[55]

In late 1957, Thomas S. Bavin, director of organization for the International Plantation Workers' Federation, visited East Africa. Springer and African labor leaders noted that the two-week visit was useful and appreciated.[56] All the East African labor unions, however, strongly opposed the ICFTU plan to appoint a plantation organizer. Following TFL protests, the ICFTU compromised by agreeing to send a representative to be posted in Mauritius, who also would be available for the TFL should they need advice.[57]

In spite of the agreement, Mpangala reported to Springer, who had by then returned to the United States, that "suddenly [the ICFTU] sent a representative here," David Barrett from the British TUC. After the TFL objected, he noted, "the ICFTU assured us that the man was not sent here to stay, but just to advise us on the plantation field for a short period and also he will be under the TFL Plantation Committee but not as boss." As a mark of Springer's influence on their relations with the ICFTU, Mpangala concluded: "We are not fools but we are watching this game. Don't worry we shall stand firm at all cost. We still keep in mind . . . what you advised us before you left."[58]

The nature of Springer's advice in this situation is not apparent. However, in other cases she tried to defuse differences between the ICFTU and African affiliates. In response to the TFL's earlier no-confidence resolution on the ICFTU representative, she stressed to them upon her arrival that October that "justice and good intentions are never all on one side and moreover the principles of the ICFTU are larger than the individual." After long deliberations at the TFL annual conference, she reported that the TFL decided to withdraw a resolution of censure for the ICFTU. She claimed not to have effected the change but noted her influence with the remark, the "trade union here know I respect them as colleagues and they are therefore amenable to suggestions from me."[59]

Resenting but using Springer's influence on labor, the government let it be known during the TFL conference that if Tanga dockworkers continued staging a strike, they would expel her from the country. She recalled, "The assumption always would be that I had something to do with it, or either was advising them." As a sign of how important the TFL considered the scholarship program and any subsequent aid that might come from the AFL-CIO, the leaders adjourned the conference so that she and Kawawa could go to Tanga. Through Kawawa's intervention, the dockworkers agreed to end the strike and try to settle their grievances through negotiation. The situation on the docks would remain volatile.[60]

The Ugandan government also resented Springer's influence on the labor movement. In the process of candidate selection, she and Mboya helped to unite the deeply divided Ugandan labor movement. Ethnic rivalries and the government's hand in perpetuating them largely fueled the personality clashes and power disputes within the Uganda TUC. Labor leaders agreed to have Springer choose the scholarship recipient out of three nominees they would submit to her. "In this way," she noted, "the onus of clan and tribal manipulation would be removed."[61]

Springer decided upon Dishan William Kiwanuka, of the Posts and Telegraphs Union, as the most acceptable candidate among the Ugandans. After she participated in the selection, the word went around in the official government circles that she was attempting to dictate policy. She reflected, "Sometimes when I read what is said about me and some of the opinions being passed out, I do not recognize the character."[62] The Special Branch also spied on her at a dance she attended at Mengo Garden, sponsored by an African-owned association. Many students from Makerere University attended this late-night function, where a local band entertained them with American jazz music. Springer and her friends were confounded by the behavior of one of the "not so secret police," who asked her to dance. She remarked, "All of us are at a loss at this. Europeans are warned not to associate socially with Africans etc etc but of course this may have been in line of duty."[63] With some amusement she accepted his offer to dance. She concluded, "It seems queer and a little silly that this man could be expected to get information from me."[64] She believed the colonial officials' efforts, however inept, were based on false assumptions about the extent of her power. She declared, "I would indeed be very powerful if I had even one tenth of the power [the Ugandan police] ascribe to me."[65]

Springer surmised that much of the unrest about the program in Uganda was connected to anxiety in government circles about the opening a few months earlier of a large U.S. consulate and information service. For this reason she made it a point to inform colonial officials that the program had nothing to do with the U.S. government. Still, her race and nationality impeded meaningful dialogue with them. Springer noted the irony in the U.S. government's coddling of colonial powers in light of settler suspicions: "The fear of American intentions hangs like a pall over these communities. Our alliance with the British government in all of the serious international commitments, our financial support under all circumstances, our votes with them for the most part in the U.N. is completely lost in African Colonies and Trust Territories. And so it is difficult for me an American, a trade unionist and a Negro or as they label me—'That busy little American Negress'—to find rapport in this 'Multi Racial Community.'"[66]

During this period Millard deemed her responsible for fomenting discontent among Africans. This judgment did not give Africans credit for forming their own opinions about ICFTU African policy and the oppressive conditions under which they lived. Although Springer understood the deep hostility that Africans had toward ICFTU policy and personnel and was herself a recipient of insults from some of its personnel, she actually encouraged Africans to maintain their affiliation. She tried to steer African discontent into channels that would redound to their benefit and ultimately to the ICFTU's.[67] She held the view that publicly railing against the ICFTU, while emotionally satisfying, would do nothing tangible to forward the interests of African labor and might even lead to further setbacks.

Springer hoped that the AFL-CIO scholarship program would help "mend strained relations" between the ICFTU and the labor federations of Ghana, Kenya, and Tanganyika. Yet she noted the limits of any program: "The ICFTU may have the best programme in the world but if the Africans neither trust or respect them, it is useless."[68] Aware that opposition was organizing to abolish the scholarship program at the upcoming AFL-CIO convention, Springer knew its demise would further undermine African commitment to the ICFTU. Her attempts to bolster the program included accelerating her travel plans in order to increase the number of trainees—not an easy task since she had to coordinate her itinerary with uncooperative colonial governments. She still hoped to get trainees from West Africa in time for the Harvard session. However, she doubted the Central African Federation would allow her entrance. Commenting on the opposition she met, Springer wrote her friend Dollie Lowther Robinson, "A simple straight forward project such as ours is enough to exercise the governments of all these countries to a degree of absurdity. I am not so tired this week, and so my sense of humor has been restored."[69]

By the time of the convention only three candidates had been selected: Arthur Aggrey Ochwada, assistant general secretary of the Kenya Federation of Labor (KFL) and the head of the Building and Construction Workers' Union; Percival Patrick Mandawa, the press and research officer and education secretary for the TFL, who also served as Springer's secretary during her stay; and Kiwanuka.[70] According to Springer, the "international politics of the project" prevented Mandawa and Kiwanuka from coming to the United States in time for the convention.[71] Aiming to have the program aborted, the British TUC if not directly involved in fostering the delays Springer experienced were at least pleased with the slow progress.

The Showdown at the AFL-CIO Convention

Springer has suggested that Walter Reuther may have wanted to select someone from the United Auto Workers (UAW) to coordinate the scholarship program. His brother Victor, who served as the UAW's director of international affairs, would have been a likely choice. Although CIO leaders originally had approved the program, presumably without regard to whether the ICFTU chose to participate, Reuther's lack of input in the final plans and the appointment of Springer, who was associated with Lovestone, help to explain their about-face. They came to view the program as part of the "independent activity" of Jay Lovestone, designed to strengthen his power base.[72]

The Reuther brothers shared with Lovestone a long history of mutual hatred and political differences. Following the merger of the AFL and CIO, they, along with James B. Carey, were successful in dissolving the Free Trade Union Committee and having Lovestone demoted to director of international publications. AFL-CIO leaders reached other compromises concerning foreign-policy personnel and practices. By 1958 Michael Ross of the CIO would replace AFL leader George Brown as international affairs director. Ironically, Lovestone preferred Ross to Brown, whom he held responsible for contributing, perhaps unwittingly, to the decision to eliminate the FTUC. In a decision blocking Victor Reuther and Irving Brown from serving as AFL-CIO representatives to the ICFTU executive board, leaders agreed that Meany and Walter Reuther would serve in these positions and that only vice presidents could serve as alternates. With these compromises Walter Reuther had managed to eliminate some of the influence of Lovestone and Irving Brown and perhaps viewed Lovestone's days as numbered.[73] Lovestone, however, maintained substantial influence over foreign policy due to his position as Meany's adviser and speech writer, his relationship with Irving Brown, and his vast international contacts. Following Ross's death in 1963, he would assume the position of international affairs director.

The groundwork for CIO opposition to the scholarship program began to be laid immediately after Springer's departure for Africa. According to Irving Brown, at an ICFTU meeting CIO leader James B. Carey defended a document Charles Millard had issued singling out the program for criticism. Moreover, Carey insisted that the ICFTU should carry out all international activities. Sir Vincent Tewson, who reportedly stated that the British TUC "had a right to be concerned about their people who carried British passports no matter where they lived in the world," specifically was not willing to forego British independent activity. Yet he was prepared to argue that the AFL-CIO should operate only through international channels, particularly in regard to the British colonies. According to Brown, Millard was willing to compromise on the question of international activities.[74]

In a letter to Randolph, however, Millard accused the AFL-CIO of not consulting with "those who after all have some experience in the African trade union field." "[O]n the spot training" in Africa, he held, was a better approach. Taking Africans away from the continent for long periods, he argued, deprived the movements of their leaders and helped to separate them from the people because of their exposure to different economic and social conditions. Moreover, he suggested that, rightly or wrongly, the Soviets would interpret the independent action of ICFTU affiliates as an extension of Western government policies, thereby giving them an excuse for their own interference and competition.[75]

Randolph disagreed. In a January 1958 letter to Millard, he deemed it insulting to expect Africans as a group to act differently from Asians, South Americans, or Europeans trained in Western schools. He asked if there was any proof these other groups had subsequently become separated from their people. Randolph stated that Millard was working under a grand illusion if he thought that the Soviets needed prompting to "carry on a program of infiltration and subversion in Africa." On the contrary, he pointed out that Africa was one of their primary targets, beginning as far back as 1928. The Soviets, he stated, were already preparing to recruit Africans to attend universities and colleges in the Soviet Union. On the issue of "on the spot training," Randolph held that leaders trained in the AFL-CIO scholarship program could cooperate with European labor organizers to develop training programs in Africa, which he deemed a more effective approach than Europeans carrying on the work alone. Randolph ended his letter by apprising Millard of the bad relations existing between Africans and those he most likely thought of as experts in the African field: "Finally, it is with deep distress and humility that I am compelled to point out that my contacts with African leaders of labor lead me to the regrettable conclusion that they have little, if any, faith in the ICFTU and that they feel strongly that the ICFTU has no faith in them. And how far can we go in the challenging great enterprise of human brotherhood, symbolized by the ICFTU, if there be no faith in one another?"[76]

Before the convention, George Brown wrote encouragingly to Springer, stating that he and Randolph were "still optimistic because we know you are doing your best." He thought it "particularly fortunate" that Ochwada was coming before the remainder of the group because he would be able to attend the convention. Expressing high confidence in Ochwada's abilities as a labor leader, Springer too believed he could help persuade those who were undecided on the merits of the program.[77] Intending to stop the program, Oldenbroek, newly elected ICFTU president Arne Geiger from Sweden, Tewson, and the British

TUC fraternal delegates attended the AFL-CIO convention held in December in Atlantic City, New Jersey.[78] In support of the program, African labor leaders and nationalists as well as Springer wrote letters to AFL-CIO leaders and the convention. Insisting that the "program could not have come at a better time," Mboya rejected British TUC paternalism and expressed a desire for the expansion of the program. He also appealed to anticommunist sentiment, arguing that by developing leadership potential in Africa, the program was helping to lay the foundation for democracy against which communism would have no answer. In praise of Springer he concluded, "We are particularly glad that the AFL-CIO chose Sister Maida Springer for this assignment. In a few days she has not only become known and respected, but has been completely accepted in our hearts and homes. Her energy, easy adaptation and deep understanding of the African situation are an asset the AFL-CIO must treasure greatly."[79]

Charles Makayu, general secretary of the troubled Uganda TUC, echoed these sentiments: "Mrs. Springer's presence in the country has definitely moved every one's heart to realize the need for cooperation. The advice received from Mrs. Springer will always be valued and followed by our movement."[80]

Nyerere also wrote in praise of Springer and the program: "In Tanganyika she is 'Sister Maida' in more than a conventional sense. She is one of them. She is equally at home in Kenya. She has already worked a near miracle in Uganda where she had helped to re-unite a labour movement which was being fragmented."[81]

Randolph's response to Nyerere acknowledged and praised Springer's commitment: "I am happy to note your observations of Sister Maida Springer. She is unquestionably a dedicated worker to the cause of Africa in particular, and all workers in general. Her whole heart is committed to the development of the African trade union movement and African freedom."[82]

In a speech Lovestone presumably wrote for the convention, countering the Communist influence was central to his argument in support of the program. It was important, he asserted, that Africans have the opportunity to visit and study in the "free world—especially the highly developed industrial countries." In these countries Africans could learn not only how a free economy functions but also observe the "functioning of strong trade union movements which are free from control by governments, employers, or any other outside forces." Lovestone was already concerned about Ghanaian moves to bring the labor movement under government direction. Since Communists often spoke about race problems in the West, he believed it was important that African trade unionists witness for themselves the progress of American blacks, especially in the labor movement.[83] In contrast to Lovestone, Springer's argument in favor of African exposure to the American racial system was not based on fostering an anticommunist outlook; rather, her emphasis was on strengthening the fight against colonialism and racism.

When the convention adjourned for the weekend, the six-member AFL-CIO executive committee and British and ICFTU leaders met all day on Saturday to work out an agreement. The Europeans were able to override the influence of Randolph, even preventing him from participating in the meeting that decided to end the program. In exchange for the AFL-CIO's agreement to halt the selection of candidates, to work only within ICFTU channels, and to give funds for international work to the ICFTU Solidarity Fund, the ICFTU agreed to allow two of the African candidates (later expanded to the three already chosen) to go through the program. They also agreed to implement immediately the long-standing request of African labor for a school in Africa. Another concession AFL leaders got from the compromise was support for Irving Brown's work. He would continue to serve as European representative, although he would spend increasing amounts of time in Africa than Europe. He also was designated as an AFL-CIO alternate to ICFTU meetings that Meany or Reuther could not attend.[84]

Based partly on Springer's arguments about the isolation of East Africa, some labor leaders pushed for the new labor school to be located in Tanganyika. The ICFTU African Labor College was actually established in Kampala, Uganda, and popularly became known as Kampala College. In a 1973 interview conducted by Springer, Randolph recalled the convention fight:

[The representatives from England] vigorously opposed my position on the fight in the interest of justice in the liberation of the African people. In fact they didn't like the idea of my calling upon the AFL-CIO to put funds into Kampala College and they didn't like the idea of my getting up on the floor and raising the question. They had one meeting where there was quite some fight about the matter. I wanted to make a speech at that meeting but the English representatives kept me from doing it. And they did it by getting some of the AFL-CIO representatives to use a parliamentary procedure in closing down the meeting before I could get the opportunity to get in and make a statement. Some of them didn't feel that was right, and they regretted it. This struggle was hot. I was insisting on young Africans going to Harvard, going to Boston College and these big eastern institutions of learning. The English representatives said that was unnecessary; this is where the conflict came in and I had the problem of trying to win the support of the AF of L leaders in backing this position. There were a large number of people who didn't think that all this money should be spent on bringing the students all the way from Africa here. The English, especially, fought the idea bitterly. I got up on the floor and supported it but they eventually prevailed.[85]

Following the decision to curtail the program, Randolph made a speech against the decision. Comparing colonialism and Southern racism, he proclaimed, "in my opinion, it is just as impossible to expect the British TUC, which is a part of the British Empire, to lead the fight against colonialism as it is impossible to expect the State of Mississippi to lead the fight for civil rights."[86] Interestingly, at the next convention, when the subject was the pace of civil rights reform, Randolph would argue that the color bar in the United States meant that American labor could not very well talk to workers in Africa and Asia about trade union democracy.[87]

Although Meany pointed out a variety of instances in which other ICFTU affiliates operated independently, he upheld the compromise and sought to minimize disputes between the AFL-CIO and the ICFTU. Contesting Randolph's complaint of having been excluded from the decision making, he stated that none of the AFL-CIO vice presidents who were not executive committee members were entitled to attend the meeting. This argument was somewhat disingenuous since Randolph was the main architect of the program and apparently the British leaders had something to do with his exclusion.[88]

Months later, Lovestone, in noting that the British TUC was still bringing Africans to Britain for study, proclaimed that although he did not oppose this practice, it contradicted Tewson's argument at the convention that Africans must receive training at home and not in other countries. "Very likely," he concluded, "Sir Vincent and his satellites think of America as 'the other countries' from which African trade unionists are to be excluded." Randolph too approved of the scholarships, which the British government was underwriting, but found the British opposition to Africans coming to the United States to be indefensible.[89]

In the interview Springer conducted with Randolph, her response to his account of the British success in curtailing the scholarship program had been, "But you won that fight." Her reference was to the establishment of Kampala College. Springer was indeed happy about the ICFTU school. Privately, however, she was also bitter and despondent about the ban on independent work. She believed that the British resented that Africans were afforded an opportunity to attend a world-class labor school like Harvard that was not under their control. She viewed the collusion of the CIO leaders for the sake of political gains within the AFL-CIO to be destructive of good relations with African labor.

On December 10, 1957, George Brown sent Springer a telegram advising her to stop all recruitment activities and await further details.[90] Trying not to give in to dejection, she remarked, "If the African trade unions gain by it, I will consider it not too high a price to pay. In the last few years we have built up goodwill, earned the respect and trust of Africa trade unionists. I hope we spend it well in the new arrangement."[91]

Africans, however, expressed outrage toward the ICFTU and particularly the British TUC. Springer reported that they were so bitter that it would have been easy for her to bring about a break with the ICFTU if she had wanted to do so.

Stating that he and others were "thoroughly disgusted with the ICFTU," Mboya conceded that disaffiliation might not be wise but insisted that he was committed to making African labor independently strong and viable.[92] Scholarship recipient Patrick Mandawa stated that the abandonment of the program was "shocking and dreadful news" for both African labor and the larger society.[93] TFL leader Rashidi Kawawa wrote that he and John Tettegah had decided to protest the ICFTU's opposition to the program and their disregard for the opinions of African labor. According to Seymour Chalfin, the labor attaché at the U.S. embassy in Ghana, Tettegah was very bitter but "reserved his criticisms" concerning the program's termination, "for the ICFTU which he felt had forced the hand of the AFL-CIO."[94]

With the ICFTU's actions fresh on their minds, the Ghana TUC executive board ratified an earlier decision of the general council to fraternize with all labor movements. Tettegah, who along with others had supported traveling to Communist countries for some time, maintained that while the Ghana TUC officers were not Communists, they nevertheless wanted to travel behind the Iron Curtain to observe conditions there.[95] Lovestone in his usual blunt way outlined for Arthur Ochwada his objections to Tettegah's stance.[96] In December 1955 the ICFTU executive board had passed a resolution against "free trade unions" exchanging delegations with trade unions lacking certain qualifications, among them freedom of association. Lovestone also faulted ICFTU European affiliates for disregarding this resolution by continuing to have contacts with communist unions.[97]

At a labor conference of East African general secretaries held a month after the AFL-CIO convention, the participants expressed regret that the program was being "abandoned." They also were disturbed that they still had not been formally notified about the Atlantic City events. Although they believed that local training was paramount, they held that opportunities to receive training overseas and outside the oppressive colonial context was of vital importance for imparting self-confidence and a wider perspective in labor activists. Thanking both Springer and Meany for their work on behalf of the program, they urged Meany to continue to exert his influence within the ICFTU.[98]

Instead of the year that Springer had planned to stay in Africa, she remained for less than four months. Thanking Randolph for his trust in her, she stated, "I have tried to discharge that trust with integrity and intelligence." Confiding her painful disappointment to her son, she held that in the compromise the United States would be the greater loser because they were closing access "to active, dedicated, and informed trade unionists who are helping to develop the economic stability of their countries." Still, she was determined not to give up hope. She remarked, "I may still be that small voice in the wilderness, but there are many other small voices, together we will be heard." On her way out of Africa, she endured a last bout of harassment at Nairobi's airport. Informed of the incident by Zainy Jamal, Nyerere wrote her stating his regrets. He looked forward to independence, when Africans and their friends would be treated courteously.[99]

Through letters and reports, the TFL kept Springer abreast of their organizational efforts, including government repression and destructive raids on their offices and a successful brewery strike and beer boycott. They also informed her of the developments in Nyerere's libel trial. Charged with libeling G.T.L. Scott, district commissioner of the Songea area, Nyerere was convicted on two counts and fined 150 pounds.[100] The end of the scholarship program, however, meant the loss of a respected adviser and a sympathethic observer of the African nationalist movements. Rashidi Kawawa wrote of his disappointment at her untimely departure: "Your presence here was too precious to us and we are absolutely dumb—no idea what to do. Your coming as usual, was at the right time for your advice which I followed without hesitation, had saved us from plunging into most serious situations. . . . I assure you that no visitor from outside Tanganyika has contributed to the country so much in so short a time."[101]

Kawawa expressed the opinion of many of his colleagues when they said that they remained hopeful that she would return to Africa.[102] TFL assistant general secretary Maynard Mpangala later wrote her: "I very well know that your heart is in Africa and you would like to hear that Africa is free from colonialism and imperialism. The people of Tanganyika have not forgotten you in their minds for the services rendered to Tanganyika. Everybody had been very happy with your stay here expecting that you will join with them in fighting slavery, but our enemies realised the future and that is why they made every effort, so that to remove you from the territory, even though the time will come when we shall have autonomy of selecting which is good for the country or for our interest."[103]

In direct reaction to Springer's stay in East Africa, the Kenyan government invited Sir Vincent Tewson of the British TUC to discuss opening an office for the region. However, African labor leaders stated categorically that they did not want a British TUC representative stationed in East Africa. Based on past experiences with British representatives, they held that such an appointment would conflict with their autonomy and hurt relations with the ICFTU.[104] If Springer or someone of her caliber were appointed, it is doubtful African labor would have objected. African American George McCray would constantly urge the AFL-CIO to link financial assistance for African labor with the assignment of a representative to the continent who would live and work with Africans and not act as a boss.[105]

Tettegah held that the ICFTU needed the influence of the AFL-CIO on its policy in Africa.[106] African labor leaders had viewed the scholarship program not in terms of Lovestone's influence but as an alternative to what they saw as ICFTU domination. Holding that ICFTU policies and programs in Africa were compromised by its European leaders' sympathies for the colonial powers, the Africans ignored the compromise by continuing to request bilateral programs with the AFL-CIO.

Although Lovestone disagreed with the compromise, he tried to promote positive relations between the ICFTU and its African affiliates. Mpangala, whom he had met through Springer, resisted his advice to appeal to the ICFTU for assistance. Influenced by the British, Mpangala argued, the ICFTU either ignored their problems or felt that it was not to their advantage to help.[107] After Lovestone sent Springer copies of his correspondence with Mpangala, she remarked that she understood Mpangala's reluctance to communicate with Brussels. "The file of rude letters [sent by] those people to the Federation takes up a good bit of their limited office space. However, strange things are happening there and your advice is constructive."[108]

After graduating from the Harvard program on May 16, 1958, the scholarship recipients spent nine months visiting different labor unions. They attended workshops, union negotiations, grievance procedures, arbitration hearings, and other labor education institutes. They also visited various departments of the AFL-CIO in Washington, and attended an NAACP convention. They then returned to their labor centers with the expectation of engaging in the work of organizing for a year with the AFL-CIO paying their salaries.[109]

Kampala College

Soon after the Atlantic City compromise, Springer worked with an ICFTU committee on plans for the ICFTU African Labor College, although she and others had doubts that the ICFTU would proceed with its creation. The ICFTU had not selected her as a committee member. Therefore, when she left Africa and unexpectedly appeared in Brussels on January 8, 1958, for the two-day meeting, her ICFTU colleagues again voiced displeasure at her presence. George Brown, the outgoing international affairs director, learned this and more when he was drawn into the ICFTU general secretary's office on the second day of meetings. There he found himself in the presence of Millard, Krane, and Oldenbroek, who incidentally was not a committee member. Brown reported on the grilling and his own sharp response:

> Millard pointed out that Maida Springer was still in Africa and that he understood that she would return to Africa after this meeting; that he did not know that she was coming to this meeting in Brussels; that he had heard a third student had been selected to come to the United States under the AFL-CIO program and that therefore, he would like to know what was going on. Since he did not raise these questions in a conversational manner, I was

rather abrupt in my reply. I explained that Maida Springer had come to Brussels because she had not had time to return to the States in order to confer with me prior to my leaving for Brussels; that the third student was included in the AFL-CIO program because we had already made a commitment prior to the decision in Atlantic City to modify our program; and that she would return to the United States when she saw fit.[110]

Since Springer could not complete the travel arrangements for the three scholarship recipients by the time of the meeting, the AFL-CIO requested that she confer with George Brown in Brussels and then return to Africa.[111] Despite this run-in, Brown noted that the committee members (which included himself and now Springer, as well as Krane, Hammerton, Millard, Hood, Hans Gottfurcht, and Alberto Nebbot) were able to work together harmoniously. Their recommendations included changing the school's location to Kampala, making the training of organizers a primary function of the school, and limiting eligibility for admissions to Africans from the English-speaking sub-Sahara. There was some discussion about establishing schools in other areas at a later date. They viewed the location in Kampala as an advantage because of its climate and the existing medical and library facilities at Makerere University College.

The committee also agreed that within a few years the African labor affiliates would administer the school and that it would be staffed entirely by Africans. Meanwhile they recommended that the second-in-command on the staff be an African, who later would become director. When Krane suggested Kawawa for the position, Brown decided to reserve his judgment since he did not know Kawawa and Springer had left Brussels by this time. His stance also reflected a certain distrust of Krane. He later learned of the general high respect for Kawawa. Kenyan Joseph Odero-Jowi, however, would serve in the position.

The concluding discussion centered on a proposal by Tewson that Hood "almost apologetically" brought before the committee. Tewson had asked him to voice his opposition to the establishment of a permanent school. Instead, he proposed that the ICFTU have a floating faculty that would travel through Africa giving seminars that would last up to six weeks. In contrast seminars at the ICFTU school would last for three months. Given the two days of work just completed, Brown remarked, "this proposal from Tewson fell with a thud." He closed the meeting by suggesting that the "proper time for Tewson to present his personal views" was at the next ICFTU executive board meeting in March.

Upset that Africans had not been informed of the ICFTU committee meeting or the decisions made, the conference of East African labor leaders passed a strongly worded resolution that the ICFTU should consult with and inform African labor about any projects or programs dealing with the continent. In relation to the school they insisted that the ICFTU should consult African labor about its structure, function, and location before any final decision was reached. During the Brussels meeting Brown had proposed that before the school was established, the ICFTU should hold a conference to solicit the "counsel and guidance" of African labor leaders. According to Brown, one committee member then suggested that a conference was unnecessary because the ICFTU was simply fulfilling the proposal Africans made at the 1957 regional conference. Still, the committee unanimously approved Brown's proposal.[112]

However, when Mboya, Kawawa, and Tettegah learned in Ghana, during the first-anniversary independence celebrations, that Hammerton was about to proceed to Uganda to discuss a site for the school with labor leaders there, they again protested the failure to consult them. More than two months later, in May 1958, Oldenbroek and Krane traveled to Kampala for a week-long conference with labor leaders to discuss the school, plantation organizing, the proposed African Regional Organization (AFRO), and ICFTU representatives for Africa.[113] Mboya wrote informing Springer that during the meeting the three African leaders rejected Hammerton as a part of AFRO and insisted on being consulted about African programs. She responded, "The least said about the ICFTU the better. Nevertheless, with you, John and Rashidi actively interested in the school and the new regional organisation, the paternalism of this group will be lessened."[114]

George McCray was the American representative on Kampala College's five-person international staff. An employee of the Illinois State Employment Agency, McCray served as president of Local 1006 (Chicago) of the Government and Civic Employees Organizing Committee and as chair of the Pan-African Labor Council of the CIO. While on a leave from his job to teach worker education in Ghana in early 1958, he became close to many African labor and nationalist leaders.[115] In response to Lovestone's proposal that he serve as director of the ICFTU school, he responded much as Springer had when Africans broached her about becoming an ICFTU representative for Africa: "Thanks very much for the vote of confidence, but surely you realize no American, unless we threaten to set up our own school in Africa, will ever be selected to head the ICFTU school, particularly if the American happens to be of such obvious African descent such as myself. But you never can tell; perhaps I am too pessimistic. But at my age one does not have many illusions left."[116]

Opening its temporary headquarters in November 1958 in an annex of the Imperial Hotel, Kampala College promptly got off to a rough start.[117] McCray noted that the European staff's inability to deal with nationalism and develop a curriculum based on African realities prevented them from being effective. He and the African teacher Joseph Odero-Jowi thought it "pure nonsense" that the British teachers, A. E. Lewis and Albert Hammerton, taught Africans to follow British procedures and patterns of organization. McCray remarked, "It is up to

Africans to study their problems carefully, . . . and then adopt, adapt or develop methods to solve their problems according to their own needs and desires. . . . If they can't do this they are lost forever for they will never be Americans or Englishmen nor anybody else except themselves."[118] Hammerton was soon withdrawn from Africa and reassigned in the ICFTU. McCray commented that this should have happened years earlier, but that the ICFTU had ignored all advice until Hammerton's usefulness was nearly depleted. Sven Fockstedt, a Swede who served as the school's principal, had a similar assessment of Hammerton. He noted that he constantly mediated in serious confrontations between McCray and Hammerton and between the students and both British teachers. Only after Hammerton's departure did Lewis develop a much more positive relationship with the students, and his relationship with McCray also improved.[119]

Hammerton's actions continued to affect the school after he left. The hotel management insisted that he and Jay Krane had acceded to their request that the students eat where the employees ate, in a noisy, crowded, and hot area next to the kitchen. McCray protested the arrangement, charging that it "smacked of discrimination" and would open the ICFTU to "disastrous criticism." The white college staff disagreed, arguing that the arrangement was for the convenience of the students and they too would eat in the designated area. In the two-month period that followed, the white staff ate all but a few times in the main dining room, while McCray and Odero-Jowi ate every day with the students.[120] Local African leaders unconnected to the school occasionally ate in the main dining hall.

The disaster that McCray predicted began to unfold when two students were rudely refused service in the main dining room and threatened with ejection. All the students then refused to eat, asked for airline tickets home, and spoke angrily about hypocritical ICFTU democracy. McCray convinced his colleagues that they should support the students unequivocally. If the administrators could not obtain integrated facilities, he argued, they should "take the damn college out into the forest, live in tents and cook with campfires." McCray reported on the speech A. E. Lewis then gave at a meeting with the students: "All the arguments I had used on him and the principal in favor of a stand uncompromisingly against discrimination, he used with resounding indignation and had the students applauding his strong stand for democratic equality. And when he said 'We will not be driven out of Kampala,' and that 'We will camp in the woods if necessary,' he almost brought the house down."[121]

This particular incident may have prompted Springer to write to Mboya in relation to Kampala College, "perhaps they are learning and I do not mean the students." The management capitulated with the understanding that students would wear the proper attire, a jacket and a tie, but pleaded that they not scatter throughout the dining room because the regular hotel guests would not sit at a "small table with strangers." The poor dress of some of the students reflected their poverty. And the traditional garb of Ghanaian men, which left one shoulder bare, offended some white female patrons.[122]

Kampala College had other problems. Against the original intent of Springer and others who favored locating the school in Uganda, the colonial government and the Colonial Office, possibly with ICFTU agreement, insisted that the Uganda TUC and those associated with Makerere University College have virtually no contact with the school or its students. The students also were unhappy with the amount of their stipend. Through McCray's efforts the stipend was increased.[123]

Despite the school's inauspicious beginning, it did evolve a curriculum to fit the African context, and it established some relations with Makerere and the Ugandan TUC. McCray eventually became the only non-African staff member. Among the school's objectives were training organizers and officials, and instructing trade-union teachers on how to administer rank-and-file training programs. The four main components of the curriculum were trade-union organization and administration, labor laws and legislation, collective bargaining and related economic problems, and African economic and social problems.[124]

The ICFTU finished construction of a large, attractive building for the school by 1961. To solve problems of isolation, the building was situated on a hill above Kampala and near Makerere. Springer reported to McCray that teachers, lawyers, government people, and others visiting the United States from Kampala gave the school the "highest praise and wonder why more of the same is not done throughout Africa." She remarked, "Considering the background and some of the hostility to the school at its inception I thought you would be interested."[125]

Articles in the ICFTU's organ, the *Free Labour World*, present a different story about the school controversy than what emerges from the documents of Springer, McCray, and Randolph. They portray an unnamed "we" of the ICFTU as being attuned to Africans' needs and having to struggle—presumably against AFL-CIO officials, although they too are unnamed—against those who are ignorant of the African context, opposed to the school, and only want to educate Africans overseas.[126]

The Question of Outside Training

At the 1957 AFL-CIO convention Meany had argued to Randolph that, based upon the experience of the British in bringing twelve Nigerian students to England for training, the scholarship program might actually hinder African labor development. After completing their training, the Nigerians had accepted jobs working for management or the government, and not the union. Fear that education would foster worker discontent with their class status was a concern that many unions, including the ILGWU, had about education programs.

Meany suggested he wanted to support African labor development by sparing the unions this fate. His position toward other foreign trade unionists who would be attending Harvard was not broached.[127]

The experience of being trained outside the African context in itself did not induce Africans to leave the labor movement, but training did open up opportunities for more lucrative and stable employment. The labor movement, with its uncertain finances and low salaries and the constant stress of harassment, could not compete. As a primary employer, colonial governments had an interest in siphoning union leaders away from the movement by offering them more lucrative employment. After Kampala College began operations, its training produced similar effects among the first graduates. The ICFTU chose to view the movement out of trade unionism and into government positions as positive. They argued that they had helped to bring trained and intelligent people into African governments and that it was beneficial to labor to have government personnel who were sympathetic to labor.[128]

Although Springer voiced concerns about labor leaders shifting into political careers, she also understood the great demand for trained and dedicated people to serve in the emerging African governments. When Patrick Mandawa informed her in April 1960 of his intention to run for a seat in Legco, along with labor leaders Rashidi Kawawa and Michael Kamaliza, she remarked: "I would rather see fewer officers of the TFL federation become members of Parliament now, for it seems to me the need for concentrated effort in learning the techniques of such a new office would consume more time than a TFL officer could possibly afford, if he is to do the large job needed to raise the standards of living of the workers in the country. But knowing as I do the temptation to serve in as many posts as possible, my opposition is not really great."[129]

The ultimate failure of the three recipients of the Harvard scholarships to live up to the expectations of the AFL-CIO or of their own labor movements cannot be attributed solely to outside training. Convicted on May 9, 1960, of misappropriating funds totaling thirty dollars from the Dockworkers and Stevedores Union, where he had worked temporarily as general secretary in early 1959, Mandawa was asked by the TFL executive committee to resign. The loss of Mandawa to the labor movement was a great blow to the TFL's educational program. Although TFL leaders considered him to be dedicated and productive, Springer later reported that his "carelessness with money" and sometimes contrary disposition forced the TFL to "support the government action against him."[130]

Mandawa denied guilt and blamed his prosecution first on the colonial government and then on TFL members who were jealous of his scholarship and stipend. However, this was not the first time Mandawa's handling of funds of the Dockworkers and Stevedores Union was questioned. In early 1957 the union put pressure on him to repay a loan and account for missing funds totaling 109 shillings that he had collected in the name of the union. Opponents of the AFL-CIO scholarship program had quietly portrayed him to the AFL-CIO as financially irresponsible when he was first selected as a trainee.[131] It should be noted that some of those who passed judgment on the integrity of Africans were colonial authorities who, with half a dozen Africans serving in their households, lived in a state of luxury and ease they could not have afforded in England. To settle the matter and allow Mandawa to participate in the scholarship program, the TFL repaid his loan. Springer, Randolph, and TFL officials still had confidence in his abilities and his dedication.[132]

Springer noted that Mandawa, while serving as her secretary during the scholarship program's recruitment phase, handled all her correspondence and her financial records without incident. Disturbed by his conviction, she still hoped that in the future the TFL might find a place for his talents. His conviction is ironic since he was the only one of the three candidates not to protest that the amount of the stipend, $150 per month, was inadequate. On the contrary, he suggested that the other two were "selfish and ungrateful."[133]

Following the All-African People's Conference held in December 1958, Arthur Ochwada renewed his campaign to topple Tom Mboya, which ultimately led to his dismissal from the KFL. Therefore, the AFL-CIO retracted the stipend he was to receive to engage in organizational work for a year. Dishan Kiwanuka faced two major problems in assuming his duties as an organizer after he completed the Harvard program. The postmaster general denied him an unpaid leave to work as an organizer without loss of seniority and his pension, and infighting and ethnic conflicts within the troubled Uganda TUC hampered finding a solution.[134] Of the candidates who participated in this exchange program, Springer later observed, "there is much to be said for improvement on this score. But this is in the nature of a new venture."[135]

Education scholarships remained a high priority of African labor movements. Inadvertently, the Atlantic City compromise, by dramatically reinforcing anti-ICFTU sentiments, helped to lay the groundwork for an African labor movement opposed to external affiliation. At the All-African People's Conference, the movement for disaffiliation gathered momentum.

Maida Springer as a young teen. Mid 1920s. Inscription reads "Lovingly to Mother from May."

Maida Springer's mother, Adina Carrington, in traditional Panamanian dress. Early 1950s.

Maida Springer and young son, Eric. Early 1930s.

Maida Springer and Charles Zimmerman. 1940s. Courtesy of the
Schomburg Center for Research in Black Culture.

Female labor-exchange delegates at a Washington, D.C., briefing with government
officers. Seated left to right: Maida Springer, Grace Woods Blackett, Julia O'Connor
Parker, Anne Murkovitch. 1945.

Mary McLeod Bethune poses with women whom the National Council of Negro Women named Outstanding Women of the Year. Springer, wearing the polka-dotted blouse, stands to the right of Pauli Murray. 1946.

Springer attends a New York State Department of Labor function as a guest of her friend Dollie Lowther Robinson, who stands beside her. 1950s. Photo by National News and Illustration Service, Inc.

Maida Springer and George Padmore in London. 1951.

Springer chairs a luncheon meeting of the Liberal Party featuring Adlai Stevenson as speaker. Eleanor Roosevelt appears at the extreme left. 1950s. Photos by Daniel Nilva.

Francis Edward Tachie-
Menson, who was responsible
for Springer's first trip to
Africa. 1955.

Arthur Ochwada (first row, second from left), Tom Mboya (fourth from left), Maida Springe
from left), and Omer Becu (seventh from left) photographed with officers of the Railway Af
Union in Kenya. February 12, 1957. Photo by "Nimmi" Photographer, Nairobi.

Delegation of Kenyan trade unionists gathered to greet A. Philip Randolph. Summer 1957. Randolph stands in the center back, on the left of the sole unknown female. Arthur Ochwada stands to the woman's right and slightly behind her.

Welcoming delegation for Maida Springer at the airport in Dar es Salaam, Tanganyika. Springer is shaking hands with an elder named Mzee Hembe. Rashidi Kawawa is between them. The branch of leaves symbolizes welcome. October 1957.

Springer gives a speech at the Tanganyika Federation of Labor's third annual conference. November 1957. TFL officers at the dais with her are, from left to right: E. E. Akena, Joseph Mpina, E.N.N. Kanyama, Michael Kamaliza, Rashidi Kawawa, and F. E. Mugodo.

At a Christmas party given by Springer on the roof of her home in Dar es Salaam. 1957. Zainy Jamal (facing the camera) is shown with Julius Nyerere (back to the camera)

At the 1957 Christmas party given by Springer on the roof of her home in Dar es Salaam. Julius Nyerere is seated on the left, and Patrick Mandawa is standing to the right.

At the 1957 Christmas party given by Springer on the roof of her home in Dar es Salaam. Springer seated with Michael Kamaliza in suit and Amir Jamal with back to the camera.

Springer (third from right) at a party for KFL scholarship recipient Arthur Ochwada (second from left). 1957.

Springer in Ethiopia with a labor delegation from the textile workers' union. 1963. The dress she is wearing was a gift from the workers.

Springer in Nigeria at a United Labor Congress celebration. Alhaji Adebola stands in the center dressed in white. Squatting in front and wearing glasses is Ezekiel O. A. Odeyemi. 1965.

Springer speaking in Nigeria at the opening of the Motor Drivers' School. Ezekiel O. A. Odeyemi is behind her (wearing glasses). Alhaji Adebola is at the far right side of the table. March 13, 1965.

U.S. Department of Labor luncheon for Springer on her retirement, January 19, 1966. Shown (left to right) are Harry Weiss, Springer, Assistant Secretary of Labor George Weaver, Ambassador William Trimbel, Agnes Douty, Edward Wiesinger, and Daniel Lazorchick

James Kemp, Springer, and A. Philip Randolph at a reception for Randolph at the Midwest office of the A. Philip Randolph Institute. December 11, 1969. Photo by Ed Jackson Studio.

Springer in Dar es Salaam, Tanzania, with Kanyama Chiume and Bibi Titi
Mohammed. 1991. Photo by the author.

Maynard Mpangala in
Dar es Salaam. 1991.
Photo by the author.

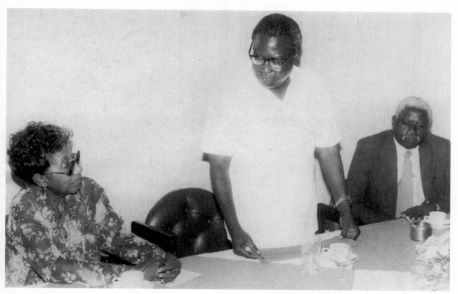

Springer in Dar es Salaam at a dinner in her honor hosted by the Tanzanian labor
federation. Also pictured are Joseph Rwegasira (standing) and Michael Kamaliza. 1991.

Jennie Silverman, Morris Milgram, and Springer gather in 1992 at New York University's Tamiment Institute for a celebration of Pauli Murray's work in connection with the publication of Richard Sherman's *The Case of Odell Waller and Virginia Justice, 1940–1942*. Photo by the author.

Maida Springer and Marty Morand (standing). Seated from left to right are Springer's goddaughter, Jan Robinson-McCray, Paul Jordan, and the author, 1995.

Brooklyn College commencement speaker Hillary Rodham Clinton congratulates Springer on the awarding of her honorary Doctor of Humane Letters degree. In the center is Vernon Lattin, President of Brooklyn College. 1995.

From left to right are Jamē McCray, Cecile and Eric Springer, Jan Robinson-McCray, Springer, Melvin McCray, Rev. Jasper Peyton (formerly of the ILGWU), and Tyi McCray, and in front is Melvin McCray, Jr. 1995.

7

The Beginning of the Affiliation Struggle

*Maida has fought an unremitting battle against the ignorance and
indifference of her friends, colleagues and contemporaries until they have begun
to take heed. She has built a liaison between the American and the African-
south-of-the-Sahara trade union movements. . . . She stands athwart two worlds,
unwilling to relinquish either and determined that both shall move
in harmony down the path of human history.[1]*

AGAINST SPRINGER'S STRONG OBJECTIONS, PAULI MURRAY
tried to influence the NAACP to award her the prestigious Springarn
Medal for 1959. Murray praised Springer's long history of involvement
with African labor, and she credited Springer with responsibility for the
resolutions on Africa passed by the AFL-CIO executive council earlier that year.
Tom Mboya joined Murray in crediting Springer and others, as well as the influence of the December 1958 All-African People's Conference (AAPC), for the passage of the 1959 resolutions, which called on the U.S. government and the
ICFTU to support African labor and independence movements. They were
deeply appreciated by many Africans but resented by Europeans.[2]

The AFL-CIO, however, was alarmed by the push for disaffiliation from the
International Confederation of Free Trade Unions (ICFTU) that began at the
AAPC. This movement marked the rupture in the world of pan-African labor.
Within the year Tom Mboya of Kenya and John Tettegah of Ghana would split
over the issue of affiliation and serve as leaders of the opposing sides. Political
pressure from Ghanaian leader Kwame Nkrumah, who played a leading role in
engineering the disaffiliation movement, was a factor in Tettegah's decision to
oppose ICFTU affiliation. Because of the deep chasm that existed between Europeans and Africans, Springer was pessimistic about the future of relations between African and Western labor.

The disaffiliation movement was connected to the trend of emerging nationalist states toward Cold War nonalignment. India's Jawaharlal Nehru helped to inaugurate this movement at the 1955 Asian-African Conference held in Bandung, Indonesia.[3] Already hostile to the Bandung conference because of the participation of Communist China, the West chafed under the delegates' strident criticism of Western oppression.

Many in the West interpreted nonalignment or neutralism as a subversive stance that would redound to the benefit of the Communist bloc of nations, commonly referred to as the East. Although A. Philip Randolph did not equate neutralism with communism, he believed that in practice it did not conform to its ideal. As an example he compared the response of Asian neutralists to the two major military aggressions of 1956: the Soviet Union's suppression of the Hungarian revolt, and the war Great Britain, France, and Israel launched against Egypt, termed the Suez crisis. However, he conceded neutralism's practical uses: "[I]t is possible to conceive of situations where a state may find it to its national interests to maintain a position of neutrality in a conflict." He also expressed hope that neutralist India could serve as a bridge between the West and the Communist world.[4]

Springer and McCray tended to view the disaffiliation movement as a strong reaction against colonialism and the subordinate status of African affiliates in the ICFTU, and as reflecting the desire of nationalist leaders to harness the labor movement in support of independence and economic development. They would cite ICFTU ineffectiveness, U.S. support of colonial powers, and later the AFL-CIO's emphasis on anticommunism as the primary reasons African labor increasingly began to support a neutralism that they held was decidedly anti-Western. Springer reflected: "I could not be as vehement about [nonalignment] as the people who were under this colonial hegemony. I understood it. I thought, like anything else, much of it went to extremes. So beyond understanding it, I never closed my eyes or closed the door on my friends, those who wanted to remain my friends, when many people I knew took a sharp position and considered me an enemy and an outsider. And I accepted that. It hurt, but I accepted it."[5]

The dual identities of African American labor leaders clashed in the context of the affiliation struggle. In a sense their position toward ICFTU affiliation reflected their stance toward involvement with U.S. labor. In the 1940s Springer urged U.S. Blacks to recognize that their destiny lay with their fellow white workers, "even with our fellow 'Cracker' workers—whose hopes and dreams, needs and sufferings, economic frustrations and ideals are pretty much the same as ours."[6] In her appeal she used language that recognized that blacks found it odious to even contemplate alliances with whites who were either unconscious of the benefits accruing to them because of race or who very consciously encouraged racist practices and policies. With the formation of the CIO, Randolph had decided to stay with the less progressive AFL in order to work against racism there. Even when delegates at AFL conventions showed contempt for him by scraping their chairs against the floor as he spoke out against racism, he remained undaunted. Moreover, Randolph's famous clash with Meany at the 1959 AFL-CIO convention over the pace of civil rights reform did not lead him to withdraw support for organized labor. Subsequently he helped form the Negro American Labor Council (NALC), an organization in which Springer was a charter member, that was dedicated to changing AFL-CIO policy.[7]

Despite the racism (and in Springer's case, sexism) they confronted within both the AFL-CIO and ICFTU, they believed that these powerful organizations were indispensable tools in the struggle for black advancement. Within the context of their anticommunism and their belief in the benefits of world association, Randolph, Springer, and McCray also held that membership in an ICFTU that Africans had helped to reform represented the best possibility for the labor movements to become stronger.[8]

During an ICFTU executive board meeting just before the AAPC, tensions were high between African and some Western labor officials. British Trades Union Congress (TUC) president Thomas Yates objected to the dissatisfaction with the ICFTU expressed in a letter Tettegah had written. Tired of what he perceived as Africans' status as beggars in the ICFTU, Tettegah argued that African affiliates would not be respected as equals and would be unable to affect ICFTU policy until they became financially strong. Particularly offended by Tettegah's reference to the ICFTU subjecting Africans to humiliations and giving mostly "lip service" to international labor solidarity, Yates viewed his own organization, the seaman's union, as having been very helpful to African labor.[9] While acknowledging that African unions appreciated the support the ICFTU and its affiliates had given, Mboya rejoined that it was no secret that labor leaders throughout Africa objected to the ICFTU's failure to consult with them and even to implement its own recommendations.[10]

The support the AFL-CIO gave African labor helps to explain why at the All African People's Conference a few weeks later, Mboya and Tettegah defended their membership in this international. Their influence on other African labor leaders was strong, and they were both well respected. Kwame Nkrumah chose Mboya to serve as chair of the conference, and Mboya also became chair of the AAPC secretariat. Tettegah served as joint secretary of both the conference and the secretariat. The AAPC was a conference of African political parties gathered to form strategies to push for the end of colonialism and white minority rule. Labor unions and other African groups supportive of independence were represented at the conference.

The relationships that Springer, McCray, and Randolph had developed with African labor contributed greatly to the positive perception of the U.S. labor movement in Africa. Before the conference McCray suggested to Randolph that, as American Negroes, their strategy should be to form strong relations between African and American labor, and between Africans and Americans in general. He urged the AFL-CIO to send a strong delegation to the AAPC, endorse the conference findings, and financially support the nationalist movements. Afterwards the AFL-CIO should convince the ICFTU to do the same.[11] The AFL-CIO sent Springer, McCray, and Irving Brown.

AAPC organizers relaxed their rule against outside financial support to allow for U.S. funds, particularly those raised by African Americans and by labor organizations. At George Padmore's request, Springer had helped raise funds to support the travels of East African labor delegates, whom he called "her boys." Nkrumah and Padmore also requested that McCray raise funds. Noting with pleasure the presence of "so many of our brothers from across the sea," Nkrumah remarked, "We must never forget they are a part of us."[12]

Attended the AAPC were over two hundred fraternal delegates and a hundred observers representing sixty-five political, nationalist, labor, youth, and women's organizations from twenty-eight countries. Springer remarked, "Many of the delegates had never been outside their own territories and had never experienced an atmosphere of freedom, democracy or non-segregation."[13] According to McCray, anticolonial fervor was so strong that no colonial government attempted to block delegates from attending. The white minority government of South Africa, however, did not allow representatives from the African National Congress or the South African Indian Congress to attend. The Belgian Congo allowed three delegates to come, one of whom was Patrice Lumumba, the future prime minister. The Israeli ambassador to Ghana, Ehud Avriel, who was close to Nkrumah, was responsible in part for Lumumba's presence. After the conference Springer traveled with Avriel and Nkrumah in Ghana. Helping with conference logistics, she served in the sensitive position of checking delegates' credentials, including those of Lumumba.[14]

Springer's first experience with the struggle of Africans in the Belgian Congo occurred in 1957, during a transit stop there on her way from East Africa to Ghana's independence celebrations. Word quickly spread that a black American was in the country. When she stopped at the U.S. liaison office to register her presence, U.S. Consul Bunsey already knew she was in the country. He warned her to be a good tourist—that is, not to involve herself with local politics. He also expressed a concern that her presence could endanger the small educational programs the liaison office was designing for Africans. However, people came to Springer, and she did not turn away from them. With her limited knowledge of the French language, Springer was unable to pick up subtle messages that Africans wanted to meet with her in secret. Finally, a couple of Africans approached her in the hotel where she was staying and told her to pretend that she was examining embroidery samples they brought, while they told her of the conditions Africans faced under colonial rule. On another stopover, Africans gave her a white paper to take out of the country to give to interested political groups abroad.

A year after Lumumba attended the AAPC, the U.S. Central Intelligence Agency prepared to assassinate him because of Cold War concerns about an independent Congo and access to its mineral resources. However, in 1961 forces loyal to the opposition in the Katanga region of the Congo murdered him first.[15] This period would represent one of the low points in Springer's activism.

By the time of the All-African People's Conference, the favorable regard Africans had toward the U.S. government had begun to erode. McCray reported that hostility toward the U.S. government was evident in the "lively discussions" between U.S. labor observers and Africans. To the African argument that the United States, through its political alliances and private and governmental investments, was becoming the principal support of colonialism and imperialism in Africa, he responded, "Of course there is some truth in this charge, but little." Two years later, in a letter to Meany, McCray would rail against the grossly exploitative practices of U.S. businesses in Liberia, which paid wages between four and six cents an hour. After his retirement, he would settle in Liberia. Despite their criticisms of official U.S. policy, Africans at the AAPC were unwilling to stereotype the actions of all Americans. When one remarked, "White or black, you Americans are all alike," the other Africans defended McCray by strongly denouncing their colleague.[16]

At this time the treatment of Guinea by the West had become a salient issue. Following Guinea's vote in September 1958 for immediate independence, and against membership in a French commonwealth of nations, France in retaliation abruptly broke off relations. As the French colonialists left the country, they destroyed whatever equipment they could not remove, leaving the country in serious economic difficulty. Western nations, not wanting to offend France, remained indifferent to Guinea's plight. While in Ghana for the All-African People's Conference, Springer observed the Parliament approve the Ghana-Guinea Union and a significant financial-aid package. The union represented the first step toward Nkrumah's vision of a united Africa. Springer recalled:

> Certainly the French government's behavior toward Sékou Touré was enough to make that government anti-Western. They ripped the telephones out. They left the country almost barren. . . . Let me tell you what happened on the occasion for Guinea to get the loan. . . . Dr. Nkrumah had Madame Sékou Touré sit in the parliament. She didn't say anything. She didn't make a speech. But as the debate went on, here was this beautiful silent woman representing her husband. The discussion at the time was of a relationship between Ghana and Guinea unifying. I want to tell you that Madame Touré sitting there was very impressive. The act went through.[17]

Springer also observed women from the French-speaking areas of Guinea, Senegal, and the Cameroons in a struggle to put issues pertinent to women's development, oppression, and inclusion on the AAPC conference agenda.

Well, the women, particularly the French-speaking women, were on fire! [They talked about] the conditions of the country, the problems that women face, the things that men have to face up to so that the women would be entirely included in the future independence of their country. Education, employment, religious and marriage customs. . . . There were men, who just couldn't quite cope with the articulateness of the women. There were a couple of instances when they tried to shout them down in some of the small committee meetings, which I did not attend. And I listened to some of the things the men said as they talked. Because they considered me nonfemale, they would say anything in my presence. They would voice their annoyance in this context, "But then what we have to fight now is colonialism. These other things cannot be our priority. They have an undertone that will be dealt with when we are free." This was the best face I could put on what some of the men were saying.[18]

Despite the fact that she was a woman working in a predominantly male arena, Springer's race, age, nationality, and position of influence within the AFL-CIO mediated against the negative feelings that could have arisen because of her gender. Still, a number of Africans were more comfortable calling her, in the language of the labor movement, "Brother" Maida. She was politically astute enough to recognize that her nationality made her an outsider, so that any public intervention on her part might undermine her influence among her male colleagues while not improving the treatment the women received. In other venues Springer did use her influence to convince male labor leaders in Africa, the United States, and other parts of the world to support equal opportunities for women.[19]

The Nasser-Nkrumah Rivalry

With only nine out of fifty-four African countries independent, and Ghana and Guinea representing the only new nations south of the Sahara, the All-African People's Conference under the leadership of Kwame Nkrumah pledged to unite in the struggle against colonialism and white minority rule.[20] Nevertheless, the exigencies of the Cold War and leadership rivalries began to impinge on that unity in both the political and labor arena. The rivalry for pan-African political leadership between Nkrumah and Gamal Abdel Nasser of Egypt had overtones of this Cold War debate.[21]

Nasser's critics in Western and African circles were leery of his affiliations with the Arab region as well as with the Soviet Union and China. The Communist powers were members of the Afro-Asian Peoples' Solidarity Organization (AAPSO) established one year earlier in Cairo. Historian Colin Legum surmises that Egypt, ostensibly a supporter of positive neutrality, felt obligated to allow the full participation of the Soviet Union in AAPSO because of Soviet support for the Aswân dam project on the Nile River. Positive neutralism represented a policy of eschewing political and military commitments, either to the Communist East or the capitalist West. Leaders of countries adhering to positive neutralism stated that they were not isolationists. Rather, they reserved the freedom to decide international issues based not on Cold War rivalries but on what was best for their nations. Egypt's increasing reliance on the Eastern bloc for economic and military assistance after the Suez crisis did not necessarily violate positive neutrality. Alliance with the Soviets on international issues in return for assistance and Soviet participation in AAPSO, however, did contravene some understandings of the meaning of neutrality. Soviet membership in AAPSO would contribute to the anxiety and suspicion that Western observers and some Africans had concerning the disaffiliation proposal and its purported goal of positive neutralism.[22]

In Egypt's relations with non-Arab African nations, the Arab-Israeli conflict was a contentious issue. As did many sub-Saharan Africans, Padmore and Ras Makonnen sympathized with Israel in this conflict; Israeli oppression of Palestinians received scant attention. Pan-Africanists looked upon the Zionist movement as akin to the black movement in its aspirations for cultural, economic, and political autonomy. Israeli foreign minister Golda Meir gave priority to building strong relationships with African nations, in large part because Israel needed allies in a region where it was surrounded by countries working for its elimination. After the 1967 Six Day War, relations between Israel and Africa began to decline. With the 1973 Yom Kippur War, most African nations broke off relations with Israel.[23] At the time of the 1958 AAPC conference, however, non-Arab Africans viewed Israel as a valuable ally.

Most delegates and Western observers looked to Nkrumah and not Nasser, who incidentally was not present, as the leading exponent of African independence. The very large and active delegation from the United Arab Republic (UAR), however, led many to view Egypt as vying to dominate the pan-African movement. Ras Makonnen, who had resettled in Ghana along with Padmore, asserted that Egypt's pan-Arab ties were detrimental to pan-Africanism. Padmore and Springer also opposed Nasser's gaining a leadership role in Africa.[24] Springer believed that the UAR had come to the conference "with the expressed purpose of preventing" the organization of the AAPC "as a permanent pan-African body." In its place, she remarked, the official and unofficial UAR delegations lobbied hard but unsuccessfully to secure an extension of AAPSO. Along with many

Western leaders, she was also concerned that the Soviet Union and China were active in AAPSO's secretariat.[25]

With the aim of allaying fears and gaining support for pan-Africanism, Springer and McCray interpreted the conference and its resolutions for a Western audience. Springer remarked that the tone of the conference, which was set by Nkrumah and maintained by Mboya, was moderate. In contrast to the Bandung conference and the Cairo conference establishing AAPSO, she recalled that the AAPC delegates "refrained from the bitter attacks on the Western powers." At the same time Nkrumah "minced no words in his support of African Freedom Movements and all necessary measures to achieve their ends." Africans, she declared, made it "unmistakably clear" that they would decide on their own standards and play their own unique role in international matters; they rejected the continent being treated as an extension of Europe. McCray explained that Africans did not feel they owed the West any gratitude. They considered their years of slavery and colonialism an "excessive price" for any benefits Africans might have received from the West.[26]

McCray and Irving Brown sought to reassure the AFL-CIO that Nkrumah's leadership should be supported, and that he was on the right side in the Cold War. Nkrumah had courted both the East and the West, alternately proclaiming that Ghana's true loyalties were with one and then the other. At the time of the AAPC, Ghana's practice of nonalignment, however, favored the West.[27]

Nkrumah's inclination toward the West for ideological or tactical reasons might explain why Soviet leader Nikita Khrushchev's two-page telegram greeting the conference delegates was never read. This apparent concession was lost on the U.S. government, which gave minimal recognition to the conference. Mc-Cray recalled that at a cocktail party Nkrumah spoke of his appreciation for the U.S. delegation's presence but "expressed sharp regret that there was no greeting from [Adlai] Stevenson or [Dwight] Eisenhower." McCray noted with bitterness that U.S. ambassador to Ghana Wilson C. Flake had refused to request that a top Washington figure send greetings, despite the strong recommendations of the embassy's political affairs officer and first secretary. It seemed to him that Flake's behavior demonstrated "shades of the ugly American."[28]

The political rivalry between Nkrumah and Nasser also surfaced in the labor debate over international affiliation. The UAR Federation of Labor was not affiliated with either of the dominant labor internationals but did help to form the International Confederation of Arab Trade Unions in 1956. The Ghana labor movement, under the influence of Nkrumah, had rejoined the ICFTU in 1954 and was one of its leading African affiliates. Political maneuvering by Nkrumah and Tettegah, some of it circumventing the labor movement's constitutional requirements, kept Tettegah in office. As general secretary of the Ghana TUC, he served on the ICFTU executive board. ICFTU affiliation, along with Nkrumah's purge of left-wing leaders from both the Convention People's Party and the labor movement, had helped to reassure the British of the respectability and responsibility of his government before the granting of independence.[29]

The Affiliation Debate

The proposal to hold a labor conference independent of the ICFTU for the purpose of forming an African international arose at a meeting of labor delegates on the last day of the conference. McCray reported that late the previous evening he had learned of the "seemingly innocent proposal" to meet. Although he viewed the proposed labor conference as inevitable, and even a good idea that the AFL-CIO should have foreseen, his suspicions were aroused when he discovered that UAR delegates, along with those from the neutral labor bodies of the All Nigerian Trade Union Federation and francophone Africa's Union Générale des Travailleurs d'Afrique Noire (UGTAN) were behind the proposal. The UAR delegates caused him particular concern because he viewed them as strongly opposed to the ICFTU.[30]

Guinean labor and nationalist leader Sékou Touré led the movement to disaffiliate the unions in francophone Africa from the French Communist labor center (Confédération Générale du Travaile, CGT) and the World Federation of Trade Unions (WFTU). In January 1957 he formed the independent UGTAN. Touré viewed UGTAN as a nucleus for a wider pan-African labor body whose main goal was support for nationalist governments. UGTAN's formation left the WFTU with few African affiliates. Since the disaffiliation movement inaugurated at the AAPC affected mostly ICFTU affiliates, the WFTU, albeit not without some reservations about neutralism, viewed the movement as a welcome change in direction.

McCray reported that he, Springer, and Brown "primed our African friends" to oppose the proposal for a pan-African labor conference by stressing that such a conference decision should only be delayed for the present moment. The high level of frustration that Tettegah and Mboya had with the ICFTU accounts for their seeming indecision on how to meet the challenge of the three labor federations initially. However, they were not ready to give up on the ICFTU, whose power they had yet to harness fully toward their ends. Tettegah and Mboya convinced the labor delegates that the proposed labor conference should happen under the auspices of the All-African People's Conference. Moreover, they defended the ICFTU against attacks, arguing that not all ICFTU affiliates were defenders of colonialism. They pointed out that they had "repeatedly received support from our 'labor friends in the AFL-CIO.'"[31] The labor delegates finally agreed to the suggestion of Arthur Ochwada, the assistant general secretary of the Kenya Federation of Labor (KFL), that they form a labor committee to coordinate activities between labor and the political parties within the framework of the

AAPC. They also agreed that a labor conference might be convened in the future. The bold stance of Tettegah, Mboya, and Ochwada on behalf of the ICFTU prompted Springer to remark, "It is ironic that three men most abused by the ICFTU were the ones to hold the line against disaffiliation."[32]

Tettegah indeed found himself in the difficult position of defending an organization with which he had serious difficulties. Moreover, according to Springer, Nigerian labor delegates had "made vicious attacks" on him earlier in the conference at a public trade-union rally, because of the Ghana TUC's affiliation with the ICFTU. Serving as chair of the final meeting of labor delegates, Tettegah answered those criticisms. He explained that his federation had withdrawn from the ICFTU in 1953 believing that the large ICFTU affiliates from the colonial powers "would hardly serve the best interests of Africans." Contact with U.S. labor, however, influenced him to rethink the affiliation issue.[33] It is unlikely that Tettegah's explanations also mentioned Nkrumah's need to appear "responsible" to the British.

Ironically, with this proposal UGTAN and its allies beat Tettegah in his own plan to unify African labor under the auspices of the ICFTU. The proposed African Regional Organization (AFRO) was to consist of three area committees. The primary reason Tettegah had hesitated in setting up AFRO's West Africa area committee was the strong presence of UGTAN in the region. He had asked Mboya not to press for the area committee's formation since there were only four ICFTU affiliates in the region, most of which were weak. To overcome these shortcomings, Tettegah consulted with the ICFTU about the Ghana TUC sponsoring an independent conference, one of whose goals would be to persuade UGTAN to affiliate with the ICFTU. The ICFTU, however, suggested that Tettegah pursue this goal at UGTAN's conference, scheduled to convene in Conakry, Guinea, in January 1959 following the AAPC. The debate at the AAPC altered the proposed plan of engagement between Tettegah and UGTAN.[34]

Mboya and Tettegah resisted the impulse to cut off their ties to the ICFTU, which had helped to sustain their leadership and had provided the struggling unions with (albeit inadequate) financial, educational, and technical assistance. It also served as a deterrent to even harsher treatment of the labor movements by colonial governments. Moreover, Western labor also aided African unions by providing financial reports and other information about Western companies with branches in Africa.[35] Africans hoped that the establishment of AFRO would give them greater influence over ICFTU policy and the means to build stronger unions. Soon, however, the advent of independence would end the ICFTU's value as a forum for anticolonial agitation. Moreover, many African governments, seeking a stable investment climate for capital, came to view the ICFTU and the independence of the African labor movements as a threat to their nation-building policies. They began to push for ICFTU disaffiliation and the incorporation of labor movements into the nationalist governments.

Clearly shocked that a disaffiliation resolution was only narrowly averted, U.S. labor viewed an African labor international forbidding outside affiliation as a move that ultimately would benefit Communists and their allies, such as the UAR. Springer in principle approved of the formation of an African labor international, particularly one that might parallel the work of the AAPC by strengthening African independence struggles. Mandatory disaffiliation, however, caused her great concern. If disaffiliation had been approved, she was sure that the rest of East and Central Africa would have withdrawn from the ICFTU, leaving only one or two small African affiliates. She asserted that the WFTU would have then filled the "vacuum in relations." The U.S. observers were well aware that if it were not for their good reputation and that of the AFL-CIO, the AAPC labor delegates would have banned outside affiliation. "At the risk of seeming immodest," Springer remarked, "I believe that the presence of three American trade unionists did much toward strengthening the hands of these three African leaders."[36]

The ICFTU Record Held Up for Censure

With a sense of urgency Springer, McCray, and Brown offered strategies to deal with what they knew would be continuing efforts to bring about disaffiliation. All faulted the ICFTU and believed U.S. labor could play a role in improving relations between Africa and the West. All realized that they faced an uphill battle.

McCray regretted that the ICFTU had no field staff in Africa who could act as interpreters for the West and help Africans find constructive channels with which to realize desires for "freedom, unity, progress and self esteem." Insisting that the ICFTU either act boldly now or pull out entirely because anything less "would be a waste of time," he suggested that the international move quickly to heal the split in Nigerian labor movement and to reassure UGTAN of its support. These moves would place the ICFTU in a better position to proceed with creating AFRO.[37]

Reporting that it was "painfully clear" to her that the ICFTU was "thoroughly unpopular" and that it needed to completely reevaluate its "attitudes, relations, and programs," Springer believed that the AFL-CIO "held the key and could play a decisive role" in this change. She correctly predicted that emerging African governments would view an African international "as a logical instrument in furthering Pan-Africanism and may encourage disaffiliation with the ICFTU."[38]

Brown specifically pointed to the role African Americans could play in building better relations. He reported that some African delegates told him, "American trade unions, and especially Negro American trade unionists could be of tremendous influence." Citing the "constant, friendly contact" that Springer and McCray had with delegates, he recommended that they spend more time in Africa and that Ed Welsh should work on the continent as well. Brown deemed it imperative to prevent African labor from moving toward a "neutral, autonomous organization and then, perhaps later, in a pro-Soviet direction." He advised Meany to write directly to Jacob Oldenbroek and Sir Vincent Tewson; he realized that his own relationship with the ICFTU was not good. "Those in Brussels," he noted "look with a jaundiced eye on anything that comes from me."[39]

Springer, McCray, and Brown knew that most Africans had no love for either the ICFTU or the WFTU. Springer reported that many African labor proponents of neutralism wanted AFL-CIO technical and financial assistance but without formal ties to the international labor movement. They would quietly make requests to her. Recognizing that neutralist practices were in a state of flux, Brown urged the AFL-CIO to refrain from any public judgments of Africans and not to dismiss even those neutralists, such as Touré, who favored the East: "It is far more important to get on with the job of working with these people, especially in terms of where people are going rather than what they are today or have been yesterday.[40]

Acknowledging receipt of Springer's report of the conference, Meany told her that he was unsure what they could do about the lack of ICFTU influence, "but we are going to try to do something."[41] Acting on Brown's suggestion, he wrote to Tewson and Oldenbroek about the deliberations of the All-African People's Conference, concerns about the UGTAN conference, and ideas about improving ICFTU relations.

By the time of the UGTAN conference, McCray expressed empathy with Mboya, who he knew felt deeply divided about his role in the affiliation struggle. Although UGTAN "literally begged" him to attend the conference, Mboya had neither the money to travel nor the time. His lack of means may also have hidden a reticence to attend. As McCray remarked, Mboya knew an African international was a "sound idea," and the ICFTU's poor record allowed him no room to bargain over the affiliation issue.[42]

As expected, the UGTAN conference endorsed the proposal to convene a labor conference that would establish an African labor international. Ironically, the UGTAN conference also signaled the beginning of the exodus of most of the francophone affiliates from UGTAN. Other West African countries became suspicious of the political work of UGTAN and were able to weaken and supplant the UGTAN unions in their countries. Although UGTAN began to weaken, the idea of an autonomous African international still had appeal.[43]

Mboya recognized that attendance at the proposed labor conference "would put some of us in a rather awkward position vis-à-vis our affiliation to the

ICFTU." Because of the international's ineffective record, he remarked, ICFTU supporters could not "very well convince others to come to our side." He complained to Randolph, McCray, and Meany of the dilemmas African ICFTU supporters faced defending an organization that he believed gave African labor short shrift. For example, the ICFTU had yet to finance an office for the East, Central, and Southern Africa area committee of the proposed AFRO.[44]

An Attempt to Circumvent the ICFTU

Springer viewed the adoption of the 1957 Atlantic City Compromise, limiting the international work of affiliates to ICFTU channels, as the final policy that set African labor on the course toward disaffiliation. The harassment she had endured in East Africa and her awareness of the bitter disappointment of Africans contributed to Springer's going into a slow mental, spiritual, and physical decline when she returned to the United States after the Atlantic City compromise. While still harboring some hope that she would again work in Africa, she kept busy with her ILGWU duties and tried to ignore her deteriorating health.

By the time of the All-African People's Conference, the direction of U.S. domestic and foreign policies also added to her pessimism. Noting that whites remained strongly resistant to expanding civil rights for blacks, Springer expressed her divided feelings about the West to Golda Meir, whom she had first met through her ILGWU activism: "Mine is a troubled spirit, for at the moment I am trying to maintain even a limited faith in the much vaunted pretensions of the Democratic West. As an American Negro I know more than most of the meaning of compromise and the acceptance of marginal gains as major victories."[45]

The resistance of European and some U.S. labor leaders to strong activism in Africa was difficult for Springer to accept. She wrote Jay Lovestone of the impasse the ICFTU policies represented: "I can only hope we are able to convince our international colleagues of the folly of a double faced approach to African development—i.e. a theoretical acceptance of the principle and a practical opposition and limitation to it. Further, there seems to be both dislike and contempt for Africans."[46]Noting her general melancholy, Lovestone, who was ordinarily not known to have sympathy for human weaknesses, responded by suggesting that perhaps he could help her if she explained the source of her despair.[47]

At its root, her depression had to do with not being able to realize her strong desire to work in Africa or to convince Western labor to work in true partnership with African labor, whose needs were so great. After Charles Zimmerman, who had recently become general manager of the ILGWU Dress Joint Board, offhandedly remarked that he did not want her to go back to Africa because she might "forget about the Union," Springer wrote him of her hopes. She explained that her trade-union roots, his confidence in her through the years, and her personal need, despite Western hostility toward Africans, to help bring forth the best traditions of democracy were the inspiration for her desire to work in Africa. For these reasons she also declined to become Local 22's educational director. Instead, at the invitation of Meir, Springer was preparing to spend close to a year gaining training and experience in Israel that she could put to use in Africa.[48]

Although Springer conceded that Israel did not always strongly support "some issues of burning importance to Africans" and that, in the United Nations, Africans and Asians often sided with Arabs, she maintained that Israel alone of the Western allies enjoyed very good relations with Africans. Unlike the rest of the West, she averred, Israel offered technical assistance with evident sincerity and humility and a sense of partnership, instead of with condescension or paternalism. She warned that its "preoccupation with the cold war" and the "technical rivalry with Russia" should not blind the West to the "equally important task of regaining the friendship and confidence of African nations." Unless the West made a rapid change in its orientation toward Africa, she proposed that inaction and lack of understanding would contribute to "the very thing we fear—that the emerging African nations will swing to the Soviet bloc." Development of projects between Africa and the West, she hoped, would display the "best traditions of Western democracy to counterbalance its worst aspects—which are the daily experience of African colonials."[49]

In addition to Meir and Israeli ambassador to Ghana Ehud Avriel, Springer had discussed her ideas for African projects with officers of the Israeli labor federation, Histadrut, during a visit to Israel following the All-African People's Conference. Although she held that African labor leaders should and would receive support, she was more concerned with the plight of the average worker and of women. These groups, she noted, needed improved material conditions in order to function as a base of support for the independent governments. Viewing African village life as conducive to cooperative methods of production, she proposed to study in Israel collective settlements and cooperative marketing operations. Dismay with the high cost of goods made in Europe from African raw materials, such as soap and textiles, led her to support small pilot projects that might encourage the development of labor-intensive, African-owned and -operated industries.[50]

Among the projects Springer envisioned was a garment vocational school that would provide scholarships for women and girls throughout the continent. Its proposed site was Ghana or Nigeria. She hoped that learning the garment trade might provide females, who had such limited opportunities, with an independent means of supporting themselves and their families. The plan called for ILGWU financial backing, Histadrut technical assistance, and close cooperation with an African government.[51]

But within a month of detailing her long-range plans to the Local 22 leadership, Springer became unavailable for work of any kind. In addition to depression she was diagnosed with echovirus, after having suffered periodic attacks that left her body weak. For some time she had ignored her doctor's advice that her "low resistance, badly fluctuating blood pressure and nervous tension" necessitated complete rest. Embarrassed and irritated about her health problems, Springer finally had to take heed. After Israel Breslow, who replaced Zimmerman as manager, read to the Local 22 executive board her letter requesting a leave of absence to attend to her health problems, he noted, "There were moments of silence and one could detect a sadness in the eyes of all those who know you well." He gave her a check as a gift and wishes for her complete recovery.[52] Her deep despondency is revealed in a letter she wrote to Lovestone from Michoacán, Mexico, where she spent some of her nine-month period of recuperation.

> Each time I have thought to write [an article for the *Free Trade Union News*], my inner self would say, what is the use no one is really interested.
>   I returned from East Africa badly shaken. The sequence of events in Africa and the culmination of those events in Atlantic City left me feeling entirely discredited in the Labor Movement. This is not said with malice, for the exigencies of the larger problem of the Movement takes its toll on unwitting and hapless victims.
>   . . . The harassment of working in a Police State, and East Africa is a police state, is the price one pays for the privilege of sharing in a social revolution. Certainly some of the consequences of my very presence in East Africa were known. The British Government and my colleagues in the TUC made no secret of how very unwelcome an American labor person and this particular one was in the area.[53]

While still recuperating, Springer began trying to find a way to return to her work on behalf of Africa. She wrote Lester Granger that he more than anyone knew of her "deep and intense desire to live and work in Africa . . . in a simple and constructive way." She estimated that she would need five thousand dollars to maintain her family, with minimal expenses for herself, while in Israel. How to raise this money, however, eluded her, and she felt it was too much of an imposition to solicit his help.[54]

Meanwhile, Springer used correspondence to stay in touch with African events. To Tanganyikan Patrick Mandawa she said, "I thirst for news of the Federation in particular and of other news in general." Israel also continued to value Springer's connections with African leaders. E. Ben-Horin of the Asian-African department of the Ministry for Foreign Affairs informed her of Israel's high esteem for Nyerere and his colleagues and hoped that they could implement constructive projects together.[55]

Ephraim Evron, the U.S. representative to Histadrut, told Lovestone that he would request that Histadrut support Springer's African projects regardless of whether the ILGWU or AFL-CIO did. Since Israel's formation in 1948, the ILGWU, reflecting its strong Jewish membership, had lent the country one million dollars, and over the years, sometimes through voluntary member donations, it provided substantial aid to various Israeli and Histadrut projects.[56] In comparison the commitments the ILGWU would give Springer for Africa were a pittance.

AFL-CIO Offensive on the ICFTU's African Policy

The leaders of the British TUC and ICFTU appear to have had a greater concern for preventing the AFL-CIO from taking a more active role in Africa than for the movement of Africans toward disaffiliation. British TUC leaders did not look favorably upon Meany's proposal for improving ICFTU relations. According to an article in the London *Daily Telegraph*, his suggestion to send "one or two competent trade unionists" from the AFL-CIO to work in Africa was interpreted to mean that he intended to send American Negroes to the continent, a group the British TUC resented even more than white Americans. Their polite acknowledgment of Meany's letter hid a steely determination to uphold the Atlantic City compromise. The same newspaper article noted that a joint meeting of the British TUC's commonwealth and international committees, which met to discuss Meany's proposals, characterized AFL-CIO concerns in Africa as "American clumsiness and interference in British affairs."[57]

Responding to the newspaper article and Tewson's letter, which indicated that differences in approach could affect future cooperation between the AFL-CIO and ICFTU, Meany stated that he regretted any misunderstanding. The AFL-CIO, he continued, had no wish to get in the way of the "internal affairs of British TUC or of British interests." However, if "European friends" and the ICFTU expected that the AFL-CIO should simply forward money to Brussels without questioning to what purpose and effectiveness it was being spent, then the labor federation would have to reconsider its relationship with the ICFTU. Debunking the British contention that they were in close touch with African labor and knew its needs best, Meany remarked that the AFL-CIO was constantly flooded with streams of requests from Africans in "desperate need of advice and assistance." Many of these letters indicated no confidence in the ICFTU.[58]

The British TUC and ICFTU at first refused to acknowledge that the African affiliates had been on the verge of disaffiliating and forming an autonomous African labor international. Oldenbroek suggested that Meany send him information about the All-African People's Conference. The ICFTU Solidarity Fund committee, scheduled to meet in Geneva in mid March, would discuss these along with the AFL-CIO proposals. Without revealing their authors' identities, Meany sent excerpts of three reports, two of which Springer and Mc-Cray had written. Given the ICFTU's hostility toward these two, knowledge of their identities would have further undermined AFL-CIO efforts to effect change.[59]

Against Oldenbroek's counsel, Meany informed the ICFTU that he planned to place before the AFL-CIO executive council meeting, scheduled for Puerto Rico in mid-February 1959, a suggestion that the federation endorse sending AFL-CIO representatives to Africa. AFL-CIO secretary-treasurer William Schnitzler and AFL-CIO vice president James B. Carey would then present the U.S. labor position before the March Solidarity Fund meeting. It was at the Puerto Rico meeting that the AFL-CIO endorsed the African resolutions that Pauli Murray had attributed to Springer's influence. These resolutions included a pledge to find competent AFL-CIO people to assist "in the development of strong African trade unions and in the promotion of ICFTU policies and programs."[60]

In the conflict about African policy, the British, ironically, subjected the AFL-CIO to red-baiting. An article in the London *Daily Telegraph* charged the AFL-CIO with making statements that resembled those made by Communists, although the federation purported to fight communism. These statements were strident denunciations of colonialism. The newspaper noted that the British TUC accepted eventual independence. Yet the 1959 resolutions rested upon a primary concern with fighting communism, reflecting the AFL-CIO leadership's Cold War stance.[61]

Lovestone held that the Solidarity Fund meeting resolved nothing in terms of African policy. The main problem, he remarked, was that "Lord Vincent Tewson fell ill and had to be flown back to London for an appendicitis operation," while Carey presented his own views and not the ones endorsed by the AFL-CIO executive council.[62] According to Schnitzler, however, the ICFTU subcommittee did resolve some contentious issues. First, they decided on a budget for the construction of the building to house the African Labor College in Kampala. Before Tewson left he restated his opposition to a permanent building, suggesting again the idea of a traveling school, which Schnitzler and others dubbed a "traveling circus." The AFL-CIO members opposed Tewson's suggestion as well as proposals to delay a decision on the building's budget. Pushing for the budget that allocated $266,000 for the building over the one allocating $96,000, the AFL-CIO agreed to lend $126,000 to the Solidarity Fund interest free. The subcommittee then accepted the higher budget and agreed to start construction immediately. In its second decisive act, the ICFTU subcommittee agreed, at least in principle, to allow U.S. labor representatives to work in Africa under the ICFTU or the ICFTU-associated International Trade Secretariats (ITS).[63]

Further changes in ICFTU policy and personnel were on the horizon by May 1959. Lobbying by McCray and by Mboya, during his spring 1959 U.S. tour, as well as fear of the rising opposition to ICFTU affiliation were factors influencing Walter Reuther, Carey, and other U.S. labor leaders to reappraise ICFTU operations.[64] Writing to Springer while she was in Mexico, Schnitzler prefaced the news of Reuther's policy shift by advising her to sit down since what he had to report would come as "quite a shock!" During the ICFTU's finance committee meeting in Brussels, Reuther joined with three Europeans in expressing dissatisfaction with ICFTU policy and personnel, particularly Oldenbroek and Charles Millard. The dissidents called for a new administration, Schnitzler stated, "to carry out an action program such as we have been pressing for years." The success of this new turn, he believed, depended on finding a new ICFTU head with "character, drive, determination and humaneness—so necessary if we intend to win the minds and hearts of people" in underdeveloped areas. In apprising her of these developments, Schnitzler remarked, "This, of course, Maida, is a little bit on the confidential side at the moment, but knowing your feelings and the many frustrations you suffered because of the little men we have in big jobs, I thought I would pass it on to you. I am sure that this news will mean more to your rapid and complete recovery than any prescription that could be written by a doctor."[65]

Although Lovestone welcomed the new developments, he treated Reuther's about-face in a sardonic fashion: "Nobody reminded our 'saintly' brother that this was a [new] line for him and that he owed it to himself as well as to us to explain why he changed his old position. Nobody raised or even mentioned the issue of so-called independent AFL-CIO work to supplement and strengthen the ICFTU activities."[66] Lovestone, however, doubted that what he perceived as the ICFTU's unwillingness to strongly oppose colonialism and communism could be resolved by a change in the top leadership and by organizational restructuring.[67] Although crediting Randolph, international affairs director Michael Ross, "and some new converts" for the AFL-CIO's new commitment to Africa, McCray too had doubts. He reflected this pessimism to Randolph: "[U]nfortunately all of this energy and determination must be squeezed through the needle's eye of the ICFTU and its timorous approach to matters. I am afraid Meany, Schnitzler, Reuther etc. will throw up their hands in disgust one of these days and say to 'hell with it.'"[68]

The uneasy truce between the AFL and CIO factions within the labor federation also continued to threaten its international work. In 1961 Michael Ross informed Irving Brown of the flare-ups between the two sides on questions of jurisdiction and relations with the Kennedy administration, with "the usual very strong carry over into the international work, and every minor difference, of course, is blown up into a major issue." He concluded intriguingly, "Sometimes, as you can imagine, a helping push is given to this by the interested people."[69]

In 1959, however, the united push by AFL-CIO leaders for a stronger influence on ICFTU African policy disturbed British TUC leaders. They struck back by sending the AFL-CIO a confidential memo detailing their grievances against African labor and pan-Africanism. The financial and organizational weakness of African labor caused them to doubt whether many of these labor centers could qualify for affiliation with the ICFTU. The idea of a pan-African labor body, they maintained, was based on negative anticolonialism, pan-Africanism, and racialism. Moreover, they argued that pan-Africanism was not even indigenous to Africa but was based on "Negro frustrations" in the United States and perpetuated by a small group of West Indian Negroes in England. Obviously attacking activists centered around George Padmore, they proclaimed, "for over 20 years [this group] operated on the fringe of British politics in London and systematically built up connections with black Africans, while assuming a lead, as 'theoreticians of Pan Africanism', which has no foundation in political experience in their own countries, the United Kingdom or in Africa." Using red-baiting in an attempt to win over the AFL-CIO, they warned that the West Indian group "include[d] a number of ex-Communists who use Communist methods of organization in support of non-Communist policies."[70]

The British TUC leaders were particularly concerned about the effect of pan-Africanism and nationalism on white workers in Africa. They excused colonialists who had formed racially separate unions by saying that they were "natural at the time of establishment." They expressed concern that Mboya's duties as chair of the All-African People's Conference, whose policies they saw as racially exclusive, would lessen his ability to integrate European and Asian labor movements in Africa.

Because of the dangers of pan-Africanism, including its "Communist methods of organization," they urged Western labor to refrain from encouraging political movements that would, like the independent government of Ghana, crush free trade unions. This danger, they asserted, had never existed under colonialism. They viewed Ghana's 1958 Industrial Relations Act and its move toward a one-party state as reflections of Communist institutions. The act gave the government strong powers over the Ghana TUC in its move to attach the labor movements to the state. Many African governments following independence adopted Ghana's pattern of government-labor relations under a one-party state. In these systems, the head of the labor movement sometimes doubled as a government official by serving as minister of labor.

The British TUC failed to recognize that the post-independence restrictions on the labor movements not only reflected Communist institutions but also had British antecedents. Under colonialism, the government restricted strike activity and labor commissioners had the dual role of being both government representatives and advisers to the labor movement. Indeed, as the 1956–57 Princess Margaret conflict demonstrated in Tanganyika, the labor commissioners catered to the interests of the government and employers over that of the unions.

In a rejoining memo the AFL-CIO took exception to many of the British TUC arguments. They criticized the British for giving Africans full blame for the weakness of trade unions and failing to acknowledge the destructiveness of colonialism, including its hostile legal systems and neglect of health and education needs.[71] The AFL-CIO also argued that, in the face of the Communist danger, the ICFTU needed to offer strong support to African labor and nationalist movements. African unions, they insisted, needed greater financial assistance, including for training programs and visits of labor leaders to Western countries. The memo concluded by charging that the British TUC memo was "grossly unfair in the judgment it passes on African unionism. It simply underestimates the difficulties faced by African labor leaders. A little more understanding, compassion and last but not least, humility would be called for."[72]

Springer objected to the notion expressed in the British TUC memo that pan-Africanism was artificial and a manipulation by outside forces. "As far back as 1897," she declared, "West Coast Africans were sending deputations to England to protest against the Colonial Administration, Laws and Policies. . . . That Pan-Africanism has received the active support and collaboration of American and West Indian Negroes is a natural consequence of their common oppression facilitated by racist theories." Any undesirable developments stemming from pan-Africanism, she maintained, could be expected in light of the "high cost which imperialism has exacted from indigenous African populations and of the revolutionary consequences of this domination" as Africans groped "for nationhood and a viable economy in a precarious world setting." With this argument she connected the colonial experience to African initiatives that Europeans viewed as negative. Springer once again despaired at the prospects of good relations between Africa and the West. She believed that the British TUC should exercise wise and experienced labor leadership by attempting to bridge the gap between Africa and the West. Instead they were widening the gap.[73]

The Growing Rift between the Ghana TUC and the West

Historian Manning Marable suggests that George Padmore's death in September 1959 helped to solidify Nkrumah's turn away from the West and toward positive neutralism. However, according to Irving Brown, Padmore along with Abdoulaye Diallo, a long-time rival of Sékou Touré and a former vice president of the WFTU, had participated in an unsuccessful attempt in May 1959 to undermine Mboya's position as chair of the Committee of the All-African People's Organization. Padmore's move against Mboya was in line with Ghana's changing position.[74] Springer, who was personally fond of both Mboya and Padmore, was unaware of this maneuvering.

The ICFTU's opposition to policies and goals advocated by Nkrumah and Tettegah was a primary factor in Ghana's about-face in regard to international affiliation. Ghana and Western labor clashed over sections of Ghana's 1958 Industrial Relations Act, legislation which had been inspired by Tettegah's study of Histadrut. Under this legislation the Ghana TUC's sixty-four affiliated unions eventually were amalgamated into ten industrial unions. During Springer's Ruskin College days, she had become aware that the proliferation of small unions was a problem in many parts of Africa. By allowing any seven people to form a union, colonial governments helped to foster the development of weak unions based on ethnic divisions and language differences. She began to understand how the International Labor Organization (ILO) convention on freedom of association could be detrimental to strong trade-union development in a colonial country. Declaring "We do not want to be bothered with Cambridge essays on imaginary ILO standards with undue emphasis on voluntary association," Tettegah defended the right of independent Ghana to deal with this particular colonial legacy.[75]

More importantly, however, the ICFTU opposed sections of the act that they held gave too much power to the ruling Convention People's Party (CPP). Under the act the government had the right to restrict strike activity, to change Ghana TUC rules and decide its membership, and, through the minister of labor, to intervene in the labor movement and its finances. These provisions were a part of the move to incorporate the Ghana TUC into the CPP.[76]

Fearing that Tettegah, who was a member of the CPP Central Executive, would oversee the institution of a labor-government alliance, some Ghana labor leaders had long opposed his leadership, despite his talents as a very able organizer. Following the passage of the 1958 legislation, moderate labor leaders, particularly of large unions, appealed to the ICFTU for help in resisting this act.[77] Radical unions in the Sekondi-Takoradi area that were politically opposed to Nkrumah also opposed the legislation. Recognizing that the ICFTU could help undermine his policies on labor and African unification, Nkrumah almost immediately after the conclusion of the All-African People's Conference pressured the Ghana TUC not only to support mandatory disaffiliation but also to take the lead in building the African labor international.

Starting at the January 1959 UGTAN conference, Tettegah would waver on this issue for most of the year. At the conference he found himself in an awkward position as he stood as a representative of the ICFTU, oversaw the affiliation of the Ghana TUC to UGTAN, and, due to the efforts of Touré, was elected first vice president of UGTAN. Although UGTAN's constitution forbade outside affiliation, Irving Brown and Tunisian labor leader Ahmed Tlili agreed with Tettegah that he should not reject the position but make it "perfectly clear to Touré that he and his organization shall remain within the ICFTU." Brown noted that UGTAN's small Communist group and WFTU observers were not happy about Tettegah's election.[78]

Although Brown often expressed admiration for Touré, at times believing him to be one of the few "sincere African neutralists," he nevertheless feared that Touré's practice of neutralism might open opportunities for Communist influence. Nkrumah, he incorrectly believed, might serve as a moderating influence on Guinea. George Meany also expressed this sentiment upon learning that Tettegah had drafted a memo for the AAPC Steering Committee concerning the formation of an African labor international under the auspices of UGTAN. He suggested getting Nkrumah's help "to check Tettegah." McCray did not learn that Nkrumah was primarily responsible for the move to develop the autonomous pan-African labor body until the end of 1959. Before that time he had doubted that Nkrumah was aware of the moves to break ICFTU affiliation.[79]

When Tettegah wrote Springer in the spring of 1959 that the Ghana TUC had decided to keep its affiliation, she responded, "As you know I am no champion of the positions taken and behavior of some of their [the ICFTU's] representatives, but have always been of the belief of the positive role this organization will and can play in trade union understanding world wide. I have been equally sure that the success of this potential is possible if my Africa Colleagues are there and participate on all levels."[80]

By September Seymour Chalfin, the labor attaché at the U.S. Embassy in Ghana, stated that Tettegah was "tottering on his throne." Informed opinion in Ghana, he noted, was that the general secretary was about to be removed for political reasons. The Ghana TUC's disaffiliation from the ICFTU came in November, and the labor center's leadership was reorganized in January 1960, presumably to facilitate its leadership in building a neutral pan-African labor body. Communist sympathizers were removed from influential positions. Tettegah was temporarily transferred to the Builders Brigade and became a roving ambassador before returning to leadership in the Ghana TUC.[81]

The continuing inaction of the ICFTU in Africa, combined with British contempt for African labor organizations, meant that the prospects for continued African affiliation to the ICFTU were dim. Concerned that Communists would take advantage of the situation, but also opposed to colonialism, the AFL-CIO sought to halt the momentum toward disaffiliation through support for Mboya and African Americans like Springer and McCray.

8

Springer Joins the AFL-CIO Department of International Affairs

WHILE SPRINGER WAS RECUPERATING IN 1959 from her bout with prolonged illness, the struggle over ICFTU affiliation had intensified. Following her recovery, she was able to realize her desire to work more closely with African labor. In April 1960 she accepted the position of AFL-CIO international affairs representative. During a six-week tour to the continent with Irving Brown in the fall of 1960, she gained a sense of where the struggle was heading and assessed the current feelings of Africans. She clearly felt that the ICFTU was its own worst enemy and that the West's increasing preoccupation with communism was detrimental to good relations with Africans. She sought to put in perspective for a Western audience the Communist and colonial models in the African context: "It is to be hoped that American foreign policy for Africa in the future can be based on a premise more acceptable to Africans than the threat of Soviet domination. This, many Africans feel, robs America of the respect and confidence this generous country might otherwise enjoy. . . . Soviet domination, though real, is less evident than the terror, violence, discrimination endured by Africans in parts of North, South, East, and Central Africa."[1]

Some of the labor literature critical of the AFL-CIO's role in Africa portrays Springer as having a divisive influence, particularly in Kenya and Southern

Rhodesia. Much of the documentation suggests, however, that in these countries Springer was respected by many in the competing groups. Ideological differences over the relationship of labor to the nationalist movements sometimes was not as strong a factor in dividing labor movements as was competition for power and limited resources within the context of colonialism, white minority rule, and the Cold War. The intrigue and collusion of Western governments in perpetuating African oppression sometimes cast a shadow over Springer's work. The Congo crisis and the assassination of Patrice Lumumba in early 1961 represented a disturbing period of her activism.

Mboya's Leadership

The AFL-CIO saw Tom Mboya as a person who might help bridge the gap between Africa and the West, despite the British TUC's objection to his political role. However, Mboya was torn by the dilemma of either supporting membership in a deeply flawed but powerful world labor organization or promoting an autonomous pan-African organization circumscribed by the exigencies of new African nations. Springer extended every effort in aid of his leadership, and not just because of his support for affiliation, which ultimately would not withstand the mounting pressure against ICFTU membership. More importantly, she was impressed by his abilities, his commitment, and his compassion for African working people. Mboya, however, faced increasing troubles in Africa. Adept at tapping into financial resources and outmaneuvering his opponents, he gained many enemies due to both ideological differences and power struggles.

Mboya's success in obtaining additional scholarships for Kenyans to study in the United States, and his role in choosing a number of the scholarship recipients, added to speculation and jealousies. He obtained forty scholarships during his second U.S. tour in 1959. This tour, like his first one in 1956, was sponsored by the American Committee on Africa (ACOA). These scholarships were not for the labor movement but were for promising young Kenyans. William X. Scheinman and George Houser of ACOA then formed the African-American Students Foundation to raise money for Airlift Africa, a project to pay for a chartered flight from Africa for these students and forty-one others who had alternative sources to finance their educations. Previously, Scheinman had financed the airfare of seventeen Kenyans after Mboya's first visit.[2]

News of these scholarships led to false rumors that Mboya had obtained them on behalf of the All-African People's Conference (AAPC) but was restricting their use to Kenyans. Tanganyika Federation of Labor (TFL) leader Patrick Mandawa wrote Springer about these rumors, including one that Mboya had been given a million dollars. He asked Springer for the truth so that he and others might defend Mboya if the information was wrong. She replied that Mboya had obtained the scholarships for Kenyans and that he did not receive a million dollars. Mandawa was also sent a letter describing the scholarships that was signed by three prominent African Americans involved with fundraising efforts for the student airlift: Harry Belafonte, Jackie Robinson, and Sidney Poitier. Mandawa's efforts to correct the false stories concerning the scholarships were unsuccessful. He asserted that the local press ignored the truth. Perhaps sensitivity to these jealousies led to the decision to include other East Africans in the 1959 airlift. The following year fund-raising efforts were successful in bringing 222 students to the United States from East and Central Africa. Yet Springer reported that some of those whose families benefited from Mboya's success resented the acclaim he received for these efforts.[3]

Within the Kenya Federation of Labor (KFL), Arthur Ochwada led the assault against Mboya. While visiting the United States on a study tour, journalist Joseph Thuo informed Springer of KFL infighting before she went to Africa to coordinate the 1957 AFL-CIO scholarship program. Noting that the friendship between Mboya and Ochwada was "evaporating," he declared that some KFL officials were trying to get rid of Mboya as general secretary. When Ochwada was in the United States as one of three recipients the ICFTU had allowed to proceed with the scholarship program, Springer had overheard him in her home strategize about ways to replace Mboya. During the AAPC, Ochwada had complained to Irving Brown about the delay in receiving his stipend from the AFL-CIO in order to carry out organization work. Noting his anger, Brown predicted that Ochwada "could become mean and nasty." Following the AAPC, Ochwada began his challenge in earnest. He began to complain to the ICFTU about Mboya's involvement in politics and his frequent absences on foreign trips. Moreover, he helped to support, although he did not sign, a petition against him. This "Memorandum of Complaints" charged Mboya with running the KFL for his own exclusive benefit.[4]

Regretting the need to take internal squabbles outside the KFL, Mboya appealed for Randolph's help. At a recent KFL general council meeting, he explained, he had pleaded against Ochwada's expulsion for his role in the petition incident. He cited Ochwada's valuable training in the scholarship program as a major reason he did not want him expelled. Concerning Ochwada's recent disappointment about not being elected general secretary, Mboya remarked, "As you know I offered to stand down in his favor but our conference insisted on my continuing in office." He believed, however, that these continued attempts to undermine him would ruin Ochwada's chance to succeed him. He asked Randolph to say a "quiet word" to Ochwada, who he believed had "come back [from the United States] with an exaggerated opinion of himself."[5]

The KFL general council voted to dismiss the six KFL executive committee members who signed the petition. Springer had, or would have, collegial relations with at least four of these leaders: Sillas S. Kweya, John Baptist Abuoga, Siangane Osore, and Clement K. Lubembe. She had met Kweya in 1957 when he was head of the Kenya garment workers. Interestingly, considering Springer's closeness to Mboya, Kweya appealed to her for support on behalf of the six, suggesting the dissidents' respect for her as well as their belief that she might influence the outcome of the dispute. But Springer only wrote Mboya that she had heard that there was some conflict within the KFL.[6] There is no evidence that she played any role in the later reinstatement of the six.

AFL-CIO international affairs director Michael Ross inquired about the internal troubles. In reply Ochwada professed innocence and implied that Mboya was paranoid. Six months later, in September, Ochwada circulated a memorandum criticizing Mboya along the same lines as the petition and also accusing him of breaking KFL constitutional rules. He reportedly ended his memorandum with a statement that connected Mboya negatively to U.S. unions, saying, "no member of this Council would like to see this Federation turned into a Teamsters' Union of America. Let us have a clean and honest federation dedicated to the good cause of the workers." When the KFL general council challenged Ochwada to prove his allegations that Mboya was guilty of a constitutional breach, he reportedly retracted this statement and apologized. Nevertheless, the seventy delegates of the KFL general council voted unanimously to expel Ochwada on charges that he had lied about Mboya.[7]

Not surprised by the outcome, Randolph assured Mboya, "I never lost an opportunity to urge Ochwada to uphold your hand and give loyalty to your leadership. I told him that he could not expect to go forward by overweening ambition at the expense of the masses." Randolph also admitted that he was wrong to have ignored Springer when she had expressed "grave doubts" about Ochwada's future in the labor movement while he was a participant in the scholarship program. Nevertheless, like Randolph, Springer expressed to Mboya her disappointment in the loss of Ochwada's services to the KFL. While she often disagreed with his approaches, she respected his abilities.[8]

Following his expulsion Ochwada formed the rival Kenya Trade Union Congress (KTUC) and eventually placed it in support of the disaffiliation movement. For more than a year, however, he continued to appeal to Western labor for support against Mboya and for the affiliation of his organization to the ICFTU. AFL-CIO representatives for the most part urged him to reconcile with Mboya, heal the split in the labor movement, and await his turn at leadership.[9]

Mboya's busy schedule during his 1959 tour provoked displeasure from other quarters. Often a critic of Mboya's, Jay Lovestone complained to Springer that those "well-meaning children who run that Committee on Africa have no idea of relative importance of people and places" and that he had not deserved the treatment he got from Mboya, who canceled two appointments. "[W]ithout violating any laws of modesty," he claimed that he and Springer had done more than any-one to see that the ICFTU and the AFL-CIO gave Mboya and the problems of Kenyan labor "the most adequate and generous consideration."[10]

In reply Springer defended Mboya and sought to placate Lovestone, praising the "quiet and effective work" he had done for African labor. She explained that the American Committee on Africa kept Mboya on a tight schedule, and that she too had seen little of him apart from one Saturday afternoon when he visited her home while someone typed a draft of the speech he was to give at Carnegie Hall. This speech was given for the first African Freedom Day celebration held April 15, 1959, a date leaders at the 1958 Conference of Independent African States set to be observed until all of Africa won independence.[11]

A year earlier Springer also had come to Mboya's defense against Lovestone concerning the decision to retain D. N. Pritt to represent him and six other African members of the Kenya Legislative Council in the conspiracy and libel case. Pritt was a highly respected British lawyer who had been honored with a commission to serve as Queen's Counsel. Lovestone, however, did not like Pritt's relations with Communists. Springer and Randolph led fund-raising efforts for the Africans' defense while Lovestone put his efforts into pressuring Mboya to change lawyers. He remarked, "No doubt Pritt is an able lawyer but as I have told Maida, Pritt is a notorious Communist and pro Muscovite."[12]

Writing Mboya about the controversy, Springer noted that Brussels and Lon-don had forwarded the news about Pritt to the AFL-CIO. While she was confi-dent he could clear up the questions that had been raised, she also reminded him that the Communist issue, coupled with the low priority given to Africa, would affect their ability to raise funds. "Those in the unofficial group understand clearly the issue at stake in the trial charges. . . . We will raise money but it will re-quire three times as much effort and produce one third the financial returns." Mboya replied that he had tried to explain to Meany and Reuther that they re-tained Pritt not because they sympathized with communism but because of his legal talents and record of success in similar cases. He hoped his "American friends" would understand.[13]

Apparently Irving Brown and Michael Ross also did not share Lovestone's view. Ross informed Brown that "the fact that Pritt was engaged as the defense lawyer was the cause for some hesitation here, but not enough." A strongly sup-portive letter from Reuther, in which he urged a substantial donation, helped to persuade Meany. The AFL-CIO grant of twenty-five hundred dollars represented the largest single donation for the defense. Although the defendants were found guilty on the charge of libel and fined a modest sum, Pritt was able to get the more serious conspiracy charge dropped. A few months later Pritt represented Nyerere in his libel trial. He had also represented Kenyatta.[14]

Mboya's opponents became increasingly successful at turning his Western support into a political liability in Kenya. They labeled him a tool or stooge of Americans. Recognizing the harm the American connection could do to Mboya's career, Brown urged that assistance to Mboya be given discreetly so as not to provide more negative propaganda for his traducers. Praising Mboya for his intelligence, the respect he commanded among African nationalists, and his strong commitment to anticommunism, Brown and McCray focused on gaining AFL-CIO support for Mboya; they believed British TUC leaders would prevent the ICFTU from providing assistance.[15]

According to Mboya, the ICFTU even controlled their gifts. The KFL had yet to be able to use a Willys station wagon that the United Auto Workers (UAW) gave them in 1956. Although ICFTU leaders had declined to provide the KFL with a vehicle, they insisted that the UAW gift go through ICFTU channels and that it be registered to the ICFTU. Then, despite KFL protests, the ICFTU representative for Kenya, David Newman, used the van for himself and locked it up when he left the country. For nearly two years the van remained locked in a garage, and Albert Hammerton, who was then the director of the ICFTU's West African Trade Union Information Center, reportedly had the keys. KFL leaders and organizers therefore had to rely on more expensive public transportation to reach workers.[16] Springer once commented that if Newman were to return, there would be no basis for a good working relationship between him and Mboya. In contrast to Newman, Kenyans had gotten along well with the previous ICFTU representative, Canadian Jim Bury.[17]

Another point of contention between the ICFTU and Mboya involved financial assistance for Solidarity House, the planned new building to house the KFL. Although the international labor confederation had turned down the union's first request for aid, Randolph in 1957 had told a highly skeptical group of KFL trade unionists of his belief that the ICFTU and the British TUC might be more inclined to give assistance. He based his assessment on conversations he had with ICFTU leader Jay Krane. But a year later, after Krane provided the KFL with information about ICFTU loans, the union decided that they could not afford the terms and conditions. Instead Mboya appealed to the ICFTU for a grant. The confederation's past missions, he reminded general secretary Jacob Oldenbroek, had recognized the need for a building. Moreover, he argued that the ICFTU and the proposed African Regional Organization (AFRO) could also make use of the building.[18]

During her 1959 leave Springer kept in touch with Mboya about the developments with the building. She described herself as "optimistic enough to believe" that the ICFTU and European labor centers would fulfill their promises to provide furnishings and equipment. Histadrut, the German labor federation (DGB), and the British TUC did make some contributions; however, the ICFTU sent nothing. Still Mboya continued to appeal for financial assistance for equipment. He commented, "Surely the ICFTU can not wish to be left completely out of this very important development in Africa."[19]

Upon the building's completion, Mboya expressed hope that Springer would soon visit Africa and see Solidarity House. Indicating that the new building had greatly heightened morale, he concluded, "It is a centre now for practically anything and everybody and it is working 24 hours a day." African workers also had made individual donations for the building based upon a plan Springer had participated in formulating. The building, however, soon became entangled in the affiliation fight. One of Mboya's opponents referred to Solidarity House as the place where plots were hatched to "sell Kenya to the Americans."[20]

The Lagos Conference

After disaffiliating from the ICFTU, the Ghana TUC called for a preparatory committee to meet in Accra in November 1959 to develop plans for the proposed All-African Trade Union Federation (AATUF). The Ghana TUC scheduled the meeting the same month that the second ICFTU African Regional Conference was to convene in Lagos, Nigeria. Moreover, the Ghana TUC for obvious reasons did not consult with Tom Mboya about the date despite his position as chair of the Committee of the All-African People's Organization, which was supposed to oversee the development of any African international. In fact, Mboya received his invitation to attend the Accra meeting after his rival in the Kenyan political arena, Oginga Odinga, received an invitation at the request of Nkrumah. Odinga, incidentally, was not a trade unionist. Although Mboya was aware that the preparatory meeting was intentionally set to overlap the ICFTU meeting, thereby forcing labor centers to make a choice, he wrote Ghana requesting the date be changed. Ghana subsequently conveyed to him that he would be considered a traitor if he did not attend the Accra conference.[21]

The top labor leaders of Ghana, Guinea, and the United Arab Republic showed up at the Accra conference, while most other labor centers sent representatives. For his decision to attend the ICFTU gathering, Mboya was excoriated in the *Ghana Times* as an "imperialist agent." In a public statement later published in the ICFTU organ, he denied that ICFTU membership committed affiliates to the policies of the West. He also made a not-so-subtle attack on the Nkrumah government, saying, "I am not unaware of dangers of other subtle forms of domination both from without and within Africa."[22]

Delegates used the Lagos conference to formulate a challenge to the ICFTU to change its African policy, to be presented at its sixth congress in Brussels the following month. The British strongly resented McCray for crafting, at the request of Mboya, what they deemed to be radical conference resolutions. Mboya remarked to Springer on the coincidence of the ICFTU's decision to provide the KFL with financial assistance for a six-month organizational drive at the same time the Lagos conference was due to meet. Clearly the confederation recognized the need to encourage its African supporters. Fear of disaffiliation also spurred the ICFTU, over the objection of the British TUC, to provide the necessary finances for AFRO's creation.[23]

It did not help the ICFTU position that several affiliates at the Lagos conference perceived few tangible benefits from their membership. Irving Brown reported that some of the delegates felt isolated, and nearly all the twenty labor centers in attendance expressed a desire for direct relationships with the AFL-CIO. They particularly continued to request scholarships to study in the United States. Aware that Africans were invited to the States by nonlabor groups, the delegates found it difficult to accept that U.S. labor would not extend the same opportunity. However, they held the British TUC responsible for the Atlantic City compromise, and were aware of the harassment Springer received while administering the AFL-CIO scholarship program. Brown added of Springer, "In all of my conversations with trade unionists from the British territories, her name was known and her work greatly appreciated." Afterwards Brown asked Springer whether she might become involved with Africa again.[24]

Following the conference, Springer sent Brown a clipping from the *Pittsburgh Courier*'s issue of December 12, 1959, which included a picture of himself addressing a cocktail party while surrounded by a group of Africans. She found humor in the caption, which incorrectly identified Brown as a North African delegate. More seriously, she hoped the conference would have a positive effect upon the upcoming ICFTU congress. She remarked, "If we could view the fledgling labor movement in Africa as we viewed the war shattered movements of Europe and address ourselves to development on this basis, it would be a mutually rewarding experience. . . . Oh well, here I go again. The political [implication] of a long term positive program in Africa is so challenging that it continues to plague me. Creature of the West that I am, the hope is there that our practices will begin to approach our ideal."[25]

Ghana's leadership in the disaffiliation movement motivated the sixth ICFTU Congress to grant greater power and more independence to its African affiliates. Despite the pleas of the British TUC to go slow, the ICFTU agreed at least in principle to support the measures Mboya had presented, and he was elected a full member of the ICFTU executive board. With the strong backing of the AFL-CIO, Mboya pressed for autonomy for African labor centers comparable to that of the U.S. and European affiliates, more financial support for Kampala College, a high-ranking leader assigned to deal with African labor, and African participation on the Solidarity Fund committee.[26]

Springer's new position in the AFL-CIO international affairs department, beginning in April 1960, represented for many African labor leaders additional bounty. With her appointment, Ross informed Mboya, "we ought to be able to give more continuous attention to African questions." Randolph wrote Springer that he and Meany had spoken of the "tremendous contribution" she would make in her new post.[27] Yet Springer had to withstand strong opposition to her work from people in both the West and in Africa. McCray remarked from Africa, "I can well imagine what consternation your entry into the Foreign Affairs Dept. has caused in certain circles. Certain people on the other side of the Atlantic Ocean seem to regard me and you as being particularly objectionable and dangerous."[28] Commenting on her position, Springer once remarked, "I had some emotional problems, not because I was asked to do anything that I disagreed with, but because I saw the drift between my colleagues in Africa and my colleagues in the United States, the hardening of the arteries."[29]

Battle Lines Drawn

Despite the Ghana TUC's disaffiliation and Ghana's steady development into a one-party state, Springer maintained positive relations in the country. The nation's limits on civil liberties troubled her, but she retained some sympathy for the problems of African governments and wanted to believe that the restrictions on the labor movement were a result of inexperience during the transition from colonialism to independence. When asked about Ghana's left leanings on the AFL-CIO public service radio program, As We See It, Springer replied that while people associated the Soviet Union with the left, she saw the country as rightist and reactionary, and she did not perceive Ghana the same way. Her sympathy for Ghana is also evident in a remark she made to Dorothy Padmore concerning Nyerere's six-week, State Department–sponsored tour of the United States in 1960. "[H]ounded at every conference" with questions of "Ghana's growing dictatorship," the Tanganyikan leader's response, she asserted, left the questioner a little defenseless.[30]

Ironically, at the time Springer made this comment, Pauli Murray, who came to view Nkrumah as a dictator, was on her way to teach the first course on constitutional and administrative law at the newly established Ghana School of Law. Following the All-African People's Conference, Springer gave Murray a clipping from the London Times advertising faculty positions at the school and urged her to apply. Murray, who had had "challenging conversations" with Mboya, Nyerere, and other nationalist leaders in Springer's home, looked forward to the experience and to exploring the "African component" of her ancestry. Informing Nkrumah and Ako Adjei (then serving as Ghana's ambassador to the UN) about Murray's application, Springer also sent Nkrumah copies of Murray's book of poetry, Dark Testament, and her legal book, States' Laws on Race and Color. She described Murray as a lawyer with superior qualifications who is also "dedicated, has a sense of history, the love of teaching and the ability to challenge searching young minds."[31] In Ghana Murray would challenge her students along lines that were critical of Nkrumah's policies.

Regarding her differences with Murray on the practices of African governments, Springer later commented, "My passionate feeling about Africa she certainly did not share. She was too cool-headed and intellectually searching and was unwilling to make any compromises for undemocratic practices in Africa. . . . We never agreed." In a speech she later gave on Murray at the University of North Carolina at Chapel Hill, Springer elaborated:

> I was so delighted with Pauli's post in Accra, I wrote to the Prime Minister — Dr. Nkrumah, advising him on what a gem he was getting — and to other friends to please show Pauli some of the wonderful African hospitality that I was still moonstruck about. . . . I returned to Accra, Ghana in the midst of one of Pauli's most uncomfortable periods; in her view, there soon would be a denial of constitutional rights. Pauli's views did not go unnoticed in Ghana Government circles, and her respect for opposition was known. One evening at dinner she attacked me for sympathy with an undemocratic leadership. We talked until late in the night and in due course she lessened her attack and we parted amicably.[32]

Ghanaian officials warned Murray that if she wrote anything critical of government policies for publication in the United States, she could face deportation. Yet it was her course at the Ghana School of Law, which dealt with Western constitutional issues, that nearly got her expelled. The course — necessarily, she reported — brought up issues of Ghana's government policies. Ghana was becoming a one-party state without provisions for separation of powers.[33]

U.S. involvement in events leading to Patrice Lumumba's assassination on January 17, 1961, may have accelerated Nkrumah's move toward authoritarianism, including mass arrests under the provisions of the 1958 Preventative Detention Act. The year of Lumumba's death, the Nkrumah government arrested Dr. Joseph D. Danquah, his long-time political opponent, because of his court defense of eight jailed opposition leaders. After being released in 1962, Danquah was rearrested in 1964 and died in prison in 1965. Nkrumah's long-time political associate Ako Adjei was arrested in 1962 on charges of complicity in a plot to assassinate him. Although Adjei was acquitted, Nkrumah kept him in jail. Adjei was released after the 1966 coup that overthrew Nkrumah.[34]

In the wake of Lumumba's murder, Murray found six members of the Criminal Investigative Department (CID) sitting in on one of her classes. It was ironic that after Springer's treatment at the hands of colonial Tanganyika's CID, Murray had a similar encounter but in Ghana and under an independent govern-

ment. Murray, however, committed a more egregious offense to the Ghana government than encouraging a respect for opposition in her classroom. Just before
she left Ghana, she and another U.S. lawyer secretly helped Danquah build a defense for the eight opposition leaders.[35]

Murray's activities caused only minimal discomfort for Springer. Her relations with the Ghana TUC were good, and she continued to regard John Tettegah as a "devoted, intelligent, and ardent champion of the trade union movement." Tettegah had returned to the position of Ghana TUC general secretary
the same month Springer joined the AFL-CIO international affairs department.
Brown remarked that Mboya and Moroccan labor leader Mahjoub Ben Seddik
believed Tettegah's replacement of Joe Fio-Meyer as general secretary signified
Nkrumah's growing commitment to the disaffiliation movement.[36]

While maintaining an outward camaraderie, Springer and McCray opposed
Tettegah over the affiliation issue. Tettegah treated them as sympathetic friends
and rather ignored their position against mandatory disaffiliation, but he lam-
basted the ICFTU for interfering with African unity. Congratulating Springer on
her new position, he appealed to the "American *brothers*" (italics mine) within
the ICFTU to act as mediators between African labor and the ICFTU European
affiliates. To McCray he argued that the differences between the two opposing
African labor groups were the result of the ICFTU's "insidious" moves to delay
the strong challenges that AATUF would present to European labor bodies. To
Springer he also remarked that the ICFTU's decision to proceed with AFRO was
a tactic designed to undermine African unity.[37] Tettegah's remarks not only reflected his long-simmering disenchantment with the ICFTU but also Nkrumah's
power over the labor movement. He forsook the uphill struggle of Africans to garner power within the ICFTU and effect policy changes in favor of developing an
autonomous pan-African labor body that was, for obvious reasons of colonial oppression, hostile to the ICFTU.

Meeting with Tettegah during her fall 1960 tour, Springer reminded him
that he now opposed the very regional organization he had demanded in 1957.
His reply was that the ICFTU's venture was "too little, too late." On the topic of
positive neutrality Springer reported, "after some talk on this nebulous subject, I
assured him that the only positively neutral people I knew were dead ones. We
both laughed at this and gave up the idea of further pursuing positive neutrality."[38] On a favorable note for the ICFTU, Springer noted that Tettegah was no
longer "inflexible" on the idea of labor centers within an African international
having "contacts" with the ICFTU. The receptions he got on his recent travels
through Africa apparently contributed to this change in position. Nkrumah sent
him on this tour to encourage labor centers to disaffiliate from the ICFTU. "The
general assumption," Springer wrote, "can be that [Tettegah's] position has soft-

ened largely because it has not been possible to command the necessary majority among the African leadership in the trade union movement."[39]

Springer's reading of Tettegah's willingness to compromise seems to have been true. From information he gathered during travels to West and North Africa in early 1960, Mboya believed that Ghana postponed the conference to form the All-African Trade Union Federation because it did not have support on the affiliation issue. He also believed that Guinean leader Sékou Touré, unlike Nkrumah, showed some flexibility on the issue. In November 1960, the same month the third ICFTU African Regional Conference convened in Tunis and formally launched AFRO, Tettegah and Mboya signed a joint declaration in which they agreed to leave the question of affiliation up to the national centers. Springer believed the declaration was "vague enough to satisfy all manner of interpretations."[40]

This compromise was soon overshadowed by another controversy. Gogo Chu Nzeribe, the general secretary of Nigeria's posts and telecommunications workers, published under the aegis of the AATUF a pamphlet entitled "The Great Conspiracy against Africa." The pamphlet got wide publicity and distribution; Springer reported that African students in the United States had copies along with other similar literature. The Soviet press and radio gave the pamphlet additional exposure. The previous year, at the ICFTU African Regional Conference in Lagos, Nzeribe had shown to conference delegates ICFTU and British TUC letters he had somehow procured which appeared to be bribing the unaffiliated TUC of Nigeria. At that time McCray described him as "a clever, energetic, and resourceful African communist."[41]

Purported to be an attachment to a British Cabinet Paper dealing with African policy, the "Conspiracy" document detailed plans to control African governments and labor movements after independence. It also supported allegations that Meany, Reuther, and Dubinsky directly, and Mboya indirectly, were carrying out U.S. State Department and CIA policy. Mboya vociferously denied the charges against him. Moreover, he held that a photostatic copy of the original document had so many errors of spelling and phraseology that it supported his contention and that of others that the document was a forgery.[42] Regardless of its authenticity, the document realistically portrayed the tensions between the United States and the British and foretold the eventual dependency of African economies on the West. For these reasons the pamphlet was damaging for ICFTU relations.

After Mboya cabled Tettegah criticizing the All-African Trade Union Federation's role in the publication, Tettegah denied that the AATUF, not yet officially formed, had sponsored the pamphlet. He also claimed to sympathize with the problems the pamphlet had caused Mboya, whom he repeatedly referred to as

"My dear Tom." Yet Tettegah in a letter to Mboya six months earlier had given credence to this document, which he stated Ghana's intelligence establishment had procured.[43]

Springer and McCray believed that the ICFTU's continued shortcomings in Africa and not propaganda would be its undoing. Discussions with Northern Rhodesia labor leaders prompted her to remark, "The usual problem of ICFTU promise and delayed performance was discussed. I hope the day will come when the ICFTU will not promise what it does not intend to comply with. This ICFTU policy of promise then delay or retraction of the original commitment has weakened the position of some of our most consistent support."[44]

The actions of the Ghana TUC demonstrated that the leadership would not capitulate easily on the affiliation issue. For example, the Ghana TUC continued to fraternize with Arthur Ochwada, who had by then repudiated the ICFTU and put the rival Kenya Trade Union Congress on the side of mandatory disaffiliation.[45]

Four months earlier, in August 1960, both Ochwada and Mboya reported that they were coming to a reconciliation. Springer first heard about the unity moves from Ochwada, whom she had not heard from since 1957. He also requested AFL-CIO assistance for payment of two thousand dollars in legal fees for a case in which he had won acquittal. Springer wrote Mboya that she was encouraged about the movements to heal the labor rift. She advised Ochwada to process his request for financial assistance through the KFL.[46]

Ochwada next communicated with Ross, suggesting that, given his history of direct contact with the AFL-CIO, the federation might make an exception regarding his direct request. Meanwhile, Mboya answered Springer's letter, confirming that Ochwada was being cooperative both in the political and labor arena. In May 1960 Mboya had won by only one vote over Ochwada the position of general secretary of the Kenya African National Union (KANU), the political party that would lead to independence. Ochwada then became deputy general secretary of the party, thus mirroring their former trade union relation. Although Mboya could not ignore the previous acrimonious association with Ochwada, he approved of any assistance that Ochwada might obtain. He concluded, "he should be given a chance perhaps he needs it." Springer subsequently urged Ross to give assistance, arguing that it could help in the unity moves, would benefit a trade unionist, and would redound to the benefit of the AFL-CIO by demonstrating the federation's ability to be impartial on urgent issues. Ross responded to Ochwada that he was pleased that he was participating in efforts toward healing the labor rift, but it is unclear whether the AFL-CIO gave him assistance.[47]

Ochwada's change in position is reflected in a confrontational letter he wrote Springer in November 1960, after she had returned from her fall tour of Africa. He bluntly asserted that, although he was opposed to a friendship turning into hatred, he had to state his case. He recalled that she had asked him during a breakfast meeting how the AFL-CIO could best help heal the split in the Kenya labor movement. Now, in response to that question, Ochwada accused the AFL-CIO of blackmail and of splitting both the labor and nationalist movements through its policy of channeling money for Kenya through the ICFTU. Moreover, he stated that the AFL-CIO was being damaged by its support of Mboya, who he claimed did not command the respect of his own people. It should be noted that two months earlier, when Ochwada was seeking unity with Mboya and financial assistance for himself, he told Ross that he was not sure he agreed with the KFL organizing secretary, who saw outside financial aid as responsible for the KFL's internal problems.[48]

Having toured Eastern bloc countries earlier in the year (with financial support from Ghana's Bureau of African Affairs) and spoken with African students there, Ochwada indicated that everyone was watching the United States to see whether it would do to Kenya what it had done in the Congo. Western corporations, the United States, and Belgium were actively involved in manipulating the crisis that enveloped the Congo following the granting of independence. Lumumba's assassination was two months away. Ochwada in part concluded that if Kenya "turned red," the fault would lie solely with the AFL-CIO and the U.S. government.[49]

In response Springer reminded Ochwada that during their breakfast conversation two months earlier, he had indicated that he and Mboya had taken steps toward unifying the labor movement, a move which the AFL-CIO would support. Offended by his blackmail charge, she retorted, "Was it blackmail when you pressed for and got an American labor scholarship for 9–10 months? Was it blackmail when American labor responded to the urgent request of the labor movement in Kenya to help them build a trade union center? You and I spent a good deal of time with your executive committee and with various government departments in Nairobi on this program which you, as deputy general secretary of the K.F.L., thought vital to the organization and self-respect in Kenya. Your claim then was that the unions were not given enough assistance from the older unions in the West."

Springer also stated that the help the ICFTU gave the plantation workers in their struggle to gain higher wages and union recognition, and their present status as the "strongest and most effective union in the Kenya labor movement," hardly supported his blackmail contention. Indeed, in the past Ochwada had expressed great appreciation for AFL-CIO support. After receiving the 1957 grant for Solidarity House, he had assured Meany that the KFL would never forget this expression of solidarity and would never disappoint the AFL-CIO.[50]

Concerning Ochwada's charge that the AFL-CIO was responsible for the split in the Kenya labor movement, Springer accused him of having division of

the labor movement "uppermost in [his] mind" as early as 1957, while he was taking part in the AFL-CIO scholarship program. She rejoined, "If, as you imply,
the unions in Kenya turned 'red' it will be because of the selfish opportunism on
the part of some leaders, rather than any overt action on our part."[51]

Although the U.S. government's role in the Belgian Congo disturbed
Springer, she did not respond directly to Ochwada's criticisms of American involvement. After spending three days in the Congo during the fall African tour,
however, she indirectly and Brown directly gave support to Alphonse R. Kithima,
whose labor federation was supportive of Lumumba. Springer indicated that the
leaders of two separate national labor federations, Cyrille Adoula and Kithima,
his brother-in-law, were finding common ground toward building the labor
movement. Kithima, in particular, Springer credited with trying to bring labor
leaders together in what she called the "lifeless city" of Leopoldville.[52] The streets
were quiet, a calm before the storm. Brown described this city of high unem-
ployement as having a "death-like air."

Since first meeting Lumumba at the All-African People's Conference,
Brown consistently urged that he and his allies in the labor movement, such as
Kithima, be supported. He cited the support that Mboya and other Africans gave
to Lumumba, and argued that it was wrong for U.S. newspapers to characterize
Lumumba as a "Kremlin-directed leader." In contrast to Lovestone, who hoped
that Lumumba would fall, Brown voiced concern that the United States was
making the same mistakes with Lumumba that it had with Sékou Touré, thereby
opening opportunities for the Soviet Union.[53]

Brown viewed Cyrille Adoula's labor and political leadership as more suspect. By the time of the third ICFTU African Regional Conference, in November 1960, Brown stated that he was "more than ever convinced" that as minister
of the interior Adoula was "too far compromised in the Congo." Following Lumumba's assassination, Brown despaired that it was perhaps too late for the
United States to make amends in the Congo. He held, however, that any future
government could only achieve stability by including the Lumumbist movement.[54] Adoula became prime minister in 1961 with covert American support.
The U.S. government also supported the notorious reign of Mobutu Sese Seko,
who came to power in 1965.

Brown later changed his mind about Alphonse Kithima. In contrast to
Springer's comments in 1961 expressing hope that Kithima would obtain "some
position of responsibility which will enable him to have both status and food,"
Brown observed in 1968 that as minister of education Kithima "appears to be getting too rich and comfortable."[55]

Because of unceasing criticism that he was being corrupted by Western aid,
Mboya publicly began to distance himself from the West. For example, during

his third U.S. tour in 1961, Springer and Ross got the impression that Mboya would prefer that Edward Welsh, whom Meany had assigned to the ICFTU to help with labor organizing, not set up base in Kenya. McCray reported that Welsh was advised not to settle in Kenya to avoid embarrassing Mboya, "who is trying to prove that he is not overly friendly with America." Instead he settled in Kampala. McCray also noted that Mboya was staying aloof from AFRO.[56] Indeed, he had not attended the third ICFTU regional conference.

By March 1961 McCray was writing Springer with concerns about Mboya's future in politics and the question of labor leadership it raised. Noting that Mboya's preoccupation with politics meant that he had "not been much good to the general African situation for about a year," McCray stated that he was trying to learn what his future intentions were. He correctly assumed that Mboya would soon leave labor altogether in exchange for a ministerial post in the independence government.[57]

With the leadership among African ICFTU affiliates faltering, McCray felt validated by Africans with whom he worked to develop new leadership. To Springer he remarked, "I have raised the question of leadership with you or rather to you, because Africans constantly raise it with me as though I were some sort of elder statesman."[58] Springer responded that African student groups in the United States constantly discussed this subject among themselves. Yet she did not offer any suggestions as to what determines a leader. She wrote, "I do not know any single formula that would supply either the need or the ingredient of character which determines ability and dedication."[59]

Before the convening of the May 1961 All-African Trade Union Federation founding conference in Casablanca, Morocco, Mboya appealed to Brown for aid. "Stupid talk" at the preparatory committee meeting, he held, suggested that the KFL was rich enough to send its own delegates. He vowed not to beg the committee for the support.[60] Just before the conference, all parties agreed to suspend previous agreements, including Tettegah and Mboya's joint declaration. Delegates approved disaffiliation toward the end of the conference after many of the ICFTU affiliates had departed amid controversy about credentials. Afterwards Tettegah delivered his famous ultimatum threatening "total war" if labor centers did not disaffiliate from outside international labor bodies within ten months.[61] Labor centers opposed to mandatory disaffiliation met in Dakar, Senegal, in January 1962 to form a rival international, the African Trade Union Confederation, which largely remained a paper organization in part because of inadequate financial resources.[62]

As the two competing African labor internationals were founded, Springer found herself "among the unwelcome people" in Ghana. Tettegah's public attacks against her work and representation particularly troubled her:

Later on when the ideological position became *tough,* John would send a message to me in the morning that he wanted to see me and talk to me. And he would say, "You are my mother." In the evening the next day he wrote a *scurrilous* article about all of the horrible things I represented. This was a part of the Hot-Cold War in Ghana and Guinea and some of the countrie that were considered to be ideologically supporting the Soviet Union poli cies. Those things happened. But in the morning John would put his arm around me and say "I love her. She's my mother. I'm going to send my wife to the United States, so that she can be with you." And in the evening . . There are books written on all of the terrible things I did to the Ghana TUC or all over Africa by John Tettegah. I never had a conversation with him *once* in my life discussing ideological purity. Never. Never.[63]

Springer continued to deflect criticisms of Mboya concerning his many ac- tivities on the political and labor fronts. His opponents, she suggested to him, were irritated that he was "too successful too often." To his friends who had ques- tioned his many roles and the ensuing conflicts, she stated, "I have suggested that this is a natural development for any changes in a social order, and that there will be conflicts, will be rivalries, will be misinterpretation of motives, but knowing your dedication and intelligent pursuance of a unified approach on the political scene as well as in the trade union movement, there is little doubt in my mind that the end you hope to achieve will be successful. I say this recognizing all of our human frailty and personal drives. I applaud your courage."[64]

Springer also admired Mboya for his fertile mind. In early 1962, when she and her mother traveled to East Africa to attend Tanganyika's independence cel- ebrations and the marriage of Tom and Pamela Mboya, they had lunch with the couple at the Kenya legislature. As he socialized with them, he also briefly en- gaged with others over political matters. Springer remarked, "He carried these off as though he was asking the waiter for a second glass of water. Whatever his sins, his virtues overcome them."[65]

Critics of Mboya resented the financial support he obtained from Western sources, including the ICFTU and the AFL-CIO. He used these funds not only to organize labor but to defeat his political and labor opponents. Ochwada's ear- lier assertion, however, that financial assistance from Western labor was responsi- ble for the split in the KFL was disingenuous, particularly in light of his long struggle to supplant Mboya's leadership and his appeals for Western assistance for his rival labor center. Ochwada had obtained assistance through Ghana and the contacts that Mboya's main rival in the political arena, Oginga Odinga, had with Communist nations. Mboya, who once labeled the opposition group aligned with Odinga as the "Mboya jealous enemies club," hinted at their hypocrisy regarding his access to U.S. money in light of the rampant rumors that they were receiving money from Eastern Europe.[66]

Ochwada's direct rivalry with Mboya ended in late 1962. The government decertified the KTUC, and Ochwada was convicted and imprisoned on forgery and theft charges in relation to his position as general secretary of the East African Federation of Building and Construction Workers' Union. Welsh informed Springer that her "old friend" had been arrested at the Nairobi airport as he was about to depart for Somalia in the company of Jomo Kenyatta and other members of the political party that would usher in independence, the Kenya African National Union.[67]

The relationship between Fred Kubai and Mboya illustrates what Springer once contended, "that Africans wore everybody's ideology and religion very lightly," although "there was a sharp feeling against the West." Kubai, who was imprisoned along with Kenyatta for nine years, joined the KFL as director of organization after his release in 1961. Although he participated in the January 1962 Dakar conference establishing the African Trade Union Confederation as a rival of AATUF, he soon became a part of the left opposition within the KFL. He began to agitate against affiliation and fraternized with members of the rival KTUC. After the KFL dismissed him, in part for overstaying his leave of absence in Europe in order to travel to Communist countries, he joined the KTUC.[68]

Perhaps as a result of her absence from the continent during the height of the Kubai-Mboya conflict, Springer did not become embroiled in the controversy. She maintained good relations with both men. In early 1962, after she had undergone exploratory surgery in Kenya to determine the cause of internal bleeding, she credited the "warmth, kindness and interest" of Kubai and others for what her doctors considered her remarkable recuperation. While on the East African trip with her mother, she became ill the day after their arrival in Tanganyika. A few months earlier she had been hospitalized in the United States with stomach ulcers. She recalled that Kubai's wife, "Mama Kubai," was very kind to her mother, who was quite worried over her health. They returned the hospitality to the couple's son, Sampson, who was studying in the United States.[69]

By 1963 Kubai and Mboya worked out some accommodation with one other. However, Kubai complained to Irving Brown that Mboya had not given him enough money to support his campaign for office in the 1963 elections preceding independence. Noting that he was doing all he could to help Mboya, whom he called "the Boy," he remarked that Mboya was too busy and that many people relied on him for help. In appealing for Western assistance, Kubai warned that temptations to seek aid "on the other side" abounded, but he was resisting this impulse. It is not clear if Brown sent him separate money, but he did win his election.[70]

Ideology, Leadership, and Outside Aid

Springer's first contact with Southern Rhodesia was in October 1960, when she and Irving Brown stopped there for two days during their African tour. Her first tangle with the white minority government, however, was through her association with Kanyama Chiume, publicity secretary of the Malawi Congress Party. She made it possible for him to publish an article in the *Free Trade Union News* about African oppression under the federation composed of Southern and Northern Rhodesia and Nyasaland. Lasting from 1953 to 1963, the federation strengthened white minority rule and the exploitation of African labor in the region's copper and agricultural sectors.

Insisting that the article was inaccurate and unfair, the minority government held that Africans were happy with the federation and glad that Joshua Nkomo's intimidating political movement, the African National Congress (ANC), had been banned.[71] Moreover, they declared that Africans like Chiume and Mboya were agitators who had little African support. As for Springer, they called her a Communist in hopes that Meany would fire her. She wrote an article supporting Chiume's arguments. Lovestone assured Meany that Springer and Chiume were factual in their representations, and the matter ended when the AFL-CIO offered federation officials a chance to rebut Chiume and gave Chiume the last word in answering them.[72]

During the 1960 stop in Southern Rhodesia, Brown went ahead of Springer to check into their hotel. She appeared as the hotel management was processing their registration, and the staff promptly reversed themselves and insisted they could not find the reservations. Anticipating that this would happen, Springer had left her luggage outside. Perhaps influenced by this incident, Brown suggested that Western labor not assign American blacks to live there.[73]

With at least one notable exception, the racist hostility carried over into the U.S. consulate. The vice consul, John (Jack) Dupont, helped put Brown and Springer in touch with labor leaders. According to Brown, Dupont contradicted the official line that his superiors in the consulate sent to Washington, which was that race relations within Southern Rhodesia were improving.[74] Dupont, who would leave foreign service by 1963, also informed Springer that one of his colleagues had described her as a black beast and worse. Springer reflected:

> I can understand, I do not respect or accept it, but I understand their position. They are in a country and deal with the leadership of the country, so they will be annoyed with anyone who comes in the country with a different view. I didn't even have to say anything. My presence suggested that I represented American labor, and that I was going to be anti whatever the govern-

ment of Southern Rhodesia was about. The fact that it required a civil war for I don't know how many years before the independence of Southern Rhodesia . . . tells its own story. The fact that a white worker doing the same job as a black worker received five times as much salary tells its own story. My very presence reflected hostility to that kind of equation. And if the American government was building their relationship with the status quo, then I, representing the American labor movement, would be an annoyance. It was not a personal thing. I was messing with the status quo.[75]

One way Springer upset the status quo was by gathering details of African oppression. At her request Knight Maripe, a journalist for the African newspaper the *Daily News* and a former labor leader of the railway workers, prepared overnight a cogent document detailing the repressive laws. Springer, who considered Maripe to have a fine analytical mind, believed that the stress associated with living under a vicious political system eventually destroyed him.

Maripe was instrumental in helping Brown and Springer to locate four African labor leaders, including Reuben Jamela, president of the Southern Rhodesia African Trade Union Congress (SRATUC), and Mark Nziramasanga, general secretary of the commercial workers. Within a year Jamela would face a powerful opposition composed of many of those who had strongly supported him at the time Springer and Brown met him. Jamela's problems were tied to the support he got and in turn gave to the ICFTU, the increasing pressure to ally formally with the liberation movement, and his inability under a hostile government and industrial boards to effect a sufficient minimum-wage increase. Springer once remarked that after the government "lured" labor into accepting bad legislation, they "completely ignored labor's pleas for the most minimum demands."[76] Jamela's opponents would constantly denounce him as a government stooge.

Struggling with a weak and beleagured labor movement, labor leaders were united in their effort to get information about their oppression to the outside world. Feeling isolated and abandoned, they indicated that Springer and Brown were the first international trade unionists to visit them. Until then international support had been negligible, and confined mainly to the British TUC's assistance in the form of literature, small grants for stationery and office equipment, and payment of correspondence classes with Ruskin College for at least one labor leader, Josias Terry Maluleke.[77]

In 1958 Maluleke, as general secretary of the commercial workers, wrote Lovestone requesting labor literature, office equipment, and especially exchange scholarships to help train organizers and equip them with negotiation, conciliation, and arbitration skills. Lovestone sent him labor literature and encouraged him to have his national center or his own union write directly to the AFL-CIO.

Yet he also informed him that, in compliance with the Atlantic City compromise, the AFL-CIO no longer gave direct scholarship aid and that he should seek training at the newly established Kampala College. After the visit of Brown and Springer, the ICFTU and affiliates such as the DGB and Histadrut became involved with African labor, and the SRATUC began sending members to study at Kampala College.[78]

At the time of Springer's visit, Maluleke was among twenty-eight men held in detention without trial since February 26, 1959. Nine were union leaders and the rest were activists from the banned ANC. They would remain in detention for over two years. These activists as well as African leaders in Nyasaland and Northern Rhodesia were arrested under the pretext of an alleged plot, supposedly orchestrated by Chiume, to kill thousands of whites. The crackdown was really an attempt to squash resistance to the Central African Federation. Moreover, in 1959 and 1960 the white minority government of Southern Rhodesia passed the Industrial Conciliation Act, the Unlawful Organizations Act, the Preventative Detention Act, and the Vagrancy Act. These laws were designed to destroy the labor and political movements, maintain white supremacy, and exploit African labor.[79]

Brown referred to Jamela and Nkomo, who were not in prison at the time, as "outstanding leaders who have suffered not only imprisonment but the worse [sic] forms of indignity to their personality." Springer too thought highly of Nkomo, who had escaped arrest because he was out of the country. Unable to meet with him before her 1960 tour, she wrote Nkomo afterwards commenting on the high esteem Jamela and others had for him. "We talked way into the night about the problems of the labor movement, your own untiring efforts and the problems of some of the present leadership in prison."[80]

The leaders with whom Springer and Brown met held that those they considered the real labor leaders were imprisoned. Springer remarked, "They told their dreadful story with much personal dignity." All the prisoners were in poor mental and physical condition, and their families suffered tremendous financial and emotional hardships. As honorary general secretary of the SRATUC, Maluleke developed an active correspondence with Springer and Lovestone, who also published his articles about labor repression in the *Free Trade Union News*.[81]

Impressed upon first hearing about Springer, Maluleke wrote her from detention, "You can imagine how I felt when I heard a lady negro trade unionist on the executive (International Affairs) had been to see our movement." He asserted that her assignment to "such a high post" was an "ideal which is yet a dream" in Southern Rhodesia. Her position reflected to him the extent to which the United States was progressing toward "true equality and freedom." Happy to note that U.S. workers identified their problems with those abroad and particularly in

Africa, he also expressed hope that her presence in his country would effect a stronger interest in trade unions among women.[82]

Gratified by Maluleke's interest in women's development, Springer had Dollie Lowther Robinson, then serving as special assistant to Esther Peterson in the U.S. Department of Labor's Women's Bureau, send him information on the problems of women workers in the United States, and low-income workers generally. Notwithstanding Maluleke's desire to increase female participation in labor unions, he accepted that certain kinds of labor should be assigned to women. For example, he described the various humiliations and hardships he and others suffered after being taken out of prison and confined to the remote and desolate Gokwe Restriction Area. He wrote in detail about the laborious and painful process of getting and carrying water. He implied that this work was humiliating on another level when he said, "Men among Africans never carry any water. It is the job for women."[83]

Although Springer responded with sympathy to the hardships they faced, she also lightly upbraided Maluleke for this comment. "I must chide you, my brother, on the remark that the arduous task of carrying water is a woman's job. The goal, its seems to me, is to evolve an economic society in which technology would release males and females from much of the existing unhealthy and arduous tasks; a society in which the minds of men and women could be more fully utilized for thinking, learning and thereby producing justice, equality and economic stability."[84]

It is not clear if Maluleke ever received this letter. He complained that authorities either confiscated or tampered with his letters, as well as the books and pamphlets he had requested from the AFL-CIO, the ICFTU, and Kampala College. The interruption in their correspondence caused both him and Springer great distress and prevented her from acting on his request that the AFL-CIO pay for correspondence courses he wanted to take with London University.[85]

During Springer and Brown's visit, Brown invited the Southern Rhodesia African Trade Union Congress to send a representative to the third ICFTU African Regional Conference in Tunis that November. The SRATUC executive council chose Jamela. The isolation, repression, and humiliations they had suffered made all the leaders very eager for the attention of the AFL-CIO and ICFTU. In a number of letters to Southern Rhodesians, Springer expressed satisfaction that Jamela would finally be able to present the labor case to international councils. The two days spent in the country, she declared, were the most rewarding of the six-week tour because they had been able to alleviate somewhat the labor leaders' feeling of isolation. Many would request that she return to help the young trade-union movement.[86]

After initially turning down the SRATUC, the ICFTU in April 1961 approved the labor center's affiliation. The African labor leaders then revised their center's name, calling it the Southern Rhodesia Trade Union Congress (SRTUC).[87] At the AATUF founding conference in May 1961, Jamela was among those who strongly opposed Tettegah on the issue of international affiliation. Tettegah at that time reportedly threatened to enter opposing countries and particularly Southern Rhodesia in order to change the tide in favor of affiliation.[88]

Like Mboya, Reuben Jamela soon came under attack over his American connections and the affiliation issue. As was the case in other African countries, trade unionists in Southern Rhodesia were involved with the political struggle. The passage in that country of the 1959 Industrial Conciliation Act forbidding labor unions from participating directly in politics marked the beginning of the divisions over political involvement in the labor movement. With both labor and political leaders under siege, the prevailing sentiment within the labor movement was that trade unionists could support the political movement but not hold office.[89]

Brown first heard rumors of a developing split between Nkomo's political movement and the labor movement in April 1961. Around this time the AFL-CIO had donated to the SRTUC a duplicator, typewriter, and a Land Rover, which helped with one of their most pressing organizing problems, lack of transportation. Maluleke expressed his appreciation to Lovestone, vowing that the Southern Rhodesian labor movement would one day repay U.S. workers for their sacrifice. Over the years various labor leaders would also rely on American labor organizations to provide them with bicycles for the task of organizing. This Land Rover, however, quickly became an object of dissension.[90]

Maluleke became aware of the political rumblings against Jamela's U.S. connections after he used the vehicle to visit him at Gokwe, and afterwards he confidentially apprised Lovestone of the situation. In his view, the political organizations wanted to be the "exclusive champions" of Africans, to control the SRTUC, and develop a one-party state. For this reason the political leaders were threatened by the help the SRTUC was getting. In language reminiscent of Lovestone's, he asserted that the trade unions represented the only serious challenge against dictatorship and totalitarianism. Months later he would also express disapproval of what he called a pan-African movement formed at the expense of world solidarity movements and non-government-controlled unions.[91]

Bemoaning that Jamela was alone in the fight against the "numerous big guns in the political party," he proposed if they "destroy[ed] him," the labor movement would not have any other strong leaders. Moreover, he held that the settler press was also involved with spreading lies aimed at making suspect any U.S. support. Part of the solution lay in the release of the detainees. He urged the AFL-CIO and ICFTU to increase the pressure for their release.[92]

Ultimately, the pressure of the political movement, combined with charges that Jamela was colluding with the minority government's labor department, influenced Nziramasanga, Maluleke, and others to split from the SRTUC, whereupon they passionately denounced Jamela and placed their support behind the All-African Trade Union Federation. As the labor movement continued to split in myriad ways, Springer often urged unity and did not press the issue of affiliation.

The Push for Bilateral Programs

Springer's arrival in the international affairs department coincided with the decision of the AFL-CIO, with the support of others within the ICFTU, to remove some of the ICFTU leaders whom Africans blamed for the ICFTU's poor record in Africa. Arne Geiger, the new ICFTU president, and Omer Bécu, its general secretary, believed that Meany placed undue emphasis on programs for Africa at the expense of Asia and Latin America. Meany and Randolph both believed that Africa should be the ICFTU's principal focus, but this emphasis did not mean that other regions did not deserve attention.[93]

Despite this disagreement, Bécu was less opposed to independent work on the part of ICFTU affiliates than his predecessor had been. In early 1961 the ICFTU and AFL-CIO worked out an agreement that in many respects overturned the Atlantic City compromise. The AFL-CIO agreed to contribute a substantial amount of money to the Solidarity Fund. In return the AFL-CIO was allowed to embark on its own programs in Africa with the cooperation of the ICFTU.[94] Springer would initiate and implement many of these programs.

9

AFL-CIO Africa Programs

S PRINGER'S PROPOSALS TO AID AFRICAN LABOR were not automatically embraced. Among her many ideas that failed to get support were proposals aimed at improving nutrition and food availability. Citing many places where African workers did not have decent midday meals, Springer wanted to institute a training program primarily for African women in nutrition and catering skills.[1] She proposed that the Caribbean would serve as an appropriate site for training African women, partly because culinary tastes there were similar to those of Africans. An earlier proposal to help build food cooperatives in Tanganyika in order to circumvent the high costs of Asian grocers was scuttled when the colonial government let her know that she would suffer reprisals for her efforts.

Springer's persistent lobbying, however, was decisive in U.S. labor's decision to support a summer employment program for African students, a garment workers' scholarship program, and two training centers, the Kenyan Institute of Tailoring and Cutting, and the Nigerian Motor Drivers' School. These centers continued to receive support through the African American Labor Center (AALC), an AFL-CIO international auxiliary founded in 1964. The AFL-CIO got positive press in the United States for these efforts; however, Springer got little public acknowledgment for her role in developing and implementing these projects and programs.[2]

Although the affiliation struggle of the early 1960s played a role in U.S. labor's approval of Springer's proposals, that approval came only after intense lobbying on her part, which sometimes took years. White rule, the affiliation struggle, and leadership rivalries helped undermine some of her efforts. Moreover, Springer's lack of authority to relinquish AFL-CIO funds for political movements and campaigns drew the ire of a few African leaders and also hampered her work.

The Great Need for Improving Skills

Springer's concern in Africa focused on the growing unemployment created by mass migration to urban areas. She held that for nation building to be a success, it had to develop a broad base of trained workers, including women. She once remarked, "if you could teach young women the beginnings of a trade, they could be self-respecting and self-supporting and help their families. And so this was my dream." Training opportunities for women would allow them to enter industry in greater numbers without depressing wages.[3]

With the garment trade representing potentially one of the largest secondary industries in Africa, Springer lobbied U.S. and international labor beginning in early 1957 to make a strong and sustained commitment to improving the prospects of garment workers. She envisioned the growth of indigenous industries to end Africans' dependency on imported cloth and ready-to-wear clothing. She knew the increasing pace of urbanization would place greater demands on this trade. East Africa particularly drew her attention because of the lack of opportunities there compared to West Africa. Comparing the plight of East African garment workers to that of U.S. garment workers fifty years previously, she considered their position worse because of the racist patterns of production. Indians were the primary employers, and they represented the bulk of the skilled labor.[4]

Government examinations in the trades and the exploitative apprenticeship system were major factors depressing wages for East African garment workers. Regardless of their skill levels, if Africans could not pass the English oral-proficiency tests, they could not qualify for a higher certification level and higher wages. In her appeals for ILGWU support, Springer reminded her union colleagues that if English language skills had been a prerequisite for higher earnings in the U.S. garment industry, many immigrants would not have fared as well as they had. It took eighteen years of work before Anselmi Karumba, the Kenyan garment workers' general secretary, could progress to the highest certification level. He remarked that many who tried all their lives were not even able to advance above the lowest level. Employers used lack of training as a reason to deny wage demands. However, Indian workers did not have to be concerned about government examinations to achieve higher wages.[5]

First S. Sillas Kweya and then his successor, Anselmi Karumba, continuously spoke to Springer about the urgent need for organizational assistance and for a training school. Founded in 1947, the garment workers' union was among the oldest in Kenya; the exploitation of Africans in the industry was so great, however, that workers barely made a living. The emergency declared by colonial authorities also wreaked havoc on the union when many union members were detained. In 1957 one white labor officer secretly let Springer know of her sympathy for African labor, admitting that she did not know how Africans survived on wages that were below subsistence level. She and an African labor officer put their careers on the line by jointly subsidizing Kweya, who had been black-listed for his union activities. They paid his rent and helped to feed his four children. One of the founders of the union and a former detainee, Karumba faced the task of having to rebuild a national union, starting from a branch in Nairobi, when he became general secretary in 1959.[6]

The London-based International Textile and Garment Workers' Federation (ITGWF), one of the International Trade Secretariats (ITS) associated with the ICFTU, consistently rejected many of the appeals of Springer and the leaders of Kenya's garment workers. In early 1957 Springer requested through the ILGWU that the garment trade secretariat open an office in Africa (she suggested Tanganyika), out of which they could operate a training program that would be run by volunteers among the skilled workers. She envisioned an office housing an information center and encouraging women to make use of its resources, whether or not they were union members. She recommended that the ITGWF finance a scholarship program to allow more advanced workers to gain experience and skills by studying and working abroad. Challenging Western labor to practice what it preached, she concluded, "This very limited kind of program would bring very large returns. We would be sharing in the experiment of the future and not among those making only high sounding declarations of peace, fraternity and brotherhood."[7] This proposal went nowhere, as did a 1959 proposal for a garment school for African women for which she sought the help of Histadrut.[8]

Following her fall 1960 tour of Africa, Springer continued to urge training for workers in all fields, particularly at the shop level and in such areas as bookkeeping and management. With Communist countries increasingly providing scholarships and other programs, she argued, "We cannot and need not compete with the grand tour techniques of Peking-Moscow. We have a labor movement worthy of open observation and, to some extent, emulation. We have leaders and workers who can, if they see fit, criticize their representatives without fear of reprisal. We have a labor force of every ethnic group in the world, unmatched by any labor movement anywhere. These are some of the assets we should be making use of now. The American labor movement can do much to help make democracy believable to Africa."[9]

By 1961 Springer got approval for both an AFL-CIO Garment Workers Scholarship Program and an AFL-CIO-sponsored summer employment program for two hundred students from Africa, India, and the Caribbean. Previously she had sought summer employment opportunities in unions for students who were Africa's potential future political leaders. She feared that without this program some students, lacking adequate financial resources, might be forced to return to Africa without completing their degrees. She also hoped that exposure to the labor movement would help them understand the problems and aspirations of labor. With the help of Caroline Ware and James Kemp, her second husband, as well as others, Springer would in future years continue to help African students.[10]

In supporting the student jobs program, AFL-CIO leaders were cognizant of the program's value in bolstering the image of the West in Africa and exposing future leaders to a "free" labor movement.[11] The affiliation struggle also influenced U.S. labor's decision to sponsor the garment workers' scholarship program. When Springer asked Dubinsky to support the training program, his first response was to rave at her for always coming to him with her unilateral ideas. Since the Atlantic City compromise, U.S. labor leaders were leery of working with international labor outside the bounds of the ICFTU or the ITSs. Undaunted, she continued to press for the program. Among the many labor leaders who had asked Springer for training opportunities was Lawrence Borha, general secretary of the Trade Union Congress of Nigeria (TUCN). In the wake of a 1960 split in his labor movement over the affiliation issue, Borha requested training for two women, a reflection of Springer's emphasis on opening opportunities for women. He also affirmed, "I cannot tell you how powerful a propaganda and really revolutionary effect this kind of arrangement will have to the advantage of the TUCN. I wish to underline that it is IMPORTANT, and urgent."[12]

Underscoring the need for urgent action, Springer included in an appeal to Dubinsky an article written by Jewell R. Mazique that originally appeared in Washington, D.C.'s *Afro-American* newspaper and was then reprinted in the *Ghanaian Times*. In this open letter to African trade unions entitled "Africa, Beware of Trade Union Imperialism," Mazique criticized U.S. labor's record on race, the ICFTU, and Tom Mboya. She praised Kwame Nkrumah for recognizing that outside forces would try "to direct Africa's destiny through 'Uncle Toms'" who would set African against African. Springer told Randolph that she found the article disturbing, particularly since she believed that Mazique, whom she otherwise viewed as dedicated and informed, distorted "everything towards which we have been bending our efforts" in Africa. To Dubinsky she concluded, "It has always been my cherished hope that the ILGWU specifically be associated with a project in Africa. Perhaps this is the time." This time Dubinsky relented. In changing his mind, he may have taken into consideration the change in ICFTU policy at the end of 1960, allowing for AFL-CIO initiatives in Africa. Dubinsky instructed Springer to talk about structuring the program with ILGWU educational director Gus Tyler. The ILGWU provided the staff, facilities, and the program. The AFL-CIO agreed to underwrite the expenses associated with bringing the trainees to the United States and supporting them.[13]

By May 1961 the garment training program had six participants hailing from Nigeria, Southern Rhodesia (Zimbabwe), Northern Rhodesia (Zambia), Kenya, and Tanganyika (Tanzania). To Charles Zimmerman, Springer remarked, "If successful, it can be the important, useful and exciting beginning of trade union association with our colleagues in Africa."[14] Similar to the 1957 scholarship program, the trainees engaged in six months of study and work. Afterwards they received a six-month stipend to organize workers in their countries.

The Pan-African and Liberation Struggle in Southern Rhodesia

Springer was pleased with Southern Rhodesia's inclusion in the AFL-CIO Garment Workers Scholarship Program. From the beginning of her relationship with the Southern Rhodesia Trade Union Congress (SRTUC), she realized the enormity of the oppression they faced, including dismally low wages that made labor organizing a herculean task. Through letters and meetings with Springer and Irving Brown, labor leaders expressed a keen desire for labor literature, access to training within and outside the country, and financial assistance to hire organizers and manage transportation.[15] Office space was also a problem. The SRTUC shared with a number of affiliates a small room in the back of a grocery store.[16]

The scholarship program, however, became entrapped in intense political rivalries. The numerous and complicated splits that soon plagued the Southern Rhodesian labor movement were directly related to the competing national liberation movements, labor's relationship with the ICFTU and the All-African Trade Union Federation, and jealousies and competition for power and limited resources. The tremendous repression the white minority regime meted out had a profound effect on both the labor and liberation struggles. The government took full advantage of splits within the movements by helping to sow discord and suspicion among rivals while repeatedly detaining political and labor leaders and banning their organizations. Throughout the turmoil of the early 1960s, the competing union leaders appealed to Springer and other AFL-CIO leaders for support. Commenting on the politics surrounding the scholarship program and the stipend, Springer remarked: "You know, a union would write to say we are unable to collect from our membership to do this, that, and the other given the restrictions. And I am sure I may have been one of those that supported the idea of a monthly stipend to the union to help the leader of the union move from here to there. I have known men, who were the leaders of the union, who have had to walk *miles* and *miles* to go from one place to the other to attend a meeting. And if this was done, it was done in that spirit. And the garment workers supported this, but that support would be used to destroy that person."[17]

Southern Rhodesian labor leaders were at first united in their support of the scholarship program and the choice of Charles Mudundo Pasipanodya as their country's trainee. Pasipanodya was the general secretary of the Southern Rhodesian Textile and Garment Workers Union (SRTGWU) and also SRTUC treasurer.[18] Detained leader Josias Terry Maluleke, who was general secretary of the commercial workers and honorary general secretary of the SRTUC, was among those who heartily welcomed the AFL-CIO program. Springer was pleased that Pasipanodya and Maluleke shared a desire to promote female labor activism.[19] Before Maluleke's release at the end of 1961, his union, the commercial workers, had turned against SRTUC president Reuben Jamela. Almost immediately after his release, Maluleke joined the attack and helped to form the rival labor center, the African Trade Union Congress (ATUC).[20]

Jamela first began facing increasing attacks in the fall of 1961, primarily charges that he was colluding with the white minority government's labor department in oppressing Africans. SRTUC deputy president Thomas E. Mswaka, who was at first perplexed by the behavior of those opposed to Jamela, soon turned against him too and supported the attacks. Less than a month before he changed positions, Springer encouragingly wrote him that she knew he was working closely with Jamela to build the labor movement. Mswaka's switch, like that of Maluleke, coincided with the intensified campaign against Jamela launched by Joshua Nkomo's Zimbabwe African People's Union (ZAPU) in December 1961.[21]

Springer believed that Nkomo misconstrued her support for Jamela to mean that she did not support his role in the liberation struggle. Following her 1960 African tour, Michael Ross, the director of the AFL-CIO international affairs department, had passed on to her a letter from Nkomo appealing for financial assistance for the political movement. She answered the letter, explaining that the AFL-CIO mainly helped trade unionists and informing him what was being done for Southern Rhodesian labor. She later believed that perhaps he thought she could have helped the liberation movement with AFL-CIO funds. Since Nkomo had better relations with some men in the AFL-CIO, she also surmised that he might have had difficulty accepting a woman as an equal.[22] In contrast, Enoch Dumbutshena, a former journalist and the London representative of ZAPU, had cordial relations with Springer. Instead of asking for AFL-CIO money, he asked her for help in making financial contacts.[23]

Nkomo also was against ICFTU affiliation. The SRTUC's affiliation to the ICFTU was interpreted as being anti-pan-African and pro-Western, and nonsupportive of party control. Moreover, Springer suggested that Nkomo opposed the anticommunist policies of the AFL-CIO and the ICFTU. After all, Western governments did not forcefully back the aspirations of the black majority. During the later guerrilla war, the Soviet Union and China, respectively, supported Nkomo's ZAPU and Robert Mugabe's Zimbabwe African National Union (ZANU), the rival liberation movements.

In January 1962 Pasipanodya arrived home from the scholarship program to discover a split national labor center and a split garment workers' union. The issues of affiliation and labor's relationship to the political struggle combined with resentment of his study tour to fuel a power struggle within the Bulawayo branch of the SRTGWU the week he returned. He wrote Springer criticizing Maluleke and Mswaka for forming the rival African Trade Union Congress. He did not inform Springer until six months later that Aaron Dunjana, who had served as acting general secretary of the garment workers while he was away, had also joined ATUC, as had his union's president.[24]

Around the time of ATUC's formation, Springer was suffering from a prolonged illness in East Africa, and she was unaware until months later of much of the correspondence. Following her recovery, she wrote Pasipanodya asking for information about the political and labor situation, and particularly about the work of the garment workers. Two months passed before he wrote to her and Joseph Shane informing them about the split in his union. Shane, the assistant manager of one the ILGWU's regional departments, was both a personal friend and a contact in the U.S. labor movement. Pasipanodya still claimed to have control of four out of five branches.[25]

Shane assured Pasipanodya of his and Springer's support. "As you also know, one of the members of our union—Maida Springer—has worked tirelessly in spite of ill health to aid and assist our African workers and their trade unions." Springer told Pasipanodya that both she and Shane agreed that a "vigorous campaign of education, information, and service to the Garment Workers Union" would be the "most effective means of combating false propaganda and misrepresentation from either union political disrupters or exploiting employers." As encouragement Shane informed Pasipanodya that the ILGWU convention had passed a resolution calling for aid to African trade unions.[26]

Inadvertently, Springer learned that Pasipanodya perhaps did not have as much support as he claimed. Because Pasipanodya no longer had control of the garment workers' mailing address, ATUC-supporter Dunjana received the AFL-CIO letter of July 14 announcing the beginning of Pasipanodya's seventy-five-dollar monthly stipend. Dunjana then wrote the AFL-CIO stating that the stipend was a "blessing" and requesting additional assistance. He also informed them that Pasipanodya had left the union, which would welcome his return.[27]

Pasipanodya's letter advising Springer to send his mail to another address crossed in the mail with the stipend letter. Requesting clarification of his status, Springer informed Pasipanodya that Dunjana had answered her letter. Pasipanodya replied that leaders of the rival garment union had labeled him an American stooge because of the stipend. However, he declared their efforts to force him out of the union and win the support of the membership had failed. A month later, after more correspondence, Springer expressed relief at receiving news from him because of the many conflicting reports about the labor movement. One report even claimed that he had joined ATUC. Assuring him that the stipend was forthcoming, she added, "I trust these funds will go toward improving workers conditions."[28]

Both Pasipanodya and Jamela appealed to Springer and other Western labor leaders for more aid, particularly for salaries and bicycles for organizers. They warned that Tettegah was helping their Communist-led ATUC rivals, while they themselves had hardly any resources. ATUC leaders also appealed to Springer and the AFL-CIO for support. Throughout 1962 and 1963, both SRTUC and ATUC leaders requested airline tickets to the United States so they could counter the "lies" of the other. ATUC officers also requested Springer's assistance in bringing pressure on the government because of its detention of labor leaders. Both Maluleke and Mswaka had been rearrested.[29]

In response to ATUC leaders asking for Springer's support and castigating Jamela, she wrote, "As a result of our interest and cooperation, the Southern Rhodesia Trade Union Congress was able to present the case of the Southern Rhodesia workers to their international colleagues. . . . In this same context, Brother Josias Maluleke's over-long detention was made known internationally, and he told me it helped him morally and otherwise. Having made some small efforts in some of these developments, the present split in the Southern Rhodesia Labor Movement and the attendant bitterness and violence is a cause for personal disappointment to me."[30]

The reported violence included a severe assault against Jamela at the funeral of the popular ZAPU deputy president, Tichafa Samuel Parirenyatwa, whom many suspected the government of killing.[31] The attack on Jamela led to two days of clashes between ZAPU and the SRTUC. A month earlier, in July 1962, ZAPU expelled Jamela and some other SRTUC leaders from the liberation movement.[32] With the government using this violence as a pretext to suppress the labor and political movements, Springer informed Pasipanodya, "All of us here are distressed over the difficult situation in Southern Rhodesia. The split in the trade union movement and the political organizations only benefit Sir Edgar Whitehead [Southern Rhodesia's premier] and Roy Welensky [premier of the Central African Federation]. I sincerely hope you all will find a way to unite your efforts and interest."[33]

To an ATUC leader Springer responded in kind, "The actions of the Southern Rhodesian Government make the need for a United Labor Movement imperative."[34] The government banned ZAPU in September and placed 243 people in restrictive custody for three months. Government repression, partly under the pretext of sympathizing with Jamela over his attack by ZAPU supporters, served to exacerbate the divisions by feeding beliefs that Jamela had been bought off by the government.[35]

Around the time of the government crackdown, the ICFTU sent Howard Robinson, an African American from the United Electrical Workers Union, to Southern Rhodesia to investigate the labor situation. Before taking a position with the ICFTU, Robinson, like many other American travelers to Africa, had sought Springer out for her knowledge of the continent. Based on Robinson's discussions with Africans, the ICFTU withdrew support from the SRTUC. It seems that both Mswaka of the ATUC and Jamela of the SRTUC were unhappy about Robinson's visit.[36] Both Pasipanodya and Jamela, however, continued to appeal to the ICFTU.

By late October 1962, Pasipanodya's assertions about his status in the garment workers' union were beginning to unravel. Using the letterhead of the Municipal and Local Government Workers Union, above which he typed the name of his own union, he wrote Dubinsky asking for quick action in getting help from the ICFTU. Two weeks later he informed Springer that at the SRTUC delegates' conference on November 10 and 11, he led a break-away movement from Jamela, whom he accused of using thugs, friends, relatives, and businessmen to ensure his reelection as president. The objective of the Unity Committee of Independent Unions, Pasipanodya claimed, was to unite all unions.[37] He requested an airplane ticket to the United States so he could explain his side and counter information the Americans might have gotten from Phineas Sithole. Sithole, who was the Bulawayo regional secretary as well as vice president of the SRTUC and leader of the Textile and Allied Workers' Union, had visited the United States in order to appear before the UN as a petitioner. Like many Africans on such a mission, he stayed at Springer's home and through her efforts met with Meany.[38]

Exasperated over the splits that had resulted in three labor centers and continuous appeals from all the groups, Springer commented, "Each group claims to speak for the workers interest. You can appreciate how difficult this is for people so far away. . . . The claims and counter claims by trade union factions do not invite confidence in requests for quick action when requested by each group." She added that Dubinsky had expressed hope that the trade union movement would become united. "In this way," she stated, "the legitimate work of the unions of Southern Rhodesia can again have the full support of the International Labor Movement." However, the ILGWU had decided against giving any financial support "in the present state of confusion."[39] The ATUC-affiliated garment workers' union received two stipend checks from the AFL-CIO before payments were stopped. In early 1963 an ICFTU mission composed of Kenyans Clement K. Lubembe, a member of the ICFTU executive board, and James Karebe, secretary of the AFRO area committee for the region, traveled to Southern Rhodesia to investigate the problems. They reported on an atmosphere filled with intrigue, suspicion, and misrepresentation, particularly against Jamela.[40]

Further union splits in 1963 were related to divisions in the liberation movement. Robert Mugabe eventually became the leader of the rival Zimbabwe African National Union. The division in the political movement began to take form at the same time that the two rival labor centers, the SRTUC and ATUC, were engaging in unity talks under pressure from the ICFTU. The ICFTU had agreed to renew financial support if the labor leaders united and remained unaligned to the nationalist movements. At the SRTUC conference in October 1963, Jamela resigned from the labor movement as part of a unity deal.[41]

A new labor center, the Zimbabwe African Congress of Unions (ZACU), affiliated with Nkomo's Zimbabwe African People's Union. ZACU accused ATUC of the same things ATUC had accused the SRTUC of under Jamela's leadership: falling prey to "imperialist agents," allying with the government, and wanting "to be insulated from and be neutral in the political struggle." ZACU opposed outside affiliation and hoped to retain friendships with all. A ZACU leader sent Springer their circulars so the AFL-CIO would have a clear understanding of the splits.[42]

ATUC leader Mswaka appealed for AFL-CIO support, explaining that although outside assistance had presented problems, they were afraid they had to continue seeking this assistance while avoiding the mistakes of the past. After receiving requests to visit the United States throughout 1963, Springer informed labor leaders that they could discuss their problems when she arrived in Southern Rhodesia after Kenya's December 1963 independence celebration.[43] On her visit she spoke with ZACU leader Francis M. Nehwati about the possibilities of unifying the divided movements. After reviewing the history of the splits with ATUC president John Dube, she concluded, "The destruction of Reuben Jamela [was] motivated by the politics on the one hand and the naiveté of the trade unionists [who] supported it on the other hand."[44]

As usual the white minority government exploited and exacerbated the crisis in the labor and political movements. Throughout 1964 and 1965, both political movements were banned and their leaders and labor allies restricted, including ZACU leader Nehwati. Curtis C. Strong, the acting labor adviser in the U.S. State Department, wrote Springer in February 1964 informing her of Nehwati's indictment. He asked her to apprise the American Federation of State, County and Municipal Employees (AFSCME) of the situation because of their connections with Nehwati's Municipal Workers Union. Strong was acting on a request from the U.S. consulate general in Salisbury. The consulate thought AFSCME

might at least want to send a message of solidarity and possibly give aid to Nehwati's defense through their affiliation with the Public Services International,
an ITS.[45]

This correspondence not only reflects the sometimes-fluid relationship between the U.S. government and labor in the international arena, but also—in relation to Springer's first visit to Southern Rhodesia—a certain shift in policy and
approach of the consulate toward the white minority government and the liberation movements. The U.S. government as a whole, however, pursued policies
that gave succor to the minority regime.

Telling Bill Lawrence, "we want to help only in those ways which will
strengthen the total work being done on behalf of the workers," Springer sought
his advice in 1964. Lawrence had come to Southern Rhodesia the previous year
as the ICFTU/ITS representative. Believing that ATUC leaders were responsible
for many of their own problems, he advised Springer not to "line up with any so
called national centre to the exclusion of the other at this stage." At this time he
thought that ZACU was gaining in popularity, particularly because of the imprisonment of Nehwati and the restrictions placed on Nkomo's movement. He also
remarked that his job was made difficult because ATUC was "suspicious that
Z.A.C.U. may be getting assistance."[46]

ATUC leaders continued to appeal to Springer for assistance in organizing
and in helping to alleviate the harsh conditions their leaders faced in detention.[47]
ATUC leader Sithole wrote her about his suspicions that ZACU was getting
WFTU assistance and noted that Lawrence had played a role in Nehwati's escape from the country. At the end of 1965, Nehwati would spend five days with
Springer as part of a delegation of African labor leaders brought to the United
States for the AFL-CIO convention and other activities. While the AFL-CIO's
strong stance against white minority rule was certainly an important factor, their
support of ZACU leaders also reflected that the losing battle over affiliation had
been superseded by efforts to maintain influence among African labor.[48]

In Springer's correspondence with Southern Rhodesians, she did not press
for ICFTU affiliation; rather, she urged unity among the competing labor movements. She saw their problems in terms not of Cold War rivalries but of the need
to withstand the opposition of a vicious white minority government. Judging
from this correspondence, these leaders disagreed with each other over outside
affiliation and labor's relationship to the nationalist movements; however, they
all valued Springer for the influence she could wield on their behalf with Western labor.

On occasion Springer heard from various leaders she had known. Returning
to the labor movement after spending a few years on his father's farm, Charles
Pasipanodya wrote her in 1968 that some workers believed that he left the union
because he was "enjoying the dollars" they thought he brought with him follow-

ing the scholarship program. He also claimed that political leaders like Mugabe admitted that they made a big mistake in destroying Jamela's leadership in ZAPU because Jamela's talent for maneuvering would have been a great asset following the government's ban on political parties.[49]

As leader of the ZANU–Patriotic Front, Mugabe established the first majority-rule government in 1980 with Nkomo's ZAPU sharing some power. Tragically, the continued rivalries, ethnic divisions, power struggles, and economic problems led Mugabe to support arrests of his opposition, using laws similar to those the white minority regime had used against the liberation movements.

The Institute of Tailoring and Cutting

When asked what she considered to be her successes in Africa, Springer responded, "I don't think I was ever satisfied with anything. Whatever you envision, you came short of the mark. But to have championed for a training school for tailors in Kenya was a reward."[50]

This school was founded over the objections of the International Textile and Garment Workers' Federation. Anselmi Karumba's participation in the 1961 garment workers' scholarship program, and his continued appeals for a training school, did not sit well with ITGWF general secretary J. Greenhalgh. The Kenyan union unanimously passed a resolution at their 1960 convention supporting the executive in efforts to find a way to establish a school. In 1961 Greenhalgh learned that the Kenyans had appealed to all of the ITGWF affiliates after a number of them wrote the trade secretariat for advice on this issue. In a letter marked "Confidential" and addressed to all the affiliates, he advised against assistance. Nevertheless, he was caught in a quandary because of the founding of the All-African Trade Union Federation that May. While acknowledging that Kenya unions needed help, he told the affiliates that he had advised the Kenyans to "drop the whole project until such times as their Union becomes more stable." Stating that the ITGWF was waiting to hear from the ITS representative in Kenya before authorizing the school, he also cautioned against working outside the ITGWF: "In any case it is obviously desirable that any assistance should be channeled through our International Federation, as it would create a very unfortunate situation if only a few affiliates made a contribution to a project of this magnitude."[51]

In a further effort to discourage any inclinations toward assistance, Greenhalgh noted that the garment union's former general secretary, who had since been dismissed, had misappropriated some funds, and other Kenya unions had misused funds as well. He pointed out that Karumba was participating in the AFL-CIO scholarship program at a time when the garment workers had been greatly weakened by an unsuccessful strike. Finally, he averred that an ITGWF member who had visited Kenya "stat[ed] quite emphatically" that, contrary to what the Kenya union said, Kenya had training facilities.[52]

In a memorandum to the ILGWU, Karumba did mention the existence of three trade schools, which provided training for males only. Of the 120 to 250 men trained in these schools, only a small number received garment training, and the training only prepared workers for certification at the lowest level. One year, out of a population of twenty-five thousand African garment workers, only eleven received training. Springer noted that twenty-two was the maximum quota for garment training in these government schools. Non-Africans found it easier to increase their skills and could also attend night training, which was not available to Africans.[53]

After Karumba returned to Kenya in January 1962, following the scholarship program, industrial disputes and strikes demanded all his attention. The disturbances were directly related to the dismally low wages Africans received. Visiting East Africa for Tanganyika's independence celebrations and Mboya's wedding, Springer observed a conflict involving a firm she had known since 1957. After the workers went on strike, a committee composed of KFL leaders and employers attempted to mediate the strike. The committee recommended a pay increase amounting to about eighty cents per month. Rejecting the recommendation, the employer proceeded to evict the 150 workers from company-owned housing, remarking flippantly, "Let your friends help you." He was referring to Irving Brown, Springer, and Edward Welsh who had recently spent time with the strikers. With the firm paying between eleven and fifteen dollars a month in wages, Springer noted that the workers' daily income, averaging between forty-four and sixty-six cents, was barely enough to purchase a day's supply of food for their families let alone other necessities. Commenting on Karumba and the other leaders, she declared, "The officers of the union are working their hearts out to build a strong union. I have known this for years and it is for this reason I have tried to help this union get a fairer hearing in the I.L.G. and other places."[54]

Six months later Karumba wrote Springer asking for help for a KFL strike concerning the issues of wages, annual leave, maternity benefits, housing allowances, and new contracts. Through Zimmerman's intercession, she was able to obtain from four ILGWU locals and the Dress Joint Board a hundred dollars each in strike support.[55]

Springer continued to push for the school, as Karumba had while in the United States for the scholarship program. To Dubinsky she insisted that the garment workers' international would act favorably only if the project had his "continued support." Rare within the context of all her correspondence regarding this project, she appealed to his anti-Communist sentiment with the statement, "This project is productive, inexpensive, and a potent anti-communist effort." Typically, Dubinsky responded, "Maida, you always come to me with your unilateral things." While he supported the school proposal, he wanted to avoid violating the protocols regarding work within an international framework.[56]

Dubinsky finally decided to have Charles Kreindler, an ILGWU vice president, present the proposal at the ITGWF executive committee meeting scheduled for September 18 in Stockholm. Meany pledged to make Springer available for the project and to solicit extra funds for the establishment of the school from the Solidarity Fund if the ITS deemed it necessary. In a letter to Kreindler, which she included with the school proposal and a memorandum on the problems of the garment workers, Springer remarked that for at least six years she had witnessed the union hamstrung in its efforts to gain better wages because of the extreme paucity of those holding certificates for the skilled classifications.[57]

Greenhalgh informed Springer and Karumba that he had "endeavoured to make a case" for the proposal at the Stockholm meeting. However, the committee had decided against the training school at its September meeting. Although Greenhalgh believed that the school could contribute to organizing the industry, he doubted that this was the best way and also contended that the school would be too costly to start and maintain. Meany's pledge was not addressed. Ignoring Springer's extensive knowledge of the union's problems, Greenhalgh acknowledged that the union needed assistance but explained that the ITGWF had decided first to "contact the ICFTU and any other organisation able to supply authentic information" and then reconsider the proposal. Under the sponsorship of five ITS's, H. M. Moulden, the president of the British Hosiery Workers Union and an ITGWF executive committee member, was preparing to visit Kenya in order to ascertain the best means of helping the garment union.[58]

Karumba took offense at Greenhalgh's statement that he was making further inquiries with people with first-hand knowledge of the problems faced by the garment union in order to determine how best to proceed. Questioning who these people were, Karumba stated that his union members were more than qualified to inform the garment workers' international about their problems and challenges. He held that if the ITGWF wanted to send an outside representative to study the situation, then his union and the KFL would work with that person. The Kenyan garment union passed a vote of thanks to both Springer and Kreindler, demonstrating their belief that these two had been working in their best interests.[59]

Not betraying her own extreme disappointment and bitterness, Springer urged Karumba not to despair because perhaps the trade secretariat would decide on equally promising ways to help the union.[60] Although she believed the ITGWF would never approve the school, she assured him that she would continue trying to find a way to implement the proposal. She later recalled:

I kept on nagging [President Dubinsky]. . . . I said I'd like to talk to some of our ILG[WU] people to see if they will make a contribution if you now feel it is OK since nothing is happening with it in the trade secretariat. He said, "All right, all right, all right." He approved it, reluctantly and said, ". . . Go talk to anybody in the ILG if you want. If anybody hears you and gives you any money to develop the program, go ahead." So I went to the Philadelphia Joint Board and spoke to them. They gave me the first ten thousand dollars to begin the Institute of Tailoring and Cutting.[61]

Springer wrote Greenhalgh thanking him for his report of the Stockholm meeting and remarking that Karumba's union and the KFL·would welcome a visit by an officer of the ITGWF secretariat. With a subtle emphasis, she let him know that she might see the officer in Kenya since she was going there to oversee the establishment of the training school that the Philadelphia Joint Dress Board had made possible.[62]

Springer and Karumba spent a busy two months working to open the institute. She exclaimed to Zimmerman that they began the effort without even a straight pin.[63] She referred to her work as "donkey-work, organization, administration, details and needling everyone to move faster to reach our objective within the scheduled time."[64]

While Springer was engaged in this work, the permanent secretary to the Ministry of Provincial Education summoned her, Karumba, and the union's education officer W. K. Mugerwa. Ironically, since the government previously had not shown any interest in expanding training in the garment field, the secretary suggested that the government could do a more efficient job with the school if the funds were given to them. Springer commented to Lovestone, "now they question this unassuming program . . . because it is underwritten by an American union." Looking to the future and surmising that Springer might be more sympathetic if the request came from an African government, Lovestone responded that he would not support turning over her project to any government, no matter who the minister of labor might be. In fact, Mboya served in that position in the transition government before the granting of independence later that year.[65]

Opening ceremonies for the school were held on March 9, 1963 and classes began two days later. Among those who showed up to take part in the four- and six-month programs were some who had spent five days traveling by bus to reach the school and others who had walked twenty miles and more. The school exceeded its limit by accepting fifty-one students. Over one hundred were put on a waiting list. Noting the enthusiasm for the school, Springer remarked, "If we had another $5000.00 we could take in three to four times the number we have now."[66]

With the ratio of men to women tailors in the industry being fifty to one,

Springer hoped that the school would give women an opening to enter the trade. The beginners' class held during the day accommodated mostly women. The evening courses were designed to help union members, who were mostly men, qualify for artisan certificates. Of the six teachers, Lucy Mark was the only woman and nonunion officer. The union had followed Springer's suggestion to hire a female teacher. At Springer's insistence, the union agreed that she would receive equal pay.[67]

Ironically, considering Springer's commitment to women's development, the women who were left out of the evening class accused her and her male colleagues of discrimination. Fifty men and nine women had registered for the evening class. Although union leaders had been told that government health regulations would allow only eighteen people for the class, they decided to admit the first thirty-one people who arrived on time on opening night. Only one among this group was a woman. When six other women subsequently arrived thereafter, they were informed that the school could not accommodate them. The women then proceeded to picket the school each night for a week. Springer recalled that the leader, whom she described as "a 90-pound doll-like figure, would point her finger at me and say in an aggrieved tone, 'You too, dada (sister)! You have joined these men, dada!'" Union leaders and Springer solved this dilemma by opening two sections of the evening class so that the six women could be admitted. Due in large measure to the support of the institute, women for the first time took the government certification tests for the garment industry.[68]

Springer continued to castigate the garment trade secretariat for its lack of support for African garment unions. To Lovestone, who had become director of the AFL-CIO international affairs department upon the death of Michael Ross, she said, "Our little school continues to be one of the best innovations in Africa. It is a serious indictment on the Garment Workers' Secretariat that they have refused to help a union which has lived up to every standard by which supposedly pure and simple trade unionists judge results. When I am less exercised about that crew I will write my views of them and their policies. When the Communists move in on this lush field they will then start howling about democracy and responsibility."[69]

A few months later she lamented, "Their lack of assistance and lack of interest in the African Garment Workers generally, and the Kenya Tailors and Textile Workers in particular, is shameful. One can only conclude that this London led group is so deeply prejudiced that even when a union demonstrates ability and initiative the secretariat remains unmoved."[70] To Charles Zimmerman she wrote, "For nine years I have been trying to speak, write, persuade whomever would listen to the importance of this sector of African workers, but to little avail." Although the AFL-CIO and the ILGWU had given some support, she asserted that more substantial help was needed.[71]

Judging from the comments of David Brombart, deputy secretary of the African American Labor Center, the relationship between African garment unions and the renamed International Textile, Garment, and Leather Workers' Federation (ITGLWF) had not improved appreciably by the late 1970s. He complained about the lack of guidance, planning, and foresight the ITGLWF displayed toward Africa: "Our impression is that the Organization's interest in the developing world is limited, that certainly the continent of Africa is not in any way a priority continent for ITGLWF. Furthermore, the ITGLWF may have a strategy, an objective, an orientation to organize workers in their profession in the developing world, but if this policy exists, it is not known to the AALC."[72]

Brombart questioned the ITGLWF for not formulating objectives for their educational seminars and for failing to evaluate the effectiveness of programs and anticipate future needs. Furthermore, he believed that the ITGLWF devoted insufficient attention to building organizational drives, assessing working conditions, gathering statistics on the textile plants and assisting unions with equipment. To correct these problems he proposed that the ITS programs be developed directly through the offices of the ILGWU instead of at the ITS headquarters, now based in Brussels. Additionally, he proposed that Springer, who served as an occasional AALC consultant, visit African textile trade unions to gather information that would help in the preparation of the AALC's program of action for 1979.[73]

Springer's five week study-tour of Zambia, Kenya, Tanzania, Malawi, and Ghana in September 1978 was carried out under the auspices of both the ITGLWF and the ILGWU. Perhaps the ITGLWF had heeded some of Brombart's comments. She was responsible for gathering information on hours, wages, and working conditions for leather and textile workers and discussing problems of mutual interest. This information would serve as a basis for making recommendations to the trade secretariat about possible new programs and ways to strengthen old programs. She visited companies with employment forces ranging from thirty-five to four thousand workers, and spoke with workers, local union leaders, officers of national labor centers, and management representatives. In general she found that workers needed better access to transportation, improved services, and better worker education programs.[74]

When Springer arrived in Kenya, officers of the Tailors and Textile Union and AALC representatives requested that she participate in the dedication ceremony for equipment that locals of the Philadelphia Dress Joint Board had donated to the Institute of Tailoring and Cutting. Since 1966 the AALC had joined the ILGWU in giving support to the school, particularly by donating needed machinery.[75] Among those attending the ceremony was a former student who had gone on to serve as a government trade testing officer for the needle trade. Fifteen years after the founding of the school, Springer was still moved by the services it provided and the sense of social responsibility it engendered. She remarked:

Present at the ceremony were about 100 daytime students, looking very smart in green uniforms with white trimmings which they had made for the occasion. In the brilliant morning sunshine, their eager young brown faces made a beautiful backdrop for the event. . . . As I made my few remarks on behalf of the Philadelphia Joint Dress Board and the ILGWU, I turned my mind's eye to an old AFL-CIO film entitled, "We are our Brothers' Keeper", which, of course, would include our Sisters' Keeper, since as trade unionists we have social conscious [sic] purposes in addition to concerns about wages, hours and conditions of service. In 1963, as in 1978, the Philadelphia Joint Board responded to a need and as one who participated from the beginning—as far back as [1957]—this was a day to remember![76]

Moreover, to Springer's delight, the government of Senegal in 1972 donated a building to house the Regional Institute of Tailoring and Cutting, a school patterned after the Kenyan institute and open to workers from all over francophone Africa. At that time the Kenyan school, with an enrollment of three hundred and four hundred more wanting to attend, had expanded to serve people from other countries, including refugees from South Africa and Namibia.[77]

The Nigerian Motor Drivers' School

At the request of the national labor movement, renamed the United Labor Congress (ULC), Springer arrived in Nigeria on November 17, 1964, to spend nearly five months advising the labor movement, helping to open the Motor Drivers' School, and working on other labor projects that the newly formed AALC was to underwrite. For many years Ezekiel O. A. Odeyemi, the general secretary of the Nigerian Motor Drivers' Union and Allied Transportation Workers, had spoken to Springer about the urgent need for a driver training school. Insufficient training was the direct cause of high accident rates among union members. Springer later commented, "Having just come from Nigeria and having survived a thousand mile road trip, I can attest to the importance" of the school.[78] In October 1963 the AFL-CIO provided a grant of twenty-five hundred dollars for the school, which was established near Lagos.[79] As a result of the appeals of Odeyemi, ULC general secretary Lawrence Borha, and others, Springer got Rudy Faupl, an international affairs representative for the International Association of Machinists (IAM), to contribute library books and tools for the school.[80] In the fall of 1964 she and Irving Brown visited Hampton Institute in Virginia to observe its vocational and technical programs and procure technical assistance for the school.[81]

With assistance from the International Labor Organization, the Austrian Federation of Labor, the IAM, the International Transport Workers' Federation (an ITS), and the AALC, the motor drivers' union was able to procure essential

materials and expand the school into its own building. The building housed facilities for a workshop, an office, and a library. The curriculum emphasized
proper driving skills, minor motor repairs, the meaning of signs, traffic regulations, geography, map reading, arithmetic to help with distance measurement,
and fundamental trade-union principles. Basic literacy was also part of the curriculum since some union members' inability to read was a direct cause of problems on the road. The school was administered entirely by union officers and
represented the only labor training center and only union-to-union project in the
entire country. It planned to train one hundred students a year.[82]

When Springer arrived in Nigeria for her five-month stay, she soon learned
of the ULC's grave financial situation. The center had to borrow money from an
ITS and from Springer. Although Meany, through the intervention of Lovestone,
had gotten the ICFTU to earmark seven thousand dollars from its Solidarity
Fund for the labor center, the payment had not arrived. Instead, the ICFTU had
requested a budget, which the ULC had provided to them. Springer requested
that the AFL-CIO cable the ICFTU to send the funds immediately. She admonished, "If the ULC dissafliates [sic] from the ICFTU it will not be for the currently popular ideological reasons but for the simple fact that a group of fairly serious and intelligent men are too often treated like children in an ungraded
class."[83]

The predecessor of the United Labor Congress, the Trade Union Congress
of Nigeria (TUCN), had split in early 1960 over the affiliation issue and disagreements about relations with Communist countries. In March 1960 TUCN president, Michael Athokhamien Ominus Imoudu, was suspended from office for
traveling to Russia and China without the consent or approval of his federation.
He and other dissidents then held a convention in April 1960, the same time the
TUCN's convention met. The dissident convention formed the Nigeria Trade
Union Congress (NTUC).[84] The United Labor Congress formed at a May 1962
conference called to unify the TUCN and NTUC. After the majority of delegates voted in favor of ICFTU affiliation and adopted the name United Labor
Congress, the NTUC, however, withdrew.

A few months earlier, the NTUC had written President John Kennedy complaining about the presence of Irving Brown and George McCray in Nigeria. At
a news conference, NTUC general secretary Mallam Ibrahim Nock expressed a
desire to have both Americans expelled. Nock charged that there was a contingent of spies operating as U.S. labor leaders and working to sabotage the unity of
the Nigerian workers. Moreover, he charged that Borha was "working with the
Pentagon and the State Department–guided AFL-CIO to sell [the Nigerian
labor movement] to American interests." McCray often traveled to the region to
implement labor seminars in his capacity as head of the Kampala College extra-
mural department. Brown was not in Nigeria at this time, but to the dismay of

Lovestone, who felt Europe needed more of his attention, he was frequently in Africa.[85] Both Brown and McCray were involved in shoring up the forces of the TUCN.

Springer's opinion of the NTUC while she was in Nigeria in 1964 was less than favorable. She reported that she had had dinner with eight executive officers of unions who had "finally been able to break away from the machinations" of the NTUC leadership. She also remarked that a number of political groups that were allied with the NTUC seemed to have access to unlimited funds from the Soviets or the Chinese.[86] The primary issue of contention Springer faced during her visit, however, was not affiliation or spy charges but who among the ULC leaders would control the African American Labor Center budget for Nigeria. Her relationship with a few labor leaders rapidly deteriorated.

On March 13, 1965, over four hundred people attended the Motor Drivers' School ceremony for the opening of its building. ULC president Alhaji Haroun Popoola Adebola introduced some of the guests and delegates, among whom were representatives of the government, foreign embassies, and ITSs.[87] The festive gathering belied the tension between Adebola and Springer that had been developing since her arrival. Adebola's grievances against her included charges that she allowed the wrong people to control the AALC budget, that she was working with the wrong union people and acting without consulting him, and that she allowed herself to be used by other people.[88] In the midst of this conflict, Springer admitted that although she was driven to finish the job assigned her, she looked forward to returning home. She felt ill and very tired.[89]

Soon after her arrival in Nigeria Springer became gravely ill. After she was found gasping for breath in her apartment, a doctor told her she had acute heart problems. Refusing this diagnosis and the prospect of "run[ning] home to enjoy poor health," she accepted a second opinion that she was suffering from extreme exhaustion, hypertension, and other symptoms that increased the possibility that she could have a stroke. Springer reported that she had been forced to admit that she could not fit a year's worth of work into three months and had cut back on her activities.[90] She would remain ill for months after her return to the United States.

Upon Springer's arrival in Nigeria, she informed Adebola that among N. Okon Eshiett, the administrative secretary, and Eric M. O. Akala, the finance officer, and Springer, any two could sign a check from the AALC budget for union work. Springer, however, was responsible for overseeing the AALC budget. Adebola did not protest this arrangement but stressed that the ULC executive committee be informed of any expenditures. In February the ULC executive committee formed a budget committee to work out a program. A month later under Adebola's leadership, the ULC decided to change the composition of the committee. Since this new committee excluded Eshiett and Akala, Adebola then informed Springer to pick two other people from the new committee who could sign AALC checks.[91]

In addition to Adebola's displeasure over the AALC financial arrangements, Springer also thought that he opposed her because she would not allow him access to AALC money to support a particular trade unionist's candidacy for the December 1964 elections, a candidate whom Springer personally liked. An Adebola supporter, V.I.M. Jack, chair of the ULC Lagos District Council, wrote that Springer "made it clear" that she could not become involved in political campaigns.[92]

E. U. Ijeh, the secretary of the ULC Western District Council and a ULC central executive committee member, joined Adebola in supporting allegations against Springer. He also charged the ULC secretariat with engaging in unorthodox procedures and making a "clandestine move" against Adebola in an effort to undermine his office.[93] Ijeh claimed that ULC deputy general secretary, Ene Henshaw, did not believe that the ULC would survive, and was therefore taking AALC money with the aim of using it in the future to support a Ghana-type organization.[94] The Ghanaian pattern of labor-government relations involved incorporating the labor movement into the government and disaffiliating from the ICFTU. Through all the infighting, ULC general secretary Borha, who had been elected to the national legislature in December 1964, was sometimes absent on political business and appears to have remained uninvolved.

All of the charges that Adebola and Ijeh made against Springer cannot be assessed thoroughly with the available documentation. Most, however, appear either to be deliberate misrepresentations or to have been blown out of proportion to their real importance.[95] Springer wrote on the bottom of one of Adebola's letters, which she sent to Lovestone along with other correspondence on this conflict, "This one was such an obvious fraud it was never sent to me." Somehow she obtained the letter anyway. In it Adebola asked her about 140 pounds she had allegedly given to a union. He felt compelled to ask her about this since he had "received similar complaints that you gave out money to some organizations."[96] On a whole the allegations against Springer indicate that Adebola's campaign against her was largely personal and centered on his lack of access to AALC funds.

Springer believed that those opposed to her gained access to her records, both in her office and at the bank. When Adebola first approached her about allegations of misconduct, she told him that she had "bent every effort to proceed within the framework of the ULC's request." She suggested that if he doubted this, she was prepared to leave the country within twenty-four hours. He replied that there had been some misunderstandings and perhaps people were giving her false information.[97]

At the end of March, when Adebola sent Springer various documents calling her work into question, he asked her to respond in writing to the ULC central executive. Stating that she welcomed his proposal, Springer also declared, "I am shocked by some of the allegations stated and implied in your letter." With Springer's friend Dollie Lowther Robinson and Murray Gross, the secretary-manager of ILGWU Local 66, due to visit the union for two days, she suggested that he and the ULC participate in the program planned for their stay. Robinson and Gross, who had run for office on the same 1942 American Labor Party ticket as Springer, were chosen as labor representatives for the East African Trade Fair sponsored by the U.S. Department of Commerce.[98]

Before the executive met, Adebola wrote two letters dated April 2 to Springer, in which he accused her of creating a wedge in the ULC by not meeting with a new committee charged with administering the AALC budget. This second committee, which he played a role in forming, supplanted the first committee. Adebola insisted that if Springer continued associating with members of the first committee who were not on the new committee, he would declare her a "persona non grata to our Congress." The second letter acknowledged receipt of her previous letter. He responded that his first impulse was not to meet with her guests because of her behavior and a previous commitment. However, after further reflection he decided to meet with them since he believed that many Americans were genuinely concerned with Nigeria.[99]

At the April 5 executive meeting, Springer charged that the allegations Adebola and Ijeh leveled at her were "without foundation or fact." She went over the charges and her expenditures in detail. To the accusation that she refused to work with the second committee, she remarked that she was not invited by the committee to participate in the one meeting it had. Stating that both AFL-CIO auditors and the U.S. Treasury Department had an interest in how she managed the AALC budget, she suggested that the ULC was not subject to such a rigorous scrutiny of their own accounts. Moreover, she held that she initiated the discussion of banking arrangements and availability of records with Adebola. In reference to the first summary report on the budget dated January 15, she stated, "To my knowledge no one has shown the slightest interest in this information."[100]

After she gave her report, shouting ensued between Henshaw and Ijeh, which developed outside into some type of a physical altercation. A few days later Henshaw wrote a letter to Adebola castigating him for his behavior toward Springer. He declared that the ULC had never authorized him "to send such hostile communications, or any communication for that matter, to a woman who has defied doctor's advice and strained her health in the interest of an organization [of] which you are supposed to be the head." Accusing Ijeh of tribalism, he also referred to him as Adebola's "boy." Ijeh responded with similar abuse and accusations.[101]

During these acrimonious exchanges Springer, having completed her assignment with the ULC, returned to the United States. However, Adebola continued to send Lovestone complaints against her. Although Springer was soon due to take a leave of absence upon her marriage to James Kemp, she wrote Borha that she was still dealing with Lagos "for the reason that the abundance of correspondence from your President makes it necessary for further documentation and discussion, if we are to proceed constructively with the work ahead."[102] Charging Springer with giving evasive answers to his questions, Adebola had informed Lovestone that if she were to return to Nigeria he would challenge her openly. Therefore, he requested that someone else be sent to do the AALC job.[103]

The AFL-CIO responded to the various charges against Springer by suggesting that Brown go to Nigeria with the objective of strengthening the labor movement and the relations between the ULC and AFL-CIO. Lovestone informed Springer, "This will, I am sure, close the matter out, and we can all forget about it." In Nigeria Brown reported that Adebola held that an atmosphere of malaise had settled around the ULC. However, Brown managed to help the leadership rally around some common objectives. And it seems an AFL-CIO donation of five thousand dollars, over ICFTU objections, toward the costs of the ULC congress scheduled for July helped to salve some feelings, in particular those of Adebola, who had felt "his presidential prerogatives had been usurped" during Springer's stay. Brown concluded, however, that there had been many misunderstandings and false accusations against Springer.[104] He remarked, "I can state without equivocation that Maida has made a real contribution during her visit and before I left Lagos everyone was united in terms of planning the work of the ULC for the future."[105] Among the individual unions voicing appreciation for Springer's stay was the largely female School Meals Caterers' Union of Nigeria.[106]

Having threatened to challenge Springer openly if she returned to his country, Adebola found himself accepting her hospitality before the year closed. He came to United States as part of an African delegation to attend the AFL-CIO convention and participate in other programs. The delegation—which included among others Alphonse Kithima, Mahjoub Ben Seddik, Francis Nehwati, Achmed Tlili, and Nana Mahomo—stayed for five days in Chicago with their host, Maida Springer, who had moved there from Washington, D.C., upon her marriage. Through the couple's contacts in the black community and with the Chicago Federation of Labor, the all-male delegation was feted.[107] The delegation also spent an evening celebrating the holidays in the Kemp home.

In 1969 Adebola used the Nigerian press as a forum to denounce George McCray and also wrote Lovestone of his complaints. At the request of Brown, who wanted McCray to work with the AALC, particularly in West Africa, McCray had resigned his ICFTU position at Kampala College in 1965. Responding to Adebola, Lovestone voiced surprise at the depth of his bitterness and asked why he brought up grievances that were a year old which he had not discussed at the time. Slightly chastising him for publicly stating his allegations instead of first allowing a discussion within labor circles, he advised him to settle the disputes with McCray during Brown's next visit. Expressing a belief that their differences could be worked out, Lovestone told Adebola that no one was perfect, but Africans in general had appreciated McCray's work over the past ten years and had gotten along with him well.[108]

Before their September 1969 conference, the ULC executive board voted to suspend Adebola from office. By an overwhelming vote, the conference sustained his suspension. Brown reported that Adebola was "discredited and humiliated," and that McCray, who delivered Meany's message to the conference, was well received. Adebola, however, was returned to office in 1971.[109]

Brown had suspected Adebola of receiving financial assistance from the Soviets and Nigerian politician Obafemi Awolowo. Back in 1965 his belief that the rival NTUC had access to both AATUF and WFTU resources had led him to call for more aid to the ULC for organizing, education, and propaganda. In the past Adebola had complained about suspected Eastern funding of the rival NTUC and about ICFTU and ITS personnel associating with Communists and their allies in the NTUC.[110] By 1976 he launched allegations against his former allies from the West. Subsequent literature critical of AFL-CIO foreign policy reported that Adebola suspected that foreign labor operating in Nigeria "had something to do with the CIA." Moreover, he is quoted as saying, "Since the advent of the African-American Labor Center in Nigeria . . . treachery and betrayal has found a comfortable asylum." In this literature his dismissal from the ULC is explained in terms of his unwillingness to submit to U.S. domination; financial assistance from the West, in particular, is viewed as damaging to African labor.[111] The problem that unmonitored financial assistance posed for leadership accountability, however, involved both the ICFTU and the WFTU. The continued factional fighting and reports of corruption led the Nigerian government to ban international affiliation in 1974.[112]

Aid from Eastern and Western sources, although badly needed, became a factor in the power struggles within labor centers and various national unions. However, African labor leaders were not mere pawns between the East and the West, nor were they pliant recipients of corrupting aid. Whether embracing ICFTU affiliation or positive neutrality, they pursued strategies that they believed would benefit their labor movements, their independent nations, or their own personal advancement. In the competition for scarce resources, complicated by the Cold War and hostile white-ruled governments, some of these labor leaders with varying degrees of social consciousness sought to perpetuate their own power.

10

Crossroads

EHUD AVRIEL, THE ISRAELI AMBASSADOR TO GHANA,
once commented to Springer about his trip to Tanganyika, "I am conscious of the value of your introduction. . . . the way I was received was
clearly because of my presence having been sponsored by you." During
his 1965 trip to Africa, ILGWU leader Murray Gross attested to the respect accorded Springer, saying that her name served as "a password in most of Africa."[1]
Her reputation remained largely unchanged even as labor centers increasingly
began to leave the International Confederation of Free Trade Unions (ICFTU).
Interested in building socialist societies, many African nations developed into
one-party states, incorporated their labor movements into the governments, and
advanced the movement for disaffiliation from the ICFTU.

The labor movement represented a possible challenge to government policies and a potentially destabilizing force on the road to nation building.[2] Desperately in need of foreign investments and development assistance, governments
put a premium on industrial peace. Governments, employers, and unions were
supposed to work as partners in decreasing unemployment and raising standards
of living. Ensuring this peace required that unions play a consultative and advisory role to the government and submit to compulsory arbitration. In this arrangement workers would be protected from lockouts and the employers from strikes.[3]

In practice, however, protecting the peace often translated into suppression of strikes and wage increases, arrests, and exile.

Springer's misgivings about disaffiliation and the circumscription of the labor movements were balanced by her sympathies for the problems African leaders faced in their efforts to bring about decent standards of living for their people. Yet she hoped African nations could find a humane and cooperative way to institute development that would not be based on either Eastern or Western models: "I believe that the independent countries cannot bear the price of capitalism exacted from people for such a long time. Neither will they stand for the harsh brutality created by Stalin's forced investment exacted from the backs of the peasants and factory workers."[4]

Although the labor movement was second only to intellectuals in promoting independence, Springer was concerned with the ignorance about the movement "in the elite and opinion making circles." She held that the newly established African American Labor Center (AALC), as well as the ICFTU, International Labor Organization (ILO), and United Nations, ought to take responsibility for educating citizens about it.[5] She also commented that labor unions must work with their governments to establish viable economies, thereby demonstrating that "national loyalty and defense of workers' rights are not incompatible."[6]

However, Springer's association with the policies of the U.S. labor movement strained some of her relations with African leaders. Her sympathies with the nation-building policies of African governments also put her increasingly at odds with the AFL-CIO over the issue of trade union independence. If she remained with the AFL-CIO International Affairs Department, Jay Lovestone and others would want her to challenge national governments' restrictions on labor movements, their associations with Communist countries, and repression against labor activists opposed to government policies. The clashes between the AFL-CIO and African governments brought her to a crossroads.

Advisor to Labor Movements

Springer's popularity in Africa in part stemmed from her services as an advisor to the young labor movements, some of which, like the Mauritius Trade Union Congress, requested her to help with programs aimed at eliciting greater participation by women.[7] In Ethiopia in December 1963, she served as one of labor's advisors during the country's first-ever labor-management agreement, which involved a sugar plantation union. Accompanying her to Ethiopia following the Kenya independence celebrations were Ed Welsh and Otto Solomon Beyene, general secretary of the newly established Confederation of Ethiopian Labor Unions (CELU). Conscious that this agreement would stand as a model,

Springer stayed up late at night reviewing the positions of the labor union and management so that she could advise the labor leaders before the start of contract negotiations. Celebrating their solidarity, Springer, Welsh, and the CELU's executive council had a small dinner party in a hotel at the end of her six-day visit. Some officers traveled seventy miles to be present. Impressed by the determination of the young leaders, she wrote, "I hope this early history of the labor movement is recorded somewhere before it is forgotten. These young boys deserve a story by themselves."[8]

With the backing of the Liberian Ministry of Labor, Springer was able to serve as an advisor in late January 1965 to Liberia's Congress of Industrial Organizations (CIO) in the country's first-ever National Industrial Relations Conference involving government, labor, and industry. Industry, which was dominated by U.S. companies, failed in its attempt to prohibit her participation. Named after the U.S. federation, the CIO was virtually hamstrung by inexperience and a government that permitted gross exploitation of workers. CIO leaders asked her to find ways of providing technical, financial, and legal assistance. Weeks later she was able to procure for them checks for two hundred dollars for automobile repairs and five hundred dollars for the partial payment of wages due to union officers.[9]

Conflict in Tanganyika

AFL-CIO leaders were generally not as interested in the dangers that Western corporations posed to the economies of independent Africa as they were in ferreting out possible sources of Communist advancement. George McCray and Springer took a different approach. McCray tried to bring the subject of neo-colonialism to the "fullest attention" of his American colleagues.[10] Springer refused to criticize the development of one-party states and the incorporation of labor movements into the governments, and helped to promote programs that she hoped would stimulate the growth of African-owned industries. Yet she found herself in a poignant position. Some of her former labor colleagues became government officials and participated in the government's suppression of trade-union demands. Beleaguered union members would complain to her.

Former AALC deputy director David Brombart recalled that Springer was among a small group within the AFL-CIO who believed that Africans would eventually change the political structure of one-party rule and government control of labor unions. Sympathetic to the problems faced by these new governments, they did not support a struggle against the African political structures, nor did they associate these structures with communism.[11] Jay Lovestone, who had a covert long-term relationship with the CIA, made a distinction between the voluntary cooperation of labor and government as two separate entities and the forced cooperation brought about by legislation that incorporated the labor movement into the party structure.

The exchanges between Lovestone and Springer concerning Tanganyikan developments illustrate how Western labor's support of freedom of association conflicted with the priorities of nation building. The new African states and Western labor figuratively spoke different languages, a consequence of their differing economic, political, and historical roots. Irving Brown understood these differences and noted that Springer's services in Tanganyika could be valuable. Regretting that illness had once again debilitated her, Brown wrote in early 1961, "If Maida were well enough, she could render a real service since she is both respected and loved here. Furthermore, she would have the flexibility to understand that due to peculiar conditions here, as in all Africa, trade unions will not be organized precisely along western lines and will have to be aligned more with parties and governments than is permitted in the West,—and especially in the U.S.A."[12]

ILGWU educational director Mark Starr, while on a UN technical assistance program to Tanganyika in early 1961, also remarked that Springer understood better than her colleagues the hardships of African labor: "The youth and scarcity of the leaders, the illiteracy of the union members . . . the lack of technical training to make Africanization of the better jobs possible, the 20 pounds per capita income per year—are all serious problems. . . . But there is friendliness, hope and expectation!"[13]

The problems of organized labor were compounded by the movement of experienced leaders into government service. While Springer bemoaned this drain on the movements and was concerned about the lack of training among the new cadre of union leaders, she also understood the need of the new governments for skilled people. Labor's hardships in Tanganyika contributed to the eruption of a series of bitter strikes in 1959 and 1960. In response the Tanganyika African National Union's move to centralize the labor movement and bring it under greater party control exacerbated tensions between the Tanganyika Federation of Labor (TFL) and TANU.[14]

Lovestone expected Randolph and Springer to oppose the moves of African governments to adopt the Ghanaian pattern of labor-government relations. Lovestone suggested to A. Philip Randolph, who was disturbed by Nkrumah's suppression of strikes in Ghana, that he write an open letter to African leaders discussing democratic rights and the proper relationship of labor unions to political parties. Although Randolph expressed interest, Lovestone later remarked that he had yet to hear from him.[15]

By late 1961 Lovestone expressed to Springer his "deep disappointment" in Julius Nyerere, whom he viewed as moving in a "dangerous" direction with the trade union movement and in his relations with China. He was particularly dis-

turbed that Nyerere might be responsible for TFL members studying in East
Germany at Bernau Workers University, arguing that they could not learn "free
trade unionism" in a Communist country. That year a delegation of TFL leaders
also attended the World Federation of Trade Unions (WFTU) congress in
Moscow.[16]

In response Springer pointed out the shortcomings of the West. Noting that
much fundamental work still had to be done to help advance trade unionism in
Africa, she wondered "how some of our international colleagues, if they really
had the African workers at heart, could have wasted so much precious effort in
acrimonious debate over who was influencing what." She also expressed hope
that Lovestone had spoken with Nyerere during his visit to New York for Tanganyika's admission into the United Nations.[17]

Through Brown, who had seen Nyerere, Lovestone learned of some of the
leader's concerns for his nation. Lovestone understood that some trade unionists
might use the labor movement in ways detrimental to the country; however, he
remained unpersuaded: "[F]ears and evil people come and go but principles stay
and principles can be advanced only if they are defended and promoted regardless of individuals who try to distort them in order to embarrass, for their own personal ambitions, Nyerere and others."[18] Springer, in turn, explained the motivations of Africans by commenting on the struggle her friends had waged for
"recognition as men, and the right to govern themselves with skill, intellect,
tenacity and humor. They are going to need these qualities and more to cope
with the internal problems they are now facing."[19]

By 1963 new legislation in Tanganyika restricted workers' right to strike and
gave greater administrative powers over the TFL to the Minister of Labor. Part of
the government's aim was to reduce waste and inefficiency and direct resources
toward unions that most needed them. The plantation workers, who prided
themselves on autonomy, and other unions defied this new legislation and went
out on strike. Noting Tanganyika's new labor laws, Springer recognized the danger industrial unrest posed for African labor movements. Concerning neighboring Kenya, she warned that if labor leaders did not operate on the basis of the industrial relations charter that Tom Mboya had played a major role in crafting, the
government might pass restrictive labor legislation of the kind "so popular in a
number of African countries." Still, her sympathies were apparent. She noted
that her Tanganyikan friends told her to pay as "much attention to the many safeguards that benefit workers" in this legislation as she did to the restrictions that
troubled her. These benefits included a minimum wage, unemployment compensation, annual leave, holidays, insurance, and one-month's notice prior to termination.[20] Unmoved, Lovestone asked why "spoil the good measures by adding
the bad ones?"

"Poor girl! You are going to have a rough time. Some of our friends apparently were very good fighters against foreign despotism. However, they must be short of breath by now and are ready to think that there can be no other despotic measures than those applied by their former colonial masters. . . .

I am afraid that our trade union friends are human beings. I am afraid they are, therefore not perfect like the rest of us. I am still more afraid that the people who have the power, who are anything but perfect will then try to take desperate and despicable advantage of mistakes and weaknesses which are inevitable in every young movement—and, yes even in an older movement.[21]

Springer's labor associates and friends expanded their contact with Communist countries. According to one report, TFL acting general secretary Alfred Cyril Tandau denied that there was forced labor or that state workers were exploited in the Soviet Union after he attended May Day celebrations there in 1963. A year earlier, while on an AFL-CIO trip to the United States, he had stayed with Springer for two weeks as her personal guest. In mid 1963 TFL deputy general secretary, Joseph Rwegasira, who also was a friend of Springer's and had received training in the Soviet Union, disaffiliated the TFL from the ICFTU. He took this action, which was without constitutional authority, in the wake of the government's plan to become a one-party state and build the East African Federation, the proposed union of the governments of Tanganyika, Uganda, and Kenya. The federation, however, was not realized.[22]

The TFL general council rejected ICFTU disaffiliation and the proposed government legislation aimed at making the TFL an integral part of the Ministry of Labor. Threats of a TFL general strike to bring down the government, and the support some leaders gave to a failed military mutiny in January 1964, led the government to dissolve the federation and detain two hundred leaders and active members. The government replaced the TFL with a new national structure named the National Union of Tanganyikan Workers (NUTA). In NUTA separate affiliates were dissolved and all workers belonged to the national center. NUTA became part of the apparatus of the political party and disaffiliated from the ICFTU. Former TFL president Michael Kamaliza, who had become Minister of Labor in 1961, was appointed general secretary of NUTA.[23]

The Tanganyikan government held that political stability was necessary in order to fight their foremost enemies: disease, poverty, and ignorance. Although concerned about the limitation on trade-union rights, Springer was equally concerned about the need for political stability. She remarked to Lovestone, "Perhaps we have not always realized the odds against which [African leaders] must work to build a functioning and developing social, political system." Politically ambitious men, she asserted, were ready take advantage of the national weakness due to unemployment and economic stagnation in order to create greater instability and insure their own rise.[24] In relation to the political movement to institute the East African Federation, she noted of the unions in the transportation sector, "Industrial strife politically induced in Tanganyika would have serious repercussions in Kenya and Uganda." Christopher Tumbo, the general secretary of the railway workers, was suspected of having encouraged the formation of a rival political movement.[25]

Springer began to consider what economic changes would make it possible for every African to have at least one pair of shoes, or for families of trade unionists to have houses with floors and running water. She held that the AFL-CIO should no longer view its role in Africa in terms of teaching traditional trade-union techniques and organizing methods. This approach would conflict with the policies of African governments. Instead the AFL-CIO could help African workers by implementing programs that would "transcend political developments and momentary instabilities of government." She favored instituting joint programs with African governments aimed at improving industrial skills, housing, and literacy among workers.[26]

After NUTA instituted a compulsory checkoff system for the collection of union dues, the government authorized 60 percent of these funds to be used to support the union's economic arm, the Workers' Investment Corporation. Springer discussed with Nyerere and Tandau the possibility of U.S. labor unions providing a loan to the government to build workers' housing. They estimated that a minimum of eighteen thousand new homes would be needed to transform the urban slums. They also saw this project as a way to help alleviate employment and add prestige to the labor movement. Springer held that if unions were to engage in this kind of "nonpolitical" work, their members "would be a less likely target for those who consider the five percent of people who are workers as a semi-privileged class."[27] However, Springer soon recognized that NUTA's creation represented an obstacle in gaining AFL-CIO support for the workers' housing plan.

During the ILO meeting held in Geneva between June 17 and July 9, 1964, Springer, Irving Brown, and Michael Kamaliza discussed the workers' housing plan and the possibility or procuring a U.S. expert on investments who could advise the Workers' Investment Corporation. Later hearing rumors that Kamaliza perceived that she and Brown had been uncivil during their meeting and had lost interest in the Tanganyikan workers, Springer became disheartened. These rumors came out of conversations Kamaliza had with U.S. embassy personnel in Tanganyika and an AFL-CIO visitor.[28]

Springer, who knew their discussions had gone badly, questioned Kamaliza about the rumors. He told her that he understood her to have said that with the changes in the labor movement, "our chances to get this loan were small since the money you hoped to raise for us comes from a 'Free Labour Financing Organisation' which, of course, finances the 'Free Labour Movement.'"[29] Western labor considered NUTA a government entity and therefore not free and autonomous. Regarding the rumors, however, he assured her that they were unfounded and that differences in approach would not interfere with their friendship.[30] Former TFL general secretary Rashidi Kawawa, now serving as second vice president of the country, agreed: "You should rest assured that in Mwalimu Nyerere, Michael and myself you have most trusted friends. And also we trust you. Your services to Tanganyika at that most crucial time will never be forgotten. You will always remain dear in our hearts. I hope whoever writes the Trade Union and Political history of Tanganyika will never forget to include your name—for it won't be complete without mentioning the very vital part you played." Asking for her understanding if governments had not developed the way she had expected, he stated that they had to develop institutions to best deal with the challenges they faced.[31]

In terms of Tanganyika's decisions about how best to promote development, Springer remarked, "The one mistake I hope I have never made, Rashidi is to use the United States' present development as the yardstick by which other developing countries are to be measured."[32] To Kamaliza she stated, "During my entire career I have been judicious in the use of such terms as 'freedom' and 'democracy', for I am among those who hold the view that this commodity is still in short supply in too many parts of the world including sections of my own country."[33] Indeed, not until after the passage of the 1964 Civil Rights Act and the 1965 Voting Rights Act did Springer say she was willing to give living in the United States a second chance.[34]

Regarding the housing plan, Springer explained that she had U.S. union pension funds in mind as the source for the loan. Although the pension funds had many legal restrictions and any proposal would be "subjected to the most rigorous scrutiny," she believed that the housing plan would have received "careful consideration" out of respect for Nyerere. Yet she knew that the creation of NUTA "raised additional difficult questions." Springer regretted that the second meeting that she and Brown were supposed to have had with Kamaliza in Geneva had not materialized. They had wanted his input concerning the tentative plans the AFL-CIO had for developing the African American Labor Center, which would engage in economic and social projects.[35]

Springer's situation continued to be conflictual. Lovestone left the decision to attend NUTA's 1965 convention up to her, but he indicated that if she went, she should be prepared to "stand by, publicize, advocate openly and energetically, the contents and policy" contained in the recent AFL-CIO executive council statements. "Sweeping differences under the rug, hiding positions or

opinions," he averred, "will never do and had best be forgotten."[36] In these statements the AFL-CIO condemned the move toward "totalitarian methods like the
one-party system, the curtailment of democratic rights and the destruction of the
independent character of the rising trade union movement in order to achieve
speedy industrial progress." The AFL-CIO held that "the experiences and plight
of the communist countries provide ample proof that totalitarian methods do not
assure sound rapid economic development."[37] Writing from Nigeria, where she
had fallen ill, Springer declined the offer. She indicated that her poor health
would not allow her to take on "such an assignment" given the expected presence of "Chinese, the Soviets, the Zanzibarians and their ilk from the people's
democracies."[38]

AATUF Collides with the AALC

As the ICFTU continued to lose influence in Africa, the AFL-CIO decided
to establish the African American Labor Center (AALC), a nonprofit private organization. Funded through the U.S. Agency for International Development,
the AALC formed a three-way partnership with African governments and the
labor centers to implement projects for the labor movements. Springer and Mc-
Cray joined the AALC with Irving Brown serving as executive director.

With Northern Rhodesia and Tanzania (the new name of Tanganyika after it
merged with the island nation of Zanzibar in 1964) joining the All-African Trade
Union Federation (AATUF) by 1964, Springer remained on good terms with
Kenneth Kaunda and Julius Nyerere, the political leaders of the two countries.
However, following the AFL-CIO's decision to establish the AALC, AATUF's
hostility toward the federation increased.[39] AATUF propagandists accused the
ICFTU, as an imperialist arm of the West, of supporting plots to overthrow the
African governments in Kenya, Uganda, and Tanzania. They accused Springer
of "using her notorious weight" to help to establish neocolonialism in Africa, and
charged McCray with being thrown out of Uganda and Brown of being a CIA
agent planning the subversion of African labor via the AALC.[40] They also accused Brown of dispensing so much money in Casablanca, when the AATUF
was established, that "[d]ollars and francs literally flowed along the streets." Due
to their increased activity AFL-CIO representatives were portrayed as being to a
greater degree than Europeans "over bearing and insidious."[41]

Believing that the AATUF was not as neutral as it professed, Western labor
speculated that AATUF supporters sometimes got more assistance from Communist countries than the West was giving to ICFTU affiliates. By at least 1964
the AATUF secretly accepted financial assistance directly from the WFTU and
began making strong pronouncements linking the African international ideologically with the WFTU. The West then viewed the AATUF's insistence on nonalignment as dishonest.[42]

Subjected to a great deal of negative press by AATUF propagandists, Kampala College became one of the casualties of the pan-African labor struggle. Like the protectorate government before, the African government instituted in 1962 viewed Kampala College as a threat. The curriculum, which McCray had a hand in shaping, was seen as too radical and tendentious, and not suited for the needs of postindependence Africa. Ugandan government officials believed that the staff helped to foster the belief that employers were enemies of the workers, thus contributing to irresponsible strikes and unrealistic demands. While this attitude was proper under colonialism, it was deemed dangerous under independent rule, as African governments sought to build a stable investment climate for foreign capital. Sven Fockstedt from Sweden, the first Kampala College principal, argued that government officials were not aware that the school's curriculum had changed to reflect the need of labor unions to work with African governments in order to serve the larger interests of their societies for economic and social development.[43] In late 1964 Brown wrote George Meany that he hoped a delegation composed of ICFTU officials and government officials of now-independent Uganda would investigate the school and "clear the air of allegation, rumors, etc."[44]

AATUF propaganda encouraged the government in its continuous efforts to take over the school. Through the control of visas, the government by 1965 made it impossible for McCray to remain employed at Kampala College as well as anyone else who was not East African. That same year Kampala College principal Reuben M. Mwilu of Kenya complained that the warnings that he and his predecessor, Joseph Odero-Jowi, had given about the dangers of AATUF propaganda had not been not heeded. The ICFTU's failure to respond to this propaganda, he maintained, gave validity to accusations that ordinarily had no merit.[45] Later that year Brown met with Ugandan prime minister Milton Obote to discuss the "labor situation, the AALC and, above all, the school." Brown reported that the meeting was friendly and that Obote was anxious to seek an amicable solution to the school problem. In 1968 the government took over the school and compensated the ICFTU on its own terms.[46] After all the battles within the ICFTU concerning the school's formation and expenses, Kampala College's termination was a great disappointment for Springer.

ICFTU affiliation quickly dwindled throughout Africa. The problems arising from competing labor centers and the decision of African governments to adopt the Ghana model contributed to the decision of some governments to force rival labor centers to unify and to sever ICFTU affiliation. In East Africa, Tanganyika led the way followed by Kenya and Uganda. In 1963, when Tanganyika first showed evidence of moving away from ICFTU affiliation, John Thalmayer, the representative in East Africa for the International Federation of Building and Wood Workers, an ITS, vented his frustration with ICFTU policy and the direction of African unions. In a letter to Arthur McDowell, director of the Upholsterers' International Union's International Labor Relations Department, he wrote: "We have given our African Brothers nothing but money and lots of fancy words—period. I swear to you, Arthur, the only ones that still listen to us are the ones on the bottom. The top has flitted away."[47]

McDowell's response, a copy of which he sent to Springer, offers insight on the relations African American labor representatives formed in Africa. He stated that European leaders, and especially the British, thought that since they had socialist beliefs, they had something in common with African leaders who advocated socialism. However, he averred:

> The lasting and binding ties [are built on] in order of importance, the individual friendships formed on basis of quality and character and principles of the individuals, common experiences in approach and solution to problems, and similar attitudes developed in terms of respect and honor for the individual and genuine love of freedom. Ideology will be weakest of all. . . . Love of a particular system of economic administration and set of doctorines [sic] and dogmas about how organizations and governments shall be set up is dry, brittle and often meaningless binding material. The ICFTU will continue to lose affiliations like that of Tanganyika, which is bad enough in view of parental sacrifice to bring movement to birth these [sic] but much worse, they will not understand why.[48]

Springer understood why. Although her activism became caught up in the atmosphere of suspicion, innuendo, propaganda, and corruption that developed out of the fierce struggle over the affiliation issue, her personal reputation largely weathered the storm.

Mboya and the "American Label"

In 1963 Lester Granger cautioned Springer against moving to Africa. Until that year she had seriously considered settling in Tanganyika. Instead, Granger urged her to accept David Dubinsky's offer of an ILGWU vice presidency. He reasoned that although the union was declining in strength, it was still stable and in a better position than most internationals because it was run with intelligence and conviction "of a sort not to be found in large areas of AFL-CIO." Holding that he had "no enthusiasm" for the prospect of her severing ties with the United States, Granger argued that the situation in Africa was "too volatile for you to have any assurances at all that there will be a place for you two or three years from now." Under Dubinsky and his successor, he concluded, Springer would have respect and a stable relationship "that simply can't be counted on in *any* African country—not even Tanganyika." Having known Springer since she was a young girl, Granger invited her to live in New York with him and his wife. He advised her to use her experience to her best advantage and reflected that she could "always find ways of keeping up with Africa."[49] Moreover, he maintained that working from a seat of power would enable her to defend herself from attacks and promote her African projects. But Springer refused the vice presidency offer, viewing it as a token position with no power. She also decided against moving to Africa.

Unable to resolve the conflicts between the AFL-CIO and African labor leaders, Springer resigned in January 1966. Her marriage to Jim Kemp, her recurring illnesses, and the health of her aging family were also factors in her decision. Two years previously her ninety-four-year-old grandmother had come from Panama to live with them. The pressure on Mboya to distance himself from his American friends and associates also had an impact on how she assessed the value of continuing her involvement in Africa. A subtle shift in her perception of her work occurred in 1963, while she was working on a housing project for Kenyan workers.

This project came about as a direct result of Mboya's influence on Springer. Radical critics later characterized Mboya as a willing collaborator with the West, a leader who perpetuated class inequalities in Kenya and underdeveloped the country through his promotion of a mixed capitalist economy. Mboya, however, had great concern for the plight of poor people and criticized the inequalities that development policies produced within countries and between poor and rich nations.[50]

On Springer's trips to Kenya, Mboya would drive her to areas where workers lived. As the two walked around, he would discuss the poor housing conditions and the limitations workers faced because of substandard earnings and poor education. Mboya had been impressed by union housing projects in the United States and wanted something similar for African workers. He also discussed housing needs with various AFL-CIO officials. George Meany eventually authorized Springer to pursue discussions about a joint venture with the German labor federation's Neue Heimat International, an organization concerned with building workers' housing. In January 1963 she traveled to Germany, where she observed their housing projects. The following month she attended a meeting in Kenya with Neue Heimat representative Herbert Weisskampf, Nairobi city treasurer A. W. Kemp, the assistant city treasurer, and the director of social services and housing. The AFL-CIO and Neue Heimat each agreed to provide a loan of 134,000 pounds to the city council for the cost of building 287 homes.[51]

Feeling enthusiastic about the progress they had made, Springer and Weisskampf went to Mboya's office to apprise him of the discussions. She understood that Mboya was always busy, but the length of time he had them wait was unusual. Moreover, he met them with an aloofness and coolness that baffled her, although he desperately wanted this project for workers. She rationalized by attributing his demeanor to the tremendous political pressure on him. His detractors, she knew, despised his success in getting education scholarships and funding for Solidarity House.

Springer continued to work on the housing project, which the AFL-CIO executive council approved in the fall of 1963. However, the AFL-CIO reversed itself and rejected the plan the following year. Extremely disappointed, Springer blamed herself, believing that she had negotiated poorly. The AFL-CIO wanted assurances that a change in the Kenyan government would not mean the invalidation of the loan, which would come from U.S. workers' pension funds. Springer suggested that her eagerness to get the housing made her discount the need to attain the proper assurances for the AFL-CIO. Walter Reuther stated that since the AFL-CIO funds were not fully insured, the federation could not make the loan.[52]

Although Springer and Mboya never discussed the critical moment that led her to question her future work in Africa, they continued to maintain friendly contact with one another. He informed her ahead of time whenever he traveled to the United States, and she would meet him at the airport. The last time they met was three months before his assassination. Traveling to Africa on a short, whirlwind assignment for the AALC, Springer stopped in Kenya to present a gift of equipment from an ILGWU local to the Institute of Tailoring and Cutting. Among the people who met her at the airport was Mboya's brother, Alphonse Okuku, who told her that Mboya wanted to speak with her. Pleading exhaustion, she asked him to allow her two hours of rest. After the allotted time, Okuku arrived at her hotel and took her to the airport to see Mboya, who was then on his way to an East African minister's conference. Upon their arrival, however, a number of young African ministers surrounded her and accused her of neglecting to inform them that she had returned to East Africa. With all the laughing and joking, time passed quickly and she was not able to speak privately with Mboya. He asked her to walk to the plane with him, hugged her at the steps, and said good-bye.

After Mboya's assassination on July 5, 1969, Springer was filled with remorse for not having gone directly to his house from the airport. His wife, Pamela, she thought in hindsight, would have made a bed for her and gotten her something to eat. It pained her that they would never have the discussion that he with some urgency had wanted. Her grief at first prevented her from writing an article about Mboya for the *Free Trade Union News*, as Jay Lovestone pressed her to do. Although she respected Lovestone, she remarked that he had ice in his veins. He was not one to understand allowing emotions to interfere with what he considered duty.

In the article she eventually wrote, Springer recalled her last meeting with Mboya, remembering "his quiet smile and thank you" after she complimented him on the efficient and courteous attention she had received at the airport. Between 1956 and 1961 the colonial immigration officers had "harassed, threatened and insulted" her dozens of times as she traveled to and from Nairobi. Mboya too had been no stranger to that harassment. She also commented on the differences that had developed between him and the Western labor. "As one who admired Tom, I do not want to leave the impression that Tom and his colleagues were always in accord. Often we were pained by the choice he made, but whatever choice he made, one was always certain it was made for the reason that he was convinced that the decision was in the best interest of his country and Africa."[53] She lamented, "an assassin's bullets, the final political tool has cheaply spent his life."[54] Mboya's death is a poignant example of actions in postindependence Africa that caused great pain for Springer. Although the assassin was arrested and subsequently executed, questions remain about the possibility of wider political involvement in planning Mboya's death. For months rumors of his impending assassination preceded the final act.

Postscript

Over the years Socialist leader Norman Thomas and Springer had supported many of the same causes. Beginning in 1958 she served with him on the board of directors of the Institute on International Labor Research. In 1966 Thomas informed her that the Institute was no longer viable and expressed his disappointment about her resignation from the AFL-CIO Department of International Affairs. The AFL's Latin American foreign policy, he held, was regrettably to the right of the *Wall Street Journal*. More recently, the AFL-CIO and the ILGWU supported the Johnson administration's invasion of the Dominican Republic.[55]

With the AFL-CIO's anticommunist policies in Africa, Latin America, and Viet Nam coming under increasingly criticism, Springer appears to have resigned at an opportune time. Charges that Lovestone and Brown had accepted CIA money, particularly for AFL activities in postwar Europe, gained credibility in 1967. However, Lovestone's longstanding close friendship and professional relationship with CIA counterintelligence official Jim Angleton remained undisclosed.[56]

After losing contact with Lovestone, Springer wrote him in 1977 to tell him that Ras Makonnen had told her of the influence Lovestone had once had on George Padmore. Neither Lovestone nor Padmore had discussed with Springer their association with one another while in the Communist Party. After Nkrumah's overthrow, Makonnen was jailed until Jomo Kenyatta engineered his release. In 1983 Menelik Makonnen informed Springer of his father's rapidly deteriorating health. As a tribute to the labor and financial resources Makonnen had dedicated to Africa's independence, many African dignitaries attended his funeral.[57]

After the AFL-CIO's determined efforts to maintain African labor organizations' affiliation with the ICFTU, the federation itself withdrew from the international in 1969. Among the reasons were the continued contacts between ICFTU affiliates and unions from Communist countries, a failure to increase and properly oversee aid to developing countries, and the ICFTU's consideration of UAW affiliation after Walter Reuther withdrew the union from the AFL-CIO in 1968. Ironically, Brown, Lovestone, and Dubinsky, three of the prominent Cold Warriors, opposed the decision to leave the ICFTU. They still held that it was better to work through the ICFTU to effect change. After an absence of twelve years, the AFL-CIO rejoined the ICFTU on January 1, 1982.[58]

Under the auspices of the Organization of African Unity, founded by African states in 1963, African labor centers united to form the Organization of African Trade Union Unity (OATUU), in April 1973. Although the former rival labor internationals, the All-African Trade Union Federation and the African Trade Union Confederation, had long since ceased to be active forces, the question of ICFTU affiliation remained a hotly contested issue. Up until the early 1990s, the small number of ICFTU affiliates within OATUU faced continuous pressure to withdraw from the ICFTU.[59]

Self-rule during the first generation following African independence was undermined by the spread of dictatorships and military rule. These in turn suppressed the labor movements. Noted for his humanism, Julius Nyerere gave up the leadership of Tanzania in 1985 and later encouraged Tanzanian leaders not to oppose the movement for multiparty democracy that had begun to sweep Africa. He informed Springer that he was aware of the danger of a one-party state "becoming slack instead of continuing to serve the people."[60]

The Cold War preoccupations of U.S. policy makers remained a disappointment to Nyerere. As late as 1986 he complained to Springer, "I can't convince your leaders in Washington that no African leader wants his country to be a puppet of the Soviet Union."[61] Mentioning his plans to visit New York under the auspices of the Council on Foreign Relations, he distinguished his feelings about U.S. policy from his relationships with Americans like Springer. "You see that in the course of time, and after succeeding in basic objectives, 'agitators' can become very respectable! Whether they will like my message any better now than they used to do has yet to be seen—but it frequently seems to me that the U.S. Administration and . . . Tanzania could hardly be further apart on the basic international questions. The important thing, however, is not to give up even when you seem to make no impact—and I am often encouraged by understanding and activity by masses of ordinary people in your country."[62]

Springer's record of service to African labor and independence movements still elicits strong praise from veteran labor and political leaders, especially in East Africa. When she spent the summer of 1991 living in Tanzania, she met with old friends including Bibi Titi Mohammed, Kanyama Chiume, Maynard Mpangala, Joseph Rwegasira, and Michael Kamaliza. Bibi Titi reflected, "Maida is by nature a very cheerful, open-hearted person and as a result we became very fond of her." Mpangala said of Springer, "Americans would not have known of us but through her."[63] During her summer stay the veterans of the labor movement and the foreign relations department of the labor center gave a dinner in her honor.

The end of the Cold War helped to facilitate the movement in Africa toward multiparty democracy and consequently weakened labor's attachment to the state. With increasing numbers of African centers joining the ICFTU, OATUU no longer served as a force against outside affiliation. By the mid 1990s the ICFTU boasted that the African Regional Organization was no longer a junior partner but had a great deal of autonomy and power within the ICFTU. In the year 2000 there were fifty-one ICFTU affiliates from forty-three African countries, including Ghana, Guinea, Kenya, South Africa, Zambia, Zimbabwe, and Tanzania. (The latter's center is now named the Tanzanian Federation of Free Trade Unions.) One of the striking absences is the Nigerian labor movement.[64]

African labor has come under renewed repression because of its opposition to dictatorships and military rule and its challenges to the policies of the International Monetary Fund and World Bank. Severe limitations on strikes in order to attract foreign investments and the social ramifications of structural adjustment policies continue to limit the effectiveness of African labor organizations. Nevertheless, Africa attracts just 5 percent of the world's investments.[65] No longer divided by the Cold War, international labor and African governments still face a formidable task in the struggle for decent living standards in a global market where developing countries are forced to compete for investments by offering a compliant and cheap labor force. The poverty of countries like Tanzania, which lack adequate medical services, is reflected in dismally high rates of infant mortality and short life expectancies.

Springer still holds hope that the resources of Africa will be used for the benefit of the masses of Africans. And she takes great pride in the tremendous investments the independent governments have put into educating the citizenry. Her contributions in these later years have included raising money with her son, Eric Springer, for the NAACP Tanzania Book Project. The project supplied the University of Tanzania with a full run of the NAACP's *Crisis* magazine. In the 1990s she personally financed the education of Tanzanian girls who ordinarily could not afford to attend secondary school. She provided these scholarships in memory of her mother.[66] Education, after all, formed the cornerstone of her work in Africa.

11

Continued Service

FOLLOWING HER RESIGNATION FROM THE AFL-CIO International Affairs Department in early 1966, Springer worked for the ILGWU as a general organizer in the South and served as Midwest director of the A. Philip Randolph Institute in Chicago. During her period of domestic labor activism she maintained ties with the African labor movements. From 1973 to 1976 she formally returned to international affairs when she joined the staff of the African-American Labor Center (AALC). Ultimately, her interest in programs designed to increase skill levels made her unattractive to the Agency for International Development (AID), the primary financial backer of the AALC programs. AID held that the best use of financial assistance was to fund institutions and infrastructure such as union headquarters, roads, and machinery.[1] However, from 1977 to 1982 she served as an occasional consultant for both the AALC and the Asian-American Free Labor Institute (AAFLI). Her work was marked by challenges, a few successes, and discouragement.

Ranking Oppressions

Springer shared with her friends Dollie Lowther Robinson and Pauli Murray a commitment to women's advancement and equality. While Robinson was working as an assistant to Esther Peterson in the Women's Bureau of the Department of Labor, she was responsible for Murray's appointment in 1962 as a member of the Committee on Civil and Political Rights, one of seven committees set up to help formulate policy for the President's Commission on the Status of Women. Other commission members included Caroline Ware and Eleanor Roosevelt, who served as chair. Murray and Springer, however, gave different weights to racial and gender oppression. Murray viewed race and sex discrimination as equivalent; Springer, who once commented "the first barrier is always race," gave her primary allegiance to the nationalist and civil rights movements.[2] Their differences were highlighted by an incident concerning A. Philip Randolph's agreement to speak before the National Press Club in connection with the 1963 March on Washington.

Springer recalled that many women protested Randolph's appearance at the Press Club because its membership was closed to women, and women attending its meetings were forced to sit in the balcony.[3] The incident added to the frustration many felt concerning the lack of meaningful female participation in the march. Responding to the criticisms, Randolph issued a statement declaring that the march leaders were committed to gender equality; then he invited Dorothy Height, president of the National Council of Negro Women (NCNW), to join the formerly all-male delegation scheduled to meet with President Kennedy on the day of the march. But no woman gave a major address at the event.[4]

Springer, who was working with the AFL-CIO International Affairs Department, lived in Washington at this time. Occupied with her duties as host to a Guinean labor delegation with whom she traveled and whom she would take to the march, Springer allowed Murray to use her apartment as a place to meet and formulate ideas for addressing the conflict. Springer described this exchange when she returned home one day:

> [Pauli] had set up a shop in the foyer and living room of my apartment as a combination of secretariat and public relations office. We greeted one another; Pauli briefed me on the project: "Maida if need be" — they were going to picket A. Philip Randolph if he spoke at the [National] Press Club. After a passionate exhortation about this unwise decision by our great man Randolph, she asked me, "You will join us, if it comes to that, won't you?" I replied, "No, I will not join you in a picket line to picket A. Philip Randolph a week before the March on Washington." Pauli fumed and said something to the effect that she had finally found my "Achilles heel." When I next came home, Pauli had cleared out of my apartment without a "by your leave."[5]

This incident led to one of several long periods of noncommunication that arose in the course of their friendship because of strong disagreements. Toward the end of Murray's life, as she was struggling with cancer, she and Springer lived in adjoining apartments in a duplex house owned by Eric Springer and his wife, Cecile.[6] Nevertheless, they never discussed the National Press Club incident. Twenty-three years after the incident and a year after Murray's death, Springer asked Bayard Rustin, the organizer of the March on Washington, how the National Press Club controversy had ended. According to Rustin, Randolph voiced his displeasure to the club, and right before he began his speech, the club invited its women guests onto the main floor.[7]

The Press Club story illustrates that Springer's reverence for A. Philip Randolph was absolute. She once commented, "If he had told me to walk the water, I would have tried. I tell you, I would have tried."[8] Although aware that women's participation in labor, civil rights, and nationalist movements did not receive the same respect or attention as that of men, Springer, nevertheless, was loyal to male leaders like Randolph because of their commitment to social change and their support of her activism.

Joined in Marriage and Commitment to Labor

Unlike the case of her first marriage, both Springer and James Horace Kemp were entrenched in the cause of labor and civil rights. Both had also been influenced by Randolph in their early careers. Kemp, known as Big Jim, stood six feet four inches tall and had no fat on his 240-pound frame. While supporting himself through law school in the 1930s, he owned a newsstand on Chicago's South Side, where he helped to organize newsstand dealers, reputedly using baseball bats to help settle disputes. When discrimination prevented him from working as a lawyer, Kemp became a policeman. One of his assignments was to spy on Randolph when he spoke in Chicago. After hearing him speak, Kemp promptly reported his assignment to Randolph and they became cordial friends.[9] Kemp went on to develop Local 189, the Building Service Employees Union, and he served as the union's president from 1946 until his death in 1983. Kemp also held many positions in the national office of the NAACP. His respect for the NAACP was formed in childhood. His parents made their house in Oklahoma a way station for traveling NAACP leaders who could not stay in Southern hotels.

Before meeting Kemp, Springer knew of his reputation for fighting for the underprivileged and standing by his convictions. She admired him for not hesitating to stand as a "majority of one." Kemp was well known to the AFL-CIO leadership for his outspokenness on civil rights issues. Springer remarked that he embarrassed labor leaders by pointing out that they put more energy into talking against discrimination than working to eradicate it.

Kemp worked within the Chicago Federation of Labor to promote equal opportunity and the activities of the NAACP. In 1966, while running for the presidency of the Building Service Joint Council no. 1, he attacked his opponent, the president of Local 66, for supporting a job-classification scheme that allowed higher pay for elevator operators working in buildings where only whites were employed. Responding to charges that he was trying to make labor organizations into civil rights organizations, Kemp asserted:

> No one knows better than this speaker, that labor organizations are not civil rights organizations, but I must insist that a labor organization or any other organization, should reflect in its daily activities, the hopes and ambitions of its constituency. Local 189 has consistently, at the risk of unpopularity and economic and political recrimination, taken the position, that if and when a representative of a segment of the house of labor, seeks elevation to a policy making position, that one of the conditions precedent, shall be that he as an individual, plus the current attitude of the local union that he represents, is unquestionably in favor of equal job opportunity for all its members, to all of the rights and privileges, irrespective of the member's race.[10]

It came as a surprise to some white labor leaders that Springer was going to marry a man they considered unreasonable. Following their engagement, Kemp was anxious that Springer complete her work for the opening of the Motor Drivers School in Nigeria and return home to marry him. Responding with impatience and humor to a delay in her departure caused by an airline strike, he suggested she take a canoe. The marriage of these two prominent labor leaders on April 29, 1965, in Louisville, Kentucky, was noted in a number of black periodicals.[11]

Springer understood that although she and Kemp shared a concern for labor and civil rights and supported each other's work, they still had many differences. He thought her commitment to Africa excessive, and she believed that the way he chose to relax was excessive.[12] Kemp adored Springer's mother, who was lighthearted and full of fun. She would join him and others for lively card games. Noting the difference in temperament between mother and daughter, he would ask Adina Stewart, Where did Maida come from?

Another difficulty between them concerned materialism and style. Having acquired some personal wealth, Kemp lavished jewelry and furs on Springer, which she resisted. Since he was generous to her personally, she was at first baffled by his behavior when she asked him to help African students in the United States, or to donate funds to her African and NCNW projects. He always complained ferociously. Later she understood that he enjoyed helping her and that being combative was an integral part of his personality. Ultimately, however, Springer was not satisfied with their relationship and decided to separate from Kemp in the late 1970s. She moved to Pittsburgh, where her son resided, but she stayed in friendly contact with Kemp.

In one of her letters to Kemp in 1981, Springer reflected on her personal misfortune over the preceding six years. Three family members had died, as well as a close family friend. Her mother had undergone four major operations and was fighting cancer when she died of a stroke in late 1976. Springer remarked, "some of the trauma of those times plus the bitter gall of the end of a marriage leaves me with the feeling that the man upstairs must have something good in store for me, or else he could not be so consistently unkind."[13]

An ambitious man, Kemp kept Springer apprised of his career advancements. After his election as one of seven NAACP vice presidents, he reflected with characteristic humor: "I have at last been relieved of the Chairmanship of the Resolutions Committee. At the present time I serve on the Personnel Committee, the Executive Committee and the Policy and Planning Committee, and the thought occurred to me, that it served no useful purpose to appear to be greedy."[14] In January 1983 Kemp was elected NAACP president for a three-year term. He died of a heart attack in his South Side home eleven months later. Although he had strenuously opposed some of the discriminatory policies and practices of the Chicago Federation of Labor, William Lee, the president of the state federation, praised him for organizing people "at the very lowest level of the economy and [bringing] them decent wages and working conditions." He remembered Kemp as "a very witty, articulate and a well informed speaker on labor, civil rights and politics."[15] Springer remembered Kemp as a gregarious, charming, handsome, strong, yet difficult man.

Coming Home to the ILGWU

Since Springer's days as a business agent, the American garment industry had been in a general state of decline. The ability of the ILGWU to command higher wages was hindered by the expansion of section work, which contributed to deskilling and the exodus of manufacturers from New York in search of cheaper wages and lower costs, particularly in the South. In efforts to stem this tide, the ILGWU put pressure on employers with Southern shops and Northern contracts, and the union used much of its financial resources to hire organizers and support strikes. In 1966 Springer decided to bring her talents to bear on this formidable problem. She became an ILGWU general organizer, working with Martin Morand, director of the Southeast Region.[16]

Morand recalled that at a General Executive Board meeting, Dubinsky bragged about Springer's return and her acceptance of a salary lower than what she had received from Meany. In Dubinsky's view, her willingness to take a pay cut was a measure of her commitment and love for the ILGWU. He did not recognize that his statement was a disservice to Springer; her years of work for the U.S. labor movement should have been enough proof of her loyalty.[17]

Initially, Springer had no immediate assignment after returning to the ILGWU. According to Morand, her stature was such that she could not be placed in a starting position; however, the ILGWU was not willing to give a woman, and a black woman at that, a position that carried real power. He remarked, "She was offered a token vice presidency and she refused to be a token." According to Morand, Springer told him that Louis Stulberg, the secretary-treasurer of the ILGWU who was soon to become president, approved of Springer's placement as an organizer in the South, expecting that as an old-timer she would help to protect the union from Morand by watching and reporting on him. Morand challenged some of Stulberg's decisions and ignored some of his instructions. He stated that Stulberg believed that he spent money too freely, did not understand the culture of the South, and was trying to turn the union over to the civil rights movement through his ties with the Southern Christian Leadership Conference (SCLC) and the NAACP. Morand, who is white, believed that Stulberg lacked the cultural sensitivity to deal with the growing black and Latino membership of the ILGWU.[18] Stulberg's assumption that Springer would disapprove of Morand's civil rights connections is both incredible and a sign of cultural insensitivity. In fact, Springer and Morand appreciated and respected one another.

Morand maintained that Stulberg, like Meany, was uncomfortable with the demonstrations and marches of the civil rights movement and was defensive about criticisms of organized labor by civil rights groups.[19] The ILGWU under Dubinsky had given support to civil rights struggles, and particularly Local 22 had always taken independent political stands. For example, in 1953 Springer served as a Local 22 delegate to the NAACP convention. In 1955 Charles Zimmerman made available to the NAACP ten thousand dollars for loans to be distributed to blacks "to help rescue [them] from the vicious persecution in Mississippi." For the 1965 March on Montgomery, the ILGWU provided a mobile health unit and in turn suffered criticism from Southern white ILGWU members.[20]

Racism and segregation in the South proved a formidable barrier to the task of union organizing. Employers threatened both whites and blacks with replacement by workers of the other race if they voted in favor of ILGWU representation.[21] In one factory in Georgia, an employer displaying a newspaper photo of Zimmerman dancing with a black woman at an NAACP event was enough to derail the organizing drive. As an organizer and troubleshooter, Springer attempted to sensitize the ILGWU staff in the South to the negative ramifications of segregation. A segregated way of thinking was so pervasive that a staff member would make separate lists of black and white workers. Morand noted that while the staff members may not have been overt racists, they worked to keep their "constituents passive if not necessarily happy." Morand also agreed with Springer's assessment that the prejudices of white unorganized workers were "too often stronger than their desire to improve their economic position."[22]

Further hampering union organizational drives and the effectiveness of unions were the so-called "right to work" laws throughout the South. Unions have termed them the "right to work for less" laws. Section 14B of the Taft-Hartley Act allows states to pass laws forbidding union security clauses in labor contracts. This means that unions cannot negotiate with employers to make union membership a condition of employment. Since all the workers do not have to share the cost of union representation, the union's ability to bring greater benefits to them is seriously impaired. Springer noted that the labor movement was "a tiny oasis in a non-union and anti-union desert."[23]

During this period Springer also studied the garment industry in Los Angeles, where sweatshops were becoming more prevalent and the workforce was increasingly black, Mexican, and Asian. Although she recognized that these newer workers were resistant to union organizing, she criticized former and present white dressmakers and cutters, who had a long tradition of union membership, for being the most effective agents of anti-unionism because of their racist attitudes. Springer recalled that some whites would say prejudicial things to her, as if she were not black. She reported that it was psychologically disadvantageous for whites to maintain that these newer workers were unorganizable and to refer to them as ethnic minorities. These new groups, she stated, represented the "present and foreseeable majority and our progress must reflect this." With less than 20 percent of garment workers organized there, Springer challenged the ILGWU to either "admit defeat and await the consequent slow disintegration of the organization" or assess the work needed to rebuild the union and set short- and long-term objectives. To Randolph she commented, "There are hours when I nearly despair and feel that there will never be meaningful dialogue between the masses of black and white citizens; and I'm not referring to the South."[24]

A year earlier Springer had recommended that the ILGWU set up training centers for workers in all the industrial centers of the nation and focus on improving the status of black garment workers in particular. Commenting on the district where she had worked as a business agent, she noted its reduced size, the diminishing skills of the workers, deterioration in working conditions, and a growing complacency toward the union and activism. With speed and manual dexterity increasingly becoming a priority over the quality of the work, she noted that the newer workers did not have the same pride in the union and their craft as did the old-timers. Although she recognized that the ILGWU might not be able to recapture the fervor of the past, she suggested that the union could instill in workers the meaning of struggle and might gain their loyalty by providing greater opportunities for them to increase their skills. Springer remarked that past ILGWU shortcomings in regard to the black worker had later repercussions: "The solidarity with the labor movement which my generation knew in the 30's was not broadly based enough to carry much weight in the late fifties and sixties. This is true because only minimally was the Negro worker drawn meaningfully into the union family and, therefore, able to transmit to the present day member-ship the heroic struggles—in this instance—the ILG waged on behalf of all of us."[25]

Much of Springer's testimony backs up charges brought by Herbert Hill and Altagracia Ortiz that the ILGWU leadership of the 1950s and 1960s was not suffi-ciently committed to improving the prospects for its black and Puerto Rican members, who continued to be concentrated largely in shops that paid lower wages and required less skill. Moreover, Hill and Ortiz charged ILGWU officials with deliberately maintaining Jewish and Italian domination of the General Ex-ecutive Board and of the lower ranks of leadership, and with trying to keep the industry in New York through a policy of wage restraint. They believed that the ILGWU should have had a more effective strategy for dealing with the problem of shops relocating to the low-wage, mostly unorganized South, one that would not have entailed a sacrifice of workers' wages in the North. They also held that ILGWU officials were helping to maintain people of color in low-wage sectors by opposing the institution of federally funded training programs connected with antipoverty programs.[26]

It should be noted that some ILGWU leaders like Martin Morand argued that the federal training programs would have primarily benefited employers. Since the government was earmarking the money for their use, employers could use these subsidies to offset their already low wage bill and pay workers sub-min-imal wages. He also stated that the training money would not have been used to increase skills but to add more workers to the already overcrowded low-wage sec-tors.[27]

This pessimistic portrait of the ILGWU leadership, however, leaves little room to understand the commitment of Springer and other activists who experi-enced racism and sexism within the union. Although Springer knew intimately of injustices perpetuated in the union, she differed from the ILGWU's critics in ascribing motivation, particularly regarding Zimmerman. Within the context of discrimination practiced by U.S. society in general and by other labor unions, she also was more willing to give credit for the ILGWU's racial advances.

Not surprisingly, considering her deep involvement with the NAACP, Springer was friends with Herbert Hill in the 1950s when she was a business agent and he worked as NAACP labor secretary. With offices located close by, they would have lunch together, and on occasion he would discuss with her the problems that black garment workers brought before him. She in turn would help to work out solutions. Springer also recalled that they discussed her views of the ILGWU's successes and shortcomings.[28]

In 1962 Congressman Adam Clayton Powell, Jr.'s House Labor and Educa-tion Committee, for which Hill served as a special consultant, investigated the status of people of color in the garment industry and in the ILGWU. In connection with this investigation, a fact-finding subcommittee chaired by New York Representative Herbert Zelenko and with the participation of Hill traveled to New York to hold hearings. In a letter to Ed Welsh, also a long-time NAACP member, Springer noted possible political reasons for Zelenko's investigation. The Liberal Party, which the ILGWU strongly influenced, had supported his opponent for office.[29]

Dubinsky requested Springer to come from Washington, where she was working for the AFL-CIO International Affairs Department, and testify on August 24 in the subcommittee hearing looking into allegations that the ILGWU provided separate pay schedules for black and white workers within the same shops. Springer was prepared to say that no documents she ever signed her name to accorded separate wage schedules. The committee had not expected her presence. Although she and Hill saw each other from different parts of the room, they did not take the opportunity to speak with one another. After a couple of people testified, the committee announced that the issue needed no further investigation and ended the session without calling Springer. Writing to Ed Welsh, Springer noted that two of her best friends, Herbert Hill and Odell Clarke, had been "looking for [her] small scalp": "I am sorry they have been spared the pleasure of scalping me because I too would have enjoyed the encounter. This is an industry I know, would never deny its sins but know enough of its virtues to be able to stand up and be counted as a member and former officer of this union."[30]

After the NAACP national board endorsed Hill's findings against the ILGWU, Zimmerman resigned in October from the NAACP Board of Trustees for the Legal Defense Fund. In his resignation speech, he castigated Hill and countered some of his charges.[31] Rancor between Hill, as labor secretary for NAACP, and Zimmerman, as chair of the AFL-CIO Civil Rights Committee, began openly as early as 1958.[32] Ironically, since both men are Jewish, the conflict between the NAACP and the AFL-CIO was characterized as a rift between blacks and Jews. In late 1959 Granger, NAACP executive secretary Roy Wilkins, and Randolph denied that there was a developing African American–Jewish conflict and held that this perception of the problem gave aid and comfort to the big offenders in the labor movement. Randolph and Wilkins averred that the differences they had with Zimmerman were not tantamount to war, and they professed a respect for his civil rights record.[33]

In a letter to the *Pittsburgh Courier* concerning the controversy, Springer suggested that without minimizing the problem of discrimination, the paper could do the black community a service by recognizing the opportunities that were available in the labor movement and encouraging blacks to participate. Specifically, she pointed out the ILGWU Training Institute, which trained people to become union officers, and the free training classes available to union members in cooperation with the Fashion Institute of Technology.[34]

Springer recognized a two-pronged problem in the relationship between organized labor and black communities throughout the nation. She not only saw the need for organized labor to be more inclusive toward blacks but also recognized that organized labor's well-known history of discrimination had fostered an anti-union bias in black communities that was difficult to overcome. Therefore, she found it gratifying when black institutions supported the efforts of the labor movement, such as in 1968–1969 during the ILGWU's successful four-month-long strike against Wentworth's garment manufacturing operations in South Carolina. The strike was about the union's efforts to encourage integrated shops by allowing the transfer of seniority status, so that black members would not lose rank if they moved to another shop. To publicize the strike, Springer helped to arrange a campaign that involved picketing major Chicago stores that did business with Wentworth. Despite their reliance on advertising from businesses such as Sears, Montgomery Ward, Marshall Field, and Carson Pirie Scott, the black mass media of Chicago supported the strike.[35]

The behavior of the South Carolina strikers demonstrated the influence that the civil rights movement sometimes had on labor operations. When the state police started arresting only black women among the strikers, some of the white women spat in the faces of the police in order to provoke their arrests too. Springer remarked that it "drove the law enforcement officials out of their minds" when the white women refused bail and integrated the jails. All the women stayed in jail for over a week. Previous to the arrests, an interracial group of strikers attended a retreat sponsored by the SCLC Citizenship Education Program and run by Dorothy Cotton and Ramelle MaCoy.[36]

Springer wrote Morand that her participation in the strike had given her the opportunity to engage in public education with the black community concerning the work of the ILGWU in assisting workers on the bottom of the economic ladder. She explained: "The misguided notion that most union members are highly paid white featherbedders is all too pervasive. In the Negro communities across the nation, the cynicism and the hostility against 'The Establishment' which includes the trade union movement is much deeper than we are prepared to acknowledge."[37]

The A. Philip Randolph Institute

Bayard Rustin, the executive director of the A. Philip Randolph Institute (APRI), requested that Springer open the institute's Midwest office and serve as director. The ILGWU continued to pay her salary. The APRI was concerned with promoting voter education, registration, and participation in elections and building a unified movement for social action between labor and communities. Upon becoming the director in April 1969, Springer continued in her efforts to instill pro-labor sentiments within black communities.[38] However, she faced an uphill battle in gaining black community support.

Some in the black community maintained that the labor movement was irrelevant to black people, and some whites concurred with that judgment. The hostility that white labor had shown toward the 1965–1966 Chicago Freedom Movement, despite the alliance of area labor leaders with the movement, made a deep impression on Chicago blacks. The black community recognized that union discrimination in employment and apprenticeship programs contributed to black unemployment and the relegation of blacks to menial jobs. They also were aware that white workers often supported housing discrimination.[39]

As a veteran in struggles against union discrimination, Springer held, "with all of organized labor's sins of commission and omission, the trade union movement [was] still the first line of defense for the economic salvation of those who are employed and those who hope to be employed." After five months of work preparing for the opening of the Midwest office, she commented that an atmosphere of skepticism and hostility surrounded their efforts.[40]

Some black trade unionists as well objected to the APRI, believing it too conservative. Historian Philip Foner suggested that Randolph by 1966 had lessened his criticism of the AFL-CIO in order to gain support for the establishment of the APRI. Randolph's resignation as president of the Negro American Labor Council, and his suggestion that the NALC cease attacking the AFL-CIO over union discrimination and instead cooperate with the federation to fight discrimination are further evidence to Foner of Randolph's accommodation to the AFL-CIO leadership. After all, George Meany had opposed the 1963 March on Washington. Yet it should also be noted that Randolph's change in tactics may have been influenced by the inclusion, at Meany's insistence, of a provision in Title 7 of the 1964 Civil Rights Act outlawing discrimination in unions.[41] Springer believed that some of the younger generation of black militants did not appreciate the pioneer struggles Randolph and others had waged: "There is so much inconsistent history and superficial intelligence today that it sometimes requires courage to remind the sudden experts that they are standing on the shoulders of those who created the climate in which they now so expertly function."[42]

The dogged criticism of the labor movement in the Chicago black media propelled Springer to write an open letter in 1971. While she did not request them to curb their criticisms of labor, she suggested that their lack of information about the important roles of black men and women in the labor movement blunted the thrust of their criticisms.[43]

One of Springer's initial projects for reaching the black community was the publication of "Profiles of Negro Pioneers in Chicago 1919–1945," a pamphlet detailing the little-known history of pioneering black labor leaders of Chicago. Although she believed that "the current demand for Negro history and Black studies courses, when removed from some of the ugly shock effect rhetoric, [was] long overdue," she was concerned that the new black studies curriculums would omit the struggles of blacks in organized labor, thus perpetuating the belief that blacks had no place in the labor movement.[44] She wanted these profiles to demonstrate that black labor leaders held onto the principles of unionism despite the obstacles of prejudice and limited opportunities. Her old friend Caroline Ware donated twenty-five hundred dollars for the APRI to publish the pamphlet. Springer noted that although the pamphlet did not attract wide public notice, it did reach some school libraries and civic groups.[45]

Springer's hope that the pamphlet would be the first in a series the APRI would sponsor in other industrial centers did not materialize. Some labor leaders were offended by the inclusion of a profile on James Kemp that Springer wrote and by the pamphlet's focus on Blacks, which in their view smacked of Black Nationalism at the expense of labor's integrationist rhetoric.[46] Although Randolph had approved the publication, the AFL-CIO never used or promoted the pamphlet. It was ironic that Kemp's participation in the labor movement and as a member of Mayor Richard Daley's political machine marked him as a conservative among some blacks, while his strong criticism of racism in the labor movement marked him as a radical among the white labor leadership.

Through her husband's contacts Springer started a weekly radio program entitled "The A. Philip Randolph Labor Forum." Devoted to educating the public about trade unions, its topics included the purpose of trade unions, labor's political work, and its role in education, housing, community projects, and civil rights, as well as the activities of union members. Among her guests were the associate director of the APRI, Norman Hill, and an ILGWU price adjuster, Melba Soloman, whom Springer had once recommended to an employer after he let slip out that he did not want a black. Anti-labor forces, however, eventually caused the termination of the program. After she hosted a radio program sympathetic to the United Farm Workers' grape boycott, program sponsors pressured the radio station to stop the broadcasts.[47]

In 1972 Springer decided to close the Midwest office after it was reported to the ILGWU that she was working full time on the congressional campaign of Paul Douglas. While it was not illegal for the APRI to campaign for an individual candidate, it was for the unions due to legal problems that had involved some of the political action committees. ILGWU assistant to the president Gus Tyler told Springer to cease working on the campaign if she wanted to remain with the ILGWU. Explaining in later years to ILGWU vice president Evelyn DuBrow the importance of the campaign to the labor movement, Springer remarked, "If my life depended on it, I could not have dropped my work for voter education and voter registration in several states."[48] She also held that the accusation against her was distorted. She denied working full time on an individual campaign. Since her work was construed in that light, however, she decided to resign.[49]

Although the office closed somewhat unceremoniously, Springer was successful in expanding the outreach of the APRI in the seven-state area under her jurisdiction.[50] Even the black groups that had opposed the APRI for ideological reasons, including opposition to a black-labor alliance, recognized that the work of the APRI in increasing voter participation could benefit the movements by mobilizing people for political action.

A Return to International Work

During Springer's tenure as APRI Midwest director, the institute hosted visiting African labor leaders.[51] On occasion she also participated in AALC projects, including a three-week visit to Africa in February 1972 and humanitarian work for refugees from colonial Angola living in Zaire (now the Democratic Republic of the Congo).[52] By 1972 U.S. labor representatives were present in thirty-one African countries serving as technical advisers in such fields as vocational training, education, and health. With her characteristic modesty in regard to her own role in promoting activism on the continent, Springer proudly wrote Randolph while she was on the 1972 AALC assignment, "The genesis of all of this activity were the programs you gave voice and support to many years ago." From Kinshasa to Nigeria, she stated, trade unionists sent him greetings and remembered his struggles on their behalf in the councils of the ICFTU.[53]

After Springer joined the AALC as a staff member in 1974, her concern for humanitarian causes continued. She became coordinator of an AALC program to aid victims of a devastating drought that affected seventeen West African countries. Sow Moussa Demba, the former leader of the Mauritanian labor movement, recalled her dedication: "I will tell you that the Mauritanian people still remember this woman who, despite her age and climate of the Sahel, after meeting with Mauritanian women in 1974 and in order to catch her flight in Dakar from Niamey (Niger), did not hesitate to take a VW "bug" to cover the distance from Nouakchott (Mauritania) to Dakar—650 kilometers—including the crossing of the Rosso ferry on the Senegal river."[54]

The National Council of Negro Women, for which Springer served as vice president from 1970 to 1974, and Jewel Frierson and other officers of the Retail, Wholesale, and Department Store Union contributed to her humanitarian projects.[55] Springer also recognized the problem of hunger in the United States. President Gerald Ford dealt with inflation and a depressed economy by severely cutting government spending on programs to help the poor and decreasing individual and corporate taxes. At a 1975 symposium at Clark College on "Feeding Americans" she applauded Andrew Young's analysis of the "administration's political gimmickry in the anti-food stamp campaign" by stating that his text should be required reading. The NCNW, she believed, was "perhaps the most active volunteer organization, fighting against hunger and malnutrition in America."[56]

The NCNW also worked with women in Africa, the Caribbean, and Latin

America to develop rural cooperative projects in their countries. Representing the NCNW at the International Women's Year Conference in Mexico City in 1974, Springer met with women from these areas, twenty-seven of whom visited the United States following the conference as guests of the NCNW. In Mississippi they observed day care centers, animal husbandry, vegetable and fruit farming, and canning. Established during a time of adversity, these initiatives had helped to sustain communities. Springer explained that the sheriff of one community, who seven years earlier had been "riding herd" on the NCNW because black and white women were meeting together to plan a day care center, had joined with the mayor in handing the keys of the city to NCNW president Dorothy Height.[57]

In her work for the AFL-CIO auxiliaries, Springer helped to formulate programs, policies, and instruments aimed at increasing female participation in labor movements. As one of the advisers to the AFL-CIO worker delegation to the January 1964 ILO Special Commission of Women Workers in a Changing World, she spoke out about the lack of opportunities for women. The International Labor Organization itself was a major offender. Springer recalled that ILO officials acted befuddled when she asked why there were no programs for women at its training facility in Turin: "The question was gently asked, observing all of the diplomatic niceties. It created consternation among some of the ILO officials. It was ironic that such a simple question could not be handled. It was tragic, especially because the emphasis of that [ILO] conference was on Third World development. I'm aware that such attitudes are not apparent now."[58]

In order to address the low level of women's activism in unions, she served as one of the coordinators of a 1977 conference jointly sponsored by the AALC and Kenya's Central Organization of Trade Unions, entitled the "Pan African Conference on the Role of Trade Union Women: Problem, Prospects and Programs." The issues discussed were reminiscent of those women attending the All-African People's Conference had raised nearly twenty years earlier. Delegates discussed the economic and social conditions of women and issues of equal rights. They expressed particular concern for the plight of the predominantly female class of agricultural workers who lived at a subsistence level. Approximately 80 percent of women lived in rural areas, and they suffered from illiteracy, lack of skills, unemployment, and underemployment. Although these workers produced the food that was the basis for foreign exchange and that fed the urban population, the majority of rural women did not have wage-earning jobs and did not have a legal right to equal pay for equal work or for paid maternity leave.[59]

Belittling the goals of the well-publicized conference in a newspaper article, one man argued that although it was good for women to come together to discuss various issues, they were "not going to gain anything by trying to devise ways of fighting for their rights through trade unions." Three of the delegates replied that their goals were not to form separate trade unions or to compete with men;

rather, they wanted to be considered partners with equal rights. Toward this end they advocated setting up women's bureaus in the national centers and in the Organization of African Trade Union Unity.[60]

Springer had hoped that the conference could be helpful in imparting self-confidence to women. She stated that during her years of travel, African women often would tell her, "We're ashamed to get up in a meeting and express ourselves; we have no sense of security about how we speak and approach a subject and we're afraid that we might be laughed at and we're afraid that we might be put down."[61] Judging from the aplomb with which these three women handled their critic, the conference boosted not only their self-confidence but their resolve to make the labor movement more meaningful to women.[62]

One of the conference participants, Joyce Alogo of the Kenyan Union of Posts and Telecommunications Employees, recalled that Springer also helped her deal with a difficult colleague. After Alogo complained to her about a woman who seemed bent on disruption and dissension, Springer advised her to give the woman substantial responsibility for a project. Soon afterwards the woman became very cooperative.[63]

As a consultant for the AAFLI, Springer also encouraged Turkish and Indonesian women to assume leadership positions and speak out on issues that concerned them. In 1979 she went to Indonesia to help the FBSI (All-Indonesian Federation of Labor) and Donell Newsom, AAFLI director for Indonesia, coordinate a seminar for women workers designed to increase female activism. Although the seminar, held in Puncak, was a success in terms of the enthusiasm of the delegates, Springer recognized that as long as the government allowed employers to pay below-poverty wages and disregard the country's labor laws with impunity, prospects for change were dismal. Particularly the widespread presence of child labor disturbed her. Ten-year-old children worked ten- to twelve-hour days in cigarette and batik factories.[64] The conditions Springer observed in Indonesia and other countries caused her to appeal to professional women to reach across class lines to help their poverty-stricken sisters who, along with their children, worked under dangerous and intolerable conditions:

> There is much work to be done, both at home and on a global scale. Oppression is a very real threat particularly in the Third World, where the intensity of the profit motive leads to appalling and dangerous work conditions. There are young women whose fingernails are eaten away and whose faces are permanently scarred by the acid in which they work, day in and day out, without protection. Seven year old children labor in textile mills and tobacco processing plants, risking crippling illnesses and bodily disfiguration as part of their daily work routine. We must not forget the great needs of our sisters elsewhere in our own search for professional satisfaction.[65]

Springer's relationship with Turkish women trade unionists began in 1977 when she planned a thirty-day educational program for Turkish garment workers, the first female delegation from Turkey to come to the United States. At that time there were no female staff members in any union in Turkey, including those with majority female memberships.[66] Springer agreed to help Turk-Is (the Confederation of Turkish Trade Unions) establish a Women's Bureau, provided that the women would be free to speak to her directly about their concerns, rather than have their views interpreted to her by men. The leaders of Turk-Is eventually and reluctantly agreed to that condition.

Springer spent two to three months a year for three years traveling in Turkey to learn about the country, the unions, and the aspirations of the female trade unionists. Nine months after her first visit to Turkey in 1978, Mark Hankin of the AAFLI complained about the slow progress in developing a liaison office for women's affairs, the first step in establishing the Women's Bureau. He suggested that male leaders were more interested in the "initial propaganda rewards from stating goals" than in actually carrying out the work. Springer once complained to Tom Riley, the AAFLI country director, that Turk-Is was making a "determined effort to sabotage the Women's Bureau" by not allowing women to perform the necessary work in the regions.[67]

Springer later stated that while the male leadership wanted to strengthen the labor movement by increasing the participation of women, they did not necessarily like what the women had to say. Turkish women spoke about similar issues that Springer had heard from women in the United States, Sweden, Indonesia, and Africa. They wanted equal opportunity, equal pay for equal work, day care provisions, family planning, and eight-hour days with no forced overtime. They also spoke out against being subjected to verbal abuse.[68]

After working on this project over a four-year period, Springer participated in the founding conference of the Turk-Is Women's Bureau in 1981. For the event, she had eight sections of Barbara Mayer Wertheimer's book, *We Were There: The Story of Working Women in America*, and "Labor Education for Women Workers" translated for the two hundred delegates. She reported that the women received the documents with great pride and enthusiasm. Seven years after the conference, AAFLI executive director Charles D. Gray wrote Springer that the Women's Bureau was "now an integral part" of Turk-Is.[69]

The Limits of AFL-CIO Anticommunism

As a consultant for the African American Labor Center, Springer again met controversy because of the AFL-CIO's preoccupation with anticommunism. The federation's policies made it almost impossible to build relationships with the leading South African trade unions. Because of the presence of Communists among the leadership of the African National Congress (ANC), the AFL-CIO insisted that South African workers separate trade unionism from politics, as the British TUC had in colonial Africa. In reference to this notion, Springer asserted, "When you are under the gun, that's very hard to differentiate."[70]

Although the AFL-CIO strongly differed with U.S. government policy regarding apartheid and had supported various boycotts and embargoes on oil and military goods, the federation was firmly against the ANC's armed liberation struggle and the divestment movement. These policies suggested to some South African trade unionists that the AFL-CIO was beholden to the interests of the U.S. government and multinational corporations.[71] Moreover, the call of the AFL-CIO for African unions to avoid politics was hypocritical since the AFL-CIO's international struggle against communism was political and tied through its funding sources to the interests of the U.S. government. Nearly 90 percent of the AALC's funding came from two government-funded institutions, the Agency for International Development, and the National Endowment for Democracy; much of the rest came from corporations. Accusations that the AFL-CIO auxiliary, the American Institute for Free Labor Development, aided and abetted right-wing dictatorships in the Americas also contributed to the negative image of the federation.[72]

The year 1962 marked the first time Springer was presented with a chance to do something tangible in support of Africans struggling against the vicious regime of South Africa. An Anglican priest, Michael Scott, and nationalist leader Sam Nujoma approached her and Brown for help in presenting the case of the exploitation of Namibian workers before the United Nations. South Africa refused to surrender Namibia (then South West Africa) to the UN Trusteeship Council and illegally held it as a colony. Springer had long known Scott, who was jailed and later ejected from South Africa for his defense of Africans and Indians. Scott, who was British, set up the Africa Bureau in London as a forum to advance justice for Africans and particularly for Namibians. While Brown helped to prepare the document, Springer approached her friend Aminu Kano, who was head of the Nigerian delegation to the UN. Through Kano's sponsorship of Nujoma as a petitioner, Nujoma was allowed to address the UN. When South Africa finally relinquished control in 1990, Nujoma was elected as Namibia's first president.[73]

Before visiting South Africa for the AALC in 1980, Springer had traveled there in 1977 as a member of the South Africa and Namibia area committee of the NAACP Task Force on Africa. This task force was composed of four different area committees. Hers was led by NAACP president Montague Cobb and included Broadus Butler, who served as chair of the task force. The developer of the task force was Margaret Bush Wilson, who had become NAACP board chair after James Kemp's strong support of her for this traditionally male position.[74]

Following the completion of the fact-finding missions, the task force wrote a report to serve as a guide in developing NAACP policy and as a source of information to the U.S. public. The report of Springer's committee was extremely critical of South Africa, to the chagrin of one of their sponsoring groups, which was supposedly independent of the government. This group made a concerted effort to veil the stark realities of apartheid. She noted that some whites in the U.S. labor movement also wanted a less critical appraisal of apartheid. Referring to the fine accommodations white South Africans denied to Africans but provided for black American visitors whom they wished to impress, Springer remarked, "I came back and said with sarcasm that I was a temporary white for three weeks. That used to offend some people in the United States who did not feel strongly about apartheid. But when it is politically expedient, they would allow you to become temporarily white and treat you with kid gloves."[75]

As an AALC consultant in 1979, Springer served as the team coordinator of a program that brought ten South African trade union leaders to the United States for a labor education program in New York City.[76] In preparation for a scheduled second course, Springer, who would serve as team coordinator again, and Lester Trachtman, the AALC deputy director, visited South Africa in April 1980 after months of delay caused in part by South Africa's initial refusal to grant visas. Their agenda included consulting with the trainees on the merits of the program and its relevance to their trade union situation, beginning the process for the selection of the second group for a course to begin in September, and learning more about the state of labor in South Africa.

Although their association with the AFL-CIO negatively affected their reception among some trade unions allied with the ANC, the report they submitted included recommendations that incorporated lessons learned from past experiences with African labor. Outlining the major concerns of both the black and nonracial unions as well as their conflicts with one another, they stressed implementing policies that would promote unity in South Africa and among the Western international labor organizations working in the country. Since the labor movement was still in a great deal of flux, they suggested that the AALC try to include all trade union groups in its education programs. Noting that "[m]utual suspicion is a virulent disease in South Africa," they held that "[n]evertheless, unity is a principle we must strongly support, though we can not enforce it." The continuation of the AFL-CIO's anticommunist and anti-ANC policy, however, marked the federation as an unlikely candidate to promote unity.[77]

In an effort to promote confidence in the AFL-CIO, Springer and Trachtman urged the federation to move away from their strong connections with J. Arthur Grobbelaar's white-dominated Trade Union Council of South Africa (TUCSA) and Lucy Mvubelo's National Union of Clothing Workers, which represented one of the separate "parallel" African unions that had belonged to

TUCSA. These two organizations, they concluded, were not representative of African labor and had not vigorously supported African labor advancement.[78]

Springer and Trachtman did not mention communism or the ANC. The only reference to politics in the AALC report was their statement that "there was no visible radical ideological orientation" in the emerging trade unions. The AALC team, however, which recognized the Federation of South African Trade Unions (FOSATU) as the strongest and most significant organization, was of course aware that FOSATU strongly supported the ANC. Perhaps the absence of discussions of communism and the ANC in their report was an indication that they did not want this sort of information to undermine their emphasis on working with all the labor unions.[79]

Springer later remarked that while most unions had welcomed them, some trade union supporters of the ANC considered them suspect. One of the critics of AFL-CIO policies whom they had met attended the subsequent 1980 AALC trade union course. While in the United States, this trainee and others voiced directly to the AFL-CIO leadership the strong disagreements and resentments they had with the AFL-CIO's policies. They also believed the AFL-CIO was in a position to put more pressure on the South African government.[80] Springer stated that she was not opposed to the South African protests and reflected that if she were in their position, she would have the same view. As for her own actions, however, she stressed that her primary concern was that South Africans should have the opportunity to come to the United States. She remarked that they could come, "have a point of view," and "continue to educate us."[81]

Three of the trainees became upset when Springer, as team coordinator of the AALC program, told them of an arranged meeting with Nana Mahomo, an AALC staff member and formerly the secretary of culture for the Pan-Africanist Congress (PAC), a black nationalist political organization that had split from the nonracial ANC in 1959 over the issue of Communist and white leadership. PAC became hopelessly faction ridden and in 1964 Mahomo was expelled. His opponents in PAC accused him of unexplained use of funds and connections with the CIA.[82] The three trainees refused to meet him.

With Barry Cohen's essay "The CIA and African Trade Unions" as the source, subsequent articles critical of AALC involvement in South Africa accused Springer of working with the CIA in East Africa and Rhodesia, and playing a role in splitting those labor movements. One of the trainees accused Springer of keeping tabs on them and intimated that she was watching to see if they would meet with ANC exiles.[83] Springer responded:

This is not true. These men and women could go where they wanted with whom they wanted. . . . I had one concern. These men and women and particularly the women—I think there were three women in the group—I did

not want to be wandering around a city that is as hectic and sometimes unpleasant as New York City, without having some sense of where they were,
how long they might be wherever they were. . . . I never asked whom they
were meeting with. I thought that that would have been an affront. They
were all adults. They were all active, young and not so young, struggling
leaders in their unions. I have been to South Africa, and I knew the hardships that they faced.

I will have to take whatever criticisms they made, but I am telling you
what was the motivation. The distrust begins from the AF of L-CIO's top-
level position not being as sharply focused as they felt it should have been.
And they said it in no uncertain terms from the president of the AF of L-CIO
on down. They spoke their mind.[84]

Other activities the delegation engaged in with Springer were apparently
pleasant. They were entertained in the home of her friend Dollie Lowther
Robinson, met Robinson's colleagues at Brooklyn College, and also attended the
christening of Robinson's granddaughter.[85]

Further opposition to the AFL-CIO arose within the South African labor
movement when the federation in September 1982 proceeded with plans to implement the AALC "Program of Action to Assist Black Unions in South Africa,"
one of Springer and Trachtman's recommendations. The AALC's appointment
of Mahomo as the officer for the program and the AFL-CIO's granting of the
George Meany Human Rights Award to Mangosuthu Gatsha Buthelezi, leader
of the Zulu-based anti-apartheid movement, Inkatha Yenkululeko ye Sizwe (the
National Cultural Liberation Movement), virtually destroyed any possibility of
working with the pro-ANC nonracial labor unions.[86] Buthelezi's professed belief
in "peaceful change" apparently applied only to the apartheid government. After
he received the human rights award, Inkatha engaged in violent clashes with the
ANC. It was discovered in 1991 that the South Africa government secretly funded
Inkatha.[87]

Springer indicated that in hindsight she could understand the reasons it was
not appropriate to give the award to Buthelezi. However, at that time and within
the context of the foreign policy limitations of the AFL-CIO, she was not opposed to granting him the award. In this controversial situation, Springer assessed
what happened from the perspective of a diplomat working within the parameters of the AFL-CIO's foreign policy.

FOSATU refused to work with the AALC's Program of Action, although
they did participate in other ways with individual U.S. unions. By 1986 a number
of forces converged to cause a change in AFL-CIO policies and strategies in
South Africa. This mounting pressure stemmed from South African trade
unions, U.S. labor groups including the Coalition of Black Trade Unionists, in-

terested members of Congress, and AID, the major AALC financial backer. The AFL-CIO changed its policy and demanded divestment and mandatory comprehensive sanctions against South Africa. Soon AFL-CIO leaders joined other AFL-CIO members in protests in front of the South African embassy, for which they were jailed.[88]

By 1991 officials of the Congress of South African Trade Unions (COSATU), a new trade union center formed from FOSATU and other non-affiliated unions in November 1985, expressed thanks to the AFL-CIO leadership for their support over the years in the struggle against apartheid.[89] As a volunteer for the AALC, Springer also that year had contact with South African trade unionists coming to the United States. She hosted in her hometown of Pittsburgh a female delegation of African women who had completed a trade union course. This delegation included two South Africans, one of whom was from COSATU. All of the women held her in high esteem.[90]

Despite the controversy surrounding some of Springer's work in Africa, perhaps her most lasting legacy is that she was a pioneer in the process of orienting the AFL-CIO to pay more attention to Africa and helping to open the door for more people of color in the United States and elsewhere to become involved in international affairs and in turn influence policy. Gemma Adaba, a Trinidadian woman, is the ICFTU permanent representative to the United Nations. For a number of years Barbara Lomax, an African-American and close friend of Springer's, headed the AALC office in South Africa. One of the recommendations for Springer and Trachtman was to have an AALC representative stationed in South Africa who could observe firsthand the labor conditions there.

A Lifetime of Struggle

Springer's zeal for promoting educational opportunities, civil rights, and trade unionism has not diminished as she enters her nineties. Her perception of unfinished business in the civil rights movement also applies to the movements for African liberation and women's rights. Noting the rollback in gains of the 1960s that she had thought were secure, in 1986 she expressed her apprehension about the future to her old friend Mwalimu Julius Nyerere: "I fear for the next and the next generations. I wish to be proven wrong in these last few years of my life, and so must try to think positively."[91] Springer remarked that the younger generations now bear the responsibility of choosing strategies to continue the struggles.

Coming of age as an international representative during the Cold War placed Springer in the midst of fierce ideological struggles and brought into relief the contradictions of a black woman working on behalf of a white male–dominated labor federation. If Springer harbors any disillusionment over how she was treated or the way world events unfolded, she chooses not to reveal it. As she has said, loyalty to the cause is more important than the price the individual pays.

Morand reported that Springer discussed with him some of her frustrations with the ILGWU, particularly in the post-Dubinsky period. The many roles she was expected to play made her constantly question how she came across to an audience. She acted, he remarked, as though she had lived like a diplomat skating on thin ice and every step had to be taken with care. David Brombart, former AALC deputy director, recalled that she preached in a hostile environment and acknowleged that AFL-CIO recognition of her contribution has come almost too late.[92]

In March 2000 the labor movement and various other organizations began to give Springer a measure of the recognition she deserves by hosting a tribute dinner in Pittsburgh. The dinner raised funds for the Institute of Tailoring and Cutting she helped found in 1963. Moreover, the Union of Needletrades, Industrial, and Textile Employees (UNITE), representing the now merged ILGWU and ACWA, and the AFL-CIO have collaborated on the creation of the Maida Springer-Kemp Fund to honor her.

The fund's purpose is to combat child labor in East Africa, which has been compounded by the growing number of HIV/AIDS orphans. A principal strategy used in this struggle is to return children to school where they may gain technical training and exposure to union principles. These tributes have been fitting since Springer otherwise eschews personal accolades.

Taking a cue from her politically conscious mother, Springer has always wanted to give something back to the community. Her own community has included the ILGWU, African Americans, Africans, and women internationally. Her respect for herself as a woman sustained her while working in the faction-ridden and male-dominated fields of domestic and international labor relations. The restrictions under which she worked, the contradictions she faced, and the political intrigue of nations and labor movements that affected her work took a heavy toll on her physically. Nevertheless, she did not lose her focus or her integrity.

NOTES

The following abbreviations are used throughout the notes to refer to manuscript collections and other document sources consulted during my research on Maida Springer-Kemp:

Amistad: MSK Papers, Amistad Research Center, Tulane University, New Orleans, Louisiana.

APR Papers: A. Philip Randolph Papers, Schomburg Center for Research in Black Culture, New York Public Library, New York, New York.

BP: Borochowicz Papers, Wagner Labor Archives, Bobst Library, New York University, New York, New York.

Brown files: Record Group 18-004, International Affairs Department, Irving Brown files, 1943–1989, George Meany Memorial Archives, Silver Spring, Maryland.

BSP: Bordentown School Papers, Bordentown Branch of the Burlington County Library, Bordentown, New Jersey.

Country Files: Record Group 18-001, International Affairs Department, Country Files, 1945–1971, George Meany Memorial Archives, Silver Spring, Maryland.

FC Papers: Frank Crosswaith Papers, Schomburg Center for Research in Black Culture, New York Public Library, New York, New York.

HSLS Papers: Hudson Shore Labor School, Wagner Labor Archives, Bobst Library, New York University, New York, New York.

IISH: International Institute for Social History, Amsterdam, The Netherlands.

ILGWU Archives: General Collection number 5780, ILGWU Archives, Kheel Center for Labor-Management Documentation and Archives, Cornell University, Ithaca, New York.

Lovestone files: Record Group 18-003, International Affairs Department, Jay Lovestone files, 1939–1974, George Meany Memorial Archives, Silver Spring, Maryland.

LP: Jay Lovestone Papers, Hoover Institution, Stanford University, Stanford, California.

Meany files: Record Group 1-027, International Affairs Department, Office of the President, Presidents' Files: George Meany, 1944–1960, George Meany Memorial Archives, Silver Spring, Maryland.

MSK PP: Maida Springer-Kemp Private Papers, Pittsburgh, Pennsylvania. (In 1999 Springer added many of her private papers, but not all, to a collection of her work already in existence at Tulane University's Amistad Center.)

RP: Microfilm edition of the A. Philip Randolph Papers, Schomburg Center for Research in Black Culture, New York Public Library, New York, New York.

Schlesinger: MSK Papers, Schlesinger Library, Radcliffe College, Cambridge, Massachusetts.

Welsh Papers: Welsh Papers, Wagner Labor Archives, Bobst Library, New York University, New York, New York.

Introduction

1. I will refer to the subject primarily as Maida Springer since this was her name during most of the period of study. After her second marriage in 1965, she changed her name to Maida Springer-Kemp.

2. Postcard by Helaine Victoria Press: Publishers and Archivists of Postcards on Women in History (Martinsville, Ind., 1985).

3. Pauli Murray, *Song in a Weary Throat: An American Pilgrimage* (New York: Harper and Row, 1987). Elizabeth Balanoff's interview of Maida Springer-Kemp was originally a project of the Twentieth Century Trade Union Woman: Vehicle for Social Change, an oral-history project of the University of Michigan–Ann Arbor, Wayne State University, and the Schlesinger Library's Black Women's Oral History Project at Radcliffe College. It is published in *The Black Women's Oral History Project*, ed. Ruth Edmonds Hill (New Providence, N.J.: K. G. Saur Verlag, 1991), 7:39–127.

4. The following are recent publications that give attention to Springer. Ted Morgan's *A Covert Life: Jay Lovestone, Communist, Anti-Communist, and Spymaster* (New York: Random House, 1999) has numerous mistakes regarding Springer's activism. Annelise Orleck's *Common Sense and a Little Fire: Women and Working-Class Politics in the United States, 1900–1965* (Chapel Hill: University of North Carolina Press, 1995) includes information from the Balanoff interview. A chapter on Maida Springer-Kemp in Brigid O'Farrell and Joyce L. Kornbluh, *Rocking the Boat: Union Women's Voices, 1915–1975* (New Brunswick, N.J.: Rutgers University Press, 1996) also includes sections of the Balanoff interview and draws liberally from my historical research.

5. Examples of scholarship concerning pan-Africanism, or the response of African Americans to U.S. foreign policy, include: Brenda Gayle Plummer, *Rising Wind: Black Americans and U.S. Foreign Affairs, 1935–1960* (Chapel Hill: University of North Carolina Press, 1996); Penny M. Von Eschen, *Race against Empire: Black Americans and Anticolonialism, 1937–1957* (Ithaca: Cornell University Press, 1997); Opoku Agyeman, *Nkrumah's Ghana and East Africa: Pan-Africanism and African Interstate Relations* (Cranbury, N.J.: Associated University Press, 1992); Esedebe P. Olisanwuche, *Pan-Africanism, The Idea and Movement, 1776–1963* (Washington, D.C.: Howard University Press, 1982); Imanuel Geiss, *The Pan-African Movement: A History of Pan-Africanism in America, Europe, and Africa* (New York: Africana Publishing Company, 1974); Colin Legum, *Pan-Africanism, A Short Political Guide* (New York: Praeger, 1965).

6. Examples of scholarship on African labor include: Paul Gray, *Unions and Leaders in Ghana: A Model of Labor and Development* (New York: Conch Magazine, 1981); Wogu Ananaba, *The Trade Union Movement in Africa: Promise and Performance* (New York: St. Martin's Press, 1979); Richard Jeffries, *Class, Power and Ideology in Ghana: The Railwaymen of Sekondi* (New York: Cambridge University Press, 1978); Anthony Clayton and Donald C. Savage, *Government and Labour in Kenya, 1895–1963* (London: Cass, 1974).

7. Daniel Cantor and Juliet Schor, *Tunnel Vision: Labor, the World Economy, and Central America* (Boston: South End Press, 1987); George Morris, *CIA and American Labor: The Sub-*

version of the AFL-CIO's Foreign Policy (New York: International Publishers, 1982); Roy Godson, American Labor and European Politics: The AFL as a Transnational Force (New York: Crane, Russak, 1976); Jeffrey Harrod, Trade Union Foreign Policy: A Study of British and American Trade Union Activities in Jamaica (Garden City, N.J.: Doubleday, 1972); Alfred O. Hero, Jr., and Emil Starr, The Reuther-Meany Foreign Policy Dispute (Dobbs Ferry, N.Y.: Oceana Publications, 1970); Ronald Radosh, American Labor and United States Foreign Policy (New York: Random House, 1969).

8. Anthony Carew, "Charles Millard, A Canadian in the International Labour Movement: A Case Study of the ICFTU 1955–61," Labour/Le Travail 37 (Spring 1996): 121–48; Beth Sims, Workers of the World Undermined: American Labor's Role in U.S. Foreign Policy (Boston: South End Press, 1992); Peter Weiler, British Labour and the Cold War (Stanford: Stanford University Press, 1988); Barry Cohen, "The CIA and African Trade Unions," in Dirty Work 2: The CIA in Africa, ed. Ellen Ray, William Schaap, Karl Van Meter, and Louis Wolf (London: Zed Press, 1980), 70–79; Don Thomson and Rodney Larson, Where Were You, Brother? An Account of Trade Union Imperialism (London: War on Want, 1978).

9. Jervis Anderson's biography of Randolph does not include information on Springer's or Randolph's work in Africa. Jervis Anderson, A. Philip Randolph, A Biographical Portrait (Berkeley: University of California Press, 1972).

10. Plummer, Rising Wind; Von Eschen, Race against Empire.

11. Springer, Morogoro (Tanganyika) meeting, Jan. 18, 1958, MSK PP.

12. Amicus curiae briefs frequently argued that the United States, in its treatment of its black citizens, should adhere to the United Nations Universal Declaration of Human Rights. Plummer, Rising Wind, 199, 201; see also Mary L. Dudziak, "Desegregation as a Cold War Imperative," Stanford Law Review 41, no. 61 (Nov. 1988): 61–120.

13. Von Eschen, Race against Empire, 145; "Labor Unit Set Up for Negro Rights: Anti-Communist Unions Form Committee to Improve Lot of Individual Workers," New York Times, March 2, 1952, reprinted in Philip S. Foner and Ronald L. Lewis, The Black Worker from the Founding of the CIO to the AFL-CIO Merger, 1936–1955, vol. 7 of The Black Worker: A Documentary History from Colonial Times to the Present (Philadelphia: Temple University Press, 1983), 580–81; Randolph to Thomas Kirksey, Feb. 27, 1953, reel 1, frames 0704–0705, RP.

14. MSK, interview by Balanoff, in Hill, ed., The Black Women's Oral History Project, 7:102, 123; Randolph, "Meaning of Human Rights," speech at the annual congress of the ICFTU in Tunis, Tunisia, 1957, MSK PP; Ghana TUC general secretary (signature is illegible) to Vincent Tewson, British TUC general secretary, Oct. 18, 1957, 21/8, Brown files.

15. Randolph to Thomas Kirksey, Feb. 27, 1953, reel 1, frames 0704–0705, RP.

16. Maida Springer-Kemp file, Freedom of Information Privacy Act no. 341. 362-001/190-71490, main investigative file 105-58437, Federal Bureau of Investigation, U.S. Department of Justice.

17. Randolph, "Meaning of Human Rights," speech at the annual congress of the ICFTU in Tunis, Tunisia, 1957, MSK PP.

18. David Brombart, interview by author, March 5, 1993; McCray to Lovestone, April 6, 1959, "McCray," box 378, LP.

19. Jay Lovestone, interview by E. Finn, New York, Aug. 30, 1978, transcript, 8–9, ILGWU Archives.

20. C. B. Jenkins (chair of Program Committee) to Jay Lovestone, Jan. 29, 1931, "Abyssinian Baptist Church, 1931," box 349, LP.

21. Randolph, interview by MSK, "Oral History Program: African American Labor History Center," June 6, 1973, in Interviews, Box 1(2), APR Papers.

22. Braden, "I'm Glad the CIA Is 'Immoral,'" *Saturday Evening Post*, May 20, 1967. Victor Reuther, *The Brothers Reuther and the Story of the UAW* (Boston: Houghton Mifflin, 1976), 423–27. For sources reporting allegations of CIA involvement with the AFL-CIO, see Sims, *Workers of the World Undermined*; Ray et al., *Dirty Work 2*; Thomson and Larson, *Where Were You, Brother?*; Philip Agee, *Inside the Company: CIA Diary* (New York: Stonehill, 1975), 75, 604; and George Morris, *CIA and American Labor: The Subversion of the AFL-CIO's Foreign Policy* (New York: International Publishers, 1967).

23. Meany to Reuther, Jan. 11, 1961, "Ross, Michael, 1956–1961," box 386, LP; Ross to Brown, May 2, 1961, 8/2, Brown files; Lovestone, interview by E. Finn, 4, 57, 59–60, ILGWU Archives; David Dubinsky and A. H. Raskin, *David Dubinsky: A Life with Labor* (New York: Simon and Schuster, 1977), 259–61.

24. Brown, who came out of the International Association of Machinists, became head of the ICFTU United Nations office in 1962, head of the AFL-CIO's African American Labor Center in 1964, AFL-CIO European representative in 1973, and head of the AFL-CIO International Affairs Department in 1982. "Irving Brown, AALC Founder, Remembered," *AALC Reporter Supplement* 24, no. 2 (1989); Burton Hersh, *The Old Boys: The American Elite and the Origins of the CIA* (New York: Charles Scribner's Sons, 1992), 239, 296, 317.

25. Springer made this comment after I showed her the People's News Service allegation, reprinted in Cohen, "The CIA and African Trade Unions," 75, 79. Until then she had not been aware of any specific allegations against her. McCray was also accused of associating with spies: "U.S. Intervention in Internal Affairs Alleged," *African Recorder*, March 12–25, 1962, 117. In 1967 an opposition member of the Kenya legislature accused Mboya of CIA involvement, which he denied. Stanley Meisler (a *Times* staff writer), "Unions Use U.S. Funds to Expand Role in Africa" (source of clipping not identified; possibly from a 1968 edition of the *New York Times*), "Africa Trade Unions," box 398, LP.

26. Brown, "Notes on Conversation Irving Brown Tom Mboya," June 7, 1959, "Brown, 1959," box 356, LP.

27. Mboya to Brown, March 12, 1961, 30/11; Kubai to Brown, Feb. 11, 1963, and Kubai to Brown, received March 11, 1963, both in 1/22; all in Brown files.

28. Pamela Mboya to Brown, June 15, 1971, 1/23, Brown files.

29. Radical critics accused Mboya of ushering in neocolonialism through his promotion of a mixed capitalist economy. David Goldsworthy, *Tom Mboya: The Man Kenya Wanted to Forget* (New York: Africana Publishing, 1982), 259.

30. Goldsworthy, *Tom Mboya*, 150; Springer, memorandum on Kenya, March 24, 1957, "Springer," box 388, LP; Springer, memorandum on Tanganyika, Feb. 19, 1957, 60/23, Lovestone files; A. Philip Randolph, report on trip to Africa (handwritten notation incorrectly dates the document in 1956; should be 1957), reel 3, frames 0543–0551, and Springer to Chief [Randolph], March 5, 1972, reel 3, frames 0026–0027, both in RP. See also Ochwada to Meany, July 26, 1957, 11/6, Country files.

31. Goldsworthy, *Tom Mboya*, 62; Springer, memorandum on Kenya, March 24, 1957, "Springer," box 388, LP; A. Philip Randolph, 1957 report on trip to Africa, reel 3, frames 0543–0551, and Springer to Chief [Randolph], March 5, 1972, frames 0026–0027, both in RP. See also Ochwada to Meany, July 26, 1957, 11/6, Country files.

32. Thomson and Larson, *Where Were You, Brother?* 18–20; Carew, "Charles Millard, A Canadian in the International Labour Movement," 136–43. See *Proceedings of the AFL-CIO Constitutional Convention*, 1957, vol. 1, 382–84, 428–33.

33. Thomson and Larson, *Where Were You, Brother?* 19.

34. Randolph, interview by MSK, June 6, 1973, in Interviews, box 1(2), APR Papers.

35. Goldsworthy also states that Mboya was "quick to approve" Ochwada as the trainee. Goldsworthy, *Tom Mboya*, 154; Clayton and Savage, *Government and Labour in Kenya*, 433; Thuo to Springer, Sept. 9, 1957, and Ochwada to Springer, June 13, 1957, both in 60/23, Lovestone files; Ochwada to Springer, July 29, 1957, and Mboya to Springer, Dec. 20, 1957, both in MSK PP; Ochwada to Springer, Sept. 7, 1957, 28/2, Brown files.

36. Cohen, "The CIA and African Trade Unions," 75–76.

37. For example, a little over a year later Brown requested that Jamela send him another receipt for five thousand dollars that he had given him. He explained that he had lost the original and needed the replacement to account for the part of the aid he had given. Brown to Jamela, Jan. 23, 1962, and Jamela to Brown, Jan. 31, 1962, both in 33/9, Brown to Ross, Oct. 31, 1960, 33/18, and July 14, 1961, 33/22, all in Brown files; Springer to Maluleke, July 21, 1961, and Nov. 20, 1961, 12/8, Country files; Cohen, "The CIA and African Trade Unions," 75.

38. MSK to Nana Mahomo, memo, Aug. 1, 1983, MSK PP.

Chapter 1: "My Wonderful Young Mother": Springer's Formative Years

1. MSK, "Mama, Maida and the United States of America," MSK PP.

2. Michael L. Conniff, *Black Labor on a White Canal: Panama, 1904–1981* (Pittsburgh: University of Pittsburgh Press, 1985), 8–9.

3. MSK, interview by author. Many of the quotes from my interviews are part of the oral-history chapters in Yevette Richards, "'My Passionate Feeling about Africa': Maida Springer-Kemp and the American Labor Movement," Ph.D. diss., Yale University, 1994.

4. According to Walter LaFeber, "the mass of Panamanians referred to the leading families as *rabiblancos*, or white tails." Walter LaFeber, *The Panama Canal: The Crisis in Historical Perspective*, 2d ed. (New York: Oxford University Press, 1989), 49–51.

5. LaFeber, *The Panama Canal*, 49–51.

6. Conniff, *Black Labor on a White Canal*, 31; Velma Newton, *The Silver Men: West Indian Labour Migration to Panama, 1850–1914* (Kingston, Jamaica: Institute of Social and Economic Research, University of the West Indies, 1984), 140–43.

7. Conniff, *Black Labor on a White Canal*, 26, 35.

8. Ibid., 30; Newton, *The Silver Men*, 134.

9. Conniff, *Black Labor on a White Canal*, 5, 39–40; Newton, *The Silver Men*, 132, 142.

10. The following information on Springer's childhood comes from MSK, "Mama, Maida and the United States of America," MSK PP.

11. With the completion of the canal in 1914, silver-roll employees declined from 38,000 in 1913 to 8,000 in 1921. Conniff, *Black Labor on a White Canal*, 49; Gilbert Osofsky, *Harlem: The Making of a Ghetto: Negro New York, 1890–1930*, 2d ed. (New York: Harper and Row, 1971), 131.

12. Under the occupation category on the S.S. *Alianza*'s manifest, both of Springer's parents are listed as tailors. Her mother's age is listed as twenty-three and her father's as thirty-four. Records of the U.S. Department of Immigration and Naturalization.

13. See, for example, Pauline Newman, transcript of 1978 interview by Barbara Wertheimer, The 20th Century Trade Union Woman: Vehicle for Social Change (Oral History Project Program on Women and Work), 2. Bentley Historical Library, University of Michigan, Ann Arbor.

14. Elizabeth Balanoff, "Maida Springer Kemp Interview," in *The Black Women Oral History Project*, vol. 7, ed. Ruth Edmonds Hill (New Providence, N.J.: K. G. Saur Verlag, 1991), 46.

15. There were ten times as many foreign-born blacks in Harlem as in any other city in the country. Osofsky, *Harlem: The Making of a Ghetto*, 131.

16. The word "integrated" was not in common use at this time. Kenneth King, ed., *Ras Makonnen, Pan-Africanism from Within* (New York: Oxford University Press, 1973), 60–69; Pauli Murray, *The Autobiography of a Black Activist, Feminist, Lawyer, Priest, and Poet* (Knoxville: University of Tennessee Press, 1987), 49; Conniff, *Black Labor on a White Canal*, 8, 9; and Osofsky, *Harlem: The Making of a Ghetto*, 132–34.

17. Others to whom Springer was exposed in the church included Roland Hayes, Ethel Waters, Bert Williams, and Florence Mills. MSK, "Bridging the Gap" (speech at Chicago's Good Shepherd Congregational Church, Oct. 10, 1970), MSK PP.

18. MSK, "Mama, Maida and the United States of America," MSK PP.

19. MSK, unnamed autobiographical sketches, MSK PP.

20. MSK, "Mama, Maida and the United States of America," MSK PP.

21. Ibid.

22. MSK, remarks made at Community College, March 31, 1989, MSK PP.

23. MSK, interview by author; see also David Levering Lewis, *When Harlem Was in Vogue*, (New York: Knopf, 1984), 111–12.

24. Eugene V. Debs was a labor and Socialist Party leader. Crosswaith was from the Virgin Islands. A. Philip Randolph and Richard Parrish, May 1, 1975, transcript. Interviews file, box 1, APR Papers.

25. Jervis Anderson, *A. Philip Randolph, A Biographical Portrait* (Los Angeles: University of California Press, 1986), 77–80 (Randolph quote, 77); Osofsky, *Harlem: The Making of a Ghetto*, 132–33.

26. Du Bois, "Close Ranks," *The Crisis* 16 (July 1918): 111; Anderson, *A. Philip Randolph*, 108, 118–119; Randolph and Owen, "Pro-Germanism among Negroes," *The Messenger*, July 1918; "Addresses Denouncing W.E.B. Du Bois" *The Negro World*, April 5, 1919, in *The Marcus Garvey and UNIA Papers*, vol. 1, ed. Robert A. Hill (Los Angeles: University of California Press, 1983), 394–400.

27. Elliott Rudwick, "W.E.B. Du Bois: Protagonist of the Afro-American Protest," in *Black Leaders of the Twentieth Century*, ed. John Hope Franklin and August Meier (Urbana: University of Illinois Press, 1982), 76–77.

28. King, *Ras Makonnen*, 66–67; Lawrence Levine, "Marcus Garvey and the Politics of Revitalization," in Franklin and Meier, *Black Leaders of the Twentieth Century*, 115.

29. Du Bois acknowledged that Garvey had "*men* [emphasis mine] of all colors and blood" in the UNIA, but still faulted him for his "'all-black'" propaganda. "Back to Africa," reprinted from *Century* magazine, Feb. 1923, in *Writings by W.E.B. Du Bois in Periodicals Edited by Others*, vol. 2, 1910–1934, ed. Herbert Aptheker (Millwood, N.Y.: Kraus-Thomson Organization, 1982), 176; William Seraile, "Henrietta Vinton Davis and the Garvey Movement," *Afro-Americans in New York Life and History* (July 1983): 7–24 (references on pp. 11, 13); George Padmore, *Pan-Africanism or Communism? The Coming Struggle for Africa* (1956; reprint, New York: Doubleday, 1971), 68–69.

30. Speech by Marcus Garvey (Royal Albert Hall, London, June 6, 1928), in *The Marcus Garvey and UNIA Papers*, 9 vols., ed. Robert A. Hill (Los Angeles: University of California Press, 1985), 4:206; "Opening Speech of the Convention by Marcus Garvey, New York, August 1, 1921," in Hill, *The Marcus Garvey and UNIA Papers*, 3:583; "Interview with Chandler Owen and A. Philip Randolph by Charles Mowbray White," Manhattan, Aug. 20, 1920, and "Interview with W.E.B. Du Bois by Charles Mowbray White," New York, Aug. 22, 1920, in Hill, *The Marcus Garvey and UNIA Papers*, 1:610, 621.

31. Anderson, *A. Philip Randolph*, 133–37; Du Bois to Domingo, Jan. 18, 1923, in *The Correspondence of W.E.B. Du Bois*, vol. 1, *Selections, 1877–1934*, ed. Herbert Aptheker (Boston: University of Massachusetts Press, 1973), 263–64; Mark Naison, *Communists in Harlem during*

the Depression (New York: Grove Press, 1984), 8; Tony Martin, *Race First: The Ideological and Organizational Struggles of Marcus Garvey and the UNIA*, The New Marcus Garvey Library no. 8 (Dover: Majority Press, 1976), 297, 300.

32. MSK, "Mama, Maida and the United States of America," MSK PP. See also Audre Lorde's experience in the 1940s at this same St. Marks School. Lorde, *Zami, A New Spelling of My Name* (Trumansburg, N.Y.: Crossing Press, 1982), 29.

33. MSK, interview by Balanoff, in Hill, ed., *The Black Women's Oral History Project*, 7:46.

34. The following information comes from MSK, "Mama, Maida and the United States of America," MSK PP.

35. MSK, interview by author.

36. MSK, "Mama, Maida and the United States of America," MSK PP; State of New Jersey Manual and Training and Industrial School for Colored Youth, *Bordentown and Its Training*, 1925). I am indebted to Richard Gross, who served as my guide in the Bordentown region, and to alumni Arthur T. Harris and Nat Hampton, and a former Bordentown teacher, Helen M. Roberts, for information and literature about Bordentown. Unrecorded collective interviews (notes only) by author, spring 1991.

37. Valentine served as principal from 1915 to 1950. Quote in W. R. Valentine, "The State Aids Negro Youth," *New Jersey Educational Review* 9, no. 2 (Nov. 1935), in BSP.

38. Clement A. Price, "Bordentown School, Tuskegee of the North, 1920–25," document 11, Quest of Racial Identity, in *Freedom Not Far Distant* (Newark: New Jersey Historical Society, 1980), 185–87, BSP.

39. State of New Jersey Manual Training and Industrial School for Colored Youth, *Bordentown and Its Training*.

40. Quotes are from a photocopy of a segment of an unlabeled 1933 Bordentown publication in BSP. See also Frances O. Grant, 1977 interview by Maurine Rothschild, in *The Black Women Oral History Project*, 10 vols., ed. Ruth Edmonds Hill (New Providence, N.J.: K. G. Saur Verlag, 1991), 4:382–83.

41. Valentine, "The State Aids Negro Youth," *New Jersey Educational Review* 9, no. 2 (Nov. 1935), BSP.

42. MSK, "Mama, Maida and the United States of America," MSK PP.

43. Granger met his future wife at the school and married her a year later. Harriet ("Lefty") Lane Granger was the school's bookkeeper from 1916 to 1951. Lester Granger, 1960 interview by William Ingersoll, transcripts, 54–81, Oral History Project, Butler Library, Columbia University, New York, N.Y.; MSK, "Mama, Maida and the United States of America," MSK PP.

44. MSK, "Mama, Maida and the United States of America," MSK PP.

45. Arthur Harris and Nat Hampton, interviewed by author; Granger, interview by Ingersoll, 55.

46. Quote from Harris and Hampton, interviews by author, spring 1991. State of New Jersey Manual Training and Industrial School for Colored Youth, "*Ironsides*," A Year Book, June 1922; *Bordentown and Its Training*, 1925; and *New Jersey Ironsides Bulletin*, 1929–1930, all from the personal collections of Bordentown alumni. Price, "Bordentown School, Tuskegee of the North," 183, BSP.

47. Ben Johnson was a famous track star with a degree from Columbia, and Charles Ray was the first black captain of the football team at Bates College. The staff held degrees from Harvard, Columbia, Temple, Rutgers, Bates, Wellesley, Radcliffe, Fisk, Morehouse, Hampton, Shaw, and Lincoln. "Salaries of Bordentown Faculty" (photocopied document), and Burrell T. Brown, "Early Schools for Blacks: Educating the head and the hands" in "Accent" (newspaper column), *Burlington County Times*, March 28, 1982, both in BSP.

48. George Haley, whose brother was the writer Alex Haley, was also a Bordentown alum-

nus. He became a lawyer and a member of the Kansas legislature, and served as a high official in the Department of Transportation under President Richard Nixon. Brown, "Early Schools for Blacks," BSP.

49. In 1922, 250 students were enrolled, whereas six years earlier there had only been 91. Springer was part of the large student influx. State of New Jersey Manual Training and Industrial School for Colored Youth, "*Ironsides*," *A Year Book*, June 1922; Valentine, "The State Aids Negro Youth," *New Jersey Educational Review* 9, no. 2 (Nov. 1935), BSP; Grant, interview by Rothschild, 4:381–82; Granger, interview by Ingersoll, 54–55.

50. Williams retired in 1946. Springer had heard that Williams's father was a janitor at Harvard. *The Ironsides Echo* (school newspaper), June 1955; Harris and Hampton, interview by author.

51. MSK, interview by author.

52. Grace B. Valentine served as preceptress and dean of girls from 1915 until her death in 1950. Carter was director of *Opportunity*, the official organ of the Urban League. Larsen was a writer of the Harlem Renaissance. Harrison was a famous elocutionist. Other distinguished visitors over the years included W. C. Handy, Nat King Cole, Duke Ellington, Carter G. Woodson, James Weldon Johnson, Roland Hayes, Mary McLeod Bethune, Benjamin Mays, Carl Van Vechten, Albert Einstein, and Eleanor Roosevelt, who gave the 1942 commencement address. *The Ironsides Echo*, June 1955; Grant, interview by Rothschild, 4:365, 385.

53. Grant, interview by Rothschild, 4:385.

54. As late as 1969 Granger remained in contact with a number of people he had known at Bordentown. He told Springer that he had given financial assistance to two former Bordentown employees who were now elderly. Granger to Springer, March 5, 1969, MSK PP; Granger, interview by Ingersoll, 84.

55. Grant, interview by Rothschild, 4:381–82; Valentine, "The State Aids Negro Youth," *New Jersey Educational Review* 9, no. 2 (Nov. 1935), BSP; and *New Jersey Ironsides Bulletin*, 1929–1930.

56. Price, "Bordentown School, Tuskegee of the North," 183, BSP.

57. MSK, "Mama, Maida and the United States of America," MSK PP.

58. Grant, interview by Rothschild, 4:386–87, 391; "School in Jersey Aids Negro Youths," *New York Times*, Nov. 21, 1948, and Lloyd E. Griscom, "'Ironsides' History Sails into County," *County Album*, Oct. 18, 1985, both in BSP.

59. By 1930 black women, representing about 10 percent of the total female population, only held 5.4 percent of manufacturing positions and .05 percent of the clerical positions open to females. Jacqueline Jones, *Labor of Love, Labor of Sorrow* (New York: Vintage Books, 1985), 162–67; Ruth Edmonds Hill, ed., *Women of Courage: An Exhibition of Photographs by Judith Sedwick* (Cambridge: Radcliffe College, 1984), 9–10.

60. MSK, interview by author.

61. MSK, "Mama, Maida and the United States of America," MSK PP.

62. Philip S. Foner, *Organized Labor and the Black Worker, 1619–1981*, 2d ed. (New York: International Publishers, 1981), 135.

63. Naison, *Communists in Harlem*, 239; Charles V. Hamilton, *Adam Clayton Powell, Jr.: The Political Biography of an American Dilemma* (New York: Atheneum and Maxwell, 1991), 61; Stephen H. Norwood, *Labor's Flaming Youth: Telephone Operators and Worker Militancy, 1878–1923* (Urbana: University of Illinois Press, 1990), 4, 42.

64. MSK, interview by Balanoff, in Hill, ed., *The Black Women's Oral History Project*, 7:142.

65. Murray, *Autobiography of a Black Activist*, 75–76.

66. MSK, interview by author.

67. Ibid.

68. Generous during her life, upon her death Walker designated two-thirds of her wealth for charitable purposes. Paula Giddings, *When and Where I Enter: The Impact of Black Women on Race and Sex in America* (New York: William Morrow, 1984), 187–89.

69. According to a U.S. Women's Bureau special study, in 1931 three-fourths of all wage earners in Harlem were unemployed. By the end of 1934, 3.5 million black families were on relief. Biographical material, box 1, folder 2, APR Papers.

70. Alice Kessler-Harris, "Organizing the Unorganizable: Three Jewish Women and Their Union," in Daniel J. Leab, ed., *The Labor History Reader* (Urbana: University of Illinois Press, 1985), 272; reprint, *Labor History* 17 (Winter 1976): 5–23.

71. The *American Labor Yearbook* of 1923–1924 estimated that 65 percent of all employed women in New York City worked in the garment industry. In 1927, 78 percent of national garment production was located in New York. Statistics from David Gurowsky, "Factional Disputes within the ILGWU, 1919–1928" (Ph.D. diss., State University of New York at Binghampton, 1978), 20, 26.

Chapter 2: "My Union Was a Very Political Union": Springer Joins Local 22

1. Granger to Zimmerman, April 6, 1937, 14/27/7; Chair of Negro Labor Committee to Local 22 (Samuel Shore), n.d., 14/28/3; and Dedication Committee of Negro Labor Committee to Zimmerman, Nov. 18, 1935, 62/1/5; all in ILGWU Archives.

2. The Harlem Advisory Committee of the Workers Education, organized by Granger, sponsored workers' education classes in Harlem for the Works Progress Administration (WPA). Randolph and Crosswaith previously were instructors at the Rand School for Social Science, a workers' school from which Crosswaith also graduated. In 1923 Crosswaith founded the Trade Union Committee for Organizing Negro Workers, which evolved into the Negro Labor Committee. He served as its head from 1935 to 1955. Program of the Twentieth Century Association, Feb. 5 and 12, 1938, FC Papers; and A. Philip Randolph and Richard Parrish, May 1, 1975, transcript, Interviews file, box 1, APR Papers.

3. MSK, interview by author.

4. Robert Laurents, "Racial and Ethnic Conflict in the New York City Garment Industry" (Ph.D. diss., State University of New York at Binghampton, 1980), 123, 129–30; Altagracia Ortiz, "'En la aguja y el pedal eché la hiel': Puerto Rican Women in the Garment Industry of New York City, 1920–1980," in Altagracia Ortiz, ed., *Puerto Rican Women and Work: Bridges in Transnational Labor* (Philadelphia: Temple University Press, 1996), 59.

5. Between 1919 and 1924 a quarter of a million Jews fled Eastern Europe and Russia for the United States. According to the union rolls of 1924, three-fourths of garment workers were born in Europe. Jews represented 63 percent of the industry and Italians, 20 percent. Only 3 percent of the workforce was American-born of other ethnicities. David Gurowsky, "Factional Disputes within the ILGWU, 1919–1928," 27; Steven Fraser, *Labor Will Rule: Sidney Hillman and the Rise of American Labor* (New York: Free Press and Maxwell, 1991), 220.

6. Charles Zimmerman, interview by David Gurowsky, Oct. 31, 1974, tape recording, Robert Wagner Labor Archives, Bobst Library, New York University, New York; Philip S. Foner and Ronald L. Lewis, eds., *The Black Worker from the Founding of the CIO to the AFL-CIO Merger, 1936–1955*, vol. 7 of *The Black Worker: A Documentary History from Colonial Times to the Present* (Philadelphia: Temple University Press, 1983), 643.

7. Silverman, interview by author, April 30, 1991.

8. Charles Zimmerman, interview by Henoch Mendelsund, 1976, transcript p. 972 (see also p. 329), ILGWU Archives.

9. "Scores Die in Triangle Blaze, Many Killed in 9-Story Leap," *The World*, n.d.; Rosey Safran, "Girl Who Escaped Sees Friends Jump to Death," *The Independent*, April 20, 1911, and Arthur E. McFarlane, "Workers Doomed by Lack of Fire Escapes," *McClure's*, Sept. 1911, all reprinted in Max D. Danish and Leon Stein, eds., *ILGWU News-History, 1900–1950: The Story of the Ladies' Garment Workers* (Atlantic City: ILGWU Golden Jubilee Convention, 1950), 35–36.

10. The General Executive Board (GEB) separated the dressmakers from Local 25 and Local 23 (which had a strong right-wing component) and placed them in the newly created Local 22 for both political and economic reasons. Local 25 now included only blousemakers, whose work in the industry was rapidly declining; and Local 23 included only skirtmakers. Zimmerman, interview by Gurowsky; Zimmerman, interview by Mendelsund, 354; Philip S. Foner, *Women and the American Labor Movement, From World War I to the Present* (New York: Free Press, 1980), 115, 160.

11. Gurowsky, "Factional Disputes within the ILGWU," xxii, xxvii, 13, 35–51, 218.

12. Will Herberg, "The ILG Civil War," *American Jewish Yearbook*, 1952, reprinted in Leon Stein, ed., *Out of the Sweatshop: The Struggle for Industrial Democracy* (New York: Quadrangle/New York Times, 1977), 214–15; Louis Levine, *The Women's Garment Workers: A History of the International Ladies' Garment Workers' Union* (New York: B. W. Huebsch, 1924), 352–54; Melech Epstein, *Jewish Labor in U.S.A.: An Industrial, Political and Cultural History of the Jewish Labor Movement*, vol. 2, 1914–1952 (New York: Ktav Publishing House, 1969), 130.

13. Zimmerman, interview by Mendelsund, 396–98; Zimmerman, interview by Gurowsky; Dubinsky and Raskin, *David Dubinsky: A Life with Labor*, 99–100.

14. Dubinsky and Raskin, *David Dubinsky*, 100–102.

15. Harry Haywood, *Black Bolshevik: Autobiography of an Afro-American Communist* (Chicago: Lake View Press, 1978), 257.

16. Haywood, *Black Bolshevik*, 246–57, 288–99, 304; Robert J. Alexander, *The Right Opposition: The Lovestoneites and the International Communist Opposition of the 1930s* (Westport, Conn.: Greenwood Press, 1981), 3–28, 121–23; Zimmerman, interview by Mendelsund, 521.

17. Known as La Pasionaria, Dolores Ibarruri Gómez (1895–1981) stood as a symbol of courage during the Spanish Civil War. Sondra Hale, "Feminist Method, Process, and Self-Criticism: Interviewing Sudanese Women," p. 135, n. 20, in Sherna Berger Gluck and Daphne Patai, *Women's Words: The Feminist Practice of Oral History* (New York: Routledge, 1991). Zimmerman, interview by Mendelsund, 535; Zimmerman, interview by Gurowsky. David Dubinsky and A. H. Raskin, *David Dubinsky: A Life with Labor* (New York: Simon and Schuster, 1977), 91, 103–4 (quote is from last page).

18. Gurowsky, "Factional Disputes within the ILGWU," 321; "Steps Taken to Rebuild the Union," c. 1928, 14/42/10, ILGWU Archives.

19. "To All Dressmakers," New York District Communist Party flyer, 14/3/12, ILGWU Archives. For more information on the Lovestoneite position, see Resolution to the New York Membership Meeting, c. 1929, and A Letter to the Plenum of the Communist Party USA (Majority Group), Nov. 27, 1930; both in 14/41/1, ILGWU Archives.

20. Zimmerman, interview by Mendelsund, 629.

21. By 1935 the left wing rarely received more than 25 percent of the vote in any of the locals. Laurents, "Racial and Ethnic Conflict," 156; Levine, *The Women's Garment Workers*, 352–54; Nancy L. Green, *Ready-To-Wear and Ready-To-Work: A Century of Industry and Immigrants in Paris and New York* (Durham, N.C.: Duke University Press, 1997), 230–33; Bert Cochran, *Labor and Communism: The Conflict That Shaped American Unions* (Princeton, N.J.: Princeton University Press, 1977), 132.

22. A large number of the original Bolshevik leadership lost their lives. Lovestone was among the approximately one-third of the members of the Comintern's Central Committee who were expelled. Letter to the Central Committee Communist Party, USA, Oct. 2, 1929; quote is from "Resolution of the New York Membership Meeting," n.d.; both in 14/41/1, ILGWU Archives.

23. Zimmerman, interview by Mendelsund, 618.

24. Zimmerman once stated that Dubinsky "treat[ed] people sometimes in a very harsh manner" and particularly treated the GEB "like a bunch of school boys," which many resented. Zimmerman, interview by Mendelsund, 1076–77; Dubinsky and Raskin, David Dubinsky, 107.

25. Zimmerman, interview by Gurowsky.

26. People solicited Zimmerman's help against persecution in the 1940s by the House Un-American Activities Committee chaired by Texas Representative Martin Dies and against persecution in the 1950s under the Smith Act. Enacted in 1940 as a tool against communism, the Smith Act made it illegal to advocate by word or deed the violent overthrow of the U.S. government. Zimmerman to the Hon. Winifred Stanley, 14/21/9, and Morton Sobell to Zimmerman, July 23, 1950, 14-5-3, both in ILGWU Archives; Zimmerman, interview by Mendelsund, 629; Cochran, Labor and Communism, 132; "Dressmakers '22' Protest Dies Fund," Justice, March 1, 1942.

27. The other FTUC officers included Meany as honorary president, Dubinsky as vice president, and William Schnitzler as honorary secretary. Ronald Radosh, American Labor and United States Foreign Policy (New York: Random House, 1969), 309.

28. The decline in union membership in the early 1920s was due to the success of the Palmer Raids and open-shop campaigns and the postwar recession. Between 1921 and 1923, the AFL lost nearly one-fourth of its membership. ILGWU membership declined from 104,000 in 1920 to 32,000 in 1929. The organized workforce in the cloak industry fell from 80 percent in 1926 to 7 percent by 1928, with 43 percent of that only nominally organized. Organized shops within the dress industry dropped from three-fourths to one-third. Gurowsky, "Factional Disputes within the ILGWU, 1919–1928," vi, 36, 267–68, 276; and Fraser, Labor Will Rule, 189.

29. Dubinsky cites the same trend but with different totals. Dubinsky and Raskin, David Dubinsky, 102, 109; Zimmerman, interview by Gurowsky; Zimmerman, interview by Mendelsund, 573–76.

30. Edith Kine, "The Garment Union Comes to the Negro Worker," reprinted in Foner and Lewis, eds., The Era of Post-War Prosperity and the Great Depression, 1920–1936, vol. 6 of The Black Worker: A Documentary History from Colonial Times to the Present (Philadelphia: Temple University Press, 1981), 179–80; Program of the Twentieth Century Association, Feb. 5 and 12, 1938, FC Papers; "The 35 Hour Week," Justice, May 1–15, 1956.

31. MSK, keynote address, Tenth Anniversary Celebration, Coalition of Labor Union Women, St. Louis, Missouri, Nov. 12, 1983, Amistad.

32. MSK to Evelyn Hoffman, memo, Perceptions of the Labor Movement, April 28, 1986, MSK PP.

33. The names of Springer's mother-in-law and sister-in-law were Beatrice Springer and Eugenia (Gene) Payne.

34. MSK, interview by author. Two other learning centers for ILGWU educational programs included Brookwood Labor College, opened in 1920, and the New Workers School, founded by Bertram D. Wolfe in 1929.

35. Welsh first began organizing workers in 1930 as a volunteer for Local 22. He went to Africa to organize workers when George Meany assigned him to the International Confederation of Free Trade Unions in 1961. In 1964 he returned to the United States and worked for the

New York City Central Labor Council. Biographical sketch, 1974 program for the Third Annual Award Dinner Dance of the Black Trade Unionists Leadership Committee of the New
York City Central Labor Council, Welsh Papers.

36. Education Department of ILGWU, *Structure and Functioning of the ILGWU*, rev. ed.
(New York: Arco Press, 1938), 30–32.

37. "The Educational Activities of Local 22, I.L.G.W.U.," 1937, "ILGWU Education Department" folder, box 487, LP.

38. Zimmerman, interview by Mendelsund, 642.

39. Lurye (Matheson) to Zimmerman, Feb. 12 and May 1944, 14/24/4, ILGWU Archives.

40. Evalyn Coppoc, "Garment Union Has Enlightened Policy," *Pittsburgh Courier*, April
22, 1944, 14/28/2, ILGWU Archives.

41. Zimmerman, interview by Mendelsund, 642; Epstein, Epstein, *Jewish Labor in the
U.S.A.*, 2:341–42.

42. MSK, interview by author.

43. Proceedings of the 10th Convention Communist Party New York State, May 20–23,
1938, and Report of Josephine Martini, Proceedings of the 10th Convention Communist Party,
both in 14/5/1, ILGWU Archives.

44. Report of Max Steinberg, Proceedings of the 10th Convention Communist Party,
14/5/1, ILGWU Archives.

45. T. Arnold Hill, "Open Letter to Mr. William Green," *Opportunity* 8 (Feb. 1930):
56–57, reprinted in Philip S. Foner and Ronald L. Lewis, eds., *Black Workers: A Documentary
History from Colonial Times to the Present* (Philadelphia: Temple University Press, 1989),
413–17; and Dubinsky and Raskin, *David Dubinsky*, 236–38.

46. ILGWU, *Report of the General Executive Board, the Nineteenth Convention of the International Ladies' Garment Workers' Union* (Boston, May 1928), 266.

47. See information about the Comintern "Black Belt" resolution in Mark Naison, *Communists in Harlem during the Depression* (New York: Grove Press, 1984), 17–25, 45–47; Haywood, *Black Bolshevik*, 227–40; George Padmore, *Pan-Africanism or Communism? The Coming
Struggle for Africa* (1956; reprint, New York: Doubleday, 1971), 284–86; and Paul Buhle, *Marxism in the United States: Remapping the History of the American Left* (London: Verso, 1987), 10,
139–42.

For views of CP operations in the South during the Third Period and Popular Front, see
Robin Kelley, *Hammer and Hoe: Alabama Communists during the Great Depression* (Chapel
Hill: University of North Carolina Press, 1990); Nell Irvin Painter, *The Narrative of Hosea Hudson: His Life as a Negro Communist in the South* (Cambridge, Mass.: Harvard University Press,
1979); and Theodore Rosengarten, *All God's Dangers: The Life of Nate Shaw* (New York: Vintage, 1974).

48. "To all Dressmakers, Members of Local 22 Int. Ladies Garment Workers Union," flyer,
n.d., 14/3/12; "Dressmakers of Local 22—Negro and White, Facts Speak Louder than Words,"
flyer, March 15, 1934, 14/28/2; both in ILGWU Archives.

49. The NTWIU put special emphasis on gaining the support of black workers. Part of
their appeal was to highlight the position of two black members of their General Executive
Board, Henry Rosemond and Virginia Allen, and to have Welsh serve as chair of at least one of
its mass meetings for dressmakers. "Negro Workers!" flyer, Feb. 21, 1929, 14/28/2, ILGWU
Archives.

50. Zimmerman to James Hubert (executive director of the Urban League), May 29, 1933,
14/27/7, ILGWU Archives.

51. MSK, interview by author.

52. Naison, *Communists in Harlem*, xvi, 38.

53. MSK, interview by author. Attesting to the prevalence of paternalism in the CP, Paul

Buhle conceded that although "the approach to race was still the noblest, and the most unique, of Communist contributions to the American left and to American society," their approach was inevitably condescending. Buhle, *Marxism in the United States*, 141–42. Robin Kelley argues that paternalism was not as much of an issue between Northern white Communists and Alabama blacks as it was in other parts of the country. Kelley, *Hammer, and Hoe*, 112. For further explanations of the gulf between the CP and the blacks it hoped to ally with the party, see Naison, *Communists in Harlem*, xvii, 68, 283; and Abner Berry, interview by Naison, July 29, 1974, tape recording, Wagner Labor Archives. Buhle, *Marxism in the United States*, 141–42; Kelley, *Hammer and Hoe*, 112.

54. Padmore, *Pan-Africanism or Communism?* 292; Buhle, *Marxism in the United States*, 145; and Naison, *Communists in Harlem*, 11.

55. MSK, interview by author.

56. Ernest Calloway, "The C.I.O. and Negro Labor," *Opportunity* 14 (Nov. 1936): 326–30, reprinted in Foner and Lewis, ed., *The Black Worker: A Documentary History from Colonial Times to the Present* (Philadelphia: Temple University Press, 1989), 459–60.

57. The vice chairmen of the Negro Labor Committee included Julius Hochman of the Dress Joint Board and Randolph. The Harlem Labor Center was at 312 West 125th Street, and the BSCP office was at 217 West 125th Street.

58. Granger to Dubinsky, March 25, 1946, and Granger to Zimmerman, April 6, 1937, both in 14/27/7, ILGWU Archives.

59. Granger to Zimmerman, March 30, 1948, 14/27/7, ILGWU Archives.

60. The Negro Labor Committee included on its letterhead the disclaimer, "No connection with any organization of similar name." The Harlem Labor Center also had to distinguish its work from that of the Harlem Labor Union, a nationalist-based organization formed in 1936 by Garveyites Ira Kemp and Arthur Reid that was opposed to organized labor. "Frank R. Crosswaith Launches Fight to Rid Harlem of Fake Union," *New York Amsterdam News*, Nov. 21, 1936, and "Crosswaith to All Affiliates of the Negro Labor Committee," circular letter, Sept. 16, 1943 (both in 14/28/3), and "Dubinsky to the Joint Boards," circular letter, Aug. 19, 1940, 14/4/7, all in ILGWU Archives; "Negro Labor Committee Has Nothing in Common with 'Victory Committee,'" July 1, 1943, *Justice*; Naison, *Communists in Harlem*, 178, 181.

61. For some perspectives on Randolph's and Crosswaith's anticommunism, see Naison, *Communists in Harlem*, 181, 245–47; Jervis Anderson, *A. Philip Randolph: A Biographical Portrait* (Los Angeles: University of California Press, 1986), 233–35; Randolph and Parrish, May 1, 1975, transcript, Interviews File, box 1, APR Papers.

62. Coppoc, "Garment Union Has Enlightened Policy," *Pittsburgh Courier*, April 22, 1944, 14/28/2, and Dedication Committee of Negro Labor Committee to Zimmerman, Nov. 18, 1935, 62/1/5, both in ILGWU Archives.

63. According to one-time vice president Jennie Matyas, Edith Ransome was the first black woman to join Local 25 around 1914–15. Matyas, interview by Corrinne L. Gilb, 1955, transcript, 208, Regional Oral History Office, Bancroft Library, University of California, Berkeley, Wagner Labor Archives; Coppoc, "Garment Union Has Enlightened Policy," *Pittsburgh Courier*, April 22, 1944, 14/28/2, ILGWU Archives.

64. Granger to Zimmerman, Sept. 20, 1948, 14/27/7, ILGWU Archives.

65. Crosswaith to Zimmerman, April 12, 1946, and May 16, 1946, both in 14/28/3, ILGWU Archives.

66. MSK, interview by author.

67. Granger to Zimmerman, April 6, 1937, 14/27/7, ILGWU Archives.

68. Granger to Zimmerman, Sept. 20, 1948, 14/27/7, ILGWU Archives.

69. According to Newman, at the time Crosswaith was the union's only black organizer. To audiences outside the ILGWU, Crosswaith consistently put a more positive face on the

union. For example, he once stated "that 'Negro delegates are in attendance at every convention. They all have their expenses paid and suffer no loss of wages. They participate fully in the deliberations at these conventions.'" George S. Schuyler, "Harlem Boasts 42,000 Negro Labor Unionists," *Pittsburgh Courier*, Aug. 21, 1937, reprinted in Philip S. Foner and Ronald L. Lewis, eds., *The Black Worker from the Founding of the CIO to the AFL-CIO Merger, 1936–1955*, vol. 7 of *The Black Worker: A Documentary History from Colonial Times to the Present* (Philadelphia: Temple University Press, 1983), 77. Pauline Newman, interview by Barbara Wertheimer, 1978, transcript, 72–75, 94, the Twentieth Century Trade Union Woman: Vehicle for Social Change, Oral History Project Program on Women and Work, Bentley Historical Library, University of Michigan, Ann Arbor.

70. Newman gives the date and place of the convention as 1946 in Cleveland, Ohio. Pesotta indicates it was in 1944 in Boston. Rose Pesotta, *Bread Upon the Waters* (1944; reprint, Ithaca, N.Y.: Cornell University, ILR Press, 1987), 395. Newman, interview by Wertheimer, 72, 75, 94; Elizabeth Balanoff, "Maida Springer Kemp Interview," in *The Black Women Oral History Project*, vol. 7, ed. Ruth Edmonds Hill (New Providence, N.J.: K. G. Saur Verlag, 1991), 139.

71. In this overwhelmingly female industry, there were too few black men to determine whether they might have had a better chance of attaining leadership positions than black and white women. However, it is clear that in the traditionally male occupations of the garment industry, they were represented in the least-skilled and lowest-paying categories. Silverman, interview by author, April 30, 1991.

72. Other than this large issue of sexist practice, Silverman viewed Dubinsky as a "fine president, bright, decent and able." Silverman, interview by author, April 30, 1991.

73. Ibid.

74. Established in 1917, the ILGWU education department featured educational, social, and recreational activities. Annelise Orlech, *Common Sense and a Little Fire: Women and Working-Class Politics in the United States, 1900–1965* (Chapel Hill: University of North Carolina Press, 1995), 169–203.

75. MSK, interview by author.

76. Orlech, *Common Sense and a Little Fire*, 196–97; Barbara Sicherman and Carol Hurd Green, eds., *Notable American Women, The Modern Period, Biographical Dictionary* (Cambridge: Belknap Press, 1980), 154–55; MSK, interview by author; quote is from MSK, keynote address, Nov. 12, 1983, Amistad.

77. Newman, interview by Wertheimer, 72–74; Orlech, *Common Sense and a Little Fire*, 201.

78. Alice Kessler-Harris quotes Pesotta in her article, "Organizing the Unorganizable: Three Jewish Women and Their Union," 284, n. 72, in Daniel J. Leab, ed., *The Labor History Reader* (Urbana: University of Illinois Press, 1985). This quote originally appeared in Pesotta, *Bread Upon the Waters*, 101.

79. MSK to Dubinsky, Nov. 23, 1965, 4/33/8; see also Granger to Zimmerman, April 6, 1937, 14/27/7; both in ILGWU Archives.

80. "Labor Movement Only Hope for Negro Workers," *Justice*, May 15, 1942; also in *Justice* see "Local 22 Continuing Race Relations Work," Jan. 1, 1947, and "How Labor Betters Race Relations," Jan. 15, 1947.

Chapter 3: The Dilemma of Race and Gender during World War II

1. Lurye (Matheson) to Zimmerman, Feb. 12, 1944, 4/24/4, ILGWU Archives.

2. MSK, Feb. 3, 1989, speech at the Anti-Defamation League of B'nai B'rith, New York

City, commemorating the issuance of the A. Philip Randolph postage stamp in the Black Heritage Series, MSK PP; "Maida Springer New Education Head in '132,'" April 1, 1943, *Justice*.

3. MSK, speech commemorating the Randolph Black Heritage stamp, MSK PP.

4. Steven Fraser, *Labor Will Rule: Sidney Hillman and the Rise of American Labor* (New York: Free Press and Maxwell, 1991), 363, 438–39.

5. David Dubinsky and A. H. Raskin, *David Dubinsky: A Life with Labor* (New York: Simon and Schuster, 1977), 244–45.

6. MSK, speech commemorating the Randolph Black Heritage stamp, MSK PP.

7. "'Union and Your Job' Talks Begin at '132'" April 1, 1944, *Justice*; MSK, interview by author. The products of the plastic, button, and novelty workers' union included buttons, buckles, apparel ornaments, jewelry, cigarette cases, compacts and lipstick cases, frames, radio cabinets, and umbrella handles. 5/24/8, ILGWU Archives.

8. MSK, interview by author.

9. Elizabeth Balanoff, "Maida Springer Kemp Interview," in *The Black Women Oral History Project*, vol. 7, ed. Ruth Edmonds Hill (New Providence, N.J.: K. G. Saur Verlag, 1991), 66.

10. MSK, interview by author.

11. Robert Weisbrot, *Father Divine and the Struggle for Racial Equality* (Urbana: University of Illinois Press, 1983), 92, 137.

12. Crosswaith, "Crosswaith Attacks Divine, Stooge of Negro Exploiters," newspaper unknown, Oct. 22, 1937; see also Ted Poston, "Harlem Emerges as Stronghold of Trade Unionism," *New York Post*, May 13, 1938, both in FC Papers.

13. Weisbrot, *Father Divine*, 138–39.

14. MSK speech, American Federation of Teachers' Women's Rights Award, Pittsburgh, Aug. 15, 1992.

15. MSK, interview by author.

16. Ibid.

17. Weisbrot, *Father Divine*, 137.

18. MSK, interview by author.

19. Weisbrot, *Father Divine*, 60–61, 73–74, 127, 139.

20. MSK, interview by author; Weisbrot, *Father Divine*, 6, 125–31.

21. Among the black lawyers who had some attachment to the Divine movement were James C. Thomas, Arthur Madison, and Ellee Lovelace. Weisbrot, *Father Divine*, 63, 66–67.

22. Crosswaith, "Crosswaith Attacks Divine, Stooge of Negro Exploiters," newspaper unknown, Oct. 22, 1937, FC Papers; Weisbrot, *Father Divine*, 137.

23. Weisbrot, *Father Divine*, 110–11.

24. MSK, interview by author.

25. One of the seminars also had participants from other ILGWU locals. "Two-Day Institute for '132' Members June 18–20 at Hudson Shore School," June 1, 1943; "'132' Group Has Big Time at Hudson Shore School Party," July 1, 1943; "Race Cooperation Highlights '132' Weekend Confab," Sept. 1, 1944; all in *Justice*.

26. MSK, interview by Balanoff, 7:70.

27. Hilda Worthington Smith, *Opening Vistas in Workers' Education: An Autobiography of Hilda Worthington Smith* (Washington: By the author, 1978), iii; MSK, interview with author.

28. See documents in HSLS Papers.

29. Dollie Lowther Robinson, interview by Bette Craig, March 1, 1977, transcript, 30, The Twentieth Century Trade Union Woman: Vehicle for Social Change, Oral History Project Program on Women and Work. Bentley Historical Library, University of Michigan, Ann Arbor.

30. John Caswell Smith, Jr., "Each Man Is an Island," *Common Ground* magazine, summer 1943, reprinted in pamphlet of the same title by Hudson Shore Labor School, HSLS Papers.

31. MSK, interview by author.

32. MSK, interview by Balanoff, 7:68.

33. MSK, autobiographical sketches, MSK PP.

34. Smith, "Each Man Is an Island," HSLS Papers.

35. Matyas, 1955 interview by Corrinne L. Gilb, 209–10, Regional Oral History Office, Bancroft Library, University of California, Berkeley.

36. Quote is from MSK, interview by Balanoff, 7:70; MSK, keynote address, tenth anniversary celebration of the Coalition of Labor Union Women, St. Louis, Nov. 12, 1983, Amistad.

37. Christman to Springer, Oct. 2, 1945, Amistad; MSK, interview by Balanoff, 7:71; Pauline Newman, "Union Health Center," Nov. 15, 1945, and "Maida Springer Broadcasts on U.S. Women in Industry," Jan. 1, 1948, both in *Justice*; Jo Freeman, "The Quest for Equality: The ERA vs. 'Other Means,'" in *Ethnicity and Women*, ed. Winston A. Van Horne, Ethnicity and Public Policy Series, vol. 5 (Madison: University of Wisconsin System, 1986), 54–56.

38. For an account of the arduous and painful work of laundry workers, see Anna Arnold Hedgeman, *The Trumpet Sounds: A Memoir of Negro Leadership* (New York: Holt, Rinehart and Winston, 1964), 35–37.

39. "Facts about Your Union," Laundry Workers' Joint Board of Greater New York, 1939, Archives Union File, no. 6046, box 139, Kheel Center for Labor-Management Documentation and Archives, Cornell University, Ithaca, N.Y.; Robinson, interview by Craig, 1–2, 45; Pauline Newman, interview by Barbara Wertheimer, 1978, transcript, 70, The Twentieth Century Trade Union Woman: Vehicle for Social Change, Oral History Project Program on Women and Work. Bentley Historical Library, University of Michigan, Ann Arbor.

40. MSK, keynote address, Nov. 12, 1983, Amistad.

41. MSK, interview by author.

42. I compiled the above essay from statements Robinson made about Adelmond in various sections of her interview. Robinson, interview by Craig, 1–3, 58–59.

43. Robinson, interview by Craig, 20.

44. MSK, interview by author.

45. Powell, circular letter, Feb. 9, 1944, 14/26/9, and Crosswaith to Zimmerman, March 6, 1944, 14/28/3, both in ILGWU Archives; "Zimmerman Blasts Outside Interference in Election," March 1, 1944, *Justice*.

46. MSK, interview by author.

47. Walter also served as the first head of the Laundry Workers Joint Board. Robinson, interview by Craig, 2, 38.

48. MSK, interview with author; Robinson, interview by Craig, 46–47.

49. Robinson, interview by Craig, quote is from pp. 3, 59.

50. Robinson, interview by Craig, 36, 47–48.

51. Esther Peterson, interview by Martha Ross, 1978, transcript, 10–11, The 20th Century Trade Union Woman: Vehicle for Social Change, Oral History Project.

52. MSK, interview by author.

53. The ALP also supported Herbert H. Lehman for governor of New York and the mayoral campaign of Fiorello La Guardia. Mark Naison, *Communists in Harlem during the Depression* (New York: Grove Press, 1984), 227, 232.

54. Dubinsky, "Russians Executed Ehrlich, Alter Despite Pleas from U.S., Britain," *Congressional Record*, April 8, 1943, and "Mass Meeting Will Protest Execution of Polish Socialists," *New York Times*, March 15, 1943, reprinted in Max D. Danish and Leon Stein, eds., *ILGWU News-History, 1900–1950: The Story of the Ladies' Garment Workers* (Atlantic City: ILGWU Golden Jubilee Convention, 1950), 102, 99; Fraser, *Labor Will Rule*, 519–20.

55. Robinson had been treasurer of the ALP in Brooklyn. Robinson, interview by Craig, 48; Dubinsky and Raskin, *David Dubinsky*, 73; "Two '22' Members are Assembly Candidates, Sept. 1, 1942, "Big '22' Meeting Pledges Aid to ALP, Dean Alfange," Oct. 1, 1942, "Getting Votes" and "Murray Gross, Maida Springer on Labor Ticket for Assembly," Oct. 15, 1942, "'22' Appeals for Support to Springer, Gross in Campaign," and "'22' Stages Big ALP Meeting for Alfange and Maida Springer," Nov. 1, 1942, all in *Justice*.

56. "Maida Springer Represents New Type of Leader," *New York Amsterdam News*, Oct. 1942, Amistad; "Unite behind the President and His War Effort, Vote Labor," box 1, folder 9, Schlesinger; and MSK, interview by author.

57. Crosswaith to All Delegates, circular letter, March 8, 1944, 14/28/3, ILGWU Archives; James H. Hagerty, "Fear Split in ALP Weakens Roosevelt Chance in New York," *New York Times*, March 2, 1944, and "Liberals vs. Commies," *Newsweek*, April 10, 1944, reprinted in Danish and Stein, *ILGWU News-History, 1900–1950*, 103; Fraser, *Labor Will Rule*, 521–22. See Naison, *Communists in Harlem*, 227–48.

58. MSK, autobiographical sketches, MSK PP.

59. "Pens to Fore in '132' V-Mail Club," July 15, 1943, and "'132' Group Issues Its Own PX Sheet," April 15, 1944, both in *Justice*; Daniel P. Woolley to Springer, April 24, 1944, MSK PP; Newman, interview by Wertheimer, 69; and MSK, keynote address, Nov. 12, 1983, Amistad.

60. MSK, keynote address, Nov. 12, 1983, Amistad.

61. MSK, autobiographical sketches, MSK PP.

62. Initially, most blacks did not benefit from New Deal legislation concerning minimum wage, maximum hours, unemployment compensation, and social security, since the fields of agriculture and domestic service were exempt from the laws. Robert W. Mullen, *Blacks in America's Wars* (New York: Monad Press, 1981), 52; Paula Giddings, *When and Where I Enter: The Impact of Black Women on Race and Sex in America* (New York: William Morrow, 1984; reprint, New York: Bantam Books, 1988), 221–22; Jacqueline Jones, *Labor of Love, Labor of Sorrow* (New York: Vintage Books, 1985), 199–200.

63. Zimmerman to Negro Labor Committee, Nov. 21, 1941, and "Fear of Disunity for War Effort Will Aid Hitler," pamphlet for conference scheduled for Feb. 7, 1942, at Columbia Teachers College, Jan. 20, 1942, both in 14/28/3, ILGWU Archives.

64. The Youth Division of the March committee, led by Richard Parrish and including Bayard Rustin (both of whom would later become strong supporters of Randolph), was vociferous in condemning the March leaders for the cancellation. In addition to Randolph, march leaders included Crosswaith, Granger, Rayford Logan, and Layle Lane. "How the Negro March Was Betrayed: Disgusted by Conduct of March Leaders," July 1941, and "Randolph Reports for the Press—But He Doesn't Report the Facts!" both in Randolph Clippings File, Schomburg Center; and Jervis Anderson, *A. Philip Randolph: A Biographical Portrait* (Los Angeles: University of California Press, 1986), 259.

65. Eight Point Program, March on Washington Movement 1943 file, box 1, APR Papers; "Race and Discrimination in America: Discussion by Norman Thomas and Randolph," Interviews file, and "A Manifesto: An Open Letter to the President," March on Washington Movement, July 4, 1943, both in APR Papers.

66. "Review of Sergeant Levy Race Protest Case Is Demanded," Sept. 15, 1943, "Alton Levy Case Review Requested by ILGWU Chief," Oct. 15, 1943, "New York Labor Acts on Levy Case; For Permanent FEPC ACT" and "Regardless of Creed, Color, Race . . ." both in Nov. 1, 1943, all in *Justice*.

67. MSK, speech commemorating the A. Philip Randolph Black Heritage stamp, MSK PP.

68. Ibid.; "Plastic Workers Aid Chinese" and "'132' First ILGWU Local to Give to China Blood Bank," both in Nov. 1, 1943, *Justice*.

69. Robinson, interview by Craig, 5–6.

70. Hedgeman, *The Trumpet Sounds*, 81.

71. Brenda Gayle Plummer, *Rising Wind: Black Americans and U.S. Foreign Affairs, 1935–1960* (Chapel Hill: University of North Carolina Press, 1996), 33, 204.

72. Pauli Murray, *The Autobiography of a Black Activist, Feminist, Lawyer, Priest, and Poet* (Knoxville: University of Tennessee Press, 1987), 150–76.

73. Ibid., 171–74.

74. MSK, interview by author.

75. Bessie Bearden was the mother of the noted artist Romare Bearden, and a one-time neighbor of Springer's. Murray, *The Autobiography of a Black Activist*, 175.

76. Ibid., 174–76. See also Sherman, *The Case of Odell Waller and Virginia Justice* (Knoxville: University of Tennessee Press, 1992).

77. The other women the NCNW honored on March 15, 1946, were: Virginia Durr, president of the National Council to Abolish the Poll Tax; Lois M. Jones, a teacher at Howard University and a renowned artist; Lt. Col. Charity Adams, leader of the Negro WACs in Europe; Helen Gahagan Douglas, Democratic congresswoman from California; Agnes Meyer, wife of the publisher of the Washington *Post*; Arenia Mallory, founder of an industrial training school in Lexington, Kentucky; J. Borden Harriman, former U.S. ambassador to Norway; Eslanda Goode Robeson, anthropologist and wife of Paul Robeson; Judge Jane Bolin, New York City Court of Domestic Relations; and Dr. Catherine Lealtad, associated with work in Germany for the United Nations Relief and Rehabilitation Administration. "Women of the Year," *Washington Evening Star*, March 16, 1946, Amistad; and "Maida Springer Put Among Outstanding Women of the Year," April 15, 1946, *Justice*.

78. As a law clerk, Eric Springer conducted research for Murray's book *States' Laws on Race and Color*. MSK speech, NCNW reception at Council House for Pauli Murray's autobiography, *Song in a Weary Throat* (reprinted as *The Autobiography of a Black Activist, Feminist, Lawyer, Priest, and Poet*), June 27, 1987, MSK PP.

Chapter 4: The National and International Struggle against the Color Line

1. "Women Labor Leaders Are Going to England In Good-Will Exchange with Four from There," *New York Times*, Jan. 10, 1945, 14/5/1, ILGWU Archives.

2. OWI press release, Jan. 13, 1945, NB-2972, Springer Clippings File, Schomburg Center; Max D. Danish, publicity director of the ILGWU, press release, Jan. 9, 1945, "British, U.S. Women on Exchange Visits," *Trade Union Record*, Jan. 20, 1945, "Women Labor Leaders Are Going to England in Good-Will Exchange with Four from There," *New York Times*, Jan. 10, 1945, and Frank Crosswaith, "Maida Springer to Represent American Labor in England," *Labor Vanguard*, Feb. 1945, all in 14/5/1, ILGWU Archives; Maida Springer Represents AFL in Britain Tour," *Justice*, Jan. 15, 1945; and "Mrs. Springer, Goodwill Delegate," *American Federationist*, Feb. 1945, MSK PP.

3. MSK, autobiographical sketches, MSK PP.

4. OWI press release, Jan. 13, 1945, N-1310, Springer Clippings File, Schomburg Center; see also Springer to Dubinsky, Feb. 22, 1945, 2/5/1B, ILGWU Archives.

5. Crosswaith to Dubinsky, Feb. 15, 1945, Randolph to Dubinsky, March 29, 1945, both in 2/5/1B; Crosswaith to Zimmerman, Feb. 16, 1945, Zimmerman to Crosswaith, April 11, 1945, both in 14/28/3; all in ILGWU Archives.

6. Keller to Dubinsky, Jan. 22, 1945, 2/5/1B, ILGWU Archives.

7. Elizabeth Balanoff, "Maida Springer Kemp Interview," in *The Black Women Oral History Project*, vol. 7, ed. Ruth Edmonds Hill (New Providence, N.J.: K. G. Saur Verlag, 1991), 80;

Crosswaith to Dubinsky, Feb. 15, 1945, and Randolph to Dubinsky, March 29, 1945, both in 2/5/1B, ILGWU Archives.

8. Dubinsky's rival, Sydney Hillman, was one of the founders of the WFTU and one of its seven vice presidents. Len De Caux, "The CIO Joins the International Labor Movement," in *The Cold War against Labor*, 2 vols., ed. Ann Fagan Ginger and David Christiano (Berkeley: Meiklejohn Civil Liberties Institute, 1987), 1:187–90.

9. Peter Weiler, *British Labour and the Cold War* (Stanford, Calif.: Stanford University Press, 1988), 5–9, 56–68.

10. MSK, interview by author.

11. Ibid.

12. Ibid.

13. "British, U.S. Women on Exchange Visits," *Trade Union Record*, Jan. 20, 1945, Crosswaith, "Maida Springer to Represent American Labor in England," *Labor Vanguard*, Feb. 1945, and "Women Labor Leaders Are Going to England in Good-Will Exchange with Four from There," *New York Times*, Jan. 10, 1945, all in 14/5/1, ILGWU Archives; OWI, press release, Jan. 13, 1945, N-1310, Springer Clippings File, Schomburg Center.

14. Anna Arnold Hedgeman, *The Trumpet Sounds: A Memoir of Negro Leadership* (New York: Holt, Rinehart and Winston, 1964), 87–88, 95; Audre Lorde, *Zami, A New Spelling of My Name* (Trumansburg, N.Y.: Crossing Press, 1983), 69–71; Mary L. Dudziak, "Desegregation as a Cold War Imperative," *Stanford Law Review* 41, no. 61 (Nov. 1988): 109–13; Brenda Gayle Plummer, *Rising Wind: Black Americans and U.S. Foreign Affairs, 1935–1960* (Chapel Hill: University of North Carolina Press, 1996), 162.

15. The Statler Hotel is now the Capitol Hilton. MSK, remarks at Community College, March 31, 1989, Amistad; MSK, international luncheon—Life Member's Guild, National Council of Negro Women, April 30, 1983, MSK PP.

16. MSK, interview by author.

17. Helen Laville and Scott Lucas, "The American Way: Edith Sampson, the NAACP, and African American Identity in the Cold War," 565.

18. MSK, remarks at Community College, March 31, 1989, Amistad.

19. MSK, interview by author.

20. Ibid.

21. Lehman was the first director of the UNRRA. "Vote Liberal Party for Mead—Lehman," Nov. 1, 1946, *Justice*.

22. Bethune was the principal adviser in Roosevelt's so-called Black cabinet. B. Joyce Ross, "Mary McLeod Bethune and the National Youth Administration: A Case Study of Power Relationships in the Black Cabinet of Franklin D. Roosevelt," in *Black Leaders of the Twentieth Century*, ed. John Hope Franklin and August Meier (Urbana: University of Illinois Press, 1982).

23. MSK, "Maida Springer Kemp on Dr. Caroline F. Ware, A Supplement to the Black Women's Oral History Project, 'Dr. Caroline F. Ware—A Majority of One, A Friend for All Reasons, for All Seasons,'" in Hill, *The Black Women Oral History Project* (hereafter MSK on Ware), 7:149.

24. MSK, interview by author.

25. Dollie Lowther, circular letter, April 9, 1945, and MSK, draft of article for the *AALC Reporter*, 1993, MSK PP. "On First Lap of Trip to England" and "Greetings Prepared for British Workers," both Feb. 1, 1945; "British Shops Seen By Maida Springer," March 1, 1945; "Maida Springer Touring England's Labor Centers," March 15, 1945; "Maida Springer Inspects Britain's Garment Plants," April 1, 1945; "Four Labor Women Coming Home with GT. Britain Sisters," April 15, 1945; "All-Day Tour of Garment Center Dazzles British, American Girl Labor Delegates," May 1, 1945; "Brigade Alerted on Black Market Peril," May 15, 1945; "Brigade Aids

Hospital Vets," July 1, 1945; and Maida S. Springer, "What I Saw in Britain" series, May 15, 1945, June 1, 1945, and July 1, 1945; all in *Justice*.

26. Ware died at the age of ninety on April 5, 1990. Quotes are from "MSK on Ware," 150–51; Springer to Mary Kate Black, Sept; 7, 1985, and "Epilogue" by Caroline Ware (on the occasion of Murray's death), c. 1985, both in MSK PP; Pauli Murray, *The Autobiography of a Black Activist, Feminist, Lawyer, Priest, and Poet* (Knoxville: University of Tennessee Press, 1987), 198–200, 233.

27. OWI press release, Jan. 13, 1945, OWI, N-1310, Springer Clippings File, Schomburg Center.

28. MSK on Ware, 150.

29. MSK, interview by author; Springer to Dubinsky, Feb. 22, 1945, 2/5/1B, ILGWU Archives.

30. OWI press release, N-1371 [no date], Springer Clippings File, Schomburg Center; MSK, interview by Balanoff, 77.

31. MSK, interview by author. OWI press release, N-1371, Springer Clippings File, Schomburg Center.

32. "Brigade Alerted on Black Market Peril," *Justice*, May 15, 1945.

33. MSK, interview by author; Wendy Craigen, Press Department of the British War Relief Society, Inc., of the U.S.A. in London, to Springer, Park Lane Hotel, March 19, 1945, MSK PP; Eric Hawkins, "The ILGWU Merchant Navy Club in London," *Chicago Sun*, Aug. 12, 1942, reprinted in Leon Stein, ed., *Out of the Sweatshop: The Struggle for Industrial Democracy* (New York: Quadrangle/New York Times Books, 1977), 252–53.

34. Loughlin also served as a member of Women's Advisory Committee of the TUC General Council and as chair of the TUC from 1942 to 1943. Loughlin to Dubinsky, April 4, 1945, 2/5/1B, ILGWU Archives.

35. OWI press release, N-1357 [no date], Springer Clippings File, Schomburg Center; George Padmore, *Pan-Africanism or Communism? The Coming Struggle for Africa* (1956; reprint, New York: Doubleday, 1971), 132.

36. Springer to Dubinsky, Feb. 22, 1945, 2/5/1B, ILGWU Archives.

37. MSK on Ware, 150.

38. For more on Marson, see Delia Jarrett-Macauley, *The Life of Una Marson* (Manchester: Manchester University Press, 1998), and Margaret Busby, ed., *Daughters of Africa: An International Anthology of Words and Writings by Women of African Descent from the Ancient Egyptian to the Present* (London: Jonathan Cape, 1992), 221. A book of Marson's poetry is entitled *Heights and Depths*.

39. MSK, interview by author; see also Kenneth King, ed., *Ras Makonnen: Pan-Africanism from Within* (New York: Oxford University Press, 1973), 123, 155.

40. MSK, interview by author.

41. Quotes are from MSK, autobiographical sketches, MSK PP; "Starr to Visit Britain in July on OWI Mission," *Justice*, May 1, 1943.

42. MSK, "Free Africa" speech, Coalition of Black Trade Unionists Free Africa Conference, Sept. 12, 1985, MSK PP. Years later Springer again met Kenyatta, who was then president of independent Kenya. Their jovial conversation started off with his recognition of her: "Oh, you girl. But you are not a small girl anymore." MSK, interview by author.

43. Padmore, *Pan-Africanism or Communism?* 131, 133, 139. Around three hundred people attended a public gathering following the March 4 Manchester meeting; there it was resolved to convene the Pan-African Congress. Imanuel Geiss, *The Pan-African Movement: A History of*

Pan-Africanism in America, Europe, and Africa (New York: Africana Publishing Company, 1974), 389–90; King, *Ras Makonnen*, 137.

44. Makonnen and Milliard were from British Guyana. Geiss, *The Pan-African Movement*, 390.

45. Plummer, *Rising Wind*, 160.

46. In August 1941 Roosevelt and Churchill signed the joint declaration on a warship off the coast of Newfoundland. Churchill later stated that the declarations on self-determination only applied to those European countries under Nazi rule and not to British colonies. Geiss, *The Pan-African Movement*, 365–66; Padmore, *Pan-Africanism or Communism?* 131.

47. George Padmore, ed., *The Voice of Coloured Labour* (1945; reprint, London: African Publication Society, 1970), 3–6.

48. MSK, remarks at Community College, March 31, 1989, MSK Papers, Amistad Center; MSK, International Luncheon—Life Member's Guild, National Council of Negro Women, April 30, 1983, MSK PP.

49. "Race and Discrimination in America: Discussion by Norman Thomas and Randolph," Interviews file, and March on Washington flyer for a National Program of Action for August 1, 1943, to July 31, 1944, March on Washington Movement file, both in box 1, APR Papers.

50. Zimmerman, long a supporter of the Fair Employment Practices Committee, had written to senators and congressmen, appealing for continued funding of the FEPC and voicing support for a permanent FEPC. Zimmerman, letters, May 22, 1944, and Feb. 15, 1945, 14/21/9, ILGWU Archives; "FEPC Law 'Crucial' Says Local 22 Head," *Justice*, July 1, 1946.

51. MSK, interview by author.

52. MSK, interview by Balanoff, 83.

53. Springer remembers the choir members numbering five hundred. New York's *New York Amsterdam News* reported that the choir had a thousand voices. "Leaders Still Hopeful FEPC Will Pass," *New York Amsterdam News*, March 9, 1946, Amistad.

54. MSK, interview by author.

55. Murray to Spingarn Medal Award Committee, April 7, 1959, 14/12/11, ILGWU Archives.

56. "Leaders Still Hopeful FEPC Will Pass," *New York Amsterdam News*, March 9, 1946, Amistad.

57. Ibid.

58. Madison Square Garden Rally paper, Feb. 28, 1946, MSK PP. After Randolph and others signed a letter aimed at bringing about the defeat of Congressman John E. Rankin of Mississippi, Rankin attempted to discredit the signers by accusing them of being part of Communist-front organizations and stating that they all had records with the Dies Committee, the FBI, and the Department of Justice. The Veteran's League of America sponsored the letter. *Congressional Record*, June 27, 1946, Randolph Clippings File, Schomburg Center.

59. Springer quote is from MSK, interview by Balanoff, 83; Murray, *Autobiography of a Black Activist*, 279–81; and MSK, "The Consummate Scholar," speech given to a conference titled "Black Women's Leadership: Challenges and Strategies," University of North Carolina, Chapel Hill, March 25, 1986, Amistad.

60. Murray, *Autobiography of a Black Activist*, 279–81; MSK, "The Consummate Scholar," March 25, 1986, Amistad; Maurice Bernhardt to Springer, Nov. 14, 1949, MSK PP.

61. Murray, *The Autobiography of a Black Activist*, 279–81.

62. In the 1954 campaign Springer served on the trade union committee of the New York branch of the NAACP. The campaign's goal was to end legal segregation and discrimination by

1963. Composed of church, labor, civic, and fraternal groups, the committee in charge of planning the 1956 rally included among its members Randolph as chairman, co-coordinator Benjamin F. McLaurin, Dollie Lowther Robinson, Charles Zimmerman, Ted Brown, Richard Parrish, Max Delson, Ella Baker, Evelyn Dubrow, Mabel Fuller, James Farmer, A. J. Muste,
Bayard Rustin, Jack Sessions, Ashley L. Totten, and Noah C. A. Walter. Springer to Zimmerman, July 12, 1954, 14/27/8, and Nov. 11, 1954, 14/26/7, both in ILGWU Archives; City-Wide
Committee to Stage Madison Square Garden Civil Rights Rally, May 24, 1956, and Springer to
Zimmerman, Sept. 19, 1958, both in MSK PP; Randolph to President Dwight D. Eisenhower,
Oct. 10, 1958, and Rocco C. Siciliano (special assistant to the President) to Randolph, Oct. 29,
1958, and Randolph to Siciliano, Nov. 19, 1958, all in White House Conference file, box 1, APR
Papers.

    63. MSK, interview by Balanoff, 90; "Maida Springer Is Named Bus. Agent N.Y. Dress
Bd.," *Justice*, March 15, 1948.

    64. Quote is from "Celebrating Black History Month: A Pioneering Unionist," *Justice*,
Feb. 1986; MSK, interview by Balanoff, 63; MSK, interview by author; Silverman, interview by
author, April 30, 1991.

    65. See "Start Dress Training Course to Meet Operator Shortage," Oct. 15, 1956, and "200
New York Dressmakers Enroll for Operators' Training Class," Dec. 1, 1956, both in *Justice*;
Springer to George S. Schuyler,editor of the *Pittsburgh Courier*, Jan. 3, 1960, 47/1/9, ILGWU
Archives.

    66. MSK, interview by author.

    67. Ibid.

    68. Silverman, interview by author, April 30, 1991.

    69. MSK to Evelyn Hoffman, memo, "Perceptions of the Labor Movement," April 28,
1986, MSK PP.

    70. Quote is from MSK, interview by Balanoff, 92; Springer, "A Day with an ILGWU
Business Agent," undated clipping from *Justice*, probably 1950s, Amistad; MSK, interview by
author; Alice Kessler-Harris, "Problems of Coalition Building: Women and Trade Unions in
the 1920s," in Ruth Milkman, ed., *Women, Work and Protest: A Century of U.S. Women's Labor
History* (Boston: Routledge and Kegan Paul, 1985), 125–26.

    71. Springer, "A Day with an ILGWU Business Agent."

    72. Heit, a member of Local 60, was employed at a shop producing for B & M Schwartz
located at 1375 Broadway. Heit to Zimmerman, Oct. 10, 1948, 14/5/1, ILGWU Archives.

    73. Heit to Zimmerman, Oct. 10, 1948, 14/5/1, ILGWU Archives.

    74. Murray, *The Autobiography of a Black Activist*, 279.

    75. Silverman, interview by author, April 30, 1991.

    76. Ibid.

    77. Fimmano was a shop chairperson at the Levenson and Mawrey Dress Shop. Fimmano
to *Justice*, Feb. 27, 1986, Amistad.

    78. "Labor Leader to Study in Scandinavia," *New York Times*, Aug. 13, 1951, 7; "Woman
Labor Aide to Study Abroad, *Philadelphia Tribune*, Aug. 18, 1951; and "Maida Springer to Study
in England, Scandinavia Lands," *Justice*, Aug. 15, 1951.

    79. MSK, interview by Balanoff, 7:63.

    80. MSK, interview by author.

    81. MSK, interview by Balanoff, 97–98. For a similar reaction of Black Mississippians in
the 1920s who did not welcome Anna Arnold Hedgeman's criticisms of the South's oppression
of blacks, see Hedgeman, *The Trumpet Sounds*, 28.

    82. MSK, interview by author.

    83. Springer remarked that in the United States, Esther Peterson had been a very success-

ful organizer. In her efforts to join workers together she used labor songs to break the ice. They could sing songs that spoke to their common experience as workers even if they did personally disliked one another. MSK, interview by author; Gunnar Hirdman to Eleanor G. Coit, Sept. 7, 1951, 14/5/1, ILGWU Archives.

84. Padmore introduced Springer to Williams, who would become the first prime minister of his country at independence. Essumen was also a student at Ruskin College. Quarshie, a principal labor officer, was studying at Oxford under an officer-training program. Quaison-Sackey received an education at Exeter, Oxford, and the London School of Economics. From 1959 until 1965 he served as Ghanaian representative to the United Nations and also as the ambassador to Cuba and Mexico. In 1964–1965 he served as the first African president of the UN General Assembly. And from 1965 until the 1966 coup, he served as the foreign minister of Ghana. In 1978 Colonel Acheampong appointed him ambassador to the United States. Daniel Miles McFarlang, *Historical Dictionary of Ghana, African Historical Dictionary* no. 39 (Metuchen, N.J.: Scarecrow Press, 1985), 151.

85. Springer, "Report to the Urban League on 1951–52 Study Abroad," box 1, folder 2, MSK Papers, Schlesinger.

86. Following the death of Springer's mother and her subsequent sale of their house, Springer in her grief discarded much important historical material, including letters from Padmore. She noted that at the time she did not have sufficient awareness of the historical importance of these papers. MSK, interview by author.

87. Memorandum, MSK to Nana Mahomo, Aug. 1, 1983, MSK PP; second quote is from MSK, interview by Balanoff, 87.

88. Springer, "Report to the Urban League on 1951–52 Study Abroad," box 1, folder 2, Schlesinger.

89. Anderson, *Imagined Communities*, 107, 127; King, *Ras Makonnen*, 155.

90. Nyerere to Springer, n.d., Amistad.

91. King, *Ras Makonnen*, 125, 163; MSK, interview by author.

92. King, *Ras Makonnen*, 143–44; Plummer, *Rising Wind*, 143–44, 208–9.

93. MSK, interview by author.

94. Springer, "Report to the Urban League on 1951–52 Study Abroad," box 1, folder 2, Schlesinger.

95. Springer to Israel Breslow (manager, Local 22), memorandum, March 22, 1959, 14/12/11, ILGWU Archives.

96. Plummer, *Rising Wind*, 109–10, 226–27, 239.

Chapter 5: Dancing on the End of a Needle: African Connections

1. Many Africans held leadership positions in both labor and political organizations. Both Kawawa and Mboya, for example, were at the head of their labor federations and served as members of the Legislative Council.

2. Dear Friend of Civil Liberties from the International League for the Rights of Man, letter, Dec. 1959, MSK PP.

3. Maida Springer, "A Distinguished American Reports: West Africa's Fight for Freedom Should Inspire U.S. Negroes," *Pittsburgh Courier*, April 13, 1957, 14/12/11, ILGWU Archives.

4. Bibi Titi Mohammed, interview by author, March 25, 1991.

5. Waiyaki Wambaa to Springer, Nov. 8, 1959, MSK PP.

6. Joseph Thuo to Adina Stewart Carrington, Dec. 6, 1957, MSK PP. Others, including Springer, referred to Adina as Madame.

7. MSK, interview by author.

8. Mpangala, interview by author, March 9, 1991.

9. Ibid.; "Ms. Springer: An African American with the Heart of a Tanzanian," *Habari Mbalimbali* (Tanzania), March 23, 1991 (translated by Susan Chematia).

10. Mpangala, interview by author, March 9, 1991; "Ms. Springer: An African American with the Heart of a Tanzanian," *Habari Mbalimbali*, March 23, 1991; Springer to Sasha [Charles Zimmerman], Dec. 7, 1957, 14/12/11, ILGWU Archives.

11. Mpangala, interview by author, March 9. 1991; MSK, interview by author.

12. MSK, interview by author.

13. Ibid. For more information on Bond and Lincoln University, see Wayne J. Urban, *Black Scholar: Horace Mann Bond, 1904–1972* (Athens: University of Georgia Press, 1992).

14. Springer, Memorandum on Tanganyika, Feb. 19, 1957, 60/23, Lovestone files; Ibrahim to Springer, Sept. 25, 1962, Amistad. C. P. Ngaiza (acting permanent representative of the Tanganyika Mission to the UN) to Springer, May 31, 1962; O. T. Hamlyn, "They Call It 'Mary's Institute'"; and Ibrahim, "And the Greatest Evil is Ignorance" (pamphlets, 1962), all in MSK PP.

15. At that time only five Tanganyikans were studying in the United States. Nyerere, "Sauti Ya TANU" (The Voice of TANU newsletter), c. 1957, 14/12/11, ILGWU Archives; "Trusteeship Council Due to Tackle Tanganyika Issues," *Africa Special Report*, 2, no. 5 (May 29, 1957); and Brenda Gayle Plummer, *Rising Wind: Black Americans and U.S. Foreign Affairs, 1935–1960* (Chapel Hill: University of North Carolina Press, 1996), 227; Kenneth King, ed., *Ras Makonnen: Pan-Africanism from Within* (New York: Oxford University Press, 1973), 168.

16. Nyerere attended Makerere University College in the years 1943–1945 and received a diploma in education. A star debater, he introduced international affairs into the discussions. In 1949 he was the first Tanganyikan "to enroll in a British University and receive a BA at Edinburgh," and in 1952 he was the first Tanganyikan to receive an M.A. degree. Laura S. Kurtz, *Historical Dictionary of Tanzania*, African Historical Dictionary no. 15 (Metuchen, N.J.: Scarecrow Press, 1978), 151–52; Nyerere to Springer, Feb. 22, 1958, Amistad; Nyerere, "Sauti Ya TANU," c. 1957, 14/12/11, ILGWU Archives; George Houser, *No One Can Stop the Rain: Glimpses of Africa's Liberation Struggle* (New York: Pilgrim Press, 1989), 22.

17. "Trusteeship Council Due to Tackle Tanganyika Issues," *Africa Special Report*; Nyerere to Springer, May 22, 1957, Amistad.

18. "Sauti Ya TANU," May 18, 1957; Nyerere, "Barriers to Democracy," and Statement to the Press by Julius Nyerere, President of TANU, June 17, 1957, all in MSK PP; *Africa Special Report*, vol. 1, no. 8 (Dec. 21, 1956) and vol. 2, no. 3 (March 29, 1957); Nyerere to Springer, May 22, 1957, Amistad.

19. John Kofi Barka Tettegah became secretary general of the Gold Coast TUC in 1954 and in 1965–66 was the secretary general of the All-African Trade Union Federation. Houser, *No One Can Stop the Rain*, 81; Tettegah to Springer, Aug. 2, 1956, MSK PP.

20. MSK, interview by author.

21. Mboya to Springer, Oct. 13, 1956, MSK PP.

22. Mboya, "Land Question—Key to Kenya Strife," *International Free Trade Union News* 11, no. 12 (Dec. 1956); George Padmore, *Pan-Africanism or Communism? The Coming Struggle for Africa* (1956; reprint, New York: Doubleday, 1971), 213; Ali A. Mazrui and Michael Tidy, *Nationalism and New States in Africa from about 1935 to the Present* (London: Heinemann, 1984), 104, 107.

23. By 1954 those labeled Mau Mau had killed 1,186 people, of whom 24 were Europeans, 17 were Asians, and 1,145 were Africans. Padmore, *Pan-Africanism or Communism?* 225, 235; Joseph Wershba, "Tom Mboya: Voice of the New Africa," *New York Post*, April 19, 1959, MSK PP; and Mboya, "Land Question—Key to Kenya Strife."

24. Mazrui and Tidy, *Nationalism and New States in Africa*, 104, 107, 121; David Goldsworthy, *Tom Mboya: The Man Kenya Wanted to Forget* (New York: Africana Publishing, 1982), 28.

25. Karumba, interview by author, March 21, 1991.

26. Elizabeth Balanoff, "Maida Springer Kemp Interview," in *The Black Women Oral History Project*, vol. 7, ed. Ruth Edmonds Hill (New Providence, N.J.: K. G. Saur Verlag, 1991), 122.

27. MSK, interview by author.

28. Gikonyo Kiano was also responsible for Mwangi's scholarship. Goldsworthy, *Tom Mboya*, 158–59, 4; Springer to Dollie Lowther Robinson, Dec. 7, 1957, MSK PP; MSK, "The Consummate Scholar," speech given to a conference titled "Black Women's Leadership: Challenges and Strategies," University of North Carolina, Chapel Hill, March 25, 1986, Amistad.

29. Mboya to Springer, Dec. 13, 1956, MSK PP.

30. "Ghanaians Chide Mboya: Kenya Leader Is Branded a Political Upstart," *New York Times*, Dec. 23, 1956, Mboya Clippings File, Schomburg Center.

31. Springer to Nyerere, Aug. 25, 1957, Amistad.

32. Springer, remarks at the African Historical Society dinner at the Carnegie Endowment Center, New York, April 18, 1959, box 1, folder 2, Schlesinger.

33. Springer to the editor of the *New York Times*, April 28, 1958, Amistad.

34. [Nyerere to Springer], Sept. 25, 1957, MSK PP.

35. Springer to Mboya, May 10, 1958, and Mboya to Springer, May 20, 1958, MSK PP.

36. Springer to the editor of the *New York Times*, April 28, 1958, Amistad.

37. Springer to the editor of the *New York Times*, Sept. 6, 1957, Amistad.

38. Springer to the editor of the *New York Times*, April 28, 1958, Amistad.

39. Springer to the editor of the *New York Times*, Sept. 6, 1957, Amistad. See also Springer to Nyerere, Sept. 6, 1957, MSK PP.

40. For Springer's reaction to *Time* magazine's coverage of East Africa, see Springer to Mboya, June 22, 1958, MSK PP. Springer to Mboya, Feb. 2, 1959, MSK PP.

41. Mboya to Springer, Feb. 18, 1959, and Springer to Mboya, March 10, 1959, MSK PP.

42. Springer to Mboya, Dec. 19, 1959, MSK PP.

43. Odero-Jowi, "The U.S. through African Eyes," *AFL-CIO Free Trade Union News* 16, no. 2 (Feb. 1961); Harry W. Flannery, "The Awakening of Africa: An Interview with Tom Mboya," *The Catholic World*, July 1959, 265, 269, Mboya Clippings File, Schomburg Center.

44. Springer, "Report to the Urban League on 1951–52 Study Abroad," box 1, folder 2, Schlesinger.

45. Springer to Mboya, April 15, 1960, 11/5; Memorandum on Conversations with Ambassador Attwood, June 7, 1963, and Ansoumane Oulare, A Summary of the Guinea Delegation Impressions on their Three Weeks Visit to the United States, both in 10/5, all in Country files.

46. Springer, "The International Trade Unions and the African Labor Movement," [no date], box 1, folder 13, Schlesinger.

47. "Tom Mboya's Future," *New Republic*, May 25, 1959, and Mboya as guest on *Meet the Press*, Sunday, April 12, 1959, transcripts, both in Mboya Clippings File, Schomburg; Paula Giddings, *When and Where I Enter: The Impact of Black Women on Race and Sex in America* (New York: William Morrow, 1984), 270.

48. Leonard Ingalls, "Moral Aid of U.S. Urged for Africa," *New York Times*, May 2, 1959; see also Flannery, "The Awakening of Africa," 269, and Tom Mboya, "Our Revolutionary Tradition: An African View," *Current History* 31, no. 184 (Dec. 1956), both in Mboya Clippings File, Schomburg Center.

49. Flannery, "The Awakening of Africa," 265, see also "Says Africa Wants No Part of Cold War," *New York Daily News*, April 16, 1965, both in Mboya Clippings File, Schomburg Center.

50. Nyerere to Springer, no date, Amistad.

51. Once when a newspaper reporter asked Mboya when he had learned to speak English so well, he quickly replied, On the plane ride over. MSK, interview with author; Springer to Michael Ross, memorandum, July 12, 1960, box 1, folder 3, Schlesinger.

52. In 1955 Roy Bryand and his half-brother J. W. Milam killed and mutilated fourteen-year-old Till beyond recognition because on a dare he flirted with Bryant's wife. After their acquittal they sold their story of the murder.

53. Don Thomson and Rodney Larson, *Where Were You, Brother? An Account of Trade Union Imperialism* (London: War on Want, 1978), 21; Anthony Clayton and Donald C. Savage, *Government and Labour in Kenya, 1895-1963* (London: Cass, 1974), 384-385.

54. Tachie-Menson to J.H. Oldenbroek, September 2, 1955, 4/17, Brown files.

55. Springer to Irving Brown, Nov. 4, 1955, 4/17, Brown files; Springer, "Progress and Problems of Gold Coast Unions," *International Free Trade Union News* 11, no. 6 (June 1956); Springer, "West Africa in Transition," *International Free Trade Union News* 11, no. 4 (April 1956).

56. Springer, "Progress and Problems of Gold Coast Unions"; Springer, "West Africa in Transition."

57. Kojo Botsio met Kwame Nkrumah in London in 1945 and helped found the Gold Coast Convention People's Party. Botsio served as the first general secretary. He would hold a number of cabinet positions in the soon-to-be-independent government. He served as Minister of Education and Social Welfare, was later Minister of Agriculture and Foreign Minister, and served as the chair of the 1958 All-Africa People's Conference. Although he was out of favor with the Nkrumah government from 1961 to 1963, he was with Nkrumah when he died in Rumania in April 1972.

58. Springer to Anne Stolt (Lovestone's secretary), Dec. 1, 1957, MSK PP; and Springer, Memorandum on the African Regional Conference, Jan. 14–19, 1957, Accra, "African Trade Unions," box 398, LP. See also letter to Sir Vincent Tewson, British TUC general secretary (signature of writer above the typed title reading "general secretary" is illegible), Oct. 18, 1957, 21/8, Brown files.

59. Arnold Beichman, "ICFTU Sparks Global Fight for Free Labor," *Justice*, Aug. 1, 1956.

60. Nkrumah worked on the ship during summer breaks from Lincoln University in the mid-to-late 1930s. He rose from dishwasher to waiter and then messenger, the highest position a black crew member could attain. Yuri Smertin, *Kwame Nkrumah* (New York: International Publishers, 1987), 14–15. "Nkrumah Pledges Freedom for Ghana Trade Unions and Recalls 'When I was a Steward,'" "World Economy Rests on Free Trade Unionism—P.M.," and "Delegates to the Conference," all in *Accra Daily Graphic*, Tues., Jan. 15, 1957; and Springer, Report on African Regional Conference, Accra, Jan. 14–19, 1957; all in 60/23, Lovestone files.

61. Springer, Report on African Regional Conference, Accra, Jan. 14–19, 1957; in 60/23, Lovestone files.

62. Ibid.; Kawawa to Springer, April 6, 1958, Mpangala to Dubinsky, Dec. 14, 1959, and Mpangala to Springer, April 24, 1960, all in MSK PP.

63. Mboya to Springer, Dec. 13, 1956, MSK PP.

64. Springer to Lovestone, Jan. 20, 1957, and "Delegates to the Conference,"*Accra Daily Graphic*, Tues., Jan. 15, 1957; both in 60/23, Lovestone files.

65. Springer, Memorandum on the African Regional Conference, Jan. 14–19, 1957, Accra, box 398, LP.

66. The deputy head of the ICFTU's economic, social, and political department, Stefan Nedzynski of Poland, learned that there would be a U.S. delegation only a few days before the

conference. In 1961 Nedzynski became an ICFTU assistant general secretary. Following World War II, Krane worked for the CIO's Paris office before joining the ICFTU in 1950. Springer, Memorandum Re ICFTU Secretariat Attitudes, Jan. 27, 1957, 60/23, Lovestone files; see also Meany to Oldenbroek, Jan. 2, 1957, MSK PP.

67. MSK, interview by author; Springer, Memorandum on the African Regional Conference, Accra, Jan. 14–19, 1957, box 398, LP; Springer, Report on African Regional Conference, Accra, Jan. 14–19, 1957, 60/23, Lovestone files.

68. Continuation of the Report on the Wednesday Session of the ICFTU Executive Board, Nov. 28, 1958, 23/6, Brown files.

69. Ibid.; and Brown memo, Nov. 18, 1959, 23/7, both in Brown files. Palm oil was one of many African resources produced for export, only to come back to Africa in finished form—in this case, soap—and sold at prices that were out of the reach of many Africans.

70. McCray to Lovestone, Jan. 11, 1959, "McCray, George," box 378, LP.

71. The quote appears in Frederick Cooper, *Decolonization and African Society: The Labor Question in French and British Africa* (New York: Cambridge University Press, 1996), 614 n. 28. Babau may have been assigned the position as delegate at the last minute. On the newspaper list of conference participants, someone wrote his name in as a delegate representing French West Africa; the paper had printed "unknown." "Delegates to the Conference," *Accra Daily Graphic*, Tuesday, Jan. 15, 1957, 60/23, Lovestone files; Springer, Memorandum on the African Regional Conference, Jan. 14–19, 1957, Accra, "Springer," box 398, LP; Springer, Report on African Regional Conference, Accra, Jan. 14–19, 1957, 60/23, Lovestone files.

72. "American Labour Greets Africa," *Ghana Worker*, Feb.–March 1957, 7, 9, 24, 25, in 60/23, Lovestone files.

73. Springer to Lovestone, Jan. 20, 1957, 60/23, Lovestone files.

74. Springer, Report on African Regional Conference, Accra, Jan. 14–19, 1957, 60/23, Lovestone files.

75. "American Labour Greets Africa," *The Ghana Worker*, Feb.–March 1957, pp. 7, 9, 24, 25, in 60/23, Lovestone files. The AFL-CIO published the speech and the U.S. Information Office published excerpts. Springer, Memorandum on the African Regional Conference, Jan. 14–19, Accra, "African Trade Unions," box 398, LP; MSK, interview by author. See also Springer to Lovestone, Jan. 9, 1957, and Springer to Anne Stolt, Lovestone's secretary, Oct. 16, 1957, in 60/23, Lovestone files.

76. Springer, Memorandum on the African Regional Conference, Jan. 14–19, 1957, Accra, "Springer," box 398, LP; MSK, interview by author; Springer to Lovestone, Jan. 20, 1957, and Springer, Memorandum Re ICFTU Secretariat Attitudes—Jan. 27, 1957, both in 60/23, Lovestone files.

77. Springer, Thumb Nail Sketch of an African Journey (c. March 1957), 14/12/11, ILGWU Archives. Also during her stay she suffered a brief but violent attack of malaria. Springer, Memorandum on Tanganyika, Feb. 19, 1957, 60/23, Lovestone files.

78. "Ms. Springer: An African American with the heart of a Tanzanian," *Habari Mbalimbali* (Tanzania) March 23, 1991.

Rashidi Mfaume Kawawa was assistant general secretary of the Tanganyika African Government Servants Association in 1951–1952 and in 1955 became president. He was the first general secretary of the TFL until 1959, and then became president. In 1958 he won a seat in Legco. In 1960 he was vice president of TANU, and in September 1960 he was appointed Minister for Local Government and Housing; in April 1961 he became Minister without Portfolio, and served from January to December 1962 as Prime Minister. Afterwards he became Vice President and leader of the National Assembly. After the union with Zanzibar he became Second

Vice President and Minister for Defense and National Service. He also served as second in command of the ruling political party, Chama Cha Manpinduzi. Kurtz, *Historical Dictionary of Tanzania*, 86–87.

79. Springer letter, Jan. 31, 1957, Dar es Salaam, 60/23, Lovestone files.

80. Springer, Memorandum on Kenya, March 24, 1957, "Springer," box 388, LP; Springer, diary entry, Feb. 20, 1957, MSK PP.

81. Springer to Lovestone, March 24, 1957, "Springer," box 388, LP.

82. Quotes are from Springer, Memorandum on Kenya, March 24, 1957, "Springer," box 388, LP. Two such articles, "Maida and the K.F.L. to Talk Dollars" and "Union Official on Inspection Visit from U.S." are in 60/23, Lovestone files. MSK, interview by author.

83. Argus, "Nairobi Roundabout; The Yankee Dollar," *Sunday Post* (Kenya), June 8, 1958; and Mboya to Sir, June 11, 1958, in 1/22, Lovestone files.

84. Goldsworthy, *Tom Mboya*, 97–98.

85. Springer, Memorandum on Tanganyika, Feb. 19, 1957, 60/23, Lovestone files; Springer, Memorandum on Kenya, March 24, 1957, "Springer," box 388, LP.

86. According to Springer's diary entry, she met on February 19 with Sir Walter Coutts, Minister of Labor, Lands, and Education, and his secretary, Sir Richard Luyt, to discuss land use (MSK PP). First quote is from Springer, Memorandum on Kenya, March 24, 1957, "Springer," box 388, LP; second quote is from Springer, Memorandum on Tanganyika, Feb. 19, 1957 60/23, Lovestone files.

87. Quote is from Springer, Memorandum on Kenya, March 24, 1957, "Springer," box 388, LP; Springer, Memorandum on Tanganyika, Feb. 19, 1957 60/23, Lovestone files; Randolph, Report on Trip to Africa, reel 3, frames 0543–0551, RP. Handwritten notation incorrectly dates the document in 1956; actual date was 1957. See also Ochwada to Meany, July 26, 1957, 11/6, Country files.

88. Springer, Memorandum on Tanganyika, Feb. 19, 1957, 60/23, Lovestone files.

89. For the greater part of the emergency, the KFL was unable to collect dues. Many of the collectors were arrested for trespassing. George Brown to Meany, July 25, 1957, 54/16, Meany files; Springer, Memorandum on Tanganyika, Jan. 31, 1957, 60/23, Lovestone files; Springer to Zimmerman, May 21, 1957, 14/12/11, ILGWU Archives.

90. George Brown to Meany, July 25, 1957, 54/16, Meany files; Springer, Memorandum on Tanganyika, Feb. 19, 1957, 60/23, Lovestone files.

91. Springer, Memorandum on Tanganyika, Feb. 19, 1957, 60/23, Lovestone files.

92. Ibid.; Mandawa, A Brief History on Labour Movement in Tanganyika, East Africa, memo, Amistad.

93. Springer, Thumb Nail Sketch of an African Journey, c. March 1957, 14/12/11, ILGWU Archives.

94. Springer, Memorandum on Tanganyika, Feb. 19, 1957, 60/23, Lovestone files.

95. Springer, Memorandum on Kenya, March 24, 1957, "Springer," box 388, LP; Springer, Thumb Nail Sketch of an African Journey, c. March 1957, 14/12/11, ILGWU Archives.

96. Springer, Memorandum on Kenya, March 24, 1957, "Springer," box 388, LP; M. M. Mpangala, Trade Union Movement in Tanganyika, April 7, 1959, 1/21, Lovestone files.

97. Springer, Memorandum on Tanganyika, Jan. 31, 1957, 60/23, Lovestone files; Susan Geiger, "Women in Nationalist Struggle: TANU Activists in Dar Es Salaam," in *International Journal of African Historical Studies* 20, no. 1 (1987); 22; Nyerere to Springer, May 22, 1957, 60/23, Lovestone files.

98. The quote is from Edna Mason Kaula, *The Land and People of Tanzania* (Philadelphia: J. B. Lippincott, 1972), 35, 130; Judith Listowel, *The Making of Tanganyika* (London: Chatto and Windus, 1965), 268; Bibi Titi Mohammed, interview by author, March 25, 1991.

99. Kurtz, *Historical Dictionary of Tanzania*, 222–23; Geiger, "Women in Nationalist Struggle," 1–26.

100. Randal Sadleir, *Tanzania: Journey to Republic* (London: Radcliffe Press, 1999); Springer, Memorandum on Tanganyika, Feb. 19, 1957, 60/23, Lovestone files; "New Tanganyikan Governor," in *Africa Special Report* 111, no. 1 (Jan. 1958): 7; Springer, Memorandum on Tanganyika, Feb. 19, 1957, 60/23, Lovestone files.

101. Kurtz, *Historical Dictionary of Tanzania*, 79–80, 230–31.

102. Quote is in Springer to Lovestone, Jan. 9, 1957, and see Springer, Memorandum on Tanganyika, Feb. 19, 1957, both in 60/23, Lovestone files; Meany to Mboya, Jan. 16, 1957, 11/4, and Meany to Mpangala, Jan. 16, 1957, 13/7, both in Country files.

103. Springer, Memorandum on Tanganyika, Jan. 31, 1957, 60/23, Lovestone files; "Newsman's Diary of the Week," *Sunday News* (Tanganyika), Jan. 27, 1957, 60/23, Lovestone files; MSK diary entry, Jan. 27, 1957, MSK PP.

104. Nyerere's ban lasted from February to September 1957. "Local Politics," *Tanganyika Standard*, Jan. 29, 1957, 60/23, Lovestone files; Springer, Memorandum on Tanganyika, Feb. 19, 1957, 60/23, Lovestone files.

105. Springer, Memorandum on Tanganyika, Feb. 19, 1957, 60/23, Lovestone files; "New Tanganyikan Governor," in *Africa Special Report* 111, no. 1 (Jan. 1958): 7.

106. "Ms. Springer: An African American with the Heart of a Tanzanian," *Habari Mbalimbali* (Tanzania), March 23, 1991.

107. Mpangala, Labour Struggle for Recognition, Feb. 11, 1957, 14/12/11, ILGWU Archives; "Odd Actions by Unions," *Sunday News* (Tanganyika), Jan. 27, 1957, and Springer, Memorandum on Tanganyika, Jan. 31, 1957, in 60/23, both in Lovestone files.

108. In Dar es Salaam the slum areas were known as Magomeni, Ilala, and Temeke. In Tanga there was Nagamiani. Springer, Memorandum on Tanganyika, Jan. 31, 1957, 60/23, Lovestone files; Maynard M. Mpangala, Labour Struggle for Recognition, Feb. 11, 1957, 14/12/11, ILGWU Archives.

109. Mpangala, "Labour Struggle for Recognition," Feb. 11, 1957, 14/12/11, ILGWU Archives. Mandawa to Springer, March 18, 1957, MSK PP.

110. Springer, Memorandum on Tanganyika, Jan. 31, 1957, 60/23, Lovestone files; Mpangala, Labour Struggle for Recognition, Feb. 11, 1957, 14/12/11, ILGWU Archives.

111. "Industrial Relations," *Tanganyika Standard*, Jan. 28, 1957, 60/23, Lovestone files.

112. "Newsman's Diary of the Week" and "Odd Actions by Unions," both in *Sunday News* (Tanganyika) Jan. 27, 1957, 60/23, Lovestone files.

113. Springer, Memorandum on Tanganyika, Feb. 19, 1957, 60/23, Lovestone files.

114. Springer letter, Jan. 31, 1957, and Springer, Memorandum on Tanganyika, Feb. 19, 1957, both in 60/23, Lovestone files; Mpangala, Labour Struggle for Recognition, Feb. 11, 1957, 14/12/11, ILGWU Archives.

115. Mpangala to Springer, May 13, 1957, 14/12/11, ILGWU Archives.

116. Springer to Randolph, April 29, 1957, MSK PP.

117. Springer to Sasha (Charles Zimmerman), May 21, 1957; Kawawa, Memorandum on Tanganyika Federation of Labor Minimum Wage; and Springer to Kawawa, telegram, May 27, 1957, all in 14/12/11, ILGWU Archives. See also Mandawa to Springer, June 28, 1957, MSK PP.

118. Kawawa to Meany, March 4, 1957, 13/7, Country files; Kawawa to Springer, May 19, 1957, 21/8, Brown files; Mpangala to Springer, May 13, 1957, 14/12/11, ILGWU Archives; Marvin Rogoff (ILGWU assistant educational director) to Kawawa, July 17, 1957, MSK PP.

119. Minya to Springer, Feb. 19, 1957, 60/23, Lovestone files; see also Mpangala to Springer, May 13, 1957, 14/12/11, ILGWU Archives.

120. Springer, Memorandum on Tanganyika, Feb. 19, 1957, 60/23, Lovestone files.

121. Letter to Sir Vincent Tewson, British TUC general secretary (signature of writer above the typed title reading "general secretary" is illegible), Oct. 18, 1957, 21/8, and Brown memo, Nov. 18, 1959, 23/7, both in Brown files; Springer to Lovestone, March 24, 1957, "Springer," box 388, LP.

122. Tettegah to Springer, Oct. 29, 1957, and Ochwada to Springer, Aug. 16, 1957, MSK PP; "Continuation of the Report on the Wednesday Session of the ICFTU Executive Board," Nov. 28, 1958, 23/6, Brown files; and Report of General Secretaries Conference held at Arusha, Feb. 15, 1958, 1/22, Lovestone files.

123. Springer to Tettegah, partial letter, c. Nov. 1957, MSK PP.

124. Among the AFL-CIO leaders with whom Springer immediately consulted following her return were Schnitzler, Ted Brown, George Brown, George Weaver, and Dan Benedict. MSK diary entry, April 12, 1957, MSK PP. Springer also wrote articles about her experiences: Springer, "Garments in Ghana," Aug. 1, 1957, *Justice*.

Chapter 6: The Atlantic City Compromise

1. Elizabeth Balanoff, "Maida Springer Kemp Interview," in *The Black Women Oral History Project*, vol. 7, ed. Ruth Edmonds Hill (New Providence, N.J.: K. G. Saur Verlag, 1991), 103.

2. Mboya to McCray, Feb. 6, 1958, 11/4, Country files.

3. The other FTUC officers included Meany as honorary president, Dubinsky as vice president, and William Schnitzler as honorary secretary. David Dubinsky and A. H. Raskin, *David Dubinsky: A Life with Labor* (New York: Simon and Schuster, 1977), 240–43; Ronald Radosh, *American Labor and United States Foreign Policy* (New York: Random House, 1969), 309; Alfred O. Hero, Jr., and Emil Starr, *The Reuther-Meany Foreign Policy Dispute: Union Leaders and Members View World Affairs* (Dobbs Ferry, N.Y.: Oceana Publications, 1970), 59, 66–70.

4. German Press Agency, Information 121, Jan. 23, 1957; see also Report from Irving Brown, May 17, 1957, both in Correspondence, Reports, Clips, Interviews, Translations, 1/57–5/57, box 1, BP. Lovestone to Brown, July 11, 1960, "Brown, 1960," box 356, LP.

5. In response to his request for advice on running their newly formed Workers Education Association, Springer sent the TFL materials on worker education programs in the United States. Springer to Rashidi Kawawa, Aug. 5, 1957, Amistad; Kawawa to Springer, May 19, 1957, 21/8, Brown files; Maynard Mpangala to Springer, May 13, 1957, 14/12/11, ILGWU Archives; and Mandawa to Springer, April 18, 1957, and Kawawa to Springer, Aug. 18, 1957, both in MSK PP.

6. Springer to Randolph, April 29, 1957, MSK PP.

7. "Ghana TUC Boss Calls for Practical Assistance," *Daily Graphic*, Jan. 15, 1957, 60/23, Lovestone files; "Kampala: Cause for Pride," *Free Labour World* 132 (June 1961): 226; Anthony Clayton and Donald C. Savage, *Government and Labour in Kenya, 1895–1963* (London: Cass, 1974), 382; Springer to Theodore E. Brown, Jan. 16, 1958, Amistad; Springer to Randolph, April 29, 1957, MSK PP.

8. Randolph would use this quote in a report to the AFL-CIO. Randolph, "An AFL-CIO Program for Awarding Scholarships to Native Africans South of the Sahara for Training in Expanding Democratic Trade Unionism in Africa," c. 1957, MSK PP; Springer, The American Labor Movement and Africa, 60/23, Lovestone files.

9. Springer to Theodore E. Brown, Jan. 16, 1958, and Springer to Schnitzler, Dec. 5, 1959, both in Amistad; Randolph, "An AFL-CIO Program for Awarding Scholarships to Native Africans South of the Sahara for Training in Expanding Democratic Trade Unionism in Africa," MSK PP; McCray to Lovestone, May 31, 1958, "McCray," box 378, LP.

10. See Randolph to Schnitzler, June 18, 1957, 14/4, Country files; Randolph, report on trip to Africa, reel 3, frames 0543–0551 (handwritten notation incorrectly dates the document in 1956; should be 1957), and Springer to Chief [Randolph], March 5, 1972, reel 3, frames 0026-0027, both in RP; Randolph, interview by MSK, "Oral History Program: African American Labor History Center," June 6, 1973, in Interviews, Box 1(2), APR Papers.

11. Randolph, Report on Trip to Africa [1957], reel 3, frames 0543–0551, RP.

12. The final decision on what institution would run the program was made after Springer arrived in Africa. Kawawa to Meany, March 4, 1957, 13/7, and Report to Meany from Randolph, 9/23, both in Country files; Kawawa to Springer, May 19, 1957, 21/8, Brown files; Randolph, Report on Trip to Africa [1957], reel 3, frames 0543–0551, RP; Randolph to Springer, Oct. 21, 1957, MSK PP.

13. Randolph, Plan for Training African Workers for Leadership of African Trade Unions, Sept. 4, 1957, MSK PP.

14. Meany to Oldenbroek, Oct. 29, 1957, reel 3, frames 0569–0570, RP; and *Proceedings of the AFL-CIO Constitutional Convention*, 2 vols., 1957, 1:433.

15. Meany to Oldenbroek, Oct. 29, 1957, reel 3, frames 0569–0570, RP; and *Proceedings of the AFL-CIO Constitutional Convention*, 1:433.

16. Diary entries, Sept. 22–Oct. 11, 1998, MSK PP; "Maida Springer, in Africa To Select Union Trainees," *Justice*, Nov. 15, 1957.

17. Springer to Anne Stolt (Lovestone's secretary), Oct. 16, 1957, 60/23, Lovestone files.

18. Also at the meeting were Bennett, the colonial officer, and Parry, the East African director. Diary entry, Oct. 15, 1957; Mother (Maida Springer) to Eric (Springer), Oct. 20, 1957, both in MSK PP; Springer to Stolt, Oct. 16, 1957, 60/23, Lovestone files; MSK, interview by author.

19. Tewson was also a former ICFTU president.

20. In a 1996 article Anthony Carew remarked that Springer snubbed the ICFTU by not informing them of her plans. Anthony Carew, "Charles Millard, A Canadian in the International Labour Movement: A Case Study of the ICFTU 1955–61," in *Labour/Le Travail* 37 (Spring 1996): 137; Springer to Stolt, Oct. 16, 1957, 60/23, Lovestone files.

21. MSK, interview by author; Mother (Maida Springer) to Eric (Springer), Oct. 20, 1957, MSK PP.

22. Springer to Nyerere, Sept. 8, 1957, and [Nyerere to Springer], Sept. 25, 1957; see also Mandawa to Springer, Oct. 1, 1957; all in MSK PP.

23. Diary entry, Oct. 18, 1957; Springer to Mama (Adina Stewart), Oct. 22, 1957. First quote is from Springer to Stolt, Nov. 7, 1957, Mother (Maida Springer) to Eric (Springer), Oct. 20, 1957; second quote is from Springer to George Brown, Oct. 24, 1957; all MSK PP.

24. Springer to Caroline Ware, Oct. 24, 1957, MSK PP.

25. Carew has stated that Springer's "application for a visitor's permit to enter East African territories was the subject of lengthy consideration, and within a matter of weeks the Secretary of State for the Colonies was actively deliberating on whether or not she should be expelled." Carew, "Charles Millard, A Canadian in the International Labour Movement," 137; Springer to Stolt, Nov. 25, 1957, MSK PP.

26. See, for example, Springer to Jean Appleton (Dubinsky's daughter), Dec. 6, 1957, MSK PP.

27. MSK, interview by author. The name of the principal immigration officer was S. C. Sinclair. An example of British harassment cloaked in polite language is found in a letter Sinclair sent her. He ended by writing, "I am, Madam, Your Obedient Servant." Sinclair to Springer, Nov. 8, 1957, Amistad; Springer to Sinclair, Nov. 8, 1957, MSK PP.

28. Although Springer wrote to her son that the hotels were full because of the coronation services for the Aga Khan, she later remarked that hotel owners had been told not to rent to her. MSK, interview by author; Mother (Maida Springer) to Eric (Springer), Oct. 20, 1957, MSK PP.

29. Springer also had informed her mother that "we" had been discussing her cooking and that the whole executive board would like to come just to see "Mama." Springer to Mama (Adina Stewart), Oct. 22, 1957, and Dec. 4, 1957, and Springer to Lester Granger, Nov. 13, 1957, MSK PP.

30. Springer to Silverman, Dec. 14, 1957, MSK PP.

31. Springer to Mama (Adina Stewart), Dec. 4, 1957, and diary entry, Oct. 22, 1957, MSK PP.

32. Springer letter, partial, c. Nov. 1957, MSK PP; Springer to [Tettegah], partial letter, c. Nov. 1957, MSK PP.

33. Springer to [Tettegah], partial letter, c. Nov. 1957, MSK PP.

34. Springer to Schnitzler, Dec. 5, 1959, Amistad; "Wind in the Sisal: A Busy Time for the Law," *Weekly News* (Tanganyika), Nov. 15, 1957, 60/23, Lovestone files; MSK, interview by author. MSK quote is from Springer to Stolt, Nov. 7, 1957, MSK PP.

35. Kamaliza, along with Kawawa and Mpangala, had helped to form the TFL. Springer to Lovestone, May 25, 1959, 60/24, Lovestone files; Springer to Stolt, Nov. 7, 1957, MSK PP.

36. Springer to Stolt, Nov. 7, 1957, and diary entries, Oct. 30–31, 1957, MSK PP.

37. Springer to Mama (Adina Stewart), Oct. 22, 1957, and Springer to Stolt, Nov. 7, 1957, MSK PP.

38. Bibi Titi Mohammed, interview by author, March 25, 1991; Springer to Silverman, Dec. 14, 1957, and Springer to Stolt, Dec. 16, 1957, MSK PP.

39. MSK, interview by author.

40. MSK, interview by author; diary entry, Dec. 18, 1957, MSK PP; Springer letter, partial, no date, MSK PP.

41. Joseph Thuo to Mama (Adina Stewart), Dec. 6, 1957, MSK PP.

42. Springer to Schnitzler, Dec. 5, 1959, Amistad.

43. Before coming to power in 1945, the Labor Party had expressed a willingness to fight against colonialism and the color bar. Pan-Africanists were disappointed by their inaction on these issues. See Kenneth King, ed., *Ras Makonnen: Pan-Africanism from Within* (New York: Oxford University Press, 1973), 159, 181; James Dennis Akumu (organizing secretary of the People's Convention Party) to Morgan Phillip (general secretary of the British Labor Party), n.d., Amistad; Hon. James Johnson, British Labour MP, "America's Role in Africa," *Africa Special Report* 3, no. 6 (June 1958): 12. See also "Who's Here This Month," *Africa Special Report* 2, no. 9 (Oct. 1957).

44. Borochowicz to Lovestone, Feb. 3, 1958, in Correspondence, Reports, Clips, Other, 1/58–12/58, box 1, BP.

45. News Summary and Report for Week Ending Aug. 17, 1958, Kampala, Uganda, ICFTU African Labor College microfilm, reel 1, IISH.

46. Kawawa, "Trade Union Suppression in Sisal Industry," Sept. 28, 1957, and Mpangala, progress report dated April 12, 1958, both in MSK PP.

47. Springer noted that Lennox Gondive, general secretary of the plantation workers, traveled fifty to seventy miles every Sunday to hold meetings. Diary entry, Dec. 29, 1957, Springer to Mama, Jan. 2, 1957 [should be 1958], and Kawawa, "Trade Union Suppression in Sisal Industry," Sept. 28, 1957, all in MSK PP; Randolph, Report on Trip to Africa [1957], reel 3, frames 0543–0551, RP.

48. Kawawa, "Trade Union Suppression in Sisal Industry," MSK PP.

49. Ibid., and Oldenbroek to Kawawa, Oct. 4, 1957, in MSK PP.

50. M. M. Mpangala, Trade Union Movement in Tanganyika, April 7, 1959, 1/21, Lovestone files; see also Mpangala, "Forerunner of Freedom: Tanganyika Labor Stirs," *AFL-CIO Free Trade Union News* 16, no. 4 (April 1961).

51. Kawawa originally had suggested to Millard that Maynard Mpangala might become the organizer. Millard wondered why J. B. Ohanga was chosen as organizer and said he preferred that Kawawa perform this work. Mpangala would later work for the ITS for plantation workers. Millard to Kawawa, July 23, 1957, MSK PP.

52. Kawawa to Millard, July 31, 1957, MSK PP; Springer to Stolt, Dec. 1, 1957, MSK PP.

53. Springer to Stolt, Nov. 7, 1957, MSK PP; quote is from Springer to Schnitzler, Dec. 5, 1959, Amistad; MSK, interview by Balanoff, 88; and MSK, interview by author; "Ms. Springer: An African American with the Heart of a Tanzanian," *Habari Mbalimbali* (Tanzania), March 23, 1991.

54. "Tanganyika: Trade Union Dilemma," *The Economist*, May 3, 1958.

55. Kawawa, "Trade Union Suppression in Sisal Industry," Sept. 28, 1957, MSK PP; Mpangala, progress report dated April 12, 1958, MSK PP.

56. Springer to Schnitzler, Dec. 6, 1957, and John B. Abuoga to Springer, Dec. 24, 1957, MSK PP.

57. Mpangala to Springer, April 24, 1958, MSK PP; Report of General Secretaries Conference held at Arusha, Feb. 15, 1958, 1/22, Lovestone files.

58. Mpangala to Springer, April 24, 1958, MSK PP; Report of General Secretaries Conference held at Arusha, Feb. 15, 1958, 1/22, Lovestone files.

59. Springer to Stolt, Dec. 1, 1957, MSK PP.

60. MSK, interview by author. The four-day conference started on November 25. The settlement talks in Tanga included union recognition and workers' problems but excluded discussions of wages. Diary entry, Dec. 2, 1957; Springer to George Brown, Dec. 2, 1957; Springer to Robinson, Dec. 7, 1957, A. P. Ndoe (general secretary of the Tanga Port Stevedores and Dockworkers Union), Union's Report, Dec. 21, 1957, and Ndoe, Secretary's Report over the Alleged Illegal Dock Strike in Tanga, Jan. 1, 1958, all in MSK PP.

61. Quote is from Springer, Memorandum on Uganda, Dec. 10, 1957, Amistad; Springer to Randolph, Nov. 3, 1957, Springer to Tewson, Nov. 25, 1957, Springer to Stolt, Nov. 25, 1957, Springer to George Brown, Dec. 2, 1957; see also C.E.S. Kabuga (general secretary of the Uganda Printing Trade Union) to Springer, Nov. 20, 1957; all in MSK PP. See also H. M. Luande (president of the Railway African Union, Uganda) to Randolph, Dec. 10, 1957, and Randolph to Luande, Jan. 14, 1957, reel 3, frames 00583–00584, RP.

62. Springer, Memorandum on Uganda, Dec. 10, 1957, Amistad; Springer to Randolph, Nov. 3, 1957, Springer to Tewson, Nov. 25, 1957, Springer to Stolt, Nov. 25, 1957, and Springer to George Brown, Dec. 2, 1957, all in MSK PP; quote is from Springer to Zimmerman, Dec. 7, 1957, 14/12/11, ILGWU Archives.

63. Diary entry, Nov. 16, 1957, MSK PP.

64. Springer to Robinson, Dec. 7, 1957, MSK PP.

65. Springer to William Schwartz (manager of the National Department), Dec. 14, 1957, MSK PP.

66. Springer to Skipper (Caroline Ware), Dec. 18, 1957, MSK PP.

67. Carew, "Charles Millard, A Canadian in the International Labour Movement," 141.

68. Springer to Stolt, Dec. 1, 1957, MSK PP; see also Springer, Memorandum on Kenya, March 24, 1957, "Springer," box 388, LP.

69. In the preceding seven weeks Springer had traveled to Dar es Salaam, Mombasa,

Tanga, Nairobi, and through parts of Zanzibar and Uganda. Springer to Robinson, Dec. 7, 1957, MSK PP.

70. In contrast to the Uganda story, Ochwada and Mandawa were selected by unanimous consent. Springer to Randolph, Nov. 3, 1957, MSK PP.

71. Springer to Stolt, Nov. 7, 1957, and Springer to Robinson, Dec. 7, 1957, both in MSK PP.

72. MSK, interview by Balanoff, 89; Don Thomson and Rodney Larson, *Where Were You, Brother? An Account of Trade Union Imperialism* (London: War on Want, 1978), 18–19.

73. Against Lovestone's advice, George Brown brought up the subject of publications, which fell under Lovestone's purview, thus precipitating a discussion of Lovestone's role within the merged federation. Lovestone to Brown, "Brown, Irving, undated," box 355, LP; German News Agency, D.P.A., Information 182, Feb. 8, 1957, in Correspondence, Reports, Clips, Interviews, Translations, 1/57–5/57, box 1, BP;; German Press Agency, Information 964, July 16, 1957, and see Minutes of Meeting, Carlton Hotel, June 5, 1956, both in Correspondence, Reports, Clips, Interviews, Translations, in 6/57–12/57, box 1, BP.

74. Carew states that Millard was frustrated by the continuation of independent British international programs. Carew, "Charles Millard, A Canadian in the International Labour Movement," 140; letter from Irving Brown, Nov. 9, 1957, 6/57–12/57, box 1, BP.

75. Millard to Randolph, Nov. 22, 1957, MSK PP.

76. Randolph to Millard, Jan. 21, 1958, MSK PP.

77. George T. Brown to Springer, Nov. 25, 1957; Springer to Mama, Dec. 4, 1957; and Springer to Silverman, Dec. 14, 1957; all in MSK PP.

78. The British TUC fraternal delegates were Joseph O'Hagen and Wilfred B. Beard. Also in attendance were British TUC president Thomas Yates, Willi Richter of the German Federation of Labor, and Donald MacDonald of the Canadian Labor Congress. *Proceedings of the AFL-CIO Constitutional Convention,* 1:18, 41, 113, 150–60, 265–71, 302–4.

79. Mboya, "Greetings From Kenya to AFL-CIO in New York," 1957, MSK PP. This letter along with Kawawa's letter of support for the program are printed in *Proceedings of the AFL-CIO Constitutional Convention,* 1:382–84.

80. Makayu to Meany, 1957, Amistad.

81. Nyerere to Randolph, Dec. 7, 1957, Amistad.

82. Randolph to Nyerere, Dec. 17, 1957, Amistad.

83. The Colonial Question (Jay's Version), 6/57–12/57, box 1, BP; [Lovestone] to Springer, Nov. 22, 1957, 60/23, Lovestone files.

84. Stanley Levey, "Labor Reshapes Foreign Policy," *New York Times,* Dec. 9, 1957, MSK PP.

85. Randolph, interview by MSK, June 6, 1973, in Interviews, Box 1(2), APR Papers.

86. *Proceedings of the AFL-CIO Constitutional Convention,* 1:428–31.

87. *Proceedings of the AFL-CIO Constitutional Convention,* 1959, volume 1, 485.

88. *Proceedings of the AFL-CIO Constitutional Convention,* 1957, 1: 432-435.

89. Ibid.; Springer to Randolph, Jan. 16, 1958, MSK PP; Lovestone to Ochwada [Boston], May 5, 1958, 1/22, Lovestone files. See Randolph's discussion of the "Colombo Plan Technical Cooperation Scheme, United Kingdom Government Offer of Study Courses for Trade Union Officials—1958," in Randolph to Millard, Jan. 21, 1958, MSK PP.

90. Brown to Springer, telegram, Dec. 10, 1957, MSK PP.

91. Springer to Stolt, Dec. 16, 1957, 60/23, Lovestone files.

92. Borochowicz to Lovestone, Feb. 3, 1958, 1/58–12/58, box 1, BP; Mboya to McCray, Feb. 4, 1958, 11/4, Country files; see also Mboya to Springer, Dec. 20, 1957, MSK PP.

93. Mandawa to Meany, April 18, 1959, Amistad.

94. Kawawa to Springer, April 6, 1958, MSK PP; Chalfin to Daniel Benedict (international representative, AFL-CIO), Jan. 14, 1958, 9/23, Country files.

95. Chalfin to Benedict, Jan. 14, 1958, 9/23, Country files

96. Lovestone to Ochwada [Boston], March 24, 1958, 1/22, Lovestone files.

97. Lovestone to McCray, June 1, 1959, 48/26, Lovestone files; address by AFL-CIO delegate William F. Schnitzler, ICFTU Congress, Tunis, July 9, 1957, 23/7, Brown files.

98. Report of General Secretaries Conference held at Arusha, Feb. 15, 1958, 1/22, Lovestone files.

99. Springer to Randolph, Jan. 16, 1958, and Springer to Eric, Dec. 23, 1957, both in MSK PP; Nyerere to Springer, Feb. 22, 1958, Amistad.

100. Springer to Mandawa, July 6, 1958, MSK PP; David Goldsworthy, *Tom Mboya: The Man Kenya Wanted to Forget* (New York: Africana Publishing, 1982), 98; News Summary and Report for Week Ending Aug. 17, 1958, Kampala, Uganda, ICFTU African Labor College microfiom, reel 1, IISH; Ross to Brown, June 19, 1958, 33/14, Brown files; Nyerere to Springer, July 5, 1958, MSK Papers, Amistad.

101. Kawawa to Springer, Jan. 31, 1958, MSK PP.

102. Kawawa to Springer, June 27, 1958, MSK PP.

103. Mpangala to Springer, Jan. 14, 1959, Amistad.

104. African labor leaders also thanked the British TUC for books and equipment they had sent in the past. Report of General Secretaries Conference held at Arusha, Feb. 15, 1958, 1/22, Lovestone files; Mboya to McCray, Dec. 6, 1958, 11/4, Country files.

105. McCray to Meany, March 3, 1959, and McCray, Basic Considerations Relative to Operations in Africa, [March 18, 1959], and McCray to Reuther, May 23, 1959, all in 48/26, Lovestone files; McCray to Meany, June 10, 1963, 13/18, Country files.

106. Tettegah to Springer, Oct. 29, 1957, and Ochwada to Springer, Aug. 16, 1957, both in MSK PP; "Continuation of the Report on the Wednesday Session of the ICFTU Executive Board," Nov. 28, 1958, 23/6, Brown files.

107. Mpangala to Lovestone, April 7, 1959, and Lovestone to Mpangala, April 23, 1959, and see Mandawa, "Memo on My Trade Union Activities, Etc.," n.d., all in MSK PP.

108. Springer to Lovestone, May 9, 1959, 60/24, Lovestone files.

109. Besides the Africans, the Harvard program included eleven students from the United States, eight from Europe, and one each from the Philippines, Peru, and Thailand. Mandawa to Meany, April 18, 1959, and Dishan William Kiwanuka, "Report on the African Trade Union Program Sponsored by the AFL-CIO," c. 1958, Amistad.

110. The following information on this committee meeting comes from George Brown to Schnitzler, Report of ICFTU Trade Union Training Program in Africa, Feb. 27, 1958, 54/12, Meany files.

111. Mandawa sent Springer, who was in Morogoro, an excerpt of the cable from the United States. Mandawa to Springer, Dec. 28, 1957; George Brown to Springer, telegram received Dec. 28, 1957; Springer to George Brown, telegram, no date, MSK PP.

112. Report of General Secretaries Conference held at Arusha, Feb. 15, 1958, 1/22, Lovestone files; George Brown to Schnitzler, Report of ICFTU Trade Union Training Program in Africa, Feb. 27, 1958, 54/12, Meany files.

113. Mboya to Meany, March 11, 1958, and Tettegah to Millard, March 5, 1958, both in "Mboya, 1958–1963," box 379, LP; Mboya to Ochwada, April 21, 1958, 1/22, Lovestone files.

114. Springer to Mboya, June 22, 1958, and Mboya to Springer, June 6, 1958, and June 11, 1958, all in MSK PP.

115. Schnitzler to Gottfurcht, May 20, 1958, and Gottfurcht to Schnitzler, June 4, 1958, 23/3, and Ross to Irving Brown, June 19, 1958, and Ross to Meany, June 19, 1958, 33/14, all in

Brown files; McCray to Randolph, Sept. 5, 1958, reel 2, frame 0104, RP. McCray's union, affiliated with the CIO, changed its name to the American Federation of State, County, and Municipal Employees (AFSCME) following the AFL-CIO merger.

116. Apparently McCray in late 1962 was under consideration as the successor to Joseph Odero-Jowi, the second principal of Kampala College, but ICFTU general secretary Omer Bécu prevented it because of "political considerations." By this time, Africanization was also an issue. See Brown to George [possibly Meany], Dec. 19, 1962, 1/23, Brown files; McCray to Lovestone, May 31, 1958, "McCray, George," box 378, LP.

117. Thirty-two students from eleven countries participated in the first four-month course. McCray to Randolph, Sept. 5, 1958, reel 2, frame 0104, RP; see also Meany to Millard, Sept. 2, 1958, 30/18, Brown files.

118. McCray, report on ICFTU African Labor College, Dec. 26, 1958, "ICFTU Regional Offices Africa," box 483, LP.

119. Ibid.; McCray to Meany, Jan. 10, 1959, "African-ICFTU African Labor College," box 397, LP; Fockstedt to Krane, Feb. 16, 1958, ICFTU African Labor College microfilm, reel 1, IISH.

120. McCray to Meany, Jan. 10, 1959, "African-ICFTU African Labor College," box 397, LP.

121. Ibid.

122. Milton Bracker, "Labor College Meets in Uganda; Hotel Dispute Is Extracurricular," *New York Times*, Feb. 7, 1959, in Labor Unions Africa, Schomburg Center Clippings File; Springer to Mboya, March 10, 1959, MSK PP; see also McCray to Ross, Sept. 8, 1959, reel 3, frames 0589–0592, RP.

123. McCray, report on ICFTU African Labor College, Dec. 26, 1958, "ICFTU Regional Offices Africa," box 483, LP; McCray to Ross, Sept. 8, 1959, reel 3, frames 0589–92, RP; Frederick Cooper, *Decolonization and African Society: The Labor Question in French and British Africa* (New York: Cambridge University Press, 1996), 440–41.

124. Agenda Item 5: Trade Union Situation in Africa, ICFTU Third African Regional Conference, Tunis, Nov. 7–11, 1960, Welsh Papers.

125. Springer to McCray, May 8, 1961, 13/19, Country files.

126. "Kampala: Cause for Pride," June 1961, 225–27; "A New Head at Kampala," Oct. 1963, 2; and "Kampala Fulfills its Promise," Oct. 1964, 4; all in *Free Labour World*.

127. *Proceedings of the AFL-CIO Constitutional Convention*, 2 vols., 1959, 1:432–35.

128. Sven Fockstedt, Findings and Observations Concerning the ICFTU Position in East Africa Made during September 9th to 18th 1964, Sept. 22, 1964, "Africa–East Africa," box 397, LP; "Kampala Fulfills Its Promise," *Free Labour World*, Oct. 1964, 4.

129. Mandawa to Springer [c. April 1960], and Springer to Mandawa, May 5, 1960, both in 13/7, Country files.

130. The general secretary of the Dockworkers and Stevedores Union was studying at the African Labor College. Mandawa to Springer, Feb. 28, 1959, MSK PP; Springer, Summary of Six Weeks in Africa, September 21–November 6, 1960, Nov. 14, 1960, 14/3, Country files.

131. Unsigned letter to Springer, Nov. 18, 1957, 60/23, Lovestone files; Kawawa to Meany, May 16, 1960, Mandawa to Springer, May 17, 1960, Springer to Mandawa, June 7, 1960, Mandawa to Springer, June 17, 1960, all in 13/6, Country files.

132. E. E. Akena (general secretary of the Dockworkers and Stevedores Union) to Mandawa, April 26, 1957, May 9, 1957, and May 15, 1957; Mandawa to Akena, May 16, 1957; Mpangala to [Akena], Nov. 12, 1957; Randolph to Springer, Nov. 22, 1957; and Springer to George Brown, Dec. 2, 1957; all in MSK PP.

133. Springer to Mandawa, June 7, 1960, 13/6, and Springer to Kawawa, June 7, 1960, 13/6, both in Country files. In his original proposal Randolph had suggested a fifty-dollar monthly

stipend, but Springer asserted that fifty dollars was not enough to support the men and their families. Randolph to Schnitzler, June 18, 1957, 14/4, Country files; Springer to Ross, Feb. 3, 1958, MSK PP; Mandawa to Springer, [c. June 1959], Amistad; see also Kiwanuka to Lovestone, Oct. 18, 1959, 1/22, Lovestone files; Springer to Theodore E. Brown, Jan. 16, 1958, Amistad; and Springer to Randolph, April 29, 1957, and Randolph, "An AFL-CIO Program for Awarding Scholarships to Native Africans South of the Sahara for Training in Expanding Democratic Trade Unionism in Africa," c. 1957, both in MSK PP.

134. Ross to A. Banyanga (Uganda TUC general secretary), 13/19, and see also Ross to Mboya, Oct. 22, 1959, 11/5, both in Country files.

135. Springer to McCray, May 8, 1961, 13/19, Country files.

Chapter 7: The Beginning of the Affiliation Struggle

1. Murray to Spingarn Medal Award Committee, letter nominating Maida Springer and Ted Poston as co-candidates for the NAACP Spingarn Medal, April 7, 1959, 14/12/11, ILGWU Archives.

2. Springer may have collaborated with Randolph in formulating the 1959 resolutions. We know that the following year, Randolph thanked her for formulating at his request the 1960 resolutions on Africa. Randolph to Springer, Sept. 13, 1960, and Mboya to Springer, March 21, 1959, both in MSK PP; Hugh Chevins, "U.S. Unions Intervene on Colonies: Africans Backed," *London Daily Telegraph*, n.d., 8/1, Brown files; "End Colonialism in Africa!" *Free Trade Union News* 14, no. 3 (March 1959).

3. George McTurnan Kahin, *The Asian-African Conference, Bandung, Indonesia, April 1955* (Ithaca, N.Y.: Cornell University Press, 1956), 23.

4. Randolph to Millard, Jan. 21, 1958, and see Millard to Randolph, Nov. 22, 1957, both in MSK PP.

5. MSK, interview by author.

6. Maida S. Springer, guest column, "The Trend in Negro Leadership," *Los Angeles Tribune*, Jan. 26, 1946, MSK PP.

7. Randolph returned Springer's check for membership in the NALC, stating that she had given more than her share to black causes. "Randolph Tells of Fight against Racial Discrimination at the AFL-CIO Convention in San Francisco," Oct. 10, 1959, and see Springer to Randolph, June 14, 1960, both in MSK PP.

8. See McCray to Lovestone, March 18, 1964, "McCray," box 378, LP.

9. Continuation of the Report on the Wednesday Session of the ICFTU Executive Board, Nov. 28, 1958, and Tettegah to Mboya, Oct. 28, 1958, both in 23/6, Brown files.

10. Ibid.

11. McCray to Randolph, July 21, 1958, reel 2, frames 0093–0096, RP.

12. McCray to Lovestone, May 31, 1958, "McCray," box 378, LP; McCray, "Observations on the All African Peoples Conference (hereafter AAPC) at Accra, Ghana December 8–13, 1958," 14/14, Country files; "People's Conference Plans Permanent Body," *Africa Special Report* 4, no. 2 (Feb. 1959): 6.

13. Springer, "Observations on the AAPC held in Accra, Ghana, December 5–13, 1958, and Its Trade Union Implications," 14/12/11, ILGWU Archives.

14. Kenneth King, ed., *Ras Makonnen: Pan-Africanism from Within* (New York: Oxford University Press, 1973), 216–17; George M. Houser, *No One Can Stop the Rain: Glimpses of Africa's Liberation Struggle* (New York: Pilgrim Press, 1989), 70; Springer notes, MSK PP.

15. For more information on CIA plans to assassinate Lumumba and the U.S. role in the Congo crisis, see Sean Kelly, *America's Tyrant: The CIA and Mobutu of Zaire* (Washington, D.C.: American University Press, 1993).

16. McCray to Meany, Jan. 30, 1961, and McCray to G. Mennen Williams (assistant secretary of state for African affairs), Jan. 31, 1961, both in 48/27, Lovestone files; David Brombart, interview by author, March 5, 1993; McCray, "Observations on the AAPC," 14/14, Country files.

17. MSK, interview by author; see also John Marcum, "French-Speaking Africa at Accra," *Africa Special Report* 4, no. 2 (Feb. 1959): 9, and Houser, *No One Can Stop the Rain*, 73.

18. MSK, interview by author; see speech by Martha Ouandie, representative of the Kamerun Women Democratic Union, 3/5, Brown files.

19. MSK, interview by author.

20. Liberia had long been nominally independent. *Africa Report* 4, no. 2 (Feb. 1959).

21. Henry S. Wilson, *African Decolonization* (London: Edward Arnold, 1994), 154–67; Houser, *No One Can Stop the Rain*, 72–73.

22. Colin Legum, *Pan-Africanism: A Short Political Guide* (New York: Praeger, 1965), 40; see Ephraim Evron (American representative to Histadrut) to Lovestone, Jan. 15, 1959, 2/247/6, ILGWU Archives; Brown to Meany, Dec. 24, 1958, 14/14, Country files.

23. There was some talk that Nkrumah, under pressure from Nasser, had delayed sending an ambassador to Israel in 1957. Unsigned letter to Springer, Nov. 18, 1957, 60/23, Lovestone files; King, *Ras Makonnen*, 235–36; George Padmore, ed., *The Voice of Coloured Labour* (1945; reprint, London: African Publication Society, 1970), 28–36; Milene Charles, *The Soviet Union and Africa: The History of the Involvement* (New York: University Press of America, 1980), 85–86; see also Olusola Ojo, *Africa and Israel: Relations in Perspective* (Boulder: Westview Press, 1988) and Joel Peters, *Israel and Africa, The Problematic Friendship* (London: British Academic Press), 1992.

24. Houser, *No One Can Stop the Rain*, 72–73; King, *Ras Makonnen*, 207, 214–15, 219.

25. Dr. Fouad M. Galal led the UAR delegation. The United Arab Republic was the name for the union of Egypt and Syria (1958–1961). Springer, "Voice of the New African," 1959, MSK Papers, Amistad; and Springer, "Observations on the AAPC," 14/12/11, ILGWU Archives. See also Peter Weiler, *British Labour and the Cold War* (Stanford: Stanford University Press, 1988), 57, and Houser, *No One Can Stop the Rain*, 71.

26. Springer, "Voice of the New African," 1959, Amistad; Springer, "Observations on the AAPC," 14/12/11, ILGWU Archives; McCray, "Observations on the AAPC," 14/14, Country files.

27. Brown to Meany, Dec. 24, 1958, 14/14, Country files; Charles, *The Soviet Union and Africa*, 85; McCray, "Observations on the AAPC," 14/14, Country files; King, *Ras Makonnen*, 245, 262–63.

28. According to McCray, when Claude Barnett, the director of the Associated Negro Press, discovered that no high-level official had sent greetings, he "cabled his friend" Vice President Richard Nixon to send a greeting. Nixon responded "in such vague generalities that the message was not used." Houser believed that it was first-term black Congressman Charles Diggs of Detroit, who attended the conference, who persuaded Nixon to send a message that, in the end, most of the Americans present were glad was not read. McCray, "Observations on the AAPC," 14/14, Country files; Houser, *No One Can Stop the Rain*, 71–72; Brown to Lovestone, Dec. 26, 1958, "Brown, 1958," box 356, LP.

29. Jean Meynaud and Anisse Salah Bey, *Trade Unionism in Africa: A Study of Its Growth and Orientation* (London: Methuen, 1967), 125. See Richard Jeffries, *Class, Power, and Ideology in Ghana: The Railwaymen of Sekondi* (New York: Cambridge University Press, 1978), 58–64; Paul S. Gray, *Unions and Leaders in Ghana: A Model of Labor and Development* (New York: Conch Magazine Limited, 1981), 26–27; and G. E. Lynd, *The Politics of African Trade Unionism* (New York: Praeger, 1968), 38–46.

30. McCray, "Observations on the AAPC," 14/14, Country files.

31. Ibid.

32. Springer, "Observations on the AAPC," 14/12/11, and see Evron to Lovestone, Jan. 15,

1959, 2/247/6, both in ILGWU Archives; and "Mr. Tom Mboya Replies to Ghana Times," n.d., 10/20, Country files.

33. In 1954 Tewson credited the ICFTU pressure for Nkrumah's turn toward anticommunism. Frederick Cooper, *Decolonization and African Society: The Labor Question in French and British Africa* (New York: Cambridge University Press, 1996), 613 n. 21; Springer, "Observations on the AAPC," 14/12/11, ILGWU Archives.

34. Continuation of the Report on the Wednesday Session of the ICFTU Executive Board, Nov. 28, 1958, 23/6, Brown files; McCray to Ross, Sept. 8, 1959, reel 3, frames 0589–0592, RP. For an account of the political maneuvering that accompanied the formation of UGTAN, see Cooper, *Decolonization and African Society*, 407–24.

35. Anthony Clayton and Donald C. Savage, *Government and Labour in Kenya, 1895–1963* (London: Cass, 1974), 380–91; McCray to Lovestone, March 18, 1964, "McCray," box 378, LP.

36. McCray, "Observations on the AAPC," 14/14, Country files, and Springer, "Observations on the AAPC," 14/12/11, ILGWU Archives.

37. McCray, "Observations on the AAPC," 14/14, Country files.

38. At the AAPC Nkrumah had spoken of the need for an African international. Meynaud and Bey, *Trade Unionism in Africa*, 140; Springer, "Observations on the AAPC," 14/12/11, ILGWU Archives.

39. Brown to Meany, Dec. 24, 1958, 14/14, Country files; see also Brown to Lovestone, Jan. 7, 1959, "Brown, 1959," box 356, LP.

40. Brown to Lovestone, Jan. 6, 1960, "Brown, 1960," box 356, LP. See also McCray to Ross, Jan. 29, 1960, and Brown, Report, Feb. 11, 1961, both in "Africa General Labor," box 397, LP.

41. Meany to Springer, Jan. 23, 1959, MSK PP.

42. McCray to Ross, Jan. 27, 1959, "Kenya," box 501, LP.

43. Legum, *Pan-Africanism*, 81–82.

44. Mboya to Randolph, Jan. 30, 1959, and see Mboya to McCray, Feb. 6, 1958, both in 11/4; and Mboya to Meany, Feb. 19, 1959, 11/5; all in Country files.

45. Springer to Meir, March 10, 1959, Amistad.

46. Springer to Lovestone, "Sunday afternoon" [c. Jan. 1959], 60/24, Lovestone files.

47. Lovestone to Springer, Jan. 19, 1959, 60/24, Lovestone files.

48. After twenty-five years as Local 22 manager, Zimmerman was elected general manager of the Dress Joint Board on June 25, 1958. Springer to Sasha, memorandum, March 15, 1959; Springer to Breslow, memorandum, March 22, 1959; and Springer, "Memorandum on Israeli-African Relations," all in 14/12/11; and Springer to Sasha, March 19, 1959, 12/247/6; all in ILGWU Archives.

49. Springer to Sasha, memorandum, March 15, 1959; Springer to Breslow, memorandum, March 22, 1959; Springer, "Memorandum on Israeli-African Relations"; all in 14/12/11, ILGWU Archives.

50. Springer to Zimmerman, March 19, 1959, 2/247/6, ILGWU Archives; Springer to Granger, July 4, 1959, Amistad.

51. Springer, "Vocational School for African Women," 1959, 14/12/11, ILGWU Archives.

52. Springer to Lovestone, May 25, 1959, 60/24, Lovestone files; Springer to Breslow, April 11, 1959, 14/12/11, ILGWU papers; Breslow to Springer, July 22, 1959, Amistad.

53. Springer to Lovestone, May 15, 1959, MSK PP.

54. Springer to Granger, July 4, 1959, Amistad.

55. Springer to Mandawa, Sept. 3, 1959; E. Ben-Horin to Springer, March 3, 1960; see also Mandawa to Springer, Dec. 16, 1959; all in MSK PP.

56. Lovestone to Springer, June 1, 1959, 60/24, LP; "Million-Dollar Loan to Israel Approved," *Justice*, June 1, 1948; "Donate $1 Million for Israeli Hospital," *Justice*, Jan. 1, 1956.

57. Hugh Chevins, "U.S. Unions Anger T.U.C.: Criticism of Africa 'Colonialism,'" *London Daily Telegraph*, Feb. 18, 1959, "Africa Trade Unions," box 398, LP.

58. Meany to Tewson, March 4, 1959, and Tewson to Meany, Jan. 19, 1959, both in 23/7; and Tewson to Oldenbroek with copy to Meany, Feb. 20, 1959, 30/18; all in Brown files.

59. Meany to Oldenbroek, Jan. 9, 1959, 33/15; Tewson to Meany, Jan. 19, 1959, and Oldenbroek to Meany, Jan. 21, 1959, and Meany to Oldenbroek, Feb. 13, 1959, all in 23/7; Tewson to Oldenbroek with copy to Meany, Feb; 20, 1959, 30/18; all in Brown files.

60. Meany to Oldenbroek, Feb. 13, 1959, 23/7, and Ross to McCray, March 5, 1959, 33/15, both in Brown files; "End Colonialism in Africa!" *Free Trade Union News* 14, no. 3 (March 1959).

61. Hugh Chevins, "U.S. Unions Intervene on Colonies: Africans Backed," *London Daily Telegraph*, n.d., 8/1, Brown files.

62. Lovestone to McCray, March 23, 1959, 48/26, Lovestone files.

63. Schnitzler to Springer, May 25, 1959, MSK PP.

64. McCray to Lovestone, April 6, 1959 and Oct. 16, 1959, both in "McCray," box 378, LP; McCray to Lovestone, May 23, 1959 and March 18, 1959; Lovestone to McCray, March 23, 1959 and June 1, 1959; McCray to Reuther, May 23, 1959; all in 48/26, Lovestone files.

65. Schnitzler to Springer, May 25, 1959, MSK PP.

66. Lovestone to Springer, June 1, 1959, 60/24, Lovestone files.

67. Lovestone to Springer, June 1, 1959, 60/24, Lovestone to McCray, June 1, 1959, 48/26, both in Lovestone files.

68. McCray to Randolph, Sept. 15, 1959, reel 3, frames 0587–0588, RP.

69. Ross to Brown, May 2, 1961, 8/2, Brown files.

70. The following information comes from Private and Confidential, Trades Union Congress, The Trade Union Situation in British Dependencies in Africa, June 1959, "African Trade Unions," box 398, LP.

71. Notes on the TUC Memorandum on African Trade Unions, c. July 1959, "African Trade Unions," box 398, LP.

72. Ibid.

73. Springer to Lovestone, July 5, 1959, 60/24, Lovestone files.

74. Diallo was a Guinean-born Sudanese labor and political leader. Although very critical of Western policies, Padmore at one time had encouraged an orientation toward Western political ideas and technology. Like A. Philip Randolph, he stressed that the West owed Africa restitution for the enslavement of millions of Africans. Had Padmore lived longer, it is questionable, based upon Makonnen's observations, whether he would have continued as Nkrumah's political advisor because of the strong antiforeign sentiment that developed within government circles. See King, *Ras Makonnen*, 255, 259, 277–83; Marable, *African and Caribbean Politics: From Kwame Nkrumah to Maurice Bishop* (London: Verso, 1987), 109–12; Brown, Notes on Conversation Irving Brown Tom Mboya, June 7, 1959, "Brown, 1959," box 356, LP; Padmore, *Pan-Africanism or Communism? The Coming Struggle for Africa* (1956; reprint, New York: Doubleday, 1971), 350–52.

75. Elizabeth Balanoff, "Maida Springer Kemp Interview," in *The Black Women Oral History Project*, vol. 7, ed. Ruth Edmonds Hill (New Providence, N.J.: K. G. Saur Verlag, 1991), 100; Springer, "Report to the Urban League on 1951–52 Study Abroad," box 1, folder 2, MSK Papers, Schlesinger; Tettegah quote is from Wogu Ananaba, *The Trade Union Movement in Africa: Promise and Performance* (New York: St. Martin's Press, 1979), 9.

76. Millard to Kwame Nkrumah (confidential letter), Dec. 22, 1958; Millard to Tettegah, Dec. 22, 1958; [Oldenbroek] to Tettegah, Jan. 12, 1959; and Oldenbroek to Ross, April 13, 1959; all in 10/2, Country files; Ananaba, *The Trade Union Movement in Africa*, 9–11.

77. In 1962 Ghana made some amendments to the act following a complaint filed by the ICFTU against Ghana's treatment of workers. United Africa Company Workers Union, The Bill, Dec. 10, 1958, 3/5, Brown files; Ananaba, *The Trade Union Movement in Africa*, 12; Lynd, *The Politics of African Trade Unionism*, 42.

78. Brown, UGTAN Congress, Conakry, Jan. 16–18, 1959, "African Trade Unions," box 398; see also Brown, Report, Feb. 11, 1961, "Africa General Labor," box 397; both in LP.

79. Brown, UGTAN Congress, Conakry, Jan. 16–18, 1959, "African Trade Unions," box 398; McCray to Ross, Dec. 11, 1959 and Jan. 29, 1960, "Africa General Labor," box 397; all in LP. Meany quote is from Supplement, Trade Union Activity in Africa, 33/15 [c. March 1959], Brown files.

80. Springer to Tettegah, May 14, 1959, MSK PP.

81. Chalfin to Ross, Sept. 16, 1959, 10/2, Country files; McCray to Ross, Jan. 29, 1960, "Africa General Labor," box 397, LP. For other examples of Tettegah's wavering on the affiliation issue see other letters in 10/2 folder, Country files.

Chapter 8: Springer Joins the AFL-CIO Department of International Affairs

1. McCray often warned AFL-CIO leaders that the preoccupation with Communist subversion was a disservice to Africa. McCray to Ross, March 4, 1959, and McCray to Meany, March 24, 1959, both in 48/26, Lovestone files; McCray to Lovestone, April 7, 1959, "McCray," box 378, LP; Springer, "Summary of Six Weeks in Africa," 14/3, Country files.

2. As political rivals, Nixon and Kennedy tried to outmaneuver one another concerning funding for these scholarships. George Houser, *No One Can Stop the Rain: Glimpses of Africa's Liberation Struggle* (New York: Pilgrim Press, 1989), 88–89.

3. Mandawa to Springer, Aug. 28, 1959, and Sept. 9, 1959, and Springer to Mandawa, Sept. 3, 1959, all in MSK PP; Belafonte, Robinson, and Poitier to Lovestone, Aug. 24, 1959, 54/12, Meany files; MSK, interview by author.

4. Thuo to Springer, Sept. 9, 1957, 60/23, Lovestone files; Brown to Lovestone, Dec. 26, 1958, "Brown, 1958," box 356, LP; Anthony Clayton and Donald C. Savage, *Government and Labour in Kenya, 1895–1963* (London: Cass, 1974), 433–34; David Goldsworthy, *Tom Mboya: The Man Kenya Wanted to Forget* (New York: Africana Publishing, 1982), 155.

5. Mboya to Randolph, Jan. 30, 1959, 11/4, Country files.

6. Osore would teach at the Institute of Tailoring and Cutting that Springer helped to found in 1963 in Kenya. Lubembe would name a daughter after Springer. The other two expelled leaders were G. S. Muhanji and W.E.C. Mukuna. Kweya to Springer, Jan. 21, 1958, and Springer to Mboya, Feb. 2, 1959, both in MSK PP.

7. Ross to Ochwada, March 5, 1959, and Ochwada to Ross, April 23, 1959, 11/6; Kenya Federation of Labor Press Statement, Sept. 28, 1959, and Kenya memo, Sept. 29, 1959, both in 11/5; all in Country files.

8. Mboya to Randolph, n.d., Randolph to Mboya, Oct. 14, 1959, Springer to Mboya, Dec. 19, 1959, all in MSK PP; MSK, interview by author.

9. See 11/6, Country files, for the numerous letters Ochwada wrote complaining about Mboya and appealing for Western assistance for his rival union. These letters are addressed to Ross, Lovestone, Oldenbroek, Springer, Mboya, and others.

10. One of Lovestone's concerns was that Mboya visit unions in non-Communist Asian countries. Lovestone to Mboya, May 18, 1959, MSK PP; Lovestone to Springer, May 18, 1959, 60/24, Lovestone files.

11. Meany and Jackie Robinson served as co-chairs of Africa Freedom Day. Houser reported on the extreme demands on Mboya's time during the 1959 tour. Among the labor lead-

ers he met with were Randolph, Dubinsky, Meany, and Walter Reuther. Lovestone met with Mboya only briefly, while riding with him to the airport. Springer to Lovestone, May 25, 1959, 60/24; and Theodore W. Kheel (chair of Africa Freedom Day celebration) to Lovestone, March 19, 1959, 1/21; both in Lovestone files. George M. Houser, "Whirlwind Tour: Mboya Visits the U.S." (reprinted from *Africa Today*, May–June 1959), 3/14, Brown files.

12. Additional discussion of this case appears in Chapter 5. Randolph and Springer to Zimmerman, May 7, 1958, 14/11/12, ILGWU Archives; Lovestone to Ochwada, May 5, 1958, and Mboya to Ochwada, April 21, 1958, both in 1/22, Lovestone files.

13. Springer to Mboya, May 10, 1958, and Mboya to Springer, May 20, 1958, both in MSK PP.

14. Additional discussion of the Nyerere trial appears in Chapter 6. Goldsworthy, *Tom Mboya*, 97–98.

15. McCray, Basic Considerations Relative to Operations in Africa, [March 18, 1959], "Africa General Labor," box 397; McCray to Ross, Jan. 27, 1959, "Kenya," box 501; McCray to Lovestone, April 9, 1959, "McCray," box 378; and Brown to Lovestone, Dec. 26, 1958, "Brown, 1958"; Brown, Notes on Conversation Irving Brown Tom Mboya, June 7, 1959, "Brown, 1959"; Brown to Lovestone, June 2, 1960, "Brown 1960"; and Brown to Lovestone, Jan. 14, 1962, "Brown, 1961–1963," all in box 356; all in LP

16. The KFL got this van through the efforts of Bill Kemsley, a Canadian who served as the ICFTU representative for the New York office. The ICFTU office in Kenya was locked when Newman was away, except for a time in 1955 when Mboya briefly ran the office. The file cabinets remained locked. The ICFTU did not act on the KFL's request to allow an African assistant for Newman so that the office might remain open when he was away. Mboya to Randolph, Jan. 30, 1959, and Mboya to McCray, Feb. 6, 1958, both in 11/4; and Mboya to Meany, Feb. 19, 1959, 11/5; all in Country files. George Brown to Meany, July 25, 1957, 54/16, Meany files. Report of General Secretaries Conference held at Arusha, Feb. 15, 1958, 1/22, Lovestone files. Abuoga to Springer, Dec. 24, 1957, MSK PP.

17. Springer, Memorandum on Kenya, March 24, 1957, "Springer," box 388, LP.

18. Randolph, report on trip to Africa (handwritten notation incorrectly dates the document in 1956; should be 1957), reel 3, frames 0543–0551, RP; Mboya to Oldenbroek and Mboya to Meany, both Nov. 27, 1958, 30/11, Brown files.

19. Goldsworthy speculates that Sir Vincent Tewson's position as chair of the ICFTU's Solidarity Fund was a factor in the decision not to provide a grant. Goldsworthy, *Tom Mboya: The Man Kenya Wanted to Forget*, 158; Mboya to Springer, Oct. 4, 1959, and Springer to Mboya, Dec. 19, 1959, both in MSK PP; Mboya to Oldenbroek, June 28, 1960, 28/2, Brown files.

20. Mboya to Springer, Aug. 30, 1960, 11/5, Country files; Clayton and Savage, *Government and Labour in Kenya*, 435.

21. Wogu Ananaba, *The Trade Union Movement in Africa: Promise and Performance* (New York: St. Martin's Press, 1979), 191–92; "Mr. Tom Mboya Replies to *Ghana Times*" [c. Nov. 1959], 10/20, Country files. Statement published as "No Conflict of Loyalties: Tom Mboya Replies to *Ghana Times*," *Free Labour World*, May 1960, 185–88.

22. "Mr. Tom Mboya Replies to *Ghana Times*."

23. Mboya to Springer, Oct. 4, 1959, MSK PP. McCray to Lovestone, Oct. 16, 1959, "McCray," box 378; McCray to Ross, Jan. 29, 1960, "Africa General Labor," box 397; and McCray, Report on ICFTU African Labor College, Dec. 26, 1958, "ICFTU Regional Offices, Africa," box 483; all in LP. Lovestone to McCray, Feb. 4, 1960, 48/27, Lovestone files.

24. Brown, Second African Regional Conference of the ICFTU, Lagos, Nigeria, November 9–14, 1959, Nov. 25, 1959, 23/6; and Brown to Springer, Dec. 19, 1959, 4/17; both in Brown files. Brown to Lovestone, n.d., "Brown, Irving, 1958," box 356, LP.

25. McCray, Randolph, Mboya, and Padmore were among a number of black leaders who called for a Marshall Plan for Africa. Springer to Brown, Dec. 11, 1959, and see Springer to Brown, Jan. 18, 1960, both in 4/17, Brown files; Manning Marable, *African and Caribbean Politics from Kwame Nkrumah to Maurice Bishop* (London: Verso, 1987), 110; McCray to Lovestone, Feb. 15, 1960, "McCray," box 378, LP; McCray to Ross, Aug. 14, 1960, 13/18, Country files.

26. Later in 1961 Mboya, as chair of AFRO, demanded that the ICFTU give "maximum autonomy for Africa," "fair representation on the executive board," and "fuller consultations." "Speech Made by Tom Mboya on 6th September, 1961," East, Central, and Southern Africa Area Committee Conference of the ICFTU African Regional Organization, Welsh Papers; Ananaba, *The Trade Union Movement in Africa*, 6; "ICFTU Allows Autonomy for African Unions," *Africa Report* 4, no. 12 (Dec. 1959).

27. Ross to Mboya, April 26, 1960, 11/5, Country files; Randolph to Springer, telegram, April 21, 1960, MSK PP; "Maida Springer Is on AFL-CIO Staff," *Justice*, May 15, 1960.

28. McCray to Springer, May 23, 1960, 13/18, Country files.

29. MSK, interview by author.

30. It is not clear what Nyerere's response was. On February 12, as part of Negro History Week celebrations, Springer and Nyerere both spoke at the Church of the Master on 125th Street in Harlem. Nyerere's talk was titled "Tanganyika Today" and Springer's, "America's Image in Africa." Flyer, MSK PP. Springer to Dorothy Padmore, Feb. 13, 1960, MSK PP; *As We See It*, AFL-CIO public service program, ABC, Sunday, Dec. 18, 1960, transcript, MSK PP.

31. Springer recalled that Murray had challenged many assumptions about the United States and black America that Africans had. MSK, "The Consummate Scholar," speech given at a conference titled "Black Women's Leadership: Challenges and Strategies," University of North Carolina, Chapel Hill, March 25, 1986, Amistad; Springer to Ambassador Ako Adjei, Feb. 13, 1960, and Springer to Nkrumah, Feb. 25, 1959, both in MSK PP; Pauli Murray, *The Autobiography of a Black Activist, Feminist, Lawyer, Priest, and Poet* (Knoxville: University of Tennessee Press, 1987), 318, 322.

32. MSK, "The Consummate Scholar," speech given to a conference titled, "Black Women's Leadership: Challenges and Strategies," University of North Carolina, Chapel Hill, March 25, 1986, Amistad.

33. Murray, *Autobiography of a Black Activist*, 333, 339; Murray, "On Teaching Constitutional Law in Ghana," *Yale Law Report* 8, no. 1 (Fall 1991).

34. Daniel Miles McFarland, ed., *Historical Dictionary of Ghana*, African Historical Dictionaries, no. 39 (Metuchen: Scarecrow Press, 1985), 71.

35. Murray, *Autobiography of a Black Activist*, 342–43.

36. Springer to I. E. Inkumsah, president of the National Union of Railway and Harbor Workers in Ghana, April 11, 1960, 9/23, Country files; Brown report, April 8, 1960, 8/1, Brown files.

37. Springer to Tettegah, Aug. 12, 1960, Tettegah to Springer, Aug. 24, 1960, and Tettegah to McCray, July 20, 1960, all in 10/2, Country files.

38. Springer, "Summary of Six Weeks in Africa," 14/3, Country files.

39. Colin Legum, *Pan-Africanism: A Short Political Guide* (New York: Praeger, 1965), 84; McCray to Ross, Aug. 9, 1960, 13/6; Springer, "Summary of Six Weeks in Africa," 14/3; Springer to J. Odero-Jowi (vice principal, ICFTU African Labor College), Dec. 16, 1960, 13/18; all in Country files.

40. Mboya to George [Houser], May 17, 1960, MSK PP. Brown, Report, May 11, 1960, 23/8, Brown files. Legum, *Pan-Africanism*, 84. McCray to Ross, Aug. 9, 1960, 13/6; Springer, "Summary of Six Weeks in Africa," 14/3; Springer to J. Odero-Jowi, Dec. 16, 1960, 13/18; all in Country files.

41. Those aligned with Nzeribe were in the minority but were well organized and suspected of being better financed by Ghana or Guinea or the WFTU. In response to these suspicions, Brown proposed giving aid discreetly and prudently to the Trade Union Congress of Nigeria (TUCN). Brown, Second African Regional Conference of the ICFTU, Lagos, Nigeria, November 9–14, 1959, Nov. 25, 1959, 23/6; [Meany] to Oldenbroek, March 1, 1960, 33/18; *ICFTU Report on Activities, 1960–1962, and Financial Reports, Seventh World Congress, Berlin, July 5–13, 1962* (Brussels: ICFTU), 66, 23/13; Brown to Lovestone, Nov. 16, 1959, 7/19; [Bécu] to Meany, April 7, 1961, and A. Braunthal to Brown, April 7, 1961, both in 23/9; and see Springer to John Davidson Cole, Gambia Workers' Union, April 21, 1961, 4/17; all in Brown files. McCray to Ross, Jan. 29, 1960, "Africa General Labor," box 397, LP. Springer to Odero-Jowi, April 13, 1961, 13/19, Country files.

42. Mboya to all ICFTU affiliates, Dec. 31, 1960, 30/11, Brown files.

43. Tettegah, press statement, Dec. 13, 1960; Mboya, Kenya Federation of Labor press statement, "The Great Conspiracy against Africa," Dec. 15, 1960; and Tettegah to Mboya, Jan. 9, 1961, all in 30/11, Brown files. Tettegah to Mboya, Dec. 14, 1960, 10/20, Country files.

44. Springer, "Summary of Six Weeks in Africa," Nov. 14, 1960, 14/3, and see McCray to Ross, Aug. 14, 1960, 13/18, both in Country files.

45. Tettegah to Mboya, Dec. 14, 1960, 10/20, Country files; see also Mboya to Brown, Nov. 4, 1960, 30/11, Brown files.

46. Springer to Mboya, Aug. 12, 1960, and Sept. 16, 1960, both in 11/5, Country files.

47. Ochwada to Ross, Sept. 8, 1960, Springer to Ross, Aug. 18, 1960, and Ross to Ochwada, Sept. 21, 1960, all in 11/6; and Mboya to Springer, Aug. 30, 1960, 11/5; all in Country files.

48. Ochwada to Springer, Nov. 24, 1960, and Ochwada to Ross, Sept. 8, 1960, both in 11/6, Country files.

49. Opoku Agyeman, *Nkrumah's Ghana and East Africa: Pan-Africanism and African Interstate Relations* (Cranbury, N.J.: Associated University Press, 1992), 134; Ochwada to Springer, Nov. 24, 1960, 11/6, Country files.

50. Springer wrote Ochwada that she had only received his letter of November 24 on January 12. Springer to Ochwada, Jan. 13, 1961, and Ochwada to Meany, July 26, 1957, both in 11/6, Country files.

51. Springer to Ochwada, Jan. 13, 1961, 11/6, Country files.

52. Adoula was leader of the Fédération Générale Travailleurs Kongolais. In 1959 he left Lumumba's party, the Mouvement National Congolais. Kithima was leader of the Confédération des Syndicats Libres du Congo. Springer, "Summary of Six Weeks in Africa," 14/3, Country files.

53. Although Lovestone did not view Lumumba as "a direct Moscow agent," he was uncomfortable with his left leanings. He thought that if the AFL-CIO did nothing or even supported the wrong position, a better and stronger group of leaders might emerge. Lovestone to Brown, Nov. 18, 1960, "Brown, 1960," box 356, LP. Brown to Lovestone, Jan. 7, 1959, "Brown, 1959," LP. Quote is from Brown to Lovestone, Nov. 14, 1960; Lovestone to Brown, July 11, 1960; see also Brown to Lovestone, July 30, 1960, all in "Brown, 1960," all in box 356, LP. Brown to Ross, Oct. 18, 1960, 33/18, and Brown report, Nov. 5, 1960, 1/22, both in Brown files.

54. Quote is from Brown to Lovestone, Nov. 14, 1960, "Brown, 1960," in box 356; Brown, Report, Feb. 11, 1961, and Notes on Africa by Irving Brown, Feb. 19, 1961, "Africa General Labor," both in box 397; all in LP.

55. Springer to Brown, June 9, 1961, 4/17, Brown files; Brown, notes on trip to Africa, November 28–December 16, 1968, "Africa General Labor," box 397, LP

56. Ross to Brown, May 2, 1961, and Brown to Ross, May 3, 1961, 8/2; and Brown to Bécu, May 2, 1961, 23/12; all in Brown files. McCray to Springer, Aug. 29, 1961, 13/18, Country files.

Welsh helped organize tea, coffee, sugar, cotton, brewery, textile, hotel, and building and con-struction workers in East Africa. "Bio Sketch of Welsh on a 1974 Program for the Third Annual Award Dinner Dance of the Black Trade Unionists Leadership Committee of the New York City Central Labor Council," Welsh Papers.

57. McCray to Springer, March 20, 1961, 13/18, Country files.

58. Ibid.

59. Springer to McCray, May 8, 1961, 13/19, Country files.

60. Mboya to Brown, May 4, 1961, 30/11, Brown files.

61. Legum, *Pan-Africanism*, 84–86; Brown to Ross, Aug. 15, 1961, "Brown, 1961–1963," box 356, LP.

62. See Arnold Beichman, "African Free Unionism Builds Solid Foundation," *AFL-CIO Free Trade Union News* 17, no. 2 (Feb. 1962).

63. MSK, interview by author.

64. Springer to Mboya, April 15, 1960, 11/5, Country files.

65. Pamela Mboya was the daughter of Kenya African Union leader Walter Odede, who served seven years in detention without trial. Mboya got to know Pamela as he looked after Odede's family during his detention. As one of the 1959 recipients of Mboya's scholarships, Pamela studied at Western College for Women in Oxford, Ohio. Goldsworthy, *Tom Mboya*, 93, 120; Springer to Lovestone, Jan. 16, 1962, "Springer" box 388, LP.

66. Goldsworthy, *Tom Mboya*, 163; Mboya, press conference, Jan. 27, 1961, and see Mboya, press statement, Jan. 27, 1961, both in 30/11, Brown files.

67. Goldsworthy, *Tom Mboya*, 201; Welsh to Springer, Aug. 1, 1962, and Springer to Welsh, Sept. 13, 1962, both in 10/20, Country files.

68. MSK, interview by author; James Karebe (KFL honorary treasurer) to Brown, Dec. 1, 1961, 28/1, Brown files; Open Letter from Philip J. Muinde (KFL president) to Kubai, no date but written in reference to Kubai's letter of Sept. 30, 1962, 10/19, Country files.

69. Lovestone to Welsh, Oct. 9, 1961, 64/9, Lovestone files; Springer to Kubai, March 20, 1962, 10/19, Country files.

70. Kubai to Brown, Feb. 11, 1963, and Kubai to Brown, received March 11, 1963, 1/22, Brown files.

71. Nkomo, formerly head of the railway workers union and a founder and first president of the Southern Rhodesia African Trade Union Congress, became the leader of the ANC in 1957.

72. W. V. Brelsford of the Federation Information Department accepted Lovestone's offer to reply to Chiume's article, after which Chiume got a chance to rebut. Brelsford to Lovestone, March 15, 1960, 12/8, Country files; Thomas J. Bray to Lovestone, Feb. 5, 1960, and Chiume, "A Rejoinder to Mr. Bray," Feb. 20, 1960, both in 2/3, Lovestone files; R. H. Hobson (director of in-formation, Federal Information Department), "A Reply to Kanyama Chiume," and Springer, "Central African Federation: Milestone or Millstone," both in *Free Trade Union News* 15, no. 9 (Sept. 1960); MSK, interview by author.

73. Brown, Notes on Africa by Irving Brown, Feb. 19, 1961, "Africa General Labor," box 397, LP; see also Brown to Ross, Oct. 31, 1960, 33/18, Brown files.

74. Brown, Notes on Africa by Irving Brown, Feb. 19, 1961, "Africa General Labor," box 397, LP.

75. MSK, interview by author.

76. Jamela came out of the Builders and Artisans Union. "Southern Rhodesia," by Howard Robinson, June 10, 1963, 12/9, Country files; Springer to Dubinsky, July 5, 1962, 2/247/5, ILGWU Archives; C. M. Brand, "Politics and African Trade Unionism in Rhodesia since Fed-eration," *Rhodesian History* 2 (1971): 97.

77. Representatives from the British TUC and ICFTU who had visited in the past evidently met only with European "legal" labor. In 1958 the country's white-controlled Federal TUC joined the ICFTU. Springer to Nkomo, Dec. 16, 1960, Nathan Shamuyarira to Springer, April 2, 1961, and Jamela to Springer, March 10, 1961, all in 12/8, Country files; Maluleke to Lovestone, Oct. 3, 1960, "Southern Rhodesia Detainees Legal Aid and Welfare Fund 1960," box 388, LP; Brand, "Politics and African Trade Unionism," 93–94.

78. Maluleke to Lovestone, Oct. 19, 1958, and Lovestone to Maluleke, Dec. 8, 1958, both in 1/22, Lovestone files; Jamela to Springer, March 10, 1961, 12/8, Country files; Maluleke to Lovestone, Oct. 3, 1960, "Southern Rhodesia Detainees Legal Aid and Welfare Fund 1960," box 388, LP.

79. Springer, Summary of Six Weeks in Africa, Nov. 14, 1960, 14/3; Shamuyarira to Springer, April 2, 1961, and Springer, Conditions in Southern Rhodesia's African Labor Movement, n.d., both in 12/8; all in Country files. Knight T. Maripe, "'Law and Order' under Smith," *Free Labour World* 191 (May 1966), 7–8, 19; Brand, "Politics and African Trade Unionism," 92–93; Ananaba, *The Trade Union Movement in Africa*, 52–53; and Houser, *No One Can Stop the Rain*, 102.

80. Brown report, Feb. 11, 1961, "Africa General Labor," box 397, LP; Springer to Nkomo, Dec. 16, 1960, 12/8, Country files.

81. Springer, Summary of Six Weeks in Africa, Nov. 14, 1960, 14/3, Country files; J. T. Maluleke, "Through the Bars: Labor Struggles in Southern Rhodesia," *AFL-CIO Free Trade Union News* 16, no. 3 (March 1961).

82. Maluleke to Springer, Sept. 10, 1961, Oct. 20, 1961, and March 22, 1961, all in 12/8, Country files.

83. Springer to Maluleke, April 5, 1961, Springer to Robinson, April 5, 1961, Robinson to Springer, April 7, 1961, and Robinson to Maluleke, April 7, 1961, all in 12/8, Country files; Maluleke to Lovestone, June 21, 1961, "Maluleke, Josias, 1960–1961," box 501, LP.

84. Springer to Maluleke, July 21, 1961, 12/8, Country files.

85. Jamela to Springer, May 1, 1961, 12/9, Country files; Springer to Maluleke, March 13, 1961, Jamela to Springer, May 28, 1961, Lovestone to Maluleke, June 8, 1961, Springer to Jamela, July 20, 1961, Springer to Maluleke, July 21, 1961, Maluleke to Springer, Sept. 10, 1961, Maluleke to Springer, Sept. 10, 1961, and Springer to Maluleke, Oct. 4, 1961, all in 12/8, Country files; Maluleke to Lovestone, Aug. 3, 1961, and Maluleke to Lovestone, Aug. 31, 1961, both in "Maluleke, Josias, 1960–1961," box 501, LP.

Springer also was very concerned with the well-being of detainee K. S. Mhizha, president of the Southern Rhodesia Transport and Allied Workers Union and treasurer of SRATUC. Springer to Maripe, Nov. 29, 1960, and Jan. 12, 1961; Springer to Jamela, March 27, 1961; Shamuyarira to Springer, April 2, 1961; all in 12/8, Country files. Jamela to Springer, May 1, 1961, 12/9, Country files.

86. Maluleke and K. S. Mhizha to ICFTU Tunis conference, Oct. 28, 1960, 33/10, Brown files; Nziramasanga and Z. Mapfumo to Lovestone, Jan. 25, 1960, Shamuyarira to Springer, April 2, 1961, Springer to Nkomo, Dec. 16, 1960, Springer to Jamela, March 27, 1961, Jamela to Springer, March 10, 1961, and see Springer to Knight Maripe, Nov. 29, 1960, all in 12/8, and Springer, "Summary of Six Weeks in Africa," 14/3, Country files.

87. Jamela to Brown, Dec. 6, 1960, 33/9, 12/8, Country files; Jamela to Brown, (c. April 1961), 33/9, Brown files; Brand, "Politics and African Trade Unionism," 94.

88. Brown, "Pan-African Trade Union Congress, Casablanca—May 25/29, 1961," "Africa Trade Unions," box 398, LP.

89. Jamela refused an executive position with the ANC successor party, the National Democratic Party (NDP). After the NDP was banned, Nkomo founded the Zimbabwe African

People's Union. Brand, "Politics and African Trade Unionism," 92, 95; Brown report, Feb. 11, 1961, "Africa General Labor," box 397, LP; Brown report, March 2, 1961, 8/2, Brown files.

90. Brown to Ross, April 4, 1961, "Brown, 1961–1963," box 356, and Brown report, Feb. 7, 1961, "Africa Trade Unions," box 398, both in LP; Maluleke to Lovestone, May 5, 1961, and Jamela to Meany, May 19, 1961, both in 12/8, Country files.

91. Maluleke to Lovestone, May 22, 1961, 12/8, Country files; Maluleke to Lovestone, Aug. 31, 1961, "Maluleke, Josias, 1960–1961," box 501, LP.

92. Maluleke to Lovestone, May 22, 1961, 12/8, Country files.

93. Brown and George McCray remarked that Africans were offended by the condescension of ICFTU leaders, who included Albert Hammerton from England, Peter de Jonge from Belgium, Charles Millard from Canada, Jay Krane from the United States, and Jacob Oldenbroek from Holland. As Brown was about to begin his post heading the ICFTU office at the United Nations in 1962, he registered his disgust with the ICFTU by stating, "I look forward to being liberated from a set-up where intrigues, untruths, and anti-Americanism plus political ignorance rule the day." Brown to George (possibly Meany), Dec. 19, 1962, 1/23, and Brown report, Dec. 7, 1960, 23/6, Brown files. See also Brown report, "Brown, 1958," and Brown to Lovestone, July 1, 1961, "Brown 1960–1963," both in box 356; McCray to Lovestone, April 22, 1964, "McCray," box 378; all in LP. Millard to Randolph, Nov. 22, 1957, and Randolph to Millard, Jan. 21, 1958, MSK PP.

94. McCray to Lovestone, Jan. 31, 1961, and Lovestone to McCray, March 6, 1961, both in 48/27, Lovestone files.

Chapter 9: AFL-CIO Africa Programs

1. Springer, A Program for Better Nutrition to Workers, n.d., MSK PP.

2. Articles highlighting the AFL-CIO work in Africa (but not mentioning Springer's role, or the fierce resistance she often encountered from colonial governments and European labor) include: "AFL-CIO Work," *New York Times*, Nov. 16, 1963, and "Hands across the Atlantic: How the AFL-CIO Helps African Nations Develop a Free Trade Union Movement," *Industrial Bulletin*, Dec. 1965; both in Labor Unions—Africa, Clippings File, Schomburg Center.

3. MSK, interview by author; Springer, Trade Union Skills, May 13, 1963, MSK PP; quote is from Elizabeth Balanoff, "Maida Springer Kemp Interview," in *The Black Women Oral History Project*, vol. 7, ed. Ruth Edmonds Hill (New Providence, N.J.: K. G. Saur Verlag, 1991), 109; [Springer], "Memorandum in Support of a Garment Workers' Training Center in Kenya, East Africa," [c. 1962], 39/20/8, ILGWU Archives.

4. Springer, The Needle Trades Potential in Africa, April 24, 1957, 60/23, Lovestone files; Springer, Thumb Nail Sketch of an African Journey, 14/12/11, [c. March 1957], ILGWU Archives.

5. Karumba, Problems Faced by Kenya Workers in the Textile Industries, n.d., 2/247/5, ILGWU Archives.

6. Renamed the Kenya Tailors and Textiles Workers' Union, the union's original name was the Tailors, Tents, Sailmakers and Garment Workers Union. Springer, Memorandum on Kenya, March 24, 1957, "Springer, Maida," box 388, LP. Karumba to Springer, May 25, 1961, 14/12/11, and Karumba, Brief historical sketch of the Textile and Garment Workers Union of Kenya, n.d., 2/247/5, ILGWU Archives.

7. Springer, The Needle Trades Potential in Africa, April 24, 1957, 60/23, Lovestone files.

8. Springer, Vocational School for African Women, March 10, 1959, 14/12/11, ILGWU Archives.

9. Springer, "Summary of Six Weeks in Africa," 14/3, Country files.

10. Ghanaian Paul Badoo worked with Springer in the effort to find summer employment for African students. "Service Spans 30 Years," *Washington Afro-American*, May 22, 1965, Amistad; Mboya to Springer, June 29, 1960, MSK PP; Springer, "Summer Jobs of African Students," *AFL-CIO Free Trade Union News* 17, no. 12 (Dec. 1962); Springer to Walter H. Uphoff (professor, University of Minnesota), Aug. 15, 1962; MSK, "Maida Springer Kemp on Dr. Caroline F. Ware, A Supplement to the Black Women's Oral History Project, 'Dr. Caroline F. Ware—A Majority of One, A Friend for All Reasons, for All Seasons,'" in Hill, *The Black Women Oral History Project*, 7:152.

11. "Jobs for African Students in U.S.," *AFL-CIO Free Trade Union News* 16, no. 7 (July 1961).

12. Springer to Dubinsky, Dec. 13, 1960, 47/1/9, ILGWU Archives.

13. Ibid.; Springer to Randolph, Nov. 28, 1960, reel 2, frame 0270, RP.

14. The trainees were Joyce Chanda of Northern Rhodesia, Charles Pasipanodya of Southern Rhodesia, Anselmi Karumba of Kenya, Flora Manjonde of Tanganyika, and Atim Williamson and Folake Johnson of Nigeria. *Justice*, Aug. 15, 1961; Springer to Matthew Schoenwald, Sept. 19, 1961, 22/8/2, and Springer to Zimmerman, March 17, 1961, 47/1/10, both in ILGWU Archives.

15. Springer to Jamela, April 4, 1961, 12/8, Country files; Jamela to Brown, May 19, 1961, and see Jamela to Brown, June 4, 1961, both in 33/9, Brown files; Jamela, "The Plight of Labor in Southern Rhodesia," *Free Trade Union News* 16, no. 9 (Sept. 1961). For numerous letters seeking assistance see 12/8, Country files

16. Brown report, March 2, 1961, 8/2, Brown files; see also Notes on Africa by Irving Brown, Feb. 19, 1961, "Africa General Labor," box 397, LP.

17. MSK, interview by author.

18. Springer to Jamela, March 27, 1961, 12/8, and Jamela to Springer, May 1, 1961, 12/9, both in Country files.

19. Pasipanodya asked Springer to help educate women on political, social, and trade-union affairs. He put her in touch with three activist women belonging to his union: Florence Chinyani, Christine Monera, and Mirian Kundodyiwa. Chinyani told Springer of the hardships working women faced and her desire to involve women in the liberation struggle. Pasipanodya to Springer, Feb. 7, 1962, Springer to Pasipanodya, March 28, 1962, Chinyani to Springer, April 16, 1962, Maluleke to Springer, March 22, 1961, all in 12/8, Country files.

20. Jamela to Brown, Dec. 30, 1961, and Brown to Jamela, Jan. 8, 1961, both in "Brown 1961–1963," box 356, LP; Jamela to Brown, Jan. 31, 1962, "Split in the T.U.C.: Maluleke, Jamela at Odds," *Daily News* (Southern Rhodesia), Jan. 16, 1962, "Gwanzura Sides with Jamela in T.U.C. Dispute," *Daily News*, Jan. 16, 1962, and telegram, Eric Gwanzura and Purivis to Jamela, received Jan. 17, 1962, all in 33/9, Brown files; see also Maluleke to Springer, Oct. 20, 1961, and "Extreme Trades Union Congress Formed in City," Jan. 31, 1962, and "ICFTU Gave SRTUC 5,342 Pounds" [c. Jan. 1962], *Evening Standard Reporter* (Southern Rhodesia), all in 12/8, Country files.

21. Mswaka to Dear Brother [c. Sept. 1961], 12/8 Country files; Mswaka to Jamela, Sept. 4, 1961, 33/9, Brown files; and Springer to Mswaka, Nov. 20, 1961, 12/8, Country files; C. M. Brand, "Politics and African Trade Unionism in Rhodesia since Federation," *Rhodesian History* 2 (1971): 96–98.

22. Apparently, at least until the end of May 1962, Nkomo did not show animosity toward Brown, who wrote Jamela that he had seen him in New York. Brown remarked, "we both felt it might be of some use if I came to your country." Brown to Jamela, July 17, 1962, 7/12, Brown files; Nkomo to Ross, Oct. 24, 1960, and Springer to Nkomo, Dec. 16, 1960, both in 12/8, Country files; MSK, interview by author.

23. On his way back to London from Brazil, Dumbutshena hoped to stop in the United States. He added, "Since I'm not a Trade Unionist I shall not bother you begging for a ticket. You have sufficient number of ticket applications already." Needing financial assistance to help buy a Land Rover to use in the election campaign, Nyerere asked Springer to get in touch with Robert Delson. Dumbutshena to Springer, Nov. 16, 1962, 12/9, Country files; Springer to Delson, March 24, 1958, MSK PP.

24. John Mtimkulu was the president of the SRTGWU. Bulawayo was a center of strong support for the rival ATUC. Brand, "Politics and African Trade Unionism," 97; Pasipanodya to Springer, Feb. 7, 1962, and Aug. 28, 1962, both in 12/8, Country files.

25. Springer to Pasipanodya, March 28, 1962, Pasipanodya to Springer, June 5, 1962, and Pasipanodya to Shane, June 5, 1962, all in 12/8, Country files.

26. Shane to Pasipanodya, June 27, 1962, and Springer to Pasipanodya, July 2, 1962, both in 39/20/8, ILGWU Archives.

27. Dunjana to Secretary [of AFL-CIO] [c. July 1962], 12/8, Country files.

28. Pasipanodya to Shane, June 5, 1962; Pasipanodya to Springer, July 24, 1962, Springer to Pasipanodya, Aug. 17, 1962, Pasipanodya to Springer, Aug. 28, 1962, all in 12/8; quote is from Springer to Pasipanodya, Oct. 29, 1962, 12/9, all in Country files. See also "Union Fight for Control of Tailors and Garment Workers Union" (newspaper unknown), Aug. 20, 1962, 39/20/8, ILGWU Archives.

29. Jamela to Brown, Jan. 31, 1962, and Feb. 5, 1962, both in 33/9, Brown files; Jamela to Springer and Jamela to Meany, both Feb. 3, 1962, and Pasipanodya to Springer, July 24, 1962, all in 12/8, Country files; Pasipanodya to Dubinsky, Oct. 25, 1962, "Messenger," ATUC First Congress, Oct. 21 and 22 (memo), Chigwendere to Springer, Oct. 17, 1962, and Aug. 16 and Aug. 28, 1963, and Springer to Chigwendere, Oct. 10, 1963, all in 12/9, all in Country files.

30. Springer included in her letter to Nziramasanga the text of an ICFTU press and radio release "condemning repression in Southern Rhodesia." Chigwendere to Springer, July 20, 1962, 12/8; Nziramasanga to Springer, Aug. 28, 1962, and Springer to Nziramasanga, Oct. 8, 1962, 12/9; all in Country files.

31. Parirenyatwa, the first African physician of the country, died on August 14 on his way to meet Nkomo. After the car was involved in an accident, the driver reported that eight Europeans dragged both of them from the car and beat them. When the driver regained consciousness, Parirenyatwa was dead. The government denied that they instructed the police to do this or to provoke trouble. "Plot to Assassinate Mr. J. Nkomo—Government's Denial," *African Recorder* (United States), Sept. 24–Oct. 7, 1962, 288.

32. An ICFTU mission reported that before ZAPU was banned, ATUC leaders at a political meeting at Chaminuka Square encouraged the crowd to attack Jamela and destroy his house. Lubembe and Karebe, Report of the Mission Sent to Southern Rhodesia by the ICFTU East, Central and Southern Area Division, January 1963, 7/12, Brown files; "Police Moved in to Stop Clashes in Harare," *Sunday Mail Reporter*, Aug. 26, 1962, 39/20/8, ILGWU Archives; Springer to Pasipanodya, Sept. 14, 1962, and Pasipanodya to Springer, Oct. 6, 1962, both in 12/9, Country files; Brand, "Politics and African Trade Unionism," 98.

33. Springer to Pasipanodya, Oct. 29, 1962, 12/9, Country files.

34. Springer to Nziramasanga, Oct. 8, 1962, 12/9, Country files.

35. Brand, "Politics and African Trade Unionism," 98–101; A. E. Abrahamson (Southern Rhodesia Minister of Labor) to Meany, Sept. 20, 1962, 12/9, Country files; Brown to Jamela, July 17, 1962, 7/12, Brown files; "UN Assembly's Call for Suspension of Southern Rhodesian Constitution," *African Recorder*, Nov. 19–Dec. 2, 1962, 337.

36. Lubembe and Karebe, Report of the Mission Sent to Southern Rhodesia by the ICFTU East, Central and Southern Area Division, Jan. 1963, 7/12, Brown files.

37. Pasipanodya to Dubinsky, Oct. 25, 1962, Pasipanodya to Springer, Nov. 5, 1962, Pasipanodya and M. B. Garah to Springer, Nov. 16, 1962, and Jamela to Stephan Nedzynski (ICFTU assistant general secretary), Nov. 16, 1962, all in 12/9, Country files.

38. Sithole to MSK, May 18, 1988, MSK PP.

39. Springer to Pasipanodya, Nov. 19, 1962, and Springer to Dubinsky, Nov. 19, 1962, and see J. Greenhalgh to Dubinsky, Dec. 11, 1962, all in 12/9, Country files.

40. Chigwendere thanked the AFL-CIO for two payments sent in Jan. 1963. Chigwendere to Brother [AFL-CIO Secretary], Feb. 15, 1963, and Harold Jack and Michael Ross letter, March 29, 1963, both in 12/9, Country files; Lubembe and Karebe, Report of the Mission Sent to Southern Rhodesia by the ICFTU East, Central and Southern Area Division, January 1963, 7/12, Brown files.

41. Sanford J. Unger, *Africa: The People and Politics of an Emerging Continent*, rev. ed. (New York: Simon and Schuster, 1989), 327; Brand, "Politics and African Trade Unionism," 99–101.

42. Maluleke and Nziramasanga had earlier split from the ATUC and formed a center they also called ATUC. After they split from one another, Maluleke formed ZALO (Zimbabwe African Labor Organization). Maluleke left ZAPU for ZANU for a short while before returning to ZAPU. Still later in the 1970s, he showed a leaning toward ZANU. Rob Cary, *African Nationalist Leaders* (Bulawayo, Zimbabwe: Books of Rhodesia, 1977), 79–81. S. Rhodesia Trades Union Report, Dec. 31, 1963, Circular Letter (ATUC), Nov. 23, 1963, and Zimbabwe African Congress of Trade Unions, Dec. 9, 1963, all in 12/9; and Zimbabwe African Congress of Unions National Trade Union Center, Jan. 20, 1964, and Aaron G. D. Ndlovu (ZACU general secretary) to Springer, Jan. 23, 1964, both in 12/10; all in Country files.

43. Mswaka to Dear Brother, Nov. 11, 1963; "Programme of Assistance: Submitted to the AFL/CIO" by ATUC Southern Rhodesia, Jan. 8, 1964; Ernest S. Lee to Mswaka, Dec. 6, 1963; Chigwendere to Springer, Aug. 16 and Aug. 28, 1963; Springer to Chigwendere, Oct. 10, 1963; all in 12/9, Country files.

44. Springer to Arnold S. Zander (president of AFSCME), Feb. 25, 1964, 12/11, Country files; quote is from Springer to Lovestone, Feb. 3, 1964, 60/26, Lovestone files.

45. Strong to Springer, Feb. 18, 1964, and Springer to Zander, Feb. 25, 1964, both in 12/11, Country files.

46. Springer to Lawrence, May 13, 1964, 12/11; Lawrence to Springer, June 17, 1964, and Alfred Braunthal (assistant general secretary of ICFTU) to Meany, Report on Rhodesia written by W. G. Lawrence, Sept. 12, 1965, both in 12/10; all in Country files.

47. Sithole to Springer, March 4, 1964, 12/10; Sithole to Springer, Feb. 3, 1964, 12/11; Mswaka to Springer, Jan. 18, 1965, 12/10; Chigwendere to Springer, April 9, 1965, misfiled in 11/22 (Nigeria 1956–1966); all in Country files.

48. Sithole to Springer, Feb. 2, 1965, 12/10, Country files.

49. In 1977 Jamela reentered the still-divided labor movement as one of the figures promoting unity. The movement continued to face factional divisions and Jamela remained a controversial figure, negatively branded as an American. After receiving a letter from Jamela at this time, Irving Brown remarked that he had not kept current with labor events in the country but was encouraged that he had rejoined the labor movement. Jamela to Brown, April 20, 1977, and Brown to Jamela, April 25, 1977, 1/26, Brown files; Wogu Ananaba, *The Trade Union Movement in Africa: Promise and Performance* (New York: St. Martin's Press, 1979), 56–57; Pasipanodya to Springer-Kemp, Aug. 17, 1968, Amistad; Brand, "Politics and African Trade Unionism," 100–101.

50. MSK, interview by author.

51. J. Greenhalgh to All Affiliated Organizations, "Subject; Kenya and Their Appeal for Assistance, *Confidential*," circular letter, Sept. 4, 1961, 2/247/5, ILGWU Archives.

52. Greenhalgh also stated that Karumba exaggerated, telling him before the strike that the union had 18,000 members and after the strike 800. In Karumba's memorandum, however, he quoted the figure of 18,000 as representing the membership before the emergency. There may have been a misunderstanding between the two. Springer estimated the membership before the emergency as 10,000. J. Greenhalgh to All Affiliated Organizations, Sept. 4, 1961, and Karumba, Brief Historical Sketch of the Textile and Garment Workers Union of Kenya, n.d., both in 2/247/5, ILGWU Archives; Springer, "Learning Skills in Kenya," *American Federationist* 70, no. 7 (July 1963): 15; Springer, "Garments in Ghana," *Justice*, Aug. 1, 1957.

53. Springer to Lovestone, Jan. 16, 1962, "Springer," box 388, LP; Karumba, Problems Faced by Kenya Workers in the Textile Industries, n.d., 2/247/5, ILGWU Archives; "ILG Garment School Fills Kenya Gap," *Justice*, April 15, 1963, 9; Springer, "Learning Skills in Kenya," 15.

54. Springer to Lovestone, Jan. 16, 1962, "Springer," box 388, LP.

55. The four were Local 22, the dressmakers; Local 155, knitgoods; Local 66 Bonnaz, embroideries, tucking, pleating, and allied crafts; and Local 23, skirtmakers and sportswear. Karumba to Springer, Aug. 20, 1962, and Zimmerman to Springer, Aug. 31, 1962, 47/1/10, ILGWU Archives; Springer to Zimmerman, Sept. 10, 1962, 10/20, Country files.

56. Springer to Dubinsky, July 5, 1962, 2/247/5, ILGWU Archives; MSK, interview by author.

57. Springer to Kreindler, Sept. 10, 1962, 10/20, Country files.

58. Greenhalgh to Karumba, Oct. 8, 1962, and Greenhalgh to Springer, Nov. 8, 1962, 10/19, Country files.

59. Greenhalgh to Karumba, Oct. 8, 1962, Karumba to Springer, Nov. 26, 1962, Karumba to Kreindler, Nov. 22, 1962, and Karumba to Greenhalgh, Nov. 26, 1962, all in 10/19, Country files.

60. Springer to Karumba, Nov. 14, 1962, 10/19, Country files.

61. MSK, interview by author.

62. Greenhalgh to Springer, Dec. 13, 1962, and see Springer to Karumba, Dec. 21, 1962, both in 10/19, Country files.

63. Springer to Sasha [Charles Zimmerman], March 22, 1963, 47/1/10, ILGWU Archives.

64. Springer to Lovestone, April 13, 1963, 10/19, Country files.

65. Springer to Lovestone, Feb. 5, 1963, and Lovestone to Springer, Feb. 11, 1963, both in 60/26, Lovestone files.

66. Robert Conley, "Nairobi Acquires Garment Center: ILGWU Opens Trade Classes in East Africa," *New York Times*, April 2, 1963, 47/1/10, ILGWU Archives; "ILG[WU] Garment School Fills Kenya Gap," *Justice*, April 15, 1963, 9; Springer, "Learning Skills in Kenya," *American Federationist* 70, no. 7 (July 1963): 17.

67. Other instructors included Owili Abaja, Geofrey Gatana, C. Gari, and S. Osore. Memorandum in Support of a Garment Workers' Training Center in Kenya, East Africa, 39/20/8, ILGWU Archives; Springer, Trade Union Skills, May 13, 1963, MSK PP; Springer to Lovestone, April 13, 1963, 10/19, Country files; MSK, interview by author; Diary entry, Feb. 8, 1963.

68. Springer, "Learning Skills in Kenya," *American Federationist* 70, no. 7 (July 1963): 17; Springer, Vocational Training in Kenya, International Affairs Department of AFL-CIO, June 10, 1963, box 1, folder 4, MSK PP, Schlesinger.

69. Springer to Lovestone, Dec. 18, 1963, "Springer" box 388, LP.

70. Springer to Lovestone, Feb. 17, 1964, 60/26, Lovestone files.

71. Springer to Zimmerman, Sept. 1, 1964, and Sept. 17, 1964, 47/1/10, ILGWU Archives.

72. Brombart to Henoch Mendelsund (ILGWU international relations department and an officer with the ITGLWF), memorandum, Feb. 28, 1978, 62/1/4, ILGWU Archives.

73. Brombart to Mendelsund, memorandum, Feb. 28, 1978, 62/1/4, ILGWU Archives.

74. Brombart to Justin D. Liabunya of TUC of Malawi, July 27, 1978, 62/1/4, ILGWU Archives; "Unions of Textile, Leather Workers Studied in 5 African Countries," AALC Reporter 13, no. 9 (Nov.–Dec. 1978).

75. The donated equipment consisted of ten sewing machines, including two high-speed industrial machines, a professional steam iron, replacement motors for three machines, office machines, and a public-address system. MSK to J. A. Ogendo (general secretary of the Tailors and Textile Workers Union), n.d., MSK PP; Brombart to Mendelsund, June 7, 1978, 62/1/4, ILGWU Archives; "U.S. Garment Workers' Gift Means Machinery for Nairobi Tailoring School," AALC Reporter 13, no. 6 (July 1978), and "Vocational Training," AALC Reporter 14, no. 2 (Feb.–March 1979).

76. Reflections on the ILGWU and the Kenya Tailors and Textile Workers Union by Springer-Kemp, Nov. 30, 1978, 62/1/4, ILGWU Archives.

77. "Hello Maida!" and "Kenya Tailoring School to Expand," AALC Reporter 7, no. 3 (March 1972).

78. Springer to Odeyemi, Jan. 31, 1964, 12/3, part 2, Country files.

79. Springer to Odeyemi, Oct. 8, 1963, and [Springer], The Nigerian Motor Drivers' Driving School, Lagos [c. Jan. 1964], both in 12/3, Country files.

80. Springer to Odeyemi, Jan. 31, 1964, 12/3, part 2, Country files.

81. Springer had hopes that Hampton Institute and the AFL-CIO would develop other training projects in Africa. Tentative Schedule for Mrs. Maida Springer and Guest during Visit to Hampton Institute, MSK PP; Springer to Lovestone, Feb. 17, 1964, 60/26, LP.

82. [Springer], The Nigerian Motor Drivers' Driving School, Lagos [c. Jan. 1964], and "AFL-CIO Helps Nigerian Trucks Roll," AFL-CIO News, April 17, 1965, both in 12/3, Country files; Prospectus, the Nigeria Motor Drivers' Driving School, n.d., 7/12, Brown files.

83. Springer to Lovestone, Nov. 25, 1964, and see N. Okon Eshiett (ULC administrative secretary) to Bécu, Nov. 16, 1964, both in 12/3, Country files.

84. Since 1949 the labor movement had suffered splits. By 1964 there were four different national labor centers. Wogu Ananaba, The Trade Union Movement in Nigeria (New York: Africana Publishing, 1970), 176, 185–86.

85. Quote is in "U.S. Intervention in Internal Affairs Alleged," African Recorder, March 12–25, 1962, 117; E. I. Ekwerike (president general of the Electrical Workers Union of Nigeria) to Springer, May 11, 1962, MSK PP; Ananaba, The Trade Union Movement in Nigeria, 217; Lovestone to Brown, Oct. 9, 1961, "Brown 1961–63," box 356, LP.

86. Springer to Lovestone, Nov. 25, 1964, and March 16, 1965, 12/3, Country files. See also G. E. Lynd, The Politics of African Trade Unionism (New York: Praeger, 1968), 129. See also Springer to Zimmerman, Sept. 17, 1964, 47/1/10, ILGWU Archives.

87. [Springer], Brief Notes—Nigeria Motor Drivers' and Mechanics School—Official Opening—Saturday, March 13, 1965, 12/3, Country files.

88. Adebola to Springer, Nov. 25, 1964, 12/2, Country files.

89. Springer to Lovestone, March 16, 1965, 11/22, Country files.

90. Springer to Lovestone, Feb. 20, 1965, "Springer," box 388, LP.

91. Adebola to Springer, Nov. 25, 1964, and March 27, 1964, and Springer to the Executive Committee of the United Labour Congress, April 5, 1965, all in 12/2, Country files.

92. MSK, interview by author; Jack to Ene Henshaw (ULC acting general secretary), April 21, 1965, 2/7, Lovestone files.

93. Ijeh to Adebola, March 27, 1965, 12/2, Country files.

94. ULC Western Nigeria, Impeachment of the Secretariat, April 5, 1965, 2/7, Lovestone files.

95. For example, on the dispute over the funding of the Ikeja office see Springer to Adebola, Jan. 25, 1965, and Adebola to Springer, Feb. 12, 1965; for the dispute over a Nigerian union's donation to the Ikeja office, see Adebola to Eshiett, March 13, 1965, and Eshiett to Adebola, n.d.; T. O. Nweama to Adebola, March 31, 1965; all in 12/2, Country files.

96. Confidential letter from Adebola to Springer, March 30, 1965, 11/22, Country files.

97. On various occasions, even while intimating that she was guilty of some misdeed, he would express gratitude for her services and the attention of the AFL-CIO. Springer to Adebola, Jan. 25, 1965, 12/2, Country files.

98. Dollie Lowther Robinson, interview by Bette Craig, March 1, 1977, transcript, 20–21, The Twentieth Century Trade Union Woman: Vehicle for Social Change, Oral History Project Program on Women and Work, Bentley Historical Library, University of Michigan, Ann Arbor; Springer to Adebola, March 30, 1965, 12/2, Country files; Springer to Robert Kinney, labor attaché, U.S. Embassy, March 30, 1965, 2/7, Lovestone files.

99. Two letters from Adebola to Springer, April 2, 1965, 12/2, Country files.

100. Springer to the Executive Committee of the United Labour Congress, April 5, 1965, 12/2, Country files.

101. Henshaw to Adebola, April 8, 1965, 12/2, Country files; Ijeh to Henshaw, April 15, 1965, and see Jack to Henshaw, April 21, 1965, both in 2/7, Lovestone files.

102. Springer to Borha, April 15, 1965, 11/22, Country files.

103. Adebola to Lovestone, April 28, 1965, and May 5, 1965, both in 2/7, Lovestone files.

104. Lovestone to Adebola, May 26, 1965, Lovestone to Springer, May 26, 1965, and Meany to Walter Reuther, May 21, 1965, all in 11/22, Country files; Brown, Memorandum for Record, June 22, 1965, 8/6, Brown files.

105. Brown, Memorandum for Record, June 22, 1965, 8/6, Brown files.

106. School Meals Caterers Union of Nigeria to Springer, May 21, 1965, MSK PP.

107. Brown to Lovestone, Nov. 30, 1965, "Brown 1964–1965," box 356, LP.

108. Brown to Lovestone, June 7, 1965, "Brown, 1964–1965," box 356, LP; Lovestone to Adebola, Aug. 11, 1969, 1/24, Brown files.

109. Brown to Meany, Results of Nigerian United Labour Congress Convention September 13, 1969, Zaria, Nigeria, "African Trade Unions," box 398, LP; Ananaba, *The Trade Union Movement in Africa*, 173.

110. Brown to [Lovestone], Sept. 7, 1969, "Brown, 1968, 1969," box 356, LP; Brown, Memorandum for Record, June 22, 1965, 8/6, Brown files; Adebola to Bécu, March 1, 1965, 11/22, Country files; see also "Indictment!" *Sunday Express* (Nigeria), Sept. 5, 1965, both in 2/7, Lovestone files.

111. Don Thomson and Rodney Larson, *Where Were You, Brother? An Account of Trade Union Imperialism* (London: War on Want, 1978), 60–62, 79–87; Barry Cohen, "The CIA and African Trade Unions," in *Dirty Work 2: The CIA in Africa*, ed. Ellen Ray, William Schaap, Karl Van Meter, and Louis Wolf (London: Zed Press, 1980); Jeremy Baskin, "AFL-CIO-AALC-CIA," *South African Labour Bulletin* 8, no. 3. (Dec. 1982): 55; "Trade Unions: America Steps In," *Work in Progress* 24 (1982): 26; Lynd, *The Politics of African Trade Unionism*, 39.

112. Ananaba, *The Trade Union Movement in Africa*, 15, 154, 159–60.

Chapter 10: Crossroads

1. Avriel to Springer, Nov. 8, 1960, "Springer," box 388, LP; Murray Gross to Lovestone, May 3, 1965, 2/7, Lovestone files.

2. William H. Friedland, "Paradoxes of African Trade Unionism: Organizational Chaos and Political Potential," and George E. Lichtblau, "The Dilemma of the ICFTU," both in *Africa Report* 10, no. 6 (June 1965).

3. Clement K. Lubembe, "Trade Unions and Nation Building," *East Africa Journal*, April 1964, 19–22; Michael Kamaliza, "Tanganyika's View of Labour's Role," *East Africa Journal*, Nov. 1964, 9–16.

4. Springer, "Pan Africanism," March 7, 1964, MSK PP.

5. Springer to Lovestone, Feb. 20, 1965, "Springer," box 388, LP.

6. Springer, "Pan Africanism," March 7, 1964, MSK PP.

7. Springer to Lovestone, Feb. 12, 1964, 60/26, Lovestone files.

8. Springer to Lovestone, Dec. 18, 1963; quote is from Springer to Ernie Lee (Meany's son-in-law and deputy international affairs director), Dec. 26, 1963, both in "Springer," box 388, LP.

9. A. Odungidie of the United Labour Congress of Nigeria also served as an advisor. Springer to Lovestone, Dec. 12, 1964, 60/26, Lovestone files; Springer to Bass, Jan. 4, 1965; "Proposed Working Paper to Be Presented by the CIO of Liberia to a Meeting on Industrial Relations Due to be Held in Monrovia in January 1965" (memorandum from CIO, Liberia), Feb. 1, 1965; Springer to Bass, Feb. 28, 1965; Springer to Hon. William V. Tubman, Jr., Feb. 15, 1965; all MSK Papers, Amistad.

10. McCray to Lovestone, Feb. 15, 1960, "McCray," box 378, LP.

11. David Brombart, interview by author, March 5, 1993.

12. Brown, Notes on Africa by Irving Brown, Feb. 19, 1961, "Africa General Labor," box 397, LP.

13. [Starr] to Springer, Oct. 17, 1961, "Springer," box 388, LP.

14. G. E. Lynd, *The Politics of African Trade Unionism* (New York: Praeger, 1968), 51.

15. Lovestone to Welsh, Oct. 12, 1961, and Oct. 17, 1961, 64/9, Lovestone files. ICFTU representative Ed Welsh also criticized Tanganyika for moving toward the Ghana pattern. Welsh to Lovestone, Oct. 1, 1961, "Welsh," box 393, LP; Lovestone to Welsh, Oct. 9, 1961, 64/9, Lovestone files.

16. Lovestone to Springer, Nov. 15, 1961, 60/24, Lovestone files; Lynd, *The Politics of African Trade Unionism*, 53; [Starr] to Springer, Oct. 17, 1961, "Springer," box 388, LP.

17. Springer to Lovestone, Dec. 16, 1961, 60/24, Lovestone files.

18. Lovestone to Springer, Dec. 22, 1961, 60/24, Lovestone files.

19. Springer to Lovestone, Feb. 11, 1962, 60/25, Lovestone files.

20. Lynd, *The Politics of African Trade Unionism*, 53–54; Springer to Lovestone, Feb. 5, 1963, 60/26, Lovestone files; "Mr. Kawawa Replies to Critics of Tanganyika's New Union," press release issued by Tanganyika Information Service, March 7, 1964, 13/9, Country files.

21. Lovestone to Springer, Feb. 11, 1963, 60/26, Lovestone files.

22. The Office of Cultural Exchange also was hosting Tandau's trip to the United States. Springer, Report on East Africa (Tanganyika and Kenya), 1962, "Africa — East Africa," box 397, LP. Excerpt from Dar es Salaam, Tanganyika, Domestic English Radio, May 15, 1963, 2/5, Lovestone files; Lynd, *The Politics of African Trade Unionism*, 55–56.

23. Laura S. Kurtz, *Historical Dictionary of Tanzania*, African Historical Dictionary no. 15 (Metuchen, N.J.: Scarecrow Press, 1978), 83–84, 213; Lynd, *The Politics of African Trade Unionism*, 53–56.

24. Springer to Lovestone, Feb. 17, 1964, 60/26, Lovestone files.

25. Springer, Report on East Africa (Tanganyika and Kenya), 1962, "Africa—East Africa," box 397, LP.

26. Springer to Lovestone, Feb. 17, 1964, 60/26; and see Lovestone to Springer, Feb. 28, 1964, 60/26; both Lovestone files.

27. Lynd, *The Politics of African Trade Unionism*, 58; Springer to Lovestone, Feb. 17, 1964, 60/26, Lovestone files.

28. Springer to Kamaliza, Aug. 28, 1964, and Kamaliza to Springer, Sept. 18, 1964, both in 13/9, Country files.

29. Kamaliza to Springer, Sept. 18, 1964, 13/9, Country files.

30. ibid.

31. Kawawa to Springer, Sept. 22, 1964, 13/9, Country files.

32. Springer to Kawawa, Oct. 5, 1964, 13/9, Country files.

33. Springer to Kamaliza, Oct. 8, 1964, 13/9, Country files.

34. Communication with Marty Morand, March 9, 2000.

35. Springer to Kamaliza, Oct. 8, 1964, 13/9, Country files.

36. Lovestone to Springer, March 4, 1965, "Springer, Maida, 1957–1976," box 388, LP.

37. "Free Trade Unions—The Keystone of African Progress," *AFL-CIO Free Trade Union News* 20, no. 3 (March 1965). Although many African governments would adopt structures similar to those of Communist governments and look to the Soviet Union as a model for rapid industrialization, many African leaders rejected such basic Communist concepts as class struggle and many moved quickly to outlaw Communist parties. Nkrumah would incredulously ask Makonnen when he spoke of African class exploitation to show him the classes in Ghanaian society. Kenneth King, ed., *Ras Makonnen: Pan-Africanism from Within* (New York: Oxford University Press, 1973), 256.

38. Springer to Lovestone, March 16, 1965, 11/22, Country files.

39. See Ras Makonnen's discussion of how an atmosphere of suspicion and intrigue in Ghana led to false representations of peoples' actions and beliefs, including his own and those of the African American ambassador to Ghana. King, *Ras Makonnen*, 233–36, 280.

40. "AATUF and African Unity: Neo-colonialist Intrigues Will Fail," (Ghana) *Evening News*, Feb. 9, 1965, 11/22, Country files.

41. "Today's Meeting of African Trade Unionists: A Decisive March in our March Towards Continental Unity," (Ghana) *Evening News*, Feb. 10, 1965, 11/22, Country files; "ICFTU Is a Threat to Labour Unity in Nigeria," (Ghana) *Daily Graphic*, Feb. 10, 1965; and see *The African Worker* 1, no. 5 (Dec. 15, 1961), 3/12, Brown files.

42. McCray to Lovestone, March 18, 1964, "McCray," box 378, LP; Opoku Agyeman, *Nkrumah's Ghana and East Africa: Pan-Africanism and African Interstate Relations* (Cranbury, N.J.: Associated University Press, 1992), 131–33.

43. Sven Fockstedt, Findings and Observations Concerning the ICFTU Position in East Africa Made during Sept. 9th to 18th 1964," Sept. 22, 1964, "Africa—East Africa," box 397, LP.

44. Brown to Meany, Nov. 13, 1964, 13/18, Country files.

45. Reuben Mwilu, Short Comments on the Position of the African Labour College, Kampala, Uganda, Confidential, Jan. 11, 1965, "African Labour College," box 399, LP.

46. Brown, Memorandum for the Record, June 22, 1965, 8/6, Brown files; *Twenty Years*, ICFTU (Brussels: ICFTU, 1969), 36. See also Robert Gabor to Brown, March 21, 1965, 1/23; Bécu to Brown, June 8, 1965, 8/6; Bécu to Brown, July 27, 1965, 8/2; all in Brown files.

47. Thalmayer to McDowell, July 25, 1963, 13/18, Country files. See also Lynd, *The Politics of African Trade Unionism*, 56–57.

48. McDowell to Thalmayer, Aug. 22, 1963, 13/18, Country files. When the ICFTU finally increased financial support, McCray faulted the West for the ill-conceived way it dispensed the aid. McCray to Meany, June 10, 1963, 13/18, Country files.

49. Granger to Springer, Feb. 24, 1963, Amistad.

50. David Goldsworthy, *Tom Mboya: The Man Kenya Wanted to Forget* (New York: Africana Publishing, 1982), 259.

51. Springer, Summary of Conclusions Arising from the Meeting Held in the City Treasurer's Office, Nairobi, Feb. 26, 1963, MSK PP; and see Springer to Mboya, Dec. 20, 1962, 10/19, and housing project documents in 11/1, both in Country files.

52. Springer to Lovestone, Feb. 17, 1964, 60/26, Lovestone files; Reuther to Alexander Bookstaver (AFL-CIO Department of Investment), April 13, 1964, 11/1; see Kenya Housing Project files, 11/1, Country files.

53. MSK, "Tom Mboya: In Memoriam," *AFL-CIO Free Trade Union News*, Aug. 1969, MSK PP.

54. Springer to Louis Stulberg (ILGWU president), July 11, 1969, 4/33/8, ILGWU papers.

55. Springer to Mboya, March 20, 1958, Thomas to Springer, Jan. 28, 1966, and Martin Morand to Springer, April 8, 1988, all in MSK PP.

56. Ted Morgan, *A Covert Life: Jay Lovestone, Communist, Anti-Communist, and Spymaster* (New York: Random House, 1999), 350–51.

57. Springer to Lovestone, Oct. 7, 1977, "Springer-Kemp," box 708, LP; Menelik Makonnen to Springer, March 22, 1983, May 9, 1983, and March 8, 1984, all in MSK PP.

58. "AFL-CIO Reaffiliates with ICFTU," *AALC Reporter* 16, no. 6 (Nov.–Dec. 1981); Lovestone, interview by E. Finn in New York, Aug. 30, 1978, transcript, 39, General Collection no. 5780, ILGWU Archives; Brown to [Lovestone], Feb. 28, 1969, "Brown 1968–1969," box 356, LP.

59. Wogu Ananaba, *The Trade Union Movement in Africa: Promise and Performance* (New York: St. Martin's Press, 1979), 137–40; Knight T. Maripe, "International Affiliation? Some Comments on the Recent OATUU Conference," *Free Labour World*, July–Aug. 1976; "Eightieth Executive Board," *Free Labour World*, March 1982; "ICFTU Opinion: African Trade Unionism," *Free Labour World*, March 19, 1985; "ICFTU Breaks Through in Africa," *Free Labour World*, Nov. 30, 1991.

60. Nyerere to MSK, April 8, 1986, MSK PP.

61. Nyerere to MSK, Dec. 6, 1985, MSK PP.

62. Nyerere to MSK, April 8, 1986, MSK PP.

63. Bibi Titi Mohammed, interview by author, March 25, 1991, and Maynard Mpangala, interview by author, March 9, 1991.

64. Hassan A. Sunmonu, former president of the Nigeria Labor Congress (1978–1984) is general secretary of the OATUU (1986 to present). Based in Accra, Ghana, the OATUU has seventy-three affiliates from fifty-three countries. With financial assistance from China, the OATUU is building the Kwame Nkrumah African Labor College. "Brief Profile of the Organisation of African Trade Union Unity (OATUU)," http://www.ecouncil.ac.cr/ngoexch/oatuul.htm, March 14, 2000; ICFTU affiliate information from Prem Fakun of the ICFTU, personal communication, March 1, 2000.

65. "African Unity—International Solidarity," *Free Labour World*, Nov.–Dec. 1974; "Afro Signals a New Beginning for African Trade Unions," *Free Labour World*, Jan. 1995; "Africa's Troublesome Adjustment," *Free Labour World*, Oct. 1995; "Right to Strike Repressed in Africa," *Free Labour World*, Jan. 1997; "Africa's Adjustment Sickness," *Free Labour World*, May 1997; "The History of the Export Processing Zone," *Behind the Wire: Anti-Union Repression in the*

Export Processing Zones (Brussels, ICFTU), http://www.icftu.org/english/tncs/tenexpzo.html, March 14, 2000.

66. Broadus and Lillian Butler to MSK, Feb. 3, 1986, and Benjamin L. Hooks (NAACP secretary) to MSK, Sept. 21, 1979, both in MSK PP.

Chapter 11: Continued Service

1. David Brombart (AALC deputy director), interview by author, March 5, 1993.

2. Pauli Murray, *The Autobiography of a Black Activist, Feminist, Lawyer, Priest, and Poet* (Knoxville: University of Tennessee Press, 1987), 347, 362. Quote is from Elizabeth Balanoff, "Maida Springer Kemp Interview," in *The Black Women Oral History Project*, vol. 7, ed. Ruth Edmonds Hill (New Providence, N.J.: K. G. Saur Verlag, 1991), 141.

3. MSK, "The Consummate Scholar," speech given to a conference titled "Black Women's Leadership: Challenges and Strategies," University of North Carolina, Chapel Hill, March 25, 1986, Amistad; MSK speech, National Council of Negro Women reception at Council House for Rev. Dr. Pauli Murray's autobiography, *Song in a Weary Throat*, June 27, 1987, MSK PP.

4. Anna Arnold Hedgeman, the only woman on the march administrative committee, tried to convince civil rights leaders, known as the "Big Six" (Randolph, Roy Wilkins, Martin Luther King, James Farmer, Whitney Young, and John Lewis), to rectify this situation and include women on the March program list of speakers. Anna Arnold Hedgeman, *The Trumpet Sounds: A Memoir of Negro Leadership* (New York: Holt, Rinehart, and Winston, 1964), 172, 178–80; Murray, *The Autobiography of a Black Activist*, 353.

5. MSK, "The Consummate Scholar," March 25, 1986, Amistad.

6. Murray letters to family and friends, Dec. 1984 and March 10, 1985, MSK PP.

7. MSK, remarks at Community College, March 31, 1989, Amistad.

8. MSK, interview by Balanoff, in *The Black Women Oral History Project*, 7:85.

9. Kemp attended John Marshall Law School (1934–1940). "James Kemp is Dead at 71; Held NAACP Presidency," *New York Times*, Dec. 9, 1983; and *Chicago Tribune*, Dec. 7, 1983, MSK PP.

10. Remarks by James H. Kemp, president of the Building Service Joint Council of Chicago, Tuesday, Feb. 1, 1966, MSK PP.

11. "Service Spans 30 Years," *Afro-American*, May 22, 1965, MSK Papers, Amistad; "Society World," *Jet*, May 13, 1965, 39, MSK PP.

12. MSK, interview by Balanoff, *The Black Women Oral History Project*, 7:133.

13. The other deaths were those of Springer's grandmother, her mother's husband, and family friend Minnie Cheevers. MSK to Kemp, June 22, 1981, MSK PP; see Murray, *The Autobiography of a Black Activist*, 433–34.

14. Kemp to MSK, April 24, 1981, MSK PP.

15. Quote from "Mass for James Kemp Friday at Corpus Christi," *Crusader*; see also "James Kemp Is Dead at 71," *New York Times*, Dec. 9, 1983; obituary, *Chicago Tribune*, Dec. 7, 1983; all in MSK PP.

16. Although Morand knew of Springer earlier, he first met her in 1961, when she served as the coordinator of the summer jobs program for African students. Morand was then the manager of the Central Pennsylvania District Council, and he hired some students at her request. Dubinsky appointed him regional director of the Southeast District in 1964. "Morand Named Head of Southeast Region," *Justice*, Nov. 15, 1964.

17. Morand, interview by author, Jan. 29, 1991.

18. Morand to Herbert Hill, May 15, 1989, MSK PP; Morand to Higdon Roberts, Feb. 5, 1992, Morand private papers; Morand, interview by author, Jan. 29, 1991.

19. Morand, interview by author, January 29, 1991; Morand to Higdon Roberts, February 5, 1992, Morand private papers.

20. The ILGWU had been active in the Little Rock desegregation case. For example, student Ernest Green had a summer job with an ILGWU local. "Education for Democracy," *Justice*, Aug. 15, 1958; Morand, interview by author, Jan. 29, 1991; Morand to Springer, April 8, 1988, MSK PP; and Morand to Higdon Roberts, Feb. 5, 1992, Morand private papers. Quote is from Zimmerman to Wilkins, April 1, 1955, 14/26/8; see also Zimmerman to Walter White, Aug. 1950, 14/26/7; Zimmerman, interview by Mendelsund, 651; all in ILGWU Archives.

21. "S'East Narrows Gap in Moulton Voting," *Justice*, Aug. 1, 1967; "NLRB Orders Ala. Hobco to Sit at Bargaining Table," *Justice*, Jan. 1, 1968.

22. Morand to Higdon Roberts, Feb. 5, 1992, Morand private papers; Morand, interview by author, Jan. 29, 1991. MSK, Summary Report of Tour of North and South Carolina, May 24–June 23," June 29, 1966, MSK PP.

23. MSK, "Summary Report of Tour of North and South Carolina, May 24–June 23," June 29, 1966, MSK PP.

24. Philip S. Foner, *Organized Labor and the Black Worker, 1619–1981*, 2d ed. (New York: International Publishers, 1981), 342; MSK to [Stulberg], July 26, 1966, Amistad; Springer to Randolph, July 20, 1966, reel 2, frame 0705, RP.

25. MSK to Dubinsky, Nov. 23, 1965, 4/33/8, ILGWU Archives.

26. Altagracia Ortiz, "Puerto Ricans in the Garment Industry of New York City, 1920–1960," in Robert Asher and Charles Stephenson, ed., *Labor Divided: Race and Ethnicity in United States Labor Struggles, 1835–1960* (Albany, N.Y.: State University of New York Press, 1990), 105–25; Herbert Hill, "Guardians of the Sweatshop: The Trade Unions, Racism, and the Garment Industry," in Adalberto López and James Petras, ed., *Puerto Rico and Puerto Ricans: Studies in History and Society* (Cambridge, Mass.: Halsted Press, 1974), 384–416.

27. Communication with Martin Morand, March 9, 2000.

28. One of the NAACP programs Springer participated in with Hill was a career conference for young blacks in Pittsburgh. Springer was the principal speaker. "Mrs. Maida Springer Speaks at Meet on Pitt Campus: 150 Youth Hear Expert Advice on Job Preparation at NAACP Career Confab," *The Pittsburgh Courier*, May 31, 1958, 7; MSK, interview by author.

29. This opponent eventually defeated Zelenko in the Democratic primary. Springer to Welsh, Sept. 13, 1962, 10/20, Country files; see also *Justice*, Sept. 1, 1962.

30. Springer to Welsh, Sept. 13, 1962, 10/20, Country files; see also "Attestant," *Justice*, Sept. 1, 1962.

31. Zimmerman, "Why I Resigned from the NAACP," *Justice*, Oct. 15, 1962.

32. "NAACP, Labor Split Growing," *Akron Beacon Journal*, Sept. 12, 1958; "Zimmerman Defends AFL-CIO on Race," *New York Amsterdam News*, March 7, 1959; address by Charles Zimmerman before the annual conference of the National Urban League, Washington D.C., Sept. 9, 1959; Don Oberdorter, "Labor Spokesman Lashes Long-Time Friend — NAACP," *Detroit Free Press*, Sept. 14, 1959; all in 47/1/9, ILGWU Archives.

33. Granger, "Manhattan and Beyond," *New York Amsterdam News*, Dec. 19, 1959; Harold L. Keith, "Will Negro, Jewish Labor Leaders War over Civil Rights?" Dec. 12, 1959, and "Randolph, Wilkins Deny 'War' But Cite 'Differences,'" Jan. 2, 1960, both in *Pittsburgh Courier*; all in 47/1/9, ILGWU Archives; Charles Zimmerman interview by Miles Gavin, AFL-CIO oral history interview no. 1 (AFL-CIO Merger), May 8, 1979, New York, New York, George Meany Center for Labor Studies Oral History Project, 1980, ILGWU Archives.

34. The ILGWU Training Institute, the only one of its kind in the nation, was established in 1950 to train future union officials. With classes held during evening hours, students would engage in six months of class instruction and six months of field work. ILGWU locals also cooperated with the High School of Fashion Industries to run courses for union members. "Arthur A. Elder Succumbs; ILG Training Institute Head," *Justice*, March 15, 1956; Education Department, ILGWU, "The Truth about the ILGWU: A Factual Reply to the 'Testimony' of Herbert Hill," 1962, 14/26/9; Springer to Sasha (Charles Zimmerman), Jan. 3, 1960, and Springer to George S. Schuyler (editor of the *Pittsburgh Courier*), Jan. 3, 1960, both in 47/1/9, all in ILGWU Archives.

35. MSK to Morand, Jan. 7, 1969, 4/33/8, ILGWU Archives; "Wentworth Gets Chicago Support," Dec. 15, 1968, and "Wentworth Faces Major S'East Pay and Medical Gains," both in *Justice*, Feb. 15, 1969.

36. Morand to Springer, April 8, 1988, MSK PP; personal communication with Martin Morand, March 9, 2000.

37. MSK to Morand, Jan. 7, 1969, 4/33/8, ILGWU Archives.

38. MSK to Stulberg, April 11, 1969, 4/33/8, ILGWU Archives.

39. MSK to Stulberg, Jan. 5, 1970, 4/33/8, ILGWU Archives; Foner, *Organized Labor and the Black Worker*, 364–65.

40. On December 11, Randolph came to Chicago to officially open the Midwest office. MSK to Stulberg, Jan. 5, 1970, 4/33/8, ILGWU Archives; see also Randolph to Springer, Dec. 30, 1969, reel 2, frame 0887, RP.

41. Morand stated that Meany was responsible for the inclusion of this provision. Morand to Higdon Roberts, Feb. 5, 1992, Morand private papers; Foner, *Organized Labor and the Black Worker*, 370–71.

42. Springer to Randolph, Sept. 23, 1969, reel 2, frames 0873–0874; and see Randolph to Springer, Oct. 23, 1969, reel 2, frame 0875, both in RP.

43. MSK, An Open Letter to the Chicago Black Media, March 5, 1971, MSK PP.

44. To the dismay of blacks who had fought against segregation, blacks attending predominantly white universities began demanding separate facilities. At Cornell University some black students began to carry handguns.

45. MSK to Stulberg, July 11, 1969, and March 6, 1970, both in 4/33/8, ILGWU Archives. Quote is from July 11 letter.

46. MSK to Morand, Oct. 21, 1991, MSK PP.

47. MSK to Dear Brother and Sister (circular letter), Oct. 13, 1969, and MSK to Stulberg, Sept. 10, 1970, both in 62/1/2; MSK to Stulberg, March 6, 1970, and list of guests, A. Philip Randolph Labor Forum, both in 4/33/8; all in ILGWU Archives. MSK, interview by author.

48. MSK to DuBrow, Nov. 13, 1986, MSK PP.

49. MSK, interview by author.

50. MSK to Stulberg, Jan. 5, 1970, 4/33/8; Bayard Rustin to Stulberg, June 4, 1971, 4/22/8; and MSK to Stulberg, Sept. 10, 1970, 62/1/2; all in ILGWU Archives.

51. In 1969 the midwest APRI hosted an informal reception for two Ghanaians, Ben Edjah, general secretary of the Industrial and Commercial Workers Union, and J. R. Baiden, general secretary of the Maritime and Dockworkers Union. In 1971 the APRI had a reception for Springer's old colleague, Lawrence Borha, then serving as the Minister of Agriculture and Information for the Mid-Western State, a region of Nigeria. MSK to Stulberg, March 6, 1970, 4/33/8, and note in file 62/1/2, both in ILGWU Archives; *AALC Reporter* 7, no. 10 (Nov. 1971).

52. "Maida, U.S. Unions Send Clothing to Exiled Angolans," *AALC Reporter* 7, no. 7 (July–Aug. 1972).

53. Springer to Randolph, March 5, 1972, reel 3, frames 0026–0027, RP.

54. Sow Moussa Demba (regional advisor to the International Labour Organisation) to Editor, *AALC Reporter*, 1992, MSK PP.

55. Picture of MSK and caption, *AALC Reporter* 9, no. 7 (July 1974), and "1974 Exchange of Views: Drought and Southern Africa Dominate Discussions," *AALC Reporter* 9, no. 8 (Aug.–Sept. 1974).

56. MSK, International Luncheon—Life Members' Guild, National Council of Negro Women, April 30, 1983, MSK PP; MSK to Bert Seidman (AFL-CIO Department of Social Security), May 1, 1975, Amistad.

57. MSK, remarks at the Community College, March 31, 1989, Amistad; MSK, interview by Balanoff, *The Black Women Oral History Project*, 7:127.

58. MSK, "Women Workers in a Changing World," MSK PP.

59. Twenty-three female delegates from nine English-speaking countries in Africa and the Caribbean met for the conference held in Nairobi July 17–27, 1977. Also present were representatives from the ILO, the United Nations Development Program, and the Economic Commission on Africa. "Pan African Meeting of Union Women, Delegates Seek to Define Women's Role," *AALC Reporter* 12, no. 7 (Aug.–Sept. 1977); "Pan African Conference on the Role of Trade Union Women: Problems, Prospects and Programs, July 17–27, 1977," and "Women Are Urged to Join Unions," *East African Standard*, July 21, 1977, both in Amistad.

60. Joram Amadin, "Talking Point," *East African Standard*, July 22, 1977; Glenys Henriette (Seychelles), Veronica Ayikwei (Ghana), and Shuweikha Rachid (Kenya), "Women Want Equal Rights," *East African Standard*, July 27, 1977, both in Amistad.

61. MSK, interview by Balanoff, *The Black Women Oral History Project*, 7:125.

62. For information on Springer's participation, see "Women Labor Leaders Study in U.S.," *AALC Reporter* 8, no. 7 (July 1973); and "Africans Study at AFL-CIO's School for Women Workers," *AALC Reporter* 25, no. 4–5 (April–May 1990).

63. Joyce Alogo, interview by author, March 21, 1991.

64. Morris Paladino (executive director of the AAFLI) to MSK, Jan. 30, 1979; MSK, "Seminar at Puncak, Sunday, Feb. 25, 1979"; and MSK to Don Newsom, March 7, 1979; all in Amistad.

65. MSK, "Black American Women Workers in the 21st Century: The Unfinished Revolution," 1985, Amistad.

66. MSK, keynote address, tenth anniversary celebration, Coalition of Labor Union Women, St. Louis, Mo., Nov. 12, 1983, Amistad; Paladino to MSK, April 11, 1977, Amistad.

67. Mark Hankin to Robert D. Wholey, Jan. 19, 1979, Amistad; Springer to Riley, n.d., MSK PP.

68. Sayg Ozturk, "Women Workers Want Solutions," in *Hurriyet* (daily newspaper), April 16, 1980, Amistad.

69. MSK, keynote address, Coalition of Labor Union Women, Nov. 12, 1983, Amistad; Gray to Springer, Feb. 1, 1998, MSK PP.

70. MSK, interview by author.

71. In 1960 the AFL-CIO supported a consumer boycott of South African imports. In 1964 they requested that the United States lead in the call in the United Nations for a complete international embargo on oil and arms shipments to South Africa. In 1981 AFL-CIO members of the U.S. worker delegation to the ILO broke with U.S. policy by supporting the ILO's position against apartheid. Two U.S. government delegations out of seven abstained. In 1982 the AFL-CIO appealed to Secretary of State Alexander Haig not to loosen the embargo on arms sales to South Africa to permit the sale of military-related items. "'Apartheid' in South Africa," *AFL-*

CIO *Free Trade Union News* 13, no. 6 (June 1958); "AFL-CIO Resolutions," *AALC Reporter* 8, no. 10 (Nov. 1973); "U.S. Worker Delegate Supports Apartheid Policy Adopted at ILO's 67th Conference in Geneva," *AALC Reporter* 16, no. 4 (July–Aug. 1981); and "U.S. Labor Movement Opposes Sale of Equipment to South African Military, Police Forces," *AALC Reporter* 17, no. 2 (March–April 1982).

72. Jay Lovestone, interview by E. Finn, Aug. 30, 1978, transcript pp. 22–23, 56, 58, 60, General Collection no. 5780, ILGWU Archives; Don Thomson and Rodney Larson, *Where Were You, Brother? An Account of Trade Union Imperialism* (London: War on Want, 1978), 42–49, 83.

73. Ralph Bunche, who served as U.S. Undersecretary for Special Political Affairs at the UN, played a large role in enabling Scott to have access to U.S. audiences. MSK to Ambassador Donald McHenry, Sept. 3, 1981, MSK PP; George Houser, *No One Can Stop the Rain: Glimpses of Africa's Liberation Struggle* (New York: Pilgrim Press, 1989), 111.

74. "NAACP Task Force Travels to Africa," *AFL-CIO Free Trade Union News* 12, no. 4 (April–May 1977).

75. MSK, interview by author.

76. The South Africans participated in five weeks of classroom study, three weeks of job training, and two weeks of travel. The courses included instruction on trade-union structure and administration, leadership skills, human relations in union and work settings, collective bargaining, and conflict resolution. There were also seminars on health and safety and an evaluation session. "AALC Holds First Program to South Africans: Ten Labor Leaders Come to U.S.," *AALC Reporter* 14, no. 3 (April–May 1979).

77. "South Africa Labor Trip Undertaken by Les Trachtman and Maida Springer, 3/31–4/11/80," MSK Papers, Amistad. See also "AALC Officials Visit South Africa, Lay Groundwork for Study Program," *AALC Reporter* 15, no. 3 (May–June 1980).

78. "South Africa Labor Trip Undertaken by Les Trachtman and Maida Springer, 3/31–4/11/80," Amistad; see also Denis MacShane et al., *Power! Black Workers, Their Unions and the Struggle for Freedom in South Africa* (Nottingham: Spokesman, 1984), 32–38; *South African Labour Bulletin* 3, no. 4 (Jan.–Feb. 1977), 30; "Southern Africa: The Struggle for Freedom," *AFL-CIO Free Trade Union News* 34, no. 7 (July 1979); "Historic Meeting in Botswana: South African Trade Unionists Speak Out," Focus on Southern Africa special issue, *AALC Reporter* 8, no. 5 (May 1973); Steven Friedman, *Building Tomorrow Today: African Workers in Trade Unions, 1970–1984* (Johannesburg: Ravan Press, 1987), 74–75.

79. "South Africa Labor Trip Undertaken by Les Trachtman and Maida Springer, 3/31–4/11/80," Amistad.

80. This second-trade union program lasted from mid October to mid December and included six courses dealing with collective bargaining, communication and leadership skills, union administration, social behavior and work, contemporary labor problems, and occupational health and safety. In addition the delegation attended bargaining sessions and executive meetings, and observed working conditions. "South African Unionists Complete Work-Study Program," *AALC Reporter* 15, no. 6 (Nov.–Dec. 1980); MSK, interview by author.

81. MSK, interview by author.

82. Under the 1960 Unlawful Organizations' Bill, the South African regime banned the ANC and the PAC. This action was taken following the Sharpeville massacre, in which police killed 69 and wounded 180 unarmed and nonviolent Africans protesting the pass laws. The government had banned the Communist Party in 1950. "Trade Unions: America Steps In," *Work in Progress* 24 (1982): 27–28.

83. See "CIA Link Feared in New Aid for Black Unions," *The Star*, Oct. 20, 1981, and Je-

remey Baskin, "AFL-CIO-AALC-CIA," *South African Labour Bulletin* 8, no. 3 (Dec. 1982): 51–67.

84. MSK, interview by author.

85. As a board member of Brooklyn College's Small College, Robinson advised older students who were returning to school. Springer to Robinson, Jan. 8, 1981, MSK PP.

86. The award was jointly conferred upon Buthelezi and the trade unionist Neil Aggett. Aggett was the forty-sixth person and the first white since 1963 to die in detention under suspicious circumstances. Buthelezi became chief of the Buthelezi tribe in 1953 and was the unelected leader of KwaZulu. "AFL-CIO Bestows George Meany Human Rights Award on Two South African Black Rights Leaders," *AALC Reporter* 17, no. 4 (July–Aug. 1982); and "Two South Africans Receive Human Rights Award," *AALC Reporter* 17, no. 6 (Nov.–Dec. 1982); Sanford J. Ungar, *Africa: The People and Politics of an Emerging Continent* (New York: Simon and Schuster, 1989), 279–80; Shelagh Gastrow, *Who's Who in South African Politics* (Johannesburg: Ravan Press, 1987), 54–56.

87. It also was revealed that Inkatha, together with the South African police, managed and controlled the United Workers' Union of South Africa. William Tordoff, *Government and Politics in Africa*, 2d ed. (London: Macmillan, 1993), 249–50.

88. Arnold M. Zack, "Evaluation of the African American Labor Center Project in the Republic of South Africa," May 12, 1986, quoted in Eileen Flanagan, draft of paper on AFL-CIO policy and South African trade unions, Yale University graduate school, 1989, 55–56.

89. "AALC Reporter Special: COSATU Officials Meet with AFL-CIO Executive Council," *AALC Reporter* 26, no. 2 (1991).

90. Personal communication of delegation with author.

91. Springer to Mwalimu (Julius Nyerere), May 15, 1986, Amistad.

92. David Brombart, interview by author, March 5, 1993.

BIBLIOGRAPHY

Books

Agee, Philip. *Inside the Company: CIA Diary*. New York: Stonehill, 1975.

Agyeman, Opoku. *Nkrumah's Ghana and East Africa: Pan-Africanism and African Interstate Relations*. Cranbury, N.J.: Associated University Press, 1992.

Ajala, Adakunle. *Pan-Africanism: Evolution, Progress and Prospects*. London: A. Deutsch, 1973.

Ananaba, Wogu. *The Trade Union Movement in Africa: Promise and Performance*. New York: St. Martin's Press, 1979.

———. *The Trade Union Movement in Nigeria*. New York: Africana Publishing, 1970.

Anderson, Benedict. *Imagined Communities: Reflections on the Origin and Spread of Nationalism*. 2d ed. London: Verso, 1990.

Anderson, Jervis. *A. Philip Randolph: A Biographical Portrait*. Berkeley: University of California Press, 1972.

Aptheker, Herbert, ed. *The Correspondence of W.E.B. Du Bois*, vol. 1, *Selections, 1877–1934*. Amherst: University of Massachusetts Press, 1973.

———. *Writings by W.E.B. Du Bois in Periodicals Edited by Others*. Vol. 2, *1910–1934*. Millwood, N.Y.: Kraus-Thomson Organization, 1982.

———. *Writings by W.E.B. Du Bois in Periodicals Edited by Others*. Vol. 3, *1935–1944*. Millwood, N.Y.: Kraus-Thomson Organization, 1982.

Arkhurst, Frederick S. *U.S. Policy toward Africa*. New York: Praeger, 1975.

Asher, Robert, and Charles Stephenson, eds. *Labor Divided: Race and Ethnicity in United States Labor Struggles, 1835–1960*. Albany: State University of New York Press, 1990.

Balanoff, Elizabeth. "Maida Springer Kemp Interview." In *The Black Women Oral History Project*, ed. Ruth Edmonds Hill, 7:39–127. New Providence, N.J.: K. G. Saur Verlag, 1991.

Bender, Gerald J., James S. Coleman, and Richard L. Sklar, eds. *African Crisis Areas and U.S. Foreign Policy*. Berkeley: University of California Press, 1985.

Blum, John, Edmund S. Morgan, Willie Lee Rose, Arthur M. Schlesinger, Kenneth M. Stamp, and C. Vann Woodward, eds. *The National Experience: A History of the United States since 1865, Part Two*. 4th ed. New York: Harcourt Brace Jovanovich, 1977.

Bryce-Laporte, Roy S., and Delores M. Mortima, eds. *Caribbean Immigration to the United States*. Research Institute on Immigration and Ethnic Studies Occasional Papers, no. 1. Washington, D.C.: Smithsonian Institution, 1976.

Buhle, Paul. *Marxism in the United States: Remapping the History of the American Left*. London: Verso, 1987.

Busby, Margaret, ed. *Daughters of Africa: An International Anthology of Words and Writings by Women of African Descent from the Ancient Egyptian to the Present*. London: Jonathan Cape, 1992.

Cantor, Daniel, and Juliet Schor. *Tunnel Vision: Labor, The World Economy, and Central America*. Boston: South End Press, 1987.

Carew, Anthony. *Labour under the Marshall Plan*. Detroit: Wayne State University Press, 1987.

Cary, Rob. *African Nationalist Leaders*. Bulawayo, Zimbabwe: Books of Rhodesia, 1977.

Charles, Milene. *The Soviet Union and Africa: The History of the Involvement*. Ed. and trans. Jo Fisher. Lanham, N.Y.: University Press of America, 1980.

Clayton, Anthony, and Donald C. Savage. *Government and Labour in Kenya, 1895–1963*. London: Cass, 1974.

Cochran, Bert. *Labor and Communism: The Conflict That Shaped American Unions*. Princeton: Princeton University Press, 1977.

Cohen, Barry. "The CIA and African Trade Unions." In *Dirty Work 2: The CIA in Africa*, ed. Ellen Ray, William Schaap, Karl Van Meter, and Louis Wolf, 70–79. London: Zed Press, 1980.

Conniff, Michael L. *Black Labor on a White Canal: Panama, 1904–1981*. Pittsburgh: University of Pittsburgh Press, 1985.

Cooper, Anna Julia. *A Voice from the South*. New York: Oxford University Press, 1988.

Cooper, Frederick. *Decolonization and African Society: The Labor Question in French and British Africa*. New York: Cambridge University Press, 1996.

Cox, Richard. *Pan-Africanism in Practice: An East African Study, PAFMECA 1958–1964*. New York: Oxford University Press, 1964.

Curtis, Alexander E. *Adam Clayton Powell, Jr.: A Black Power Political Educator*. New York: E.C.A. Associates, 1983.

Danish, Max D., and Leon Stein, eds. *ILGWU News-History, 1900–1950: The Story of the Ladies' Garment Workers*. Atlantic City: ILGWU Golden Jubilee Convention, 1950.

Dubinsky, David, and A. H. Raskin. *David Dubinsky: A Life with Labor*. New York: Simon and Schuster, 1977.

Dubofsky, Melvyn, and Warren Van Tine, eds. *Labor Leaders in America*. Urbana: University of Illinois Press, 1987.

Duster, Alfreda M., ed. *Crusade for Justice: The Autobiography of Ida B. Wells*. Chicago: University of Chicago Press, 1970.

Epstein, Melech. *Jewish Labor in U.S.A.: An Industrial, Political and Cultural History of the Jewish Labor Movement, Two Volumes in One*. Vol. 2, 1914–1952. New York: Ktav Publishing House, 1969.

Fanon, Frantz. *Wretched of the Earth: The Handbook for the Black Revolution That Is Changing the Shape of the World*. 1963. Reprint, New York: Grove Press, 1968.

Foner, Philip S. *Organized Labor and the Black Worker, 1619–1981*. 2d ed. New York: International Publishers, 1981.

——. *Women and the American Labor Movement: From World War I to the Present*. New York: Free Press, 1980.

——, ed. *History of the Labor Movement in the United States*. Vol. 9, *The TUEL to the End of Gompers*. New York: International Publishers, 1991.

Foner, Philip S., and Ronald L. Lewis, eds. *Black Workers: A Documentary History from Colonial Times to the Present*. Philadelphia: Temple University Press, 1989.

——. *The Era of Post-War Prosperity and the Great Depression, 1920–1936*. Vol. 6, *The Black Worker: A Documentary History from Colonial Times to the Present*. Philadelphia: Temple University Press, 1981.

Foner, Philip S., and Ronald L. Lewis, eds. *The Black Worker from the Founding of the CIO to the AFL-CIO Merger, 1936–1955*. Vol. 7, *The Black Worker: A Documentary History from Colonial Times to the Present*. Philadelphia: Temple University Press, 1983.

Franklin, John Hope, and August Meier, eds. *Black Leaders of the Twentieth Century*. Urbana: University of Illinois Press, 1982.

Fraser, Steven. *Labor Will Rule: Sidney Hillman and the Rise of American Labor*. New York: Free Press and Maxwell, 1991.

Friedman, Steven. *Building Tomorrow Today: African Workers in Trade Unions, 1970–1984*. Johannesburg: Ravan Press, 1987.

Gaines, Kevin K. *Uplifting the Race: Black Leadership, Politics, and Culture in the Twentieth Century*. Chapel Hill: University of North Carolina Press, 1996.

Gastrow, Shelagh. *Who's Who in South African Politics*. 2d ed. Johannesburg: Ravan Press, 1987.

Geiss, Imanuel. *The Pan-African Movement: A History of Pan- Africanism in America, Europe, and Africa*. New York: Africana Publishing, 1974.

Getty, J. Arch, and Roberta T. Manning, eds. *Stalinist Terror: New Perspectives*. New York: Cambridge University Press, 1993.

Giddings, Paula. *When and Where I Enter: The Impact of Black Women on Race and Sex in America*. 1984. Reprint, New York: Bantam Books, 1988.

Ginger, Ann Fagan, and David Christiano, eds. *The Cold War against Labor*. Vol. 1. Berkeley: Meiklejohn Civil Liberties Institute, 1987.

Gitlow, Benjamin. *I Confess: The Truth about American Communism*. New York: E. P. Dutton, 1940.

Gluck, Sherna Berger, and Daphne Patai. *Women's Words: The Feminist Practice of Oral History*. New York: Routledge, 1991.

Goldsworthy, David. *Tom Mboya: The Man Kenya Wanted to Forget*. New York: Africana Publishing, 1982.

Gray, Paul. *Unions and Leaders in Ghana: A Model of Labor and Development*. New York: Conch Magazine, 1981.

Green, Nancy L. *Ready-To-Wear and Ready-To-Work: A Century of Industry and Immigrants in Paris and New York*. Durham, N.C.: Duke University Press, 1997.

Hamilton, Charles V. *Adam Clayton Powell, Jr.: The Political Biography of an American Dilemma*. New York: Athenaeum and Maxwell, 1991.

Harris, William H. *Keeping the Faith: A Philip Randolph, Milton Webster, and the Brotherhood of Sleeping Car Porters, 1925–37*. Urbana: University of Illinois Press, 1977.

Haywood, Harry. *Black Bolshevik: Autobiography of an Afro- American Communist*. Chicago: Liberator Press, 1978.

Hedgeman, Anna Arnold. *The Trumpet Sounds: A Memoir of Negro Leadership*. New York: Holt, Rinehart and Winston, 1964.

Hero, Alfred O., Jr., and Emil Starr. *The Reuther-Meany Foreign Policy Dispute*. Dobbs Ferry, N.Y.: Oceana Publications, 1970.

Hersh, Burton. *The Old Boys: The American Elite and the Origins of the CIA*. New York: Charles Scribner's Sons, 1992.

Hill, Robert A., ed. *The Marcus Garvey and UNIA Papers*. 4 vols. Los Angeles: University of California Press, 1983–1985.

Hill, Ruth Edmonds, ed. *Women of Courage: An Exhibition of Photographs by Judith Sedgwick*. Cambridge, Mass.: Radcliffe College, 1984.

Horne, Gerald. *Black and Red: W.E.B. Du Bois and the Afro-American Response to the Cold War, 1944–1963*. Albany: State University of New York Press, 1985.

Houser, George. *No One Can Stop the Rain: Glimpses of Africa's Liberation Struggle*. New York: Pilgrim Press, 1989.

Hutchinson, Louise Daniel. *Anna Julia Cooper: A Voice from the South*. Washington, D.C.: Smithsonian Institution Press, 1982.

International Confederation of Free Trade Unions. *Twenty Years, ICFTU*. Brussels: ICFTU, 1969.

International Labor Research and Information Group. *Solidarity of Labor: The Story of International Worker Organizations*. Salt River, South Africa, 1984.

International Ladies' Garment Workers' Union. Educational Department. *Structure and Functioning of the ILGWU*. Rev. ed. New York: Arco Press, 1938.

International Ladies' Garnment Workers Union. *Report of the General Executive Board the Nineteenth Convention of the International Ladies' Garment Workers' Union*. Boston: ILGWU, 1928.

Jarrett-Macauley, Delia. *The Life of Una Marson*. Manchester: Manchester University Press, 1998.

Jeffries, Richard. *Class, Power and Ideology in Ghana: The Railwaymen of Sekondi*. New York: Cambridge University Press, 1978.

Johnson, Daniel M., and Rex R. Campbell. *Black Migration in America: A Social Demographic History*. Durham, N.C.: Duke University Press, 1981.

Jones, Jacqueline. *Labor of Love, Labor of Sorrow: Black Women, Work and the Family, From Slavery to the Present*. New York: Vintage Books, 1985.

Kahin, George McTurnan. *The Asian-African Conference, Bandung, Indonesia, April 1955*. Ithaca, N.Y.: Cornell University Press, 1956.

Kaula, Edna Mason. *The Land and People of Tanzania*. Philadelphia: J. B. Lippincott, 1972.

Kelley, Robin. *Hammer and Hoe: Alabama Communists during the Great Depression*. Chapel Hill: University of North Carolina Press, 1990.

Kelly, Sean. *America's Tyrant: The CIA and Mobutu of Zaire*. Washington, D.C.: American University Press, 1993.

Kenneally, James J. *Woman and American Trade Unions*. St. Albans, Vt.: Eden Press Women's Publications, 1978.

King, Kenneth, ed. *Ras Makonnen: Pan-Africanism from Within*. New York: Oxford University Press, 1973.

Kousser, J. Morgan, and James M. McPherson, eds. *Region, Race and Reconstruction: Essays in Honor of C. Vann Woodward*. New York: Oxford University Press, 1982.

Kurtz, Laura S. *Historical Dictionary of Tanzania*. African Historical Dictionaries, no. 15. Metuchen: Scarecrow Press, 1978.

Kwong, Peter. *Chinatown, New York: Labor and Politics, 1930–1950*. New York: Monthly Review Press, 1979.

LaFeber, Walter. *The Panama Canal: The Crisis in Historical Perspective*. 2d ed. New York: Oxford University Press, 1989.

Leab, Daniel J., ed. *The Labor History Reader*. Urbana: University of Illinois Press, 1985.

Legum, Colin. *Pan-Africanism: A Short Political Guide*. New York: Praeger, 1965.

Levine, Barry B., ed. *The Caribbean Exodus*. New York: Praeger, 1987.

Levine, Louis. *The Women's Garment Workers: A History of the International Ladies' Garment Workers' Union*. New York: B. W. Huebsch, 1924.

Lewis, David Levering. *When Harlem Was in Vogue*. New York: Knopf, 1984.

Listowel, Judith. *The Making of Tanganyika*. London: Chatto and Windus, 1965.

López, Adalberto, and James Petras, eds. *Puerto Rico and Puerto Ricans: Studies in History and Society*. Cambridge, Mass.: Halsted Press, 1974.

Lorde, Audre. *Zami, A New Spelling of My Name*. Trumansburg, N.Y.: Crossing Press, 1983.

Lynd, G. E. *The Politics of African Trade Unionism*. New York: Praeger, 1968.

MacShane, Denis. *Power! Black Workers, Their Unions and the Struggle for Freedom in South Africa*. Nottingham: Spokesman, 1984.

Marable, Manning. *African and Caribbean Politics from Kwame Nkrumah to Maurice Bishop*. London: Verso, 1987.

Martin, Tony. *Pan-African Connection: From Slavery to Garvey and Beyond.* 1983. Reprint, Dover: Majority Press, 1985.

———. *Race First: The Ideological and Organizational Struggles of Marcus Garvey and the Universal Negro Improvement Association.* Dover: Majority Press, 1976.

Mayer, Arno J. *Why Did the Heavens Not Darken? The "Final Solution" in History.* New York: Pantheon Books, 1988.

Mazrui, Ali A., and Michael Tidy. *Nationalism and New States in Africa from about 1935 to the Present.* London: Heinemann, 1984.

McFarland, Daniel Miles, ed. *Historical Dictionary of Ghana.* African Historical Dictionaries, no. 39. Metuchen: Scarecrow Press, 1985.

Meynaud, Jean, and Anisse Salah Bey. *Trade Unionism in Africa: A Study of Its Growth and Orientation.* London: Methuen, 1967.

Milkman, Ruth, ed. *Women, Work and Protest: A Century of U.S. Women's Labor History.* Boston: Routledge and Kegan Paul, 1985.

Moore, James Thomas, Jr. *A Search for Equality: The National Urban League, 1910–1961.* University Park: Pennsylvania State University Press, 1981.

Morgan, Ted. *A Covert Life: Jay Lovestone, Communist, Anti-Communist, and Spymaster.* New York: Random House, 1999.

Morris, George. *CIA and American Labor: The Subversion of the AFL-CIO's Foreign Policy.* New York: International Publishers, 1982.

Mullen, Robert W. *Blacks in America's Wars: The Shift in Attitudes from the Revolutionary War to Vietnam.* New York: Monad Press, 1981.

Murray, Pauli. *The Autobiography of a Black Activist, Feminist, Lawyer, Priest, and Poet.* Knoxville: University of Tennessee Press, 1987.

———. *Song in a Weary Throat: An American Pilgrimage.* New York: Harper and Row, 1987.

Murray, Pauli, and Leslie Rubin. *The Constitution and Government of Ghana.* London: Sweet and Maxwell, 1961.

Naison, Mark. *Communists in Harlem during the Depression.* New York: Grove Press, 1984.

Newton, Velma. *The Silver Men: West Indian Labour Migration to Panama, 1850–1914.* Kingston, Jamaica: Institute of Social and Economic Research, University of the West Indies, 1984.

Nielsen, Waldemar A. *The Great Powers and Africa.* New York: Praeger, 1969.

Noer, Thomas J. *Cold War and Black Liberation: The United States and White Rule in Africa, 1948–1968.* Columbia: University of Missouri Press, 1985.

Norwood, Stephen H. *Labor's Flaming Youth: Telephone Operators and Worker Militancy, 1878–1923.* Urbana: University of Illinois Press, 1990.

Nye, Joseph S. *Pan-Africanism and East African Integration.* Cambridge: Harvard University Press, 1965.

O'Farrell, Brigid, and Joyce L. Kornbluh. *Rocking the Boat: Union Women's Voices, 1915–1975.* New Brunswick, N.J.: Rutgers University Press, 1996.

Ojo, Olusola. *Africa and Israel: Relations in Perspective.* Boulder, Colo.: Westview Press, 1988.

Olisanwuche, Esedebe P. *Pan-Africanism: The Idea and Movement, 1776–1963.* Washington, D.C.: Howard University Press, 1982.

Orlech, Annelise. *Common Sense and a Little Fire: Women and Working-Class Politics in the United States, 1900–1965.* Chapel Hill: University of North Carolina Press, 1995.

Ortiz, Altagracia, ed. *Puerto Rican Women and Work: Bridges in Transnational Labor.* Philadelphia: Temple University Press, 1996.

Osofsky, Gilbert. *Harlem: The Making of a Ghetto, Negro New York, 1890–1930.* 2d ed. New York: Harper and Row, 1971.

Padmore, George. *Pan-Africanism or Communism? The Coming Struggle for Africa*. 1956. Reprint, New York: Doubleday, 1971.

———, ed. *The Voice of Coloured Labour*. London: African Publication Society, 1970.

Pesotta, Rose. *Bread Upon the Waters*. 1944. Reprint, Ithaca, N.Y.: ILR Press, 1987.

Peters, Joel, *Israel and Africa, The Problematic Friendship*. London: British Academic Press, 1992.

Plummer, Brenda Gayle. *Rising Wind: Black Americans and U.S. Foreign Affairs, 1935–1960*. Chapel Hill: University of North Carolina, 1996.

Radosh, Ronald. *American Labor and United States Foreign Policy*. New York: Random House, 1969.

Rasmussen, R. Kent. *Historical Dictionary of Rhodesia/Zimbabwe*. African Historical Dictionaries, no. 18. Metuchen: Scarecrow Press, 1979.

Reuther, Victor. *The Brothers Reuther and the Story of the UAW*. Boston: Houghton Mifflin, 1976.

Robinson, Archie. *George Meany and His Time: A Biography*. New York: Simon and Schuster, 1981.

Roediger, David. *Towards the Abolition of Whiteness: Essays on Race, Politics and Working Class History*. New York: Verso, 1994.

Rothschild, Maurine. "Frances O. Grant, Interview." In *The Black Women Oral History Project*, ed. Ruth Edmonds Hill, 4:361–421. New Providence, N.J.: K. G. Saur Verlag, 1991.

Sadleir, Randal. *Tanzania: Journey to Republic*. London: Radcliffe Press, 1999.

Shepherd, George W., Jr. *Nonaligned Black Africa*. Lexington, Mass.: D. C. Heath, 1970.

Sherman, Richard B. *The Case of Odell Waller and Virginia Justice, 1940–1942*. Knoxville: University of Tennessee Press, 1992.

Sicherman, Barbara, Carol Hurd Green, Ilene Kantrov, and Harriette Walker, eds. *Notable American Women, The Modern Period, Biographical Dictionary*. Cambridge, Mass.: Belknap Press, 1980.

Sims, Beth. *Workers of the World Undermined: American Labor's Role in U.S. Foreign Policy*. Boston: South End Press, 1992.

Smertin, Yuri. *Kwame Nkrumah*. New York: International Publishers, 1987.

Smith, Hilda Worthington. *Opening Vistas in Workers' Education: An Autobiography of Hilda Worthington Smith*. Washington, D.C.: By the author, 1978.

South Africa Department of Foreign Affairs and Information. *Official Yearbook of the Republic of South Africa*. 12th ed. Pretoria: Department of Information, 1986.

———. *Official Yearbook of the Republic of South Africa*. 15th ed. Pretoria: Department of Information, 1989–1990.

South African Labour Bulletin 3, no. 4 (Jan.–Feb. 1977).

South African Labour Bulletin 8, no. 3 (Dec. 1982).

State of New Jersey Manual Training and Industrial School for Colored Youth. *Bordentown and Its Training*. Bordentown, N.J.: 1925.

———. *Bordentown*. Bordentown, N.J.: May 1936.

———. *"Ironsides": A Year Book*. Bordentown, N.J.: June 1922.

———. *Ironsides Echo*. Anniversary Picture Section. Vol. 21, no. 1. Bordentown, N.J.: October 1936.

———. *Ironsides Echo*. Historical Edition. Vol. 39, no. 5. Bordentown, N.J.: June 1955.

———. *New Jersey Ironsides Bulletin*. Bordentown, N.J.: 1929–1930.

———. *Views of the Manual Training and Industrial School*. Bordentown, N.J.: 1920.

Staupers, Mabel Keaton. *No Time for Prejudice: A Story of the Integration of Negroes in Nursing in the United States*. New York: Macmillan, 1961.

Stein, Leon, ed. *Out of the Sweatshop: The Struggle for Industrial Democracy*. New York: Quadrangle/New York Times, 1977.

Stevens, Richard P. *Historical Dictionary of Botswana*. African Historical Dictionaries, no. 5. Metuchen: Scarecrow Press, 1975.

Thelen, David, ed. *Memory and American History*. Bloomington: University of Indiana Press, 1990.

Thomson, Don, and Rodney Larson. *Where Were You, Brother? An Account of Trade Union Imperialism*. London: War on Want, 1978.

Tordoff, William. *Government and Politics in Africa*, 2d ed. London: Macmillan, 1993.

Ungar, Sanford J. *Africa: The People and Politics of an Emerging Continent*. Rev. ed. New York: Simon and Schuster, 1989.

Urban, Wayne J. *Black Scholar: Horace Mann Bond, 1904–1972*. Athens: University of Georgia Press, 1992.

Van Horne, Winston A., ed. *Ethnicity and Women*. Ethnicity and Public Policy Series, vol. 5. Madison: University of Wisconsin System, 1986.

Von Eschen, Penny M. *Race against Empire: Black Americans and Anticolonialism, 1937–1957*. Ithaca, N.Y.: Cornell University Press, 1997.

Ware, Susan, ed. *Forgotten Heroes: Inspiring American Portraits from our Leading Historians*. New York: Free Press, 1998.

Weiler, Peter. *British Labour and the Cold War*. Stanford, Calif.: Stanford University Press, 1988.

Weisbrot, Robert. *Father Divine and the Struggle for Racial Equality*. Urbana: University of Illinois Press, 1983.

Wertheimer, Barbara M. *We Were There: The Story of Working Women in America*. New York: Pantheon Books, 1977.

Wertheimer, Barbara M., and Anne H. Nelson. *Trade Union Women: A Study of Their Participation in New York City Locals*. New York: Praeger, 1975.

Wilson, Henry S. *African Decolonization*. Great Britain: Edward Arnold, 1994.

Windmuller, John P. *American Labor and the International Labor Movement, 1940–1953*. Ithaca, N.Y.: Institute of International Industrial and Labor Relations, Cornell University, 1954.

Unpublished Papers and Dissertations

Flanagan, Eileen. Draft of paper on AFL-CIO policy and South African trade unions. History Department, Yale University, 1989.

Gurowsky, David. "Factional Disputes within the ILGWU, 1919–1928." Ph.D. diss., State University of New York at Binghampton, 1978.

Laurents, Robert. "Racial and Ethnic Conflict in the New York City Garment Industry." Ph.D. diss., State University of New York at Binghampton, 1980.

Richards, Yevette. "An Examination of Race, Sex among Eight Black Club Women of Washington, D.C." Master's thesis, Yale University, 1988.

———. "'My Passionate Feeling about Africa': Maida Springer-Kemp and the American Labor Movement." Ph.D. diss., Yale University, 1994.

Articles in Periodicals

"Africa Divides: African Union Unity Collapses with a Shove from the U.S." *International Labour Reports* (May–June 1986): 19–22.

Barrett, James, and David Roediger. "Inbetween Peoples: Race and Nationality and the 'New Immigrant' Working Class." *Journal of Ethnic History* 16, no. 3 (Spring 1997): 3–44.

Baskin, Jeremy. "AFL-CIO-AALC-CIA." *South African Labour Bulletin* 8, no. 3 (Dec. 1982): 51–67.

Blair, Iain. "Setting the Record Straight." *Film and Video*, Sept. 1992, 49–53.

Brand, C. M. "Politics and African Trade Unionism in Rhodesia since Federation." *Rhodesian History* 2 (1971): 89–109.

Carew, Anthony. "Charles Millard, A Canadian in the International Labour Movement: A Case Study of the ICFTU 1955–61." *Labour/Le Travail* 37 (Spring 1996): 121–48.

Dudziak, Mary L. "Desegregation As a Cold War Imperative." *Stanford Law Review* 41, no. 61 (Nov. 1988): 61–120.

Ellis, Mark. "W.E.B. Du Bois and the Formation of Black Opinion in World War I: A Commentary on 'The Damnable Dilemma.'" *Journal of American History* 81, no. 4 (March 1995): 1584–90.

Geiger, Susan. "Women in Nationalist Struggle: TANU Activists in Dar Es Salaam." *International Journal of African Historical Studies* 20, no. 1 (1987): 1–26.

Kamaliza, Michael. "Tanganyika's View of Labour's Role." *East Africa Journal* (Nov. 1964): 9–16.

Laville, Helen, and Scott Lucas. "The American Way: Edith Sampson, the NAACP, and African American Identity in the Cold War." *Diplomatic History* 20, no. 4 (Fall 1996): 565–90.

Lubembe, Clement K. "Trade Unions and Nation Building." *East Africa Journal* (April 1964): 19–22.

"Ms. Springer: An African American with the Heart of a Tanzanian." *Habari Mbalimbali* (Tanzania), March 23, 1991.

Seraile, William. "Henrietta Vinton Davis and the Garvey Movement." *Afro-Americans in New York Life and History* (July 1983): 7–24.

"Trade Unions: America Steps In." *Work in Progress* 24 (1982): 21–28.

Oral Histories and Interviews

Butler Library, Columbia University, New York, N.Y., Oral History Project

Granger, Lester. Interview by William Ingersoll, 1960

ILGWU Archives. General Collection no. 5780, Kheel Center for Labor-Management Documentation and Archives, Cornell University, Ithaca, N.Y.

Lovestone, Jay. Interview by E. Finn, August 30, 1978

Zimmerman, Charles. Interview by Henoch Mendelsund, 1976

Interviews by the Author (private collection)

Alogo, Joyce. March 21, 1991, Nairobi, Kenya

Brombart, David. March 5, 1993, Washington, D.C.

Chiume, Kanyama. March 20, 1991, Dar es Salaam, Tanzania

Mohammed, Bibi Titi. March 20, 1991, Dar es Salaam, Tanzania

Morand, Martin. January 29, 1991, Pittsburgh, Pennsylvania

Mpangala, Maynard. March 9, 1991, Dar es Salaam, Tanzania

Silverman, Jennie. April 30, 1991, New York, New York

Robert Wagner Labor Archives, Bobst Library, New York University, New York

Berry, Abner. Interviews by Mark Naison, July 29, 1974, July 5, 1977, and December 2, 1977
Matyas, Jennie. Interview by Corrinne L. Gilb, 1955

Regional Oral History Office, Bancroft Library, University of California, Berkeley

Zimmerman, Charles. Interview by David Gurowsky, 1974

The Twentieth Century Trade Union Woman: Vehicle for Social Change. Oral History Project Program on Women and Work. Bentley Historical Library, University of Michigan, Ann Arbor
Newman, Pauline. Interview by Barbara Wertheimer, 1978
Peterson, Esther. Interview by Martha Ross, 1978
Robinson, Dollie Lowther. Interview by Bette Craig, 1977

Manuscript Sources

Amsterdam, The Netherlands

International Institute for Social History. Microfilm on the ICFTU African Labor College

Bordentown, New Jersey

Bordentown Branch of the Burlington County Library. File on Bordentown Manual and Industrial School for Colored Youth

Cambridge, Massachusetts

Schlesinger Library, Radcliffe College. Maida Springer-Kemp Papers

Ithaca, New York

Kheel Center for Labor-Management Documentation and Archives, General Collection number 5780, Cornell University. ILGWU Archives

New Orleans, Louisiana

Amistad Center, Tulane University. Maida Springer-Kemp Papers

New York, New York

Schomburg Center for Research in Black Culture
Frank Crosswaith Papers
Hudson Shore Labor School Papers
Tom Mboya Clippings File
A. Philip Randolph Clippings File
A. Philip Randolph Papers
Microfilm edition of the A. Philip Randolph Papers
Maida Springer-Kemp Clippings File
Wagner Labor Archives
Edward K. Welsh Papers

Pittsburgh, Pennsylvania

Maida Springer-Kemp Private Papers

Silver Spring, Maryland

George Meany Memorial Archives, AFL-CIO
AFL-CIO International Affairs Department Country Files
Irving Brown Files
Jay Lovestone Files
George Meany Files

Stanford, California

Hoover Institution, Stanford University. Jay Lovestone Papers

Organs and Official Journals

AALC Reporter, AFL-CIO
AFL-CIO Free Trade Union News (also called the *International Free Trade Union News*)
Africa, Special Report, African-American Institute, Washington, D.C.
African Recorder, Asian Recorder, New Delhi, India
Free Labour World, ICFTU, Brussels, Belgium
Justice, International Ladies' Garment Workers Union
Negro World, UNIA

INDEX

Abada, Gemma, 282
Adebola, Alhaji Haroun Popoola, 241–45
Adelmond, Charlotte, 67–70, 74
Adjei, Ako, 133, 207
Adoula, Cyrille, 212
AFL-CIO: African American leaders in, 102; anticommunist stance of, 192, 254, 259; Atlantic City convention, 144–51; British TUC rivalry, 127; Communist countries and, 101; corruption in, 119; delegation to AAPC, 179; donation from, 244; grants from, 107, 115, 119, 202, 239; housing project loan, 258; racial harmony in, 131; racism in, 178; Randolph and, 272; Springer's work with, 205–6; women in, 275
AFL-CIO, Africa programs, 222–45; Adebola and, 241–45; garment trade, 222–26; Institute of Tailoring and Cutting, 233–39; Nigerian Motor Drivers School, 239–40, 241; in Southern Rhodesia, 226–33
AFL-CIO, and International Confederation of Free Trade Unions. See ICFTU, AFL-CIO and
AFL-CIO, role in Africa, 1–12, 198; CIA funding of, 7–8; foreign policy of, 4; Kenyan labor movement and, 210–11; Lovestone and, 6; in Nigeria, 239–45; Solidarity House grant by, 9–10; South African unions and, 277–82, 280, 344n.71; in Southern Rhodesia, 10–11; in Tanganyika, 126, 137, 252, 253–54
AFL-CIO scholarship program, 10, 157. See also Trade Union Scholarship Program for Africans, AFL-CIO
Africa: African American bond with, 129, 131, 146, 178–79; and global market, 261; sexism in, 96; West and, 189. See also East Africa; independence, African; pan-Africanism; and specific country
Africa, AFL-CIO in. See AFL-CIO, Africa programs; AFL-CIO, role in Africa
African American Labor Center (AALC), 222,

254–55; South African program of, 278, 279, 281; Springer's work for, 1, 238, 241–43, 262, 274
African Americans: African view of, 110; bond with Africa, 129, 131, 146, 178–79; and Carribean blacks, 18; Communist party and, 5–6; Jewish conflict, 270; as labor leaders, 4, 177–78, 186–87; mixed-race children of, 98, 99. See also black community; racism; segregation
African-American Students Foundation, 199
African Labor College, 147, 151, 192. See also Kampala College
African labor leaders, 100–101, 150, 152–53, 213, 229. See also specific leaders
African labor movement, 88, 100–128; Cold War and, 108–13; ICFTU and, 112–13, 128, 143
African National Congress (ANC), 216, 278, 280
African Regional Organization (AFRO), 186, 188, 203, 213, 261; African unity and, 208; financing of, 205; ICFTU proposal for, 114, 116, 153, 185, 203, 261; launching of, 209
African Trade Union Confederation (ATUC), 227–32
African Trade Union Movement, 11
African women: opportunities for, 181; political activism of, 122–23; trade unions and, 121; training for, 222, 223–24. See also black women; women
Africa Trade Union Confederation, 215
Afro-Asian Peoples' Solidarity Organization (AAPSO), 182–83
Agency for International Development (AID), 262, 278
Airlift Africa, 199–200
Akala, Eric M.O., 241
Alfange, Dean, 71
Alice Foote MacDougall restaurant, 32
All-African People's Conference (AAPC), 157, 176, 182–83, 194, 200; African labor and, 178–79, 183–84, 186

357

All-African Trade Union Federation (AATUF), 204, 208, 209, 215, 221, 254–55
All-Indonesian Federation of Labor, 276
Alogo, Joyce, 276
Alter, Victor, 70–71
Amalgamated Clothing Workers of America (ACWA), 58, 64, 71
American Committee on Africa (ACOA), 105, 199
American Federation of Labor (AFL), 130
American Federation of Labor-Congress of Industrial Organizations. See AFL-CIO
American Federation of State, County and Municipal Employees (AFSCME), 231–32
American Labor Party, 70, 71, 243
American Red Cross, 73–74
Anderson, Benedict, 97
Anderson, Eliza, 14–15
Andrews, Freida Louise, 89
Andrews, William T., 71
anticolonialism, 5, 100, 108. See also colonialism; independence, African
anticommunism, 6–7, 8, 55, 277; Lovestone's, 41–42, 130, 146. See also Cold War
apartheid, 278, 279, 282
A. Philip Randolph Institute (APRI), 271–74
Arab-Israeli conflict, 182
Asian-American Free Labor Institute (AAFLI), 262, 276, 277
Asian Railway Workers Union, 121–22
Asians, voting rights of, 123
As We See It (radio program), 206
Atlantic City compromise, 129–57; AFL-CIO convention, 144–51; and AFL-CIO scholarship program, 129, 130–34; colonial government reaction to, 134–39; conflict resolution and, 139–44; and Kampala College, 151–55; training program controversy, 155–57
Avriel, Ehud, 179, 189, 246

Babau, Marcel, 116, 117
Back to Africa movement, 14
Barrett, David, 141
Bavin, Thomas S., 141
Bécu, Omer, 126, 221
Belgian Congo, 116, 179. See also Congo
Belgian Labor Movement (FGBT), 115, 116
Bethune, Mary McLeod, 76, 81, 82
Beyene, Otto Solomon, 247
Bintou, Raphael, 116
black community: ethnic and class division in, 18; labor movement and, 270–71, 272
Blackett, Grace Woods, 79

black leadership, 37, 213; ILGWU alliance with, 47–52
black women, employment of, 30–33, 44, 92. See also African women
black workers, garment industry, 268–71
blood drives, 73–74
Bond, Horace, 104
Bordentown Manual and Industrial School, 25–30, 56
Borha, Lawrence, 225, 239, 240, 242
Boruchowitz, Joseph, 39
Botsio, Kojo, 113, 310n.57
Braden, Thomas, 7
Breslow, Israel, 93, 190
Britain. See Great Britain
British Trade Union Congress (TUC), 5, 137, 192, 203, 205; AFL-CIO rivalry with, 4, 127, 130, 138–39, 144–45; African labor disatisfaction with, 148, 150; grants from, 217; leaders of, 79, 191, 194–95; opposition to US study programs of, 132, 148; paternalism of, 129, 146; Tanganyikan strike and, 125, 126
Brombart, David, 6, 238, 248, 283
Brotherhood of Sleeping Car Porters (BSCP), 18–19, 36, 50
Brown, George, 145, 148, 151–52, 153
Brown, Irving, 11, 186–87, 195, 212, 216, 252; anti-Communism of, 7, 8; complaints against, 254, 259; as European field rep, 114, 130; and funding of Mboya, 8, 203; at Lagos conference, 205; and Nigerian unions, 240–41, 244, 245; on Nyerere, 250; on Springer, 249; and SRATUC, 219; support for, 147; tour of Africa, 198; and training programs, 239; on UGTAN, 196–97
Brown v. Board of Education, 30
Bukharin, Nikolai, 40, 41
Bunsey (U.S. Consul), 179
Bury, Jim, 203
Buthelezi, Mangosuthu Gatsha, 281

Cameroons, 181
Camps and Schools for Unemployed Women, 64
Carew, Anthony, 10
Carey, James B., 64, 144, 192
Carribean blacks, 18
Carrington, Darymple, 17
Central African Federation, 110, 216, 218. See also Nyasaland; Southern Rhodesia
Central Intelligence Agency (CIA), 7–8, 9, 180, 248, 259
Chalfin, Seymour, 149, 197

Charter of Labor for the Colonies, 87–88
Chicago Freedom Movement, 272
childhood, Springer's. *See* formative years
child labor, 276, 283
children, mixed-race, 98
China, 112, 228, 249
Chinese blood bank, 74
Chiume, Kanyama, 216
Christman, Elizabeth, 67
"CIA and African Trade Unions, The" (Cohen), 280
civil rights, 5, 91, 110; colonialism and, 78, 148
civil rights movement, 264–65, 267, 271; and anticolonialism, 5, 108
Clarke, Odell, 270
class hierarchy, 15, 18, 32
Claudius Ash and Son (firm), 34
Clayton, Anthony, 10
Cohen, Barry, 8, 10, 11, 280
Cohn, Fannia M., 50, 54–55, 67
Cold War, 2, 177, 245, 260; AFL-CIO policies during, 4, 6–8, 9; African labor and, 108–13; colonialism and, 109; Nasser-Nkrumah rivalry during, 181–84; segregation and, 80, 110, 111
colonial governments: Cold War and, 109; employment by, 155–56; and labor movement, 194–95; reaction to training programs, 134–39; Springer and, 123–24, 142–43. *See also* white minority rule
colonialism, 87–88, 99, 102, 177, 195; British, 14, 104–5, 129; civil rights and, 78, 148; Communism and, 109; labor opposition to, 100–101; neocolonialism, 248
Colonial Laundry strike (1937), 67
color consciousness, 32. *See also* racism; segregation
Comintern (Communist International), 39, 40, 47, 71
Communist countries, 130, 224, 251; AFL-CIO relations with, 101; African unions and, 249–50; Cold War in Africa and, 109, 112. *See also* Soviet Union; *and specific countries*
Communist Party (CP): African Americans and, 5–6; black support of, 47–52; ILGWU and, 38–43; Lovestone and, 37, 41; Springer's opinion of, 49–50
Communists, 79, 202, 245; civil rights alliance with, 108
Confederation of Ethiopian Labor Unions (CELU), 247–48
Congo, 109, 116, 179–80, 211, 212
Congress of Industrial Organizations (CIO),

7–8, 47, 100, 129–30, 177; in Liberia, 248. *See also* AFL-CIO
Congress of South African Trade Unions (COSATU), 282
Conniff, Michael, 14
Convention People's Party (Ghana), 196
Cooper, Barnet, 41
corruption, of unions, 119
Coutts, Walter, 137
Crosswaith, Frank, 20–21, 37, 46, 51, 52, 69, 78; and Divine movement, 60, 62
Curtis, Sam, 90

Danquah, Joseph D., 207, 208
Davis, Benjamin, 6
Davis, Henrietta Vinton, 22
Davis, Minnie E., 25, 27
Davis, Oscar, 75
Demba, Sow Moussa, 274
democracy, 111, 261
Democratic Party, 72, 91
Denmark, 95
development, in Tanganyika, 253, 254
Diallo, Abdoulaye, 195
discrimination, 15; in employment, 30–33, 36; and unions, 55–56, 272; war effort and, 72–73. *See also* racism
Divine movement, 60–63
Doña Luisa. *See* Anderson, Eliza
Dockworkers and Stevedores Union, 156–57
domestic life, 33–35. *See also* family life; marriage
Drew, Charles, 73
Dubinsky, David, 37, 42, 53, 54, 58, 270; and AFL-CIO Africa programs, 225–26; as anticommunist, 234–35; Springer and, 78, 79, 256, 266; support for Roosevelt, 70, 71
DuBois, W.E.B., 5–6, 21, 22, 88
Dumbutshena, Enoch, 227
Dunjana, Aaron, 228
Dupont, John (Jack), 216

East Africa: garment trade in, 223–26; ICFTU affiliation in, 255–56; multiracial labor system in, 131–32; Springer's activism in, 117–22, 190; training programs in, 133; U.S. interest in, 111. *See also specific country*
East African Federation, 251. *See also* Kenya; Tanganyika; Uganda
Economist (magazine), 141
education, 18, 19, 23–30; African labor school, 10, 131–34; of Africans in west, 97; for blacks in Panama, 16; Bordentown school, 25–30;

education (cont.)
concerns about programs for, 155–57; English language, 16, 17, 223; ILGWU movement for, 44–46, 63–66; interracial programs, 53, 64–66; NAACP project for, 261; opportunities for, 103–4, 107; program, 279; Tuskegee model for, 26, 29; for women, 189, 236–37. See also Kampala College; scholarship programs; training programs
educational director, Springer as, 59
Egypt, 181–82
Ehrlich, Henryk, 70–71
Eisenberg, Samuel, 61
employment: discrimination, 30–33, 36, 44; opportunities, 48, 73, 92, 155–56, 225
England. See Great Britain
English (language) education, 16, 17, 223
Equal Rights Amendment (ERA), 67
Eshiett, N. Okron, 241
Ethiopia, 247
ethnic conflict, in unions, 59–60
European labor leaders, 100–101, 115–17, 147, 203. See also specific leaders

Fair Employment Practices Committee (FEPC), 73, 88–90
family life: in Harlem during WWI, 17–22; in Panama, 14–16. See also marriage
Federation of South African Trade Unions (FOSATU), 280, 282
Feldman, Martin, 61, 62
financial aid, 214, 245, 262; for labor movements, 248; for worker's housing, 257–58. See also AFL-CIO, grants from
Fio-Meyer, Joe, 208
Flake, Wilson C., 183
Fockstedt, Sven, 154, 255
Foner, Philip S., 272
formative years: Springer's, 13–35; domestic affairs, 33–35; education, 23–30; employment discrimination, 30–33; family life in Panama, 14–16; Harlem during WWI, 17–22
Foster, William, 40
France, 180
Free Trade Union Committee (FTUC), 8, 130, 144

garment industry: in East Africa, 223–26; in Kenya, 233–39; people of color in, 268–71; Springer's activism in, 34–35; training school, 189. See also International Ladies' Garment Workers Union
Garvey, Marcus, 14, 21, 22

Geiger, Arne, 145, 221
Geiger, Susan, 123
gender. See race, and gender
General Executive Board, ILGWU, 38–39
Germany, 58, 257
Ghana, 114, 117, 179, 180, 194; ICFTU affiliation in, 183–84, 205; independence of, 102, 184; labor model in, 255; Murray's post in, 206–8; Springer unwelcome in, 213–14
Ghana Trade Union Congress (TUC), 108, 113, 127, 149, 208; and ICFTU affiliation, 185, 194, 195–97, 210
global market, Africa and, 261
Gold, Ben, 40
Goldsworthy, David, 9
government, labor and, 248. See also colonial government; U.S. government; white minority rule
Granger, Lester, 27, 28, 37, 51, 64, 256–57; on black education, 29, 53
Grant, Frances Olivia, 28, 29
Great Britain, 97–99, 143, 184, 256; colonialism of, 14, 104–5, 129; Springer's labor-exchange trip to, 77–80; war effort in, 83–85. See also British Trades Union Congress
"Great Conspiracy against Africa, The" (Nzeribe), 209
Green, Nancy L., 41
Green, William, 78
Greenhalgh, J., 233, 235, 236
Gross, Murray, 243, 246
Guinea, 180, 181, 197, 204, 214

Hammerton, Albert, 118, 126, 127–28, 134, 140, 153–54, 203
Hankin, Mark, 277
Harlem Labor Center, 37, 44, 45, 50, 51–52, 53
Harlem (NYC): 1935 riot, 32; organized labor in, 50–51, 79; in WWI, 17–22
Harrison, Hubert, 14
Harvard Labor-Management Industrial Relations Center, 131–32
Harvard scholarships, 151, 156
Haskel, Hanna, 78
Hastie, William, 28
health, Springer's, 188, 189–90, 215, 241, 254
Hedgeman, Anna Arnold, 74, 89
Height, Dorothy, 263
Heit, Leo, 94
Henshaw, Ene, 242, 243
Hill, Herbert, 269, 270
Hillman, Bessie, 70, 71, 74
Hillman, Sidney, 58, 70

Hirdman, Gunnar, 96
Histadrut (Israeli labor federation), 189, 190–91, 203, 218, 224
Hood, Walter, 118, 126, 127, 133, 152
Houser, George, 199
housing plan, 252, 253, 257–58
Hudson Shore Labor School, 44, 63–66
Huxley, Elspeth, 109

Ibrahim, Mary Theresa, 104
ICFTU, 10, 100, 130, 143, 211, 245; African disaffection with, 145; African nationalism and, 112–13; African Regional Conferences, 204–6, 209, 212; AFRO and, 114, 116, 153, 185, 203, 261; Atlantic City compromise and, 147; criticism of, 208, 210, 254; Hammerton and, 127–28; Kampala College and, 151–55; Nigerian ULC and, 240; paternalism of, 129; Solidarity Fund committee, 191–92; Springer's conflict with, 113–17, 118, 128, 246; Tanganyikan unions and, 103, 139–41
ICFTU, affiliation with, 148–49, 176–97, 213; and AFL-CIO offensive, 191–95; attempt to circumvent, 188–91; debate on, 184–88; and Ghana TUC, 185, 194, 195–97, 210; Nkomo's opposition to, 227–28; and Nkrumrah/Nasser rivalry, 181–84; Southern Rhodesian labor and, 219–20, 230; struggle over, 198; Tanganyika unions, 255–56
ICFTU, AFL-CIO and, 100, 187, 221, 260; rivalry, 115, 117, 129, 148, 191–95; and scholarship programs, 132, 133–34, 135, 143, 150–51
Ijeh, E. U., 242, 243
immigration experience, 17–18
Imoudu, Michael Athokhamien Ominus, 240
independence, African, 4, 99, 101–2, 178, 185–86, 260; in Ghana, 102, 184; Kenyan, 110; labor movement and, 247; Tanganyikan, 124. See also nationalist movements, African
Indians, in Africa, 121–22, 123, 223
Indonesia, 276
Industrial Conciliation Act (Southern Rhodesia, 1959), 220
Industrial Relations Act (Ghana, 1958), 194, 196
Inkatha Yenkululeko ye Sizwe (National Cultural Liberation Movement), 281
Institute of Tailoring and Cutting, 233–39
International Confederation of Free Trade Unions. See ICFTU
International Council of Women, 137–38
International Labor Organization (ILO), 196, 275
International Ladies' Garment Workers' Union (ILGWU), 71, 266–71; African training pro-
gram, 226, 238, 239; aid to Africa by, 228, 230; aid to Israel by, 191; and colonialism, 87; General Executive Board, 38–39, 53; limited liberalism of, 52–56; local 132, 57; mass-education movement of, 44–46; and Merchant Navy Club, 84; people of color in, 268–71; Springer and, 91–94, 273; in U.S. South, 266, 267–68, 271; war effort and, 58, 72; white male dominance of, 37, 38, 53–54; women in leadership of, 53–55
International Ladies' Garment Workers' Union (ILGWU), local 22, 36–56, 57, 267; alliance with black leadership, 47–52; Lovestoneite influence on, 38–43, 46–47; and union's rebirth, 43–47
International League for the Rights of Man, 101
International Plantation Workers' Federation (IPWF), 139, 140
International Textile, Garment and Leather Workers' Federation (ITGLWF), 224, 233, 235, 238
International Trade Secretariat (ITS), 140, 192, 224, 235, 238
International Transportworkers Federation (ITF), 126
International Women's Year Conference (1974), 275
international work, Springer's, 274–77
interracial marriage, 22
interracial relationships, 98
interracial strikers, 271
Israel, 182, 189, 190–91
Isthmian Canal Commission (ICC), 15

Jamal, Amir Habib, 123
Jamal, Zainy, 123, 137–38
Jamela, Reuben, 217, 218, 220, 229, 233; charges against, 11, 227, 231
Jewish-African American conflict, 270
Jim Crow system, 15–16, 72, 75
Johnson, James, 138–39
Justice (ILGWU newsletter), 73, 74, 82, 93

Kamaliza, Michael, 137, 251, 252, 261
Kampala College, 147, 148, 151–55, 156, 192, 218, 255
Kano, Aminu, 278
Karebe, James, 231
Karumba, Anselmi W., 107, 223–24, 233–34, 235
Kawawa, Rashidi Mfaume, 149, 150, 152, 311n.78; on Springer, 127, 253; TFL and, 118, 125, 130, 134, 139, 142
Keenan, Joseph, 132

Keller, Mildred A., 78–79
Kemp, A.W., 257
Kemp, James Horace (husband), 225, 244, 257, 264–66, 274
Kenya, 9, 198; colonial government of, 104, 106–7, 118–21; garment workers in, 223–24; housing project in, 257–58; independence of, 110; Indian-African relations in, 121–22; labor movement in, 210–11; labor movement restrictions in, 120–21; Mboya's scholarship work in, 199; tailor training school in, 233–39
Kenya Africa National Union (KANU), 210, 215
Kenya African Union (KAU), 106–7
Kenya Federation of Labor (KFL), 9, 10, 103, 115, 215; grant for, 107; internal conflict in, 200–201, 203
Kenyatta, Jomo, 86–87, 99, 106–7, 259
Kessler-Harris, Alice, 34
Kikuyu anticolonial movement, 105, 106, 118
Kiruka, S.J. Nasero, 135
Kithima, Alphonse R., 212
Kiwanuka, Dishan William, 142, 143, 157
Krane, Jay, 115, 116, 137, 152, 154, 203
KTUC, 201, 210, 215
Kubai, Fred, 215
Kweya, S. Sillas, 201, 224

Labor College. *See* Kampala College
labor crisis, in Tanganyika, 124–26
labor-exchange trip, 77–80
labor legislation, 218, 220, 250, 268
labor movement: black community and, 270–71, 272; and family life, 34–35; laws restricting, 218, 220; nation-building and, 246–47; racism in, 78, 131, 178; Springer as advisor to, 247–48; Springer's activism, 36–37; women in, 35, 275–77. *See also* strikes; unions
LaFeber, Walter, 15
Lagos (Nigeria) Conference, 204–6
La Guardia, Fiorello, 67
Larson, Rodney, 10
laundryworkers' strike, 67, 69
Lawrence, Bill, 232
Lazorchick, Dan, 2
leadership, black, 37, 74–52, 213. *See also* African labor leaders; *and specific leaders*
Lee, William, 266
legislation, labor, 218, 220, 250, 268
Legislative Council (Legco), 119, 137
Legum, Colin, 182
Lemon, Vivian Odems, 89
Lethman, Herbert, 82
Levy, Alton, 73

Lewis, A.E., 153, 154
Liberal Party, 71, 90–91
Liberia, 248
Lincoln University, 104
Lomax, Barbara, 282
Loughlin, Anne, 84–85
Lovestone, Jay, 40, 144, 149, 151, 236, 248–49; AFL-CIO policy and, 6–8, 253–54; anticommunism of, 42–43, 130, 146; CIA and, 259; Communist party and, 37, 41; defense of Mc-Cray, 244–45; on Mboya, 201–2, 258; on Nyerere, 250; on Reuther, 193; on scholarships, 148, 217–18; on trade unions, 250–51
Lovestoneites, 37, 38–43, 44–45, 46–47
Lubembe, Clement, 231
Lumumba, Patrice, 179, 180, 207, 212
Lurye, Minnie, 41, 45–46, 47, 57

Madison Square Garden rally, 88, 89, 91
Maendeleo ya Wanawake (Women's Progress), 121
Mahomo, Nana, 280, 281
Major, Louis, 115–16
Makayu, Charles, 146
Makonnen, Ras, 86, 98, 102, 182, 259
Malawi/Nyasaland, 216, 218
Mali, 1
Malone, Annie M. Turnbo, 33, 34
Maluleke, Josias Terry, 11, 217, 218–19, 227, 229
Mandawa, Percival Patrick, 143, 149, 156–57, 199
Manual Training and Industrial School for Colored Youth (Bordentown, NJ), 25–30
Marable, Manning, 195
March on Washington Movement, 52, 73, 76, 88, 263
Maripe, Knight, 217
marriage: interracial, 22; Springer's, 33–34, 244, 264, 265; women activists and, 123
Marson, Una, 83
Martini, Josephine, 46–47
mass-education movement, ILGWU, 44–46
Matyas, Jennie, 66
Mau Mau rebellion, 105, 106–7
Mauritania, 274
Mauritius Trade Union Congress, 247
Mazique, Jewell R., 225
Mboya, Pamela, 8, 214, 258
Mboya, Tom, 7, 115, 120, 142, 146, 204; AAPC and, 178, 183; assassination of, 8–9, 108, 258, 259; character of, 107; CIA and, 8; criticism of, 209; distancing of, 212–13, 257; ICFTU affiliation and, 149, 176, 185, 187–88; leadership of, 199–204; Ochwada rivalry with, 10,

200–201, 210, 214–15; Padmore and, 195; press and, 109, 111; Springer's support of, 103, 214, 257–59; Tettegah and, 105–6

McCray, George, 3, 6, 131, 150, 183, 203; on African-American relations, 179, 180; African liberation and, 5; complaints against, 244, 254; on FGTB, 116; funding of Mboya and, 8; ICFTU affiliation and, 177, 184, 186; Kampala College and, 153, 154, 255; at Lagos conference, 204; on Mboya, 213; on neocolonialism, 248; and Nigerian unions, 240–41; pessimism on AFL-CIO, 193; on Springer, 206; U.S. labor movement and, 10–11

McDowell, Arthur, 255–56

McLaurin, Ben, 89, 90

McNulty (teacher), 24

Means, Gardner, 83

Meany, George, 69, 148, 149, 202, 257, 272; and AFL-CIO training programs, 132, 133; anticommunism of, 130, 197; CIA funding and, 7, 8; and ICFTU relations, 187, 191–92, 221; pledge of aid by, 235; and Randolph, 178; Springer and, 216

Meir, Golda, 182, 189

Meyer, Joseph-Fio N., 108, 131

Millard, Charles, 140, 143, 144, 145

Minya, Aggrey, 127

miscegenation, 22

Mohammed, Bibi Titi, 102, 123, 137, 261

Morand, Martin, 266, 267, 269

Mowrer, Jack, 119

Mpangala, Maynard, 103, 125, 126, 140, 141, 151; Springer and, 150, 261

Mswaka, Thomas E., 227

Mugabe, Robert, 233

Murkovich, Anne, 79

Murray, Dora, 18

Murray, Pauli, 1, 32, 83, 90–91, 176, 262; disagreement with Springer, 263–64; Ghana post of, 206–8; Mboya and, 106; on Springer, 89, 94; Waller case and, 75, 76

Muslim women, 122–23

Mwangi, Kamau, 107

Myrdinn-Evans, Sir Guildhamm, 134

Naison, Mark, 51

Namibia, 278

Nasser, Gamal Abdel, 181–84

National Association for the Advancement of Colored People (NAACP), 87, 91, 94, 270; Kemp's role in, 264, 266; Springer and, 267, 269; Tanzania Book Project, 261; Task Force on Africa, 278–79

National Council of Negro Women (NCNW), 76, 83, 274–75

National Endowment for Democracy, 278

National Industrial Recovery Act (1933), 43

nationalist movements, African, 68, 101, 112–13, 194, 199. See also independence, African

National Press Club, 263–64

National Union of Tanganyikan Workers (NUTA), 251, 252–53

Needle Trades' Workers Industrial Union (NTWIU), 40, 41, 48

Negro American Labor Council, 178, 272

Negro Labor Committee, 36–37, 50, 51, 52, 53; war effort and, 72–73

Nehwati, Francis M., 231–32

neocolonialism, 248. See also colonialism

Neue Heimat International, 257

Neuman, Pauline, 53, 54, 67

neutralism, 177, 182, 184, 187, 195–96

Newman, David, 203

New Negro radicals, 14

Newsom, Donell, 276

New York Telephone Company, 30–31

New York Times, 109

Nigeria, 209, 239–45; ICFTU conference in, 204–6; labor movement in, 136, 186, 239, 240–45

Nigerian Motor Drivers School, 239–40, 241

Nigeria Trade Union Congress (NTUC), 240–41, 245

Nkomo, Joshua, 216, 218, 227–28, 233

Nkrumah, Kwame, 114, 116, 131, 185, 195–96, 206–7; AAPC and, 178, 179; ICFTU affiliation and, 176, 208; Nasser rivalry, 181–84

nonalignment, 177. See also neutralism

Northern Rhodesia, 216, 218

Nujoma, Sam, 278

Nyasaland/Malawi, 216, 218

Nyerere, Julius, 97, 122, 150, 249–50, 260, 308n.16; colonial government and, 123, 124; friendship with Springer, 103–5, 134, 137, 146; on role of U.S. in Africa, 111–12

Nzeribe, Gogo Chu, 209

Nziramasanga, Mark, 217

Obote, Milton, 255

Ochwada, Arthur Aggrey, 9, 120, 143, 145, 184; AFL-CIO and, 210–11; rivalry with Mboya, 10, 157, 200–201, 214–15

Odero-Jowi, Joseph, 152, 153, 255

Odinga, Oginga, 204, 214

Oldenbroek, Jacob, 126, 129, 139–40, 145

Operation Anvil, 106

Organization of African Trade Union Unity (OATUU), 260, 261
Orlech, Annelise, 54, 55
Ortiz, Altagracia, 269
Owen, Chandler, 14, 21

Padmore, George, 22, 179, 182, 194, 206; death of, 195; as pan-African mentor, 77, 86, 97
Pan African Conference on the Role of Trade Union Women (1977), 275
pan-Africanism, 11, 183, 186, 194, 195; network for, 85–88; Padmore and, 77, 86, 97
Pan-Africanist Congress, 87, 280
Panama, family life in, 14–16
Parirenyatwa, Tichafa Samuel, 229
Parker, Julia O'Connor, 79–80
Parrish, Richard, 20
Pasipanodya, Charles Madundo, 227, 228–29, 230, 232–33
Perkins, Frances, 67, 81, 88
Pesotta, Rose, 53, 55
Peterson, Esther, 67, 70, 74, 83, 95, 96
Peterson, Oliver, 95, 96
Philadelphia Dress Joint Board, 238, 239
Pins and Needles (play), 46
plantation workers unions, 139–41, 250
Plummer, Brenda Gayle, 4, 87, 98, 99
political activism, 71, 88–91, 273
political stability, 251–52
poll tax, 75, 76
Powell, Adam Clayton, Jr., 69, 269
prejudice, 5. See also discrimination; racism
President's Commission on the Status of Women, 263
press coverage, of Springer, 136
Princess Margaret Incident, 124–26, 195
Pritt, D.N., 202
"Profiles of Negro Pioneers in Chicago 1919–1945," 272–73

race, and gender, 57–72, 263; and racism education, 63–66; and religious conflict in local 132, 59–63; and women's circles, 66–72. See also women; sexism
race riots, 21
racial hierarchy, 15, 17–18, 32
racial pride, 22, 30
racism, 11, 36, 267; in Britain, 98; colonialism and, 148; Communist party and, 47, 48; educating against, 63–66; in labor movement, 37, 78, 131, 178; in school system, 24; and war effort, 58, 72–75. See also discrimination; segregation

Randolph, A. Philip, 3, 10, 14, 78, 203, 249; African concerns and, 5; allegiance to AFL, 177–78; on Atlantic City compromise, 147–48; civil rights projects of, 91; on Crosswaith, 20–21; distrust of Communists, 6, 52; FEPC and, 88–90; Kemp and, 264; on Lovestone, 7; March on Washington and, 52, 73, 88, 263; on Mboya's leadership, 201; on neutralism, 177; racism and, 36, 131; Springer and, 22, 37, 58, 146, 264; tour of East Africa, 131–32; on training programs, 145; U.S. labor movement and, 10–11
Ransome, Edith, 91
Red Summer of 1919, 21
religious conflict, in unions, 60–63
Reuther, Victor, 7, 144
Reuther, Walter, 7, 64, 144, 202, 258, 260; ICFTU and, 132, 193
"Revolt of the Twenty Thousand," 38
Rhodes House, 97
Rhodesia. See Northern Rhodesia; Southern Rhodesia; Zimbabwe
Rhodesia African Trade Union Congress (SRATUC), 217, 218
right to work laws, 268
Robeson, Paul, 5, 29
Robinson, Dollie Lowther, 67, 68, 74, 83, 281; labor activism of, 219, 243, 262
Robinson, Howard, 230
Roosevelt, Eleanor, 64, 67, 72, 75, 82, 263
Roosevelt, Franklin, 58, 63, 70, 71, 72, 75
Ross, Michael, 144, 193, 201, 202
Ruskin Labour College (Oxford University), 95, 96
Rustin, Bayard, 264, 271
Rwegasira, Joseph, 251, 261

Sadleir, Randal, 123
St. Marks Catholic School, 18, 19, 23
Sampson, Edith, 81
Savage, Donald C., 10
Scheinman, William X., 107, 199
Schneiderman, Rose, 64, 67
Schnitzler, William, 114, 116–17, 192, 193
scholarship programs, 10, 139, 155, 157, 199–200; AFL-CIO and ICFTU struggle over, 132, 133–34, 135, 143, 150–51; in Southern Rhodesia, 226–27; Trade Union Scholarship Program for Africans, 129, 130–34, 142, 143, 144–48; in U.S., 151, 156, 205
Scott, Michael, 133, 278
Scottsboro Boys, 49
Seddik, Mahjoub Ben, 208

segregation, 5, 80–83, 110, 111, 267
Seko, Mobutu Sese, 212
Senegal, 181, 239
Seraile, William, 22
sexism, 11, 37, 38, 95–96
Shane, Joseph, 228
Silverman, Jennie, 38, 41, 53–54, 93, 94
sisal industry unions, 120, 139–41
Sithole, Phineas, 230, 232
Smith, Hilda Worthington, 64, 67
Smith, John Caswell, Jr., 66
Socialism, 256
Socialist Party, 52
Solidarity House, 120, 137, 203, 204; AFL grant for, 9–10, 107, 115, 119
Soloman, Melba, 92, 273
Song in a Weary Throat (Murray), 1
South Africa, 104, 179, 344n.71; trade unions in, 277–82
Southern Rhodesia, 10–11, 198–99, 216–20; repression in, 229–30
Southern Rhodesia Africa Trade Union Congress (SRATUC), 218, 219
Southern Rhodesia Trade Union Congress (SRTUC), 219–21, 226–31
South (US), ILGWU in, 267–68, 271
Soviet Union, 71, 79, 182, 212, 228; Cold War and, 111; domination by, 198; training in, 145, 251
Spanish language, 23
Spencer, Howland, 63
Springer, Eric (son), 34, 106, 133, 261
Springer, Owen (husband), 33–34, 48, 49, 72, 83–84; divorce from, 99; opposition to labor activism, 44, 55
Stalin, Joseph, 40, 41–42, 70
Starr, Mark, 46, 50, 54, 64, 86, 249
Sterling, Nana, 13, 14
Stewart, Adina (mother), 13, 14, 30, 102, 107, 265; character of, 32; employment history of, 31, 33; political activism of, 20; as single parent, 17; Springer's education and, 23, 24–25
Stewart, Harold (father), 14, 15, 16–17
Stewart, Hélène (sister), 16
strikes: dressmakers, 43; government suppression of, 246–47; ILGWU, 38, 39, 60–63, 271; in Kenya, 234; laundryworkers 19, 37, 67, 69; legislation to restrict, 250; in Tanganyika, 124–25, 139, 142, 249
Strong, Curtis C., 231
Student jobs program, 225
Stulberg, Louis, 267
Sweden, 95–96

Tachie-Menson, Francis Edward, 113, 114, 121
Taft-Hartley Act (1947), 94, 268
Tandau, Alfred Cyril, 251
Tanganyika Africa National Union (TANU), 103, 122–24, 249
Tanganyika Federation of Labor (TFL), 103, 133, 150, 249, 251; AFL-CIO scholarship program and, 142; British TUC and, 118; financial straits of, 120; labor crisis and, 124–26; Mandawa and, 156–57; and plantation workers unions, 139–41; Springer's impressions of, 135–37
Tanganyika Standard (newspaper), 124, 125
Tanganyika/Tanzania, 118, 130, 195, 222, 260; development in, 253, 254; housing plan for, 252, 253, 257–58; ICFTU affiliation and, 255–56; labor conflict in, 103–5, 124–26, 248–53; labor movement restrictions in, 120–21; Muslim women in, 122–23; poverty in, 261; sisal industry unions in, 120, 139–41; U.S. interest in, 111–12
Teamsters' union, 119
Tettegah, John, 113, 127, 149, 150, 183, 196–97; attack of Springer by, 213–14; ATUC and, 229; friendship with Springer, 208–9; on ICFTU affiliation, 176, 178, 185; Mboya and, 105–6
Tewson, Sir Vincent, 133, 150, 152, 191, 192; scholarship program and, 144, 145, 148
Thalmayer, John, 255–56
Thomas, Norman, 69, 73, 101, 259
Thomson, Don, 10
"Those Draftin' Blues" (song), 19
Thuo, Joseph, 102, 138, 200
Tlili, Ahmed, 196
Touré, Sékou, 180, 187, 195, 209, 212; UGTAN and, 184, 196–97
Trachtman, Lester, 279, 280, 281
Trade Union Congress of Nigeria (TUCN), 225, 240
Trade Union Council of South Africa (TUCSA), 279–80
Trade Union Education League, 38–39
trade unions: *See* ICFTU; labor movement; unions; *and specific trade unions*
Trade Union Scholarship Program for Africans, AFL-CIO, 129, 130–34, 142, 143, 144–48
training programs, 44, 92, 269; AFL-CIO sponsored, 129, 130–34; for African women, 222, 223–24; controversy about, 155–57; for Kenyan tailors, 233–39; for Nigerian motor drivers, 239–40, 241
Triangle Shirtwaist Company fire, 38
Truman, Harry, 80, 90–91

Tumbo, Christopher, 252
Turkey, 277
Turk-Is Women's Bureau, 277
Turnbull, Sir Richard G., 124
Tuskegee model, 26, 29
Twining, Sir Edward, 104, 105, 124

Uganda, 147, 155, 255; Trades Union Congress (TUC), 142, 146, 155, 157
Union Générale des Travailleurs d'Afrique Noire (UGTAN), 184, 185, 187, 196–97
unions: activism, 36, 56; discrimination and, 55–56, 272; ethnic conflict in, 59–60; leadership of, 37, 38, 53–55; women in, 53–55, 121, 219. See also labor movement; strikes, and specific unions
United Arab Republic (UAR), 182, 184, 204
United Auto Workers (UAW), 107, 203, 260
United Labor Congress (ULC, Nigeria), 240, 241–45
U.S. Congress, FEPC and, 89–90
U.S. Supreme Court, 30
U.S. government: AAPC and, 183; AFL-CIO and, 278; African hostility toward, 180; in Belgian Congo, 212; Cold War policy of, 260; colonial governments and, 142–43; hypocrisy of, 80–83; role in Africa, 111–12; and segregation, 110, 111; white minority governments and, 232
United Women of Tanganyika (UWT), 123
Universal Negro Improvement Association (UNIA), 20, 21–22
urbanization, 223
Urban League, 51

Valentine, Grace B., 29
Valentine, William R., 25, 26, 28, 29
Von Eschen, Penny M., 4, 5

wages: differential, 15, 95–96; in East Africa, 120, 121, 125, 234; garment industry, 223–24, 266, 269, 270; minimum, 217
Walker, Madame C.J., 34
Waller, Odell, 74–75, 76
Walter, Noah C.A., 69
war. See World Wars
Ware, Caroline, 64, 83, 90, 225, 263, 273
Ware, Robert L., 120, 137

Washington, Booker T., 26
Weiler, Peter, 79
Weisbrot, Robert, 60–62, 63
Weisskampf, Herbert, 257
Welsh, Edward, 40, 44–45, 187, 213, 215, 247
West: African confidence in, 189; Cold War and, 111, 112; criticism of, 177; Ghana TUC and, 195–97; Mboya's distancing from, 212–13. See also specific countries
White, Walter, 94
White Man's Burden, 97. See also colonialism
white minority rule, 109, 110, 216, 218, 231–32
Williams, Thomas Calvin, 28
women: education/training of, 189, 222, 223–24, 236–37; employment of black, 30–33, 44, 92; equality of, 262; exclusion of, 263–64; in ILGWU, 38, 39, 53–55, 267; in labor movement, 35, 275–77; Muslim, 122–23; opportunities for, 181; organizations for, 137–38, 274–75; pay rates for, 95–96; price of activism for, 123; self-confidence of, 276; trade unions for, 121, 219. See also sexism
women's circles, 66–72
Women's Trade Union League (WTUL), 58, 64, 66–67
Workers' Investment Corporation, 252
World and Africa, The (DuBois), 6
World Federation of Trade Unions (WFTU), 100, 184, 186, 245, 250, 254
World War I, 19, 20–21
World War II, 58, 72–75, 83–85
Wortis, Rose, 40

Yates, Thomas, 178

Zelenko, Herbert, 270
Zimbabwe African Congress of Unions (ZACU), 231, 232
Zimbabwe African National Union (ZANU), 228, 233
Zimbabwe African People's Union (ZAPU), 227, 228, 229–30, 233
Zimmerman, Charles "Sasha," 37, 38, 39, 78, 91–92, 126; black leaders and, 47–48, 50; Communist Party and, 40–41, 42; Hill's accusations and, 270; loans to NAACP, 267; Powell and, 69; on racist union practises, 72–73; on union revival period, 45